Campanologists Companion

Guide to Traditional Bell-Ringing around the World

Copyright©Kevin Jones 2002.

ISBN: 0-9543191-0-9

Compiled by Kevin Jones.

Designed by Kevin Jones.

Edited by Kevin Jones.

Published by Kevin Jones.

Written by Kevin Jones.

Printed and bound in Great Britain
By Antony Rowe Ltd, Chippenham, Wiltshire.

First Edition 2002.

Introduction.

This book is the A – Z guide to traditional ways of ringing bells throughout the world.
Full circle ringing (English Style), (Italian Style), (Spanish Style) from one to twelve bells.
Carillons that are automatic carillon or operated by a baton keyboard, clavier keyboard, electronic keyboard, traditional keyboard carillon.
Chimes that are automatic or automatically swing chimed, baton keyboard chimed, Chimestand chimed, clapper chimed, clock chimed, electric keyboard chimed, ellacumbe chimed, lever chimed, swing chimed, zvon chimed. I may not have every tower but what I do have maybe enough to keep everyone interested and when you go on holiday places to visit. Maybe the information in this book could help get more towers actively rung and not disused or abandoned.

I would like to thank these people for all the information they have sent me to make this book possible : John Hearn, Ruth Ball, Anthony Brickell, George Bonham, Peter Ellis, James White, Adam J Beer, Nick Bowden, Robert Havard, David Bagley, Mike Fradd, Andrew Aspland, John Long, Owen Borlase, Eric Kangas (Ottawa), Dick van Dijk and Dirk van Tellingen (Netherlands), Jack Cummins and Elizabeth Hill (Australia), Petra (Hong Kong), Garry Barr, Peter Minchin, David and Mary Creaser.

I would also like to thank Darren Lee Hodges, Andrew Middlicott and Dave Andrews for Fixing my computer so I could finish this book, Jim and Cathy Main for the use of the printer, and Jeremy Slater-Brown for proof-reading my finished book.

If you have any information or alterations for the book please write to:

Campanologists Companion,
126 Willowfield Drive,
Marlpool Gardens,
Kidderminster,
Worcestershire,
DY11 5HA.
England,

Or E-Mail me "Campanologists Companion" at: kevscabs@hotmail.com

I have listed the towers by country, place and dedication in alphabetical order. The first tower in the book is in **ENGLAND** and is called *Abberley* in the county of Worcestershire. The name of the tower is Abberley Hall School and there are five bells in this tower. The biggest bell normally called the tenor weighing 20 cwt with a note of D. I have included a ordinance survey grid reference number on some towers for example of *OS: SK 723 229* which may be useful in finding a church or tower. If the towers are in bold like **Ab Kettleby** they are hung for full circle ringing but if they are in italics for example *Abberley* these bells are chimed, If these bells are in a combined bold with italics the tower has full circle and chimed bells. Also I have included interesting information in this book after the weight of the Tenor. The towers abroad are described in the same way but they are named as area or state instead of county. Where I have put (G.F.) is Ground Floor, (R.C.) Roman Catholic Church.

| Total Rings of Three (English Style): | 1048 |
| Total Towers in over 60 Countries: | 6632 |

2

Description of the Weights of the Bells.

There are 0-0-28lbs in a quarter which is written as 0-1-0. There are four quarters to 1-0-0 which is also written as 1 cwt. To assist you I have included the following conversion chart.

CWT.		K.G.		LBS.
0-0-1	=	0.44	=	1
0-0-2	=	0.89	=	2
0-0-3	=	1.33	=	3
0-0-4	=	1.78	=	4
0-0-5	=	2.23	=	5
0-0-6	=	2.67	=	6
0-0-7	=	3.12	=	7
0-0-8	=	3.57	=	8
0-0-9	=	4.01	=	9
0-0-10	=	4.46	=	10
0-0-20	=	8.92	=	20
0-0-27	=	12.05	=	27
0-1-0	=	12.50	=	28
0-2-0	=	25.00	=	56
0-3-0	=	37.50	=	84
1cwt / 1-0-0	=	50.00	=	112
2cwt / 2-0-0	=	100.00	=	224
3cwt / 3-0-0	=	150.00	=	336
4cwt / 4-0-0	=	200.00	=	448
5cwt / 5-0-0	=	250.00	=	560
10cwt / 10-0-0	=	500.00	=	1120
20cwt / 20-0-0	=	1000.00	=	2240
30cwt / 30-0-0	=	1500.00	=	3360
40cwt / 40-0-0	=	2000.00	=	4480

Index.	Page Number.
England:	5
Wales:	59
Scotland:	61
Ireland:	62
Overseas Towers:	64
Antigua and Barbuda:	64
Argentina:	64
Australia:	64
Austria:	69
Belgium:	69
Bermuda:	71
Brazil:	71
Canada:	72
Chile:	75
Costa Rica:	75
Cuba:	76
Denmark:	76
Dominican Republic:	79
El Salvador:	77
Finland:	77

France:	77
Germany:	81
Guatemala:	82
Guyana:	82
Honduras:	82
Hong Kong:	82
Iceland:	82
India:	82
Israel:	83
Italy:	83
Jamaica:	99
Japan:	99
Korea:	100
Lithuania:	100
Malawa:	100
Malta:	100
Mexico:	100
Netherlands:	101
Netherlands Antilles:	105
New Zealand:	105
Nicaragua:	107
Norway:	107
Pakistan:	107
Peru:	107
Poland:	108
Portugal:	108
Puerto Rico:	108
Russia:	108
Slovakia:	108
Slovenia:	108
South Africa:	108
South Korea:	109
Spain:	109
Suriname:	152
Sweden:	152
Switzerland:	153
Trinidad:	154
Uruguay:	154
United States of America:	154
Venezuela:	183
West Indies:	183
England County List:	184
Wales Tower List:	189
Scotland Tower List:	189
Overseas Tower List:	189
Summary of Rings:	190

George Henry William Jones   1906 - 1999
Mary Jones   1915 - 2001
Emma Cannon Main   1981 - 2001

Who have moved away for a new life in a new existence
best wishes with all my heart to your future
you will be remembered with adoration and admiration.

ENGLAND.

Abberley , Worcs, Abberley Hall School, 5, 20 cwt in D. - *Clock Chime, The weights of the bells are 2 cwt, 3 cwt, 4 cwt, 10 cwt & 20 cwt, The three trebles were cast as a chiming profile & the two tenors were cast as a ringing profile , All the bells still retain there crowns & headstocks, This tower would be ideal to have a ring of bells installed or have the present bells rehung for change ringing there is plenty of room in the belfry with the bells housed in a small part of the wooden frame & there are two possible ringing chambers, This Detached tower used to house 20 Bells with a Tenor of 78-2-0 until 1939 when they were removed and sold for scrap I presume for the war effort, All the bells were cast by Taylors in 1884, This tower is 161 feet high and can be seen from Six Counties.*
Abberley , Worcs, St Mary the Virgin, 6, 9-1-14. in Ab. - *Chimed Only.*
Abbots Bickington, Devon, St James, **3**, 5cwt. - ***OS: SS 385 133.***
Abbots Ripton, Cambs, St Andrew, (G.F.), **3**, 6cwt. in B. - ***OS: TL 231 780.***
Abenhall, Glos, St Michael, **3**, 8cwt. in Ab. - Unringable, Tenor Cracked. , ***OS: SO 671 174.***
Abingdon , Oxon, St Michael, 3, 2-1-8. - *Chimed Only, OS: SU 492 973.*
Abington, Northants, St Peter and St Paul, **3**, 7cwt. in C. - Unringable. - ***OS: SP 733 619.***
Ab Kettleby, Leics, St James, **3**, 6-2-0. - ***OS: SK 723 229.***
Abthorpe, Northants, St John the Baptist, **1** , 2-2-0. in G#.
Accrington, Lancs, St John the Baptist, **1**, 6cwt.
Acklam, N.Yorks, **3**, 1-3-0.
Acton Beauchamp, Herefords, St Giles, **3**, 5-2-0. in C. - ***OS: SO 679 503.***
Addington, Bucks, St Mary the Virgin, **3**, 7-2-9. - Also Sanctus Bell Hung for Ringing 0-0-15. ***OS: SP 743 286.***
Addlestone , Surrey, St Paul, 8, 3-1-18. in E. - *Chimed Only.*
Addlethorpe, Lincs, St Nicholas, (G.F.), **1**, 2-2-7. - Also **6**, 10-2-12. in F., ***OS: TF 551 691.***
Adel , W.Yorks, St John the Baptist, 3, 3-0-22, Automatically Chimed Only, OS: SE 275 402.
Adstock, Bucks, St Cecilia, **2**, 7-2-9. - Unringable., Derelict.
Ainsworth, Lancs, **1**, 3cwt. - Steel Bell.
Aintree, Mers, Hartley's Jam Factory, 1, 30-0-10., - *Chimed Only.*
Aintree , Mers, St Giles, 8, 6-2-4. in Bb. - *Chimed Only.*
Aisholt, Som, All Saints, **3**, 8-2-0. ***OS: ST 194 357.***
Aldbrough, Humbs, 3, 13-2-9., - *These Bells were rehung Dead by Taylors.*
Alderbury, Wilts, St Mary, **1**, 3-1-0.
Alderley, Glos, St Kenelm, **1**, 9cwt. in Bb. - ***OS: ST 769 908.***
Alderney, C.I., Old Church, **2**, - Only the tower Remains of the Church.
Alderney, C.I., (R.C.), **3**, - *Automatically Chimed Only, Plus a **Separate Bell** hung for Ringing.*
Aldingbourne, W.Sussex, St Mary the Virgin, (G.F.), **3**, 3-3-0.
Aldwincle, Northants, All Saints, **1**, 7-1-4. in B.
Aldworth, Berks, St Mary, (G.F.), **3**, 8-3-0 in Ab. - Rehung in 1957. , ***OS: SU 555 794.***
Alfreton , Derbys, (Methodist), Watchorn Memorial Church, 12, 12-2-19. in G. - *Chimed Only.*
Alkborough, Humbs, St John the Baptist, (G.F.), **3**, 12cwt. in F#. - ***OS: SE 882 219.***
Allerston, N.Yorks, St John the Evangelist, (G.F.), **3**, 4-3-16. - ***OS: SE 878 829.***

5

Allerton Mauleverer, N.Yorks, St Martin, **3**, 5cwt., - Unringable, Two of the Bells are Cracked, Redundant Church, *OS: SE 416 580.*
Allestree, Derbys, St Nicholas, **3**, 8-0-26. in A. - Anti-Clockwise. - *OS: SK 348 397.*
Allington, Wilts, St John the Baptist, **3**, - The Tenor Bell was Cast by the Salisbury Foundry in 1350.
Alne, N.Yorks, 3, 5-3-3. - *Hung Dead, Chimed Only.*
Alnmouth, Nothumb, St John the Baptist, 5, 6-0-4. in C. - *Hung Dead, Clock Bells.*
Alsop-en-le-Dale, Derbys, St Michael and All Angels, **1**, 3-2-20. - *OS: SK 160 551.*
Alston, Cumb, St Augustine, 10, 10-3-1. in Ab. - *Chimed Only.*
Altham, Lancs, St James, 8, 23-2-27. in D. - *Chimed Only.*
Althorpe, Humbs, St Oswald, 3, 15cwt. in F#. - *Chimed Only, OS: SE 834 096.*
Alton, Hants, All Saints, **3**, 12-2-0. *Sun 10 am, Fri 7.30 pm.* - *OS: SU 714 390.*
Alton Barnes, Wilts, St Mary, **2**, 3-2-0.
Alton Priors, Wilts, All Saints, **3**, 5-3-14. in C. - Derelict Church.
Alverdiscott, Devon, All Saints, **3**, 8cwt. - Unringable, Derelict, *OS: SS 520 252.*
Alverthorpe, W.Yorks, St Paul, 13, 11-1-0. in G. - *Chimed Only.*
Alvingham, Lincs, St Adelwold, (G.F.), **3**, 9cwt. in A. - Anti-Clockwise. - *OS: TF 368 913.*
Amcotts, Humbs, St Mark, **3**, 4-3-10. - *OS: SE 854 141.*
Ampleforth, N.Yorks, (R.C.), Ampleforth Abbey, 1, 92-2-8., - *Swing Chiming Only.*
Ampleforth, N.Yorks, St Hilda, (G.F.), **3**, 5cwt. - *OS: SE 583 787.*
Ampney, Glos, St Peter, **2**, 2-2-0. in C. - *OS: SP 085 019.*
Ancroft, Northumb., St Anne, **1**, 7cwt. - *OS: NT 002 452.*
Anwick, Lincs, St Edith, (G.F.), **3**, 6-1-0. in C. - *OS: TF 115 508.*
Arkengarthdale, N.Yorks, St Mary, **3**, 7cwt., -, These Bells were Cast by Bradwell of Richmond and are Weird Shaped. *OS: NZ 003 027.*
Armitage, Staffs, St John the Baptist, **3**, - Unringable. - *OS: SK 077 163.*
Armthorpe, S.Yorks, St Leonard and St Mary, 3, 3-1-13. - *Lever Chimed Only, OS: SE 622 049.*
Arncliffe, N.Yorks, St Oswald, (G.F.), **3**, 18cwt. - *OS: SD 933 720.*
Arundel, W. Sussex, (R.C.), Arundel Cathedral, 1, - *Chimed Only.*
Arundel, W.Sussex, (R.C.), Arundel Castle Chapel, **3**.
Ascot, Berks, Priory Church, **1**, 52-1-8. - No Stay or Slider.
Ashbourne, Derbys, St John the Baptist, **1**, 7-3-25. - *OS: SK 180 469.*
Ashbury, Devon, St Thomas of Canterbury, **3**, 5cwt. - Unringable., No2 on the floor. – *OS: SX 507 980.*
Ashby cum Fenby, Humbs, St Peter, 3, 7cwt. - *Chimed Only, OS: TA 255 010.*
Ashby Magna, Leics, St Mary (G.F.), **3**, 7-2-10. - *OS: SP 564 905.*
Ashby Parva, Leics, St Peter, **3**, 6cwt. - Unringable. - *OS: SP 525 887.*
Ashcombe, Devon, St Nectan, 3, 9cwt. - *Swing Chiming Only On Half Wheels Unringable., Derelict*, *OS: SX 914 796.*
Ashdown Forest, E.Sussex, Convent of Notre Dame, 5, 21-2-22. in E. - *Clock Chime.*
Ashen, Essex, St Augustine, (G.F.), **3**, 8-2-0. in A. - *OS: TL 747 423.*
Ashendon, Bucks, Nativity of the Blessed Virgin Mary, **3**, 5-3-19. in B. - The Bells are a complete set Cast By Henry Bagly 1st in 1658., Derelict. - *OS: SP 705 143.*
Ashley, Wilts, St James the Greater, **3**, 4cwt. - Unringable., The Treble is a 14th Century Bell and the Tenor was cast by the Gloucester Foundry in 1360. - *OS: ST 816 684.*
Ashorn Hill, Warwicks, Musical Museum, 18, 0-3-0. in C. - *Chimed Only, These Bells are Dutch.*
Ashmansworth, Hants, St James, 3, - *Swing Chiming Only.*
Ashurst, Kent, Parish Church, 3, 4cwt. - *Swing Chiming Only, OS: TQ 512 391.*
Askham, Notts, St Nicholas, **3**, - Unringable.
Aslackby, Lincs, St James the Great, **3**, 7cwt. in A. - *OS: TF 083 304.*
Asthall, Oxon, St Nicholas, (G.F.), **3**, 6-1-16. in B. - Tenor Cast early 15th Century. – *OS: SP 287 114.*
Aston, S.Yorks, All Saints, **3**, 9-2-2. - Unringable. - *OS: SK 465 853.*

6

Aston cum Aughton, S.Yorks, All Saints, 3, 9-2-2. - *Chimed Only, OS: SK 468 852.*
Aston Magna, Glos, St John, 1, - *OS: SP 202 357.*
Aston Sandford, Bucks, St Michael, 3, 6cwt. - Unringable. - *OS: SP 757 079.*
Astwood, Bucks, St Peter, 3, 10-0-13. - Derelict. - *OS: SP 950 474.*
Aswarby, Lincs, St Denis, 3, 8cwt. in A. - *Chimed Only, OS: TF 068 399.*
Attleborough, Warwicks, Holy Trinity, 3, - *Hung Dead.*
Atworth, Wilts, St Michael and All Angels, 3, - Unringable, The Treble was cast by the Bristol Foundry in 1350.
Aubourn, Lincs, St Peter, 3, 8-0-9. - *Clock Bells.*
Aunsby, Lincs, St Thomas a Becket, 3, 10cwt. in G#. - *Chimed Only, OS: TF 044 389.*
Axmouth, Devon, St Michael, 3, 8cwt. - *OS: SY 256 910.*
Aycliffe, Durham, St Andrew, 3, 3-2-6. - *OS: NZ 283 222.*
Aylburton, Glos, St Mary, 1, 5cwt. in C. - *OS: SO 618 019.*
Aylesbury, - *See Walton.*
Aylesby, Humbs, St Laurance, 3, 8cwt. in Bb. - *Hung Dead, OS: TA 203 077.*
Ayot, Herts, St Peter, 6, 5cwt. - *Chimed Only.*
Bacton, Norfolk, St Andrew, 5, 7cwt. - *Chimed Only.*
Badminton, Glos, 3.
Bagendon, Glos, St Margaret, 5, 2-3-19 in E. - *Chimed only except* **One Bell** *the* **Tenor** *is only Hung for Ringing. OS: SP 012 067.*
Baildon, W.Yorks, St John the Evangelist, 8, 11-3-26. in G. - *Chimed Only.*
Baldersby, N.Yorks, St James, 8, 25-3-19. in C#., - *Chimed Only.*
Balderstone, Lancs, 1, 10cwt.
Ballingham, Herefords, St Dubricus, 3, 7-2-0. - *OS: SO 57 31.*
Bamburgh, S.Yorks, St Peter, 3, 8cwt. in A. - *OS: SE 484 032.*
Banbury, Oxon, (R.C.), St John, 3, 1-2-8. in Bb.- No Stays or Sliders. - *OS: SP 455 404.*
Barcheston, Warwicks, St Martin, 3, - *Hung Dead, The Tenor was cast by Bartholomew Atton of Buckingham in 1596. OS: SP 266 399.*
Bardon, Leics, St Peter, 3, 8-1-17. - Unringable, 2 Bells Broken, Derelict, - *OS: SK 450 127.*
Bardsey, W.Yorks, All Hallows, 3, - Unringable. *OS: SE 365 432.*
Barford St Michael, Oxon, St Michael, 2, 6-1-0.
Barholme, Lincs, St Martin, 3, 6-0-11. - No Stays or Sliders. - *OS: TF 090 110.*
Barmston, Humbs, All Saints, 1.
Barnacre, Cumb, 1, 7cwt.
Barnetby Le Wold, Humbs, St Mary and St Barnabus, 3, 7cwt. in Bb. - Unringable, Redundant Church, Derelict, - *OS: TA 05 09.*
Barningham, Suff, St Andrew, 3, 10cwt., - Unringable, The Tenor was cast in 1722 and the rest are Pre Reformation Bells, *OS: TL 968 769.*
Barnoldswick, Lancs, St Mary Le Gill, 3, 4cwt., *OS: SD 877 468.*
Barnsley, S.Yorks, St Peter and St John the Baptist, 1, 3-2-0. - *OS: SF 351 059.*
Barrow-in-Furness, Cumb, (R.C.), St Mary of Furness, 1, 11cwt.
Barrow-on-Trent, Derbys, St Wilfred, (G.F.), 3, 10-2-0. - *OS: SK 353 285.*
Barton, Cumbs, St Michael, 2, 8cwt. - Both Bells are the same note, *OS: NY 488 263.*
Basingstoke, Hants, (R.C.), 1, - *Chimed Only.*
Baswich See Stafford.
Batchott. - *See Richards Castle.*
Bath, Avon, (R.C.), St John the Evangelist, 8, 19cwt. in F. - *Chimed Only.*
Bath, Avon, St Luke, 5, 7cwt. - *Chimed Only.*
Bath, Avon, St Stephen, 3, 6cwt. - Unringable, *OS: ST 751 656.*
Batheaston, Avon, St Katherine, 6, 12cwt. in F#. - *Chimed Only.*
Batley, W.Yorks, Market Hall, 1, 30cwt., - *Chimed Only.*
Batley Carr, W.Yorks, Holy Trinity, 6, 11-2-21. in G#. - *Chimed Only.*
Baumber, Lincs, St Swithin, 3, 13cwt. - Unringable, Bells on Chuch floor, *OS: TF 222 744.*

Baverstock, Wilts, St Editha, **3**, 7cwt., The Treble and Tenor were cast by the Bristol Foundry around 1350. *OS: SU 029 316.*
Baxendon, Lancs, St John the Baptist, 6, *9cwt. - Chimed Only.*
Baydon, Wilts, St Nicholas, (G.F.), **3**, 5cwt. in C., *OS: SU 282 780.*
Beamish, Dur, St Andrew, 11, 16-2-3. in F. *- Chimed Only.*
Bearley, Warwicks, St Mary the Virgin, **1**, 2-2-0. - Unringable.
Bear Wood, Berks, St Catherine, **2**, 10-0-13. in A. *- OS: SU 697 839.*
Beaudesert, Warwicks, St Nicholas, **3**, 5cwt. - Unringable, The Treble and Second were cast in 1350 *OS: SP 154 661.*
Beaworthy, Devon, St Alban, 3, *- Chimed Only, All these Bells were cast by Taylors in 1820.*
Beckbury, Salop, St Milburga, (G.F.), **3**, 6-2-15., *OS: SJ 765 016.*
Beckenham, Kent, Christ Church, 8, 4-1-9. in E. *- Chimed Only.*
Beckingham, Notts, All Saints, (G.F.), **3**, 9-2-0 in Bb. *Mon.*, *OS: SK 779 902.*
Becontree, Essex, St Alban, 10, 4cwt. in Eb. *- Chimed Only.*
Bedford, Beds, Bedford High School for Girls, **1**, 5-0-11. in D. *- OS: TL 053 505.*
Bedford, Beds, Bedford School for Boys, **1**, 5cwt. in D.
Bedford, Beds, Cemetery Chapel, **1**, 10-0-16. in C. *- OS: TL 048 512.*
Bedford, Beds, Pax House, 14 Ellis Road (G.F.), **1**, 1-1-0. - This Bell is Rung in the Hall and is hung in the Loft.
Bedford, Beds, St Cuthbert, **1**, 10-0-25. in A. *- OS: TL 053 499.*
Bedford, Beds, St John, **1**, 6-2-15. in C. *- OS: TL 042 492.*
Bedworth, Warwicks, (R.C.), **3**, - Tenor only Ringable.
Beeby, Leics, All Saints, **3**, 9cwt. - Unringable, Redundant Church, *OS: SK 664 084.*
Beech Hill, Berks, St Mary the Virgin, 3, 2-3-0. *- Chimed Only., OS: SU 697 644.*
Beechingstoke, Wilts, St Stephen, **2**, 2-0-26. - Both the bells were cast by Taylors in 1909. *OS: SU 083 590.*
Beeford, Humb, **3**, 5cwt.
Beeley, Derbys, St Anne, (G.F.), **3**, 6-0-11. in A#., *OS: SK 265 677.*
Beer Hacket, Dorset, St Michael, **3**, 6-2-0 in D. - Unringable, *OS: ST 599 118.*
Beesby, Lincs, St Andrew, 5, 4cwt. *- Chimed Only, OS: TF 464 802.*
Begbroke, Oxon, St Michael, **1**, 3-1-17. - No Stay or Slider.
Belford, Northumb., St Mary, **2**, 11cwt. *- OS: NU 108 340.*
Belleau, Lincs, St John the Baptist, 3, 6cwt. *- Chimed Only, OS: TF 401 786.*
Belmont, Lancs, St Peter, 6, 10-1-17. in G. *- Chimed Only, Steel Bells.*
Belmont. - See Hereford.
Belvoir, Leics, Belvoir Castle Chapel, (G.F.), **1**.
Benniworth, Lincs, St Julian, (G.F.), **3**, 4-3-12. in D. *- OS: TF 209 818.*
Berwick Bassett, Wilts, St Nicholas, (G.F.), **3**, 6-1-0. *- OS: SU 098 734.*
Berwick St Leonard, Wilts, St Leonard, **2**, 6-0-12.
Bethnal Green, Gtr London, St John, **3**, 10-0-1. in G., *OS: TQ 350 827.*
Betteshanger, Kent, St Mary the Virgin, (G.F.), 3, 4cwt. in E. *- Chimed Only, OS: TR 312 526.*
Beverley, Humbs, Minster Church of St John the Evangelist, (S.W. Tower), **1**, 140-3-1 This Bell is named "Great John" - Swing Chiming Only, (N.W. Tower), **10**, 41-1-20. in C., *- OS: TA 037 392.*
Beverstone, Glos, St Mary, **2**, 4-2-0. *- OS: ST 802 940.*
Bickerstaffe, Lancs, Holy Trinity, 8, 8-1-0. *- Chimed Only.*
Bicknor, Kent, **3**, - Steel Bells and Steel Wheels.
Biddlestone, Wilts, St Nicholas with St Peter, 2, *- Lever Chimed, OS: ST 862 736.*
Bilborough, Humb, **3**, 7cwt.
Bilborough, Notts, St Martin of Tours, **1**, 4-1-18. *- OS: SK 520 418.*
Billingford, Norfolk, St Leonard, **1**, 2-2-0.
Billingham, Cleve, 3, *Chimed Only.*
Billinghay, Lancs, St Michael, **3**, 9cwt. in C. *- OS: TF 158 549.*
Bilsthorpe, Notts, St Margaret, **2**, *- OS: SK 646 605.*

Binbrook, Lincs, St Mary, **3**, 11cwt. in F#. - *OS: TF 212 939.*
Bincombe, Dorset, Holy Trinity, **2**, 6cwt. - *OS: SY 686 845.*
Binton, Warwicks, St Peter, **1**, 4cwt. - Unringable.
Birchencliffe, W.Yorks, St Philip the Apostle, **1**, 3-3-0. - *OS: SE 119 188.*
Birdsall, N.Yorks, **3**., - Derelict Church.
Birkenhead, Mers, Town Hall, **5**, 35-3-00., - *Chimed Only.*
Birkin, W.Yorks, **3**, 7cwt., - Derelict Church.
Birley, Herefords, St Peter, **3**, 4-1-0. in C#. - *OS: SO 453 534.*
Birmingham, W.Mids, Birmingham Art Gallery, **5**, 66-2-0., - *Clock Chime.*
Birmingham, W.Mids, Birmingham Cemetery Chapel, **1**, 21-1-12., - Cast by Taylors in 1862.
Birmingham, W.Mids, Birmingham University, **5**, 121-2-11., - *Clock Chime.*
Birmingham, W.Mids, St Peter, **1**, 21-0-24., - This Bell was cast by James Barwell in 1902.
Birtley, Tyne and Wear, St John the Evangelist, **6**, 12cwt. in G. - *Chimed Only.*
Bisbrook, Leics, St John the Baptist, **1**, 1-1-0.
Bisham, Berks, All Saints, **3**, 6-0-2. in Bb. - Rehung in 1955 in a Six Bell Frame. – *OS: SU 848 854.*
Bishop Burton, Humb, **3**, 12cwt.
Bishop Monkton, N.Yorks, St John the Baptist, **8**, 5-2-4. in C. - *Chimed Only.*
Bishop Norton, Lincs, St Peter, **3**, 9-1-14. - Hung Dead, *OS: SK 983 927.*
Bishops Stortford, Herts, Holy Trinity, **2**, 0-3-0., - *Lever Chimed Only.*
Bishopstone, Wilts, St John the Baptist, **3**, 7-1-0. - The Treble and Second were cast at the Salisbury Foundry in 1587.
Bishopstrow, Wilts, St Aldrum, **1**, 7-1-0. -This Bell was cast by Robert Wells in 1785. *OS: ST 893 434.*
Bishops Tachbrook, Warwicks, St Chad, **3**, 6-3-10. in Bb. - The Treble was cast by John Martin of Worcester in 1653, The Second was cast by Richard Sander of Stratford in 1719 and the Tenor was cast by William Brooke of Bromsgrove in 1740. *OS: SU 314 614.*
Bishop Wilton, Humbs, **3**, 10cwt.
Bitchfield, Lincs, St Mary Magdalene, **3**, 9cwt. in A. - Hung Dead, *OS: SK 982 284.*
Bitterne, Hants, (R.C.), Christ the King, **2**, - *Chimed Only.*
Blackburn, Lancs, (R.C.), St Alban, **3**.
Blackburn, Lancs, St Jude, **8**, 6-0-25. in Db. - *Chimed Only.*
Blackburn, Lancs, St Mark, **1**, 6cwt. - Unringable.
Blackburn, Ewood, Lancs, **3**, 3cwt. - *Chimed Only.*
Blackburn, Feniscowles, Lancs, Emmanuelle, **1**, 6cwt. in Zb.- No Stay or Slider.
Blackford, Som, Holy Trinity, **3**, - Unringable, *OS: ST 658 262.*
Blackfordby, Leics, St Margaret of Antioch, **1**, 8-1-0. - *OS: SK 330 181.*
Blandford, Dorset, St Mary, **3**, 8cwt. in A#. - *Chimed Only, OS: ST 892 053.*
Blatherwycke, Nothants, Holy Trinity, **1**, 9-3-7. in G#.
Blaydon, Wilts, St Nicholas, **3**, 5cwt. in C. - *OS: SU 283 780.*
Bleasby, Notts, St Mary the Virgin, **2**, 2-2-0. - *OS: SK 718 497.*
Blendworth, Hants, Holy Trinity, **5**, 7-2-2. - Clock Bells the **Tenor** is only hung for Ringing. *OS: SU 711 136.*
Blore, Staffs, St Bartholomew, **3**, - Unringable, *OS: SK 137 493.*
Bloxworth, Dorset, St Andrew, **2**, 6cwt. in C. - *OS: SY 881 946.*
Blubberhouses, N.Yorks, St Andrew, (G.F.), **3**, 3-2-0. - Rehung in June 2001, All these Bells were cast by Taylors in 1878.
Bluntisham, Cambs, St Mary the Virgin, **8**, 13-2-10. in F. - *Chimed Only.*
Blyborough, Lincs, St Alkmund, **1**, 9-0-12. - *OS: SK 933 946.*
Blymhill, Staffs, St Mary, **3**, 5-1-0. in Eb. - Unringable, *OS: SJ 809 122.*
Blyth, Nothumb, St Cuthbert, **8**, 8-1-0. - *Chimed Only.*
Boddington, Glos, St Mary Magdalene, **3**, 9cwt. - *Chimed Only, OS: SO 894 252.*
Boldre, Hants, St John, **8**, 7cwt. in B. - *Chimed Only.*

9

Bole, Notts, St Martin, **3**, 5-2-0. - Unringable, *OS: SK 793 871*.
Bolton, *Gtr Man, Town Hall, 1, 82-0-13., - Clock Bell.*
Bolton-by-Bowland, Lancs, St Peter and St Paul, (G.F.), **3**, 13-3-0., *OS: SD 785 495*.
Bolton-le-Sands, Lancs, Holy Trinity, **3**, 14cwt., *OS: SD 484 688*.
Bolton on Dearne, *S.Yorks, St Andrew the Apostle, 3, 12cwt. - Chimed Only, OS: SE 456 025*.
Bolton Percy, N.Yorks, **3**, 8cwt., - Unringable.
Bolton upon Dearne, S.Yorks, St Andrew, **3**, 12cwt. - Unringable, Derelict, *OS: SE 457 025*.
Bonby, Humbs, St Andrew, **3**, 7cwt., *OS: TA 003 156*.
Boothby Graffoe, Lincs, St Andrew, (G.F.), **3**, 8-1-24. in A. - *OS: SK 987 599*.
Boothby Pagnell, Lincs, St Andrew, **3**, 6-2-0. in B. - *OS: SK 972 308*.
Bootle*, Mers, (R.C.), St James, 1, 30cwt. - This tower also contains Nine Chiming Bells with a Tenor weighing 23-1-0. in F., These are Irish Bells.*
Boscombe. - *See Bournemouth.*
Boscombe, Wilts, St Andrew, **1**, - Unringable, This Bell is in the Church.
Botley, Hants, All Saints, **3**, 6cwt. ***Sun 9 am.***
Botolphs, W. Sussex, St Botolph, **3**, 5-2-0 in Bb., - Medieval Ring of three by the same founder.
Bottesford, Humbs, St Peter, **3**, 6-3-03., - *OS: SE 899 070*.
Bottesford, Lincs, St Peter ad Vincula, **3**, 7-0-21. - Rehung in a Six Bell Frame, *OS: SE 898 070*.
Boughton, Norf, All Saints, **3**, - Unringable, *OS: TF 699 022*.
Boughton Malherbe, Kent, St Nicholas, **3**, 8-2-0. - Unringable, *OS: TQ 882 496*.
Boultham, *Lincs, Holy Cross, 8, 2-2-27. in E. - Chimed Only.*
Bourton-on-Dunsmore, Warwicks, St Peter, **3**, 5-1-12. in Bb. - Unringable, The Treble and Second were both cast by Thomas Newcombe of Leicester in 1580, Also the Tenor was cast by Taylor and Sons of Oxford in 1827. *OS: SP 436 703*.
Bournemouth, *Dorset, College of Further Education, 1, 30cwt., - Chimed Only.*
Bournemouth, Dorset, Holy Epiphany, **1**, 8-2-24. in Bb. - *OS: SZ 093 944*.
Bournemouth, Boscombe, Dorset, (R.C.), Corpus Christi, **1**, 20-2-26.
Bournemouth, Boscombe, Dorset, St Clement, **1**, 17-2-17. in F#. - *OS: SZ 116 906*.
Bournemouth, Ensbury Park, Dorset, (R.C.), Our Lady of Victories and St Bernadette, **1**, 4cwt.
Bournemouth, *Moordown*, *Dorset, St John the Baptist, 8, 6cwt. - Chimed Only.*
Bournemouth, *Throop*, *Dorset, 10, 4cwt. - Automatic Chiming.*
Bournemouth, Westbourne, Dorset, St Ambrose, **1**, 19-1-7. in Eb. - *OS: SZ 071 909*.
Bournville, *W.Mids, Bournville Schools, 48, 64-0-18. in A#. - Carillon.*
Bournville, W.Mids, (Greek Orthodox), St Lazar, **3**, 9-1-23. in Ab., - These Bells are recessed in to the Headstock and are Counterbalanced with No Stays or Sliders, Cast by Taylors in 1967, *OS: SP 034 809*.
Boveney, Berks, St John the Baptist, **3**, 7-2-9. - Unringable.
Boveney, Bucks, St Mary Magdelen, **3**, 5cwt. - *OS: SU 940 776*.
Bovingdon, *Herts, 3, - Hung Dead.*
Bowerchalke, Wilts, Holy Trinity, **3**, 18cwt. - The Second and the Tenor were both cast by the Salisbury Foundry. *OS: SU 021 233*.
Bowers Gifford, Essex, St John and St Margaret, (G.F.), **3**, 9cwt. - *OS: TQ 755 873*.
Boxworth, Cambs, **1**. Unringable.
Brackenfield, Derbys, Holy Trinity, (G.F.), **3**, 5-0-25. in D#. - Unringable., *OS: SK 373 590*.
Brackley, Northants, St James, **1**, 3cwt. in G.
Bradenham, *Bucks, St Botolph, 3, 4cwt. - Chimed Only, OS: SU 828 972.*
Bradfield St Clare, *Suffolk, St Clare, (G.F.), 3, 8-1-01. in G#. - Chimed Only, OS: TL 910 578.*
Bradford, *W. Yorks, (R.C.), St Patrick, 5, 3-0-7., - Chimed Only.*
Bradford, *W.Yorks, Town Hall, 13, 87-0-7. in A. - Chimed Only.*
Bradley, W.Yorks, Gymnasium, Formally St Thomas, **1**, 13-2-26. in F. - *OS: SE 172 202*.
Bradwell, *Derbys, St Barnabas, 8, 39-1-5. in B. - Chimed Only.*
Bradwell, Norfolk, St Nicholas, (G.F.), **3**, 10-0-19. in G. - Round tower. - *OS: TG 503 038*.
Braishfield, Hants, All Saints, **3**, 3cwt.

Braithwell, S.Yorks, St James, 3, 5-1-26. - *Chimed Only, OS: SK 534 947.*
Bramcote, Notts, St Michael and All Angels, (G.F.), **3**, 5-2-22. in B
Bramerton, *Norfolk, St Peter, (G.F.),* **8**, *5-1-0. in C.* - *The Back* **Three** *are only hung for Ringing the rest are Chimed Only.* **OS: TG 296 047.**
Bramfield, *Herts, St Andrew, 2, 5cwt. in B.* - *Unringable, The* **Tenor** *is only Hung for Ringing.*
Brampton, *Derbys, St Thomas, 8, 17cwt. in F.* - *Chimed Only.*
Brampton Abbots, Herefords, St Michael, **3**, 5-1-0. in D. - *OS: SO 601 265.*
Bramshall, Staffs, St Laurance, 3, - *OS: SK 061 332.*
Bramshaw, Hants, St Peter, **2**, 2-1-0. - The Treble was cast in 1250.
Brandesburton, Humbs, **3**.
Branksome, *Dorset, (R.C.), 1, - Chimed Only.*
Brantingham, *Humbs, 3, 9-3-17.* - *Hung Dead, Chimed Only.*
Bratoft, Lincs, St Peter and St Paul, (G.F.), **3**, 8cwt. - Anti-Clockwise., *OS: TF 474 641.*
Brattleby, *Lincs, St Cuthbert, 3, 4cwt.* - *Chimed Only, OS: SK 948 818.*
Braunstone, Leics, St Peter, **3**, 2-3-9. - *OS: SK 555 029.*
Brayton, N.Yorks, **3**.
Breage, *Corn, St Breaca, 8, 6-0-10. in C.* - *Chimed Only.*
Bream, Glos, St James, **1**, 4cwt. - *OS: SO 601 056.*
Brean, Somerset, St Briget, (G.F.), **3**.
Brenzett, Kent, St Eanswith, **3**, 11-2-0. in Ab. - Unringable., *OS: TR 005 277.*
Brentford, *Middlesex, St Paul, 6, 7-1-8. in A.* - *Chimed Only.*
Brentwood, *Essex, (R.C.), Brentwood Cathedral, 1, 20cwt., - Swing Chimed Only.*
Brereton, *Staffs, St Michael and All Angels, 5, 10cwt.* - *Hung Dead, Chimed Only.*
Bressington, *Norfolk, St John the Baptist, 5, 12cwt.* - *Chimed Only.*
Bretby, *Derbys, St Wystan, 5, 4cwt.* - *Chimed Only.*
Bricklehampton, Worcs, **3**.
Bridge, Kent, St Peter, **3**, 10cwt. in G. - Unringable., *OS: TR 183 541.*
Bridge Sollers, Herefords, St Andrew, **2**, 3cwt. in F. - *OS: SO 414 425.*
Bridlington, Humbs, Christ Church, **1**.
Bridlington, Humbs, Holy Trinity, **3**, 14cwt.
Briercliffe, Lancs, **1**, 4cwt.
Brierfield, Lancs, **1**, 5cwt. - Metal wheel No Stay or Slider.
Brierley, S.Yorks, St Paul, **1**, 6cwt. in D#. - *OS: SF 411 111.*
Brigham, Cumb, St Bridget, **3**, - *OS: NY 087 309.*
Brighton, E.Sussex, St Paul, **1**, 41-1-13., - This Bell was cast by Mears in 1853.
Brighton, Preston, E.Sussex, St Peter, (G.F.), **3**, 5cwt. in B. - Anti-Clockwise, *OS: TQ 306 066.*
Brigsley, *Humbs, St Helen, 3, 6-0-13.* - *Hung Dead, OS: TA 255 019.*
Brimfield, Herefords, St Michael, **3**, 7-2-0. in A. - *OS: SO 527 676.*
Brimington, Derbys, St Michael and All Angels, **1**, - Steel Bell., Unringable, *OS: SK 405 736.*
Brindle, Lancs, (R.C.), St Joseph, **1**, - This bell is Hung Outside on the Roof of the Building.
Brinsop, Herefords, St George, **3**, 6-2-0. in Db. - *OS: SO 442 448.*
Bristol, *Avon, Cathedral Church with St George, (Central Tower) 4, 20cwt., - Swing Chimed Only These Bells were cast by Purdue in 1670, (N.W. Tower) 8, 21-0-1. in Eb.*
Bristol, *Avon, St George, 3, - Clock Bells, Also 1, - Service Bell and 10, 20cwt. in Eb.*
Bristol, *Avon, St Nicholas, 1, 29-3-22., - Chimed Only.*
Bristol, Clifton, *Avon, (R.C.), Clifton Cathedral, 2, - Automatic Chiming Only.*
Bristol, Clifton, Avon, Christ Church, **1**, 4-0-16. in F. - Unringable, *OS: ST 570 734.*
Bristol, Clifton, Avon, *College Chapel, 5, 3-3-0. in E.* - **Tenor** *only Hung for Ringing the rest are Hung Dead. OS: ST 572 737.*
Bristol, Easton, Avon, Greek Orthodox, St Peter and St Paul, **1**, 2-3-0. in F#.
Bristol, Portland Square, Avon, St Paul, **1**, 26cwt. in Db.
Bristol, Sea Mills, Avon, St Edyth, **1**, 12-2-10. in F#.
Bristol, Two Mile Hill, Avon, St Michael, **1**, 1-3-0. in G#.

Bristol , Tyndale , Avon, Baptist Chapel, 5, 9cwt. in G. - Hung Dead, Clock Chime.
Bristol, Avon, Bristol University, **1**, 191-1-19. - (Great George) This Bell is Counterbalanced with No Stay or Slider, Also this Bell was cast by Taylors in 1925.
Brixton Deverhill, Wilts, St Michael, **1**, - This Bell was cast by the Salisbury Foundry in 1400. *OS: ST 862 388.*
Brocco Bank, S.Yorks, St Augustine, 5, 14cwt. - The **Tenor** *is only Hung for Ringing the rest are Hung Dead.* *OS: SK 333 859.*
Brockhall, Northants, St Peter and St Paul, **3**, 3cwt. - *OS: SP 633 627.*
Brockham Green , Surrey, Christ Church, 8, 6-3-16. in B. - Chimed Only.
Brockhampton, Herefords, All Saints (Old Church), **3**, 5cwt. in Eb. - *OS: SO 595 312.*
Brockhampton, Herefords, All Saints (New Church), **2**, 7-0-15. - *OS: SO 595 322.*
Brocklesby, Lincs, All Saints, **1**, 8-1-7. - *OS: TA 140 113.*
Brockley , Gtr London, St Peter, 5, 7cwt. in B. - Chimed Only.
Brockley, Suffolk, St Andrew, **3**, - *OS: TL 834 704.*
Brodsworth, S.Yorks, St Michael and All Angels, **3**, 4-1-0. - Unringable, *OS: SE 507 073.*
Brokenborough, Wilts, St John the Baptist, **1**, - This Bell was cast by John Rudhall in 1801. *OS: ST 918 896.*
Bromley , Kent, 6, 2cwt. in G#. - Chimed Only.
Brompton, N.Yorks, St Thomas, **3**, 7cwt. - *OS: SE 373 964.*
Brook , Kent, St Mary, 3, 6-2-0. - Hung Dead, OS: TR 066 443.
Brook Green , Gtr London, (R.C.), 8, 13-3-5. in F., - Chimed Only.
Brookthorpe, Glos, St Swithin, **2**, 17cwt. in E. - *OS: SO 834 123.*
Brotherton, N.Yorks, **3**, 6cwt., - Unringable.
Broomfield, Kent, St Margaret, (G.F.), **3**, 4-2-0. in C#. - *OS: TQ 840 525.*
Brougham , Cumb, 2, 1-2-0., - Lever Chimed Only.
Broughton, Oxon, St Mary the Virgin, 5, 17-0-21 in F. - The **Tenor** *is only Hung for Ringing the rest are Chimed.* *OS: SP 419 383.*
Broughton Gifford, Wilts, St Mary, **1**, 10-?-0. - *OS: ST 875 641.*
Broughton with Elslack, N.Yorks, All Saints, (G.F.), **3**, 8cwt. - *OS: SD 934 505.*
Broxbourn, Herts, Council Offices, **1**, 2cwt.
Bruntingthorpe, Leics, St Mary, **3**, 5-2-0. - *OS: SP 601 898.*
Brushford, Devon, St Mary the Virgin, **3**, 9cwt. - Unringable, Bells taken Down, *OS: SS 670 070.*
Brushford Barton, Devon, St Nicholas, **3**, 9cwt. - *OS: SS 677 077.*
Buckfastleigh, Devon, (R.C.), Buckfast Abbey of St Mary, **1**, 149-0-18. - This Bell is Counterbalanced with No Stay or Slider and is called "Hosannah", **14**, 41-1-3. in C. Including a Sharp Second and Flat Sixth., *OS: SX 741 674.*
Buckland, Bucks, All Saints, (G.F.), **3**, 5cwt. - *OS: SP 888 125.*
Buckland , Herts, St Andrew, 6, 6-2-22. in B#. - Chimed Only.
Buckland in Dover , Kent, St Andrew, 6, 2-3-27. - Chimed Only.
Bucknell , Oxon, St Peter, 3, 9cwt. - Chimed Only.
Bucknell, Salop, St Mary, (G.F.), **3**, - Anti-Clockwise.
Budbrooke , Warwicks, St Michael, 3, 5cwt. - Swing Chiming, The Tenor was cast by Edward Newcombe and Hugh Watts of Leicester in 1600., OS: SP 258 656.
Buildwas, Salop, Holy Trinity, **3**, 3cwt. - Anti-Clockwise., *OS: SJ 637 048.*
Bulford, Wilts, St John the Evangelist, **1**, 11cwt. - *OS: SU 167 433.*
Bulkworthy, Devon, St Michael, **2**, 2cwt. - Unringable., These Bells were cast in the 14th Century, *OS: SS 395 142.*
Bullington, Hants, St Michael and All Angels, **3**, - Derelict.
Bulmer, Herefords, St John the Baptist, **3**, 5-3-0. in C. - *OS: SO 397 429.*
Bulmer, N.Yorks, St Martin, (G.F.), **3**, 4cwt. - *OS: SE 699 677.*
Buntingford, Layston, Herts, St Bartholomew, **3**, 10-2-0. in G., - Unringable, *OS: TL 369 301.*
Buntingford , Herts, (R.C.), St Richard, 2, 5-5-13., - Swing Chimed Only, Steel Wheels.
Burcombe , Wilts, St John the Baptist, 1, 3cwt. - Chimed Only, OS: SU 071 308.

Burford, Salop, St Mary, 5, 7cwt. - *Chimed Only.*
Burghwallis, S.Yorks, St Helen, **3**, 6cwt. - Unringable., *OS: SE 537 121.*
Burley, Leics, Holy Cross, **1**, - Bell Cracked.
Burnby, Humbs, **3**.
Burnley, Habergham, Lancs, **1**, 16cwt.
Burnley, Lancs, St John, **1**, 22cwt.
Burnley, Lancs, Town Hall, *1, 24-1-21., - Chimed Only.*
Burpham, W.Sussex, St Mary, *5, 21-1-3. in Eb. - Chimed Only.*
Burslem, Staffs, (R.C.), St Joseph, **1**, 40cwt.
Burton Lazers, Leics, St James, (G.F.), **2**, - *OS: SK 768 169.*
Burton-Le-Coggles, Lincs, St Thomas a Becket, (G.F.), **3**, 8-0-27. in Ab. - *OS: SK 979 259.*
Burton Overy, Leics, St Andrew, *3, 8-2-0. - Chimed Only, OS: SP 678 982.*
Burton Pidsea, Humb, **3**, 10cwt.
Burton upon Trent, Staffs, Unknown, **1**, 22cwt. - *OS: SK 23 23.*
Bury, Cambs, The Holy Cross, (G.F.), **3**, 7cwt. - *Sun 10.45-11.15 am (1st & 3rd), Thurs 7.30 pm., OS: TL 287 838.*
Burythorpe, N.Yorks, **3**.
Bury St Edmunds, Suffolk, St Mary, *8, 23-3-0. - Chimed Only.*
Bush End, Essex, St John the Evangelist, **3**, 2-2-0. in F. - No Stays or Sliders., *OS: TQ 548 200.*
Bushey, Herts, Royal Masonic School, *3, 4-3-13. in C#., - **The Tenor** is Hung for Ringing and the rest are Hung Dead.*
Bussage, Glos, St Michael and All Angels, **1**, 4-2-0. - *OS: SO 883 036.*
Butterleigh, Devon, St Matthew, (G.F.), **3**, 5cwt. - *OS: SS 975 082.*
Buttermere, Wilts, St James, **1**, - Hung in the Central Turret, *OS: SU 340 609.*
Byford, Herfords, St John the Baptist, **3**, 5-3-0. in C., - *OS: SO 397 429.*
Cadeby, Leics, All Saints, *3, 2-1-6. - Chimed Only., OS: SK 427 023.*
Cainscross, Glos, St Matthew, **1**, 3-2-0. - *OS: SO 832 049.*
Caldbeck, Cumb, St Mungo, **3**, - *OS: NY 325 399.*
Caldecote, Cambs, St Michael and All Angels, **3**, - Unringable, *OS: TL 348 563.*
Caldecote, Warwicks, St Theobald and St Chad, *3 - Chimed Only, Steel Bells, These Bells were All cast By Naylor Vickers of Sheffield in 1868.*
Calder Vale, Lancs, St John the Evangelist, **1**, - *OS: SD 538 463.*
Calow, Derbys, St Peter, *6, 5cwt. in C. - Chimed Only.*
Camberley, Surrey, (R.C.), St Tarcisius, *12, 1-2-7. in C. - Chimed Only.*
Cambo, Northumberland, Holy Trinity, **1**, 10cwt.
Cameley, Avon, St James, *5, 10cwt. - Chimed Only.*
Cambridge, Cambs, All Saints, **3**, - *OS: TL 451 587.*
Cambridge, Cambs, St Matthew, **3**, - Unringable, *OS: TL 461 585.*
Canon Frome, Herefords, St James, **3**, 6-1-0. in C. - *OS: SO 645 435.*
Cantley, S.Yorks, St Wilfred, *3, 4-3-18. - Lever Chimed Only, OS: SE 618 015.*
Canturbury, Kent, Cathedral and Metropolitical Church of Christ, (Arundel Tower), *5, 9-2-2. in F#. Clock Chime, Also 1, 62-2-9., Automatically Swing Chimed Only, (Central Tower), 1, 8cwt. in B., Hung Dead, (Oxford Tower), 14, 34-3-4. in C#., Including a Extra Treble and Flat Sixth.*
Canturbury, Kent, St Gregory the Great, *3, 2-0-2. - Lost Chime the Bells were transferred to Wormshill, OS: TR 155 582.*
Canterbury, Kent, St Margaret, *3, 6cwt. in F. - Chimed Only, OS: TR 158 577.*
Canterbury, Kent, St Martin, *3, 6cwt. in Bb. - Chimed Only, OS: TR 159 578.*
Canterbury, Kent, St Paul, *3, 6-2-7. in C. - Chimed Only, OS: TR 154 577.*
Canwick, Lincs, All Saints, **2**, 4-2-0. in E. - *OS: SK 988 698.*
Capel St Mary, Suffolk, St Mary the Virgin, *5, 9-3-11. in G. - Chimed Only.*
Carlby, Lincs, St Stephen, **1**, 3cwt. - *OS: TF 049 139.*
Carleton in Craven, N.Yorks, St Mary the Virgin, *3, 8cwt. - Hung Dead., OS: SD 973 498.*
Carlisle, Cumb, St Aiden, **2**.

13

Carlton, S.Yorks, St John the Evangelist, 1, 14-2-14. in G. - *OS: SF 366 102.*
Carlton Curlieu, Leics, St Mary the virgin, 3, 5-2-0. - Unringable, *OS: SP 693 972.*
Carlton-le-Moorland, Lincs, St Mary the Virgin, 3, 5-2-7. in C#. - *OS: SK 908 589.*
Carlton-in-Lindrick, Notts, St John the Evangelist, 3, 9-2-0. - *OS: SK 588 839.*
Carlton Scroop, Lincs, St Nicholas, 3, 8cwt. in Bb. - *Chimed Only, OS: SK 947 451.*
Carnaby, Humbs, 3.
Carrington, Lincs, St Paul, 1, 5cwt. - *OS: TF 113 552.*
Carshalton, Surrey, (R.C.), Convent of the Daughters of the Cross, 8, 2-1-8. in G., Chimed Only.
Casterton, Cumb, Holy Trinity, (G.F.), 6, 8cwt. in Bb. - *Chimed Only exept the front Three Bells with a Tenor of 6cwt but Unringable, OS: SD 63 79.*
Castle Bytham, Lincs, St James, 3, 7-1-06. in B. - *OS: SK 988 183.*
Castle Combe, Wilts, St Andrew, 1, 32cwt. - This Bell was cast by Thomas Rudhall in 1766, Also there is a Service Bell cast in 1380 and weights 1-1-0. , *OS: ST 845 776.*
Castleford, N.Yorks, St Michael, 3, 1-3-0. - *Swing Chiming Only, These Bells were All Cast by Taylors in 1929. OS: SE 420 253.*
Castle Frome, Herefords, St Michael, 3, 5-2-0. in C. - *OS: SO 667 458.*
Castlethorpe, Bucks, St Simon and St Jude, 1, 5-2-6. - No Stay or Slider.
Caton, Lancs, St Paul, 8, 8-3-4. in A. - *Chimed Only.*
Catsfield, E.Sussex, 6, 9-2-12. in F#. - *Chimed Only.*
Catthorpe, Leics, St Thomas, 3, 6cwt. - *OS: SP 552 781.*
Caunton, Notts, St Andrew, (G.F.), 3, 7-3-9 in Ab.
Caversham, Berks, (R.C.), Our Lady and St Anne, 4, 5-2-0. in C. - *The Tenor is only Hung for Ringing the rest are Chimed Only. OS: SU 719 748.*
Cayhurst, Bucks, St Peter, 1, 6-2-9. in Bb.
Cayton, N.Yorks, St John the Baptist, (G.F.), 3, 9-3-24. in G#., **Tues,** *OS: TA 057 833.*
Chaddesden, Derbys, St Mary, 3, 10cwt. in G. - Anti-Clockwise, Unringable., *OS: SK 384 369.*
Chadwell, Leics, St Mary, (G.F.), 3, 6-3-0. in Bb., - Unringable, *OS. SK 782 247.*
Chaldon, Surrey, St Peter and St Paul, 6, 6cwt - *Chimed Only.*
Chaldon Herring, Dorset, St Nicholas, 3, 6-2-0. in C. - Unringable, *OS: SY 790 831.*
Chalk, Kent, St Mary, 3, 6cwt.
Chalton, Hants, St Michael and All Angels, (G.F.), 3, 6cwt. - *OS: SU 732 159.*
Chalvington, E.Sussex, St Bartholomew, (G.F.), 3, 2cwt. - *OS: TQ 519 093.*
Charfield, Avon, St James, 1, 15-2-0. - Redundant Church, *OS: ST 719 911.*
Charlton, Wilts, All Saints, 2, 1-1-0.
Charlton Musgrove, Som, St John, 3, 9cwt. - *OS: ST 730 318.*
Charmouth, Dorset, St Andrew, 3, 9-2-0. in A. - Anti-Clockwise., *OS: SY 364 936.*
Charsfield, Suffolk, St Peter, 5, 10cwt. - *Chimed Only.*
Cawood, N.Yorks, 3.
Chearsley, Bucks, St Nicholas, (G.F.), 3, 10-0-10. in A. - Also Service Bell Pre Reformation., *OS: SP 720103.*
Chelsham, Surrey, 1.
Cheltenham, Glos, Christ Church, 1, 17-1-0. - *OS: SO 939 223.*
Cheltenham, Glos, (R.C.), St Gregory, 2, - *Swing Chiming Only.*
Cheltenham, Glos, St Luke and St John, 1, 3cwt. - *OS: SO 952 218.*
Cheltenham, Glos, St Paul, 1, - *OS: SO 941 234.*
Cheltenham, Pittville, Glos, All Saints, 1, 11-0-10. - *OS: SO 948 232.*
Chelwood, Somerset, St Leonard, (G.F.), 1, 8cwt. in A.
Cherhill, Wilts, St James, 3, 10cwt. - The Second was cast by the Bristol Foundry in 1450. *OS: SU 041 703.*
Cherry Burton, Humb, 3, 6cwt.
Chesham Bois, Bucks, St Leonard, 3, 5-1-0 in C#. - No Stays or Sliders, Tenor Cast in 1470-1480., *OS: SU 969 999.*
Cheshunt, Herts, Broxbourne Council Offices, 1, 2cwt.

14

Chessington, Surrey, St Mary the Virgin, 8, 6cwt. in B. - *Chimed Only.*
Chester, Ches, Cathedral Church of Christ and the B.V.M., (Central Tower), **1**, (Detatched tower), **13**, 24-3-0. in D., Including a Flat Sixth, *OS: SJ 406 664.*, *Monday.*
Chester, Ches, St John the Baptist, 8, 14cwt. - *Chimed Only.*
Chester Le Street, Durham, St Mary and St Cuthbert, **1**, - Also in the tower, **8**, 19-0-2. in E.
Chesterton, Cambs, St Michael, (G.F.), **3**, 8cwt. in B. - Anti-Clockwise., *OS: TL 126 954.*
Chesterton, Oxon, St Mary, **3**, 11-2-23. in F#. - Anti-Clockwise. - *Wed*, *OS: SP 562 214.*
Chesterton, Warwicks, St Giles, **3**, 8-2-0. - Unringable, All these Bells were cast by Abraham Rudhall in 1705, *OS: SP 358 582.*
Chetnole, Dorset, St Peter, (G.F.), **3**, 8cwt. in A, *OS: ST 603 083.*
Chettle, Dorset, St Mary, **3**, 8-2-0. in A. - Unringable, *OS: ST 952 133.*
Cheveley, Cambs, St Mary and the Holy Cross of Heaven, 5, 14-0-17. in F. - *Chimed Only.*
Chichester, W.Sussex, Cathedral Church of the Holy Trinity, (Central Tower), **1**, - Swing Chiming Only, (Detached Tower), *1, 73cwt., - Clock Bell, Also 8, 18-1-12. in Eb.*
Chicklade, Wilts, All Saints, **1**, 2-1-0.
Chilbolton, Hants, St Mary the Less, (G.F.), **3**, 7cwt. in B. - Ropes fall in a straight line, *OS: SU 394 402.*
Chilton, Bucks, Blessed Virgin Mary, **3**, 7-3-14. in A, - Ropes fall in a straight line, *OS: SP 687 116.*
Chingford, Gtr London, St Peter and St Paul, 6, 5-0-13. - *Chimed Only.*
Chislehampton, Oxon, **2**.
Chorleywood, Herts, Christ Church, **1**, 2-0-3. in G.
Christ Church, Glos, Christ Church, **1**, 5-2-0. in C#. - *OS: SO 572 130.*
Christon, Som, Blessed Virgin Mary, **2**, - *OS: ST 379 573.*
Church Knowle, Dorset, St Peter, (G.F.), **3**, 5-2-0 in C. - The Treble was cast by James Wells of Aldbourne, Wilts in 1804. Also The Second and the Tenor were Recast by Henry Bond 11 and Thomas Bond of Burford, Oxon in 1928. **Mon 7.30pm and Sun 9am (1st) 6pm (4th),** *OS: SY 941 819.*
Church Westcote, Glos, St Mary the Virgin, (G.F.), **3**.
Cinderford, Glos, St John the Evangelist, 8, 8-1-14. - *Chimed Only.*
Cinderhill, Notts, **3**, - Unringable.
Clanfield, Hants, **2**.
Clannaborough, Devon, St Petrock, 8, 7-3-11. in B. - *Chimed Only.*
Clapham, N.Yorks, St James the Apostle, (G.F.), **3**, 10-3-21. in G., *OS: SD 746 695.*
Clarborough, Notts, St John the Baptist, (G.F.), **3**, 10cwt., *OS: SK 734 834.*
Claydon, Oxon, St James the Great, (G.F.), **3**, 6-1-19 in Bb, *OS: SP 456 501.*
Clay Coton, Northants, St Andrew, **3**, 7-2-0. in Bb. - Unringable, *OS: SP 593 770.*
Clayhanger, Devon, St Peter, 3, 8cwt. - *Swing Chiming Only on Half Wheels, Unringable, Derelict Church*, *OS: ST 022 229.*
Clayton, W.Sussex, **2**.
Clayton Le Moors, Lancs, **1**, 12cwt. - Unringable.
Cleckheaton, W.Yorks, White Chapel, 8, 2-1-18. in F#. - *Chimed Only.*
Cleethorpes, Humbs, St Peter, **1**, 7cwt. - *OS: TA 305 087.*
Cleethorpes, - *See Old Clee.*
Clifton, - *See Bristol.*
Clifton Campville, Staffs, St Andrew, 6, 9-2-9. in G. - *Chimed Only.*
Clifton Hampden, Oxon, St Michael and All Angels, 5, 6-2-16. in B. - *Chimed Only.*
Climping, W.Sussex, **2**.
Clipsham, Leics, St Mary, **3**, 6cwt. - Unringable., *OS: SK 970 164.*
Clitheroe, Lancs, St James, 10, 7-0-19. in B. - *Chimed Only.*
Cloford, Som, St Mary, **3**, 7cwt. in B. - Unringable, *OS: ST 727 440.*
Clopton, Nothants, St Peter, **1**.
Cloughton, N.Yorks, 3, 2cwt., - *Lever Chimed Only.*

Clumber, Notts, St Mary the Virgin, **1**, 30-0-1. in D. - *OS: SK 627 756.*
Clungunford, Salop, St Cuthbert, **3**, 7cwt.
Clyst St Mary, Devon, 3, - *Hung Dead, Chimed Only.*
Coates, Glos, St Mary, **2**, 11cwt.
Coates, Glos, St Matthew, **1**, 9cwt. - *OS: SO 973 010.*
Coberley, Glos, St Giles, **3**, 6cwt. - *OS: SO 966 158.*
Cockfield, Suffolk, St Peter, 6, 12cwt. - *Chimed Only.*
Codford St Mary, Wilts, St Mary, **3**, - *OS: ST 971 396.*
Codnor, Derbys, St James, **1**, 1-3-0. - Derelict Church, *OS: SK 418 488.*
Cogges, Oxon, St Mary, **2**, 5-3-19.
Colan, Cornwall, **3**.
Colchester, Essex, Town Hall, 1, 25cwt., - *Chimed Only.*
Colchester, Stanway, Essex, All Saints, 3, 6-3-8. in G. - *This Church is now in Ruins in the middle of Colchester Zoo the Bells were transferred to Shrub End.*
Cold Brayfeild, Bucks, St Mary, **3**, 3-3-24. - Unringable. - *OS: SP 929 523.*
Cold Overton, Leics, St John the Baptist, (G.F.), **3**, 10cwt. in G#. - Anti-Clockwise., *OS: SK 810 102.*
Collyweston, Northants, St Andrew, **1**, 5-2-4.
Colne, Lancs, Christ Church, **1**, 4cwt.
Coln Rogers, Glos, St Andrew, **3**, 6cwt. in B. - *OS: SP 088 097.*
Colwich, Staffs, (R.C.), St Mary's Abbey, 8, 2-0-24. in F#. - *Chimed Only.*
Combe, Berks, St Swithin, **3**, 8cwt. in A. - *OS: SU 368 607.*
Combe Pyne, Devon, St Mary the Virgin, **3**, 5cwt. - *OS: SY 290 924.*
Combe Raleigh, Devon, St Nicholas, (G.F.), **3**, 7cwt. - *OS: ST 158 022.*
Combrook, Warwicks, 3, 2-1-16. - *Hung Dead, All Cast by Mears and Stainbank of London in 1867.*
Combwich, Som, St Peter, 5, 8cwt. - *Chimed Only.*
Compton, Hants, All Saints, (G.F.), **3**, 3-?-9. in C#. *Sun 10.10 am (2nd, 3rd and 4th), 6.10 pm (1st and 4th)., OS: SU 468 256.*
Compton, Surrey, St Nicholas, (G.F.), **3**, 6cwt.
Compton Beauchamp, Oxon, St Swithin, **1**, 3-1-17. in F. - 14th Century Bell.
Compton Dundon, Som, St Andrew, 5, 19-3-0. - *Chimed Only.*
Compton Pauncefoot, Som, Blessed Virgin Mary, **3**, 3-2-0. - Unringable, *OS: ST 645 262.*
Cookbury, Devon, St John the Baptist and the Seven Maccabes, **3**, 7cwt. in Ab. - *OS: SS 407 060.*
Cooling, Kent, St James, 3, 6cwt. - *Chimed Only, Redundant Church, OS: TQ 756 759.*
Coombe, Wilts, St Swithin, **3**, 8cwt. in A. - Second Early 15th Century.
Copthorne, W.Sussex, St John the Evangelist, 6, 6-3-14. in B. - *Chimed Only.*
Cornard Magna, Suffolk, St Andrew, 5, 8-3-25. - *Chimed Only.*
Corsham, Wilts, St Mary, **3**, 3-3-0. - The Treble was cast by the Salisbury Foundry in 1603.
Corston, Wilts, All Saints, **2**, - The Treble is a Ancient Bell. *OS: ST 925 844.*
Cossal, Notts, St Catherine, **2**, 2cwt. - *OS: SK 483 423.*
Coston, Leics, St Andrew, **3**, 6-1-25. - Unringable, *OS: SK 848 222.*
Cothall, Herts, 2, - *Lever Chimed Only.*
Cotham, Notts, St Michael, **2**, 3-0-1. in D#. - *OS: SK 796 474.*
Cotmanhay, Derbys, Christ Church, **1**, 2-0-11. - *OS: SK 460 438.*
Cotton, Staffs, (R.C.), 1, - *Chimed Only.*
Coulston, Wilts, St Thomas a Becket, **1**, - *OS: ST 950 541.*
Countisbury, Devon, St John the Evangelist, **3**, 6cwt. - Unringable, *OS: SS 747 498.*
Covenham St Bartholomew, Lincs, St Bartholomew, 3, 5cwt. - *Chimed Only, Redundant Church, OS: TF 337 947.*
Covenham St Mary, Lincs, St Mary, 3, 7cwt. - *Chimed Only, OS: TF 340 943.*
Coverham, N.Yorks, Holy Trinity, **3**, 7cwt., - Unringable, Redundant Church.
Covington, Cambs, All Saints, (G.F.), **3**, 7cwt. in G. - Anti-Clockwise. - *OS: TL 054 708.*

Coventry, W.Mids, St John the Baptist, **5**, 9-3-21. - *Chimed Only, The Third Bell was cast by John Hose in 1350 and the Fourth Bell was cast by John of Stafford in 1360.*
Coventry, Foleshill, W.Mids, St Laurance, **3**, 8cwt. - Unringable, All these Bells were cast by Hugh Watts of Leicester, The Treble in 1635, The Second and Tenor in 1616.
Cowes, Isle of White, Holy Trinity, **8**, 10-2-0. - *Chimed Only.*
Cowfold, Parkminster, *W.Sussex, (R.C.), (Carthusian Order), Charter House of St Hugh,* **1**, *21-3-11. in Eb. - Also Five Clock bells with the Tenor weighing 14-2-20. in F.*
Cowling, N.Yorks, Holy Trinity, **5**, 3-2-0. - *The* **Tenor** *is only Hung for Ringing the Rest are Hung Dead.* ***OS: SD 968 432.***
Cowthorpe, N.Yorks, St Michael, **3**, 2cwt. - *Swing Chiming, Redundant Church.*
Cowton, N.Yorks, **3**, 7cwt.
Coxwold, N.Yorks, St Michael, **3**, 8cwt. - Unringable, ***OS: SE 533 772.***
Cradley Heath, W.Mids, (Methodist Church), Graingers Lane, **8**, 12-0-19. - *Chimed Only.*
Cragg Vale, W.Yorks, St John the Baptist, **1**, 4-2-0.
Crakehall, N.Yorks, St Gregory, **6**, 1-2-0. - *Chimed Only.*
Crambe, N.Yorks, **3**.
Cranoe, Leics, St Michael, **2**, 3cwt. - Unringable, ***OS: SP 761 953.***
Cranwell, Lincs, Royal Air Force College, **6**, 24-2-16. in Eb. - *Automatic Chiming.*
Craswall, Herefords, St Mary, **1**, 1-2-0. - ***OS: SO 281 363.***
Crathorne, N.Yorks, All Saints, **3**, 6-3-03. in C., Also Sanctus Bell Hung for Ringing., ***OS: NZ 443 075.***
Crayke, N.Yorks, **3**, 4cwt., - Unringable.
Credenhill, Herefords, St Mary, **3**, 6cwt. in C. - ***OS: SO 451 439.***
Cressage, Salop, Christ Church, **8**, 3-3-19. - *Chimed Only.*
Cressbrook, Derbys, St John the Evangelist, **2**, - Unringable, ***OS: SK 171 732.***
Cricklade, Wilts, St Mary, **3**, - All the Bells were Cast by the Gloucester Foundry by Thomas Rudhall in 1779. ***OS: SU 099 935.***
Croft, Herefords, St Michael, **1**, 3-2-0. in E. - ***OS: SO 450 606.***
Croft, N.Yorks, St Peter, **3**, 5-3-10. - Unringable, ***OS: NZ 289 099.***
Cromford, Derbys, St Mary, **1**, - Unringable.
Cromwell, Notts, St Giles, (G.F.), **3**, 8-2-0. - ***OS: SK 799 615.***
Crook, Cumb, **2**, - One Bell Cracked.
Crook, Durham, (R.C.), Our Lady Immaculate and St Cuthbert, **8**, 12cwt. in G. - *Only the* **Number** *Seven is Hung for Ringing the rest are Chimed.* ***OS: NZ 168 358.***
Crosby Ravensworth, Cumbria, St Laurence, **3**, 8cwt. - ***OS: NY 622 144.***
Crowle, Humbs, St Oswald, **3**, 12cwt. in F. - Unringable, ***OS: SE 772 130.***
Croxley Green, Herts, All Saints, **2**, - Lever Chimed Only.
Croydon, Surrey, Town Hall, **5**, 37-0-4., - *Chimed Only.*
Crudwell, Wilts, All Saints, **5**, 9-3-18. in G. - *Chimed Only.*
Crundale, Kent, St Mary the Virgin, **3**, 8cwt. in A. - Manual Chime, Tenor is Hung for Ringing, ***OS: TR 086 486.***
Cullmington, Salop, All Saints, **3**, 7-1-01. - ***OS: SO 493 820.***
Cumrew, Cumbs, St Mary, **1**, 7cwt. - ***OS: NY 549 507.***
Curdworth, Warwicks, St Nicholas and St Peter, **3**, 7-2-0. in A. - Tenor cast by a Midlands Bell Founder in 14th Century, The Treble was cast by John Martin of Worcester in 1663. ***OS: SP 177 928.***
Cusop, Herefords, St Mary, **6**, 3-1-23. in G. - *Chimed Only.*
Cuxham, Oxon, Holy Rood, **1**, 3-1-17. in F.
Dacre, Cumb, St Andrew, **2**, - ***OS: NY 460 267.***
Dalbury, Derbys, All Saints, **2**, 2cwt. - No Stays or Sliders, ***OS: SK 263 343.***
Dalston, Gtr London, (R.C.), Our Lady and St Joseph, **8**, 6-0-15. in C. - *Chimed Only.*
Dalston, Gtr London, St Jude, **1**, - Unringable.
Dalton Holme, N.Yorks, **3**.

17

Danby, N.Yorks, St Hilda, **3**, 6-1-12. - *OS: NZ 707 086.*
Danby Wiske, N.Yorks, Parish Church, **3**, 5-2-5. in Bb., **Mon,** *OS: SE 338 984.*
Darenth, Kent, St Margaret, 3, 4-3-24. in C#. - Swing Chiming Levers, OS: TQ 561 713.
Darley Abbey, Derbys, St Matthew, **1**, 2-3-0. - *OS: SK 351 38.*
Darlton, Notts, St Peter, **3**, 5-2-0. - *OS: SK 779 737.*
Dartmouth, Devon, Dartmouth Naval College, 1, 20-2-26., - Chimed Only.
Darwen, Lancs, St Cuthbert, 5, 10cwt. - Hung Dead, Ellacombe Chimed.
Davington, Kent, Priory of St Mary Magdalene and St Laurance, **3**, 2-0-12. in F, - Unringable, *OS: TR 011 618.*
Deal, Kent, R M Barracks, St Albans Chapel, 3, 2cwt. - Chimed Only, OS: TR 374 515.
Denford, Berks, Holy Trinity, **1**, 1-2-8. in B. - *OS: SU 363 694.*
Denstone, Staffs, College, 8, 6cwt. - Hung Dead, Clock Chime.
Denton, Northants, St Margaret, **3**, 5cwt. in C. - Unringable, *OS: SP 838 580.*
Denton, N.Yorks, St Helen, **1**.
Deptford, Gtr London, St Luke, 8, 3-1-19. in F. - Chimed Only.
Deptford, Kent, St Paul, **3**, 11-2-0. in A. - Unringable., *OS: TQ 373 775.*
Derby, Derbys, Holy Trinity/Church of the First Born, **1**, 7-1-15. - *OS: SK 358 366.*
Derby, Derbys, (R.C.), St Mary, **1**, 18-1-7. in Eb. - Derelict Church, *OS: SK 345 366.*
Devizes, Wilts, St Peter, **1**, - *OS: ST 996 617.*
Dewlish, Dorset, All Saints, 3, 5-0-17. in C. - Chimed Only, OS: SY 775 982.
Dewsbury, W.Yorks, St Mark, **1**, 15-1-14. in F#. - *OS: SF 229 234.*
Dewsbury, W.Yorks, Town Hall, 5, 35-0-12., - Chimed Only.
Dewsbury Moor, W.Yorks, St John the Evangelist, 8, 5-1-24. in C#. - Chimed Only.
Didcot, Oxon, All Saints, (G.F.), **3**, 4-3-0. in C#. - Treble and Second Cast in the Workinham Foundry in the 14th Century., These Bells have been recently rehung., *OS: SU 519 905.*
Diddington, Cambs, St Lawrence, (G.F.), **3**, 7cwt. in A. - Unringable., *OS: TL 190 659.*
Didmarton, Glos, St Laurance, **1**, - *OS: ST 821 876.*
Digby, Lincs, St Thomas a Becket, 3, 6-0-22, - Chimed Only, OS: TF 081 541.
Dilton Marsh, Wilts, Holy Trinity, **2**, - *OS: ST 014 315.*
Dinedor, Herefords, St Andrew, **3**, 4cwt. in B. - *OS: SO 534 367.*
Dinton, Wilts, St Mary, **2**, 1-3-0. - The Tenor is a 13th Century Bell. *OS: SU 014 315.*
Ditton, Kent, St Peter ad Vincula, 3, 3cwt. - Chiming Only, OS: TQ 703 570.
Docking, Norfolk, St Mary the Virgin, **6**, 14-1-0 in E. - The **Tenor** is only Hung for Ringing the rest are Chimed. *OS: TF 764 370.*
Doddiscombsleigh, Devon, St Michael, (G.F.), **3**, 7cwt. - The Treble and Second were cast by Taylors in 1961., *OS: SX 858 866.*
Dolphinholme, Lancs, St Mark, **1**, 3cwt. - *OS: SD 517 534.*
Donington on Bain, Lincs, St Andrew, (G.F.), **3**, 3cwt. - Unringable, *OS: TF 236 830.*
Donisthorpe, Leics, St John the Evangelist, **1**, 8cwt. - *OS: SK 315 139.*
Donnington, Glos, St Mary, **1**, 3-2-0. - *OS: SP 193 283.*
Donnington, Herefords, St Mary, **1**, 3-2-0. - *OS: SO 709 347.*
Donton, Bucks, St Martin, **3**, 5-3-19. - Derelict.
Dorchester, Dorset, (R.C.), 1, - Chimed Only.
Dormington, Herefords, St Peter, (G.F.), **3**, 3-2-0. in D. - *OS: SO 583 402.*
Dorrington, Lincs, St James, (G.F.), **3**, 9-3-25. in F. - *OS: TF 076 534.*
Dorrington, Salop, St Edmund King and Confessor, 6, 6-0-9. in C. - Chimed Only.
Dorton, Bucks, St John the Baptist, **3**, 7-1-9. - Unringable., *OS: SP 679 139.*
Douglas. - *See Isle of Man.*
Dowdeswell, Glos, St Michael, **3**, 7cwt. - *OS: SP 001 199.*
Down Hartherley, Glos, St Mary of Corpus Christi, **1**, 3cwt. - *OS: SO 868 225.*
Downhead, Som, All Saints, **3**, - Unringable, *OS: ST 692 463.*
Downside Abbey - *See Stratton-on the-Fosse.*
Downton on the Rock, Herefords, St Giles, **3**, 13cwt. in G. - Steel Bells, *OS: SO 437 733.*

Dowsby, Lincs, St Andrew, **3**, 7-2-0. in A. - *OS: TF 113 293.*
Draycot Cern, Wilts, St Peter, **1**, - *OS: ST 930 782.*
Draycott, Derbys, St Mary, **1**, 0-2-5. - *OS: SK 444 332.*
Drayton, Oxon, St Peter, (G.F.), **3**, 7-2-3. in A. - *OS: SP 428 416.*
Drayton Beauchamp, Bucks, St Mary, **3**, 11cwt. - Chimed Only, OS: SP 902 118.
Driffield, Glos, St Mary, **3**, 5cwt. in C#. - *OS: SU 074 998.*
Droitwich, Worcs, (R.C.), The Church of the Sacred Heart and St Catherine of Alexandria, **1**, 10cwt. This Bell is Recessed into the Headstock with No Stay or Slider and was installed in 1946, Also This Church is decorated inside with mosaics covering every inch of the Church inside.
Drybrook, Glos, Holy Trinity, **1**, 12cwt. - *OS: SO 648 166.*
Duddington, Northants, St Mary, **6**, 6-2-19. in B. - Chimed Only.
Dulwich, Gtr London, College Chapel, **8**, 5-2-0. in C. - Chimed Only.
Dunchideock, Devon, St Michael and All Angels, **3**, 7cwt. - *OS: SX 876 876.*
Dunnington, N.Yorks, **3**, 5cwt. - No Stays or Sliders.
Dunsop Bridge, Lancs, (R.C.), **1**, - Chimed Only.
Dunstall, Staffs, St Mary, **3**, 9-3-4. in G. - *OS: SK 817 206.*
Dunterton, Devon, All Saints, **3**, 7cwt. - These Bells were Re-Hung in 2001, The Tenor is Late Mediaeval and was cast before 1600. *OS: SX 376 793.*
Duntisbourne Rouse, Glos, St Michael and All Angels, **2**, 3-3-0. in D. - *OS: SO 985 061.*
Dunton, Beds, St Mary Magdelin, **5**, 6cwt. - Chimed Only.
Dunton, Bucks, St Martin, **3**, 5cwt. - *OS: SP 824 244.*
Dunton Bassett, Leics, All Saints, **3**, 7-2-23. in G., - *OS: SP 548 904.*
Durham, Dur, St Giles, **3**, - Hung Dead.
Durham, Dur, St Margaret, **3**, - Hung Dead.
Durley, Hants, Holy Cross, **3**, - Chimed Only, OS: SU 506 170.
Dymchurch, Kent, St Peter and St Paul, **3**, 4-2-0. - Hung Dead, OS: TR 103 298.
Eakring, Notts, St Andrew, (G.F.), **3**, 7-2-0. in G#. - *OS: SK 675 622.*
Ealing, Gtr London, St John, **8**, 7-3-25. in Bb. - Chimed Only.
Earley, Berks, St Peter, **1**, 1-1-0. in B. - *OS: SU 745 722.*
Earl Sterndale, Derbys, St Michael and All Angels, **3**, 10-1-2. in Bb. - Chimed Only, OS: SK 091 671.
Earsham, Norfolk, All Saints, (G.F.), **3**, 11-2-0. in G. - *OS: TM 327 888.*
Easington, Cleveland, All Saints, **8**, 5-3-19. in C#. - Chimed Only.
Easington, Durham, St Mary the Virgin, **3**, 8-2-22. in A.
East Acton, Gtr London, (R.C.), **9**, 5-3-27. in C., - Chimed Only.
East Barkwith, Lincs, St Mary, **3**, 7cwt. in C#. - Chimed Only, OS: TF 166 815.
East Clandon, Surrey, St Thomas of Canterbury, (G.F.), **3**, 9cwt. - *OS: TQ 060 518.*
East Cowton, N.Yorks, All Saints, **3**, - *OS: NZ 307 034.*
East Dean, E.Sussex, St Simon and St Jude, **5**, 5-0-25. in Bb. - Swing Chiming Only.
East Gilling, N.Yorks, The Church of the Holy Cross, (G.F.), **3**, 12cwt. - Unringable, These Bells were Cast in 1667, 1701 and 1773 The Oldest Bell was given by Charles Fairfax the 5th Viscount.
East Grimstead, Wilts, St Nicholas, **1**, - *OS: SU 225 279.*
East Halton, Humbs, St Peter, **3**, 8cwt. - Unringable, All the Bells are Cracked, *OS: TA 139 198.*
East Hardwick, W.Yorks, St Stephen, **3**, 2-3-0. - Steel Bells, *OS: SE 463 186.*
East Hauxwell, N.Yorks, **3**, 9cwt., - Unringable.
East Hendred, Oxon, (R.C.), **1**, - Chimed Only.
East Heslerton, N.Yorks, St Andrew, **3**, 13-3-0. - Unringable, *OS: SE 926 767.*
Easthope, Salop, St Peter, **6**, 5cwt. in D. - Chimed Only.
East Huntspill, Som, All Saints, **8**, 4-0-27. in E. - Chimed Only.
East Keswick, W.Yorks, St Mary Magdelene, **3**, 1-0-25. - Hung Dead., OS: SE 358 444.
East Kirkby, Lincs, St Nicholas, **2**, 9-0-9. in G. - *OS: TF 332 630.*
Eastleach Martin, Glos, St Martin, **3**, 6cwt. in F#. - *OS: SP 202 054.*
Eastleach Turville, Glos, St Andrew, **2**, 3-2-0. in E. - *OS: SP 202 054.*

East Lulworth , Dorset, St Andrew, 3, 9-0-24. in G. - Chimed Only, OS: SY 853 821.
East Marton, N.Yorks, St Peter, (G.F.), **3**, 7cwt. - Unringable, *OS: SD 908 507.*
East Norton , Leics, All Saints, 3, 3-2-0. - Chimed Only, OS: SK 783 003.
Eastoft , Humbs, St Bartholomew, 3, 2-0-27. - Chimed Only, OS: SE 805 166.
Easton, - See Bristol.
Easton Grey, Wilts, **3**, - Unringable, The Treble was Cast by the Gloucester Foundry in the 14th Century. *OS: ST 881 877.*
Easton Royal, Wilts, Holy Trinity, **3**, 6-1-0. - *OS: SU 205 602.*
East Reynham, Norfolk, St Mary the Virgin, **3**, 10cwt. in G. - Unringable, *OS: TF 879 255.*
East Tisted, Hants, St James, (G.F.), **3**, 7cwt. - *OS: SU 701 323.*
East Wellow , Hants, St Margaret, 3, 8cwt. - Chimed Only, OS: SU 303 203.
Eastwick, Herts, St Botolph, (G.F.), **3**, 6-2-0. in B. - *OS: TL 433 117.*
East Wickham , Kent, St Michael, Old Church, 3, 4cwt. in D#. - Disused manual chime Bells lowered from frame - OS: TQ 468 177.
Eaton, Ches, Christ Church, **3**, 5-0-8. - *OS: SJ 870 654.*
Eaton , Ches, Eaton Hall, 28, 40-0-15. in C. - Carillon, These Bells were cast in Belgium.
Ebberston, N.Yorks, St Mary, (G.F.), **3**, 7cwt. - *OS: SE 892 833.*
Ebchester , Dur, St Ebba, 6, 7cwt. in C. - Chimed Only.
Ecchinswell, Hants, St Lawrence, **3**, 7cwt. - *OS: SU 501 598.*
Eccles , Norfolk, St Mary the Virgin, 3, - Chimed Only, OS: TM 019 894.
Eddystone , Devon, Lighthouse, 2, 41-3-14., - Chimed Only, These Bells were cast by Gillett and Bland in 1881 and the treble weights 40-3-11, This Lighthouse is 14 Miles of the Coast of Plymouth, There has been a Lighthouse here for 300 years and was rebuilt in 1882.
Edenfield , Lancs, 8, 6-2-9. in Bb. - Chimed Only.
Edenhall, Cumb, St Cuthbert, **3**, 2cwt. - *OS: NY 569 321.*
Edgcott, Bucks, St Michael and All Angels, (G.F.), **3**, 7-1-9. in Ab. Anti-Clockwise, Also Service Bell Hung for Ringing 0-1-15., *OS: SP 680 228.*
Edlington, Lincs, St Helen, (G.F.), **3**, 7 1-0. - *OS: TF 233 715.*
Edmonsham, Dorset, St Nicholas, **3**, 6-2-0. in B. - Unringable, *OS: SU 062 116.*
Edmonthorpe, Leics, St Michael, **3**, 10cwt. - Unringable, *OS: SK 858 176.*
Edvin Loach, Herefords, St Mary, **3**, 5-0-13. in D. - *OS: SO 662 584.*
Edwalton, Notts, The Holy Rood, (G.F.), **3**, 5-1-1. in C.
Edworth, Beds, St George, (G.F.), **3**, 9cwt. in G. - *OS: TL 222 407.*
Effingham , Surrey, St Lawrence, 5, 7-0-3. - Hung Dead but Ellacombe Chimed.
Eggborough, N.Yorks, **3**.
Eggesford, Devon, All Saints, (G.F.), **3**, 9cwt. - The Treble and Second were cast by Pennington in 1637 and the Tenor was cast in 1613. *OS: SS 686 112.*
Egginton, Derbys, St Wilfred, (G.F.), **3**, 7-0-7. in A#. - *OS: SK 268 279.*
Egham, Surrey, Royal Holloway College, 1, 35-2-8., - This Bell was cast by Gillett and Bland in 1883.
Egloskerry, Cornwall, St Keri and St Petroc, (G.F.), **2**, 2-2-22 in E. - *OS: SX 273 867.*
Egmanton, Notts, Our Lady of Egmanton, (G.F.), **3**, 8-0-5. in A. - *OS: SK 736 689.*
Egton, N.Yorks, **3**, 4cwt.
Egton Bridge , N.Yorks, (R.C.), 1, - Chimed Only.
Elkesley, Notts, St Giles, **3**, 6cwt. - Unringable., *OS: SK 689 755.*
Ellington, Cambs, All Saints, **3**, 9cwt., There is also a Treble for a ring of Four but it is Un-Hung at present, *OS: TL 160 717.*
Ellingham , Norfolk, St Mary, 5, 10-1-27. in G. - Chimed Only.
Elmstone , Kent, Parish Church, 3, 5-3-0. in B. - Hung Dead, OS: TR 262 603.
Elmton, Derbys, St Peter, (G.F.), **3**, 6-3-10. - Unringable. - *OS: SK 504 734.*
Elstead, Surrey, St James, (G.F.), **3**, - *OS: SU 903 434.*
Ely , Cambs, Cathedral Church of the Holy and Undivided Trinity, 4, 13cwt. - Chimed Only, There is also a Medieval Bell in the Cathedral to look at.

Emmington, Oxon, St Nicholas, **3**, 6-1-19. in B. - Very Derelict., *OS: SP 742 024.*
Enborne, Berks, St Michael, **2**, 2cwt. in F. - Treble was cast in the early 14th Century., No Stays or Sliders.
Enfield, Middlesex, St John the Baptist, 8, 3-0-6. in F#. - Chimed Only.
Etchilhampton, Wilts, St Andrew, **2**, 1-1-0. - Unringable, The Tenor is Cracked, *OS: SU 045 604.*
Eton, Berks, College Lupton Towers, 3, 17cwt. - Hung Dead, Clock Chime, OS: SU 967 779.
Etton, Cambs, St Stephen, **3**, 6-0-15. in A. - *OS: TF 141 066.*
Etton, Humb, **3**, 7cwt.
Evedon, Lincs, St Mary, **3**, 6cwt. in B. - *OS: TF 093 476.*
Everthorpe, Humbs, **3**.
Evesbatch, Herefords, St Andrew, **3**, 2-0-14. in Bb. - *OS: SO 696 482.*
Exeter, Devon, Cathedral Church of St Peter, 1, 80cwt., - Swing Chimed Only, Also **14**, 72-2-2. in Bb., Including Extra Treble and Flat Sixth.
Exeter, Heaveritree, Devon, (R.C.), Church of the Blessed Sacrament, 1, 77-0-12. - Chimed Only.
Exeter, Devon, (R.C.), Sacred Heart, **1**, 20cwt., - This Bell was cast by John Murphy in 1884.
Exeter, Devon, St Stephen, **3**, 6cwt. - *OS: SX 921 925.*
Exeter, Devon, St Mary Arches, **3**, 6cwt. - *OS: SX 918 922.*
Exeter, Devon, St Michael, **1**, 26cwt., - This Bell was cast by Taylors in 1867.
Exmouth, Devon, Holy Trinity, **5**, 26-0-2 in D. - The **Tenor** is only Hung for Ringing the rest are Hung Dead. *OS: SY 003 813.*
Eye, Cambs, St Matthew, **3**, 8cwt. - *OS: TF 228 028.*
Faccombe, Hants, St Barnabas, **3**, - Unringable.
Fairfield, Kent, St Thomas a Becket, (G.F.), **3**, 3-0-11. in G. - *OS: TQ 966 265.*
Fairlight, E.Sussex, St Andrew, 8, 10-3-20. in Ab. - Chimed Only.
Faldingworth, Lincs, All Saints, **3**, 10cwt. in A. - Also Sanctus Bell hung for Ringing , *OS: TF 067 848.*
Falmouth, Corn, King Charles the Martyr, 8, 8-0-25. in A. - Chimed Only.
Falmouth, Corn, (R.C.), 1, - Chimed Only.
Farcet, Cambs, St Mary, **3**, - Unringable, *OS: TL 202 946.*
Fareham, Hants, (R.C.), Sacred Heart, 1, - Chimed Only.
Farewell, Staffs, St Bartholomew, **3**, 3-2-0. - Unringable, *OS: SK 083 116.*
Farley, Wilts, All Saints, **2**, 8cwt. - *OS: SU 218 291.*
Farley Chamberlayne, Hants, St John, (G.F.), **3**, 6cwt. - No Stays or Sliders, *OS: SU 397 275.*
Farmington, Glos, St Peter, **3**, 7cwt. - *OS: SP 136 154.*
Farnborough, Gtr London, St Giles, **1**.
Farnborough, Hants, (R.C.), St Michael's Abbey, 6, 5-3-11. in C. - Swing Chiming Only, This Abbey was built for the Empress Eugenie in Memory of Napoleon III and there Son, There Bodies rest in a Crypt under the Abbey.
Farnham, Dorset, St Laurance, **2**, 3-2-0. in F. - *OS: ST 957 151.*
Farnham, N.Yorks, St Oswald, (G.F.), **3**, 4-3-0. - Unringable, No Stays or Sliders, *OS: SE 347 606.*
Farnley, N.Yorks, All Saints, **1**.
Farrington Gurney, Avon, St John the Baptist, **3**, 4cwt. - Unringable, *OS: ST 636 557.*
Farway Street, Devon, St Michael and All Angels, **3**, 11-2-0 in A., - Medieval Tenor., *OS: SY 186 953.*
Faversham, Preston, Kent, St Catherine, **3**, 2-2-0. in G#. - Unringable, *OS: TR 017 608.*
Fawley, Berks, St Mary, **3**, 4-1-24. in D. - Tenor was cast in the early 15th Century, No Stays or Sliders, Tower Unsafe., *OS: SU 392 814.*
Fawley, Bucks, St Mary the Virgin, **3**, 9cwt., - *OS: SU 753 867.*
Featherstone, W.Yorks, All Saints, **3**, 11-0-17. in G. - *OS: SE 422 221.*
Feltham, Gtr London, St Dunstan, **3**, 6-2-16. - *OS: TQ 098 722.*
Felton, Herefords, St Michael the Arch Angel, 5, 6-0-20. in C#. - Chimed Only.
Feltwell, Norf, St Mary, **3**, - Unringable, *OS: TL 715 907.*

Fence, Lancs, **1**, 6cwt. - Unringable.
Fen Drayton, Cambs, **1**, Unringable.
Feniscowles, - *See Blackburn.*
Fenny Bentley, Derbys, St Edmund King and Martyr, **3**, 3-2-0. - Unringable., *OS: SK 178 494.*
Fenny Compton, Warwicks, St Peter and St Clare, (G.F.), **3**, 7cwt. in Bb. - Unringable, The Treble and Tenor were cast by Henry Bagley I in 1636 and 1663, Also the Second was cast by John Appowell of Buckingham in 1560. *OS: SP 417 522.*
Fenton, Lincs, All Saints, **3**, 9cwt. in A. - *OS: SK 878 507.*
Fernhurst, W.Sussex, St Margaret of Antioch, **3**, 6cwt. in C., *Sun 9.35 am., OS: SU 899 285.*
Fewston, N.Yorks, St Michael and St Laurence, **3**.
Field Dalling, Norfolk, St Andrew, 5, 8-1-17. in Ab. - *Chimed Only.*
Fifehead Magdalen, Dorset, St Mary Magdalen, **3**, 8-2-0. in A#. - *OS: ST 783 211.*
Fifield, Oxon, St John the Baptist, (G.F.), **3**, 4-2-21. in D. - Anti-Clockwise., Second Cast in the 14th Century, Derelict., *OS: SP 240 188.*
Fifield Bavant, Wilts, St Martin, **1**, - This Bell is Hung inside the Roof of the Church, *OS: SU 017 251.*
Figheldean, Wilts, St Michael, **3**, 13cwt. - *OS: SU 153 469.*
Fimber, Humbs, **3**.
Finmere, Oxon, St Michael, (G.F.), **3**, 10-2-0. in A. - Tenor Cast in 1470., *OS: SP 663 332.*
Finningley, Notts, Holy Trinity and St Oswald, **3**, 2cwt., - Unringable., *OS: SK 669 991.*
Firvale, S.Yorks, St Cuthbert, 8, 5-0-10. in C. - *Chimed Only.*
Fiskerton, Lincs, St Clement, 3, 7cwt. in Bb. - *Chimed Only, OS: TF 048 720.*
Fledborough, Notts, St Gregory, **2**, 5cwt. - *OS: SK 812 722.*
Fleetwood, Lancs, (R.C.), St Wulstan, 8, 5-1-0. in C. - *Chimed Only.*
Flixton, Gtr Man, Flixton Hall, 1, 27-1-14., - *Chimed Only.*
Foleshill, - *See Coventry.*
Folkstone, Kent, Holy Trinity, 8, 2-3-27. in F. - *Chimed Only.*
Folkstone, Kent, St Saviour, 3, 4cwt, in D. - *Hung Dead, OS: TR 228 376.*
Folkton, N.Yorks, **3**.
Fonthill Bishops, Wilts, All Saints, **2**, 7-2-0. - The Tenor is dated around 1320. *OS: ST 936 330.*
Fonthill Gifford, Wilts, St Nicholas, **1**, - *OS: ST 924 321.*
Forcet, N.Yorks, St Cuthbert, **3**, 3cwt. - Unringable, *OS: NZ 175 123.*
Forcett. - *See Forcet.*
Forest Hill, Oxon, St Michael, 3, 3cwt. - *Chimed Only, OS: SP 584 077.*
Fosdyke, Lincs, All Saints, **1**, 5-0-8. - *OS: TF 315 333.*
Foston, Lincs, St Peter, 3, 9cwt. in A. - *Chimed Only, OS: SK 858 430.*
Foston, N.Yorks, **3**.
Fotherby, Lincs, St Mary, **3**, 6cwt. in Bb. - Unringable, Derelict Church, *OS: TF 317 917.*
Foulridge, Lancs, St Michael and All Angels, 10, 12-0-22. in Ab. - *Chimed Only.*
Foxham, Wilts, St John the Baptist, **2**, - Both Cast by Warners in 1879. *OS: ST 975 722.*
Foxholes, N.Yorks, St Mary, (G.F.), **3**, 4cwt. - Anti-Clockwise., *OS: TA 010 732.*
Foxley, Wilts, Mortuary Chapel at Cowage Farm, **1**, 2cwt.
Fradswell, Staffs, St James the Less, 8, 2-3-18. in F. - *Chimed Only.*
Fretherne, Glos, St Mary, **1**, 9cwt. - *OS: SO 733 092.*
Fridaythorpe, Humbs, St James, **2**, - *OS: SF 875 593.*
Friesthorpe, Lincs, St Peter, 3, 3cwt. - *Chimed Only, OS: TF 072 834.*
Frimley, Surrey, St Peter, 12, 12-3-0. in G. - *Chimed Only.*
Fringford, Oxon, St Michael, (G.F.), **3**, 9-0-1. in Ab. - Unringable., *OS: SP 606 292.*
Fritton, Norfolk, St Catherine, (G.F.), **3**, 8cwt. in A. - Round Tower., *OS: TM 218 926.*
Frolesworth, Leics, St Nicholas, **3**, 11cwt. - Unringable, *OS: SP 503 906.*
Froxfield, Wilts, All Saints, **2**, 2-3-0. - *OS: SU 294 678.*
Fugglestone, Wilts, St Peter, **3**.
Fulbrook, Oxon, St James the Great, (G.F.), **3**, 4-3-21. in C., *OS: SP 258 131.*

Full Sutton, Humbs, **3**.
Fulwood , S.Yorks, Christ Church, 8, 16-2-0. in F#. - Chimed Only.
Fyfield, Wilts, **2,** 8-2-0. - Unringable, *OS: SU 148 688.*
Ganton , N.Yorks, St Nicholas, 3, 5cwt. - Lever Chimed Only, OS: SE 990 776.
Garstang, Lancs, New Church, **1,** - Unringable.
Garstang, Lancs, (R.C.), **1.**
Garston , Mers, (R.C.), St Francis of Assisi, 8, 13-3-21. in F#. - Chimed Only.
Garthorpe, Leics, St Mary, **3,** 6-2-0. - Unringable. - *OS: SK 832 209.*
Garton on the Wolds, Humbs, **3**.
Gate Burton, Lincs, St Helen, **6**, 5cwt. - The **Three Largest Bells** which are **Steel** are Hung for Ringing the rest are Chimed. *OS: SK 839 829.*
Gate Helmsley, N.Yorks, **3**.
Gerrards Cross , Bucks, St James, 5, 10cwt. in G. - Hung Dead.
Gidea Park , Essex, St Michael and All Angels, 6, 5-3-17. in C. - Chimed Only.
Gilling , N.Yorks, St Agatha, 3, 6cwt. - Swing Chiming Only, OS: NZ 182 052.
Gilston, Herts, St Mary, (G.F.), **2**, 5cwt. in C.
Gissing , Norfolk, St Mary the Virgin, 5, 9-2-0. in G. - Swing Chiming Only, This Tower is Round.
Gittisham, Devon, St Mary, **3**, 12cwt. - *OS: SY 134 984.*
Glandford , Norfolk, St Martin, 12, 11-1-17. in G. - Chimed Only.
Glapthorn, Northants, St Leonard, (G.F.), **3**, 5-2-0. in B. - *OS: TL 021 902.*
Gloucester , Glos, Baker Shop, Practical Watchmaker Jeweller and Optician, 5, 1cwt., - Hung Dead, Chimed Only by Five Lifestyle and Decorative Statues above the Shop face.
Gloucester , Glos, Cathedral Church of the Holy and Indivisible Trinity, 3, 59-3-14. The Tenor is Automatically Swing Chimed Only and the rest are Hung Dead, Also **12**, 23-3-14. in D.
Gloucester , Glos, Eastgate Shopping Centre, 12, 0-2-6. in G. - Hung Dead, These Bells are Automatically Chimed and are Dutch Bells.
Gloucester, Kingsholme, Glos, St Mark, **1**, 2-3-0. - *OS: SO 845 191.*
Glympton , Oxon, St Mary, 5, 5cwt. - Chimed Only.
Goadby Marwood, Leics, St Denys, **3**, 5-2-0. - Unringable, Derelict Church, *OS: SK 779 263.*
Goathland , N.Yorks, The Blessed Virgin Mary, 5, 9cwt. in A. - Hung Dead and Ellacombe Chimed.
Gobowen , Salop, All Saints, 8, 3-3-26. in E. - Chimed Only.
Godington, Oxon, Holy Trinity, **1**, 3-1-17. in F.
Golcar, W.Yorks, St John the Evangelist, **3**, 4-2-0., - Unringable, The **Tenor** is only Hung for Ringing the rest are Clock Bells, *OS: SF 097 159.*
Golders Green , Gtr London, St Alban, 10, 5cwt. - Chimed Only.
Goldsborough , N.Yorks, St Mary, 3, 6cwt. - Lever Chimed Only, OS: SE 384 561.
Gomersal, W.Yorks, St Mary, **1**, 16cwt.
Goodmanham, Humbs, All Hallows, (G.F.), **3**, 6cwt. - *OS: SE 890 432.*
Gosforth, Cumb, (R.C.), Sacred Heart of Jesus, St Mary, **3**, - *OS: NY 069 035.*
Grafham, Cambs, All Saints, (G.F.), **3**, 10cwt. - *OS: TL 159 692.*
Grange over Sands, Cumb, **1**.
Grange over Sands , Cumb, Clock Tower, 3, - Hung Dead.
Grainsby , Lincs, St Nicholas, 3, 5cwt. - Chimed Only, OS: TF 278 996.
Grainthorpe, Lincs, St Clement, (G.F.), **3**, 19cwt. in F., **Alternate Wed,** *OS: TF 388 965.*
Grantchester, Cambs, St Andrew and St Mary, **3**, - Unringable, *OS: TL 434 556.*
Grasmere, Cumbria, St Oswald, (G.F.), **3**, 15cwt. - *OS: NY 336 074.*
Grassendale , Mers, St Mary the Virgin, 6, 10-0-6. - Automatically Chimed Only.
Graveney, Kent, All Saints, (G.F.), **3**, 6-3-19. in B. - *OS: TR 053 627.*
Grayingham, Lincs, St Radegunda, **3**, 8cwt. - *OS: SK 935 962.*
Great Badminton, Avon, St Michael, **3**, 8cwt. in Ab. - *OS: ST 807 828.*
Great Bealings , Suffolk, 5, 7cwt. in A. - Chimed Only.
Great Billing, Northants, St Andrew, **3**, 13cwt. in G. - *OS: SP 808 629.*

23

Great Bourton, Oxon, All Saints, **1**, 4-1-24. - Hung in a Gate House, *OS: SP 456 456.*
Great Chesterford, *Essex, All Saints, 3, - Hung Dead, Also 6, 10-1-0. in G., Unringable.*
Great Clacton, *Essex, St John the Baptist, 6, 8-2-24. in G#. - Chimed Only.*
Great Eversden, Cambs, St Mary, **3**, - Unringable, *OS: TL 367 534.*
Great Gonerby, *Lincs, St Sebastian, 3, 9cwt. in A. - Chimed Only, OS: SK 898 391.*
Great Hampton, Bucks, St Mary Magdalene, (G.F.), **3**, 8-2-4. - No Stays or Sliders., *OS: SP 848 024.*
Great Harrowden, Northants, All Saints, **3**, 9cwt. in G. - Unringable, *OS: SP 880 719.*
Great Harwood, Lancs, St Bart, **1**, 11cwt.
Great Harwood, Lancs, (R.C.), **1**, 17cwt.
Great Houghton, *Northants, St Mary, 6, 8-0-25. - Chimed Only.*
Great Limber, *Lincs, St Peter, 3, 9-1-16. - Chimed Only, OS: TA 135 086.*
Great Malvern, Worcs, Christ Church, **3**, 12cwt.
Great Oakley, Northants, St Michael, (G.F.), **3**, 5-2-18. in B. - *OS: SP 872 848.*
Great Ouseburn, N.Yorks, **2**.
Great Warley, *Essex, St Mary, 8, 5-0-17. in D. - Chimed Only.*
Great Warley, *Essex, Barracks, 13, 16cwt. - Chimed Only.*
Greatworth, Northants, St Peter, **3**, 6-2-0. in C. - *OS: SP 553 425.*
Greengates, *W.Yorks, St John the Evangelist, 6, 10-2-0. in G#. - Chimed Only.*
Greetland, W.Yorks, St Thomas, **1**, 6-3-0., - Unringable.
Grendon Underwood, Bucks, St Leonard, **3**, 15-1-16. in F#. - Rehung by Taylors in 1998, *OS: SP 677 210.*
Greywell, Hants, St Mary the Virgin, (G.F.), **3**, 6cwt. - *OS: SU 718 510.*
Grimoldby, *Lincs, St Edith, 3, 11cwt. - Chimed Only, OS: TF 392 880.*
Grimston, Leics, St John the Baptist, **3**, 9-2-0. - Unringable., *OS: SK 685 219.*
Grizedale, Lancs, **1**.
Groton, *Suffolk, St Bartholomew, 5, 10-3-11. in G. - Chimed Only.*
Guernsey, Castle, C.I., St Mary Du Castle, **3**, 13 2-0. in F#. - Unringable, All the Bells were Cast by Thomas Mears of London in 1811.
Guernsey, *C.I., (R.C.), Notre Dame du Rosaire, 3, - Automatic Swing Chiming Only.*
Guernsey, C.I., (R.C.), St Joseph and St Mary, **11**, 10-1-25. in G. - The **Number Seven** is Only Hung for Ringing the rest are Chimed Only. *OS: WV 33 78.*
Guernsey, *C.I., St Andrew, 3, 7-2-0. in Bb. - Chimed Only, All the bells were Cast by Chapman of London in 1778.*
Guernsey, C.I., St Marrinde La Bellouse, **3**, 8-2-0. in Ab. - Unringable, All the bells were Cast by Jean Baplish Brocard of Lorraim 1730-1736.
Guernsey, *St Peter Port, C.I., The Holy Trinity, 3, Hung for Chiming in the Turret.*
Guernsey, St Peter Port, C.I., St James, **1**, 10-2-0. - Unringable.
Guernsey, St Peter Port, C.I., St John, **3**, 7cwt. in Bb. - The Bells were Cast by John Warner in 1887.
Guernsey, C.I., St Philip du Torteval, **3**, 4cwt. in C#. - Round Tower, No Stays or Sliders, The Second is the Lightest Bell and Cast by a French Bellfounder in 1432.
Guernsey, *C.I., St Pierre Du Bois, 3, 15-2-0. in F. - Swing Chiming Only, These Bells are Hung with Half Wheels and The Treble was Cast in the 15th Century, Also 10, 11-1-0. in F#..*
Guernsey, C.I., St Sampson, **1**, 11cwt. in A. - No Stay, Slider or Pulley Wheel.
Guernsey, C.I., St Savior, **3**, 17cwt. in E.
Gumley, Leics, St Helen, (G.F.), **3**, 7-3-15., - *OS: SP 680 903.*
Gunby, Lincs, St Nicholas, **3**, 2-3-15. in F., - *OS: SK 913 215.*
Habergham, - *See Burnley.*
Habrough, Humbs, St Margaret, (G.F.), **3**, 6cwt. - *OS: TA 154 143.*
Hacheston, *Suffolk, All Saints, 5, 9cwt. - Chimed Only.*
Hackness, N.Yorks, **3**, 9cwt., - Unringable.
Haddon, Cambs, St Mary, (G.F.), **3**, 6-2-0 in C#. - *OS: TL 134 925.*

Hail Weston, Cambs, St Nicholas, (G.F.), **3**, 13cwt. - Anti-Clockwise., *OS: TL 165 621.*
Hainton, Lincs, St Mary, (G.F.), **3**, 7cwt. - Anti-Clockwise., *OS: TF 180 845.*
Halifax, W.Yorks, St Jude, **5**, 10cwt. in A. - *The Tenor is Only Hung for Ringing the rest are Hung Dead*. *OS: SE 086 241.*
Halifax, W.Yorks, Town Hall, **1**, 59cwt., - *Clock Bell.*
Haltham on Bain, Lincs, St Benedict, **3**, 7cwt. - *Chimed Only*, *OS: TF 247 638.*
Halton on Lune, Lancs, St Wilfrid, **3**, *Chimed Only*, *OS: SD 499 647.*
Hamble-le-Rice, Hants, Priory Church of St Andrew, **3**, - *Chimed Only.*
Hambleton, N.Yorks, **3**.
Hammersmith, Gtr London, St Peter, **5**, 7-3-0. - *Chimed Only.*
Hammersmith, Gtr London, (R.C.), Holy Trinity, **8**, 13-3-5. in F. - *Chimed Only.*
Hampstead, Gtr London, Christ Church, **3**, 6-0-13. in D. - *OS: TQ 265 861.*
Hampstead Marshall, Berks, St Mary, **2**, 5-2-0. in C.
Hampsthwaite, N.Yorks, St Thomas a Becket, (G.F.), **3**, 10-0-8. in G. - *OS: SE 483 054.*
Hampton Gay, Oxon, St Giles, **2**, 0-3-17. - The Treble Weight is 1-0-3., No Stays or Sliders.
Hampton Hill, Middlesex, St James, **6**, 14cwt. in F#. - *Chimed Only.*
Hampton Lucy, Warwicks, St Peter ad Vincula, **1**, 10cwt., - Unringable, This bell was cast by T Mears of London in 1826 at the same time as the Church was built. The Bellframe is made from wood from Ship's Timbers, This tower would be ideal for a future light ring of six.
Hampton Wick, Middlesex, St John the Baptist, **10**, 2-1-24. in A. - *Chimed Only.*
Hannington, Hants, All Saints, (G.F.), **3**.
Harbledown, Kent, St Michael, **3**, 6cwt. - *Chimed Only*, *OS: TR 132 581.*
Harborne, W.Mids, St Faith with St Laurence, **9**, 6-1-21. in C. - *Chimed Only.*
Harborough Magna, Warwicks, All Saints, **3**, 5cwt. - Unringable., The Second and Tenor were cast by Bryan Eldridge of Coventry in 1657.   *OS: SP 478 783.*
Harbridge, Hants, All Saints, **3**, - *OS: SU 144 101.*
Harden Huish, Wilts, St Nicholas, **1**.
Hardmead, Bucks, St Mary, **3**, 8cwt. - *OS: SP 935 477.*
Hardwick, Northants, St Leonard, **1**, 8-2-0.
Harewood, W.Yorks, All Saints, **3**, 10cwt. - Redundant Church.
Harford, Devon, St Petroc, **3**, 8cwt. - *OS: SX 638 595.*
Harlaston, Staffs, St Matthew, **3**, 4-2-0. in F. - *OS: SK 214 110.*
Harley, Salop, St Mary, **3**, 4cwt. - Anti-Clockwise., *OS: SJ 596 015.*
Harlington, Beds, St Mary the Virgin, **5**, 11-2-0. in F#. - *Chimed Only.*
Harlton, Cambs, Assumption of the Blessed Virgin Mary, (G.F.), **3**, 7cwt. - *OS: TL 388 525.*
Harnhill, Glos, St Michael and All Angels, **2**, 3cwt. in D. - *OS: SP 069 005.*
Harold Wood, Essex, St Peter, **8**, 6-1-3. in C. - *Chimed Only.*
Harpham, Humbs, St John of Beverley, **3**, 10cwt. - *OS: TA 092 616.*
Harrington, Lincs, St Mary, **3**, 2-3-17. - Rehung in August 2000 in a Six Bell Frame. *OS: TF 367 719.*
Harrogate, N.Yorks, Christ Church, **3**, 22-1-0.
Harrogate, N.Yorks, St Mary, **8**, 16-3-0. in F. - *Chimed Only.*
Harrow, Middlesex, St Alban, **8**, 6-1-13. - *Chimed Only.*
Hart, Cleveland, St Mary Magdalene, (G.F.), **3**, - *Chimed Only*, *OS: NZ 470 352.*
Harteshead, N.Yorks, **3**, 4cwt. - Tenor only Hung for Ringing the other Two are Unhung.
Hartham Park, Wilts, Chapel, **3**, 7-2-9. in Bb., - *OS: ST 864 715.*
Hartington, Derbys, St Giles, **3**, 10cwt. in G. - Unringable., *OS: SK 129 604.*
Harlebury, Bishops Wood, Worcs, St John, **6**, 0-1-0. in Bb. - *Hung Dead in Wooden Church but Ellacombe Chimed Only these Bells are Belgian Bells.*
Hartlepool, Cleveland, (R.C.), The Immaculate Conception, **8**, 15-2-26. - *Chimed Only.*
Hartlepool, Dur, **3**, - *Chiming Only.*
Harwood Dale, N.Yorks, **3**.

Haseley, Warwicks, St Mary, 3, 4cwt. - Swing Chiming Only, The Treble is a Medieval Bell and the Second was cast by Thomas Newcombe of Leicester in 1565.
Haselor, Warwicks, St Mary, 2, 6cwt. - Unringable, The Tenor was cast by Edward Newcombe of Leicester in 1610.
Haugham, Lincs, All Saints, 2, 5cwt. - *OS: TF 336 814.*
Hauxton, Cambs, St Edmund, 3, - Unringable, *OS: TL 436 522.*
Haveringland, Norfolk, St Peter, (G.F.), 3, 8cwt. - Round Tower., *OS: TG 152 209.*
Haversham, Bucks, Nativity of the Blessed Virgin Mary, (G.F.), 3, 7-2-9. - *OS: SP 828 428.*
Hawbridge, Bucks, St Mary, 2, 1-2-8. - No Stays or Sliders.
Hawkstow - *See Horkstow.*
Hawksworth, Notts, St Mary and All Saints, 3, 10-2-0. in A. - *OS: SK 753 435.*
Hawling, Glos, St Edward, 3, 6-2-0. - *OS: SP 063 230.*
Hawstead, Suffolk, All Saints, 3, 10cwt. - *OS: TL 855 593.*
Hauxwell, N.Yorks, St Oswald, 3, 6-2-0. - Unringable.
Hayes, Hillington, Middlesex, (R.C.), The Immaculate Heart of St Mary, 9, 4cwt. in E. - Chimed Only.
Hayle, Cornwall, 1, 12cwt.
Hayling Island, North Hayling, Hants, St Peter, 3, - Swing Chimed Only with Half Wheels, OS: SU 731 032.
Hayton, Humbs, St Martin, 2, - *OS: SE 821 461.*
Hayton, Notts, 3, - Hung Dead.
Hazelton, Glos, St Andrew, 1, 4-3-0. - *OS: SP 080 183.*
Hazlemere, Bucks, Holy Trinity, 8, 11-2-0. in G. - Chimed Only.
Headbourne Worthy, Hants, St Swithun, 3, 8cwt. - *OS: SU 493 323.*
Headley, Hants, All Saints, 8, 4-2-7. in D. - Chimed Only.
Headley, Surrey, St Mary, 8, 10-2-21. in G#. - Chimed Only.
Healaugh, N.Yorks, St John the Baptist, 3, - *OS: SE 499 480.*
Heaton, W.Yorks, St Barnabas, 8, 4-3-18. in C. - Chimed Only.
Heavitree, Devon, (R.C.), Church of the Blessed Sacrament, 1, 77-0-12.
Hebden Bridge, W.Yorks, St James the Great, 5, 7cwt. - Hung Dead, Clock Chime.
Heckmondwike, W.Yorks, St James, 1, 5-1-0, - Unringable, *OS: SF 218 235.*
Hedgerley, Bucks, St Mary the Virgin, 6, 5-3-7. - Chimed Only.
Helmsley, N.Yorks, 3, 1-2-0., - Lever Chimed Only.
Helperthorpe, N.Yorks, 3, 4-3-14., - Unringable.
Helpston, Cambs, St Botolph, 3, 6cwt. - Unringable, *OS: TF 122 056.*
Hemingby, Lincs, St Margaret, 3, 6cwt. in B. - *OS: TF 237 744.*
Henley-on-Thames, Oxon, Holy Trinity, 3, 3cwt. - Chimed Only, OS: SU 760 823.
Henley-on-Thames, Oxon, Toad Hall, 3, 14cwt. - Hung Dead, Clock Chime.
Hereford, Belmont, Herefords, (R.C.), Abbey Church of St Michael and All Angels, 9, 20-0-7. in E. Chimed Only.
Herriard, Hants, St Mary, 3, 7cwt. - Anti-Clockwise., *OS: SU 664 460.*
Heston, Middlesex, (R.C.), Our Lady Queen of the Apostles, 12, 6-0-11. in C. - Chimed Only.
Hethe, Oxon, St Edmund and St George, 1, 3-1-17. - Unringable.
Heworth, Tyne and Wear, St Mary, 3.
Heythrop, Oxon, St Nicholas, 3, 3-2-24. - *OS: SP 352 277.*
Heywood, Gtr Man, St James, 1.
Hibaldstow, Humbs, St Hibald, 3, 7-3-0. in A., **Tues,** *OS: SE 979 027.*
Hickleton, S.Yorks, St Wilfred, (G.F.), 3, 6-2-24. in Ab. - *OS: SE 483 058.*
Higham, Kent, St Mary, Old Church, 3, 3-1-9. - Hung Dead, Redundant Church, OS: TQ 713 715.
Highampton, Devon, Holy Cross, (G.F.), 3, 8cwt. - The Treble and Second were cast in Exeter in 1450 and the Tenor was cast in 1550. *OS: SS 489 047.*
Highbrook, W.Sussex, All Saints, 9, 12cwt. in G - the **Flat Second** is Only Hung for Ringing the rest are Chimed. *OS: TQ 363 302.*

Highgate, Gtr London, St Michael, **1**, 20cwt. - Unringable.
High Hurstwood, W.Sussex, **2**.
High Melton, S.Yorks, St James, **3**, 7cwt. - *OS: SE 509 018.*
Highnam, Glos, Holy Innocents, **3**, 25-1-0. in D. - Unringable, These Bells are 1, 8 and 10 of a ring of Ten., *OS: SO 797 196.*
Highway, Wilts, St Peter, **2**, - *OS: SU 041 744.*
Hildersham, Cambs, Holy Trinity, (G.F.), **3**, 10-3-4., - Unringable, *OS: TL 545 489.*
Hill, Avon, St Michael, **1**, 6cwt. in C. - *OS: ST 649 952.*
Hillsboroughm , S.Yorks, (R.C.), The Sacred Heart, 8, 25-0-8. in D. - Chimed Only.
Hinchley Wood , Surrey, St Christopher, 6, 3-2-4. in Eb. - Chimed Only.
Hinkley , Leics, (R.C.), St Peters Priory, 8, 5-3-27. in B. - Chimed Only.
Hinton Ampner, Hants, All Saints, **3**, 7cwt. - Unringable., *OS: SU 598 276.*
Hinton in the Hedges, Nothants, Holy Trinity, **2**, 6-1-0. in B.
Hitchin , Herts, St Savior, 3, 2-2-26., - Lever Chimed Only.
Hittisleigh , Devon, St Andrew, 3, - Hung Dead, Chimed Only.
Hoath, Kent, Holy Cross, **3**, 4-3-0. in C. - Unringable., *OS: TR 203 642.*
Hockerton, Notts, St Nicholas, (G.F.), **3**, 5cwt. in C. - *OS: SK 716 565.*
Hockworthy, Devon, St Simon and St Jude, **3**, 7cwt. - Unringable, Derelict Church, *OS: ST 040 195.*
Hoggeston, Bucks, Holy Cross, **3**, 6-2-19. - Unringable., *OS: SP 808 250.*
Hognaston , Derbys, St Bartholomew, 3, 3cwt. - Chimed Only, OS: SK 236 506.
Holbrook , Suffolk, Holbrook Royal Hospital School, 1, 21-1-22., - Chimed Only.
Holdenby, Northants, All Saints, **2**, 17cwt. in E.
Hollacombe, Devon, St Petrock, (G.F.), **3**, 7cwt. - *OS: SS 633 112.*
Holmbridge, W.Yorks, St David, **1**, 5-2-0. - *OS: SE 121 068.*
Holmbury St Mary , Surrey, St Mary, 8, 4-3-17. in D. - Chimed Only.
Holme, Notts, St Giles, **1**, 4cwt. in C.
Holme on the Wolds, Humbs, **3**, 11-2-16.
Holtby, N.Yorks, **3**.
Holton, Oxon, St Bartholomew, **3**, 8cwt. in A. - *OS: SP 605 064.*
Holton , Som, St Nicholas, 3, - Hung Dead, OS: ST 685 268.
Holton Beckering , Lincs, All Saints, 3, 15cwt. - Chimed Only, OS: TF 117 813.
Holton le Clay , Lincs, St Peter, 3, 6cwt. - Chimed Only, OS: TA 286 028.
Holwell , 2, - Lever Chimed Only.
Holybourne, Hants, Holy Rood, (G.F.), **3**, 8cwt. - *OS: SU 732 412.*
Homerton, Gtr London, St Barnabas, **3**, 5cwt. in C. - Anti-Clockwise., *OS: TQ 358 852.*
Homington, Wilts, St Mary, **1**, - *OS: SU 892 822.*
Honeychurch, Devon, St Mary, (G.F.), **3**, 6cwt. - *OS: SS 629 029.*
Honley, W.Yorks, St Mary, **2**, 19-3-5. - *OS: SE 136 116.*
Hooton Pagnell, S.Yorks, All Saints, 9, 14cwt. - Including Flat Fourth, There are **Three Bells** *in this Tower what are Ringable the* **Three, Four and Five** *of the Octave with a Tenor weight of 6-1-6. in B. The rest are Chimed. Wed, OS: SE 486 080.*
Hooton Roberts , S.Yorks, St John the Baptist, 3, 5cwt. - Chimed Only, OS: SK 484 971.
Hope under Dinmore, Herefords, St Mary, **3**, 8cwt. in B. - *OS: SO 501 529.*
Horden , Dur, St Mary, 8, 5-0-11. in C. - Chimed Only.
Horkstow, Humbs, St Maurice, **3**, 6cwt. - *OS: SE 987 183.*
Hornblotton, Som, St Peter, (G.F.), **3**, 6cwt. in C. - Unringable, Anti-Clockwise, *OS: ST 591 342.*
Horndon on the Hill , Essex, St Peter and St Paul, 5, 2-5-0-11. - Chimed Only.
Horninghold, Leics, St Peter, **3**, 8-2-0. - *OS: SP 807 971.*
Hornsea, Humbs, 8, 10-0-14., - Chimed Only, These Bells used to be hung as a Ring of Three until they were augmented and rehung.
Hornsea , Humbs, St Nicholas, 8, 15-1-27. in F. - Chimed Only.

Horsehouse, N.Yorks, St Botolph, (G.F.), 3, 2-1-0., - Lever Chimed Only, The Tenor is Cracked, *OS: SE 047 813*.
Horsenden, Bucks, St Michael, **1**, 3-2-24. - Oldest Declared Bell in Bucks Cast in 1582., Unringable Will only go half way up due to a stopper on the Rope.
Horwood, Devon, St Michael, **3**, - *OS: SS 498 270*.
Hougham, Kent, St Laurence, 3, 5-2-0. in C. - Hung Dead, Clocked, *OS: TR 278 400*.
Houghton, Cambs, St Giles, **3**.
Houghton, Hants, All Saints, **3**, - Unringable., *OS: SU 341 326*.
Hound, Hants, St Mary the Virgin, 3, - Chimed Only, *OS: SU 470 088*.
Hounslow, Middlesex, Holy Trinity, 12, 8-3-5. in A. - Chimed Only.
How Caple, Herefords, St Andrew and St Mary, **3**, 6cwt. in C. - The **Tenor** is Hung for Ringing, *OS: SO 612 305*.
Howsham, Humbs, 4, 5cwt., - Lever Chimed Only, These Bells were cast by Warners in 1860.
Hoxton, Gtr London, St John the Baptist, 8, 4-0-25. in E. - Chimed Only.
Hubberholme, N.Yorks, **3**, - Two of the Bells are hung in a Three Bell frame and the Third Bell is not Hung.
Huddersfield, W.Yorks, St Stephen, **1**, 4-2-0. - Unringable, *OS: SE 118 181*.
Huddersfield, W.Yorks, St Thomas the Apostle, **5**, 8-2-0. in Ab. - The **Tenor** is Only Hung for Ringing the rest are Hung Dead. *OS: SE 138 163*.
Huggate, Humbs, St Mary, **2**, 4cwt.
Huish, Devon, St James the Less, (G.F.), **3**, 7cwt. - Unringable, *OS: SS 533 111*.
Huish, Wilts, St Nicholas, **1**, - *OS: SU 146 634*.
Hulcot, Bucks, St Mary, **3**, 4-0-10. - Unringable., *OS: SP 854 167*.
Hullavington, Wilts, St Mary, **2**, 7-1-0. *OS: SU 892 822*.
Humbleton, Humbs, **3**.
Hundleby, Lincs, St Mary, (G.F.), **3**, 11-3-0. - *OS: TF 399 666*.
Hungarton, Leics, St John the Baptist, 3, 7-2-0. - Chimed Only, *OS: SK 691 072*.
Hunmanby, N.Yorks, **3**.
Huntshaw, Devon, St Mary Magdalene, **3**, 9cwt. - *OS: SS 506 229*.
Hurley, Berks, St Mary, **3**, 7-2-0. in A. - Unringable, *OS: SU 826 841*.
Hurst Green, Lancs, Cemetery (G.F.), **1**, 14cwt., - Hung in the roof gable at on end of the building and it is rung from outside.
Husthwaite, N.Yorks, **3**, 8cwt.
Huttoft, Lincs, St Margaret, **3**, 7-1-15. - *OS: TF 512 764*.
Hutton Buscel, N.Yorks, St Matthew, (G.F.), **3**, 9cwt. - *OS: SE 973 841*.
Hyde, Gtr Man, Holy Trinity, 8, 15-1-10. in F. - Chimed Only.
Hyde, Gtr Man, Town Hall, 1, 20-1-13., - Chimed Only.
Hylton, Tyne and Wear, St Mary, 8, 2-3-13. in F. - Chimed Only.
Ickford, Bucks, St Nicholas, **3**, 8-2-10. - *OS: SP 645 074*.
Idbury, Oxon, St Nicholas, **3**, 8-2-24. in A. - Second and Tenor Cast by the Worcester Foundry between 1400-1420., Unringable., *OS: SP 237 201*.
Ilford, Essex, St Mary the Virgin, **1**, - Also **8**, 7-0-22. in Ab., *OS: TQ 448 868*.
Ilmer, Bucks, St Peter, 3, 9cwt. - Chimed Only, *OS: SP 769 055*.
Impington, Cambs, St Andrew, (G.F.), **3**, 10cwt. in A, - *OS: TL 448 632*.
Ince, Ches, St James, **3**, - *OS: SJ 450 764*.
Inglesham, Wilts, St John the Baptist, **2**, - These Bells are hung in a Double Belcote at the West End of the Church. *OS: SU 205 984*.
Ingoldsby, Lincs, St Bartholomew, 3, 8cwt. - Chimed Only, *OS: TF 010 300*.
Ingrow, W.Yorks, St John, 5, 4-1-0. in D. - Hung Dead, Clock Chime.
Ings, Cumb, St Anne, **3**, 7cwt. - *OS: SD 446 987*.
Inkpen, Berks, St Michael, **3**, 7-2-0. in A.
Inskip, Lancs, St Peter, 8, 6-0-14. in B. - Chimed Only.
Instow, Devon, All Saints Chapel (St John the Baptist), **3**, 8cwt. - *OS: SS 480 310*.

Ipswich, *Suffolk, St Peter*, **3**, *9cwt.* - *There are Five Bells in Total in this Tower but the Trebles are only Chimed and the Back **Three** Bells are only Hung for Ringing.*
Ipswich, Suffolk, St Stephen, **3**, 6cwt. in B.
Irby in the Marsh, Lincs, All Saints, (G.F.), **3**, 5cwt. - Anti-Clockwise., *OS: TF 468 638.*
Irby upton Humber, Lincs, St Andrew, **3**, *12cwt.* - *Chimed Only, OS: TA 196 049.*
Irthington, *Cumbria, St Kentigern*, **5**, *9-1-0 in Bb.* - *The **Tenor** is Only Hung for Ringing the Rest are Hung Dead. **OS: NY 499 617.***
Isle of Man, *Government Chapel*, **5**, *12cwt.* - *The **Tenor** is Only Hung for Ringing the rest are Hung Dead. **SC 448 045.***
Isle of Man, Douglas, Government Chapel of St Mary, **1**, 12cwt. - *OS: SC 265 674.*
Isle of Man, *Douglas, St Thomas the Apostle*, **8**, *12-3-7. in F#.* - *Chimed Only.*
Isles of Scilly, Bryher, Scilly Isles, Unknown, **1**, - *OS: SU 880 149.*
Isles of Scilly, Hugh Town, Scilly Isles, St Mary the Virgin, (G.F.), **1**, 8cwt. - *OS: SU 970 107.*
Isles of Scilly, St Marys, Scilly Isles, St Marys Church, **1**.
Islington, *Gtr London, (R.C.)*, **1**, - *Chimed Only.*
Itchen Abbas, *Hants, St John*, **3**, *2cwt.* - *Lever Chimed, OS: SU 534 327.*
Jersey, Coin Varin, *C.I., (R.C.), St Matthieu*, **2**, - *Chimed Only.*
Jersey, St Aubin, C.I., (R.C.), Sacred Heart, **3**.
Jersey, St Helier, *C.I., (R.C.), St Thomas*, **5**, *51-2-17. in B.* - *Automatic Swing Chiming Only, Also these Bells were cast in France by Paccard in 1930.*
Jersey, *C.I., St Mary the Virgin*, **5**, *11cwt.* - *Hung Dead, Clock Chime.*
Jersey, *C.I., St Matthew*, **8**, *7-2-18. in B.* - *Chimed Only.*
Jersey, *C.I., St Luke*, **8**, *5-3-6.*, - *Hung Dead, Automatic Chime in Detached Steel Tower.*
Jersey, *C.I., St Saviour*, **9**, *11-0-3. in B.* - *Five of the Bells are Hung Dead and Four of the Bells are Automatic Chiming Only.*
Keelby, *Lincs, St Bartholomew*, **3**, *7cwt. in B.* - *Chimed Only, OS: TA 165 100.*
Keighley, *W.Yorks, Keighley Institute*, **1**, *25-1-1.*, - *Chimed Only.*
Keinton Mandeville, Som, St Mary Magdalene, **3**, 6cwt. - Unringable, *OS: ST 548 301.*
Kelham, Notts, St Wilfred, (G.F.), **3**, 7-2-0. - *OS: SK 773 554.*
Kellbrook, Lancs, **2**, 3cwt. - Unringable.
Kellington, *W.Yorks*, **3**, *7cwt.* - *Lever Chimed.*
Kelshall, *Herts, St Faith*, **5**, *12-0-9. in G.* - *Chimed Only.*
Kelstern, *Lincs, St Faith*, **3**, *6cwt. in Bb.* - *Chimed Only, OS: TF 252 890.*
Kencot, Oxon, St George, **2**, 4-3-21. in G#. - Unringable.
Kendal, *Cumb, (R.C.), Brettargh Holt Chapel*, **1**, - *Chimed Only.*
Kendal, *Cumb, Town Hall*, **11**, *44-1-0. in C.* - *Chimed Only.*
Kenilworth, *Warwicks, St John*, **10**, *9-2-4. in G#.* - *Chimed Only, All the Bells were cast by John Taylor and CO between 1949/1950.*
Kenley, Gtr London, All Saints, (G.F.), **3**, 5-3-0. - *OS: TQ 325 598.*
Kennerleigh, *Devon, St John the Baptist*, **3**, *2-0-19. in F#.* - *There are Eight Bells in Total in this Tower but the Back **Three** Bells are Hung for Ringing the rest are Chimed Only. **OS: SS 820 075.***
Kennett, Cambs, St Nicholas, **3**.
Keswick, Cumb, **3**.
Kettlethorpe, *Lincs, (R.C.), St Peter and St Paul*, **3**, *9cwt.* - *Chimed Only, OS: SK 848 757.*
Kettlewell, N.Yorks, St Mary, (G.F.), **3**, 9-1-0. - *OS: SD 972 723.*
Keyham, Leics, All Saints, **3**, 4-0-19. - *OS: SK 670 065.*
Keyingham, Humb, **3**, 4cwt.
Keyworth, Notts, St Mary Magdelene, (G.F.), **3**, 6-2-23. in G#.
Kidderminster, *Worcs, (R.C.), St Ambrose*, **5**, *6-3-0.* - *The **Tenor** is Hung for Ringing but Unringable the other Four Bells are disused. **OS: SO 838 768.***
Kidderminster, *Worcs, St George*, **6**, *6-1-9. in B.* - *Hung Dead.*
Kidderminster, Worcs, St John the Baptist, **1**, - Unringable.
Kiddington, Oxon, St Nicholas, **3**, 6-2-19. in B. - Unringable., *OS: SP 411 229.*

Kilburn, Gtr London, St Augustine, **1**, 23-0-7. - Also **8**, 8-1-0. in A., **Mon**, *OS: TQ 255 831.*
Kilburn, N.Yorks, St Mary, (G.F.), **3**, 12cwt. - *OS: SE 514 797.*
Kilnwick, Humbs, **3**.
Kilve, Som, St Mary the Virgin, **2**, - *OS: ST 146 439.*
Kimpton, Hants, St Peter and St Paul, **3**, - Hung Dead, OS: SU 281 446.
Kingscote, Glos, St John the Baptist, **1**, 11-1-0. - *OS: ST 819 962.*
Kingsholme. - *See Gloucester.*
Kingsland, Gtr London, (R.C.), **8**, 6-0-15. in C., - Chimed Only.
Kingsey, Bucks, St Nicholas, **3**, 10-2-0. - Chimed Only, OS: SP 744 067.
Kingston, Cambs, All Saints and St Andrew, **3**, - Unringable, *OS: TL 346 553.*
Kingston upon Hull, Humbs, **1**, 38cwt., - Clock Bell.
Kingswear, Devon, St Thomas of Canterbury, (G.F.), **3**, 10cwt. - These Bells are Hung in a Six Bell Frame, *OS: SX 882 510.*
Kington, Worcs, St James, **3**, 4cwt. in D#. - Unringable, *OS: SO 990 559.*
Kinson, Dorset, St Andrew, **1**, 6-1-0. in B. - *OS: SZ 073 963.*
Kirkburn, Humbs, St Mary, **3**, 12cwt. - *OS: SE 980 551.*
Kirkby cum Osgodby, Lincs, St Andrew, **3**, 9-3-7. - Chimed Only, OS: TF 063 928.
Kirby Fleetham, N.Yorks, St Mary, **3**, 8cwt. - Unringable.
Kirby Grindalythe, N.Yorks, St Andrew, **3**, 9cwt. - Unringable. - *OS: SE 904 676.*
Kirby Knowle, N.Yorks, St Wilfred, **3**, 1-2-0. -, *OS: SE 468 873.*
Kirkby La Thorpe, Lincs, St Denys, (G.F.), **3**, 6cwt. in B. - *OS: TF 099 461.*
Kirkby Laythorpe - *See Kirkby La Thorpe.*
Kirkby Malham, N.Yorks, St Michael Archangel, (G.F.), **3**, 19cwt. in E., - **Fri**, *OS: SD 894 610.*
Kirkby Misperton, N.Yorks, **3**.
Kirkby Overblow, N.Yorks, All Saints, (G.F.), **3**, 8-3-5. in G. - These Bells are Hung in a Four Bell Frame. *OS: SE 324 493.*
Kirkby Thorpe, Cumb, St Michael, **1**, - *OS: NY 638 260.*
Kirkby Underwood, Lincs, St Mary and All Saints, **3**, 4-1-4. in D. - *OS: TF 069 271.*
Kirkby Wharfe, N.Yorks, **3**.
Kirk Fenton, N.Yorks, **3**, 8cwt., - Hung Dead.
Kirk Hallam, Derbys, All Saints, (G.F.), **3**, 4-2-3. in C. - Unringable, Anti-Clockwise, Ropes fall in a straight line., *OS: SK 458 406.*
Kirk Ireton, Derbys, Holy Trinity, **3**, 6-0-13. - *OS: SK 269 502.*
Kirkleatham, N.Yorks, **3**.
Kirk Leavington, N.Yorks, **3**.
Kirklington, Notts, St Swithin, **3**, 5-2-0. - *OS: SK 679 576.*
Kirklington, N.Yorks, St Michael the Archangel, **3**, 9-2-0.
Kirkshall, W.Yorks, St Stephen, **8**, 8cwt. in Ab. - Chimed Only.
Kirk Smeaton, N.Yorks, **3**, 8cwt., - Unringable.
Kirmington, Humbs, St Helen, **1**, - *OS: TA 105 113.*
Kneesall, Notts, St Bartholomew, **3**, 10-0-2. in F#. - *OS: SK 703 642.*
Kneeton, Notts, St Helen, (G.F.), **3**, 6-0-20. in C.
Knill, Herefords, St Michael and All Angels, (G.F.), **3**, 2-1-0. in C. - Unringable, Tenor Cracked, *OS: SO 292 604.*
Kniveton, Derbys, St Michael and All Angels, **2**, 4cwt. - No Stays or Sliders, *OS: SK 211 503.*
Knossington, Leics, St Peter, **1**, 5cwt. - Unringable, *OS: SK 801 088.*
Kynnersley, Salop, St Chad, (G.F.), **3**, 5cwt. - *OS: SJ 673 167.*
Laindon, Essex, St Nicholas, **5**, 12cwt. - Chimed Only.
Laleham, Middlesex, All Saints, **8**, 7-3-24. in Bb. - Chimed Only.
Lambeth, Gtr London, Town Hall, **1**, 37-3-18., - Chimed Only.
Lamesley, Tyne and Wear, St Andrew, **3**, - Chimed Only, OS: NZ 253 580.
Lamyatt, Som, St Mary and St John, **3**, 9cwt. - Unringable, *OS: ST 661 362.*
Lancaster, Lancs, (R.C.), St Joseph, **1**, 15cwt.

Lancaster , Lancs, Town Hall, **1**, *56cwt.*, - *Clock Bell.*
Lancaster, Warton, Lancs, **3**, 15cwt. - Unringable.
Langford , Beds, St Andrew, (G.F.), **3**, - *Swing Chiming Only, OS: TL 185 414.*
Langford, Essex, St Giles, **3**, 5cwt. - *OS: TL 838 091.*
Langford, Notts, St Bartholomew, **1**, 7-0-15. in B.
Langford , Som, Langford House, **8**, *2-1-9 - Chimed Only.*
Langton Long, Dorset, All Saints, (G.F.), **3**, 3-3-0. in F. - *OS: ST 898 059.*
Langwathby , Cumb, **2**, *1cwt., - Lever Chimed Only.*
Larkfield , Kent, Holy Trinity, **3**, *2-2-2. - Chimed Only, OS: TQ 704 592.*
Lastingham, N.Yorks, St Mary, (G.F.), **3**, 6cwt. - *OS: SE 728 905.*
Laughton by Blyton , Lincs, All Saints, **3**, *12cwt. - Chimed Only, OS: SK 849 973.*
Laughton-en-le-Morthen, S.Yorks, All Saints, **3**, 12cwt. - Unringable, *OS: SK 517 883.*
Laverstock, Wilts, St Andrew, **2**, 2-2-0. - The Treble and Tenor are both the same weight. *OS: SU 158 306.*
Laxton, Northants, All Saints, **1**, 3cwt.
Leake , N.Yorks, **3**, *- Hung Dead.*
Lea Marston, Warwicks, St John the Baptist, **3**, 6-1-8. in B. - *OS: SP 204 927.*
Leamington Spa , Warwicks, St Mary, **8**, *6-3-3. - Chimed Only, All the Bells were cast by Mears and Stainbank in 1945.*
Leamington Spa , Warwicks, St Paul, **3**, *- Hung Dead.*
Leavesden , Herts, All Saints, **8**, *7-3-5. in B. - Chimed Only.*
Leckhampton, Glos, St Philip and St James, **1**, 5-2-0. - *OS: SO 943 194.*
Ledsham, W.Yorks, All Saints, (G.F.), **3**, 8-1-25. in A. - *OS: SE 456 298.*
Lee , Gtr London, St Margaret, **16**, *6-0-10. in C. - Chimed Only.*
Lee , Kent, St Mildred, **3**, *- Chimed Only, OS: TQ 398 737.*
Leeds, W.Yorks, St George, **3**, 13cwt. - Unringable.
Leeds, W.Yorks, St John the Evangelist, **3**, 13-0-4. in F#. - Unringable, Redundant Church, *OS: SE 302 339.*
Leeds, W.Yorks, St John New Briggate, **3**, 4-3-26. in C#. - Wed, *OS: SE 338 872.*
Leeds, W.Yorks, St Philip, **3**, *9cwt. - Church Demolished.*
Leeds , W.Yorks, Town Hall, **1**, *81-0-11., - Clock Bell.*
Leicester, Leics, Holy Trinity, **1**, 5-1-0. - Unringable, *OS: SK 592 039.*
Leicester, Leics, St Nicholas, **1**, 20-3-14., - This Bell was cast by Gillett and Johnson in 1949.
Leicester, Leics, St Peter, **1**, 20-2-0. - Unringable, *OS: SK 599 039.*
Leicester , Leics, Town Hall, **1**, *20-3-2., - Chimed Only.*
Leigh, Wilts, All Saints, **3**, - The Second was cast by the Bristol Foundry in 1450. *OS: SU 063 922.*
Leigh Delamere, Wilts, St Margaret, **1**, - *OS: ST 884 792.*
Leigh-on-Sea , Essex, (R.C.), Our Lady of Lourdes and St Joseph, **8**, *15cwt. in F., Swing Chiming Only.*
Leighterton, Glos, St Andrew, **2**, 6cwt. - *OS: ST 823 911.*
Leighton, Salop, St Mary the Virgin, **3**, 4-2-0. - Anti-Clockwise., *OS: SJ 613 052.*
Lenton, Lincs, St Peter, **3**, 7cwt. in Bb. - *OS: TF 025 303.*
Letchworth, Herts, St Mary, **1**.
Letcombe Basset, Berks, St Michael, (G.F.), **3**, 5cwt. in C., *OS: SU 374 849.*
Letton, Herefords, St John the Baptist, **3**, 8cwt. in Ab. - *OS: SO 335 465.*
Levens , Cumb, **3**, *- Steel Bells, Hung Dead under a canopy in the Church Yard.*
Leverstock Green , Herts, **2**, *- Lever Chimed Only.*
Lew, Oxon, Holy Trinity, **1**, 2-1-8. - No Stay or Slider.
Lexden , Essex, St Leonard, **12**, *2-3-4. in F. - Chimed Only.*
Leysters, Heref, St Andrew, (G.F.), **3**, 4-2-0. in C#. - The Treble was cast by Richard Le Belyetere of Worcester in 1450 and the Tenor cast by the Medieval Worcester Bell Foundry between 1400 - 1420, *OS: SO 568 633.*

Leystone , Herts, 3, - *Chimed Only.*
Lichfield, Staffs, Christ Church, **1**.
Lightwater , *Surrey, All Saints,* **6**, *1-0-18. in C.* - *Chimed Only.*
Lillingstone Dayrell, Bucks, St Nicholas of Bari, **3**, 6cwt. - *OS: SP 706 398.*
Lillingstone Lovell, Bucks, St Nicholas, **3**, 4-3-21.
Limehouse , *Gtr London, (R.C.), Our Lady Immaculate,* **9**, *20-2-0. in E.* - *Chimed Only.*
Limehouse , Gtr London, (R.C.), St Mary Immaculate, **1**, 20-1-21.
Limpley Stoke, Wilts, St Edith, **1**, - Unringable, This Bell was cast by William Purdue in 1596. *OS: ST 778 607.*
Lincoln, Lincs, All Saints, **1**, - *OS: SK 987 725.*
Lincoln , *Lincs, Cathedral Church of the Blessed Virgin Mary, (Central Tower),* **5**, *108cwt. in A.,Clock Bells, (N.W Tower)* **2**, *20cwt., Hung Dead, (St Hugh's Tower)* **13**, *23-2-13. in D., Including a Flat Sixth.*
Lincoln , *Lincs, (R.C.), St Hugh,* **3**, *6cwt.* - *Chimed Only, OS: SK 980 720.*
Lincoln, Lincs, St Swithin, **1**, 4-0-21. - *OS: SK 977 713.*
Linthwaite, W.Yorks, Christ Church, **1**, 4cwt. in F. - *OS: SE 102 145.*
Linton in Craven , *N.Yorks, (G.F.),* **4**, *3cwt. in C.,* - *Hung Dead, Ellacombe Chimed Only, Hemispherical Bells, All these Bells were cast by Mears and Stainbank in 1930, There is also a conventional Bell on Display in the Church is was cast by Smith of York and weights about 3cwt.*
Little Addington, Cambs, St Mary the Virgin, **3**, 8cwt. in G#. - Unringable, *OS: TL 958 736.*
Little Amwell, Herts, Haileybury College, **1**, 5-3-1.
Little Barrington, Glos, St Peter, **3**, 5-2-0. in C#. - Anti-Clockwise, *OS: SP 209 128.*
Little Birkhampsted , *Herts,* **3**, - *Hung Dead in 1960.*
Little Bredy , *Dorset, St Michael and All Angels,* **6**, *8cwt. in Bb.* - *Chimed Only.*
Little Brickhill, Bucks, St Mary Magdalene, (G.F.), **3**, 6-3-19., - Anti Clockwise., *OS: SP 911 325.*
Little Bytham, Lincs, St Medard, **3**, 6cwt. - *OS: TF 013 181.*
Little Cheverell, Wilts, St Peter, **2**, - The Treble was cast in the 14th Century and the Tenor was cast in 1450. *OS: ST 988 536,*
Little Dalby, Leics, St James, (G.F.), **3**, 7-0-15. in G#. - Ropes fall in a straight line, *OS: SK 775 137.*
Little Gransden, Cambs, **3**, Unringable.
Little Hereford, Herefords, St Mary Magdalene, **3**, 7-2-0. in Bb. - *OS: SO 563 680.*
Little Langford, Wilts, St Nicholas, **1**, - *OS: SU 049 362.*
Little Lever , *Gtr Man, St Matthew,* **6**, *66-3-3. in Bb.* - *Chimed Only.*
Little Linton, Wilts, St Mary, **3**, 5cwt. - The Treble was cast by the Aldbourne Foundry and the Tenor was cast by the Bristol Foundry in 1500.
Little Marlow, Bucks, St John the Baptist, **3**, 7-2-9. - Unringable., *OS: SU 874 878.*
Littlemore, Oxon, St Mary and St George, **1**, 7-2-9. - Unringable.
Little Oakley, Northants, St Peter, **1**, 6-0-6.
Little Ouseburn, N.Yorks, **2**, - Unringable.
Little Rissington, Glos, St Peter, **1**, - *OS: SP 190 200.*
Little Sodbury, Avon, St Adeline, **1**, 3cwt. - *OS: ST 758 833.*
Little Somerford, Wilts, St John the Baptist, **3**, 9cwt. - Unringable, *OS: ST 968 844.*
Little Steeping , *Lincs, St Andrew,* **3**, *12cwt. in G.* - *Chimed Only, OS: TF 432 636.*
Little Tew , *Oxon, St John the Evangelist,* **6**, *8cwt. in A.* - *Chimed Only.*
Little Thurlow , *Suffolk, St Peter,* **5**, *12-1-0. in F#.* - *Chimed Only.*
Littleton , *Hants, St Catherine,* **6**, *1-2-0.* - *Chimed Only.*
Littleton Drew, Wilts, All Saints, **3**, - Unringable, The Treble was cast by the Bristol Foundry in the 14th Century. *OS: ST 832 808.*
Little Walsingham , *Norf ,Shrine Church of our Lady of Walsingham,* **12**, *1-0-8. in C#.* - *Chimed Only.*
Little Wilbraham, Cambs, St John, **3**, - Unringable, *OS: TL 545 587.*

Little Woolstone, Bucks, Community Music Centre, Ex Holy Trinity, **3**, 5-2-16., *OS: SP 876 393.*
Little Wymondly - *See Little Wymondsey.*
Little Wymondsey, Herts, Blessed Virgin Mary, (G.F.), **3**, 3-2-0. - *OS: TL 217 273.*
Liverpool, Mers, Cathedral Church of Christ, **1**, 295-2-2. in C#., - Hung in the Centre of the Radial Frame with No Stay or Slider, Also **13**, 82-0-11 in Ab. Including Sharp Second. *OS: SJ 354 894.*
Liverpool, Mers, Christ Church, **1**, 28cwt., - This Bell was cast by John Rudhall in 1798.
Liverpool, Mers, *(R.C.), Metropolitan Cathedral, 4, 91-2-6., - Chimed Only except the Tenor that is Automatic Swing Chiming, Also the Bells are named Matthew, Mark, Luke and John.*
Liverpool, Mers, Municipal Buildings, **5**, 40cwt. in B. - **Tenor** hung for Chiming and the **Fourth Bell** which is 13-3-11. is Hung for Ringing the other Three Bells are Hung Dead.
Liverpool, Mers, *(R.C.), St Mary, 8, 13cwt. in G. - Chimed Only.*
Liverpool, Mers, *Liverpool University, 5, 45-1-23., - Clock Chime.*
Llanyblodwell, *Salop, St Michael, 8, 8-3-9. in A. - Chimed Only.*
Loddington, Leics, St Michael and All Angels, **3**, 6cwt. - Unringable, *OS: SK 787 021.*
Loddington, Northants, St Leonard, (G.F.), **3**, 6-0-8. in B. - *OS: SP 815 784.*
Lolworth, Cambs, All Saints, (G.F.), **3**, 5cwt. - *OS: TL 369 642.*
Londesborough, - *See Longesborough.*
London, Gtr London, St Pauls Cathedral, (S.W. Tower), 3, 104cwt. in Ab. - These are Clock Bells and the Tenor is called "Great Tom", There is also a 334-2-19. in Eb. Swing Chiming Bell called "Great Paul", Also in the (N.W. Tower) **12**, 61-2-12. in Bb., *OS: TQ 319 811.*
London, Aldersgate, Gtr London, St Botolph, **2**, 12cwt. - *OS: TQ 322 825.*
London, Barking by the Tower, *Gtr London, All Hallows, 18, 41-3-0. in C. - Chimed Only.*
London, Bread Street, Gtr London, All Hallows, **2**, 12cwt. in F#. - *OS: TQ 330 815.*
London, Bread Street, *Gtr London, St Mildred, 1, 2-2-0. in C. - Church Demolished,* *OS: TQ 325 811.*
London, *Gtr London, Caledonian Market, 1, 30-1-18., - Chimed Only.*
London, Cannon Street, Gtr London, St Mary Abchurch, **1**, 6cwt. in C#. - *OS: TQ 313 811.*
London, Coleman, Gtr London, St Katherine, **2**, 8cwt. - *Church Demolished,* *OS: TQ 326 814.*
London, Cornhill, Gtr London, St Peter, **1**.
London, Eastcheap, Gtr London, St Clement, **1**, 7cwt. - *OS: TQ 325 813.*
London, Eastcheap, *Gtr London, St Mary at Hill, 3, 12cwt. in F#. - Hung Dead, OS: TQ 331 809.*
London, Fleet Street, Gtr London, St Brides, **1**, 15-0-21. in F.
London, Gresham Street, Gtr London, St Anne and St Agnes, **1**, 3cwt. - *OS: TQ 317 812.*
London, Hatton Garden, Gtr London, Italian Church, **1**, 70cwt., - Steel Bell, This Bell was cast by Vickers in 1862.
London, *Gtr London, Hounsditch Warehouse, 10, 4-1-0. in E. - Chimed Only.*
London, Lombard Street, Gtr London, St Mary Woolnoth, **3**, 12cwt. in G., *OS: TQ 332 888.*
London, London Wall, Gtr London, St Alphage, **2**, 14cwt. - *OS: TQ 320 815.*
London, Lothbury, *Gtr London, St Margaret, 3, 9-1-22. in A. - Hung Dead, OS: TQ 327 815.*
London, Ludgate Hill, Gtr London, St Martin, **2**, - Unringable, Derelict Church, *OS: TQ 321 811.*
London, Old Jewry, Poultry, Gtr London, St Olive, **3**, 11cwt. - *Church Demolished.,* *OS: TQ 326 811.*
London, Oxford Street, *Gtr London, Selfridges, 1, 58-3-14., - Clock Bell.*
London, Queen Victoria Street, *Gtr London, St Andrew by the Wardrobe, 3, 8-0-8, Hung Dead, OS: TQ 319 810.*
London, *Gtr London, Royal Courts of Justice, 5, 68cwt., - Clock Chime.*
London, *Gtr London, Royal Exchange, 13, 33-0-7. in C#. - Chimed Only.*
London, Strand, Gtr London, St Mary le Strand, **1**.
London, Undershaft, *Gtr London, 6, 13-2-6. in F#. - Chimed Only.*
London, Upper Thames Street, Gtr London, St James Garlickhythe, **2**, 6cwt. in C#., *OS: TQ 324 808.*

London, Wood Street, Gtr London, St Alban, **2**, 5cwt. - Church Demolished, *OS: TQ 325 813.*
London Colny, Herts, (R.C.), **1**.
Londonthorpe, Lincs, St John the Baptist, **3**, 6-2-4. in Bb. - Hung Dead, *OS: SK 952 381.*
Longesborough, Humbs, **3**, 9cwt.
Longford, W.Mids, St Thomas, **8**, 4-1-8. - Chimed Only, All Cast by John Taylor and Co in 1904.
Longhurst, Northumb., St John the Evangelist, **8**, 12-3-0. in F#. - Chimed Only.
Long Marston, Herts, **1**., - Has a Small Wheel.
Long Marston, N.Yorks, **3**.
Long Marston, Warwicks, St James the Great, **1**, 7-0-24. in B. - Unringable, *OS: SP 152 481.*
Long Marton, Cumb, St Margaret and St James, **3**, - *OS: NY 666 240.*
Long Preston, N.Yorks, St Mary the Virgin, (G.F.), **3**, 9cwt. - *OS: SD 837 582.*
Longridge, Lancs, St Lawrence, **8**, 4-2-18. in D. - Chimed Only.
Longridge, Lancs, (R.C.), St Wilfred, **1**, 8cwt. - Requires a Rope.
Long Riston, Humbs, St Margaret, (G.F.), **3**, 5-1-25. - *OS: TA 123 427.*
Longstowe, Cambs, **1**, Unringable.
Long Whatton, Leics, All Saints, **3**, 13-0-8. in G#. - Ropes fall in a straight line, *OS: SK 482 233.*
Loose, Kent, All Saints, (G.F.), **3**, 8-3-21. in Ab. - Anti-Clockwise., *OS: TQ 757 521.*
Loppington, Salop, St Michael and All Angels, **3**, 8-1-4. - *OS: SJ 472 293.*
Loughborough, Leics, War Memorial Campanile, 47, 82-3-16. in A. - Carillon.
Louth, Lincs, St Michael, **1**, 3cwt. in Eb. - *OS: TF 333 872.*
Loversall, S.Yorks, St Katherine, **3**, 5cwt. - Unringable, *OS: SK 575 987.*
Lovington, Somerset, St Thomas a Becket, **3**, 10cwt. - *OS: ST 597 308.*
Low Catton, Humbs, **3**.
Lower Brixham, Devon, All Saints, 10, 4-3-21. in D. - Chimed Only.
Lower Cumberworth, N.Yorks, **3**, 2-0-21. - Lever Chimed Only.
Lower Halstow, Kent, St Margaret, **3**, 6cwt. - Unringable, Derelict Church, *OS: TQ 860 675.*
Lower Shuckburgh, Warwicks, St John the Baptist, **1**, - Chimed Only, This Tower used to have Three Bells but Two were Sold in 1999.
Lower Swell, Glos, St Mary the Virgin, **3**, - Hung in open Bell Cote, *OS: SP 174 258.*
Lowesby, Leics, All Saints, (G.F.), **3**, 10-2-6. in G. - *OS: SK 723 075.*
Lowestoft, Suffolk, Christ Church, 6, 10cwt. - Chimed Only.
Low Marnham, Notts, St Wilfred, **3**, 5-3-0. - Redundant Church, *OS: SK 806 694.*
Lowick, Cumb, St Luke, (G.F.), **3**, 2cwt. - Steel Bells. - *OS: SD 289 860.*
Lowick, Northumb., St John the Baptist, **3**, - *OS: NU 012 397.*
Loxbeare, Devon, St Michael and All Angels, (G.F.), **3**, 7cwt. - *OS: SS 911 161.*
Loxley, Warwicks, St Nicholas, **2**, 5cwt.
Loxwood, W.Sussex, St John the Baptist, **8**, 4-0-9. in D#. - Chimed Only.
Ludborough, Lincs, St Mary, **3**, 5-0-12. in B. - *OS: TF 295 955.*
Luddesdown, Kent, St Peter and St Paul, 6, 6-3-0. in A. - Chimed Only.
Luddington, Humbs, St Oswald, 3, 9cwt. in A. - Chimed Only, OS: SE 835 173.
Luddington, Northants, St Margaret, **2**.
Luddington, Warwicks, All Saints, **3**, - Chimed Only.
Luffincott, Devon, St James, **3**, 6cwt. - *OS: SX 333 946.*
Lurgashall, W.Sussex, St Lawrence, **8**, 6-0-20. in B. - Chimed Only.
Luton, Beds, Town Hall, **1**, 45-2-20., - Clock Bell.
Lyme Regis, Dorset, (R.C.), **1**, - Chimed Only.
Lyndhurst, Hants, (R.C.), **3**, - Swing Chiming Only.
Lytchett Heath, Dorset, St Aldhelm, 8, 5-2-0. - Chimed Only.
Lyford, Oxon, St Mary, (G.F.), **3**, 2-1-24. in G. - *OS: SU 390 943.*
Mackworth, Derbys, All Saints, **3**, 8-2-0. in G. - Unringable, *OS: SK 310 378.*
Maddingly, Cambs, St Mary Magdelen, **3**, - Unringable, *OS: TL 394 602.*
Maddington, Dorset, St Mary, **3**, - The Treble was cast by the Salisbury Foundry. *OS: SU 063 060.*

34

Maghull, Mers, St Andrew, 8, 13-2-22. in F#. - *Chimed Only.*
Maidenhead, Berks, St Andrew and St Mary Magdalene, **2**, 6-2-0. - ***OS: SU 889 813.***
Maidenhead, Berks, St Peter, **1**, 4-2-0. in E. - ***OS: SU 876 826.***
Maidford, Northants, St Peter and St Paul, **2**, 7-2-0. in Bb.
Malden, Gtr London, St John the Baptist, **1**, 7cwt. in B.
Maltby, S.Yorks, St Bartholomew, **3**, 6cwt. - Rung from the Vestry, ***OS: SK 528 919.***
Maltby le Marsh, Lincs, All Saints, **3**, 5-0-3. in B. - *Chimed Only,* OS: TF 462 813.
Mamhead, Devon, St Thomas the Apostle, 5, 9cwt. in A. - *Chimed Only.*
Manby, Lincs, St Mary, 3, 13cwt. - *Chimed Only,* OS: TF 399 867.
Manchester, Gtr Man, (R.C.), The Holy Name, 15, 14-2-9. in G. - *Chimed Only.*
Manchester, Gtr Man, Town Hall, 23, 42-2-5 in B., - Automatic Carillon, **Thirteen** of these Bells are also **hung for Ringing** including a Sharp Second, These Bells were cast by Taylors in 1936, There is also a Hour Bell called " Great Abel " which weights 162-3-3. in F#., **Wed,** ***OS: SJ 838 981.***
Manchester, Gtr Man, Methodist College, 5, 10cwt. - Hung Dead, Clock Chime.
Manchester , Chorlton-cum-Hardy, Gtr Man, St Clement Bishop of Rome, 5, 14cwt. - *Chimed Only.*
Manchester, Gtr Man, St Paul, **1**, 36cwt., - This Bell was cast by Taylors in 1879.
Manfield, N.Yorks, All Saints, **3**, 6cwt. - ***OS: NZ 223 134.***
Manningford Bohune, Wilts, All Saints, **1**, - Hung in open Belcote. ***OS: SU 137 577.***
Manningford Bruce, Wilts, St Peter, **2**, - The Tenor was cast in 1592. ***OS: SU 137 588.***
Mansfield, Notts, St John the Evangelist, **1**, 5-1-14. - ***OS: SK 535 614.***
Mansfield, Notts, St Laurance, **1**, 9-0-13. in A. - ***OS: SK 53 61.***
Manton, Leics, St Mary the Virgin, **2**, 3-0-9.
Maplebeck, Notts, St Radegund, **3**, 4-2-0. - ***OS: SK 711 608.***
Mareham Le Fen, Lincs, St Helen, **3**, 11-2-25. in F. - ***OS: TF 278 613.***
Marholm, Cambs, St Mary the Virgin, **1**.
Market Stainton, Lincs, St Michael and All Angels, (G.F.), **3**, 6cwt. - ***OS: TF 228 799.***
Markyate, Herts, **1**., - Unringable.
Marnham, Notts, **3**, 5-3-0.
Marnhull, Dorset, (R.C.), 1, - *Chimed Only.*
Marr, S.Yorks, St Helen, (G.F.), **3**, 6cwt. - ***OS: SE 514 054.***
Marrick, N.Yorks, **3**.
Marshchapel, Lincs, St Mary the Virgin, (G.F.), **3**, 13-0-18., **Wed (Alt)**, ***OS: TF 360 988.***
Marston Meysey, Wilts, St James, **1**.
Marston Montgomery, Derbys, St Giles, (G.F.), **3**, 3-3-0. - Unringable, Anti-Clockwise, ***OS: SK 134 378.***
Martin, Hants, All Saints, **3**, - ***OS: SU 072 194.***
Marton, Ches, St James, 6, 4-1-27. in E. - *Chimed Only.*
Marton, Lincs, St Margaret, 3, 7cwt. - Hung Dead, Clocked, OS: SK 840 818.
Marton, Warwicks, St Espris, **3**, 9cwt. - Unringable, All these Bells were cast by Hugh Watts of Leicester, The Treble in 1624, The Second in 1623 and the Tenor in 1616. ***OS: SP 407 689.***
Marton in Craven, N.Yorks, St Peter, **3**, 7cwt. - Unringable, ***OS: SD 908 507.***
Martyr Worthy, Hants, St Swithun, **3**, 7cwt. - Unringable, ***OS: SU 515 328.***
Maryvale, W.Mids, (R.C.), The Assumption, 8, 7-2-22. in Bb. - *Chimed Only.*
Matfen, Northumb, Holy Trinity, **3**, 4cwt. - ***OS: NZ 031 718.***
Matlock, Derbys, St Giles, **1**, - Also **8**, 14cwt. in F., **Thurs**, ***OS: SK 301598.***
Mavis Enderby, Lincs, St Michael, **3**, 6cwt. in Bb. - ***OS: TF 363 667.***
Mawnan, Cornwall, St Maunan and St Stephen, **3**, 6-2-0.
Medmenham, Bucks, St Peter and St Paul, (G.F.), **3**, 7-2-10. - Derelict., ***OS: SU 805 845.***
Mellor, Lancs, St Mary, 10, 20-1-3. - *Chimed Only.*
Melplash, Dorset, Christ Church, **2**, 3-1-9. in F. - ***OS: SY 484 976.***
Meltham Mills, W.Yorks, St James, **1**, 15-2-14. in F#. - ***OS: SE 108 109.***

Merton, Norf, St Peter, (G.F.), **3**, 8cwt. in Ab., - Unringable, Anti-Clockwise and Round Tower, *OS: TL 912 981.*
Methley, W.Yorks, St Oswald, **3**, 14-1-12. - Unringable. *OS: SE 391 266.*
Mexborough, S.Yorks, St John the Baptist, **3**, 6-3-02. in A., **Thurs**, *OS: SE 473 006.*
Michaelchurch on Arrow, Herefords, St Michael, **1**, 2-2-0. - *OS: SO 522 256.*
Michaelstow, Corn, St Michael and All Angels, 6, 7-2-16. in A. - *Chimed Only.*
Michelmersh, Hants, St Mary, **3**, 9cwt. - Unringable.
Mickleham, Surrey, St Michael, 6, 11cwt. in G#. - *Chimed Only.*
Mickleover, Derbys, All Saints, **3**, 7cwt. - Unringable, *OS: SK 305 332.*
Middle Chinnock, Som, St Margaret, (G.F.), **3**, 4cwt. in D. - *OS: ST 472 131.*
Middle Clayton, Bucks, All Saints, **3**, 7cwt. - *OS: SP 718 254.*
Middlesbrough, Cleve, Church House, All Saints, 8, 11-0-25. in G#. - *Automatically Chimed Only.*
Middlesbrough, Cleve, (R.C.), Cathedral, 2, - *Chimed Only.*
Middlesbrough, Cleve, (R.C.), St Philomena and Sacred Heart, 11, 8-0-26. in A. - *Chimed Only.*
Middlesbrough, Cleve, Town Hall, 1, 47-1-16., - *Clock Bell.*
Middleton, Warwicks, St John the Baptist, **3**, 8-3-1. in G. - All the Bells were cast by Thomas Mears of Whitechapel in 1826, *OS: SP 177 984.*
Middleton-in-Teeside, Dur, St Mary the Virgin, 3, 7-3-14. - *Swing Chiming Only, Hung in a Detached Tower which resembles a Yorkshire Dales Barn.*
Middleton-on-the-Hill, Heref, St Mary the Virgin, **3**, 7-1-0. in B. - The Treble was cast by Richard Le Belyetere of Worcester in 1450, Also the Second and Tenor were cast by the Medieval Worcester Bell Foundry between 1400 - 1410. *OS: SO 540 646.*
Middleton Tyas, N.Yorks, St Michael and All Angels, **3**, 4cwt. - Unringable, *OS: NZ 235 056.*
Midhurst, W. Sussex, (R.C.), 1, - *Chimed Only.*
Milstead, Kent, St Mary, **3**, 6cwt. - Unringable.
Milston, Wilts, St Mary, 1, Lever Chimed, This Bell was cast in the 13th Century. *OS: SU 162 450.*
Milton, Cambs, All Saints, **3**, - Unringable, *OS: TL 480 629.*
Milton, Notts, Mausoleum Chapel, **1**, 5cwt. - *OS: SK 715 730.*
Milton Abbas, Dorset, St James, **1**, 8-2-0. in A. - *OS: ST 806 018.*
Milton Abbey, Dorset, St Sampson, 3, - *Clock Bells, Also 8, 11cwt. in G., OS: ST 798 022.*
Milton Bryan, Beds, St Peter, (G.F.), **3**, 9cwt. in A. - Anti-Clockwise, *OS: SP 972 308.*
Milton Damerel, Devon, Holy Trinity, 3, 9cwt. - *Chimed Only, OS: SS 385 107.*
Milton-next-Bloxham, Oxon, St John the Evangelist, **2**, 3-1-17. - No Stays or Sliders.
Minster Lovell, Oxon, St Kenelm, **3**, 9cwt. in G. - *OS: SP 324 114.*
Miserden, Glos, St Andrew, **1**, 18cwt. in E. - *OS: SO 936 090.*
Misterton, Notts, All Saints, (G.F.), **3**, 11-3-17. in F#. - *OS: SK 764 948.*
Mitcham, Surrey, (R.C.), **3**.
Mitford, Northumb, St Mary Magdalen, 8, 17-1-0. in F. - *Chimed Only.*
Mixbury, Oxon, All Saints, (G.F.), **3**, 10-2-14. in G. - *OS: SP 609 340.*
Moccas, Herefords, St Michael, **2**, 2-3-0. in F. - *OS: SO 357 433.*
Molesworth, Cambs, St Peter, (G.F.), **3**, 7cwt. - *OS: TL 070 758.*
Monkton, Kent, St Mary Magdalene, **3**, 5-0-3. in B. - Unringable, *OS: TR 279 653.*
Monkton Combe, Avon, St Michael and All Angels, 8, 13cwt. - *Chimed Only.*
Monkton Deverhill, Wilts, **2**, 6-2-0. - *OS: ST 857 376.*
Monkton Farleigh, Wilts, St Peter, (G.F.), **3**, 7cwt. in Ab. - The Second weights 12cwt. *OS: ST 807 652.*
Monkwearmouth, Tyne and Wear, St Peter, **2**, - This Church was built in 674.
Monyash, Derbys, St Leonard, (G.F.), **3**, 8-3-1. in A. - *OS: SK 151 665.*
Mooredown. - See Bournemouth.
Moor Monkton, N.Yorks, **1**.
Morecambe, Lancs, Emanuel, 1, - *Swing Chimed Only.*
Mordiford, Hereford, The Holy Rood, (G.F.), **1**, 10cwt. in Bb.

36

Moreland, Cumb, St Laurance, **3**, - *OS: NY 598 227.*
Moreleigh, Devon, All Saints, **3**, 9cwt. - *OS: SX 762 527.*
Moreton , Staffs, St Mary, 6, 4-1-1. in Eb. - Chimed Only.
Moreton Morrel , Warwicks, Holy Cross, 3, - Hung Dead, All these Bells were cast by Edward Newcombe of Leicester, The Treble and Second in 1616, and the Tenor in 1609.
Morgans Vale, Wilts, St Birinus, **1**, 1-1-0. - *OS: SU 197 212.*
Morley, Derbys, St Matthew, (G.F.), **3**, 5cwt. in C#. - *OS: SK 397 409.*
Morton, Notts, St Denys, **2**, 1-1-6. - *OS: SK 727 514.*
Moseley , W.Mids, St Anne, (G.F.), 4, 5cwt. in C#., - Lever Chiming Only.
Mossley Hill , Mers, St Matthew and St James, 5, 39-1-7. - Hung Dead, Clock Chime.
Moulsford, Oxon, St John the Baptist, (G.F.), **3**, 5cwt. in C. - *OS: SU 590 837.*
Mount St Bernard, Leics, (R.C.), St Bernard's Abbey, **1**, 30cwt. - The was the First Catholic Abbey to be founded after the Reformation between 1133 - 1538., *OS: SK 458 162.*
Mourton-in-Marsh, Glos, Toll House, **1**, 0-3-0. - Unringable, This is hung in a open Belcote on top of the Toll House.
Murston , Kent, All Saints, 5, 10-3-0. in G. - Automatic Chiming Only.
Myddle, Salop, St Peter, (G.F.), **3**, 7cwt. - *OS: SJ 468 236.*
Myton on Swale, N.Yorks, **3**, - Unringable.
Nacton , Suffolk, St Martin, 5, 5cwt. - Chimed Only.
Nafferton, N.Yorks, **3**, 13cwt.
Nailstone , Leics, All Saints, 3, 12-0-24, Chimed Only, OS: SK 418 071.
Neen Sollars, Salop, All Saints, **3**, 11cwt. - Unringable, *OS: SO 660 724.*
Nelson Great Marsden, Lancs, **1**, - Metal Wheel, Unringable.
Nelson Little Marsden, Lancs, **1**, - Metal Wheel, No Stay or Slider.
Nether Broughton, Leics, St Mary the Virgin, **3**, 8-1-15. in A. - *OS: SK 695 262.*
Netherhampton, Wilts, St Catherine, (G.F.), **3**, 4cwt. in Eb. - *OS: SU 108 298.*
Nether Hoyland , S.Yorks, St Peter, 3, 5cwt. - Chimed Only, Derelict Church, OS: SE 37 00.
Nether Worton, Oxon, St James, **1**, 3-1-17. - No Stay or Slider.
Nettleden, Herts, **3**, - These Bells were rehung by Whites but they hit the Frame.
Nettleton , Lincs, St John the Baptist, (G.F.), 3, 10cwt. in A. - Chimed Only, OS: TA 111 002.
New Bolingbroke , Lincs, St Peter, 6, 1-1-0. in Bb. - Chimed Only.
Newborough, Cambs, St Bartholomew, **2**.
Newburn on Tyne, *Tyne and Wear, St Michael and All Angels, 1, - Medieval Bell hung for Chiming Only 6, 16-1-9. in Eb.,* **OS: NZ 167 654.**
Newbury , Bucks, (R.C.), St Joseph, 1, - Chimed Only.
Newcastle upon Tyne *, Tyne and Wear, Cathedral Church of St Nicholas, 1, 118-2-0. - Swing Chiming Only, Also 3, - Medieval Bells, Also 13, 37-2-17. in Db.,* **Tues, OS: NZ 250 640.**
Newcastle upon Tyne , Tyne and Wear, St Andrew, 6, 16-2-12. in F. - Automatically Chimed Only.
Newcastle upon Tyne , Tyne and Wear, Civic Centre, Edith Adamson Memorial Carillon, 25, 71-1-13. in A. - Carillon.
Newcastle upon Tyne , Tyne and Wear, Northern Goldsmiths, 8, 10-2-17. in G. - Clock Chime.
Newchurch in Pendle, Lancs, **1**, - Metal wheel No Stay or Slider.
Newhaven , E.Sussex, St Michael and All Angels, 10, 10cwt. in A. - Chimed Only.
Newington Bagpath, Glos, St Bartholomew, **1**, 10cwt. - Redundant Church, *OS: ST 816 949.*
Newnham, Hants, St Nicholas, **3**, 5cwt. in C.
Newport , Humbs, St Stephen, 8, 8cwt. - Chimed Only.
Newton, Cambs, St Margaret, **5**, - Unringable, *OS: TL 435 491.*
Newton, Herefords, St John the Baptist, **1**, 3-3-0. in Db. - *OS: SO 347 329.*
Newton Aycliffe, Durham, **3**.
Newton Blossomville, Bucks, St Nicholas, **3**, 9-0-1. - *OS: SP 926 517.*
Newton Green , Suffolk, All Saints, 5, 7cwt. in A. - Chimed Only.
Newton Kyme, N.Yorks, St Andrew, (G.F.), **3**, 4-0-9. - *OS: SE 466 449.*
Newton on Ouse , N.Yorks, 3, 10cwt., - Hung Dead, Chimed Only.

Newton Regis, Warwicks, St Mary, **3**, 9-0-5. in G. - *OS: SK 279 075.*
Newton St Petrock, Devon, St Petrock, (G.F.), **3**, 10cwt. - Unringable, *OS: SS 411 122.*
Newton Solney, Derbys, St Mary the Virgin, **3**, 5-3-11. in A. - *OS: SK 279 258.*
Newton Tracy, Devon, St Thomas a Becket, *3, 11cwt. - Swing Chiming Only on 3/4 Wheels, Unringable, OS: SS 529 269.*
Newton-upon-Trent, Lincs, St Peter, *3, 7-1-8. in A. - Chimed Only, OS: TF 048 362.*
New Milton, Warwicks, St Mark, **1**, 11cwt.
New Milverton, *Warwicks, St Mark,* **5**, *14-2-11. The* **Fourth** *Bell is Hung for Ringing and which Weights 9-3-15. - OS: SP 310 663.*
Nidd, *N.Yorks, St Paul and St Margaret, 5, 6-0-19. in C. - Chimed Only.*
Nonington, Kent, St Mary, **3**, 9cwt. - Unringable - *OS: TR 255 546.*
Norbury, *Gtr London, St Oswald, 6, 2-2-17. in F#. - Chimed Only.*
Norby, Derbys, St Mary and St Barlok, (G.F.), **3**, 8cwt. - Rung from Porch, *OS: SK 125 414.*
Normanby by Spital, *Lincs, St Peter, 3, 7cwt. - Chimed Only, OS: TF 001 882.*
Normanby le Wold, *Lincs, St Peter, 3, 8cwt. - Chimed Only, OS: TF 123 947.*
Normanton, Lincs, St Nicholas, (G.F.), **3**, 13cwt. in F. - *OS: SK 948 463.*
Normanton, W.Yorks, All Saints, **3**, 15cwt. - *OS: SE 387 225.*
Normanton Le Heath, Leics, Unknown, **2**, - *OS: SK 378 128.*
Normanton on Trent, Notts, St Matthew, (G.F.), **3**, 6cwt. - Unringable, *OS: SK 791 690.*
Northampton, Northants, (R.C.), St Mary and St Thomas Cathedral, **1**, 6-3-0. - *OS: SP 753 617.*
Northampton, Northants, Holy Trinity, **1**, 11cwt. - *OS: SP 755 625.*
Northampton, Northants, St Alban the Martyr, **1**, 9-0-19. - *OS: SP 777 630.*
Northampton, Northants, St Laurance, **1**, 4-3-18. - *OS: SP 758 612.*
Northampton, *Northants, St Matthew, 12, 13-1-8. in F#. - Chimed Only.*
Northampton, Northants, St Michael and All Angels, **1**, 3-2-0. - *OS: SP 765 614.*
Northampton, Northants, St Paul, **1**, - *OS: SP 712 618.*
Northbourn, Berks, St Peter, **1**, 4-0-10. in E.
North Carlton, *Lincs, St Luke, 3, 5cwt. - Chimed Only, OS: SK 944 777.*
Northchapel, W.Sussex, St Michael and All Angels, **3**, Anti-Clockwise.
North Clifton, Notts, St George, **3**, 7-2-0. - *OS: SK 812 722.*
North Cockerington, *Lincs, St Mary, 3, 4cwt. - Chimed Only, OS: TF 372 907.*
North Cotes, *Lincs, St Nicholas, 3, 5-1-13. in D. - Chimed Only, OS: TA 350 008.*
North Cray, Gtr London, St James, **3**, 4-2-0., - Unringable, Derelict, *OS: TQ 484 718.*
North Dalton, Humbs, **3**.
North Featherstone, W.Yorks, All Saints, **3**, 11-0-17. in G. - *OS: SE 421 221.*
North Frodingham, Humbs, St Elgin, **3**, 10-2-25. - *OS: TA 090 535.*
Northington, Hants, St John the Evangelist, **3**, 6cwt. in A. **Sun 10.30 am (1st).**, *OS: SU 564 374.*
North Kelsey, Lincs, All Hallows, (G.F.), **3**, 9cwt. in C. - Anti-Clockwise, *OS: TA 044 015.*
North Leverton, Notts, St Martin, **3**, 6cwt. - Unringable, *OS: SK 787 822.*
North Mundham, *W.Sussex, St Stephen, 5, 9cwt. - Chimed Only.*
North Newbold, Humbs, **3**, 12cwt., - Unringable.
North Runcton, Norfolk, **3**.
North Scarle, Lincs, All Saints, (G.F.), **3**, 7cwt. - Anti-Clockwise, *OS: SK 848 668.*
North Somercotes, *Lincs, Locksley Hall, 3, 0-3-0. - Chimed Only, OS: TF 413 958.*
North Somercotes, Lincs, St Mary, (G.F.), **3**, 9-2-18. in Ab., **Wed (alt)**, *OS: TF 422 958.*
North Stoke, Oxon, St Mary the Virgin, (G.F.), **3**, 7-1-9. in Bb. - Anti-Clockwise., Unringable, *OS: SU 608 862.*
North Thoresby, Lincs, St Helen, **3**, 10-1-02. in Ab. - *OS: TF 290 987.*
North Willingham, Lincs, St Thomas, **3**, 5-2-12. in C#. - Anti-Clockwise, *OS: TF 163 883.*
North Witham, *Lincs, St Mary, 3, 11cwt. in G. - Chimed Only, OS: SK 928 219.*
North Woolwich, *Gtr London, St John the Evangelist, 5, 4cwt. - Chimed Only.*
North Wooton, Som, St Peter, **3**, 7cwt. in B. - *OS: ST 564 418.*
North Wraxhall, Wilts, St James, **1**, 10-2-0.

<u>Norwich</u>, Norfolk, Cathedral Church of the Holy and Undivided Trinity, 5, 14cwt. in F#. - Swing Chimed Only, *OS: TG 234 089*.
<u>Norwich</u>, Norfolk, City Hall, 1, 54-2-12., - Clock Bell.
<u>Norwich, Mile Cross</u>, Norfolk, St Catherine, 6, 5-3-6. in Bb. - Chimed Only.
<u>Norwich</u>, Norfolk, St Clement Colegate, 3, - Hung Dead.
Norwich, Norfolk, St Stephen, **3**, 4cwt., - *OS: TG 229 083*.
<u>Norwich, Tombland</u>, Norfolk, St George, 5, 10cwt. in G#. - Chimed Only.
Norton Malreward, Avon, Holy Trinity, (G.F.), **2**, 6cwt. in C. - *OS: ST 603 641*.
Notgrove, Glos, St Bartholomew, **3**, 7cwt. in Bb. - *OS: SP 110 200*.
<u>Nottingham</u>, Notts, Nottingham Exchange, 5, 207-0-27., - Clock Bells.
<u>Nottingham</u>, Notts, Nottingham University, 1, 20-0-24., - Chimed Only.
Nottingham, Notts, St Nicholas, **1**, 5-3-21. in C#. - *OS: SK 572 396*.
<u>Nottingham, Carlton</u>, Notts, St John the Baptist, 10, 8-2-25. in Ab. - Chimed Only.
<u>Nuneaton</u>, Warwicks, Courtaulds Works, 1, 30-1-21., - Chimed Only.
<u>Nun Monkton</u>, N.Yorks, St Mary, 3, 8cwt. - Chimed Only, OS: SE 512 580.
Nunnington, N.Yorks, All Saints and St James, (G.F.), **3**, 4-2-0. - *OS: SE 661 796*.
<u>Nunthorpe</u>, Cleve, St Mary the Virgin, 8, 9-1-11. in A. - Chimed Only.
Nunton, Wilts, St Andrew, (G.F.), **3**, 6-2-0. -Anti-Clockwise,Tenor was cast by William Purdue in 1641.
<u>Nutfield</u>, Surrey, St Nutfield, 5, 3-2-0. - Chimed Only.
<u>Nuthurst Cum Hockley Heath, Umberslade</u>, W.Mids, (Baptist Church), Christ Church, 8, 8-0-10. in Ab. - Chimed Only.
Nympsfield, Glos, St Bartholomew, **1**, 8cwt. - *OS: SO 801 002*.
Oakley, Bucks, St Mary and St Matthew, **3**, 7-2-16. in A. - *OS: SP 643 123*.
Oakley, Oxon, St Mary, **3**, 7cwt.
Oakridge, Glos, St Bartholomew, **1**, 1-2-0. - *OS: SO 913 034*.
Oakworth, W.Yorks, **1**, 12cwt. - Steel Bell., Unringable.
Oare, Som, Blessed Virgin Mary, **3**, 5cwt. - *OS: SS 802 473*.
Ocle Pychard, Herefords, St James the Great, **3**, 18cwt. in A. - *OS: SO 596 452*.
Oddington, Oxon, St Andrew, **3**, 9cwt. in Ab. - *OS: SP 552 148*.
Odstock, Wilts, St Mary, **3**, The Treble was cast in 1636, the Second was cast in 1624 and the Tenor was cast by John Barber.
<u>Offham</u>, Kent, St Michael, 3, 7cwt. in G. - Chimed Only, OS: TQ 661 581.
Offord Darcy, Cambs, St Peter, **3**, 11cwt., - Unringable, Derelict, *OS: TL 216 664*.
Old, Wilts, **3**, 7-2-0.
<u>Oldberrow</u>, Worcs, 3, - Swing Chimed Only.
<u>Old Buckenham</u>, Norfolk, All Saints, 6, 8-2-0. in G#. - Chimed Only.
Oldbury on Severn, Avon, St Arlida, **1**, 5-2-0. - *OS: ST 608 919*.
Oldbury on the Hill, Glos, St Arlida, **1**, 5-2-0. in B. - *OS: ST 819 883*.
Old Clee, Cleethorpes, Humbs, Holy Trinity and St Mary, (G.F.), **3**, 13-0-11. in F., *OS: TA 290 084*.
Old Malden, Surrey, St John the Baptist, **6**, 7cwt in B. - The **Tenor** is Only hung for ringing the rest are Chimed. *OS: TQ 211 661*.
Old Malton, N.Yorks, St Mary the Virgin, **3**, 8cwt. - *OS: SE 798 727*.
Old Milverton, Warwicks, St James, **3**, 6cwt. - Unringable, Tower Unsafe, The Tenor was cast by Henry Jordon of London in 1460.
Old Romney, Kent, St Clement, **3**, 7-2-0. in B. - Unringable, *OS: TR 035 252*.
Old Sodbury, Avon, St John the Baptist, **1**, 15cwt. - *OS: ST 755 818*.
Old Whitacre, Warwicks, **2**.
Ollerton, Notts, St Giles, **1**, 13-1-16. - *OS: SK 653 674*.
Orby, Lincs, All Saints, (G.F.), **3**, 10cwt. - *OS: TF 491 673*.
Orcheston, Wilts, St Mary, **3**, 7-1-25. - These Bells were All cast by Taylors in 1916. *OS: SU 058 457*.

Orlestone, Kent, St Mary the Virgin, 3, 5cwt. in C. - Anti-Clockwise, *OS: TR 000 348.*
Ormseby St Michael, Norfolk, St Michael, 5, 7-3-20. in G. - *Chimed Only.*
Orton, Northants, Orton Trust, 1, 2cwt.
Orton Longueville, Cambs, 1, Unringable, Awaiting work to be done.
Osbournby, Lincs, St Peter and St Paul, 3, 8-0-2. - *Chimed Only, OS: TF 068 399.*
Osmondthorpe, N.Yorks, 3, 9cwt., - Unringable.
Osmotherley, N.Yorks, St Peter, 3, 8cwt. - Unringable, *OS: SE 455 972.*
Oswaldkirk, N.Yorks, 2.
Otham, Kent, St Nicholas, 3, 7-1-11. in A. - *OS: TQ 789 541.*
Otterham, Corn, St Dennis, 3.
Otteringham, Humb, 3, 5cwt.
Oulton, Staffs, (R.C.), St Marys Abbey, 11, 14cwt. - *Chimed Only.*
Ovenden, W.Yorks, 3, 3cwt., - Hung Dead.
Over Kellet, Lancs, St Cuthbert, (G.F.), 3, 11cwt. - Unringable, *OS: SD 512 695.*
Over Peover, Cheshire, St Lawrence, 3, 5cwt. - *OS: SJ 773 736.*
Overstone, Northants, St Nicholas, 3, 5-3-3. - *OS: SP 806 661.*
Over Whitacre, Warwicks, 2.
Over Winchendon, Bucks, St Mary Magdalen, 3, 6-3-19. - *OS: SP 746 145.*
Oving, Bucks, All Saints, 3, 7-2-16. - *OS: SP 783 214.*
Ovingham, Tyne and Wear, St Mary the Virgin, 3.
Owlpen, Glos, Holy Cross, 1, 8-2-0. - *OS: ST 800 984.*
Owmby by Spital, Lincs, St Peter and St Paul, 3, 4cwt. - *Chimed Only, OS: TF 000 873.*
Owston, Leics, St Andrew, (G.F.), 3, 7-0-18. - *OS: SK 774 080.*
Owston, W.Yorks, All Saints, 6, 9-2-0. in G#. - *Chimed Only.*
Owthorpe, Notts, St Margaret, 1, 5cwt. - *OS: SK 672 334.*
Oxenhall, Glos, St Anne, 3, 7cwt. in B. - Unringable, Tower Cracked, *OS: SO 711 267.*
Oxenton, Glos, St John the Baptist, 1, 6-3-0. - *OS: SO 958 315.*
Oxford, Oxon, Great Tom Tower, 1, 124-2-24., - *Swing Chiming Only, Counterbalanced and it maybe possible to ring it Full Circle, Also it was cast by Christopher Hodson in 1680.*
Oxford, Oxon, St Edward's School, 5, 14-2-11. in F. - *The* **Treble and Second** *are Hung for Ringing the rest are Hung Dead.*
Oxford, Oxon, The Claredon Press, 3, 5-2-26. - *The* **Second** *Bell is Hung for Ringing weighing 3-0-17. the Treble and Tenor are Clock Bells only.* - *OS: SP 515 065.*
Oxford, Oxon, St Michael at the North Gate, 6, 13cwt. in F#. - *Chimed Only.*
Oxford, Oxon, Trinity College, 3, 3cwt. - *Chimed Only, OS: SP 514 065.*
Paddington, Gtr London, St James, 1, 30-2-12., - Cast by Gillett and Johnson in 1920.
Paddington, Gtr London, St Matthew, 5, 10cwt. in A. - *Hung Dead, Clock Chime.*
Paddockhurst, Sussex, (R.C.), Worth Priory, 8, 24-2-23. in Eb. - *Chimed Only.*
Panfield, Essex, St Mary and St Christopher, (G.F.), 3, 5-2-0. - Tower Unsafe, *OS: TL 739 254.*
Pannal, N.Yorks, 3, 10cwt.
Papplewick, Notts, St James, 3, 5-1-19. in C.
Papworth Everard, Cambs, 1, Unringable.
Parkend, Glos, St Paul, 1, 6cwt. - *OS: SO 620 077.*
Parkgate, Ches, Mostyn House School, War Memorial Carillon, 37, 18-2-25. in E. - *Carillon.*
Parkminster, Sussex, (R.C.), Parkminster Priory, 5, 21-3-11., - *The* **Tenor** *is Only Hung for Ringing the Rest are hung Dead as a Clock Chime.*
Parracombe, Devon, Christ Church, 6, 8cwt. in Bb. - *The Back* **Three** *Bells are Hung for Ringing the rest are Chimed. OS: SS 669 449.*
Partney, Lincs, St Nicholas, 3, 9cwt. - *Chimed Only, OS: TF 411 683.*
Parwich, Derbys, St Peter, 1, 5cwt. - *OS: SK 188 543.*
Paston, Cambs, All Saints, 3, 6cwt. - Unringable, *OS: TF 181 023.*
Patley Bridge, - *See Ramsgill.*
Patrick Brompton, N.Yorks, St Patrick, 3, 7cwt. - Unringable. *OS: SE 219 907.*

Patrixbourne, Kent, St Mary, **3**, 4-3-25. in D. - Unringable, *OS: TR 190 552.*
Patterdale , Cumb, St Patrick, **8**, 7-2-12. *in Bb. - Chimed Only.*
Pauntley , Glos, St Anne, **3**, 4cwt. *- Swing Chiming Only.*
Pelton , Dur, Holy Trinity, **6**, 5-3-17. *in C. - Chimed Only.*
Pencoyd, Herefords, St Denys, **3**, 5-3-0. in Bb. - *OS: SO 517 266.*
Pendock, Worcs, **1**.
Penn Street, Bucks, Holy Trinity, **3**, 10-0-13. - Unringable, Ropes fall a 35 Foot Draght with No Rope Guides - *OS: SU 923 963.*
Penwood, Wilts, St Peter, **1**, - This Bell was cast around the end of the 13th Century.
Peover Superior. *- See Over Peover.*
Peper Harow, Surrey, St Nicholas, (G.F.), **3**, 3-3-23. in Bb. - *OS: SU 935 440.*
Perranuthnoe, Corn, St Piran and St Michael, **3**, 3cwt. - *OS: SW 547 296.*
Perry Hill, Kent, St George, **1**, 9cwt. - Unringable, *OS: TQ 367 729.*
Peterborough, Cambs, (R.C.), All Souls, **1**, - *OS: TL 192 991.*
Peterborough, Cambs, Christ the Carpenter, **1**, - *OS: TL 200 012.*
Peterborough, Cambs, St Mark, **1**, - *OS: TL 190 990.*
Pewsey, Wilts, St Peter, **3**, 5-1-0. - The Treble was cast by the Salisbury Foundry. *OS: SU 162 599.*
Philleigh, Cornwall, **3**.
Pickhill, N.Yorks, All Saints, (G.F.), **3**, 8cwt. - *OS: SE 347 837.*
Pidley, Cambs, **3**, Have No Stay's and Sliders at present.
Pilham, Lincs, All Saints, **1**, - *OS: SK 863 938.*
Pillerton Hersey, Warwicks, St Mary the Virgin, (G.F.), **3**, 8cwt. in A, Unringable, The Tenor was cast by Edward Newcombe of Leicester in 1602, *OS: SP 298 489.*
Pilling, Lancs, St John the Baptist, **3**, 14-3-7. in F. - Anti-Clockwise.
Pitcombe, Som, St Leonard, (G.F.), **3**, 8-2-0. - *OS: GR 674 327.*
Pitstone, Bucks, St Mary, **3**, 8-2-4. - Unringable, *OS: SP 942 149.*
Pitton, Wilts, St Peter, **3**, 3cwt. - *OS: SU 210 313.*
Pittville. *- See Cheltenham.*
Plaistow , Gtr London, West Ham Central Mission, **10**, 9-1-26. *in A. - Chimed Only.*
Pleasley Hill, Notts, St Barnabas, **1**, 3-1-21. in E. - *OS: SK 508 639.*
Plumpton, Northants, St John the Baptist, **1**, 3cwt. in F.
Plungar, Leics, St Helen, **2**, 4cwt. - Unringable, *OS: SK 769 341.*
Plymouth, Devon, (R.C.), Cathedral Church of St Mary and St Boniface, **1**, 15cwt.
Pool, Canford Cliffs , Dorset, The Transfiguration, **9**, 11-2-6. *in G. - Chimed Only.*
Pool Keynes, Glos, St Michael, **1**, 1-0-0. - This Bell was cast by Abel Rudhall in 1756. *OS: ST 999 955.*
Portchester, Hants, St Mary, **3**, 11-2-0. in G. *Mon 6.30 pm., OS: SU 625 045.*
Portsmouth , Hants, Guild Hall, **1**, 78-2-12., *- Clock Bell.*
Portswood. *- See Southampton.*
Postling , Kent, St Mary and St Radigund, **3**, 9-3-0. *in G. - Hung Dead, OS: TR 145 391.*
Potern End , Herts, **3**, 0-3-14., *- Lever Chimed Only.*
Potterhanworth, Lincs, St Andrew, (G.F.), **3**, 6-3-25. in B. - *OS: TF 054 661.*
Poulshot, Wilts, St Peter, **3**, - The Treble was cast by the Bristol Foundry, and the Second and Tenor were both cast in 1606. *OS: ST 968 593.*
Poulton, Glos, St Nicholas, **2**, - *OS: SP 102 010.*
Pouny, Wilts, St Swithin, **3**, - The Second was cast around 1500.
Poyntington, Dorset, All Saints, **3**, 9cwt. in A. - Unringable, *OS: ST 560 199.*
Preston, *- See Brighton.*
Preston, *- See Faversham.*
Preston, Humbs, **3**, 4cwt., - Derelict Church.
Preston, Lancs, (R.C.), St Augustine, **1**, 5cwt. - Steel Bell and wheel, Unringable.
Preston , Lancs, (R.C.), St Ignatious, **3**, Automatic Swing Chiming.

Preston, Lancs, (R.C.), St Walburghe, **1**, 31-0-26. - This Bell is Counterbalanced to reduce the sway on the Tower and was cast by Mears in 1860.
Preston Bisset, Bucks, St John the Baptist, **1**, 4-0-10.
Preston Deanery, Northants, St Peter and St Paul, **1**, 1-3-0.
Preston-on-Stour, Warwicks, St Mary, **3**, 8cwt. in Bb. - The Second and Tenor were both cast by Henry Bagley in 1635, and the Treble was cast by Abraham Rudhall I in 1713,**Sun 9-9.30am** *OS: SP 203 499.*
Priddy, Somerset, St Lawrence, (G.F.), **3**, 8cwt. in F#.
Priors Hardwick, Warwicks, St Mary the Blessed Virgin, (G.F.), **3**, 8cwt. in A. - The Treble and Tenor were cast by Henry Bagley in 1670, The Second was cast by Thomas Newcombe in 1580, These Bells were Re-Hung in 1922 in a two tier frame by Frederick Webb of Kiddlington, *OS: SP 472 562.*
Princes Risborough, Bucks, **1**, 7cwt. - Unringable.
Princethorpe, Warwicks, (R.C.), Benedictine Priory of our Lady of the Angels,(Princethorpe College), (Original Chapel), 3, 2-2-0. - Unringable,(Big Tower), 1, 3cwt. - Swing Chiming Only, Also 8, 10cwt. in G., Hung Dead, Ellacombe Chimed., These Bells were cast by John Warner in 1899, OS: SP 395 710.
Prinknash , Glos, (R.C.), Abbey of Our Lady and St Peter, 8, 21-3-1. in E. - Chimed Only.
Puddington, Devon, St Thomas a Becket, **3**, 4cwt. - Unringable, Derelict Church, *OS: SS 833 107.*
Puncknowle, Dorset, St Mary the Blessed V , (G.F.), **3**, 8-2-0. in A. - Anti-Clockwise, *OS: SY 535 887.*
Purse Caundle, Dorset, St Peter, (G.F.), **3**, 10cwt. in G. - Unringable, Two Bells Cracked, *OS: ST 697 177.*
Putley, Herefordshire, Unknown, (G.F.), **3**, 3-2-0. in Bb. - *OS: SO 637 377.*
Puttenham, Herts, St Mary, (G.F.), **3**, 10cwt. in A. - *OS: SP 884 149.*
Quarley , Hants, St Michael and All Angels, 3, - Hung Dead outside Church, OS: SU 424 348.
Quarndon, Derbys, **1**.
Quarr , Isle of White, (R C.), Quarr Abbey, 4, 50cwt., - Swing Chiming Only.
*Quarrington, Lincs, St Botolph, 8, 5-2-0. in C. - The **Seventh and Tenor** are Hung for Ringing the rest are Chimed. OS: TF 053 446.*
Quatford, Salop, St Mary Magdalene, (G.F.), **3**, 6-2-0. - *OS: SO 732 908.*
Quethiock, Cornwall, St Hugh, (G.F.), **3**, 7cwt. - *OS: SX 313 647.*
Quy , Cambs, St Mary the Virgin, 5, 6cwt. - Chimed Only.
Radbourne, Derbys, St Andrew, (G.F.), **3**, 4cwt. in C., **Thurs (5th),** *OS: SK 286 360.*
Radclive, Bucks, St John the Evangelist, **3**, 7-1-9. - Derelict Church, *OS: SP 676 339.*
Raddington, Som, St Michael, **3**, 9-2-0. - *OS: ST 021 260.*
Radford, Notts, St Peter, **2**, 4cwt. - *OS: SK 552 407.*
Radley , Oxon, St Peters College, 3, 30-0-2. - Hung Dead, Clock Chime, OS: SU 522 995.
Radstone, Northants, St Laurance, **2**.
Ragdale, Leics, All Saints, **3**, 3-3-05. in C#. - *OS: SK 661 199.*
Ramsbotton , Gtr Man, St Andrew, 5, 7cwt. - Chimed Only.
Ramsbotton, Lancs, St Andrew, **1**, 7cwt.
Ramsden, Oxon, St James, **3**, 3-1-0. - *OS: SP 357 152.*
Ramsey, Cambs, St Mary, **2**, Unringable but awaiting work to be done on them.
Ramsey , Essex, St Michael, 5, 13-1-1. in F. - Chimed Only.
Ramsgill, Patley Bridge, N.Yorks, St Mary, **3**, 3-3-0. - Unringable. *OS: SE 119 709.*
Ranby, Lincs, St German, (G.F.), **3**, 7-0-23. in B. - *OS: TF 228 791.*
Rand, Lincs, St Oswald, **2**, 6cwt. - *OS: TF 107 791.*
Rashcliffe, W.Yorks, St Stephen, **1**, 4-2-0., - Unringable.
Raskelf, N.Yorks, St Mary the Virgin, (G.F.), **3**, 8cwt. - *OS: SE 490 708.*
Raithby by Louth, Lincs, St Peter, **2**, 5cwt. - *OS: TF 311 847.*
Ratcliffe on the Wreake , Leics, (R.C.), College, 8, 2-1-21. in F. - Automatically Chimed Only.

Ratley, Warwicks, St Peter ad Vincula, 3, - Unringable, *OS: SP 383 473.*
Ravensden, Beds, 3, Hung Dead, Ellecombe Chimed Only.
Ravenstone, Bucks, All Saints, 3, 8-3-24. in G. - the Second was Cast in the 14th Century, Derelict and Rough Going, *OS: SP 851 509.*
Ravenstone, Leics, St Michael and All Angels, (G.F.), 3, 6-1-8. - *OS: SK 402 139.*
Ravenstonedale, Cumbria, St Oswald, 3, 8cwt. - *OS: NY 722 033.*
Rawcliffe, N.Yorks, St James, 3, 2cwt. - Lever Chimed Only, Steel Bells, OS: SE 581 537.
Reading, Berks, (R.C.), St James, 1.
Reading, Berks, St John the Evangelist, 1, 2-2-0. in E. - *OS: SU 724 734.*
Reading, Berks, St Mary (Castle Street), 1, 4-3-21. in C. - *OS: SU 724 736.*
Reading, Berks, Town Hall, 9, 7-2-25. in Ab. - Chimed Only.
Reading ,Greyfriars, Berks, 3, 3cwt. - Chimed Only, OS: SU 713 736.
Reading, Berks, Reading University, 1, 51-0-16., - Chimed Only.
Redbrook, Glos, St Saviour, 1, 2-2-0. - *OS: SO 538 099.*
Redcar, N.Yorks, 3.
Redlynch, Wilts, St Mary the Virgin, 1, - *OS: SU 203 207.*
Redmile, Leics, St Peter, 1, - *OS: SK 797 354.*
Rearsby, Leics, St Michael, 3, 7-3-11. - *OS: SK 651 146.*
Rede, Suffolk, All Saints, (G.F.), 3, 6cwt. - *OS: TL 805 559.*
Reed, Herts, 1, - Hung Dead, Two of the Bells were Scrapped in 1976.
Reepham, Lincs, St Peter and St Paul, 1, 6-1-18. - *OS: TF 039 739.*
Reigate, Surrey, St Mark, 3, - Steel Bells, *OS: TQ 255 509.*
Remenham, Berks, St Nicholas, 3, 3-3-16. - Chimed Only, OS: SU 771 843.
Richards Castle, Batchott, Salop and Herefords, New Church, All Saints, 1, 41-2-5.
Richards Castle, Herefords and Salop, Old Church, St Bartholomew, 3, 7cwt. in B. - Detatched Tower *OS: SO 495 695.*
Ridge, Herts, St Margaret, (G.F.), 3, 11cwt. in G.
Rilby, Lincs, St Edward, 3, 9cwt. - Chimed Only, OS: TA 185 075.
Rillington, N.Yorks, St Andrew, (G.F.), 3, 5-3-16. in Bb. - *OS: SE 853 744.*
Rimpton, Som, Blessed virgin Mary, (G.F.), 3, 6cwt. - Unringable, *OS: ST 611 218.*
Ringmore, Devon, All Hallows, 3, 7cwt. - *OS: SX 922 720.*
Ripley, N.Yorks, All Saints, 3, 9cwt. in G. - Swing Chimed Only, OS: SE 283 605.
Risborough, Bucks, St Mary Princess, 1, 7-2-9.
Risley, Derbys, All Saints, 6, 3-0-26. in Eb. - Chimed Only.
Riston, Lancs, (R.C.), St Charles, 1.
Rochdale, Gtr Man, Town Hall, 1, 55-1-07., - Chimed Only.
Rockbeare, Devon, St Mary, 6, 12cwt. - Chimed Only.
Rockhampton, Glos, St Oswald, 1, 10cwt. - *OS: ST 655 933.*
Rockingham, Northants, St Leonard, 1, 5-2-20.
Rodborough, Glos, St Mary Magdalene, 1, 20cwt. - *OS: SO 843 045.*
Rodbourne, Wilts, Holy Rood, 1, - This Bell was cast in 1654. *OS: ST 938 835.*
Rodmarton, Glos, St Peter, 3, 10-1-0. - *OS: ST 943 981.*
Roehampton, Gtr London, 1.
Roehampton, Gtr London, (R.C.), St Joseph, 13, 8cwt. - Chimed Only.
Rollerstone, Wilts, St Andrew, 1.
Romaldkirk, Dur, St Romald, 3, 7-1-23. - Chimed Only. - OS: NY 995 222.
Rosliston, Derbys, St Mary, (G.F.), 3, 4-3-0. - Unringable, *OS: SK 243 169.*
Rossington, S.Yorks, St Michael, 3, 5cwt. - *OS: SK 642 984.*
Rotherby, Leics, All Saints, 3, 6cwt. - Chimed Only, OS: SK 675 165.
Rotherfield Peppard, Oxon, All Saints, 3, 4-2-14. - Chimed Only, OS: SU 714 816.
Rotherhithe, Gtr London, Norwegian Church, St Olive, 2, - *OS: TQ 353 792.*
Rothwell, Lincs, St Mary, (G.F.), 3, 8-3-02. - *OS: TF 149 994.*
Rothwell, Nothants, (R.C.), St Barnadette, 1.

Roundhay, W.Yorks, St John, **3**, 4-3-26. in C#., **Wed**, *OS: SE 338 372.*
Rowlestone, Herefords, St Peter, **3**, 5-3-0. - *OS: SO 374 271.*
Roxbourne, Middlesex, St Andrew, 8, 9-2-6. in A. - Chimed Only.
Roxby, Humbs, St Mary, 3, 7cwt. - Chimed Only, OS: SE 920 171.
Rudston, Humbs, **3**.
Rufforth, N.Yorks, All Saints, **3**, 5cwt. - *OS: SE 528 516.*
Rugby, *Warwicks, (R.C.), St Marie, **1**, 5-3-21. - Hung in a Saddleback Tower this Bell was cast by Mears in 1847, Also in the other Tower there is Eight Bells All cast by Mears and Stainbank in 1871 with a Tenor weight of 14-3-2. in F. Hung for Chiming Only.* ***OS: SP 502 745.***
Rugby, Warwicks, School Chapel, **1**, 64-2-20. in Bb. - Counterbalanced Bell, No Stay or Slider, This bell was cast by Taylors in 1914.
Rugeley, Staffs, (R.C.), **1**.
Runcton Holme, Norfolk, St James, 3, 7cwt. in G. - Swing Chiming Only, OS: TF 619 095.
Runnington, Som, St Peter and St Paul, **2**, - *OS: ST 119 219.*
Ruscome, Berks, St James, **2**, 4-3-21. in C#. - Treble cast by the Workingham foundry in the 14th Century, *OS: SU 798 763.*
Rushall, Norfolk, St Mary the Virgin, **1**, 4-3-0.
Rushall, Wilts, St Michael, **3**, - The Treble was cast by the Salisbury Foundry and the Tenor was cast in 1606. *OS: SU 123 556.*
Ruston, N.Yorks, **3**, 6cwt.
Ryarsh, Kent, St Martin, 3, 7-1-22. in Bb. - Chimed Only, OS: TQ 672 591.
Ryde, Isle of White, (R.C.), St Mary, 8, 2cwt., - Chimed only.
Ryhill, W.Yorks, St James, 8, 1-2-0. - Chimed Only.
Ryhope, Tyne and Wear, St Paul, 6, 5-2-0. in C. - Chimed Only.
Rylstone, N.Yorks, St Peter, **3**, 7-2-20. in C., **Tues**, *OS: SD 972 589.*
Ryme Intrinseca, Dorset, St Hippolytus, (G.F.), **3**, 9cwt. in A. - *OS: ST 582 108.*
St Albans, Herts, Clock Tower, **2**, 18cwt., - The Tenor is Hung for Ringing but Unringable and the Treble is a Clock Bell.
St Albans, Herts, St Saviour, **1**, - Rehung in 1951.
St Anne's on the Sea, Lancs, St Thomas, 5, 15cwt. in F. - Hung Dead, Clock Chime.
St Gunwalloe, Corn, St Winwallow, 6, 4-2-14. in Eb. - Chimed Only.
St Helens, Mers, (R.C.), Lowe House, St Mary, 47, 84-2-20. in A. - Carillon.
St Ives, Cambs, United Reform Church, Free Church, **1**.
St Just in Penwith, Cornwall, St Just, **3**, 8-3-7. in G. - *OS: SW 371 315.*
St Lawrence, Isle of White, St Lawrence, 8, 2-1-19. in G. - Chimed Only.
St Leonards on Sea, E.Sussex, St Ethelburga, 5, 5-0-4. in D. - Hung Dead, Clock Chime.
St Levan, Cornwall, St Levan (G.F.), **3**, 5cwt. in B. - The Treble Ringer has to Stand on a 5 Foot High Safe. *OS: SW 381 223.*
St Margaret at Cliffe, Kent, St Margaret, 8, 6-0-2. in C. - Chimed Only.
St Margarets, Herefordshire, St Margaret, (G.F.), **3**, 6cwt. in Bb. - *OS: SO 353 372.*
St Mary in the Marsh, Kent, St Mary the Virgin, 3, 10-1-10. in G. - Hung Dead, OS: TR 064 280.
St Marylebone, Gtr London, Baker Street, Abbey House, 8, 7-3-4. in B. - Hung Dead, Clock Chime.
St Michael on Wyre, Lancs, St Michael, (G.F.), **3**, 6cwt., - Unringable, *OS: SD 46 41.*
St Michaels Mount, Corn, St Michael, 6, 9cwt. - Chimed Only.
St Pancras, Gtr London, St Pancras, 8, 26cwt. in C#. - Chimed Only.
St Paul's Cray, Kent, St Paulinus, **3**, 7cwt. - Unringable, *OS: TQ 474 691.*
Sacomb, Herts, St Catherine, **3**, 6cwt. in Bb. - Two of the Bells go most of the way up and the other is totally Unringable.
Salcombe Regis, Devon, St Mary and St Peter, **3**, 12cwt. - *OS: SY 148 888.*
Sale, Gtr Man, St Paul, **8**, 10-1-0 in G. - The **Tenor** is only Hung for Ringing the rest are Chimed. *OS: SJ 795 916.*
Salisbury, Wilts, Bishops Palace Chapel, **1**, 8cwt. in Bb.

44

Salisbury, Wilts, Cathedral Church of the Blessed Virgin Mary, 5, 25cwt. in D. - Clock Chime.
Salisbury, Wilts, St Mark, **1**.
Salisbury, Wilts, St Nicholas Hospital, **1**, 0-3-16. - This Bell was Cast in 1623.
Salisbury, Wilts, (R.C.), St Oswald, 1, - Chimed Only.
Salisbury, Wilts, Town Hall, **1**.
Salisbury, Wilts, Workhouse, 2, 0-2-0. - Chimed, The Treble is a Long wasted Bell.
Saltfleetby All Saints, Lincs, All Saints, 5, 8cwt. - Chimed Only.
Saltley, W.Mids, (R.C.), Our Lady of the Rosary, 23, 17-0-14. in F#. - Carillon.
Sancton, Humbs, All Saints, (G.F.), **3**, 5-1-20. - Octagonal Tower, *OS: SE 900 395*.
Sandford-on-Thames, Oxon, St Peter, 3, 3-3-0. - Chimed Only, OS: SP 534 017.
Sand Hutton, N.Yorks, **3**.
Sandwich, Kent, St Peter, **1**, 15-2-19 in F.
Sapperton, Glos, St Kenelm, **3**, 7cwt. in A. - *OS: SO 948 035*.
Sark, C.I., St Peter, **1**, This Bell was cast in 1580.
Satterleigh, Devon, St Peter, 3, 3cwt. - Swing Chiming on Half Wheels, OS: SS 668 225.
Saunderton, Bucks, St Mary, **3**, 4-3-21. - No Stays or Sliders, *OS: SP 796 018*.
Saul, Glos, St James, **1**, 7cwt. - *OS: SO 749 095*.
Sausthopre, Lincs, St Andrew, **3**, 5cwt. - *OS: TF 382 681*.
Saxby, Leics, St Peter, 3, 5-2-0. - Chimed Only, OS: SK 814 201.
Saxby All Saints, Humbs, All Saints, **3**, 6cwt. - *OS: SE 992 167*.
Saxelbye, Leics, St Peter, (G.F.), **3**, 7-2-5. in Bb. - *OS: SK 691 210*.
Saxton, N.Yorks, All Saints, **3**, 10-3-0. - *OS: SE 475 369*.
Scalford, Leics, St Egelwin the Martyr, (G.F.), **3**, 8-1-22. in A. - *OS: SK 763 242*.
Scampton, Lincs, St John, 3, 4cwt. - Chiming Only, OS: SK 948 794.
Scraptoft, Leics, All Saints, 3, 5-1-17. - Chimed Only, OS: SK 648 055.
Scarrington, Notts, St John of Beverley, **3**, 6cwt. in Bb. - Unringable, *OS: SK 735 417*.
Scartho, Humbs, St Giles, **3**, 10-0-5. in Ab. - *OS: TA 267 064*.
Scawby, Humbs, St Hybald, **3**, 7-3-16. in Eb. - Ropes fall in a straight line, *OS: SE 969 057*.
Screveton, Notts, St Wilfred, **3**, 10cwt. - Unringable, *OS: SK 729 434*.
Scorborough, Humbs, **3**, 7-2-26, - Derelict Church.
Scrooby, Notts, St Wilfred, **3**, 4-2-0. - Unringable, *OS: SK 653 907*.
Scropton, Derbys, St Paul, (G.F.), **3**, 2-1-23. in D#. - *OS: SK 192 932*.
Scruton, N.Yorks, 3, 5-3-16., - Lever Chimed Only.
Seagrave, Leics, All Saints, **3**, 7-2-0. - *OS: SK 620 176*.
Seagry, Wilts, St Mary, **1**.
Seaham Harbour, Dur, St John the Evangelist, 8, 9-0-12. in B. - Chimed Only.
Seamer, N.Yorks, St Martin, (G.F.), **3**, 13cwt. - *OS: TA 015 834*.
Seaton Ross, Humbs, **3**.
Sedgebrook, Lincs, St Laurence, 3, 8cwt. - Chimed Only, OS: SK 857 381.
Selby, N.Yorks, St James the Apostle, 10, 6-3-8. in B. - Chimed Only.
Selside, Cumb, **1**.
Semington, Wilts, St George, **1**.
Sessay, N.Yorks, **3**.
Settle, Stainforth, N.Yorks, **3**, 6cwt. - Unringable.
Settrington, N.Yorks, All Saints, **3**, 9cwt. - Unringable, *OS: SE 839 702*.
Sevenhampton, Glos, St Andrew, **3**, 7cwt. in A. - *OS: SP 033 218*.
Sewerby, Humbs, St John the Evangelist, 6, 3-3-5. in Eb. - Chimed Only.
Shackerstone, Leics, St Peter, **3**, 9-2-11. - Unringable, Derelict Church, *OS: SK 374 067*.
Shadingfield, Suffolk, **1**.
Shaftesbury, Dorset, Grammar School, **3**, - Steel Bells and Steel Wheels.
Shaftesbury, Dorset, (R.C.), 8, - Chimed Only, Hemispherical Bells.
Shamley Green, Surrey, Christ Church, 6, 1-2-26. in Bb. - Chimed Only.
Shaw, Wilts, Christ Church, **1**.

Sheepscombe, Glos, St John, **1**, 2-2-0. - *OS: SO 892 101.*
Sheldon, Devon, St James the Greater, **3**, 3cwt. - *OS: ST 120 086.*
Shenley , Herts, St Martin, 6, 10-0-4. in G. - Chimed Only.
Shepherds Bush, Gtr London, St Simon, **8**, 9cwt. - *The Tenor is only Hung for Ringing the rest are Chimed.* **OS: TQ 236 798.**
Shepton Montague, Som, St Peter, **3**, 9-0-18. - *OS: ST 682 318.*
Sherbourne , Dorset, (R.C.), 1, - Chimed Only.
Sherburn, Oxon, All Saints, **1**, 4-3-21.
Sheriff Hutton, N.Yorks, St Helen and the Holy Cross, (G.F.), **3**, 8cwt. - *OS: SE 658 673.*
Sherrington , Wilts, St Michael, 1, - Lever Chimed Only, Medieval Bell.
Shilton, Oxon, Holy Rood, (G.F.), **3**, 4-3-21. in C#. - Anti-Clockwise, *OS: SP 267 083.*
Shipton by Beningborough , N.Yorks, 3, 4cwt., - Swing Chiming Only, Steel Wheels.
Shipton Bellinger, Hants, St Peter, **3**, 9cwt. - Unringable, *OS: SU 233 453.*
Shirley, Derbys, St Michael, **3**, 4-3-0. - Unringable, *OS: SK 219 417.*
Shirley , Hants, (R.C.), St Boniface, 1, - Chimed Only.
Shirley , Surrey, St John the Evangelist, 6, 6-0-4. in C. - Hung Dead, Clock Chime.
Sholden , Kent, St Nicholas, 3, 5-2-0. in B. - Chimed Only, OS: TR 359 522.
Shrewsbury , Salop, Holy Cross Abbey, 8, 21cwt. - Chimed Only.
Shrewsbury , Salop, (R.C.), The Cathedral Church of Our Lady Help of Christians and Saint Peter of Alcantara, 1, - Chimed Only.
Shrewsbury , Salop, St Julians Arts and Crafts Centre, 6, 13-1-0. in F#. - Chimed Only.
Shurdington, Glos, St Paul, **1**, 1-1-0. - *OS: SO 921 189.*
Siddal, W.Yorks, St Mark, **5**, 7-3-24. in A# - *The Tenor is Only Hung for Ringing the rest are Hung Dead.* *OS: SE 098 239.*
Sigglesthorne, Humbs, **3**, 12cwt., - Unringable.
Singleton, W.Sussex, **2**.
Sinnington, N.Yorks, **3**, 1-1-0., - These bells were rehung in 1990.
Sithney, Cornwall, St Sithney, **3**, 10cwt. - *OS: SW 637 290.*
Sittingbourne , Kent, (R.C.), The Sacred Heart, 8, 2-2-5. in F. - Chimed Only, Cast in Belgium.
Sixhills, Lincs, All Saints, **3**, 9cwt. - Anti-Clockwise, *OS: TF 170 871.*
Sispenny Handley, Dorset, St Mary, **3**, 7cwt. in B. - Unringable, *OS: ST 995 173.*
Skegby, Notts, St Andrew, **3**, 4-2-24. in C#. - Unringable, Ringing Chamber converted to a Kitchen, *OS: SK 492 610.*
Skegby, Notts, All Saints, **3**, - *OS: SK 783 811.*
Skelbrook, S.Yorks, St Michael and All Angels, (G.F.), **3**, 3cwt. - *OS: SE 511 122.*
Skelton, N.Yorks.
Skendleby , Lincs, St Peter and St Paul, 3, 6-3-0. - Chimed Only, OS: TF 433 698.
Skipsea, Humbs, **3**, 11-2-4.
Skipwith , N.Yorks, St Helen, 6, 8cwt. in Bb. - Chimed Only.
Skirwith, Cumb, St John the Evangelist, **3**, - *OS: NY 618 327.*
Slaithwaite, W.Yorks, St James, **5**, 16cwt. - *The Tenor is Only Hung for Ringing the rest are Hung Dead.* *OS: SE 078 141.*
Slapton , Northants, St Botolph, 3, 6cwt. Chimed Only, The Priest Bell was cast in 1312. the other two are also Pre-reformation.
Slaughterford, Wilts, St Nicholas, **2**, 0-1-0. - The Treble weights 3-2-0.
Slawston, Leics, All Saints, **3**, 6-2-0. - Unringable, *OS: SP 781 945.*
Sledmere, Humbs, St Mary, (G.F.), **3**, 8cwt. - Unringable, Anti-Clockwise, *OS: SE 930 646.*
Sleights, N.Yorks, **3**.
Slingsby , N.Yorks, 3, - Hung Dead.
Smalley, Derbys, St John the Baptist, **5**, 40-1-2. in B. - *The Treble is Hung for Ringing it weighs 2cwt. the rest are Chimed Only.* *OS: SK 406 446.*
Smisby, Derbys, St James, **2**, 5cwt. - *OS: SK 348 192.*
Snargate , Kent, St Dunstan, 3, 8-2-0. in B. - Swing Chiming Only, OS: TQ 991 287.

Snave, Kent, St Augustine, **3**, 8cwt. - Unringable.
Sneinton, Notts, St Stephen, **3**, 4cwt. - Unringable, *OS: SK 585 395.*
Snelston, Derbys, St Peter, (G.F.), **3**, 5cwt. - *OS: SK 155 434.*
Snettisham , Norfolk, St Mary the Virgin, 6, 8-0-23. in A. - Chimed Only.
Somerby , Lincs, St Margaret, 3, 4cwt. - Chimed Only, OS: TA 063 066.
Somerford Keynes, Glos, All Saints, **3**, 7cwt. - The Treble and Tenor were Cast by the Bristol Foundry between 1500-1540, Also the Service Bell was Cast by the Bristol Foundry between 1500-1540.
Somersal Herbert, Derbys, St Peter, **1**, 6-0-2. in C#. - *OS: SK 136 352.*
Sopworth, Wilts, St Mary, **1**, 6-2-0. - *OS: ST 828 683.*
Southampton , Hants, Civic Centre, 9, 67-2-10. in Bb. - Hung Dead, Clock Chime.
Southampton, Portswood, Hants, Christ Church, **1**, 7cwt. - *OS: SU 425 146.*
South Anston, S.Yorks, All Saints, **3**, 9-2-0.
South Ascot, Berks, All Souls, **1**, 7-2-1. in C.
South Bank , Cleve, (R.C.), St Peter, 6, 12cwt. - Chimed Only.
South Barrow, Som, St Peter, (G.F.), **3**, 8cwt. - *OS: ST 603 279.*
Southborough*,* Kent, St Peter, **6**, 7-1-21. in B. - The **Tenor** is Only Hung for Ringing the rest are Chimed. *OS: TQ 477 428.*
South Carlton, Lincs, St John the Baptist, **2**, 4-3-5. - *OS: SK 951 767.*
South Cave, Humbs, **3**, 12cwt., - Unringable.
South Cockerington, Lincs, St Leonard, (G.F.), **3**, 11cwt. in G. - *OS: TF 381 887.*
South Cowton, N.Yorks, St Mary, (G.F.), **3**, 8cwt. - *OS: NZ 293 027.*
South Crosland, W.Yorks, Holy Trinity, **1**, 4cwt. - *OS: SF 118 128.*
South Dalton, Humbs, **3**.
South Darley , Derbys, St Mary the Blessed Virgin, 8, 5cwt. - Chimed Only.
South Elkington , Lincs, All Saints, 3, 9-3-26. - Chimed Only, OS: TF 293 883.
South Elmsall, W.Yorks, **3**.
South Ferriby , Lincs, St Nicholas, 3, 3-1-0. - Chimed Only, OS: SE 988 208.
Southampton , Hants, (R.C.), LSU College Chapel, 1, - Chimed Only.
Southampton, Hants, (R.C.), St Edmund, **1**.
South Hinksey, Oxon, St John, **3**, 8cwt. - *OS: SP 509 040.*
South Kelsey , Lincs, St Mary, 3, 9cwt. in G#. - Chimed Only, OS: TF 041 982.
South Leverton, Notts, All Saints, **3**, 10-2-0. - *OS: SK 783 811.*
South Littleton, Worcs, St Michael, **3**, 8-1-1. in A. - Treble and Tenor were both cast at the Mediaeval Worcester Bell Foundry in 1410, Also these Bells were Re-Hung by Taylors in 1966 in a Six Bell Frame *OS: SO 076 463.*
South Malling , E.Sussex, St Michael the Archangel, 8, 2-2-0. - Chimed Only.
South Muskham, Notts, St Wilfred, **3**, 9-3-21. in G#. - *OS: SK 793 573.*
South Otterington, N.Yorks, **3**.
Southowram, W.Yorks, St Anne in the Grove, 6, 11-3-16. in F. - Chimed Only.
Southport, Mers, Holy Trinity, **1**, 40-1-21. - *OS: SD 342 175.*
South Shields , Tyne and Wear, Municipal Buildings, 1, 47-3-14., - Chimed Only.
South Somercoates , Lincs, St Peter, 3, 15cwt. - Chimed Only, Redundant Church, OS: TF 8 3.
South Stoke , Avon, St James the Greater, 3, 8cwt. - Chimed Only, OS: ST 746 613.
South Stoneham , Hants, St Mary, 3, Chimed Only, OS: SU 440 155.
South Warnborough, Hants, St Andrew, (G.F.), **3**, 6-3-0. in Bb. - Anti-Clockwise. **Sun 10.30-11 am, Mon 7-8 pm.,** *OS: SU 721 472.*
South Willingham , Lincs, St Martin, 3, 12cwt. - Chimed Only, OS: TF 195 833.
Southwell, Notts, Holy Trinity, **1**, 3-2-0. - *OS: SK 697 535.*
Spalding , Lincs, St Holland Centre, 23, 5-0-11. in C. - Carillon.
Sparham, Norfolk, St Mary, (G.F.), **3**, 12cwt. -, *OS: TG 071 198.*
Sparkford, Som, St Mary Magdalene, **3**, - Unringable, *OS: ST 609 257.*
Sparkhill , W.Mids, (R.C.), English Martyrs, 8, 7-3-26. - Chimed Only.

47

Spencers Wood, Berks, St Michael, **1**, - *OS: SU 715 666.*
Spennithorne, N.Yorks, St Michael, **3**, 10cwt. -, *OS: SE 137 889.*
Spennithorpe - *See Spennithorne.*
Sproxton, *Leics, St Bartholomew, 3, - Hung Dead, Also (G.F.) 8, 8-2-15. in A., - OS: SK 856 249.*
Stafford, Staffs, St Mary, Castle Church, (G.F.), **3**, 8cwt. in Bb. - These Bells were cast by Charles Carr in 1902, The Treble weighs 5cwt in D and the Second weights 6-2-0 in C., *OS: SJ 905 222.*
Stafford, Baswich, Staffs, Holy Trinity, **3**, 5-2-0. in Db. - Anti-Clockwise, - *OS: SJ 944 223.*
Staincliffe, W.Yorks, Christ Church, **1**, 20-0-14. in Eb., - Ex Worcester Cathedral Tenor, *OS: SF 231 236.*
Stainforth, - *See Settle.*
Stainland, *W.Yorks, St Andrew, 6, 5-0-15. in C. - Chimed Only.*
Stainton, N.Yorks, **3**.
Stainton, *S.Yorks, St Peter, 3, 4-3-1. - Hung Dead, OS: SK 555 936.*
Staintondale, N.Yorks, **3**.
Stamfordham, Northumb, St Mary the Virgin, **1**, - *OS: NZ 076 720.*
Stamor St Bernard, Wilts, All Saints, **2**, 7-1-0. - Both Cast by the Bristol Foundry around 1500.
Stanbridge, *Dorset, St John, 6, 4-1-12. in D. - Chimed Only.*
Stanbrook, *Worcs, (R.C.), St Marys Abbey, 9, 6-1-21. - Chimed Only.*
Stanford Bishop, Herefords, St James, **2**, 5cwt. in C#. - *OS: SO 682 516.*
Stannington, *Northumb, St Mary the Virgin, 8, 30-1-16. in D. - Chimed Only.*
Stanstead Abbots, Herts, St James, (G.F.), **3**, 8-1-0. in A. - *OS: TL 387 122.*
Stanstead Abbots, *Herts, St Margerats, 4, 4-3-18., - Hung Dead.*
Stanton by Bridge, *Derbys, St Michael, 3, 2-0-3. - Chimed Only, OS: SK 367 271.*
Stanton Long, Salop, St Michael and All Angels, **3**, 1cwt. - *OS: SO 572 907.*
Stanton St Quintin, Wilts, St Giles, **1**.
Stanway. - *See Colchester.*
Stanwick - *See Stanwick-St-John.*
Stanwick-St-John, N.Yorks, St John the Baptist, **3**, 6-2-0. in Bb. Unringable, Redundant Church, *OS: NZ 185 120*
Stapehill, Dorset, (R.C.), Heritage Centre, Formerly Stapehill Abbey, **3**.
Staplefield, *W.Sussex, St Mark, 5, 4-1-10. in Eb. - Chimed Only.*
Stapleford, *Herts, 2, - Swing Chimed Only.*
Stapleford, Leics, St Mary Magdalene, **6**, 10cwt. The **Tenor** is Only Hung for Ringing the rest are Chimed.
Stapleton, Leics, St Martin, **1**, 6-0-17. - *OS: SP 435 984.*
Staveley, N.Yorks, All Saints, **3**, 2-2-0. - Unringable, Steel Bells with Steel Wheels on Treble and Second Bells, *OS: SE 362 627.*
Staverton, *Glos, St Catherine, (G.F.), 4, - Chimed Only exept the front* **Three Bells** *with a Tenor of 9cwt in Ab. But Unringable, OS: SO 890 236.*
Staverton, Wilts, St Paul, **1**.
Steeple Gidding, Cambs, St Andrew, **3**, 7cwt. - *OS: TL 132 814.*
Stelling, Kent, St Mary, **3**, 7-2-0. - Unringable.
Stickford, Lincs, St Helen, **1**, 7-2-0. - *OS: TF 352 600.*
Stillingfleet, N.Yorks, **3**.
Stillington, N.Yorks, St Nicholas, (G.F.), **3**, 5-3-0. in C. - Anti-Clockwise, *OS: SE 583 678.*
Stilton, Cambs, **2**, Unringable.
Stockcross, *Berks, St John, 3, 6-3-19. - Only The* **Treble and Tenor** *are Hung for Ringing Also Weight of the Treble is: 1-1-3. - OS: SU 434 684.*
Stockerston, Leics, St Peter, **3**, 8-2-0. - Unringable, *OS: SP 834 975.*
Stocking Pelham, Herts, **1**.
Stockleigh Pomeroy, Devon, St Mary the Virgin, (G.F.), **3**, 5-1-22. in B. - *OS: SS 887 306.*
Stocklynch Ottersay, Som, St Mary Magdalene, **3**, 4-2-0. - Unringable, *OS: ST 387 171.*

48

Stockport, Gtr Man, St Thomas, **5**, 22-1-14. - The **Tenor** is Only Hung for Ringing the rest are Hung Dead. *OS: SJ 898 898.*
Stockton, Warwicks, St Michael and All Angels, **3**, 9cwt. - Unringable, The Treble was cast by Edward Newcombe of Leicester in 1608, *OS: SP 438 636.*
Stoke at Hoo, Kent, St John the Baptist, 3, 5-2-22. in Bb. - Swing Chiming Only, OS: TQ 823 751.
Stoke Charity, Hants, St Michael, 3, 7cwt. - Chimed Only.
Stoke Dry, Leics, St Andrew, **1**, 9cwt.
Stoke Gifford, Glos, St Michael, **3**, 10cwt. in Ab. - Unringable, Anti-Clockwise, *OS: ST 623 797.*
Stoke Hammond, Bucks, St Luke, (G.F.), **3**, 10-1-19., - Rung from the Chancel, *OS: SP 879 298.*
Stokenchurch, Bucks, St Peter and St Paul, **3**, 7-1-2. in Bb. - *OS: SU 760 965.*
Stoke Lyne, Oxon, St Peter, **3**, 8-3-8. in A. - Hung in a Four Bell Frame., *OS: SP 566 284.*
Stoke on Trent, Burslem, Staffs, (R.C.), St Joseph's, **1**, 40-0-22.
Stoke on Trent, Tunstall, Staffs, (R.C.), **1**, 50-0-23.
Stoke Pero, Som, Unknown, **3**, 7cwt. - *OS: SS 878 436.*
Stoke Row, Oxon, St John the Evangelist, **1**, 3-1-17. - No Stay or Slider.
Stoke St Michael, Som, St Michael, (G.F.), **3**, 6cwt. - Unringable, *OS: ST 664 470.*
Stoke Talmage, Oxon, St Mary Magdelan, **2**, 4-0-10. - Treble Cast in 1350 and Tenor Cast in 1360, No Stays or Sliders.
Stonegrave, N.Yorks, **3**, 8cwt.
Stonesby, Leics, St Peter, 3, 9cwt. - Chimed Only, OS: SK 822 247.
Stoney Middleton, Derbys, St Martin, (G.F.), **3**, 5cwt. in Eb. - Anti-Clockwise, Ropes fall in a straight line, Unringable, *OS: SK 232 755.*
Storrington, W.Sussex, (R.C.), Our Lady of England, (G.F.), **3**, 8-2-0. - *OS: TQ 093 145.*
Stoughton, W.Sussex, St Mary, (G.F.), **3**, 10cwt. in A
Stourmouth, Kent, All Saints, 3, 5cwt. in C. - Chimed Only, OS: TR 256 629.
Stowe, Salop, St Michael and All Angels, (G.F.), **3**, 4cwt. - *OS: SO 310 737.*
Stowell, Glos, St Leonard, **1**, 3cwt. - *OS: SP 088 131.*
Stowell, Som, St Mary Magdalene, (G.F.), **3**, 8cwt. - *OS: ST 687 224.*
Stradsett, Norfolk, St Mary, **3**, 6cwt. - Unringable, *OS: TF 668 057.*
Stratford Sub Casmo, Wilts, St Laurence, **2**, 4-3-0.
Stratford Tony, Wilts, St Mary, **3**, 7-2-0.
Stratford-upon-Avon, Warwicks, Bell Court Shopping Centre, 1, 12cwt, - Hung Dead in the Entrance of the Shopping Centre, In Storage at Present during renovation of Shopping Centre.
Stratford-upon-Avon, Warwicks, Saint Peters Mission, 1, 0-1-0., - Hung Dead in Belcote.
Stratford-upon-Avon, Warwicks, St Andrews, 1, 0-1-0., - Chimed Only in a Belcote.
Stratford-upon-Avon, Warwicks, (R.C.), St Gregory's, 1, 0-1-0., - Chimed Only in a Belcote.
Stratford-upon-Avon, Warwicks, The Collegiate Church of the Holy Trinity, 1, 4-2-18., - Hung Dead, This Bell used to be Hung for Ringing in the Cemetery Chapel on the Evesham Road and was cast by Warners in 1881, There is also in this tower, **10**, 19-0-2. in E., These Bells were cast by Taylors in 1948. and the weights of the bells are 5-1-2, 5-1-10, 5-1-6, 5-3-14, 6-3-18, 8-0-16, 10-0-23, 11-3-1, 14-2-2, 19-0-2., **Tues**.
Stratford-upon-Avon, Warwicks, The Guild Chapel, 2, 27-3-2. in D., - The Tenor is Automatically Swing Chimed Only and was cast by Hugh Watts II in 1633. The Treble is Hung Dead and Electronically Chimed Only also this Bell was cast by Robert Wells in 1782 with a weight of 3cwt,There was also a Proposal in 1721 to Scrap the Bell and put a New Ring of Six cast by Richard Sanders who had a Bellfoundry in Stratford-upon-Avon at the time.
Stratton-on-the-Fosse, Som, (R.C.), 5, 5cwt., - Chimed Only.
Stratton-on-the-Fosse, Som, (R.C.), Downside Abbey (G.F.), **1**, 106-3-0. - This Bell is Counterbalanced and also has No Stay or Slider., Also this Bell is Called "Great Bede".
Stratton-on-the-Fosse, Som, St Vigor, (G.F.), **3**, 4-2-0. - Unringable, *OS: ST 659 508.*
Strelley, Notts, All Saints, **1**, 6-2-2. - *OS: SK 506 422.*
Stretton-en-le-Field, Leics, St Michael, **2**, 6-3-0. - Unringable, *OS: SK 304 119.*
Strickland, Cumb, 3, 2cwt. - Lever Chimed Only.

49

Stringston, Som, Unknown, **3**, 7cwt. - Unringable, *OS: ST 176 425.*
Strixton, Nothants, St John, **1**.
Strood, Kent, St Nicholas, **3**, 8-2-0. *- Swing Chiming Only, OS: TQ 736 693.*
Stroxton, Lincs, All Saints, **3**, 7-1-13. in B. - *OS: SK 903 311.*
Stubton, Lincs, St Martin, **2**, 6cwt. in B. - *OS: SK 874 488.*
Studley, Wilts, St John, **1**.
Stuntney, Cambs, Holy Cross, **3**, - Unringable, *OS: TL 556 783.*
Sudbury, Middx, (R.C.), St George, **1**, 20-2-24., - Cast by Mears and Stainbank in 1938.
Sulham, Berks, St Nicholas, 6, 7-1-11. in Bb. - Chimed Only.
Sulhamstead Abbots, Berks, St Mary, **3**, 5cwt. in C.
Sunderland, Tyne and Wear, Town Hall, 1, 78-0-11., - Chimed Only.
Sunninghill, Berks, St Michael and All Angels, **3**, 3-2-24. in E. - *OS: SU 940 686.*
Sutton, - *See Wansford.*
Sutton Mandeville, Wilts, All Saints, **3**.
Sutton Montis, Som, Holy Trinity, (G.F.), **3**, 7-2-0. - *OS: GR 624 248.*
Sutton on Sea, Lincs, St Clement, (G.F.), **3**, 10cwt. - *OS: TF 519 818.*
Sutton on the Forrest, N.Yorks, 3, - Lever Chimed Only.
Sutton St Edmund, Lincs, St Edmund, **1**, - *OS: TF 368 132.*
Sutton St Michael, Herefords, St Michael, **2**, 3-1-0. in F#. - *OS: SO 527 458.*
Sutton upon Derwent, Humbs, St Michael and All Angels, **3**, 6-2-11., - *OS: SE 705 473.*
Swallowcliffe, Wilts, St Peter, (G.F.), **3**, 6cwt. - The Treble was Cast in 1632.
Swanley, Kent, St Paul, 3, 6-1-11. in C. - Chimed Only, OS: TQ 530 698.
Swarkestone, Derbys, St James, **3**, 4-0-20. - Unringable, *OS: SK 372 287.*
Swaton, Lincs, St Michael, 3, 7cwt. in Bb. - Chimed Only, OS: TF 135 376.
Swayfield, Lincs, St Nicholas, **3**, 7cwt. in Bb. - *OS: SK 993 227.*
Swettenham, Cheshire, St Peter, **3**, 7-2-15. - *OS: SJ 801 627.*
Swillington, W.Yorks, St Mary, 3, - Hung Dead, Also 8, 12-0-22. in G., **Mon**, OS: SE 384 305.
Swinbrook, Oxon, St Mary, (G.F.), **2**, 2-3-13. - *OS: SP 280 121.*
Swindon, Wilts, St Augustine, **1**.
Swindon, Wilts, St Banabus, **1**.
Swindon, Wilts, St Paul, **1**.
Swythamley Park, Staffs, 8, 13cwt. - Chimed Only.
Syde, Glos, St Mary, **3**, 5cwt. in C#. - *OS: SD 949 108.*
Sydenham, Oxon, St Mary, **3**, 7cwt. in Bb. -Anti-Clockwise.
Syston, Lincs, St Mary, (G.F.), **3**, 10-0-9. - *OS: SK 930 409.*
Sywell, Northants, St Peter and St Paul, **3**, 6-0-13. in Bb. - *OS: SP 821 672.*
Tadlow, Cambs, St Giles, (G.F.), **3**, 7cwt. in Bb. - *OS: TL 279 477.*
Talbot Village, Dorset, St Mark, **12**, 3-2-2 in F. - The **Tenor** is Only Hung for Ringing the rest are Chimed. *OS: SZ 070 930.*
Tallington, Lincs, St Laurence, 3, 8-2-14. - Chimed Only, OS: TF 091 078.
Tankersley, S.Yorks, St Peter, **3**, 7cwt. - Unringable, *OS: SK 350 997.*
Tansor, Northants, St Mary, (G.F.), **3**, 7cwt. in A. - *OS: TL 053 909.*
Taplow, Bucks, St Nicholas, **1**, 16-2-0. in E. - *OS: SU 912 822.*
Tarrant Crawford, Dorset, St Mary, (G.F.), **3**, 7cwt. in Bb.
Tarrant Gunville, Dorset, St Mary, **3**, 9-2-25. in A#. - *OS: ST 926 127.*
Tatenhill, Staffs, St Michael, **3**, 6-3-0. in A. - Unringable, *OS: SK 205 220.*
Tatham, Lancs, St James the Less, (G.F.), **3**, 9-1-21. in B., *Wed 7.30 pm., OS: SD 605 694.*
Tatham Fells, Lancs, **1**.
Taunton, Som, (R.C.), St George, - Chiming Only, Tubular Bells.
Taunton, Som, St Mary Magdelan, 3, - Chimed Only, Semitone Bells, **12**, 29-3-20. in C#., **Mon**.
Teddington, Glos, **2**.
Tedstone Delamere, Herefords, St James, **5**, 3-1-23. - The **Tenor** is Only Hung for Ringing the rest are Chimed. *OS: SO 695 585.*

50

Teffont Evias, Wilts, **3**.
Teigh, Leics, Holy Trinity, **3**, 8cwt. - *OS: SK 865 160*.
Telford, Salop, St George, St George, 8, 8cwt. - *Chimed Only*.
Temple Grafton, Warwicks, St Andrew, **1**, 4cwt. - Unringable.
Temple Sowerby, Cumb, St James, **1**, - *OS: NY 612 272*.
Templeton, Devon, St Margaret, (G.F.), **3**, 8cwt. - *OS: SS 888 140*.
Tenterden, Kent, St Michael and All Angels, 6, 10cwt. - *Chimed Only*.
Terrington, N.Yorks, All Saints, (G.F.), **3**, 9cwt. - *OS: SE 672 708*.
Teston, Kent, St Peter and St Paul, **3**, 6cwt. in B. - Unringable, *OS: TQ 705 535*.
Tetney, Lincs, St Peter and St Paul, **3**, 11cwt. in G. - *OS: TA 316 009*.
Thatcham, Berks, (R.C.), Cold Ash Retreat Centre, **3**.
Theddlethorpe St Helens, Lincs, St Helen, (G.F.), **3**, 12-2-0. in G#. - *OS: TF 477 889*.
The Leigh, Wilts, All Saints, **3**, 5-2-0 in A.
Therfield, Herts, St Mary the Virgin, 6, 12-0-9. in G. - *Chimed Only*.
Thirkleby, N.Yorks, All Saints, **3**, 5-2-7. - *OS: SE 473 787*.
Thisleton, Leics, St Nicholas, **1**, - *OS: SK 913 180*.
Threlfield, Herts, 6, 14cwt., - *Rehung for Chiming in 1911 in a Ringing Frame*.
Thormanby, N.Yorks, **3**.
Thornbury, Herefords, St Anna, **3**, 7-2-0. in A. - *OS: SO 622 547*.
Thornhill Lees, W.Yorks, Holy Innocents, **2**, 8-3-0. in Ab. - Unringable, *OS: SF 247 195*.
Thornton, Bucks, St Michael and All Angels, **3**, 16-3-9. - Treble and Tenor cast in 1400, *OS: SP 753 362*.
Thornton, Leics, St Peter, **3**, 8-2-7. - *OS: SK 468 077*.
Thornton Dale, N.Yorks, All Saints, (G.F.), **3**, 8cwt. - *OS: SE 838 832*.
Thornton Watlass, N.Yorks, St Mary, **3**, 10cwt. - Unringable.
Thoroton, Notts, St Helena, **2**, 6-2-0. - *OS: SK 764 426*.
Thorp Arch, W.Yorks, All Saints, (G.F.), **3**, 5-0-3. - Anti-Clockwise, *OS: SE 437 461*.
Thorpe, Derbys, St Leonard, (G.F.), **3**, 4-3-26. in B. - *OS: SK 155 502*.
Thorpe, Notts, St Laurance, **2**, 4-2-0. - *OS: SK 767 501*.
Thorpe Arch, - *See Thorp Arch*.
Thorpe Langton, Leics, St Leonard, **3**, 6-3-10. - Unringable, *OS: SP 740 925*.
Thorpe Mandeville, Northants, St John the Baptist, (G.F.), **3**, 6-2-26. in B. -*OS: SP 533 449*.
Thorpe-Next-Haddiscoe, Norfolk, St Matthias, **2**, 4-2-0. - *OS: TM 436 981*.
Thorpe on the Hill, Lincs, St Michael, 3, 4-1-19. - *Chimed Only*, OS: SK 908 655.
Thorpe St Peter, Lincs, St Peter, 3, 16cwt. - *Chimed Only*, OS: TF 485 607.
Thorpe Salvin, S.Yorks, St Peter, **3**, 7cwt. - Unringable, *OS: SK 521 812*.
Threekingham, Lincs, St Peter, 3, 11cwt. in G. - *Chimed Only*, OS: TF 089 367.
Throop. - *See Bournemouth*.
Thurgarton, Notts, Priory Church of St Peter, **3**, 7-2-9. in A.
Thurlby, Lincs, St German, 3, 6cwt. - *Chimed Only*, OS: TF 098 169.
Thurnham, Kent, St Mary the Virgin, (G.F.), **3**, 6cwt. in B. - *OS: TQ 804 577*.
Thursley, Surrey, St Michael and All Angels, (G.F.), **3**, - Rung from side aisle, *OS: SU 901 394*.
Thurstonland, W.Yorks, St Thomas, **1**, 5-1-0. in D#. - Unringable, *OS: SE 166 108*.
Tibberton, Glos, Holy Trinity, (G.F.), **3**, 7cwt. in Bb. - **Sun 10.15 am, Wed 8 pm.**, *OS: SO 757 219*.
Tickencote, Leics, St Peter, **2**, 4-0-2.
Tidcombe, Wilts, St Michael, **3**, 7cwt.
Tidmarsh, Berks, St Laurance, (G.F.), **3**, 5cwt. in B. - Tenor Cast in the Reading Foundry in 1510., Unringable, *OS: SU 634 745*.
Tidmington, Warwicks, Unknown, (G.F.), **3**, 6cwt. - Unringable, *OS: SP 260 395*.
Tiffield, Northants, St John the Baptist, (G.F.), **3**, 7cwt. in Bb. - *OS: SP 699 517*.
Tilbrook, Cambs, **3**, 7cwt. - Unringable, Bells taken down into Church, *OS: TL 081 693*.
Tile Cross, W.Mids, St Peter, 6, 4-0-9. in D. - *Chimed Only*.

Tilshead, Wilts, St Thomas, **3**, 7cwt. - Unringable, Cast as a Complete set by Thomas Bilbie in 1764.
Tingrith, Beds, St Nicholas, **3**, - *Chimed Only, OS: TL 006 325.*
Tinsley, S.Yorks, St Lawrence, **3**, 1-3-6. - *Lever Chimed Only, OS: SK 403 907.*
Tissington, Derbys, St Mary, (G.F.), **3**, 7cwt. in B. - Ropes fall in a straight line, *OS: SK 176 522.*
Titley, Herefords, St Peter, **1**, 4cwt. in F. - *OS: SO 332 696.*
Titsey, Surrey, **1**.
Tittensor, Staffs, St Luke, 6, 7-3-0. in A. - *Chimed Only.*
Tixover, Leics, St Luke, **1**.
Tockwith, N.Yorks, **3**, 5cwt., - Unringable.
Todwick, S.Yorks, St Peter and St Paul, (G.F.), **3**, 4-0-6. - *OS: SK 497 842.*
Tolland, Som, St John the Baptist, **3**, 6-2-0. - Unringable, *OS: ST 101 323.*
Tollerton, Notts, St Peter, **3**, 6cwt. - Unringable, *OS: SK 615 348.*
Tonbridge, Kent, St Stephen, **3**, 5cwt. in E. - Unringable, *OS: TQ 587 457.*
Tong, Kent, St Giles, **3**, 5-3-0. in Bb. - Unringable, *OS: TQ 959 562.*
Tong, Salop, St Bartholomew (G.F.), **1**, 46-1-0. - Rung from Chancel, Also **6**, 12-0-17. in F., *OS: SJ 796 074.*
Tooting, Gtr London, Holy Trinity, **2**, - *OS: TQ 279 726.*
Torksey, Lincs, St Peter, 3, 11cwt. in Bb. - *Chimed Only, OS: SK 837 789.*
Torquay, Devon, (R.C.), St Mary Church, **1**.
Toxteth, Mers, St Michael in the Hamlet, 5, 9cwt. - *Hung Dead, Clock Chime.*
Toynton All Saints, Lincs, All Saints, 3, 6cwt. - *Chimed Only, OS: TF 393 638.*
Toynton St Peter, Lincs, St Peter, **1**, 10cwt. - *OS: TF 404 624.*
Treborough, Som, St Peter, **3**, 7cwt. - *OS: ST 011 364.*
Tresswell, Notts, St John the Baptist, **3**, 7-2-0. - Unringable, *OS: SK 782 794.*
Trimingham on Sea, Norfolk, St John the Baptist's Head, 6, 5-0-25. in C. - *Chimed Only.*
Troutbeck, Cumb, Jesus Chapel, 6, 5-0-26. in C#. - *Chimed Only.*
Trowbridge, Wilts, Holy Trinity, **1**.
Truro, Cornwall, Cathedral of St Mary (Green Tower), **1**, 17cwt., Also 5, 14-3-3. in E., Clock Bells, Also 10, 33-3-10. in Db., **Tues**, *OS: SW 826 449.*
Trusthorpe, Lincs, St Peter, **3**, 6-2-0. in Bb. - *OS: TF 514 836.*
Tudeley, Kent, All Saints, 3, 5-2-0. - *Hung Dead.* - OS: TQ 622 455.
Tunbridge Wells, Kent, St Luke, 8, 14-0-25. in F#. - *Chimed Only.*
Tunstall, Lancs, St John the Baptist, (G.F.), **3**, 12cwt. - *OS: SD 604 739.*
Tunstall, Staffs, (R.C.), Sacred Heart, **1**, 50cwt.
Turkdean, Glos, All Saints, **2**, 5cwt. - *OS: SP 108 175.*
Turnham Green, Gtr London, Christ Church, 8, 8-0-11. in A. - *Chimed Only.*
Turnworth, Dorset, St Mary, (G.F.), 3, 6-2-0. in B. - *Chimed Only, OS: ST 821 075.*
Twitchen, Devon, St Peter, **3**, 8cwt. - *OS: SS 789 304.*
Twycross, Leics, St James the Greater, **3**, 7-2-0. - Unringable, *OS: SK 339 049.*
Twyford, Derbys, St Andrew, **3**, 5cwt. in C. - Unringable, *OS: SK 328 287.*
Tytherington, Wilts, St James, **1**, - This Bell hangs in a open Turret in the West End of the Church.
Tytherington, Wilts, St Nicholas, **1**, - This Bell was Cast in the 13th Century and is the Oldest Bell in Wiltshire.
Ufton, Warwicks, St Michael and All Angels, **3**, 6cwt. - Unringable, All these Bells were cast by Matthew Bagley in 1779. *OS: SP 379 395.*
Ugglebarnby, N.Yorks, All Saints, (G.F.), **3**, 11cwt. in G. - *OS: NZ 880 072.*
Uley, Glos, St Giles, **1**, 15cwt. - *OS: ST 782 987.*
Ullingswick, Herefords, St Luke, 5, 2-3-0. in E. - *Chimed Only.*
Umberslade, Warwicks, (Baptist Church) Christ Church, 8, 8-0-10. in Ab. - *Hung Dead, Chimed Only, All these Bells were cast by Gillet and Bland in 1878.*
Upcerne, Dorset, 6, 1-2-0. - *Chimed Only.*

Upper Hardres, Kent, St Peter and St Paul, **3**, 8-1-0. in G. - Unringable, *OS: TR 153 507.*
Upper Helmsley , N.Yorks, St Peter, (G.F.), 3, 1cwt. -, Ellacombe Chimed, OS: SE 695 570.
Upper Heyford, Oxon, St Mary, **3**, 8-2-4. in A. - Derelict Church, *OS: SP 495 259.*
Upper Hopton, W.Yorks, St John the Evangelist, **1**, 9-1-0. in B. - Unringable, *OS: SE 197 186.*
Upper Tooting, Gtr London, Holy Trinity, (G.F.), **2**.
Uppingham , Leics, Uppingham School, 1, 20-1-24., - Chimed Only.
Upton, Cambs, St Michael and All Angels, (G.F.), **2**, 8cwt. - *OS: TF 005 110.*
Upton, Northants, St Michael, **1**, 5-1-0. in D.
Upton Lovell, Wilts, St Mary Magdelane, **3**, 4-3-0.
Upton Scudamore, Wilts, St Mary, **3**, - These Bells were All Cast by Warner and Sons in 1882, Also they are Hung on a Three Tear Frame.
Upwood, Cambs, St Peter, (G.F.), **3**, 8cwt. in E. - Unringable, Anti-Clockwise, *OS: TL 259 827.*
Utterby, Lincs, St Andrew, (G.F.), **3**, 5cwt. - *OS: TF 305 933.*
Venn Ottery, Devon, St Gregory, (G.F.), **3**, 5cwt. - The Second Bell is Cracked, *OS: SY 079 912.*
Vowchurch, Heref, St Bartholomew, (G.F.), **3**, 4-3-11. in Eb. - The Treble and Second were both cast by W.Blews and Sons of Birmingham in 1871, The Tenor was cast by Thomas Rudhall in 1770.*OS: SO 362 365.*
Waddington , Lincs, St Mary and St Peter, 3, 9cwt. - Chimed Only, OS: SK 987 964.
Wadesmill , Herts, 4, - Chimed Only.
Wainfleet , Lincs, All Saints, 8, 4-2-0. - Chimed Only.
Waithe , Lincs, St Martin, 3, 8cwt. in Bb. - Chimed Only, OS: TA 283 008.
Wakerley, Northants, St John the Baptist, **3**, 9cwt. in G#. - Church Closed, *OS: SP 957 993.*
Wakefield , W.Yorks, St John the Baptist, 8, 22-3-24. in Eb. - Chimed Only.
Wakefield , W.Yorks, Town Hall, 1, 54-2-12., - Chimed Only.
Wales , S.Yorks, St John the Baptist, 3, 6-3-9. - Hung Dead, OS: SK 488 827.
Walesby , Lincs, All Saints, 8, 3-3-12. - Chimed Only.
Walesby, Lincs, St Mary, **1**, 3-3-12. - *OS: TF 123 923.*
Walesby, Notts, St Edmund King and Martyr, (G.F.), **3**, 5-2-6. in C. - *OS: SK 685 708.*
Walkeringham, Notts, St Mary Magdalene, (G.F.), **3**, 12-2-2. in F. - *OS: SK 771 922.*
Wallingford, Oxon, St Leonard, **1**, 4-3-26. in D. - *OS: SU 608 891.*
Wallingford, Oxon, St Peter, **1**, 3-2-24. in Eb. - *OS: SU 609 895.*
Wallsend, Tyne and Wear, St Peter, **3**.
Walmersley , Gtr Man, Christ Church, 9, 8-2-17. in A#. - Chimed Only.
Walsall , W.Mids, Town Hall, 14, 16-0-22. in F. - Chimed Only.
Walton , W.Yorks, 3, 6cwt., - Hung Dead, Chimed Only.
Walton, Aylesbury, Bucks, Holy Trinity, **3**, 3-0-21. - Unringable.
Walton-on-Trent, Derbys, St Laurance, **3**, 8-2-16. - Unringable, *OS: SK 213 185.*
Wansford, Sutton, Cambs, St Michael and All Angels, **1**, - *OS: TL 095 988.*
Wandsworth, West Hill, Gtr London, (R.C.), St Thomas a Becket, **1**, 41-0-4.
Wansford, Humbs, **3**.
Wappenbury, Warwicks, St Mary the Virgin, **3**, 10cwt. - Unringable, The Second was cast by Edward Newcombe in 1600. *OS: SP 378 693.*
Wardley, Leics, St Botolph, **2**, 4-2-0. in C.
Waresley, Cambs, St James the Great, **3**, 11cwt. in F#. - *OS: TL 249 546.*
Warkworth, Northants, St Mary, **2**, - *OS: SP 486 407.*
Warlaby, Humbs, St Clement, **3**, - *OS: TA 105 140.*
Warley Town, W.Yorks, St John the Evangelist, **2**, 1-1-0. - *OS: SF 065 250.*
Warmington, Warwicks, St Michael, **3**, 10cwt. - Unringable, The Tenor was cast by Edward Newcombe in 1602. *OS: SP 410 475.*
Warminster , Wilts, St Laurence, 3, - Chimed Only.
Warminster, Wilts, St John, **1**.
Warrington , Cheshire, St Elphin, 8, 18-2-8. in F. - Chimed Only.

Warrington, Cheshire, (R.C.), St Mary's Priory, **8**, 12-3-25 in G. - The **Tenor** is Only Hung for Ringing the rest are Chimed. **OS: SJ 609 883.**
Warter, Humb, **3**, 6cwt.
Warthill, N.Yorks, **3**, 3cwt., - Unringable.
Warton, - See Lancaster.
Wartnaby, Leics, St Michael and All Angels, **2**, 3-2-0. - Unringable, **OS: SK 713 232.**
<u>Warwick</u>, Warwicks, (R.C.), St Mary Immaculate, 1, - Chimed Only.
Water Newton, Cambs, St Remigius, (G.F.), **3**, 10cwt. in Ab. - **OS: TL 108 974.**
Waterperry, Oxon, St Mary, **2**, 2-3-19. in E. - No Stays or Sliders.
<u>Waterstock</u>, Oxon, St Leonard, 6, 7-3-21. in Bb. - Chimed Only.
<u>Water Stratford</u>, Bucks, St Giles, 3, 4-1-11. - Chimed Only, OS: SP 653 344.
<u>Water Stratford</u>, Bucks, Water Stratford House, 9, 2-2-0. - Chimed Only.
<u>Watford</u>, Herts, St Andrew, 5, 3-1-6. - Hemispherical Bells, Hung Dead, Chimed Only, Cast by Mears & Stainbank 1883.
<u>Watford</u>, Herts, St Michael, 3, 5-1-4., - Hung Dead, Chimed Only.
<u>Watford</u>, Herts, St Michael and All Angels, 8, 3-2-15. in G#. - Chimed Only.
Watford, Herts, Old Orphanage, **1**, 2-3-17., - Hung by Taylors in 1870.
Wawne, Humbs, **3**.
Weaverthorpe, N.Yorks, **3**.
Weeting, Norfolk, Blessed Virgin Mary, **3**, - Unringable, Round Tower, **OS: TL 776 892.**
Weeton, N.Yorks, St Barnabus, **3**, 9-3-3. in G. - Wed, **OS: SE 284 460.**
Welham, Leics, St Andrew, **2**, 7cwt. - Unringable, **OS: SP 765 924.**
Well, N.Yorks, St Michael and All Angels, **3**, 13-3-7. in F#. - **OS: SE 268 821.**
<u>Well</u>, Herts, Garden City, Digswell, 3, - Hung Dead in 1956.
Wellington, Salop, Christ Church, **1**, 40-0-16. in B. - **OS: SJ 655 112.**
Wellington Heath, Herefords, Christ Church, **1**, 7cwt. in C. - **OS: SO 332 602.**
Wellow, Notts, St Swithin, **3**, 7-2-0. - Unringable, **OS: SK 671 661.**
<u>Welton</u>, Humbs, St Helen, 4, - Hung Dead, Ellacombe Chimed Only.
Welton Le Wold, Lincs, St Martin, (G.F.), **3**, 6cwt. in Bb. - **OS: TF 273 873.**
Wembworthy, Devon, St Michael, **3**, 9cwt. - **OS: SS 663 099.**
<u>Wendlebury</u>, Oxon, St Giles, 3, 7-2-0. - Chimed Only.
Wendling, Norfolk, St Peter and St Paul, **3**, 10-1-0. - **OS: TF 932 132.**
Wensley, N.Yorks, Holy Trinity, **3**, 12cwt. - Unringable, **OS: SE 895 093.**
<u>Wentbridge</u>, W.Yorks, St John the Evangelist, 6, 5-2-26. in B. - Chimed Only.
West Ashby, Lincs, All Saints, **3**, 8cwt. - **OS: TF 265 725.**
<u>Westbere</u>, Kent, All Saints, 3, 2-1-15. - Hung Dead, OS: TR 193 611.
West Bretton, W.Yorks, St Bartholomew, **3**, 5cwt. - Unringable, **OS: SE 289 139.**
Westbourne. - See Bournemouth.
<u>West Bradley</u>, Som, Unknown, 3, - Chimed Only, OS: ST 558 369.
Westbury, Bucks, St Augustine, **3**, 5-3-19. in C#. - Limited Ringing, **OS: SP 623 356.**
<u>West Chiltington</u>, W.Sussex, St Mary, 5, 7-2-23. in B. - Chimed Only.
Westcote, Glos, St Mary the Virgin, **3**, 6cwt. - **OS: SP 220 206.**
Westcott Barton, Oxon, St Edward the Confessor, (G.F.), **3**, 6-2-19. in B. - Ropes fall in a straight line and the Second Bell Cast in 1490, **OS: SP 431 257.**
West Derby, Mers, St Mary, **5**, 33cwt. in C. - the **Third** Clock Bell is Hung for Ringing and it weights 15cwt. the rest are hung Dead, **OS: SJ 412 929.**
West Drayton, Gtr London, St Martin, **1**, 18-1-3. in F. - **OS: TQ 061 796.**
Westerdale, N.Yorks, Christ Church, (G.F.), **3**, 8cwt. - **OS: NZ 664 058.**
Westerfield, Suffolk, St Mary Magdalene, (G.F.), **3**, 5-1-0. - Anti-Clockwise, **OS: TM 175 477.**
West Farleigh, Kent, All Saints, **3**, 5-1-20. in C. - Unringable, Anti-Clockwise, OS: **TQ 715 536.**
West Gilling, N.Yorks, **3**, 6cwt. - These have New Wheels but no Stays or Sliders.
West Grinstead, Wilts, **1**, - **OS: SU 206 265.**
<u>West Halton</u>, Humbs, St Ethelreda, 3, 4-3-16. - Chimed Only, OS: SE 904 209.

54

Westham, Dorset, (R.C.), 1, - *Chimed Only.*
West Harnham, Wilts, St George, **2**, 1cwt. in Eb.
Westhead, Lancs, **3**, 8cwt.
West Horsley, Surrey, St Mary, (G.F.), **3**, 10cwt. - *OS: TG 088 527.*
Westhide, Herefords, St Bartholomew, **3**, 9-1-0. in Bb. - *OS: SO 587 442.*
West Mersea, *Essex, St Peter and St Paul, 6, 5-3-27. in Bb. - Chimed Only.*
Westminster, *Gtr London, Westminster Abbey (Colligate Church of St Peter), 3, - These are Three Bells of the Original Six Bells, Also 10, 30-0-15. in D., OS: TQ 300 795.*
Westminster, *Gtr London, 24 Bond Street, J Fox and Co, The Atkinson Carillon, 23, 12-0-16. in G#. - Carillon.*
Westminster, *Gtr London, Houses of Parliament, 5, 270-3-15. - Clock Chime, The Tenor Bell and Bell Tower are commonly known as " Big Ben ", This Bell sounded above London for the first time on the 31st of May 1859 and Parliament had a special sitting to decide the name for the great bell, These Bells were cast by Warners in 1856 with the original Tenor weighing 331-2-20 before recasting by Mears and Stainbank in 1857.*
Westminster, *Gtr London, New Coventry Street, Swiss National Tourist Office, 27, 5-0-15. in C. - Hung Dead, Automatically and Manually Operated Carillon with a Piano Style Keyboard, Also these Bells were cast in Switzerland.*
Westminster, *Gtr London, (R.C.), Westminster Cathedral, Lady Chapel, 3, - Chimed Only, There is Also a **Bourdon Bell** called "Big Edward" which weighs 52-0-10.*
Westminster, Strand, Gtr London, St Mary Le Strand, **1**.
Weston, Lincs, St Mary, **3**, 4cwt. - *Anti-Clockwise, Chimed Only, OS: TF 292 252.*
Weston, Notts, All Saints, **3**, 10-0-9, - *OS: SK 774 680.*
Weston, N.Yorks, All Saints, **1**.
Weston Bampfylde, Som, Holy Cross, **3**, 6cwt. - Unringable, *OS: ST 611 249.*
Weston-on-Avon, Warwicks, All Saints, (G.F.), **1**, 7-2-0. in Bb. - Cast about 1450, *OS: SP 726 666.*
Weston on Trent, Derbys, St Mary the Virgin, (G.F.), **3**, 5-3-6. in D. - *OS: SK 409 275.*
Weston Subedge, Glos, St Lawrence, **1**, 8-2-0. - *OS: SP 128 407.*
Weston under Lizard, Staffs, St Andrew, **3**, 4-1-6. in Eb. - *OS: SJ 806 106.*
West Ogwell, Devon, St Bartholomew, **3**, 5cwt. - *OS: SX 818 702.*
Westow, N.Yorks, **3**, 18cwt., - Unringable.
West Peckham, Kent, St Dunstan, (G.F.), **3**, 5-0-26. in B. - *OS: TQ 656 625.*
Westport, Wilts, St Mary, **1**, - This Bell was Cast by Abraham Rudhall in 1739.
West Rasen, Lincs, All Saints, **3**, 8cwt. - *Chimed Only, OS: TF 064 895.*
West Raynham, Norfolk, St Mary the Virgin, **3**, 10cwt. in G. - *OS: TF 873 253.*
West Rudham, Norfolk, St Peter, (G.F.), **3**, 6cwt. - *OS: TF 819 276.*
West Stafford, Dorset, St Andrew, (G.F.), **3**, 6-2-0. in B. - *OS: SY 725 896.*
West Stour, Dorset, St Mary, **3**, 8cwt. in A. - *OS: ST 785 229.*
West Tytherley, Hants, St Peter, **3**, 4cwt. - Unringable.
West Wickham, *Kent, St Francis, 8, 6-1-22. in C. - Chimed Only.*
West Witton, N.Yorks, St Bartholomew, (G.F.), **3**, 6-2-0. in B. - *OS: SE 062 885.*
West Woodhay, Berks, St Laurance, **2**, 6cwt. in C. - *OS: SU 391 631.*
Wetton, Staffs, St Margaret, **3**, - *OS: SK 109 553.*
Wetwang, Humbs, St Nicholas now St Michael, (G.F.), **3**, 7-3-16. - Anti-Clockwise, *OS: SE 933 591.*
Wexham, Berks, St Mary, **1**, 2-1-8. - No Stay or Slider.
Whaddon, Cambs, St Mary the Virgin, **3**, - Unringable, *OS: TL 349 465.*
Whaddon, Wilts, St Mary, **2**, - Both these Bells were both Cast by Lleweuins and James of Bristol.
Whatcote, Warwicks, St Peter, **3**, 6cwt. in C. - *OS: SP 296 455.*
Wheldrake, *N.Yorks, St Helen, 6, 7cwt. in B. - Chimed Only.*
Whenby, N.Yorks, St Martin, (G.F.), **3**, 3cwt. - *OS: SE 631 699.*

Whitby, N.Yorks, **3**.
Whitchurch, Somerset, St Nicholas (Old Church), **1**, 13-2-0. in F. - Rung from Chancel.
Whitechapel, Gtr London, Whitechapel Bellfoundry, (G.F.), **1**, 4cwt. - Rung in the Tuning Shop and is not for Public use Staff Only.
Whiteparish, Wiltshire, All Saints, **3**, 10cwt. in Ab. - *OS: SU 246 236.*
Whiteshill, Glos, St Paul, **1**, 7cwt. - *OS: SO 841 068.*
Whitfield , Northumb, Holy Trinity, 8, 3-1-3. in E. - Chimed Only.
Whitgift, Humbs, St Mary Magdalene, (G.F.), **3**, 12-1-10. in Ab. - *OS: SE 809 227.*
Whitkirk, W.Yorks, St Mary, **3**, 6cwt. - Unringable, *OS: SE 363 336.*
Whitmore, Staffs, St Mary and All Saints, **3**, 2-2-0. - *OS: SJ 810 410.*
Whittingham, Tyne and Wear, St Bartholomew, **2**.
Whitton , Humbs, St John, 3, 5cwt. - Chimed Only, OS: SE 902 246.
Whitwell, Derbys, St Laurance, **3**, 6cwt. - Unringable, *OS: SK 526 769.*
Whitwick , Leics, (R.C.), Holy Cross, 15, 10-0-17. in G#. - Chimed Only.
Whitwood, Hightown, W.Yorks, All Saints, **3**, 5-1-0. - All the Bells were cast by James Harrison in 1830 *OS: SE 420 253.*
Wicken Bonhunt, Essex, **3**, - Unringable due to the tower being cracked these bells are 1, 7, 8 of a Eight.
Wickenby, Lincs, St Peter and St Laurance, **3**, 3-2-0. in E. - *OS: TF 088 820.*
Wickersley, S.Yorks, St Alban, (G.F.), **3**, 5cwt. - *OS: SK 478 917.*
Wickham, Berks, St Swithin, **1**, 3-2-15. in E. - No Stay or Slider, Unringable, *OS: SU 395 715.*
Widdington, Essex, St Mary, (G.F.), **3**, 14-2-0. - *OS: TL 540 319.*
Wigan, Goose Green , Gtr Man, St Paul, 5, 6-1-17. in C. - Hung Dead, Clock Chime.
Wighill, N.Yorks, All Saints, **3**, 6cwt. - *OS: SE 473 466.*
Wilberfoss , Humbs, 3, 5cwt., - Lever Chimed Only.
Wilcot, Wilts, Holy Cross, **1**.
Willen , Bucks, St Mary Magdalen, 3, 6cwt. - Chimed Only, OS: SP 878 413.
Willerby , N.Yorks, St Peter, 3, 6cwt. - Lever Chimed Only, OS: TA 008 793.
Willey, Warwicks, St Leonard, **3**, 4-2-0. - Unringable, The Tenor was cast by Hugh Watts II of Leicester in 1617.   *OS: SP 497 848.*
Willian , Herts, All Saints, 6, 6-1-23. - Chimed Only.
Wilmington , Kent, St Michael and All Angels, (G.F.), 3, 6-2-0. in B.- Swing Chiming with Half Wheels, OS: TQ 538 725.
Wilsford, Lincs, St Mary, (G.F.), **3**, 7-2-21. in Ab. - *OS: TF 006 430.*
Wilsford, Wilts, St Nicholas, **3**, - The Treble was cast in 1585.
Wilshaw, W.Yorks, St Mary, **1**, 12-3-0. in F#. - *OS: SE 116 098.*
Wimbledon , Gtr London, Christ Church, 6, 13-0-12. in G#. - Chimed Only.
Wimbotsham, Norfolk, St Mary, **3**, - Unringable, *OS: TF 622 049.*
Wimbourne , Dorset, (R.C.), 1, - Chimed Only.
Winchester , Weeke, Hants, St Matthew, 3, 5cwt. - Lever Chimed, Treble cracked and not hung, OS: SU 468 305.
Winchfield, Hants, St Mary, (G.F.), **3**, 6cwt. in Db.
Winchmore Hill , Gtr London, Holy Trinity, 8, 5-0-22. in Bb. - Chimed Only.
Windermere , Cumb, St Mary the Virgin, 8, 13-3-14. in F. - Chimed Only.
Windsor , Berks, Holy Trinity, 8, 7-3-15. in A. - Chimed Only.
Windsor , Berks, Windsor Castle, (Clock Tower), **3**, 32cwt. in C., Hung Dead, Clock Chime , The Clock Tower is in the Royal Quadrangle Gateway, OS: SU 967 770, (Round Tower), **1**, 17-1-21.- This Bell was Cast in Russia in the 17th Century, No Stay or Slider, Only Rung for the Death of a Monarch and is called the " Raven ", *OS: SU 970 770,* (Curfew Tower), H.M. Free Chapel of St George (G.F.), **8**, 26cwt. in D., Anti-Clockwise, *OS: SU 968 770.*
Winforton , Herefords, St Michael, 5, 8cwt. in A. - Chimed Only.
Winfrith Newburgh , Dorset, St Christopher, 6, 9cwt. in G. - Chimed Only.

Wingfield, Wilts, St Andrew, **3**, 5cwt. - The Tenor was cast by the Bristol Foundry between 1500-1550.
Winsley, Wilts, St Peter, (G.F.), **3**, 5-1-18. in Db. - Unringable, Anti-Clockwise.
Winterbourne, Berks, St James, **1**, - *OS: SU 451 719.*
Winterbourne Abbas, Dorset, St Mary, **3**, 7-2-0. in A. - *OS: SY 618 904.*
Winterbourne Basset, Wilts, St Katharine and St Peter, **3**, 9cwt., The Treble was cast in 1583.
Winterbourne Gunner, Wilts, St Gunner, **2**, 3cwt. - The Tenor was cast by the Old Salisbury Foundry.
Winterbourne Houghton, Dorset, St Andrew, **3**, 8cwt. in A#. - *OS: ST 821 044.*
Winterbourne Stickland, Dorset, St Mary, (G.F.), **3**, 7-2-0. in Bb. - *OS: ST 834 046.*
Wintringham, N.Yorks, St Peter, **3**, 7cwt. - *OS: SE 887 733.*
Winwick, Northants, St Michael and All Angels, (G.F.), **3**, 7cwt. in Bb. - *OS: SP 627 738.*
Wisbech , Cambs, Working Mens Club and Institute, 13, 3-0-26. - Chimed Only.
Wishaw, Warwicks, St Chad, **3**, 6-0-6. in Bb. - The Treble and Second were both cast by John Martin of Worcester in 1650 and the Tenor was cast by Thomas Mears of Whitechapel in 1799.*OS: SP 177 946.*
Wistow, N.Yorks, All Saints, **3**, 12-1-15. - *OS: SE 592 357.*
Witherslack , Cumb, 3, 6cwt. - Swing Chiming Only, OS: SD 432 843.
Withiel Florey, Som, St Mary Magdalene, **3**, 6cwt. in Bb. - *OS: SS 987 333.*
Withington , Gtr Man, St Paul, 8, 11-2-0. - Chimed Only.
Wolferslow, Herefords, *St Andrew, 3, 5cwt. in B. - Only The* **Second and Tenor** *Bell are Hung for Ringing,* **OS: SO 668 617.**
Wombwell , S.Yorks, St Mary with St George, 8, 4-1-21. in C#. - Chimed Only.
Womersley, N.Yorks, St Martin, **3**, 9-3-16. in G. - *OS: SE 532 190.*
Woodborough, Wilts, St Mary Magdalene, **1**, 2cwt. in G.
Woodbury Salterton, Devon, Holy Trinity, **3**, - *OS: SY 013 891.*
Woodford , Gtr Man, Christ Church, 8, 7-1-0. in Bb. - Chimed Only.
Woodford Bridge, Gtr London, St Pauls (G.F.), **1**, 2cwt.
Woodford Wells , Gtr London, All Saints, 8, 10-2-13. in Ab. - Chimed Only.
Woodhouse, W.Yorks, Christ Church, **1**, 11-1-17. in G#. - *OS: SE 381 222.*
Woodhurst, Cambs, **1**, Unringable.
Woodland, Devon, St John the Baptist, **3**, 7cwt. - *OS: SX 791 687.*
Woodlands St Mary, Berks, St Mary, **1**, - *OS: SU 334 750.*
Woodley , Berks, St John the Evangelist, 3, 3cwt. - Chimed Only, OS: SU 766 729.
Woodmansterne , Surrey, St Peter, 9, 3-2-14. - Chimed Only.
Woodnesborough , Kent, St Mary the Blessed Virgin, 5, 14cwt. - Chimed Only.
Woodnewton, Northants, St Mary, **2**, 10-0-22. in G.
Woodside , Beds, St Andrew, 5, 2-1-27. in F. - Chimed Only.
Woodstock , Oxon, Blenheim Palace, 8, 8cwt. - Hung Dead, Clock Chime, OS: SP 441 162.
Woodthorpe, Notts, St Mark, **1**, 6-1-18. in B. -*OS: SK 581 443.*
Woolfardisworthy, Devon, St Mary, **3**, 6cwt. - Unringable, Derelict Church, *OS: SS 827 086.*
Woolhampton , Berks, St Peter, 3, 4cwt. - Chimed, OS: SU 577 677.
Wootton, Oxon, St Peter, **1**, 1cwt. - *OS: SU 476 017.*
Worcester, Worcs, Cathedral Church of Christ and the Blessed Virgin Mary, **1**, 82-3-24. in A., Also **15**, 49-2-0. in B., Including a Sharp Fifth, Flat Sixth and Sharp Ninth., **Wed,** *OS: SO 850 545.*
Worcester, Worcs, St Mary, **1**.
Worksop, Notts, St John the Evangelist, **1**, 11-2-9. - *OS: SK 585 796.*
Worlaby, Humbs, St Clement, **3**, 5cwt. - *OS: TA 105 140.*
Wormbridge, Herefords, St Peter, **1**, 5cwt. in Eb. - *OS: SO 428 306.*
Wormersley, N.Yorks, St Martin, **3**, 9-3-16.
Worminghall, Bucks, St Peter and St Paul, **3**, 5cwt. - *OS: SP 643 081.*
Wormington, Glos, St Catherine, **1**, 3-2-0. - *OS: SP 039 364.*

Wormleighton, Warwicks, St Peter, (G.F.), **3**, 8cwt. - Unringable, Anti-Clockwise, The Second was cast by Robert Mellour of Nottingham in 1500. *OS: SP 448 539.*
Worsbrough, S.Yorks, St Mary, **3**, 5cwt. - Unringable, Derelict Church, *OS: SE 354 036.*
Worstead, Norfolk, St Mary, 6, 17-0-21. in E. - Hung Dead.
Worth, Kent, St Peter and St Paul, **3**, 5cwt. in B. - The Tenor is Hung Dead, The **Treble and Second** are Hung for Ringing but are Chimed, *OS: TR 337 561.*
Worth, W. Sussex, (R.C.), Abbey, 8, 24-2-23. in Eb., - Chimed Only.
Worthington, Leics, St Matthew, (G.F.), **3**, 2-1-1. - *OS: SK 409 204.*
Worth Matravers, Dorset, St Nicholas, **3**, 6-0-6. in C.
Worton, Wilts, Christ Church, **1.**
Worlaby, Humbs, St Clement, **3.**
Wrawby, Humbs, St Mary the Virgin, (G.F.), **3**, 11cwt. - *OS: TA 010 086.*
Wroxall, Warwicks, St Leonard, **3**, 9cwt. - Unringable, The Second was cast by Edward Newcombe in 1600 and the Tenor was cast by Thomas Bullisdon of London in 1500. *OS: SP 222 708.*
Wyberton, Lincs, St Leodegar, 3, 11cwt. - Chimed Only, OS: TF 328 408.
Wycombe and Chadwell, Leics, St Mary, **3**, 6-3-0. - Unringable, *OS: SK 783 247.*
Wyfordby, Leics, St Mary, **2**, 3cwt. - Unringable, *OS: SK 793 189.*
Wyke, W.Yorks, St Mary the Virgin, 10, 7-0-18. in B. - Chimed Only.
Wysall, Notts, Holy Trinity, **3**, 7-0-16. in A#. - Unringable, *OS: SK 604 271.*
Wytham, Oxon, All Saints, 8, 9-1-17. in A. - Chimed Only.
Yarburgh, Lincs, St John the Baptist, (G.F.), **3**, 8cwt. in Ab. - *OS: TF 351 930.*
Yarlington, Somerset, Blessed Virgin Mary, (G.F.), **3**, 8cwt. - *OS: GR 655 293.*
Yarm, N.Yorks, **3.**
Yelling, Cambs, Holy Cross, **3**, 7cwt. in B., - *OS: TL 262 625.*
Yelverton, Norfolk, St Mary, (G.F.), **3**, 8cwt. - *OS: TG 292 022.*
York, N.Yorks, Cathedral and Metropolitan Church of St Peter (Minster), (N.W. Tower), **1**, 216-2-22 in Eb,-"Great Peter" This Bell is Counter Balanced and has No Stay or Slider, This Bell was cast by Taylors in 1927, 6, 60-1-17. in Bb. Clock Chime. These Bells were cast by Taylors in 2000.(S.W Tower) 14, 59-1-23. in Bb. Including a Extra Treble and Flat Sixth, These Bells were cast by Taylors in 1925. 11, 23-1-19. in D. These Bells were cast by Taylors in 1933., - Chimed Only, **1**, 4cwt, Dumb Bell, **6**, 4lbs 2 1/4 Oz. in A. This Model Ring was cast by Mears and Stainbank in 1930. *OS: SE 603 522.*
York , N.Yorks, Former St Sampson Church, Now St Sampson Social Centre for the Over 60's, **1**, 8cwt. in Bb., This Bell was cast by Richard Blakey of York in 1501.
York , N.Yorks, Former St Saviour Church, Now York Archaeological Resource Centre, **2**, 3-2-0. in F#., The Tenor was cast by Edward Seller II of York in 1730.
York, N.Yorks, St Denys, **3**, 8cwt., - Unringable, The Treble was cast by James Smith and William Cureton in 1658, The Second was cast by Edward Seller I of York in 1718 and the Tenor was cast by William Oldfield in 1621.
York, N.Yorks, (R.C.), St George, 2, 2cwt., - Lever Chimed Only.
York, N.Yorks, St Helen, 2, - Chimed Only.
York, N.Yorks, St Michael le Belfrey, 1, 3-2-0., - Chimed Only, This bell was cast by Warners in 1883.
York, N.Yorks, The Kings Manor, 1, 0-2-0., - Swing Chimed Only.
York, Castlegate, N.Yorks, St Mary, **3**, 7-1-0., - The Treble was cast by Samuel Smith I of York in 1682, The Second and Tenor was cast by Samuel Smith II of York in 1730 and 1718, Octagonal Tower.
York, Goodramgate, N.Yorks, Holy Trinity, **3**, 4-2-0. in C. - Unringable, The Treble was cast by Robert Quarmbie and Henry Oldfield I of Nottingham in 1580, The Second was cast by William Oldfield in 1626, The Tenor was cast by the York Foundry in 1500.
York, North Street, N.Yorks, **2**, 5cwt. in C.

York, Micklegate, N.Yorks, Holy Trinity, **2**, 5-1-0. in C#., - The Tenor was cast by John Potter of York in 1370.
York, Micklegate, N.Yorks, St Martin Cum Gregory, **2**, 7-3-0. in A., - The Treble was cast by Samuel Smith I of York in 1697 and the Tenor was cast by Robert Mot of Whitechapel in 1579.
York, Pavement, N.Yorks, All Saints, **3**, 15cwt. in F#. - Unringable, The Treble and Second were both cast by the York Bell Foundry in the 15th Century, Also the Tenor was cast by William Oldfield of York in 1633.
York, Pavement, N.Yorks, St Crux, 2, 5-2-0. in B. - The Tenor was cast by Samuel Smith of York in 1673 and the other Bell the Sanctus was cast by a German Bell Founder in 1523, This Church was Demolished in 1884 to 1887 and the Bells were transferred to Bishopthorne Church.
York, Peaseholme, N.Yorks, St Cuthbert, **2**, 2cwt., - Cast by Samuel Smith I of York in 1673 and 1693.

WALES.

Aberavon, Port Talbot, (R.C.), St Joseph, **1**, 30cwt., - Cast by Matthew O'Byrne in 1931.
Aberdovey, Gwynedd, St Peter, *10, 9-2-0. - Chimed Only.*
Angle, Dyfed, **2**.
Bangor, Gwynedd, Cathedral, **3**, 30cwt.
Bangor (Upper Bangor), Gwynedd, St James, *6, 7cwt. - Chimed Only.*
Barry, S.Glam, All Saints, *10, 18-1-18. in F. - Chimed Only.*
Bersham, Clwyd, St Mary, *8, 10-1-2. in G. - Chimed Only.*
Bethesda, Gwynedd, **1**, - *OS: SR 625 667.*
Bettisfield. - See Bettisford.
Bettisford, Clwyd, St John the Baptist, (G.F.), **3**, 5-1-7. in D., *Wed 7.30-8.30 pm., OS: SJ 461 361.*
Bettws Cedewain, Powys, St Beuno, **3**, 7cwt. - Unringable, - *OS: SO 123 968.*
Bettws Y Coed, Snowdonia, (R.C.), **1**.
Bodfari, Clwyd, St Stephen, **3**, 9cwt., *OS: SJ 093 701.*
Bodfuan, Gwynedd, St Buan, *6, 5cwt. - Chimed Only.*
Bosherston, Dyfed, St Michael, **3**, 4cwt. - *OS: SR 966 948.*
Bridgend (Nolton), M.Glam, St Mary, *9, 21-2-13. in E. - Chimed Only.*
Bronington, Clwyd, **1**.
Broughton, Clwyd, **1**.
Caergwrie, Clwyd, St Michael, **3**, 8cwt. - *OS: SJ 307 575.*
Cardiff, S.Glam, City Hall, *5, 51-0-14., - Chimed Only.*
Cardiff (Lisvane), S.Glam, St Denys, **3**, - Unringable, *OS: ST 192 831.*
Cardiff (Roath), S.Glam, (R.C.), St Peter, *8, 24-3-4. in Eb. - Chimed Only.*
Carno, Powys, St John the Baptist, **3**, 6-2-0. - Unringable., *OS: SN 963 965.*
Castle Caereinion, Powys, St Garmon, **3**, 4cwt. - Unringable, *OS: SJ 163 055.*
Cilgerran, Dyfed, St Llanwiddog, **3**, 9cwt. - Unringable, *OS: SN 191 431.*
Cilybebyll, W.Glam, St John the Evangelist, (G.F.), **3**, 5cwt. - The Second Bell is Pre-Reformation and is Cracked, **Tues,** *OS: SN 744 047.*
Clynnog Fawr, Gwynedd, St Beuno, (G.F.), **3**, 18-0-5. in E. - *OS: SH 414 497.*
Crickhowell, Powys, St Edmund St Katherine and St Mary, *8, 10cwt. - Chimed Only.*
Cwmbach Llechryyhyd, Powys, St John the Evangelist, *5, 4cwt. - Chimed Only.*
Deganwy, Gwynedd, All Saints, **1**, 12-2-0. - There is also Six Chiming Bells with a Tenor weight of 4-1-14. in Db. in the same Tower. *OS: SH 783 791.*
Evancoyd, Powys, St Peter, **3**, 8-0-20. - *OS: SO 262 627.*
Gorsedd, Clwyd, **1**.
Gwenddwr, Powys, St Dubricius, **3**, - Unringable, *OS: SO 065 433.*
Henllys, Gwent, St Peter, **3**, 5-3-0. - *OS: ST 267 910.*
Kerry, Powys, St Michael and All Angels, **3**, 11cwt. - Unringable, *OS: SO 147 901.*

Kidwely, Dyfed, St Mary, 6, 9-3-26. in G. - *Chimed Only.*
Lisvane. - *See Cardiff.*
Llanafan Fawr, Powys, St Afan, 5, 6cwt. in B. - *Chimed Only.*
Llanbedrog, Gwynedd, St Pedrog, **3**, 4-0-26. in C. *Fri 7-8 pm., OS: SH 299 215.*
Llandeilo Graban, Powys, St Teilo, (G.F.), **3**, 6cwt. - Unringable, *OS: SO 093 447.*
Llandygwydd, Dyfed, St Tydwdd, 6, 13-0-10. in G#. - *Chimed Only.*
Llanedeyrn, S.Glam, St Edeyrn, 5, 6-2-0. in Bb. - *Chimed Only.*
Llanegwad, Dyfed, St Egwad, 8, 4cwt. - *Chimed Only.*
Llanfair Caerinion, Powys, St Mary, 6, 8-0-18. - *Chimed Only.*
Llanfairfechan, Gwynedd, St Mary, **2**, - *OS: SR 681 747.*
Llangefni (Isle of Anglesey), Gwynedd, St Cyngar, **3**, 6cwt. - Anti-Clockwise., *OS: SH 468 759.*
Llangennech, Dyfed, St Cennych, 8, 11-3-4. - *Chimed Only.*
Llangwm Uchaf, Gwent, St Heirome, **3**, 6-2-0. - *OS: SO 433 007.*
Llanvapley, Gwent, St Mabel, **2**, - Unringable.
Llanvetherine, Gwent, St James the Elder, **2**, - Unringable, *OS: SO 364 172.*
Maenclochog, Dyfed, St Mary, 5, 0-3-0. - *Chimed Only.*
Maesteg, M.Glam, St Michael and All Angels, 8, 18cwt. in F. - *Chimed Only.*
Marchwiel, Clwyd, St Deiniol, 8, 10-0-6. in A. - *Chimed Only.*
Meifod, Powys, St Mary, **3**, 8-3-0. - Unringable, *OS: SJ 154 132.*
Minera, Clwyd, St Mary, 10, 5cwt. - *Chimed Only.*
Mitchell Troy, Gwent, St Michael and All Angels, (G.F.), **3**, 6cwt. in B., Ropes fall in a straight line *OS: SO 493 102.*
Monkton, Dyfed, St Nicholas, 8, 10cwt. - *Chimed Only.*
Mountain Ash, M.Glam, St Margaret, 6, 9cwt. - *Chimed Only.*
Narberth, Dyfed, St Andrew, 6, 10cwt. - *Chimed Only.*
Neath, W.Glam, St David, 11, 7-3-1. in Bb. - *Chimed Only.*
Newport, Gwent, St Mark, **5**, 7-1-5. - The **Tenor** is Only Hung for Ringing the rest are Chimed. *OS: ST 310 880.*
Newport, Stow Hill, Gwent, (R.C.), St Mary, 8, 20cwt. - *Clock Chime.*
Oystermouth, W.Glam, All Saints, 3, - Spanish Bells, Hung Dead, OS: SS 616 880.
Panteg, Gwent, St Mary, **3**, 5cwt. - *OS: ST 310 991.*
Pembroke. - *See Monkton.*
Pembroke Dock, Dyfed, St John the Evangelist, 8, 9-3-22. - *Chimed Only.*
Penally, Dyfed, St Teilo, 5, 7cwt. - *Chimed Only.*
Pennant, Powys, St Mary on the Hill, **3**, 8-3-0. - *OS: SN 882 974.*
Plas Power, Clwyd, Clwyd Estate, 8, 10-2-0. in Ab. - *Chimed Only.*
Pont Bleiddyn, Clwyd, Christ Church, 10, 5cwt. in C. - *Chimed Only.*
Porth, M.Glam, St Paul, 8, 16cwt. - *Chimed Only.*
Prestatyn, Clwyd, Christ Church, 5, 5-2-6. in C. - *Chimed Only.*
Roath. - *See Cardiff.*
Rockfield, Gwent, St Cenedlon, (G.F.), **3**, 6-3-0. - *OS: SO 482 148.*
Rudry, Mid Glam, St James, **3**, 7-1-0. - Unringable, *OS: ST 193 865.*
St Asaph, Clwyd, St Asaph Cathedral, **2**, 25cwt. - The Smallest Cathedral in Great Britan.
Sealand, Clwyd, **1**, 8-1-21.
South Stack, Anglesey, Lighthouse, 1, 41-2-24., - *Chimed Only.*
Talacre, Clwyd, (R.C.), Abbey, 8, 4-0-19. in D. - *Chimed Only.*
Trefeglwys, Powys, St Michael, (G.F.), **3**, 7-2-0. - *OS: SN 971 905.*
Upper Bangor. - *See Bangor.*
Wenvoe, S.Glam, St Mary, (G.F.), **3**, 7-2-0. in A. - *OS: ST 122 727.*
Whitford, Clwyd, St Mary, **3**, 9-2-15. in Ab. - Unringable, Anti-Clockwise, OS: *SJ 146 782.*
Wolvesnewton, Gwent, St Thomas a Becket, (G.F.), **3**, 5-1-3. in C#. - *OS: ST 454 997.*
Wrexham, Clwyd, (R.C.), Cathedral, **1**.

Ysciefiog, Clwyd, St Mary the Virgin, **3**, 6-3-0. - *OS: SJ 153 715.*
Ystrad Mynach , M.Glam, Holy Trinity, 8, 9-2-0. - *Chimed Only.*

SCOTLAND.

Aberdeen , Grampian, Marischal College, 1, 31cwt., - *Chimed Only.*
Aberdeen , Grampian, St Nicholas, 48, 89-3-26. in G#. - *Carillon.*
Aboyne, Grampian, St Thomas, (G.F.), **2**.
Advie , Highland, Tormore Distillery, 8, 3-2-0. in Eb. - *Hung Dead, Clock Chime.*
Ayr , Ayrshire, Town Hall, 1, 22-0-16., - *Chimed Only.*
Bothwell , Strathclyde, Parish Church, 5, 15cwt. - *Hung Dead, Clock Chime.*
Braemar , Grampian, Former Parish Church, 5, 8-0-22. - *Chimed Only.*
Brechin , Tays, Cathedral, 3, 11cwt. - *Two Bells are Hung Dead and the other is hung for Swing Chiming, These Bells were cast by Whitechapel in 1780., There is a Round tower attached to the Cathedral which was originally free standing, A Celtic Culdee Architecture built around 990 A.D.*
Bridge of Weir , Strathclyde, Orphan Homes of Scotland, 12, 10-3-18. in Ab. - *Chimed Only.*
Broughty Ferry , Tayside, (R.C.), Our Lady of Good Counsel, 9, 8-0-17. in Ab. - *Chimed Only.*
Burntisland , Fife, (Episc), 5, 6-0-5. in C. - *Hung Dead, Clock Chime.*
Carbisdale , Highland, Carbisdale Castle, 6, 31-3-20. - *Chimed Only.*
Cardross , Strathclyde, Parish Church, 6, 6cwt. - *Chimed Only.*
Clydebank , Strathclyde, Town Hall, 8, 14-1-8. in G. - *Chimed Only.*
Dumbarton, Strathclyde, (R.C.), St Patrick, **1**, 19-3-0. - Also there is a Carillon of Twenty-three Bells with a Tenor weight of 16-2-24. in F#. in the same Tower. *OS: NS 39 75.*
Dumfries , Dumfries and Galloway, (R.C.), St Joseph's College, 8, 3-1-23. in E. - *Chimed Only.*
Dundee , Tayside, St Andrew, 16, 12-2-0. in F#. - *Chimed Only.*
Dundee , Tayside, (R.C.), St Mary, 9, 12cwt. - *Chimed Only.*
Dunecht , Grampian, Duneecht House, 8, 12cwt. - *Chimed Only.*
Dunfermline , Fife, Abbey, 2, - *Swing Chiming Only These Bells are 18th Century and There is also a Carillon of Twenty-five Bells with a Tenor weight of 13-2-12. in F#. in the Tower.* *OS: NT 090 874.*
Dunfermline , Fife, Dunfermline Corporation, 1, 33cwt., - *Chimed Only.*
Edinburgh, Colinton, Lothian, St Cuthbert, **3**, 3cwt. - Cast by Barwell around 1883., *OS: NT 217 698.*
Edinburgh , Lothian, St Giles, **1**, 27-2-0.
Edinburgh, Portobello , Lothian, (R.C.), St John, 8, 12-2-0. - *Chimed Only.*
Edinburgh, Easter Road , Lothian, Claremont Church, 8, 8-2-0. in G#. - *Chimed Only.*
Edinburgh, Shandwick Place , Lothian, St George's West Church, 5, 19cwt. -, *Clock Chime.*
Falkirk , Central, Old Church, 13, 26-2-22. in D. - *Chimed Only, These Bells were cast in the United States of America by McShane in 1926.*
Forres , Grampian, St Lawrence, 8, 2-2-9. - *Chimed Only.*
Fort Augustus , Highland, St Benedict's Monastery, 9, 20cwt. - *Chimed Only.*
Fort William , Highland, St Mary, 8, 24cwt. - *Chimed Only.*
Fraserburgh , Grampian, West Parish Church, 5, 12-1-2. in G#. - *Hung Dead, Clock Chime.*
Glasgow , Strathclyde, Bellahouston Parish Church, 8, 9-0-21. in A. - *Chimed Only.*
Glasgow , Strathclyde, Blackfriars Church, 5, 12-0-4. - *Chimed Only.*
Glasgow , Strathclyde, Cathedral, **1**, 22cwt., - This Bell was cast by John Wilson in 1896.
Glasgow , Strathclyde, Cross Steeple, 16, 12-1-2. - *Chimed Only.*
Glasgow, Strathclyde, Free Church, **1**, 26-2-19., - This Bell was cast by Mears in 1845.
Glasgow , Strathclyde, Glasgow Corporation, 3, 10cwt., - *Hung Dead, Clock Chime, These Bells were cast by Whitechaple in 1839.*
Glasgow , Strathclyde, (Congregational), Trinity Church, 6, 12cwt. - *Chimed Only* , *Steel Bells.*
Glasgow, Botanical Gardens , Strathclyde, Kelvinside Church, 8, 12cwt. - *Chimed Only.*
Glasgow, Strathclyde, Kinning Park Free Church, **1**, 20-1-21., - Cast by Taylors in 1881.

<u>Glasgow, Possil Park</u>, Strathclyde, (R.C.), St Teresa, 8, 10-1-6. in G#. - Chimed Only.
<u>Glasgow</u>, Strathclyde, Glasgow University, 1, 57-3-0., - Chimed Only.
Golspie, Highland, Dunrobin Castle, **3**, 25-3-4., - These Bells were cast by Mears in 1850.
<u>Greenock</u>, Strathclyde, St George, 10, 18-1-7. in F. - Chimed Only.
<u>Helensburgh</u>, Strathclyde, (Episc), St Michael and All Angels, 8, 12-2-9. in G. - Chimed Only.
<u>Helensburgh</u>, Strathclyde, Parish Church, 5, 12-0-9. in G. - Hung Dead, Clock Chime.
Iona, Isle of Iona, St Columba Abbey, **1**, 21cwt.
<u>Johnstone</u>, Strath, 3, - Chiming Only.
<u>Kilmarnock</u>, Strathclyde, Henderson Church, 8, 10-3-20. in Ab. - Chimed Only.
<u>Kilmarnock</u>, Strathclyde, St Marnock, 30, 12-2-1. in G. - Carillon.
<u>Kirkcaldy</u>, Fife, St Bricedale Parish Church, 11, 14-0-10. in F. - Chimed Only.
Kirkcudbright, Southwick, Dumfries and Galloway, **3**.
<u>Kirkwall</u>, Orkney Islands, St Magnus Cathedral, 3, - Chimed Only.
<u>Lamlash</u>, Strathclyde, Kilbride Parish Church, 9, 7-1-7. - Chimed Only.
<u>Largs</u>, Strathclyde, Clark Memorial Church, 5, 22cwt. - Automatic Chiming Only.
<u>Lerwick</u>, Shetland Isles, Town Hall, 11, 11-2-4. in G. - Chimed Only.
<u>Lochbee</u>, Tayside, West Church, 8, 8cwt. - Chimed Only.
Millport, Isle of Cumbrae, **3**, 8cwt., - These Bells were cast by Whitechapel in 1914.
<u>Newton Stewart</u>, Dumfries and Galloway, 3, - Hung Dead.
<u>Old Kilpatrick</u>, Strathclyde, Parish Church, 8, 14-0-23. in F. - Chimed Only.
Paisley, Strathclyde, High Kirk, **1**, 20cwt., - This Bell was cast by James Duff in 1872.
<u>Paisley</u>, Strathclyde, Town Hall, 10, 19-2-8. in Eb. - Chimed Only.
<u>Peebles</u>, Border, Old Parish Church, 13, 30-0-9. in C. - Chimed Only.
Perth, Central, St John Baptist, **35**, 28-0-14 in D. - The **Tenor** Bell is Hung for Ringing the rest are operated as a Carillon, Also there is Thirteen disused Bells hung at the top of the Tower and Fifteen Miscellaneous Bells on Display. **OS: NO 119 235.**
<u>Port of Menteith</u>, Central, Parish Church, 8, 17cwt. - Chimed Only.
<u>Renton</u>, Strathclyde, Parish Church, 6, 7cwt. - Chimed Only.
<u>Rhu</u>, Strathclyde, Parish Church, 5, 14-3-5. - Hung Dead, Clock Chime.
<u>Rossie</u>, Tayside, Priory, 5, 6-2-0. in C. - Chimed Only.
<u>St Andrews</u>, Fife, Holy Trinity, 23, 31 1 12. in D. - Carillon.
St Andrews, Fife, University of St Andrews, St Salvatore's Chapel, **2**, - **OS: NO 512 169.**
<u>Sanquhar</u>, Dumfries and Galloway, St Bride, 10, 8-3-17. in A#. - Chimed Only.
<u>Stirling</u>, Central, Tolbooth, 16, 0-2-4. in D. - Automatic Chiming Only.
<u>Stirling</u>, Central, Municipal Buildings, 8, 19-0-10. in E. - Chimed Only.
Strenton, Lothian, **1**, - **OS: NT 622 743.**
<u>Troon</u>, Strathclyde, (R.C.), Our Lady and St Meddan, 8, 7-3-15. in Bb. - Chimed Only.
<u>Wemyss Bay</u>, Strathclyde, (Episc), Chapel of Lord Inverclyde, 8, 15-1-2. - Chimed Only.
Wemyss Bay, Strathclyde, Parish Church, **1**, - No Stay or Slider.

IRELAND.

<u>Armagh</u>, Armagh, (R.C.), Cathedral of St Patrick, 39, 43-0-14. in C. - Carillon.
Armagh, Armagh, (C.I.), Cathedral of St Patrick, **8**, 19-2-14 in E. - The **Tenor** is Only Hung for Ringing the rest are Chimed.
Ballaghadereen, Rosc, (R.C.), Cathedral of the Annunciation and Nativity, **9**, 34-1-0. - The **Tenor** is only hung for Ringing the rest are Chimed.
<u>Ballyshannon (Kilbarron)</u>, Doneg, (C.I.), 8, 23-1-24. in Eb. - Chimed Only.
Banbridge, Seapatrick, Down, (C.I.), Holy Trinity, **10**, 19-1-13. in Eb. - The **Tenor** is Only Hung for Ringing the rest are Chimed.
<u>Belfast</u>, Antrim, Albert Memorial Clock Tower, 1, 27-2-23., - Clock Bell.
<u>Belfast</u>, Antrim, (Prebyt), Assembly Buildings, 12, 41-3-5. in C. - Chimed Only.
<u>Belfast</u>, Antrim, (R.C.), Pro-Cathedral of St Peter, 9, 26cwt. in D. - Chimed Only.

Belfast, Antrim, (R.C.), St Peter's Cathedral, **1**, 26cwt.
Belfast, Finaghy, Antrim, St Polycarp, 8, 5-3-25. in B. - Chimed Only.
Belfast, Antrim, (Prebyt), Sinclair Seamen's Church, 8, 7-2-6. in Bb. - Chimed Only.
Belfast, Antrim, The Lourdes Grotto, St Mary, 6, 10-1-21. in G#. - Automatic Chiming Only.
Cardonagh, Donegal, (R.C.), Parish Church, 5, 15cwt. in F#. - Hung Dead, Clock Chime.
Carrickmacross, Monagh, (R.C.), St Joseph, 12, 17-0-1. in F#. - Chimed Only.
Castlerea, Rosc, (C.I.), Kilkeevin, Trinity, 8, 4-2-19. - Chimed Only.
Castlerock, Derry, (C.I.), Christ Church, 8, 14-1-7. - Chimed Only.
Clogher, Tyrone, (R.C.), Cathedral of St Macartan, 8, 5-3-25. in B. - Chimed Only.
Clones, Monagh, (R.C.), Sacred Heart, 5, 30cwt. in D. - Hung Dead, Clock Chime.
Cobh, Cork, (R.C.), St Colman's Cathedral, St Colman's Carillon, 47, 67-2-22. in A. - Carillon.
Collooney, Sligo, (C.I.), St Paul, 5, 7cwt. - Chimed Only.
Cork, Shandon, Cork, (C.I.), St Ann, 8, 27-1-9. in D. - Chimed Only.
Cork, Cork, (C.I.), St Nicholas, 8, 16cwt. in E. - Chimed Only.
Delgany, Wicklow, (C.I.), Christ Church, 8, 3-0-21. in F. - Chimed Only.
Drogheda, Louth, (R.C.), St Peter, **1**, 53cwt. - This Bell was cast by Matthew O'Byrne in 1894 and There is also Eight Chiming Bells in the Tower with a Tenor weight of 20cwt. in Eb.
Drumberg, Down, (C.I.), St Patrick, 8, 12-3-7. in F#. - Chimed Only.
Dublin, Dub, Lighthouse, 1, 42-3-08., - Chimed Only.
Dublin, Dub, Post Office, 1, 43cwt., - Chimed Only.
Dublin, Dub, (C.I.), St Bartholomew, 8, 15-0-26. in F. - Chimed Only.
Dublin, Dub, (R.C.), St Mary, **1**, 50cwt., - This Bell was cast by Matthew O'Byrne in 1907.
Dublin, Arran Quay, Dub, (R.C.), St Paul, 8, 15-1-0. in F. - Chimed Only.
Dublin, Mount Argus, Dub, (R.C.), St Pauls Retreat, 8, 10-2-0. - Chimed Only.
Dublin, Ringsend, Dub, (R.C.), St Patrick, 5, 23-1-21. - Hung Dead, Clock Chime.
Dublin, Dub, Trinity College, **1**, 36-0-2., - This Bell was cast by Abel Rudhall in 1744.
Dublin, Dub, Water Tower, 1, 44-0-12., - Chimed Only, This Bell was cast by Van Aerschodt in 1880.
Dundalk, Louth, (R.C.), Cathedral of St Patrick, 5, 42-2-9. in C. - Hung Dead, Clock Chime.
Dundalk, Louth, (R.C.), St Joseph Redemptorist Church, 10, 25cwt. in D. - Chimed Only.
Galway, Gal, (C.I.), St Nicholas Collegiate Church, 10, 18-2-14. in F. - Chimed Only.
Garron Point, Antrim, (R.C.), St Macnissi's College, 8, 10-2-21. in G#. - Automatically Chimed.
Glengery, Dub, (C.I.), St Paul, 9, 15-2-21. - Chimed Only.
Hannahstown, Antrim, (R.C.), St Teresa, 9, 23-0-11. in D. - Chimed Only.
Kilkea, Kildare, (C.I.), Chapel of Ease, 8, 14cwt. - Chimed Only.
Killaloe, Clare, (C.I.), Cathedral of St Flannan, 8, 11-0-14. - Chimed Only.
Killylea, Armagh, (C.I.), St Mary, 5, 9-2-1. in G#. - Hung Dead, Clock Chime.
Killyman, Tyrone, (C.I.), St Andrew, 8, 10cwt. - Chimed Only.
Kinawley, Ferman, (C.I.), Trinity Church, 8, 7cwt. - Chimed Only.
Letterkenny, Donegal, (R.C.), Cathedral of St Eunan, 12, 41cwt. in C. - Chimed Only.
Limerick, Lim, (R.C.), St Augustine, **1**, 30-2-0. - There is also a 8, 9-2-0. in G#., - Chimed Only.
Lismore, Waterford, (C.I.), Cathedral and Parish Church of St Carthagh, 12, 42-1-12. - Chimed Only.
Londonderry, Derry, (R.C.), Cathedral of St Eugene, **10**, 51-0-3 in C. - The **Tenor** is Only Hung for Ringing the rest are Chimed.
Londonderry, Derry, Guildhall, 1, 46cwt., - Chimed Only.
Longford, Longf, (R.C.), Cathedral of St Mel, 12, 42-0-8. in C. - Chimed Only.
Magheralin, Down, (C.I.), Holy and Undivided Trinity, **8**, 14-3-2. in F. - The **Seventh Bell** is Only Hung for Ringing it weights 6cwt. and the rest are Chimed.
Monaghhan, Monagh, (R.C.), Cathedral of St Macartan, **10**, 51-1-14. - The **Tenor** is Only Hung for Ringing the rest are Chimed.
Mullingar, Westmeath, (R.C.), Cathedral of Christ the King, 5, 20cwt. in Eb. - Clock Chime.
Newry, Down, (C.I.), Cathedral of St Patrick, 11, 32-2-0. in C. - Chimed Only.

63

Portadown, *Armagh, (C.I.), St Mark, 15, 9-3-18 in A. - Only the **Tenor** is Hung for Ringing the rest are Chimed.*
Sligo , Sligo, (R.C.), Cathedral of the Immaculate Conception, 9, 28-1-0. in D. - Chimed Only.
Strabane , Tyrone, (C.I.), Camus-j-Mourne, Christ Church, 8, 5-1-21. in C. - Chimed Only.
Toome , Co Antrim, (R.C.), Our Lady of the Lourdes, 1, 50cwt.
Westport , Co. Mayo, (R.C.), St Mary, 9, 20-0-21. in Eb. - Chimed Only.
Whitehouse , Antrim, (R.C.), Parish Church, 10, 33-2-16. in Db. - Chimed Only.

OVERSEAS TOWERS.

ANTIGUA and BARBUDA.

Antigua , British West Indies, (Anglican), Cathedral Church of St John the Divine, (North West Tower), 14, in C, - Chimed Only, Cast by Vanbergen in 1960, (South West Tower), 2, - Chimed Only.

ARGENTINA.

Buenos Aires , Mercado, 23, in C, - Carillon, All these Bells were cast by Paccard in 1912.
Buenos Aires , Municipio, Torre del Consejo Deliberante, 30, in A, - Hung Dead, Automatic Carillon, All the Bells were cast by Schilling in 1930.
La Merced , 23, in C, - Hung Dead, Automatic Carillon, All these Bells were cast by Paccard.
Mercedes , San Patricio, 24, in G#, - Carillon, All the Bells were cast by Schilling in 1931.

AUSTRALIA.

Adelaide , South Australia, General Post Office, 5, 49cwt., - Chimed Only, Cast by Taylors in 1874.
Adelaide , South Australia, Holy Trinity, 2, - Hung Dead, Clock Bells.
Adelaide, South Australia, St Peter's College, School Chapel , **1**, 5cwt., - This Bell was cast by Taylors in 1922.
Albury, New South Wales., St Matthew, **1**, 24-0-6. in D. - Also **8**, 7-3-21. in Ab., **Thurs 6.30pm**.
Albury, New South Wales, St Patrick, **2**, 14cwt., - The Tenor was cast in Dublin in 1923 and the Treble was cast by Whitechapel in 1907.
Alice Springs, Northern Teritory, **3**, 4-1-0., - These Bells were cast by Taylors in 1969.
Appotsford, Victoria, (R.C.), Good Shepheard Convent, **3**, - These Bells were cast in Dublin.
Ararat, Victoria, Holy Trinity, **1**, 6cwt., - This Bell was cast by Whitechapel in 1912.
Armidale, New South Wales, St Nicholas, **1**, - This Bell was cast by Whitechapel in 1861.
Armidale, New South Wales, (R.C.), St Mary's Cathedral, **1**, 12cwt., - This Bell was cast by P.N. Russell and Co. Sydney in 1872.
Arncliffe, New South Wales, (R.C.), **1**, 17-2-0., - This Bell was cast in Dublin in 1931.
Ashbury, New South Wales, **1**, 7-2-0., - This bell was cast by Whitechapel in 1954.
Badu Island, Queensland, St Mark, **1**, 5-3-0., - This Bell was cast by Taylors in 1961.
Bakewell, Northern Teritory, **1**, 1-0-20. in C#., - This Bell was cast by Gillett and Johnson in 1924.
Ballarat , Victoria, City Fire Station, 2, 16cwt., - Chimed Only, Steel Bells, These Bells were cast by Vickers of Sheffield in 1860 and 1862.
Ballarat, Victoria, (R.C.), Ballarat Monastery, **3**, 4-1-0., - Cast by Whitechapel in 1899.
Ballarat *, Victoria, Town Hall, 15, 3cwt., - Hung Dead, Automatic Chime in a Detached Tower to the Right of the Town Hall, Cast by Whitechapel in 1869, Also 8, 22-0-10. in D. Hung in the Town Hall.*
Balmain, New South Wales, St John the Evangelist, **1**, 2-3-0., - This Bell was cast by Taylors in 1986.

Baranald, New South Wales, (R.C.), 1, 8cwt., - This Bell was cast in Dublin in 1927.
Bathurst, New South Wales, All Saints Cathedral, 6, 9-2-0., - Chimed Only, All the Bells were cast by Warners in 1855, These Bells were hung for Ringing until news came in that we had Captured Sebastopol on the 10th of September 1855 everyone was so happy they all ran up the Tower and hit the Bells with Hammers, Bars or anything to hand until cracking the Tenor.
Bathurst, New South Wales, (R.C.), 1, 10cwt., - This Bell was cast by Murphy of Dublin in 1853.
Bathurst, New South Wales, St Michael and St John, 2, 15-2-24. in F#., - Both these Bells were cast by Whitechapel in 1856 and 1861.
Bathurst, New South Wales, Soldiers Memorial, 35, 31cwt., - Carillon, Cast by Taylors in 1929.
Belora, New South Wales, St James, 1, 2-3-0., - This Bell was cast by Tanner.
Benalla, Victoria, (R.C.), 1, 14cwt., - This Bell was cast in Dublin in 1904.
Bendigo, Victoria, St Kilian, 1, 15cwt., - This Bell was cast by Murphy of Dublin in 1869.
Berowra, New South Wales, St Joseph, 1, 3cwt., - This Bell was cast by Whitechapel in 1899.
Bombala, New South Wales, St Patrick, 1, 7cwt., - This Bell was cast in Dublin in 1958.
Bondi North, New South Wales, St Anne's Shrine, 1, 4-3-0., - Cast by Whitechapel in 1963.
Boorowa (or Old Name for Town: Burrowa), New South Wales, (R.C.), 2, 15cwt., - The Tenor was cast in 1891 and the Treble was cast in 1906 in Dublin.
Boorowa, New South Wales, St Joseph's Convent, 1, 3cwt., - Cast by Whitechapel in 1899.
Bowral, New South Wales, St Simon and St Jude, 1, 5cwt., - This Bell was cast by Taylors in 1938.
Branxton, New South Wales, (R.C.), 1, - This Bell was cast in 1900.
Brisbane, Queensland, Church of Assumption, 1, 12-1-14., - This Bell was cast by Whitechapel in 1947.
Brisbane, Queensland, St Stephen's Cathedral, 1, 35-1-27., -This Bell was cast by Whitechapel in 1887.
Bundaberg, Queensland, St Andrew, 11, 9cwt., - Chimed Only, Tubular Bells, All these Bells were cast by Taylors in 1932.
Burnside, South Australia, St David, 1, 8cwt., - This Bell was cast by Taylors in 1966.
Burwood, New South Wales, (Presbyterian), St James, 5, 8cwt., - Chiming Only, All these Bells were cast by Wilson of Glasgow.
Camberwell, Victoria, (R.C.), 2, 30cwt., - The Tenor was cast in Dublin in 1938 and the Treble was cast by Gillett and Johnson in 1925.
Camberwell South, Victoria, St Mary, 1, 5cwt., - This Bell was cast by Taylors in 1962.
Camden, New South Wales, St John, 8, 14cwt., - Chimed Only, Cast by Whitechapel in 1896.
Campsie, New South Wales, School, 1, 2cwt., - This Bell was cast by Taylors in 1927.
Canberra, Australian Capital Territory, Lake Burley Griffin, National Carillon, 53, 118-2-19., Carillon, All These Bells were cast by Taylors in 1970.
Canberra, Australian Capital Territory, St Andrew, 8, 10-1-0., - Chimed Only, All these Bells were cast by Taylors in 1968.
Canberra, Australian Capital Territory, St John, 8, 12-3-0., - Chimed Only, All These Bells were cast by Taylors in 1964.
Carisbrook, Victoria, (R.C.), St Kevin's Church, 1, - This Bell was cast by J.C. Wilson in 1868.
Casino, New South Wales, (R.C.), 1, 10cwt., - This Bell was cast in Dublin in 1916.
Cessnock, New South Wales, (R.C.), 1, 10cwt., - This Bell was cast in Dublin in 1926.
Clayfield, Queensland, (R.C.), St Agitha, 1, 12-2-0., - This Bell was cast by O'Byrne in Dublin in 1933.
Cobargo, New South Wales, (R.C.), 1, 12cwt., - This Bell was cast by Warners in 1858.
Colac, Victoria, St John, 1, 7-2-0., - This Bell was cast by Whitechapel in 1901.
Col. Light Gardens, South Australia, All Saints, 1, 4-1-0., - This Bell was cast by Whitechapel in 1963.
Concord, New South Wales, St Mary, 1, 12cwt., - This Bell was cast by Taylors in 1928.
Condoblin, New South Wales, St Joseph, 1, 5-1-0., - This Bell was cast by Taylors in 1937.

Cooktown, Queensland, (R.C.), **2**, 6cwt. - The Treble was Cast before 1916 and the Tenor was cast in 1922 and they were both cast by O'Byrne of Dublin.
Cunnamulla, Queensland, (R.C.), **1**, 5cwt., - This Bell was cast by Taylors in 1952.
Dalby, Queensland, (R.C.), **1**, 7cwt., - This Bell was cast in Dublin in 1922.
Darlinghurst , New South Wales, Sacred Heart Church, 5, - These Bells disappeared around 1916.
Darwin , Northern Teritory, (R.C.), St Marys Cathedral, 4, - Chimed Only.
Dee Why, New South Wales, St John, **1**, 5cwt., - This bell was cast by Taylors in 1957.
Drayton, Queensland, St Mary, **1**, 1-2-0., - This Bell was cast by Whitechapel in 1965.
Eaglehawk, Tasmania, **1**, 3cwt. - This Bell was cast by Whitechapel in 1900.
Firle, South Australia, St Barnabus, **1**, 4-1-0., - This Bell was cast by Taylors in 1960.
Fitzroy North, Victoria, (R.C.), **1**, 12-2-0., - This Bell was cast in Dublin in 1922.
Fitzroy North, Victoria, Town Hall, **1**, 4-2-9., - This Bell was cast by Gillett and Johnson in 1938.
Fortitude Valley, Queensland, (R.C.), **1**, 20cwt., - Steel Bell, This Bell was cast by Vickers in 1886.
Fremantle, Western Australia, Scots Church, **2**, 6-2-0., - The Treble was cast in 1890 and the Tenor was cast in 1906 by Taylors.
Ganmain, New South Wales, (R.C.), **1**, 14cwt., - This bell was cast in Dublin in 1928.
Gawler , South Australia, St George, 8, 3-2-0. - Chimed Only, Hemispherical Bells, All these Bells were cast by Taylors in 1921.
Geelong, Victoria, All Saints, **1**, 5cwt., - This Bell was cast by Whitechapel in 1911.
Gippsland, Victoria, **1**, 5-3-0., - This Bell was cast in 1920.
Glebe , New South Wales, St John, 10, - Chimed Only, Hemispherical Bells, All these Bells were cast by Wm. Taylor of Pyrmount in 1910.
Goulburn, New South Wales, St Peter and St Paul, **1**, 17cwt., - This Bell was cast by Murthy of Dublin in 1869, This Bell was first Rung on the 5th of April 1890.
Goulburn, New South Wales, House of Ascension, **1**, 30cwt., - This Bell was cast by Taylors in 1936.
Grenfell, New South Wales, (R.C.), **1**, 14cwt., - This Bell was cast in Dublin in 1926.
Gulgong, New South Wales, (R.C.), **1**, 12cwt., - This Bell was cast by Taylors in 1900.
Guildford, Western Australia, (R.C.), **1**, 10cwt., - This bell was cast in Dublin in 1912.
Gunning, New South Wales, (R.C.), Catholic School, **1**, - This Bell was cast in 1914.
Haberfield, New South Wales, (R.C.), **1**, - This Angelus Bell was cast in 1913.
Hamilton, New South Wales, Sacred Heart Church, **1**, 18cwt., - This Bell was cast by Taylors in 1930.
Hamilton, Queensland, St Augustine, **1**, 8-3-0., - This Bell was cast by Whitechapel in 1966.
Hawthorne, Victoria, St Briged, **1**, 12-2-0., - This Bell was cast in Dublin in 1891.
Henty, New South Wales, Lutheran Church, **1**, - This Bell was cast by Vickers Riwolt-Adams of Moorabbin in 1963.
Highgate, Western Australia, St Alban, **1**, - This Bell was cast by Whitechapel in 1806.
Hobart , Tasmania, Scot's Church, 1, - Clock Bell, This Bell was cast by Whitechapel in 1839.
Hobart, Tasmania, (R.C.), St Joseph, **1**, 8cwt., - This Bell was cast by Whitechapel in 1859.
Ipswich , Queensland, Post Office, 1, 9-2-21., - Chimed Only, Cast by Gillett and Johnson in 1901.
Ipswich, Queensland, (R.C.), St Mary, **2**, 30cwt., - The Tenor was cast in Dublin in 1873 and the Treble was cast in Dublin in 1927.
Jervis Bay, New South Wales, Naval College, **1**, 2-2-0., - This Bell was cast by Taylors in 1958.
Kangaroo Point, Queensland, St Joseph, **1**, 10cwt., - This Bell was cast in Dublin in 1923.
Kangaroo Point, Queensland, St Mary, **1**, 10-1-0., - This Bell was cast by Whitechapel in 1928.
Kalgoolie, Western Australia, Town Hall, **3**, 6-3-21. in B., - These Bells were cast by Gillett and Johnson between 1899 - 1900.
Kempsey, New South Wales, (R.C.), **1**, 12cwt., - This Bell was cast in 1903.
Kiama , New South Wales, Christ Church, 8, 3-2-0., - Chimed Only, All these Bells were cast by Whitechapel in 1976.
Kogarah, New South Wales, (R.C.), **1**, 17-2-0., - This Bell was cast in Dublin in 1935.

Latrobe, Tasmania, (R.C.), **1**, - This Bell was cast by Whitechapel in 1881.
Launceston, *Tasmania, Church of the Apostles, 19, 6-3-0., - Chimed only, Cast by Taylors in 1988.*
Launceston, *Tasmania, Post Office, 5, 40-0-6., - Chimed Only, Cast by Gillett and Johnson in 1909.*
Leederville, Western Australia, (R.C.), **1**, 10cwt., - This Bell was cast in Dublin in 1927.
Leederville, *Western Australia, Convent of Good Shepherd, 4, 3-2-16., - Hung Dead, Chimed Only, All these Bells were cast by Gillett and Johnson in 1952.*
Lewisham, New South Wales, St Thomas, **1**, 19cwt., - This Bell was cast by Taylors in 1933.
Lindfield, *New South Wales, Uniting Church, 13, - Chimed Only, Tubular Bells, All Cast in 1936.*
Lismore, *New South Wales, St Carthage Cathedral, 12, 43cwt., - Chimed Only, All these Bells were cast in Dublin in 1908, There is Also an* ***Angelus Bell*** *Hung for Ringing and weight's 29cwt.*
Liverpool, New South Wales, St Lukes Anglican Church, **1**, - Unringable at present but will be Ringable Again Soon.
Lutwyche, *Queensland, St Andrew, 13, 6cwt., - Chimed Only, Cast by Taylors in 1927.*
Maitland, New South Wales, (R.C.), **1**, 30cwt., - This Bell was cast in 1865.
Maitland, *New South Wales, St Mary, 5, 45cwt., - Hung Dead, Clock Bells, Cast by Taylors in 1886.*
Malvern East, Victoria, St John the Evangelist, **1**, 5-2-0., - This Bell was cast by Taylors in 1958.
Manly, *New South Wales, St Patrick's College, 1, 10-2-0., - Automatic Chiming Only, This Bell was cast by Whitechapel in 1955.*
Marrickville, *New South Wales, St Clement, 8, 8cwt., - Chimed Only, All Cast by Taylors in 1926.*
Melbourne, Victoria, **3**, 5cwt., - These Bells were cast by Whitechapel in 1896.
Melbourne, Victoria, **3**, 7cwt., - These Bells were cast by Whitechapel in 1899.
Melbourne, Victoria, Jesuit Church, **1**, 12cwt., - This Bell was cast in Dublin.
Melbourne, Victoria, St Briged, **1**, 6cwt., - This Bell was cast by Whitechapel in 1907.
Melbourne, *Victoria, Town Hall, 12, - Chimed Only.*
Michelago, New South Wales, (R.C.), **1**, 8-3-0., - This Bell was cast in 1882.
Mitcham, Victoria, St Pauls Evangelical Church, **1**, 4cwt., - This Bell was cast in W.Germany in 1962.
Mittagong, New South Wales, St Stephen, **1**, 3cwt., - This Bell was cast by Taylors in 1926.
Moree, New South Wales, All Saints, **1**, 3cwt., - This Bell was cast by Whitechapel in 1895.
Mount Gambier, South Australia, (R.C.), **1**, 12-2-0., - This Bell was cast in Dublin in 1893.
Mount Leonora, Western Australia, (R.C.), **3**.
Mudgee, New South Wales, St Mary, **2**, 15cwt., - Both these Bells were cast by Whitechapel in 1859 and 1896 they also are the Same weight.
Murrumbeena, Victoria, St Peter, **1**, 4-1-0., - This Bell was cast by Taylors in 1962.
Murrurundi, *New South Wales, St Paul, 1, 18cwt., - Steel Bell, This Bell was cast by Vickers of Sheffield in 1877, There is Also a Chime of Ten Bells in the Same Tower with a Tenor of 4cwt and they were cast by Warner's in 1883.*
Mussellbrook - *See Muswellbrook.*
Muswellbrook, New South Wales, **4**, 7cwt., - All these Bells were cast by Taylors in 1914.
Narrandera, New South Wales, (R.C.), **1**, 14cwt., - This Bell was cast in Dublin in 1909.
Nedlands Park, Western Australia, (R.C.), **1**, 15cwt., - This Bell was cast in Dublin in 1951.
Neutral Bay, New South Wales, St Augustine, **1**, 5cwt., - This Bell was cast by Taylors in 1928.
Newcastle, *New South Wales, Christ Church Cathedral, 6, 12cwt., - Automatic Swing Chiming Only, These Bells were cast in Holland in 1977, There is Also a Service Bell that is also hung for Automatic Swing Chiming Only and was cast by Taylors in 1903.*
New Norcia, *Western Australia, Benedictine Monastery, 4, - Chimed Only, All these Bells were cast between 1768 and 1849 by a foundry in Madrid.*
Newtown, *New South Wales, St Stephen, 20, 4cwt., - Chimed Only, Hemispherical Bells, These Bells were cast by Whitechapel in 1880.*
Northam, Western Australia, (R.C.), **1**, 15cwt., - This Bell was cast in Dublin in 1949.

Northcote, Victoria, Church of the Epiphany, 1, 11cwt., - This Bell was cast by Taylors in 1927.
Norwood, South Australia, (R.C.), 1, 10cwt., - This Bell was cast in Dublin.
Norwood, South Australia, Town Hall, 1, 16-2-14. in F#, - Cast by Gillett and Johnson in 1889.
Paddington, New South Wales, St Matthias, 1, 2-4-0., - Cast by the Russell Foundry in Sydney.
Parkes, New South Wales, Council Chambers, 1, 6-1-0., - This Bell was cast by Taylors in 1956.
Parramatta, *New South Wales, King's School, 8, 11-3-0., - Chimed Only, All these Bells were cast by Whitechapel in 1974.*
Parramatta, *New South Wales, St John, 13, 10cwt., - Chimed Only, All these Bells were cast by Taylors in 1923, Also there is a Clock Bell in the Tower cast by Whitechapel in 1820.*
Parramatta, New South Wales, St Patrick, 1, 17-2-2., - This Bell was cast in Dublin in 1904.
Parramatta Park, Queensland, St Mary, 1, 17-2-0., - This Bell was cast in Dublin in 1904.
Perth, Western Australia, 3, 1-2-25., - Cast by Gillett and Johnson between 1932 - 1934.
Perth, *Western Australia, (R.C.), St Mary's Cathedral, 13, 9-2-0. - Chimed Only, These Bells were cast by Gillett and Johnson in 1951, There is Also Bell in the Entrance of the Cathedral which was cast in Spain in 1676.*
Perth, Western Australia, Wesley Church, 1, - This Bell was cast by Whitechapel in 1864.
Plympton, South Australia, Good Shepherd, 1, 4-3-0., - This Bell was cast by Whitechapel in 1963.
Portland, Victoria, St Stephen, 1, 10-3-3., - This Bell was cast by Whitechapel in 1857.
Pymble, New South Wales, Sacred Heart (This Tower is no Longer a Church), 1, 13cwt., - This Bell was cast by Taylors in 1937.
Quirindi, New South Wales, War-Memorial Tower, 1, 4cwt., - This Bell was cast by Taylors in 1925.
Red Hill, Queensland, St Mark, 1, 14cwt., - This Bell was cast in Dublin in 1924.
Richmond, Victoria, St Ignatius, 1, 16cwt., - This Bell was cast in Dublin in 1927.
Rockhampton, *Queensland, St Paul's Cathedral, 8, 12-0-19. - Chimed Only, All these Bells were cast by Gillett and Johnson in 1946.*
Rockhampton, Queensland, St Joseph's Cathedral, 1, 42cwt., - This Bell was cast in Dublin in 1904.
Rockhampton North, Queensland, (R.C.), 3, 2cwt., - These Bells were cast in 1893.
Rose Bay, New South Wales, Sacred Heart Convent, 1, 4cwt., - Cast by Whitechapel in 1901.
St Lucia, Queensland, St Mary, 1, 3cwt., - This Bell was cast by Whitechapel in 1962.
Sale, Victoria, (R.C.), 1, 10cwt., - This Bell was cast in Dublin in 1907.
Sandgate, Queensland, Town Hall, 3, - These Bells were cast in 1923.
Scone, New South Wales, St Luke, 2, 5cwt., - Cast by Whitechapel between 1855 - 1856.
Shepparton, Victoria, St Augustine, 1, 3cwt., - This Bell was cast by Taylors in 1928.
Smithtown, New South Wales, (R.C.), 1, 10cwt., - There used to be Two Bells in this Church but one was lost in a Flood, They were cast in Dublin the lost one was cast in 1901 and the present Bell was cast in 1923.
South Brisbane, Queensland, (R.C.), 1, 15cwt., - This Bell was cast by Whitechapel in 1914.
Stanley, Tasmania, (R.C.), 1, 5cwt., - This Bell was cast in Dublin in 1912.
Stanmore, New South Wales, St Augustine, 1, 2cwt., - This Bell was cast by Taylors in 1964.
Strathalbyn, South Australia, Christ Church, 1, 8cwt., - This Bell was cast by Taylors in 1950.
Strathfield, New South Wales, St Anne, 1, 18cwt., - This Bell was cast by Taylors in 1948.
Strathfield, New South Wales, St Martha, 1, 12cwt., - This Bell was cast by Taylors in 1927.
Sydney, New South Wales, All Hallows Church, 2, 12-2-0., - Cast by Whitechapel in 1965.
Sydney, New South Wales, C. of E. Girls Grammar School, 1, 3-2-0., - Cast by Taylors in 1955.
Sydney, New South Wales, Presbyterian Church, 1, 3cwt., - This Bell was cast by Whitechapel in 1879.
Sydney, New South Wales, (R.C.), St Patrick's, 1.
Sydney, New South Wales, St James, 1, 5cwt., - This bell was cast by Taylors in 1891.
Sydney, New South Wales, St John's College (Sydney University College), 1, 10cwt., - This Bell was cast by Taylors in 1921.

Sydney, *New South Wales, Town Hall, 5, 30-0-14., - Chimed Only, Cast by Gillett & Johnson in 1884.*
Sydney, New South Wales, Trinity Garison, **2**, 3-1-0., - These Bells were cast by Taylors in 1970.
Sydney, *New South Wales, University of Sydney, War Memorial Carillon, 54, 84cwt. in G., - Carillon, All the Bells were cast by Taylors.*
The Barton, South Australia, (R.C.), **1**, 21cwt., - This Bell was cast in Dublin in 1920.
Toorak, *Victoria, St John, 13, 10cwt. - Chimed Only, These Bells were cast by Whitechapel in 1920.*
Toowoomba, Queensland, (R.C.), Cathedral, **1**, 30cwt., - This Bell was cast in Dublin in 1933.
Toowoomba, Queensland, Town Hall, **3**, 24-2-2., - Cast by Gillett and Johnson in 1901.
Townsville, Queensland, (R.C.), Cathedral, **1**, 12cwt., - This Bell was cast by Whitechapel in 1901.
Tumut, New South Wales, (R.C.), **2**, 16cwt., - The Treble was cast by Taylors in 1865 and the Tenor was cast in Dublin in 1918.
Ulverstone, Tasmania, (R.C.), **1**, 10cwt., - This Bell was cast in Dublin in 1925.
Unley, *South Australia, St Augustine, 13, 15cwt., - Chimed Only, Cast by Taylors in 1933.*
Vaucluse, *New South Wales, St Michael, 8, 7-2-2. in Bb., - Chimed Only, All these Bells were cast by Gillett and Johnson in 1938.*
Waanambool, Victoria, Christ Church, **3**, 10-2-0., - Cast by J.J. Radler and Sons in Hannover.
Wagga Wagga, New South Wales, (R.C.), **1**, 17-2-0., - This Bell was cast in Dublin in 1924.
Wahroonga, New South Wales, Dominican Priory, **1**, 15cwt., - Unringable, This Bell is on the Floor and was cast by Murphy of Dublin.
Wangaratta, Victoria, (R.C.), **1**, 14cwt., - This Bell was cast in Dublin in 1923.
Warwick, *Queensland, 8, 28-2-0., - Chimed Only, All These Bells were cast by Taylors in 1961.*
Watson Bay, New South Wales, Our Lady Star of the Sea, **1**, 20cwt., - Cast by Taylors in 1965.
Wauchope, New South Wales, Soldiers Memorial Tower, **1**, 7cwt., - Cast by Taylors in 1928.
Waverley, New South Wales, Mary Immaculate Church, **1**, 20cwt., - Cast by Taylors in 1930.
Wellington, New South Wales, St Patrick, **2**, 12cwt., - Cast by Taylors in 1858 and 1926.
West Maitland, New South Wales, **1**, 13cwt., - This Bell was cast by Whitechapel in 1929.
West Terrace, South Australia, (R.C.), **1**, 4cwt., - This Bell was cast in Dublin in 1893.
West Tamworth, New South Wales, St Paul, **1**, 6-2-0., - This Bell was cast by Taylors in 1929.
West Wyalong, New South Wales, (R.C.), **1**, 14cwt., - This Bell was cast in Dublin in 1936.
West Wyalong, New South Wales, St Barnabus, **1**, 18cwt., - This Bell was cast by Taylors in 1937.
Winchelsea, Victoria, (R.C.), **1**, 14cwt., - This Bell was cast in Dublin in 1923.
Yass, New South Wales, St Augustine, **1**, 15cwt., - This Bell was cast by Murphy of Dublin in 1836.
Yarrawonga, Victoria, (R.C.), **1**, 14cwt., - This Bell was cast in Dublin in 1924.
Yarrawonga, *Victoria, Coombs Cottage, On the Corner of Melba and Maroondah Highways, 1, 3-0-13., - Chimed Only, This Bell was cast by Gillett and Johnson in 1909.*

AUSTRIA.

Bell Salzburg, *Parish Church, 3, Hung Dead, These Bells were cast by Josef Pfundner in 1927.*
Innsbruck, *Dom Sct. Jakob, 48, - Carillon.*
Zisterzienserabter, *Stift Heiligenkreuz, 35, - Carillon.*

BELGIUM.

Aalst, *Oost-Vlaanderen, Belfort, 52, - Carillon.*
Antoing, *Hainaut (Henegouwen), Kerk, 25, - Carillon.*
Antwerpen, *Antwerpen, O.L. Vrouwe Kathedraal, 49, - Carillon.*
Antwerpen (Kiel), *Antwerpen, Sint-Catharina Toren, 47, - Carillon.*

<u>Ath (Aat)</u>, Hainaut (Henegouwen), Sint-Julien Toren, 46, - Carillon.
<u>Beauraing</u>, Namur (Namen), Sint-Martin Toren, 29, - Carillon.
<u>Binche</u>, Hainaut (Henegouwen), Beffroi, 25, - Carillon.
<u>Borgerhout</u>, Antwerpen, Districtshuis Toren, 47, - Carillon.
<u>Braine-le-Comte</u>, Hainaut (Henegouwen), Sint-Gery Toren, 47, - Carillon.
<u>Bruges</u> - See Brugge.
<u>Brugge</u>, West-Vlaanderen, Belfort, 47, - Carillon.
<u>Brussel</u>, Brabant, Paleis der Natie, 37, - Carillon.
<u>Brussel</u>, Brabant, Sint-Michiels Kathedraal, 49, - Carillon.
<u>Bruxelles</u> - See Brussel.
<u>Burcht</u>, Antwerpen, Openluchtbeiaard, 37, - Carillon.
<u>Charleroi</u>, Hainaut (Henegouwen), Beffroi, 47, - Carillon.
<u>Damme</u>, West-Vlaanderen, Stadhuis Toren, 39, - Carillon.
<u>Deinze</u>, Oost-Vlaanderen, O.L. Vrouwe Toren, 48, - Carillon.
<u>Dendermonde</u>, Oost-Vlaanderen, Belfort, 49, - Carillon.
<u>Diest</u>, Vlaams-Brabant, Sint-Sulpitius-en-Dionysius Kerk, 47, - Carillon.
<u>Diksmuide</u>, West-Vlaanderen, Belfort, 30, - Carillon.
<u>Eeklo</u>, Oost-Vlaanderen, Belfort, 25, - Carillon.
<u>Enghien (Edingen)</u>, Hainaut (Henegouwen), Sint-Niklaas Toren, 51, - Carillon.
<u>Florenville</u>, Luxembourg, Notre Dame, 49, - Carillon.
<u>Gembloux (Gembloers)</u>, Namur (Namen), Beffroi, 47, - Carillon.
<u>Genk</u>, Limburg, Sint-Martinus Toren, 52, - Carillon.
<u>Gent</u>, Oost-Vlaanderen, Belfort, 54, - Carillon.
<u>Geraardsbergen</u>, Oost-Vlaanderen, Sint-Bartholomeus Kerk, 49, - Carillon.
<u>Grimbergen</u>, Vlaams-Brabant, Sint-Servaas Basiliek, 49, - Carillon.
<u>Haaltert</u>, Oost-Vlaanderen, Sint-Goriks Toren, 44, - Carillon.
<u>Halle</u>, Vlaams-Brabant, O.L. Vrouwe Basiliek, 54, - Carillon.
<u>Harelbeke</u>, West-Vlaanderen, Sint-Salvator Toren, 50, - Carillon.
<u>Hasselt</u>, Limburg, Sint-Quintinus Kathedraal, 54, - Carillon.
<u>Herentals</u>, Antwerpen, Belfort, 49, - Carillon.
<u>Herzele</u>, Oost-Vlaanderen, Schepenhuis, 28, - Carillon.
<u>Hoogstraten</u>, Antwerpen, Sint-Catharina Toren, 50, - Carillon.
<u>Huy (Hoei)</u>, Liege, Notre Dame, 49, - Carillon.
<u>Ieper</u>, West-Vlaanderen, Belfort, 49, - Carillon.
<u>Izegem</u>, West-Vlaanderen, Sint-Hilonius Toren, 47, - Carillon.
<u>Kortrijk</u>, West-Vlaanderen, Belfort, 48, - Carillon.
<u>Kortrijk</u>, West-Vlaanderen, Sint-Maartens Toren, 49, - Carillon.
<u>La Louviere</u>, Hainaut (Henegouwen), Sint-Jozefs Toren, 47, - Carillon.
<u>Lede</u>, Oost-Vlaanderen, Sint-Martinus Toren, 24, - Carillon.
<u>Leuven</u>, Vlaams-Brabant, Sint-Geertrui Toren, 49, - Carillon.
<u>Leuven</u>, Vlaams-Brabant, Sint-Pieters Kerk, 49, - Carillon.
<u>Leuven</u>, Vlaams-Brabant, Centrale Bibliotheek Universiteit, American Engineers Memorial Carillon 63, - Carillon.
<u>Liege</u>, Liege, Sint-Barthelemy Toren, 40, - Carillon.
<u>Liege</u>, Liege, Sint-Jan-de-Evangelist Kerk, 34, - Carillon.
<u>Liege</u>, Liege, Sint-Paulus Kathedraal, 49, - Carillon.
<u>Lier</u>, Antwerpen, Sint-Gummarus Toren, 47, - Carillon.
<u>Lokeren</u>, Oost-Vlaanderen, Sint-Laurentius Toren, 49, - Carillon.
<u>Lommel</u>, Limburg, Sint-Pietersbanden Kerk, 63, - Carillon.
<u>Malmedy</u>, Liege, Sint-Petrus-en-Paulus-Kathedraal, 40, - Carillon.
<u>Mechelen</u>, Antwerpen, Hof van Busleyden, 49, - Carillon.
<u>Mechelen</u>, Antwerpen, O.L. Vrouwe-over-de-Dijle Toren, 50, - Carillon.
<u>Mechelen</u>, Antwerpen, Sint-Rombouts Toren, 49, 177-2-12. - Carillon, Cast by Eijesbouts.

Meise , *Vlaams-Brabant, Sint-Martinus Kerk, 47, - Carillon.*
Menen , *West-Vlaanderen, Belfort, 49, - Carillon.*
Mol , *Antwerpen, Sint-Petrus-en-Paulus Toren, 49, - Carillon.*
Mons (Bergen) , *Hainaut (Henegouwen), Belfort, 49, - Carillon.*
Namur (Namen) , *Namur, Sint-Albanus Kathedraal, 47, - Carillon.*
Nederbrakel (Brakel) , *Oost-Vlaanderen, Sint-Pieters Kerk, 49, - Carillon.*
Nieuwpoort , *West-Vlaanderen, O.L. Vrouwe Toren, 67, 28-0-14. in Eb. - Carillon, All these Bells were cast by Marcel Michiels Jr. a Bell Founder in Doornik in 1952 and the Tuning was executed according to the Pythagorean scale.*
Ninove , *Oost-Vlaanderen, Stadhuis, 30, - Carillon.*
Nivelles (Nijvel) , *Waals-Brabant, Sinst-Gertrudis Toren, 47, - Carillon.*
Oostende , *West-Vlaanderen, Feest-en-Cultuurpaleis, 49, - Carillon.*
Oudenaarde , *Oost-Vlaanderen, Sint-Walburga Toren, 49, - Carillon.*
Peer , *Limburg, Sint-Trudokerk, 51, - Carillon.*
Poperinge , *West-Vlaanderen, Sint-Bertinus Toren, 47, - Carillon.*
Postel (Mol) , *Antwerpen, Norbertijnerabdij, 49, - Carillon.*
Roeselare , *West-Vlaanderen, Sint-Michiels Toren, 49, - Carillon.*
Ronse , *Oost-Vlaanderen, Sint-Hermes Kerk, 49, - Carillon.*
Scherpenheuvel , *Vlaams-Brabant, O.L. Vrouwe Basiliek, 49, - Carillon.*
Sint-Niklaas , *Oost-Vlaanderen, Stadhuis Toren, 49, - Carillon.*
Sint-Truiden , *Limberg, Belfort, 41, - Carillon.*
Sint-Truiden (Kortenbos) , *Limberg, O.L. Vrouwe-Hemelvaart Basiliek, 27, - Carillon.*
Soignies (Zinnik) , *Hainaut (Henegouwen), Sint-Vincentius Kerk, 47, - Carillon.*
Steenokkerzeel , *Vlaams-Brabant, Sint-Rumoldus Toren, 49, - Carillon.*
Temse , *Oost-Vlaanderen, Gemeentehuis, 23, - Carillon.*
Thuin , *Hainaut (Henegouwen), Beffroi, 31, - Carillon.*
Tielt , *West-Vlaanderen, Belfort, 35, - Carillon.*
Tienen , *Vlaams-Brabant, Sint-Germanus Toren, Stadsbeiaard, 54, - Carillon.*
Tongeren , *Limburg, O.L. Vrouwe Basiliek, 42, - Carillon.*
Tournai (Doornik) , *Hainaut (Henegouwen), Belfort, 43, - Carillon.*
Turnhout , *Antwerpen, Sint-Pieters Toren, 52, - Carillon.*
Verviers , *Liege, O.L. Vrouwe-der-Recollecten Kerk, 40, - Carillon.*
Veurne , *West-Vlaanderen, Sint-Niklaas Toren, 48, - Carillon.*
Wavre (Waver) , *Waals-Brabant, Sint-Jan-de-Doper Toren, 49, - Carillon.*
Wingene , *West-Vlaanderen, Sint-Amandus Toren, 37, - Carillon.*
Zottegem , *Oost-Vlaanderen, O.L. Vrouwe-Hemelvaart Kerk, 49, - Carillon.*
Zoutleeuw , *Vlaams-Brabant, Sint-Leonardus Kerk, 39, - Carillon.*

BERMUDA.

Pembroke , *Main Island, St John the Evangelist Anglican Church, 25, in G, - Traditional Keyboard, Carillon, All the Bells were cast by Taylors in 1970.*
Smith's Parish , Main Island, (Anglican), Church of St Mark the Apostle, **10**, in C, - Unringable, Cast by Taylors.

BRAZIL.

Belo Horizonte , *Minas Gerais Cathedral, 38, in E, - Traditional Keyboard Carillon,Cast by VanBergen.*
Brasilia , *(R.C.), 18, in C, - Chimed Only, All the Bells were cast by VanBergen.*
Sao Paulo , *Vila Formosa, (R.C.), 47, in D#, - Traditional Keyboard, Carillon, Unplayable Keyboard is disconnected. All the Bells were cast by Eijsbouts in 1951.*

Sao Paulo, Cathedral Metropolitan de Sao Paulo, 61, in A, - Traditional Keyboard Carillon, Cast by Petit & Fritsen in 1959, This Cathedral also contains the largest pipe organ in South America.

CANADA.

Banff, Alberta, St George-in-the-Pines, 11, in G#, - Baton Keyboard Chimed, Cast by Taylors in 1927.
Brampton, Ontario, Holl. Christian Homes, 23, in G, - Automatic Carillon, Cast by Eijsbouts in 1986.
Brandon, Manitoba, St George's Anglican Cathedral, 14, in A, - Chimed Only, Including a Sharp Fourth and Flat Seventh, These Bells were cast by Gillett and Johnson in 1931.
Brockville, Ontario, Trinity Church, 11, in D, - Chimestand Chimed, Cast by Taylors in 1925.
Calgary, Alberta, City Hall, 1, - Hung Dead, Clock Bell.
Calgary, Alberta, (R.C.), St Mary's Cathedral, 4, - Tenor Hung for Automatic Swing Chiming Only and The Front Three Bells are Hung for Ringing but only have Swing Chiming Ropes with no Tail End, All these Bells were cast in France in the 19th Century.
Chatham, Ontario, First Presbyterian Church, 11, - Chimed Only, These Bells were cast by McShane.
Cobourg, Ontario, St Peter's Anglican Church, 10, 16-1-14 in F#, - Chimed Only, Cast by Meneely of Watervliet in 1905.
Cornwall, Ontario, Trinity Anglican Church, 9, in F, - Chimestand Chimed, Cast by McShane in 1885.
Edmonton, Alberta, City Hall, (Friendship Tower), 23, 60 cwt. in C, - Electric Keyboard, Carillon, These bells were cast by Petit and Fritsen in 1991.
Erin Mills, Ontario, Shopping Mall, 15, in F, - Automatic Chiming Only, Cast by Eijsbouts in 1989.
Exeter, Ontario, Trivitt Memorial (Anglican) Church and Precious Blood (R.C.) Mission, 10, 16-0-22. in F. - The front Four Bells are Hung Dead and the Back Six Bells are Hung Veronese Style, Counterbalanced, No Stay or Slider, These Bells can be Rung to Changes and also these Bells were cast by Mcshane Bell Foundry in 1890, Sat 1-4pm, Sun 10.30am-10.35am.
Fredericton, New Brunswick, Christ Church Cathedral, 15, in A, - Electric Keyboard Chimed, Cast by Warner in 1911, Originally there was a Full Circle Ring of Eight Bells in this Tower Cast by Whitechapel in 1852 but destroyed by a fire in 1911.
Fredericton, New Brunswick, University of New Brunswick, (Lady Beaverbrook Residence Hall), 8, in G#, - Chimed Only, Cast by Taylors in 1930, The Clock Plays " The Jones Boys " at 12pm and 6pm.
Georgetown, Ontario, Knox Presbyterian Church, (N.E. Tower) Lawson Memorial Chimes, 8, in G#, - Chimed Only, These Bells were cast by Taylors in 1922.
Guelph, Ontario, St George's Church, Cutton Memorial Carillon, 23, in F#, - Traditional Keyboard, Carillon, These Bells were cast by Gillett and Johnson in 1926.
Halifax, Nova Scota, (R.C.), St Agnes Church, 18, - Automatic Chime, Cast by Eijsbouts in 1967.
Halifax, Nova Scotia, St John's Church, 13, in F, - Chimed Only, Cast by Gillett and Johnson in 1920.
Halifax, Nova Scotia, (R.C.), St Mary's Cathedral Basilica, 11, 10-2-15. in F#, - Electric Keyboard Chimed, Including Flat Seventh, These Bells were cast by Gillett and Johnson in 1920.
Halifax, Nova Scota, The United Memorial Church, 10, in F#, - Chimed Only, These Bells were cast by Meneely of Troy in 1921.
Hamilton, Ontario, (R.C.), Cathedral of Christ the King, 23, 84-2-26 in G#, - Traditional Keyboard, Carillon, These Bells were cast by Whitechapel in 1933.
Hamilton, Ontario, Hamilton Memorial Clock Tower, King and Jarvis Streets, 14, 8 cwt, - Chimed Only, These Bells were cast by Petit and Fritsen in 1988, Detatched Tower.
Hamilton, Ontario, St Giles United Church, 11, in D#, -Chimestand Chimed, Cast by McShane in 1913.

Hamilton, Ontario, St Paul's Presbyterian Church, 11, in E, - Chimestand Chimed, These Bells were cast by Meneely of Watervliet in 1906, This Church has the Tallest Stone Spire in Canada.
Hope, Ontario, St Paul's Presbyterian Church, 11, - Ellacombe Chimed.
Kingston, Ontario, 9, in E, - Chimed Only, Including a Flat Seventh, Cast by Gillett & Johnson in 1911.
Kitchener, Ontario, St Peter's Evangelist Lutheran Church, 12, in D#, - Chimed Only, These Bells were cast by Meneely of Watervliet in 1901, This town changed its name to Kitchener from Berlin.
Kitchener, Ontario, Kitchener-Waterloo Oktoberfest, 23, in G, - Traditional Keyboard, Carillon, Cast by Eijsbouts in 1976, The town of Kitchener was originally called Berlin.
London, Ontario, St John the Evangelist Church, 14, in D#, - Automatic Chime, Ten Bells Cast by Petit and Fritsen in 1996, The other two were cast in 1902 & 1955.
London, Ontario, (Anglican), St Pauls Cathedral, 11, in E, - Baton Keyboard Chimed, This Tower used to have a Ring of Six Bells cast by Mears and Stainbank in 1851 and were Rung until 1901 when they were All recast and rehung in 1935 by Gillett and Johnson.
London, Ontario, Saint Peter's Cathedral Basilica, 35, - Electric Keyboard, Carillon, Cast by Petit & Fritsen.
Lunenburg, Nova Scota, St John's Anglican Church, 10, 20 cwt in F, - Chimed Only, These Bells were cast by Meneely of Watervliet in 1902, Also another bell cast by Mears & Stainbank in 1813, All the Bells have been removed from the tower due to a arson attack on the 1st of November 2001 which destroyed the Church.
Markham, Ontario, (Byzantine Slovak), Cathedral of the Transfiguration, 10350 Woodbine Avenue, 3, 380 cwt. in C, - Automatically Swing Chimed, Cast by Paccard in 1986, Treble weighs 120 cwt. in G, Second weights 200 cwt. in E.
Marystown, Newfoundland, (R.C.), Sacred Heart Church, **1**, 3-2-1.
Montreal, Quebec, (R.C.), Notre-Dame Basilica, **10**, 52-2-10. in B. - Unringable, These Bells used to Rung but are now Ellacombe Chimed Only, All the Bells were cast by Whitechapel, The Eighth was cast in 1892, The Ninth was cast in 1862, The Tenor was cast in 1863 and the rest were cast in 1843, Also there is a **Bourdon Bell** in the Tower that is Rung only at Easter that is Swing Chimed, Corpus Christi and Christmas it was cast in 1847 and weights 221-0-25.
Montreal, Quebec, Oratoire St-Joseph du Mont-Royal (St Joseph's Orarory), 56, in D#, - Traditional Keyboard, Carillon, These Bells were cast by Paccard in 1956.
Montreal, Quebec, St Georges Anglican Church, 10, in E, - Electric Keyboard Chimed, Cast by Gillett and Johnson in 1901.
Montreal, Quebec, (Anglican), Church of St James the Apostle, 10, in D#, -Chimed Only,Cast by Meneely of Troy in 1889.
Montreal, Quebec, St Patricks Basilica, **10**, 20-0-26. in E. - Unringable, The Ropes, Wheels and Clappers Removed, These Bells were cast by Mears and Stainbank in 1910.
Moose Jaw, Saskatchchewan, (Anglican), St John's Church, 8, in F#, - Chimed Only, Cast by Taylors in 1910.
Newcastle, New Brundswick, St James and St John United Church, 11, in A, - Electric Keyboard Chimed, Including Sharp Fourth & Flat Seventh, These Bells were cast by Gillett and Johnson in 1947.
New Westminster, British Columbia, Holy Trinity Cathedral, 8, 24-0-18. - Cast by Mears and Stainbank in 1861 but were Destroyed by a fire in 1898 but fortunately only One Bell Survived.
Niagara Falls, Ontario, Rainbow Bridge, The Rainbow Tower Carillon, 55, 178cwt. in E. - Traditional Keyboard, Carillon, All these Bells were cast by Taylors in 1948.
Niagara Falls, Ontario, Christ Church, 10, in E, - Chimed Only, Cast by McShane in 1912.
Niagara-on-the-Lake, Ontario, St Mark's Anglican Church, 9, - Chimed Only, The Back Three Bells were Cast by Meneely of Watervliet in 1917, The front Six Bells were cast in 1877.
North York, Ontario, Office Building, City Square, 14, in D#, - Automatic Chiming Only, These Bells were cast by Eijesbouts in 1986.

Oakville, Ontario, St Jude's Anglican Church, **9**, in F, - Ellacombe Chimed Only exept the **Tenor** which is Hung for Ringing, Including a Flat Seventh, These Bells were cast by Whitechapel in 1906.
Oliver, British Columbia, St Edward the Confessor, 8, 6-1-0 in B, - Baton Keyboard Chimed, Cast by Whitechapel in 1952, The Tower is built in a Norman Style.
Oshawa, Ontario, St George Memorial Anglican Church, Memorial Tower, 15, 52 cwt in B, - Baton Keyboard Chimed, Including Sharp Fourth, Flat Seventh, Flat Ninth, Flat Tenth, These Bells were cast by Whitechapel in 1924.
Ottawa, Ontario, All Saints Anglican Church, 9, - Chimed Only.
Ottawa, Ontario, Concordia Building, 8, in D, - Chimed Only, Cast by Taylors in 1990.
Ottawa, Ontario, Eglise St-Jean-Baptiste, 47, in C, - Traditional Keyboard, Carillon, These Bells were cast by Michiels in 1940.
Ottawa, Ontario, Houses of Parliament, Peace Tower, 53, 201-2-4 in E. - Traditional Keyboard, Carillon, All these Bells were cast by Gillett and Johnson in 1927.
Ottawa, Ontario, St Bartholomew, **3**, 4-3-18. in F#.- The Princess Louise who was a Daughter of Queen Victoria and the Wife to the Governor General of Canada the Marquis of Lorne presented the Three Bells to the Church. The Bells were Cast by the Meneely Bell Foundry in New York, U.S.A. and Stamped 1878 & 1879. The Treble 1-3-24. in C. and the Second 2-2-0. in D, These Bells were Rehung in 1952 by Gillett & Johnson, Also the Tower and Porch were rebuilt in 1985, Ringing of the Bells is Restricted.
Peterborough, Ontario, (Anglican), Christ Church, 11, - Chimed Only, Cast by Meneely of Watervliet.
Peterborough, Ontario, St John's Anglican Church, 19, 28-2-10. in C# - Chimed Only,Cast by Taylors.
Petrolia, Ontario, (Anglican), Christ Church, 11, in D#, - Chimed Only, Cast by Meneely of Watervliet in 1909.
Port Hope, Ontario, St Paul's Presbyterian Church, 11, in F, - Chimed Only, Cast by Meneely of Watervliet in 1912.
Quebec, Quebec, (R.C.), Basilica, **3**.
Quebec, Quebec, l'Eglise Saint-Dominique, rue Grande-Allee, 10, - Chimed Only.
Regina, Saskatchewan, Knox-Metropolitan United Church, Darke Memorial Port Chimes, 12, 40 cwt in C, - Chiming Only, Rung by individual Ropes attached to the Clappers which fall in a circle in the Ringing Chamber, Cast by Mears & Stainbank in 1927, The local band practice Change Ringing.
Regina, Saskatchewan, Wascana Place, Wascana Chimes, 8, - Tubular Bells, Ellacumbe Chimed.
Richmond, British Columbia, (Bota), Fantasy Garden World, 10800 No 5 Road, 23, in C,, - Hung Dead, Automatic Carillon, These Bells were cast by Eijsbouts in 1984.
Saint Catharines, Ontario, St George's Anglican Church, 23, - Carillon.
Saint John, New Brunswick, St John at St John, **1**, 12cwt.
Saint John, New Brunswick, Trinity Church Anglican Parish of Saint John, **9**, 19 cwt, - Unringable but now Electric Keyboard Chimed, The Tenor is inscribed "In Memoriam the Loyalists 1783: Faithful alike to God and King". All the Bells were cast in 1882.
Simcoe, Ontario, Norfolk County War Memorial, 23, 23 cwt. in F#, - Traditional Keyboard, Carillon, Cast by Gillett and Johnson in 1925, Detatched Tower.
St John's, Newfoundland, (R.C.), Cathedral Basilica of St John the Baptist, 200 Military Road, (East Tower), 1, 40 cwt. - Hung Dead, Clock Bell, Cast by James Murphy in 1850, (West Tower), **8**, - Unringable, Three Bells were cast by James Murphy in 1854 & 1857, Five Bells were cast by Matthew O'Byrne in 1906.
Stratford, Ontario, St James Anglican Church, **11**, 16 cwt. in E, - Chimestand Chimed Only exept the **Tenor** which is Hung for Ringing, No Stay or Slider, Including Sharp Fourth & Flat Seventh, Cast by Meneely of Watervliet in 1909, The Chimestand is made of Quarter Sawn Oak.
Sydney Mines, Nova Scota, St Andrew's Perspiration Church, 10, in E, - Chimed Only, These Bells were cast by McShane in 1911.

74

Thunder Bay, Ontario, St Paul's Anglican Church, 10, in F#, - Chimestand Chimed, Cast by Meneely of Watervliet in 1909, Thunder Bay was formed by a merger of the two towns Fort William & Port Arthur.
Toronto, Ontario, Old City Hall, 3, 104 cwt. in A, - Clock Chimed, Cast by Gillett & Johnson in 1900.
Toronto, Ontario, The Exhibition Place Carillon, 50, in D#, - Traditional Keyboard, Carillon, Cast by Eijsbouts in 1974.
Toronto, Ontario, The Promenade Shopping Centre, 15, in C, - Automatically Chimed Only, These Bells were cast by Eijsbouts in 1986.
Toronto, Ontario, Metropolitan United Church, 54, in A, - Traditional Keyboard, Carillon, Twenty-three Bells were cast by Gillett and Johnson in 1922, Twelve bells by Petit and Fritsen in 1960 and the rest by Paccard in 1971.
Toronto , Ontario, St James Cathedral, (Upper Belfry), 10, in C#, - Electric Keyboard Chimed Only, These Bells were cast by Meneely of Watervliet in 1865 and 1928, (Lower Belfry), **12**, 21-2-10 in D., These Bells were cast by Whitechapel in 1828 and 1996.
Toronto, Ontario, (Anglican), Church of St John the Baptist Norway, 8, in A, - Baton Keyboard Chimed, These Bells were cast by Gillett and Johnson in 1926.
Toronto, Ontario, Streetside Clock Tower, 101 Yorkville Avenue, 12, in C, - Automatically Chimed Only, These Bells were cast by Eijsbouts in 1977.
Toronto, Ontario, Timothy Eaton Memorial United Church, 21, in A, - Chimestand Chimed, Cast by Warner in 1914.
Toronto, Ontario, University of Toronto, Soldiers Tower, 51, in A#, - Traditional Keyboard, Carillon, Twenty-three Bells were cast by Gillett & Johnson in 1927, The rest were cast by Petit & Fritsen in 1975, Detatched Tower.
Truro, Nova Scotia, St John's Anglican Church, 10, in F#, - Chimed Only, Cast by Meneely of Watervliet in 1906.
Vancouver, British Columbia, St James Church, 8, in C, - Chimestand Chimed, Cast by Taylors in 1938.
Victoria, British Columbia, Centennial Carillon Tower, 62, in D, - Traditional Keyboard, Carillon, Visiting Times 3pm Sunday April-Dec & 7pm, Friday July-Aug, Cast by Petit & Fritsen in 1967 & 1971.
West Toronto, Ontario, St John's Anglican Church, 10, 24-0-10 in D#, - Chimed Only, Cast by Gillett & Johnson in 1924.
Winnipeg, Manitoba, Osbourne Village Square, 14, - Chimed Only.
Winnipeg, Manitoba, Portridge Place, 20, in F, - Automatically Chimed Only, Cast by Eijsbouts in 1987.
Winnipeg, Manitoba, St Luke's Anglican Church, 8, - Chimed Only, Cast by Gillett & Johnson in 1919.
Winnipeg, Manitoba, Knox United Church, 16, in C, - Chimed Only, Cast by Warner in 1912.
Woodstock , Ontario, New St Paul's Church, **10**, - Unringable, only Ellacumbe Chimed from hammers on the outside of the bells, These Bells were cast by Taylors in 1910.
Yarmouth, Nova Scotia, Holy Trinity Anglican Church, 11, in E, - Chimed Only, Cast by Meneely of Watervliet in 1908.

CHILE.

Santiago, San Pedro Tower, 25, in C, - Automatic Carillon, All the Bells were cast by Mabilon.

COSTA RICA.

Cartago, Almacen Gonzalez, 12, in C, - Chimed Only, All the Bells were cast by Petit and Fritsen.

CUBA.

Havana, Our Lady of Lourdes Church, 49, in C, - Traditional Keyboard Carillon All the bells were cast by Petit and Fritsen in 1958.

DENMARK.

Aalborg, Domkirken Sct. Budolfi, 48, 25cwt. in D#. - Carillon, Cast by Petit and Fritsen in 1970.
Arhus, Radhuset, 43, 48cwt. in D. - Carillon, Detatched Steel Tower.
Astrup (Ning Herred), Kirken, 24, 5-1-12. in C. - Hung Dead, Automatic Carillon, All the Bells were cast by Eijesbouts in 1986.
Ballerup, Vestkirken, 24, 8cwt. in A#. - Hung Dead, Automatic Carillon, All the Bells were cast by Eijsbouts in 1973.
Billund, Kirken, 29, 8cwt. in A#. - Hung Dead, Automatic Carillon, All the Bells were cast by Eijesbouts in 1981.
Brondby, Strand Kirke, 48, 26-1-2. in D#. - Carillon, Cast by Petit and Fritsen in 1986.
Esbjerg, Zions Kirke, 5, - Hung Dead, Clock Chime, All the Bells were cast by Taylors in 1920.
Faborg, Klokketam, 38, 6-1-12. in h1. - Carillon, Also the Tower is painted Yellow and All the Bells were cast by Petit and Fritsen in 1960.
Frederiksburg, Radhuset, 47, 26cwt. in F. - Hung Dead, Automatic Carillon.
Frederikshavn, Kirke, 24, 1-2-18. in G. - Carillon, Cast by Petit and Fritsen between 1984 - 1985.
Godthab (Gronland), Hans Egeds Kirke, 26, 7-2-26. in A#. - Hung Dead, Automatic Carillon, All the Bells were cast by Petit and Fritsen in 1975.
Hadsund, Kirken, 23, 3-2-16. in D. - Hung Dead, Automatic Carillon, Cast by Eijesbouts in 1991.
Hasseris, Kirken, 26, 18-1-20. in F. - Hung Dead, Automatic Carillon
Herning, Kirke, 48, 27-2-0. in D#. - Carillon.
Hillerod, Frederiksborg Slot, 27, 15cwt. in G. - Carillon.
Hjorring, Sct. Catharinae, 25, 10-1-12. in A#. - Hung Dead, Automatic Carillon.
Holbaek, Sct. Nicolai Kirke, 37, 7-2-0. in A#. - Carillon.
Holstebro, Sct. Jorgens Kirke, 48, 30-2-14. in D. - Carillon, Cast by Eijesbouts in 1974.
Holstebro, Norrelandskirke, 48, 9-2-14. in A. Carillon.
Holte, Sollerodgard, 26, 3-1-12. in E. - Hung Dead, This Automatic Carillon is in a Large White House, All the Bells were cast by Michiels between 1928 - 1929.
Ikast, Kirken, 29, 5-1-12. in C. - Hung Dead, Automatic Carillon, All the Bells were cast by Eijesbouts.
Kobenhavn, Helligandskirke, 42, 60cwt. in C#. - Carillon, All the Bells were cast by Sorensen in 1947.
Kobenhavn, Vor Frelsers Kirke, 48, 43cwt. in C. - Carillon, All the Bells were cast by Petit and Fritsen in 1982, Also the Tower has a very decorative Spiralling Spire.
Kobenhavn, Magrethe Kirke, 38, 4-1-12. in C#. - Carillon, Cast by Petit and Fritsen in 1970.
Kolding, Sct Nicolai Kirke, 48, 25-1-10. in D#. - Carillon, Cast by Petit and Fritsen in 1973.
Logumkloster, Kong Frederik IX's Klokkespil, 49, 36cwt. in C#. - Carillon, All the Bells were cast by Petit and Fritsen in 1973, Also Detatched Hexagonal Steel Tower.
Nykobing Falster, Kirken, 26, 9-0-8. in A. - Hung Dead, Automatic Carillon, All the Bells were cast by Petit and Fritsen in 1969.
Odder, Kirken, 26, 6-1-12. in h1. - Hung Dead, Automatic Carillon, All the Bells were cast by Petit and Fritsen in 1968.
Odense, Domkirken Sct. Knud, 48, 12-2-24. in G. - Carillon, Cast by Petit and Fritsen in 1989.
Ramsing, Kirken, 25, 12-2-24. in G. - Hung Dead, Automatic Carillon, Cast by Eijesbouts in 1992.
Randers, Sct. Mortens Kirke, 49, 7-2-16. in F. - Carillon, Cast by Petit and Fritsen in 1994.
Silkeborg, Kirke, 42, 6-1-12. in h1. - Carillon, All the Bells were cast by Petit and Fritsen in 1966.

Sonderborg, Sct. Maria Kirke, 24, 5-1-2. in C. - Hung Dead, Automatic Carillon.
Svendborg, Vor Frue Kirke, 27, 9-1-16. in A. - Carillon, Cast by Petit and Fritsen in 1958.
Thorshavn (Faeroerne), Domkirken, 24, 2-0-24. in F. - Hung Dead, Automatic Carillon, All the Bells were cast by Eijesbouts in 1988.
Ulfborg by, Ulfkjaer Kirke, 36, 7-2-4. in A#. - Hung Dead, Automatic Carillon, All the Bells were cast by Eijsbouts in 1974.
Varde, Sct. Jacobi Kirke, 42, 5-0-6. in C. - Carillon, Cast by Petit and Fritsen in 1963.
Vejle, Sct. Nicolai Kirke, 48, 27-2-0. in D#. - Carillon.

DOMINICAN REPUBLIC.

Higuey, Altagracia, Catedral Basilica de Nuestra SeOora, 45, in D, - Hung Dead, Automatic Carillon, All the Bells were cast by Paccard in 1977.

El SALVADOR.

San Salvador, Iglesia Maria Auxiliadora, 35, in G, - Traditional Keyboard Carillon, All Cast by Petit and Fritsen in 1963.

FINLAND.

Kouvola, Radhuset, 18, 8cwt. in A. - Automatically Chimed, Cast by Pfunder (Wien) in 1966.

FRANCE.

Agde, Herault, 14, - Automatically Chimed Only, All the Bells were cast by Paccard in 1900.
Agen, Lot-et-Garonne, 12, - Chimed Only.
Albi, Tarn, La Madeleine, 9, - Chimed Only.
Albi, Tarn, Notre Dame de la Dreche, 28, - Carillon.
Albi, Tarn, St Salvy, 8, - Automatically Chimed Only.
Allegre, Gard, 10, - Chimed Only.
Annecy, Haute-Savoie, Couvent de la Visitation, 37, - Carillon.
Arques, Aude, 16, - Chimed Only.
Aspet, Haute-Garonne, 12, - Chimed Only.
Auterive, Haute-Garonne, 9, - Automatically Chimed Only.
Avesnes sur Helpe, Nord, Collegiale St. Nicolas, 48, - Carillon.
Avignon, Vaucluse, 17, - Automatically Chimed Only.
Avignonet-Lauragais, Haute-Garonne, 13, - Chimed Only.
Ax-les-Thermes, Ariege, 7, - Automatically Chimed Only.
Bailleul, Nord, Beffroi de l'Hotel de Ville, 35, - Carillon.
Baraigne, Aude, 3, - Chimed Only, Hung in a Trangular Bellcote.
Baziege, Haute-Garonne, 25, - Hung Dead, Automatic Carillon.
Beaune, Cote d'Or, Les Hospices, 23, - Carillon.
Bellegarde du Razes, Aude, 12, - Chimed Only.
Belmontet, Lot, 11, 6-2-4., - Automatically Chimed Only.
Belpech, Aude, 7, - Chimed Only.
Berat, Haute-Garonne, 13, - Chimed Only.
Bergues, Nord, Beffroi Communal, 50, - Carillon.
Bethune, Pas-de-Calais, Beffroi Communal, 38, - Carillon.
Blois, Loir et Cher, Basilique Nore Dame de la Trinite, 48, - Carillon.
Bordeaux, Gironde, St Michel, 22, - Chimed Only.
Bouloc, Haute-Garonne, 7, 6-2-0., - Automatically Chimed Only.
Boulogne-sur-Gesse, Haute-Garonne, 16, - Chimed Only.

Bourg-St-Bernard, Haute-Garonne, 11, - Automatically Chimed Only.
Buglose, Landes, St Vincent de Paul, 60, - Carillon, On the Four Corners at the top of the Tower there are Trumpeting Angels.
Cambo-les-Bains, Pyrenees-Atlantiques, Chapelle des Thermes, 12, - Automatically Chimed Only.
Cambrai, Nord, Hotel de Ville, 32, - Carillon.
Cappelle-la-Grande, Nord, Beffroi Communal, 58, - Carillon.
Caraman, Haute-Garonne, 8, - Automatically Chimed Only.
Carbonne, Haute-Garonne, 10, - Chimed Only.
Carcassonne, Aude, Basilique St. Nazaire, 37, - Carillon.
Carcassonne, Aude, Eglise St. Vincent, 54, - Carillon.
Cassagne, Haute-Garonne, 5, - Chimed Only.
Castanet-Tolosan, Haute-Tolosan, 8, - Chimed Only.
Castans, Aude, 7, - Chimed Only.
Castelnaudary, Aude, Collegiale St. Michel, 35, - Carillon.
Castelnau-Magnoac, Hautes-Pyrenees, 8, - Automatically Chimed Only.
Castres, Tarn, Eglise Notre Dame de la Trinite, 33, 6-1-24. - Carillon.
Cazeres, Haute-Garonne, 15, - Chimed Only.
Cenne, Aude, (R.C.), Monastery, 9, - Automatically Chimed Only, Cast by Martin in 1903.
Chalons Sur Marne, Marne, Eglise Notre Dame en Vaux, 56, - Carillon.
Chambery, Savoie, Chateau des Ducs de Savoie, 70, - Carillon.
Champagney, Haute-Saone, Eglise, 35, - Carillon.
Chateau-Gombert, Bouches du Rhone, Musee ATP, 10, - Chimed Only.
Chatellerault, Vienne, Eglise St. Jacques, 52, - Carillon.
Cilaos, Eglise (Ile de la Reunion), 48, - Carillon.
Coursan, Aude, 8, - Automatically Chimed Only.
Decazeville, Aveyron, 10, - Automatically Chimed Only.
Dijon, Cote d'Or, Cathedrale St. Benigne, 63, - Carillon.
Douai, Nord, Hotel de Ville, 62, - Carillon.
Dunkerque, Nord, Beffroi, 48, - Carillon.
Espira de l'Agly, Pyrenees-Orientales, 8, - Automatically Chimed Only, Cast by Bollee in 1964.
Fanjeaux, Aude, 10, - Chimed Only.
Fendeille, Aude, 8, - Chimed Only, All these bells were cast by Vinel in 1892.
Fonsorbes, Haute-Garonne, 11, - Chimed Only.
Fontiers Carbades, Aude, 17, - Chimed Only.
Forcalquier, Alpes-de-Haute-Provence, 18, - Chimed Only.
Gaillac-Toulza, Haute-Garonne, 11, - Chimed Only.
Gaulene, Tarn, 11, - Chimed Only.
Gourdon, Lot, 24, - Carillon, All the Bells were cast in 1988 and are very wide in the Mouth, These Bells are Hung in a Museum or Hotel on the Ground Floor Level.
Hazebrouck, Nord, Eglise St. Eloi, 48, - Carillon.
Hondschoote, Nord, Eglise Saint Vaast, 61, - Carillon.
Ille-sur-Tet, Pyrenees-Orientales, 15, - Automatically Chimed Only.
La Bastide de Bousignac, Ariege, 8, - Automatically Chimed Only.
La Cassaigne, Aude, 8, - Automatically Chimed Only, All these bells were cast by Fourcade in 1939.
La Dreche, Tarn, Notre Dame, 29, - Carillon.
Lagarde-Lauragais, Haute-Garonne, **19**, - the Back **Five** Bells are Rung Full Circle on Counterbalanced Bells with No Wheels, Stays or Sliders. These Bells are on the Roof of the Church in a Triangular Bellcote the rest are Chimed Only.
Lanta, Haute-Garonne, 14, - Automatically Chimed Only.
Lareole, Haute-Garonne, 12, - Automatically Chimed Only.
Larressingle, Gers, 2, - Chimed Only.
Larroque d'Olmes, Ariege, 8, - Automatically Chimed Only.

Launaguet , Haute-Garonne, 9, - Chimed Only.
Laure Minervois , Aude, 10, - Automatically Chimed Only, These bells were cast by Arragon in 1890.
Lauzerte , Tarn-et-Garonne, 4, - Chimed Only.
Le Creusot , Saone et Loire, Eglise St. Henri, 24, - Carillon.
Le Fousseret , Haute-Garonne, 11, - Automatically Chimed Only.
Le Mas Rillier (Miribel) , Ain, Sanctuaire Notre Dame du Sacre-Coeur, 50, - Carillon.
Le Quesnoy , Nord, Hotel de Ville, 48, - Carillon.
Lezat-sur-leze , Ariege, 14, - Hung Dead, Keyboard Chimed Only, Hexagonal Shaped Tower.
Liesse , Aisne, Basilique Notre Dame de Liesse, 31, - Carillon.
Lille , Nord, Cathedrale Notre Dame de la Treille, 37, - Carillon.
Lille , Nord, Eglise du Sacre-Coeur, 36, - Carillon.
Lisieux , Calvados, Basilique Sainte Therese, 49, - Carillon.
L'isle-Jourdain , Gers, Eglise, 9, 6-1-2., - Hung Dead, Keyboard Chimed Only, Round Tower, The Bourden Bell was cast in 1864 and weighs 3-0-18., The Other Eight Bells were cast by Paccard in 1982 and weigh in order of Treble to Tenor 0-3-7, 1-0-4, 1-1-26, 2-0-18, 3-0-4, 3-0-16, 4-2-0, 6-1-2.
L'isle-Jourdain , Gers, Musee d'art Campanaire (Bell Museum), (Place de l'hotel de ville), 23, Carillon, This Museum has lots of Bells and is only 15F entrance fee.
Lyon , Rhone, Hotel de Ville, 65, - Carillon.
Magalas , Heraut, Musee des Cloches et des Campanes, 40, - Carillon.
Martres-Tolosane , Haute-Garonne, 12, - Chimed Only.
Mas Carbades , Aude, 10, - Chimed Only.
Mas-Grenier , Tarn-et-Garonne, 9, - Automatically Chimed Only.
Massat , Ariege, 12, - Automatically Chimed Only.
Maubeuge , Nord, Eglise St. Pierre et St. Paul, 28, - Carillon.
Mauzac , Haute-Garonne, 11, - Chimed Only.
Mende , Lozere, Cathedrale, 9, - Chimed Only.
Millau , Aveyron, Notre Dame, 10, - Automatically Chimed Only.
Millau , Aveyron, Sacre-Coeur, 21, - Chimed Only.
Miremont , Haute-Garonne, 12, - Chimed Only.
Mirepoix , Ariege, 15, - Chimed Only.
Moissac , Tarn et Garonne, Eglise St. Pierre l'Abbaye, 24, - Carillon, Six of the Bells were cast in 1707 and the other Eighteen bells were cast by Paccard in 1984.
Molandier , Aude, 11, - Automatically Chimed Only, Hung outside in Three Triangular style Belcote.
Molitg-les-Bains , Pyrenees-Orientales, 15, - Automatically Chimed Only.
Montbel , Ariege, 8, - Automatically Chimed Only.
Montclar, Haute-Garonne, **5**, - Rung Full Circle , Counterbalanced with No Wheels, Stays or Sliders.
Montech , Tarn-et-Garonne, 17, - Chimed Only.
Montferrier , Ariege, 9, - Chimed Only.
Montpellier , Herault, 26, - Hung Dead, Automatic Carillon.
Narbonne , Aude, Cathedrale St. Just, 36, - Carillon.
Nice , Alpes-Maritimes, 25, - Chimed Only.
Noe , Haute-Garonne, 10, - Automatically Chimed Only.
Nuits St. Georges , Cote d'Or, Eglise St. Symphorien, 37, - Carillon.
Onet , Aveyron, le Chateau, 10, - Chimed Only.
Orchies , Nord, Eglise Notre Dame de l'Assomption, 48, - Carillon.
Pamiers , Ariege, Cathedrale St. Antonin, 49, - Carillon. The base of the Tower is Square with a walk through archway above there is a Fortress style Battlement under the Octagonal shaped Tower.
Pamiers , Ariege, Notre Dame du Camp, 21, - Carillon.

<u>Paris</u>, Eglise Sainte Odile, 23, - Carillon.
<u>Paris</u>, Cathedrale de Notre-Dame de Paris, (North Tower), 4, - Chimed Only, These Bells were cast in 1856 with Bronze taken from the Imperial Russian Army at there defeat of Sebastopol, The Bells bear the names and coats of arms of archbishops and there patrons the Bells are named: Angelique-Francoise, Antoinette-Charlotte, Hyacinthe-Jeanne and Denise-David, (South Tower), 1, 260cwt., - Chimed Only.
<u>Pau</u>, Pyrenees-Atlantiques, Notre Dame, 10, - Automatically Chimed Only.
<u>Pau</u>, Pyrenees-Atlantiques, St Martin, 28, - Hung Dead, Automatic Carillon.
<u>Paulhac</u>, Haute-Garonne, 12, - Chimed Only.
<u>Perpignan</u>, Pyrenees-Orientales, Cathedrale Saint-Jean-Baptiste, 46, 32-2-4. -, Carillon, The Tenor is called " Antoinette ".
<u>Perigueux</u>, Dordogne, 17, - Automatically Chimed Only.
<u>Peyreleau</u>, Aveyron, 5, - Chimed Only.
<u>Pibrac</u>, Haute-Garonne, 7, - Chimed Only.
<u>Pointis-Inard</u>, 14, - Chimed Only.
<u>Portet sur Garonne</u>, Haute-Garonne, Eglise (Carillon de Timbres), 24, - Carillon.
<u>Poucharramet</u>, Haute-Garonne, 11, - Chimed Only.
<u>Pradelles Carbades</u>, Aude, 10, - Chimed Only.
<u>Puy l'Eveque</u>, Lot, 15, - Automatically Chimed Only.
<u>Rabastens</u>, Tarn, 8, - Automatically Chimed Only.
<u>Reims</u>, Marne, Eglise St. Nicaise, 35, - Carillon.
Renneville, Haute-Garonne, 4, - Rung Full Circle ,Counterbalanced with No Wheels, Stays or Sliders.
<u>Rieumes</u>, Haute-Garonne, 14, - Automatically Chimed Only.
<u>Roubaix</u>, Nord, Eglise St. Martin, 38, - Carillon.
<u>Rouen</u>, Seine Marittime, Cathedrale Tour de Beurre, 56, - Carillon.
<u>Saint-Amand-les-Eaux</u>, Nord, Tour de l'ancienne Abbaye, 48, - Carillon.
<u>Saint-Amans</u>, Tarn, Val Toret, 10, - Automatically Chimed Only.
<u>Saint-Bertrant-de-Comminges</u>, Haute-Garonne, 5, - Chimed Only.
<u>Saint-Gaudens</u>, Haute-Garonne, Eglise, 36, - Carillon.
<u>Saint-Leon</u>, Haute-Garonne, 10, - Chimed Only.
<u>Saint-Lys</u>, Haute-Garonne, 11, - Chimed Only.
<u>Saint-Quentin</u>, Aisne, Hotel de Ville, 37, - Carillon.
<u>Saint-Sardos</u>, Tarn-et-Garonne, 8, - Automatically Chimed Only.
<u>Saint-Sulpice-sur-Leze</u>, Haute-Garonne, 14, - Chimed Only.
<u>Saint-Thomas</u>, Haute-Garonne, 11, - Chimed Only.
<u>Salles sur l'Hers</u>, Aude, 6, - Automatically Chimed Only, All the bells were cast by Granier in 1964.
<u>Seclin</u>, Nord, Collegiale St. Piat, 42, - Carillon.
<u>Segoufielle</u>, Gers, 10, - Chimed Only.
<u>Selongey</u>, Cote d'Or, Eglise, 48, - Carillon.
<u>Sete</u>, Herault, 12, -, Automatically Chimed Only, All these Bells were cast by Paccard in 1915.
<u>Seurre</u>, Cotre d'Or, Eglise St. Martin, 47, - Carillon.
<u>St Michel de Lannes</u>, Aude, 9, - Automatically Chimed Only.
<u>Taninges</u>, Haute-Savoie, Eglise Paroissiele, 26, - Carillon.
<u>Tarascon</u>, Ariege, Notre Dame de Sabart, 11, - Chimed Only.
<u>Thil</u>, Haute-Garonne, 10, - Automatically Chimed Only.
<u>Toulouse</u>, Haute-Garonne, Basilique Notre Dame la Lardenne, 5, - Automatically Chimed Only.
<u>Toulouse, Capitole</u>, Haute-Garonne, Hotel de Ville, 4, - Automatically Chimed Only.
Toulouse, Haute-Garonne, Cathedrale Saint Etienne, **21**, 78-0-2., - **Five** of the Bells are Rung Full Circle including the **Tenor** Counterbalanced with No Wheels, Stays or Sliders the rest are ChimedOnly.
<u>Toulouse</u>, Haute-Garonne, Immaculee Conception, 5, - Automatically Chimed Only.

Toulouse, Haute-Garonne, Notre Dame du Taur, 13, - Chimed Only, These Bells are Hung in a Bellcote.
Toulouse, Haute-Garonne, Notre Dame la Dalbade, 13, - Chimed Only.
Toulouse, Haute-Garonne, St Aubin, 9, - Automatically Chimed Only.
Toulouse, Haute-Garonne, St Exupere, 14, - Hung Dead, Unplayable Keyboard Chime, Octagonal Tower.
Toulouse, Haute-Garonne, St Francois-de-Paulie, 17, - Chimed Only.
Toulouse, Haute-Garonne, St Jerome, 10, - Chimed Only.
Toulouse, Hante-Garonne, St Joseph, 10, - Chimed Only.
Toulouse, Hante-Garonne, St Madeleine, 5, - Chimed Only.
Toulouse, Haute-Garonne, St Madeleine, eglise de Pouvourville, 14, - Chimed Only.
Toulouse, Haute-Garonne, St Martin du Touch, 9, - Chimed Only.
Toulouse, Haute-Garonne, St Michel Ferrier, 9, - Automatically Chimed Only.
Toulouse, Haute-Garonne, St Nicholas, 17, - Chimed Only, One of the Bells was cast in 1397.
Toulouse, Haute-Garonne, St Pierre-des-Chartreux, 16, - Chimed Only.
Toulouse, Haute-Garonne, St Sernin, **24**, - **Eight** of the Bells are Rung Full Circle, Counterbalanced with No Wheels, Stays or Sliders, the rest are Chimed Only.
Toulouse, Haute-Garonne, St Simon, 5, - Chimed Only.
Tourcoing, Nord, Eglise St. Christophe, 61, - Carillon.
(Transportable), Nord and Pas de Calais, Cloche de l'Europe, 50, 10-3-6., - All these Bells were cast by Paccard in 1989, The Tenor is inscribed " Fondue en l'an 1989 en commemoration du Bicentenaire de la Revolution Francaise, je sonne l'espoir de l'Europe ".
Valentine, Haute-Garonne, 9, - Chimed Only.
Venerque, Haute-Garonne, 14, - Chimed Only.
Verfeil, Haute-Garonne, 13, - Chimed Only.
Villefranche, Aveyron, de Rouergue, 37, - Hung Dead, Automatic Carillon.
Villefranche, Haute-Garonne, de Lauragais, 9, - Automatically Chimed Only.
Villegailhenc, Aude, 15, - Automatically Chimed Only.
Villegly en Minervois, Aude, 14, - Chimed Only.
Villelongue, Pyrenees-Orientales, de la Salanque, 11, - Chimed Only, All the Bells were cast by Paintandre Freres in 1896.

GERMANY.

Aachen, Nordrhein-Westfalen, Rathaus, 49, - Carillon.
Altenburg, Thuringen, Katholische Kirche, 24, - Carillon.
Aschaffenburg, Bayern, Schlossturm, 48, - Carillon.
Bad Godesburg, Nordrhein-Westfalen, Stadtpark, 23, - Carillon.
Berlin, Berlin, Nicolaikirche, 41, - Carillon.
Berlin, Berlin, Franzosischer, 60, - Carillon.
Berlin, Berlin, Carillon am Haus der Kulturen der Welt, 68, 156cwt. - Carillon, Detatched Tower, All these Bells were cast by Eijesbouts in 1987.
Bonn-Beuel, Nordrhein-Westfalen, St. Josephskirche, 62, - Carillon.
Chemnitz, Sachsen, Rathaus, 28, - Carillon.
Duren, Nordrhein-Westfalen, St. Annakirche, 37, - Carillon.
Emmerich, Nordrhein-Westfalen, St. Aldegundiskirche, 43, - Carillon.
Eppingen, Baden-Wurttemburg, Katholische Stadtkirche, 49, - Carillon.
Erfurt, Thuringen, Bartholomausturm, 60, - Carillon.
Frankfurt (Main), Hessen, Alte Nicolaikirche, 47, - Carillon.
Gera, Thuringen, Rathaus, 36, - Carillon.
Halle / Saale, Sachsen-Anhalt, Roter Turm, 76, 160cwt. - Carillon, Cast by Apolda and Metz.
Hamburg, Hamburg, St. Nikolaiturm, 51, - Carillon,
Hamburg, Hamburg, Christianskirche, 42, - Carillon.

Hannover, Niedersachsen, Henriettenstifttung, 49, - Carillon.
Heidelberg, Baden-Wurttemberg, Neues Rathaus, 26, - Carillon.
Kassel, Hessen, Karlskirche, 47, - Carillon.
Kiel, Schleswig-Holstein, Klosterturm, 45, - Carillon.
Koln, Nordrhein-Westfalen, Alter Rathausturm, 48, - Carillon.
Lossnitz, Sachsen, Johanneskirche, 23, - Carillon.
Magdeburg, Sachsen-Anhalt, Rathaus, 47, - Carillon.
Muhlhausen, Thuringen, Kommarktkirche, 41, - Carillon.
Munchen, Bayern, Olympiapark, 48, - Carillon.
Offenburg, Baden-Wurttemberg, Altes Rathaus, 25, - Carillon.
Potsdam, Brandenburg, Ehrenhain, 24, - Carillon.
Rostock, Mecklenburg-Vorpommern, Universitatsplatz, 32, - Carillon.
Saalfeld, Thuringen, Bergfried-Park, 25, - Carillon.
Schirgiswalde, Sachsen, Katholische Pfarrkirche, 29, - Carillon.
Schwerin, Mecklenburg-Vorpommern, Schlachtermarkt, 26, - Carillon.
Wechselburg, Sachsen, Katholische Stiftskirche, 36, - Carillon.
Wiesbaden, Hessen, Marktkirche, 49, 44cwt. in C. - Carillon.

GUATEMALA.

Guatemala City, 99, in C, - Carillon, All the Bells were cast by Michiels in 1932.

GUYANA.

Georgetown, Sacred Heart Catholic Church, 10, in C, - Chimestand Chimed, Cast by Meneely of Watervliet in 1905.

HONDURAS.

Tegucigalpa, Basilica de Suyapa, 42, in E, - Traditional Keyboard Carillon, Cast by Petit & Fritsen in 1960.

HONG KONG.

Causeway Bay, St Mary's Church, 2, - Chimed Only.
Hong Kong, St John's Cathedral, 8, - Hung Dead, Ellacombe Chimed, These Bells were donated in 1953 by the Hong Kong and Shanghai Banking Corporation to commemorate the Corination of Queen Elizabeth the Second and they were all cast by Gillett and Johnson, These Bells replaced the Old Ring of Four Bells cast by Whitechapel in 1845 and 1869 which were first Rung on New Years Day in 1870 were they were Rung until the Tower was Damaged in World War II,
Wanchai, St James Settlement, 1, - Chimed Only.

ICELAND.

Reykjavik, Hallgrimskirkja, 29, 5-2-12. in C. - Hung Dead, Automatic Carillon, All these Bells were cast by Eijesbouts in 1971.

INDIA.

Colaba, Bombay, Afghan Mission of St John, **8**, 14-0-22. in F. - Unringable.
Pune, Panch Howd, The Holy Name, **8**, 25-0-18. in E. - Unringable, Detatched Tower.

ISRAEL.

Jerusalm , YMCA-migdal, 35, - Carillon.

ITALY.
In northern Italy they ring the bells full circle, The bells are counterbalanced with no stays or sliders, they ring to music rather than methods, Also they do not like visiting bands but individual ringers would be welcomed.

Affi, Vr, St Pietro in Vincoli, **5,** 19cwt. in Eb., - Counterbalanced, No Stays or Sliders.
Albare , Vr, Costermano, St Lorenzo Martire, 5, 6cwt. in B., - Automatically Swing Chimed Only.
Albaredo D'Adige, Vr, St Maria Assunta, **6,** 26cwt. in D., - Counterbalanced, No Stays or Sliders.
Albaro, Vr, Ronco all'Adige, St Andrea Apostolo, **5,** 9-2-4. in G., - Counterbalanced, No Stays or Sliders.
Albettone , Vi, Nativita di Maria, 6, 21-2-0. in Eb., - Automatically Swing Chimed Only.
Albisano , Vr, Torri del Benaco, St Martino di Tours, 6, 8-0-20. in G., - Automatically Swing Chimed Only.
Alcenago, Vr, Grezzana, St Clemente, **5,** 13-0-20. in E., - Counterbalanced, No Stays or Sliders.
Almisano di Lonigo , Vi, 5, 24cwt. in Db., - Automatically Swing Chimed Only.
Alpo, Villafranca di Verona, St Giovanni Battista, **6,** 13cwt. in E., - Counterbalanced, No Stays or Sliders.
Altavilla Vicetina , Vi, 3, 24cwt. in D., - Automatically Swing Chimed Only.
Altissimo, Vi, **6,** 6cwt. - Counterbalanced, No Stays or Sliders.
Altissimo, Vi, **9,** 13cwt. - Counterbalanced, No Stays or Sliders.
Altissimo, Vi, St Nicola, **10,** 25-1-4. in Db. - Counterbalanced, No Stays or Sliders.
Angiari, Vr, St Michele, **5,** 20-1-12. in D., - Counterbalanced, No Stays or Sliders.
Anson di Minerbe , Vr, Minerbe, 3, 3-1-12. in Db., - Automatically Swing Chimed Only.
Aracoeli, Vi, Vicenza, **3,** 12-1-12. in F#., - Counterbalanced, No Stays or Sliders.
Arbizzano, Vr, Negrar, St Pietro, **6,** 14-1-12. in E., - Counterbalanced, No Stays or Sliders.
Arcella , Pd, Padova, 8, 34cwt. in C., - Automatically Swing Chimed Only.
Arcole, Vr, St Giorgio, **5,** 32cwt. in C., - Counterbalanced, No Stays or Sliders.
Arcugnano , Vi, 4, 24cwt. in D., - Automatically Swing Chimed Only.
Arsiero, St Michele Arcangelo, **6,** 39-0-10. in C., - Counterbalanced, No Stays or Sliders.
Arzignano, Vi, Duomo di Ognissanti, **9,** 42-2-16. in Bb., - Counterbalanced, No Stays or Sliders.
Aselogna, Vr, Cerea, St Maria Bambina, **5,** 8-0-18. in Ab., - Counterbalanced, No Stays or Sliders.
Asiago , Vi, Duomo di St Matteo, 6, 57-1-0. in Bb., - Automatically Swing Chimed Only.
Asigliano Veneto, Vi, **3,** 14cwt. in F., - Counterbalanced, No Stays or Sliders.
Asparetto , Vr, Cerea, St Nicolo, 5, 6-2-4. in Ab., - Automatically Swing Chimed Only.
Avesa, Vr, Verona, St Martino, **9,** 29-2-14. in Db., - Counterbalanced, No Stays or Sliders.
Azzago, Vr, Grezzana, St Pietro in Vincoli, **5,** 16cwt. in E., - Counterbalanced, No Stays or Sliders.
Azzano , Vr, Castel d'Azzano, St Nome Di St Maria, 5, 5-0-16. in Bb., - Automatically Swing Chimed Only.
Badia Calavena , Vr, 3, 25cwt. in Db., - Automatically Swing Chimed Only.
Badia Calavena , Vr, St Vito St Modesto e Crescenzia, 5, 30cwt. in Db., - Automatically Swing Chimed Only.
Bagnolo, Vr, Nogarole Rocca, St Martino, **6,** 10-1-12. in F#., - Counterbalanced, No Stays or Sliders.
Baldaria di Cologna Veneta , Vr, Cologna Veneta, 3, 14-1-12. in E., - Automatically Swing Chimed Only.
Barbarano Vicentino, Vi, St Maria Assunta, **6,** 16-2-4. in Eb., - Counterbalanced, No Stays or Sliders.
Bardolino , Vr, St Nicolo e St Severo, 5, 10-2-24. in F#., - Automatically Swing Chimed Only.

Bassano Angarano, Vi, St Michele, **5**, 3-2-6. in C., - Counterbalanced, No Stays or Sliders.
Bassano del Grappa , Vi, St Croce, 5, 13cwt. in F., - Automatically Swing Chimed Only.
Bassano del Grappa, Vi, Tempio Ossario, **5**, 36cwt. in Db., - Counterbalanced, No Stays or Sliders.
Beccacivetta, Vr, Castel d'Azzano, **5**, 14-2-14. in E., - Counterbalanced, No Stays or Sliders.
Begosso , Vr, Terrazzo, St Lorenzo Martire, 5, 12-1-12. in F., - Automatically Swing Chimed Only.
Belfiore , Vr, Nativita di Nostro Signore, 5, 14-0-20. in E., - Automatically Swing Chimed Only.
Belluno Veronese, Vr, Brentino-Belluno, St Giovanni Battista, **5**, 10-2-24. in F#., - Counterbalanced, No Stays or Sliders.
Belvedere di Villaga , Vi, 5, - Automatically Swing Chimed Only.
Bevadro, St Leonardo, **6**, 21cwt. in Eb., - Counterbalanced, No Stays or Sliders.
Bevilacqua, Vr, St Antonio Abate, **3**, 3-2-24. in C., - Counterbalanced, No Stays or Sliders.
Bionde, Vr, Salizzole, St Caterina, **5**, 10cwt. F#., - Counterbalanced, No Stays or Sliders.
Bolca, Vr, Vestenanuova, St Giovanni Battista, **6**, 25-0-14. in D., - Counterbalanced, No Stays or Sliders.
Bolzano Vicentino , Vi, 3, 24cwt. in D., - Automatically Swing Chimed Only.
Bonaldo , Vr, Zimella, St Apollinare, 5, 28cwt. in Db., - Automatically Swing Chimed Only.
Bonavicina , Vr, St Pietro di Morubio, St Filippo e St Giacomo, 5, 16-1-8. in E., - Automatically Swing Chimed Only.
Bonavigo , Vr, St Giovanni Battista, 6, 15-2-4. in E., - Automatically Swing Chimed Only.
Bonferraro, Vr, Sorga, St Maria e St Giuseppe, **6**, 11-0-20. in F., - Counterbalanced, No Stays or Sliders.
Borghetto Sul Mincio, Vr, Valeggio Sul Mincio, St Marco, **5**, 3-1-12. in Db., - Counterbalanced, No Stays or Sliders.
Borgo di Bonavicina, Vr, St Pietro di Morubio, **3**, 3-1-10. in Db., - Counterbalanced, No Stays or Sliders.
Borgo Nuovo, Vr, Verona, St Maria, **6**, 6-1-6. in A., - Counterbalanced, No Stays or Sliders.
Borgo Primo Maggio , Vr, Verona, Gesu Divino Lavoratore, 9, 10-1-12. in F#., - Automatically Swing Chimed Only.
Borgo Trieste, Vr, Verona, St Maria Addolorata, **6**, 23-2-8. in Eb., - Counterbalanced, No Stays or Sliders.
Borgo Venezia , Vr, Verona, St Giuseppe Fuori le Mura, 8, 25-2-4. in Db., - Automatically Swing Chimed Only.
Boschi St Anna, Vr, St Anna, **5**, 18cwt. in Eb., - Counterbalanced, No Stays or Sliders.
Bosco di Nanto , Vi, St Salvatore, 5, 13cwt. in F., - Automatically Swing Chimed Only.
Bosco di Zevio, Vr, Zevio, St Nome di St Maria, **5**, 7-0-20. in A., - Counterbalanced, No Stays or Sliders.
Boscochiesanuova, Vr, St Benedetto e St Tommaso, **6**, 33cwt. in C., - Counterbalanced, No Stays or Sliders.
Bovolone, Vr, St Giuseppe, **10**, 28cwt. in C., - Counterbalanced, No Stays or Sliders.
Breganze, Vi, **10**, 56-2-4. in Bb. - Counterbalanced, No Stays or Sliders.
Brendola , Vi, 6, 31-3-6. in Db., - Automatically Swing Chimed Only.
Brentino, Vr, Brentino-Belluno, St Virgilio, **6**, 14cwt. in E., - Counterbalanced, No Stays or Sliders.
Brenton di Ronca , Vr, Ronca, 3, 10-1-12. in F#., - Automatically Swing Chimed Only.
Brenzone , Vr, St Giovanni Battista, 5, - Automatically Swing Chimed Only.
Breonio , Vr, Fumane, St Marziale, 5, 20cwt. in D., - Automatically Swing Chimed Only.
Brogliano , Vi, 5, 13cwt. in F., - Automatically Swing Chimed Only.
Brognoligo, Vr, Monteforte d'Alpone, St Stefano, **9**, 40-0-6. in B., - Counterbalanced, No Stays or Sliders.
Bure, Vr, St Pietro in Cariano, St Martino, **5**, 6-0-22. in A., - Counterbalanced, No Stays or Sliders.
Bussolengo , Vr, Cristo Risorto, 6, 21-2-0. in Eb., - Automatically Swing Chimed Only.

Bussolengo, Vr, Maddona di Perpetuo Socorsso (Frati), **5**, 6cwt. in A., - Counterbalanced, No Stays or Sliders.
Bussolengo , *Vr, St Maria Maggiore, 9, 30cwt. in C., - Automatically Swing Chimed Only.*
Buttapietra , *Vr, St Croce, 5, 7-2-4. in Ab., - Automatically Swing Chimed Only.*
Ca' Degli Oppi, Vr, Oppeano, St Maria e St Girolamo, **6**, 6-2-4. in Ab., - Counterbalanced, No Stays or Sliders.
Ca di David, Vr, Verona, St Giovanni Battista, **9**, 48-0-26. in Bb., - Counterbalanced, No Stays or Sliders.
Cagnano di Poiana Maggiore , *Vi, Poiana Maggiore, St Pietro, 8, 14-1-12. in E., - Automatically Swing Chimed Only.*
Caldierino (Rota), Vr, Caldiero, St Antonio, **3**, 3-2-24. in C., - Counterbalanced, No Stays or Sliders.
Caldiero, Vr, St Pietro e St Matteo, **3**, 10cwt. in G., - Counterbalanced, No Stays or Sliders.
Caldogno , *Vi, 3, 24cwt. in D., - Automatically Swing Chimed Only.*
Calmasino , *Vr, Bardolino, St Michele Arcangelo, 5, 15cwt. in E., - Automatically Swing Chimed Only.*
Caltrano , *Vi, 3, 50cwt. in Bb., - Automatically Swing Chimed Only.*
Caluri, Vr, Villafranca di Verona, **5**, 2-2-18. in Db., - Counterbalanced, No Stays or Sliders.
Camilliani Villa, Vr, Verona, Frati, **3**, 1-2-24. in E., - Counterbalanced, No Stays or Sliders.
Camisano Vicentino , *Vi, 6, 38cwt. in C., - Automatically Swing Chimed Only.*
Campanella, Vi, Altissimo, **6**, 4-0-20. in B., - Counterbalanced, No Stays or Sliders.
Campiano, Vr, Cazzano di Tramigna, St Bernardo, **6**, 8-1-12. in G., - Counterbalanced, No Stays or Sliders.
Campiglia dei Berici , *Vi, 3, 24cwt. in D., - Automatically Swing Chimed Only.*
Campofontana, Vr, Selva di Progno, St Giorgio, **5**, 16-2-24. in Eb., - Counterbalanced, No Stays or Sliders.
Campolongo, Vi, St Germano dei Berici, **3**, 3-1-2. in Db., - Counterbalanced, No Stays or Sliders.
Camporovere , *Vi, Roana, 3, 17-1-12. in E., - Automatically Swing Chimed Only.*
Camposilvano, Vr, Velo Veronese, St Carlo, **5**, 4-0-20. in B., - Counterbalanced, No Stays or Sliders.
Canale, Vr, Rivoli Veronese, St Luca, **5**, 13cwt. in F., - Counterbalanced, No Stays or Sliders.
Cancello, Vr, Verona, St Salvatore, **5**, 13-2-4. in F., - Counterbalanced, No Stays or Sliders.
Canove, Vr, Legnago, St Agostino Vecovo, **5**, 6-2-4. in A., - Counterbalanced, No Stays or Sliders.
Canove di Roana , *Vi, Roana, 5, 19-2-4. in Eb., - Automatically Swing Chimed Only.*
Caprino Veronese, Vr, St Maria Maggiore, **6**, 22-2-24. in Db., - Counterbalanced, No Stays or Sliders.
Carpi , *Vr, Villa Bartolomea, St Margherita, 6, 21-0-20. in D., - Automatically Swing Chimed Only.*
Cartigliano , *Vi, 7, 36cwt. in C., - Automatically Swing Chimed Only.*
Casaleone, Vr, St Biagio, **6**, 13cwt. in F#., - Counterbalanced, No Stays or Sliders.
Caselle, Vr, Isola della Scala, St Pietro, **5**, 4-0-20. in B., - Counterbalanced, No Stays or Sliders.
Caselle , *Vr, Pressana, St Maria Maddalena, 5, 12-2-24. in F., - Automatically Swing Chimed Only.*
Caselle di Nogara , *Vr, Nogara, St Pietro, 5, 16-3-12. in Eb., - Automatically Swing Chimed Only.*
Caselle di Sommacampagna, Vr, Sommacampagna, Santissimo Redentore, **10**, 21-2-26. in Eb., - Counterbalanced, No Stays or Sliders.
Casoni , *Vi, Mussolente, 5, 25-2-4. in D., - Automatically Swing Chimed Only.*
Casotto di Valdastico , *Vi, 5, 13-2-4. in F., - Automatically Swing Chimed Only.*
Cassone, Vr, Malcesine, St Benigo e St Caro, **5**, 11-2-4. in F., - Counterbalanced, No Stays or Sliders.
Castagnaro , *Vr, St Nicola, 6, 19-2-4. in D., - Automatically Swing Chimed Only.*

Castagne, Vr, Mezzane di Sotto, St Ulderico, **5,** 17-2-4. in Eb., - Counterbalanced, No Stays or Sliders.
Castegnero , Vi, St Giorgio, 5, 21-2-0. in Eb., - Automatically Swing Chimed Only.
Castel d'Azzano , Vr, St Maria Annuciata, 5, 14-2-14. in F., - Automatically Swing Chimed Only.
Caselbrenzone , Vr, Brenzone, St Maria Assunta, 5, 14-1-12. in E., - Automatically Swing Chimed Only.
Castelcerino, Vr, Soave, **6,** 11-2-4. in F#., - Counterbalanced, No Stays or Sliders.
Castelgomberto , Vi, 3, 25-2-6. in D., - Automatically Swing Chimed Only.
Castellaro , Vi, 5, 13cwt. in F., - Automatically Swing Chimed Only.
Castelletto , Vr, Brenzone, St Carlo Borromeo, 5, 13cwt. in F., - Automatically Swing Chimed Only.
Castello, Vi, Arzignano, St Maria ed St Elisabetta, **9,** 25cwt. in Db., - Counterbalanced, No Stays or Sliders.
Castello di Montecchia , Vr, Montecchia, 3, - Automatically Swing Chimed Only.
Castello de St Giovanni Ilarione , Vr, St Giovanni Ilarione, St Giovanni Battista, 5, 30cwt. in C., - Automatically Swing Chimed Only.
Castelnovo di Isola Vicentino , Vi, 5, 25-1-20. in D., - Automatically Swing Chimed Only.
Castelnuovo del Garda, Vr, St Maria, **6,** 33-1-10. in Db., - Counterbalanced, No Stays or Sliders.
Castelrotto, Vr, St Pietro in Cariano, St Ulderico, **3,** 4cwt. in C., - Counterbalanced, No Stays or Sliders.
Castelvecchio , Vi, Valdagno, 5, 23-2-12. in D., - Automatically Swing Chimed Only.
Castelvero, Vr, Vestenanuova, St Salvatore e St Biagio, **5,** 24cwt. in D., - Counterbalanced, No Stays or Sliders.
Castiglione, Vr, Verona, St Rocco, **3,** 3-1-12. in Db., - Counterbalanced, No Stays or Sliders.
Castion Veronese , Vr, Costermano, St Maria Maddalena, 5, 15-2-4. in E., - Automatically Swing Chimed Only.
Cattignano , Vr, St Giovanni Illarione, 5, 19cwt. in D., - Automatically Swing Chimed Only.
Cavaion, 5, 32cwt. - Counterbalanced, No Stays or Sliders.
Cavaion Veronese, Vr, St Giovanni Battista, **6,** 29-2-4. in C., - Counterbalanced, No Stays or Sliders.
Cavalcaselle, Vr, Castelnuovo del Garda, St Filippo e St Giacomo, **9,** 17cwt. in E., - Counterbalanced, No Stays or Sliders.
Cavalo, Vr, Fumane, St Zeno, **5,** 21-0-20. in D., - Counterbalanced, No Stay or Slider.
Cavazzale, Vi, **6,** 24cwt. in D., - Counterbalanced, No Stays or Sliders.
Cavreca, Vi, Valli Del Pasubio, **3,** 9cwt. in G., - Counterbalanced, No Stays or Sliders.
Cazzano di Tramigna, Vr, St Giorgio Martire, **6,** 20cwt. in Eb., - Counterbalanced, No Stays or Sliders.
Cellore, Vr, Illasi, St Zeno, **6,** 15cwt. in E., - Counterbalanced, No Stays or Sliders.
Centrale di Zugliano , Vi, Zugliano, 6, - Automatically Swing Chimed Only.
Centro, Vr, Tregnago, St Ermagora e St Fortunato, **5,** 12-2-24. in F., - Counterbalanced, No Stays or Sliders.
Ceraino, Vr, Dolce, St Nicolo, **5,** 6-2-4. in A., - Counterbalanced, No Stays or Sliders.
Cerea , Vr, St Maria Assunta, **5,** 15-0-20. in E., - Counterbalanced, No Stays or Sliders.
Cereda di Cornedo Vicentino , Vi, Cornedo Vicentino, 3, 36-0-10. in C., - Automatically Swing Chimed Only.
Cerna, Vr, St Anna d'Alfaedo, St Giovanni Battista, **6,** 17cwt. in E., - Counterbalanced, No Stays or Sliders.
Cerro Veronese, Vr, St Osvaldo, **6,** 19-1-2. in Eb., - Counterbalanced, No Stays or Sliders.
Cervrese St Croce , Pd, 3, 45cwt. in B., - Automatically Swing Chimed Only.
Cesuna , Roana, 3, 29-2-6. in Db., - Automatically Swing Chimed Only.
Chiampo, Vi, Maddona delle Grazie, **6,** 5cwt. in B., - Counterbalanced, No Stays or Sliders.
Chiampo , Vi, St Martino, 8, 19-0-4. in Eb., - Automatically Swing Chimed Only.
Chiampo , Vi, Santuario della Pieve, 9, 30-0-2. in Db., - Automatically Swing Chimed Only.

Chievo, Vr, Verona, St Antonio Abate, **9**, 21cwt. in Eb., - Counterbalanced, No Stays or Sliders.
Chiuppano, Vi, St Michele Arcangelo, 6, 19cwt. in Eb., - Automatically Swing Chimed Only.
Cimitero Monumentale, Vr, Verona, Cappella del Redentore, **3**, 4-1-18. in B., - Counterbalanced, No Stays or Sliders.
Cisano, Vr, Bardolino, St Maria, **6**, 6-0-20. in A., - Counterbalanced, No Stays or Sliders.
Cismon del Grappa, Vi, 6, 30cwt. in Db., - Automatically Swing Chimed Only.
Cogollo, Vr, Tregnago, St Biagio, **6**, 17-2-4. in E., - Counterbalanced, No Stays or Sliders.
Cola, Vr, Lazise, St Giorgio Martire, 6, 15-0-20. in E., - Automatically Swing Chimed Only.
Colloredo, Vi, Sossano, 5, 21cwt. in D., - Automatically Swing Chimed Only.
Cologna Veneta, Vr, Duomo di St Maria Nascente, 5, 29-2-10. in D., - Automatically Swing Chimed Only.
Colognola ai Colli, Vr, St Fermo e St Rustico, **9**, 40-1-12. in Bb., - Counterbalanced, No Stays or Sliders.
Colze di Montegalda, Vi, Montegalda, 5, 14cwt. in F., - Automatically Swing Chimed Only.
Concamarise, Vr, St Lorenzo e St Stefano, 5, 10-2-4. in Gb., - Chimed Only.
Corbiolo, Vr, Boscochiesanuova, St Maria Ausiliatrice, 6, 21-3-4. in Eb., - Automatically Swing Chimed Only.
Coriano, Vr, Albaredo D'Adige, St Filippo e St Giacomo, 5, 9-0-20. in F#., - Automatically Swing Chimed Only.
Cornedo Vicentino, Vi, St Giovanni Battista, 6, 25cwt. in D., - Automatically Swing Chimed Only.
Corno, Bussolengo, St Giovanni Battista, 5, 2-2-24. in D., - Chimed Only.
Correzzo, Vr, Gazzo Veronese, St Giovanni Battista, **5**, 11-1-26. in F#., - Counterbalanced, No Stays or Sliders.
Corrubio di Lugo, Vr, Grezzana, St Carlo Borromeo, **6**, 5cwt. in Bb., - Counterbalanced, No Stays or Sliders.
Cortivo, Vi, Altissimo, Beata Vergine della Salute, **5**, 3cwt. in Db., - Counterbalanced, No Stays or Sliders.
Costabissara, Vi, 3, 24cwt. in D., - Automatically Swing Chimed Only.
Costalunga, Vr, Monteforte d'Alpone, St Brizio, 6, 22-2-24. in Db., - Automatically Swing Chimed Only.
Costeggiola, Vr, Soave, St Antonio Abate, **5**, 9-1-12. in F#., - Counterbalanced, No Stays or Sliders.
Costermano, Vr, St Antonio Abate, **6**, 10cwt. in G., - Counterbalanced, No Stays or Sliders.
Costozza, Vi, Longare, 3, 36cwt. in C., - Automatically Swing Chimed Only.
Creazzo, Vi, **6**, 36cwt. in C., - Counterbalanced, No Stays or Sliders.
Crespadoro, Vi, St Andrea, 3, 21cwt. in D., - Automatically Swing Chimed Only.
Crespano del Grappa, Vr, **3**, 67cwt., - Counterbalanced, No Stays or Sliders.
Crosare di Pressana, Vr, Pressana, 4, - Automatically Swing Chimed Only.
Cusinati di Rosa, Vi, 5, - Automatically Swing Chimed Only.
Custoza, Vr, Sommacampagna, St Pietro in Vincoli, **6**, 12-1-24. in F., - Counterbalanced, No Stays or Sliders.
Dolce, Vr, St Lucia, **6**, 11-2-4. in F#.; - Counterbalanced, No Stays or Sliders.
Dossobuono, Vr, Villafranca di Verona, St Maria Maddalena, **9**, 17-2-18. in Eb., - Counterbalanced, No Stays or Sliders.
Dueville, Vi, 3, 24cwt. in D., - Automatically Swing Chimed Only.
Durlo di Crespadoro, Vi, Crespadoro, 5, 30cwt. in Db., - Automatically Swing Chimed Only.
Enego, Vi, St Giustina, 6, 37cwt. in C., - Automatically Swing Chimed Only.
Engazza, Vr, Salizzole, St Maria Assunta, **5**, 10-1-12. in F#., - Counterbalanced, No Stays or Sliders.
Erbe, Vr, Madonna, 3, 2cwt. in E., - Chimed Only.
Erbe, Vr, St Giovanni Battista, 5, 12cwt. in F., - Automatically Swing Chimed Only.
Erbezzo, Vr, St Filippo e St Giacomo, **5**, 20-1-12. in D., - Counterbalanced, No Stays or Sliders.
Eremo Camaldolese, Vr, Bardolino, **3**, 7cwt. in A., - Counterbalanced, No Stays or Sliders.

Fagnano, Vr, Trevenzuolo, St Nome di St Maria, **6**, 11-1-12. in F#., - Counterbalanced, No Stays or Sliders.
Fane, Vr, Negrar, St Giorgio e St Antonio, **6**, 11-0-14. in F., - Counterbalanced, No Stays or Sliders.
Fara Vicentino, *Vi, 3, 24cwt. in D., - Automatically Swing Chimed Only.*
Fellette di Romano d'Ezzellino, *Vi, Romano d'Ezzellino, 3, 33cwt. in C., - Automatically Swing Chimed Only.*
Ferrara di Monte Baldo, Vr, **3**, - Counterbalanced, No Stays or Sliders.
Ferrazze, Vr, San Martino Buon Albergo, St Maria della Neve, **6**, 10-0-20. in F#., - Counterbalanced, No Stays or Sliders.
Finetti, Vr, Tregnago, St Maria della Salute, **5**, 8-2-24. in G., - Counterbalanced, No Stays or Sliders.
Forette, *Vr, Vigasio, St Martino, 8, 7cwt. in A., - Automatically Swing Chimed Only.*
Foza, *Vi, 6, 29-1-6. in Db., - Automatically Swing Chimed Only.*
Fumane, Vr, St Zeno Vecovo, **6**, 18cwt. in Eb., - Counterbalanced, No Stays or Sliders.
Gaium, Vr, Rivoli Veronese, St Michele Arcangelo, **6**, 8cwt. in Ab., - Counterbalanced, No Stays or Sliders.
Gallio, *Vi, 4, 50cwt. in Bb., - Automatically Swing Chimed Only.*
Gambellara, *Vi, 6, 21-2-10. in Eb., - Automatically Swing Chimed Only.*
Garda, *Vr, St Maria Assunta, 5, 15cwt. in E., - Automatically Swing Chimed Only.*
Gardone, *Br, 5, 14cwt. in F., - Automatically Swing Chimed Only.*
Gargagnago, Vr, St Ambrogio di Valpolicella, St Maria della Misericordia, **6**, 15-0-20. in E., - Counterbalanced, No Stays or Sliders.
Gargnano, *Br, 5, 15-2-4. in E., - Automatically Swing Chimed Only.*
Gazzo Veronese, Vr, St Maria, **5**, 6-0-20. in Ab., - Counterbalanced, No Stays or Sliders.
Gazzolo, *Vr, Arcole, 5, 32-3-8. in C., - Automatically Swing Chimed Only.*
Giare, Vr, St Anna d'Alfaedo, Madonna del Carmine, **5**, 5-2-4. in A., - Counterbalanced, No Stays or Sliders.
Giazza, Vr, Selva di Progno, St Giacomo, **5**, 16-2-4. in E., - Counterbalanced, No Stays or Sliders.
Golosine, Verona, Madonna della Fraternita, **6**, 3-1-12. in Db., - Counterbalanced, No Stays or Sliders.
Grantorto Padovano, Pd, **4**, 22-2-24. in D., - Counterbalanced, No Stays or Sliders.
Grezzana, *Vr, St Maria e St Elisabetta, 5, 19-0-26. in D., - Automatically Swing Chimed Only.*
Grezzano, Vr, Mozzecane, St Lorenzo, **6**, 9-2-4. in G., - Counterbalanced, No Stays or Sliders.
Grisignano di Zocco, *Vi, 3, 24cwt. in D., - Automatically Swing Chimed Only.*
Illasi, Vr, St Bartolomeo, **10**, 21-3-10. in Eb., - Counterbalanced, No Stays or Sliders.
Illasi, Vr, Villa Trabbuchi, St Marco, **6**, 3-1-6. in Db., - Counterbalanced, No Stays or Sliders.
Isola della Scala, *Vr, Madonna delle Bastia, 5, 4-2-0. in C., - Automatically Swing Chimed Only.*
Isola della Scala, *Vr, St Stefano, 5, 19-2-4. in D., - Automatically Swing Chimed Only.*
Isola Rizza, Vr, St Pietro e St Paolo, **6**, 22-2-14. in Db., - Counterbalanced, No Stays or Sliders.
Isola Vicentina, *Vi, 5, 36cwt. in C., - Automatically Swing Chimed Only.*
Isolalta di Vigasio, Vr, Vigasio, **3**, 4-1-12. in B., - Counterbalanced, No Stays or Sliders.
Lago di Velo d'Astico, *Vi, Velo d'Astico, 5, 11cwt. in G., - Automatically Swing Chimed Only.*
Laverda, *Vi, Breganze, 4, 18-2-2. in Eb., - Automatically Swing Chimed Only.*
Lazise, *Vr, St Zenone e St Martino, 6, 16-2-24. in E., - Automatically Swing Chimed Only.*
Legnago, *Vr, Duomo di St Martino, 6, 19-2-8. in D., - Automatically Swing Chimed Only.*
Lerino di Torri di Quartesolo, *Vi, Torri di Quartesolo, 3, 24cwt. in D., - Automatically Swing Chimed Only.*
Lisiera di Bolzano Vicentino, *Vi, 5, 11cwt. in G., - Automatically Swing Chimed Only.*
Lobia, *St Bonifacio, St Luca, 5, 13cwt. in F., - Automatically Swing Chimed Only.*
Locara, Vr, St Bonifacio, St Giovanni Battista, **5**, 17cwt. in Eb., - Counterbalanced, No Stays or Sliders.
Lonato, *Br, Lonato, 5, 15cwt. in E., - Automatically Swing Chimed Only.*

Longa di Schiavon, Vi, Schiavon, 5, 36cwt. in C., - *Automatically Swing Chimed Only.*
Lonigo, Vi, St Quirico e St Giulitta, **9**, 22-2-24. in Eb., - Counterbalanced, No Stays or Sliders.
Lovertino, Vi, Albettone, 6, 10-1-24. in G., - *Automatically Swing Chimed Only.*
Lugagnano, Vr, Sona, St Anna, 5, 15-0-8. in E., - *Chimed Only.*
Lughezzano, Vr, Boscochiesanouva, St Bernardo da Chiaravalle, **6**, 10-2-24. in F#., - Counterbalanced, No Stays or Sliders.
Lugo, Vr, Grezzana, St Apollinare, **6**, 29-0-10. in C., - Counterbalanced, No Stays or Sliders.
Lumignano, Vi, Longare, 6, 35-0-24. in C., - *Automatically Swing Chimed Only.*
Lumini, Vr, St Zeno di Montagna, St Eurosia, **5**, 8-2-0. in Ab., - Counterbalanced, No Stays or Sliders.
Lusiana, Vi, St Giacomo Apostolo, **5**, 67cwt. in Ab., - Counterbalanced, No Stays or Sliders, The Tenor was cast in 1890.
Maccacari, Vr, Gazzo Veronese, St Fabiano e St Sebastiano, **5**, 8cwt. in Ab., - Counterbalanced, No Stays or Sliders.
Maderno, Br, 5, 23cwt. in D., - *Automatically Swing Chimed Only.*
Madonna del Frassino, Vr, Peschiera del Garda, Madonna del Frassino, **9**, 17-2-10. in E., - Counterbalanced, No Stays or Sliders.
Madonna di Campagna, Vr, Verona, St Maria della Pace, **5**, 7cwt. in A., - Counterbalanced, No Stays or Sliders.
Madonna di Dossobuono, Vr, Verona, Madonna della Salute, **6**, 4-1-8. in C., - Counterbalanced, No Stays or Sliders.
Madonna di Lonigo, Vi, Lonigo, Madonna dei Miracoli, **6**, 7-2-24. in Ab., - Counterbalanced, No Stays or Sliders.
Magugnano di Brenzone, Vr, Brenzone, St Giovanni Battista, 5, - *Automatically Swing Chimed Only.*
Maguzzano, Br, Lonato, 6, 19cwt. in Eb., - *Automatically Swing Chimed Only.*
Malavicina, Mn, Roverbella (MN), St Francesco, **9**, 25cwt. in Db., - Counterbalanced, No Stays or Sliders.
Malcesine, Vr, St Stefano, 5, 17-2-4. in Eb., - *Automatically Swing Chimed Only.*
Malo, Vi, 3, 36cwt. in C., - *Automatically Swing Chimed Only.*
Mama d'Avio, Tr, Avio (TR), **5**, 6-1-12. in A., - Counterbalanced, No Stays or Sliders.
Mambrotta, Vr, San Martino Buon Albergo, St Giuliano, **6**, 12-1-12. in F., - Counterbalanced, No Stays or Sliders.
Manerba del Garda, Br, 5, 14cwt. in F., - *Automatically Swing Chimed Only.*
Marana, Vi, Crespadoro, 5, 16-2-4. in Eb., - *Automatically Swing Chimed Only.*
Marano di Valpolicella, Vr, St Pietro e St Paolo, **5**, 30-1-26. in C., - Counterbalanced, No Stays or Sliders.
Marcellise, Vr, San Martino Buon Albergo, Cattedra di St Pietro, **6**, 27cwt. in Db., - Counterbalanced, No Stays or Sliders.
Marcemigo, Vr, Tregnago, **3**, 3-2-4. in C., - Counterbalanced, No Stays or Sliders.
Marciaga, Vr, Costermano, St Filippo e St Giacomo, **5**, 5-1-12. in A., - Counterbalanced, No Stays or Sliders.
Marega, Vr, Bevilacqua, St Giorgio Martire, **5**, 9-1-12. in G., - Counterbalanced, No Stays or Sliders.
Marniga del Garda, Vr, Brenzone, 5, 12-0-20. in F., - *Automatically Swing Chimed Only.*
Marola, Vi, Torri di Quartesolo, 3, 30cwt. in Db., - *Automatically Swing Chimed Only.*
Marzana, Vr, Verona, Ognissanti, **6**, 7-1-12. in A., - Counterbalanced, No Stays or Sliders.
Mason Vicentino, Vi, 3, 24cwt. in D., - *Automatically Swing Chimed Only.*
Mazzano, Vr, Negrar, St Marco Evangelista, **5**, 4-3-4. in B., - Counterbalanced, No Stays or Sliders.
Mazzantica, Vr, Oppeano, Nativita di St Maria, **5**, 7-2-4. in Ab., - Counterbalanced, No Stays or Sliders.

Mazzurega, Vr, Fumane, St Bartolomeo Apostolo, **5**, 11-1-12. in F., - Counterbalanced, no Stays or Sliders.
Meledo , Vi, Sarego, 5, 36cwt. in C., - Automatically Swing Chimed Only.
Mena , Vr, Castagnaro, St Anna, 6, 18-0-20. in Eb., - Automatically Swing Chimed Only.
Mezzane di Sopra, Vr, Mezzane di Sotto, St Fermo e St Rustico, **5**, 11cwt. in F#., - Counterbalanced, No Stays or Sliders.
Mezzane di Sotto, Vr, St Maria Assunta, **9**, 31cwt. in B., - Counterbalanced, No Stays or Sliders.
Michellorie, Vr, Albaredo D'Adige, St Maria della Salute, **5**, 7-0-20. in Ab., - Counterbalanced, No Stays or Sliders.
Miega, Vr, Veronella, St Antonio Abate, **5**, 9-1-22. in G., - Counterbalanced, No Stays or Sliders.
Minerbe, Vr, St Lorenzo, **6**, 39-2-12. in B., - Counterbalanced, No Stays or Sliders.
Mistrorighi, Vi, Chiampo, St Antonio, **6**, 9-2-4. in F#., - Counterbalanced, No Stays or Sliders.
Mizzole, Vr, Verona, St Pietro e St Paolo, **5**, 5-1-12. in Bb., - Counterbalanced, No Stays or Sliders.
Molina, Vr, Fumane, St Urbano, **5**, 8-2-4. in G., - Counterbalanced, No Stays or Sliders.
Molino, Vi, Altissimo, St Francesco d'Assisi, **9**, 9-2-20. in F#., - Counterbalanced, No Stays or Sliders.
Moniga del Garda , Br, 5, 13-2-4. in F., - Automatically Swing Chimed Only.
Monte, St Ambrogio di Valpolicella, St Nicolo, **5**, 14-2-24. in E., - Counterbalanced, No Stays or Sliders.
Monte di Malo , Vi, 6, 25cwt. in D., - Automatically Swing Chimed Only.
Monte Magre di Schio , Vi, 5, 19cwt. in Eb., - Automatically Swing Chimed Only.
Montebello Vicentina , Vi, 9, 35-2-22. in C., - Automatically Swing Chimed Only.
Montecchia di Crosara, Vr, St Maria, **6**, 19cwt. in Eb., - Counterbalanced, No Stays or Sliders.
Montecchio di Negrar, Vr, Negrar, Maternita della B.V. Maria, **6**, 14-1-12. in E., - Counterbalanced, No Stays or Sliders.
Montecchio Maggiore, Vi, St Maria e St Vitale, **10**, 37-1-2. in C., - Counterbalanced, No Stays or Sliders.
Montecchio Precalcino , Vi, 3, 24cwt. in D., - Automatically Swing Chimed Only.
Monteforte d'Alpone, Vr, St Maria Maggiore, **9**, 34-0-26. in C., - Counterbalanced, No Stays or Sliders.
Montegalda , Vi, St Giustina, 6, 37-2-12. in C., - Automatically Swing Chimed Only.
Montegaldella, Vi, **12**, 33-2-26. in Db., - Counterbalanced, No Stays or Sliders.
Monticello Conte Otto , Vi, 5, - Automatically Swing Chimed Only.
Montorio, Vr, Verona, St Giuseppe in Santa Maria, **10**, 22-1-4. in Db., - Counterbalanced, No Stays or Sliders.
Montorso Vicentino , Vi, St Biagio, 5, 32cwt. in C., - Automatically Swing Chimed Only.
Monzambano, Mn, St Michele, **6**, 16cwt. in E., - Counterbalanced, No Stays or Sliders.
Moruri, Vr, Verona, St Zenone, **5**, 16-2-4. in Eb., - Counterbalanced, No Stays or Sliders.
Mossano , Vi, 3, 24cwt. in D., - Automatically Swing Chimed Only.
Mozzecane, Vr, St Pietro e St Paolo, **6**, 19cwt. in Eb., - Counterbalanced, No Stays or Sliders.
Mussolente , Vi, Santuario Madonna dell Acqua, 3, 30cwt. in Db., - Automatically Swing Chimed Only.
Muzzolon di Cornedo Vicentino , Vi, 5, 19cwt. in Eb., - Automatically Swing Chimed Only.
Negrar, Vr, St Martino, **6**, 29-1-20. in C., - Counterbalanced, No Stays or Sliders.
Nichesola , Vr, Terrazzo, St Pietro Celestino, 5, 7-1-12. in Ab., - Automatically Swing Chimed Only.
Nogarole Rocca, Vr, St Lorenzo, **5**, 12cwt. in F#., - Counterbalanced, No Stays or Sliders.
Nogarole Vicentino , Vi, St Simone e St Giuda, 5, 19cwt. in Eb., - Automatically Swing Chimed Only.
Novaglie, Vr, Verona, St Maria Maddalena, **6**, 13cwt. in F., - Counterbalanced, No Stays or Sliders.

Novare di Negrar, Vr, Negrar, Villa Fattori - Mosconi, **3**, 2-2-24. in Db., - Counterbalanced, No Stays or Sliders.
Nove , *Vi, St Pietro e St Paolo, 5, 36cwt. in C., - Automatically Swing Chimed Only.*
Noventa Vicentina , *Vi, St Vito St Modesto e St Crescenzia, 5, 44-0-8. in B., - Automatically Swing Chimed Only.*
Oliero , *Vi, 3, 36cwt. in C., - Automatically Swing Chimed Only.*
Oliosi, Vr, Castelnuovo del Garda, St Maria Assunta, **3**, 5-1-12. in A., - Counterbalanced, No Stays or Sliders.
Oltre Adige, Vr, Verona, St Pancrazio, **3**, 3-1-2. in C., - Counterbalanced, No Stays or Sliders.
Oppeano , *Vr, St Maria e St Giovanni Battista, 5, 12-1-12. in F#., - Automatically Swing Chimed Only.*
Oratorio San Biagio, Vi, Chiampo, **3**, 1-1-20. in F#., - Counterbalanced, No Stays or Sliders.
Orgiano , *Vi, 3, 24cwt. in D., - Automatically Swing Chimed Only.*
Orti, Vr, Bonavigo, **3**, 10cwt. in G., - Counterbalanced, No Stays or Sliders.
Orti di Bonavigo, Vr, Bonavigo, St Tommaso, **3**, 1-3-10. in E., - Counterbalanced, No Stays or Sliders.
Ossenigo, Vr, Dolce, St Andrea Apostolo, **5**, 9cwt. in G., - Counterbalanced, No Stays or Sliders.
Ostiglia , *Mn, Assuzione della B.V. Maria, 10, 51-2-16. in Bb., - Automatically Swing Chimed Only.*
Pacengo , *Vr, Lazise, St Giovanni Battista, 6, 11-0-20. in F., - Automatically Swing Chimed Only.*
Padenghe del Garda , *Br, 5, 16cwt. in E., - Automatically Swing Chimed Only.*
Pai, Vr, Torri del Benaco, St Marco Evangelista, **5**, 3-3-6. in C., - Counterbalanced, No Stays or Sliders.
Palazzina, Vr, Verona, St Andrea Apostolo, **6**, 13-2-4. in F#., - Counterbalanced, No Stays or Sliders.
Palazzolo, Vr, Sona, St Giacomo e St Giustina, **5**, 15-0-22. in E., - Counterbalanced, No Stays or Sliders.
Palesella di Cerea, Vr, Cerea, **3**, 1-2-24. in E., - Counterbalanced, No Stays or Sliders.
Palu, Vr, St Zenone, **6**, 7-2-4. in Ab., - Counterbalanced, No Stays or Sliders.
Pampuro di Nogara, Vr, Nogara, **3**, - Counterbalanced, No Stays or Sliders.
Parona, Vr, Verona, St Filippo e St Giacomo, **6**, 18-1-26. in Eb., - Counterbalanced, No Stays or Sliders.
Pastrengo, Vr, St Croce, **6**, 14cwt. in E., - Counterbalanced, No Stays or Sliders.
Pazzon, Vr, Caprino Veronese, St Vito St Modesto e St Crescenzia, **5**, 19cwt. in D., - Counterbalanced, No Stays or Sliders.
Pedescala , *Vi, 4, 24cwt. in D., - Automatically Swing Chimed Only.*
Pelaloco , *Mn, Castiglione Mantovano, 5, 3-2-4. in B., - Automatically Swing Chimed Only.*
Pellegrina , *Vr, Isola della Scala, St Pellegrino, 6, 9-1-8. in G., - Automatically Swing Chimed Only.*
Perarolo di Arcugnano , *Vi, 3, 27-3-0. in Eb., - Automatically Swing Chimed Only.*
Peri, Vr, Dolce, St Filippo e St Giacomo, **6**, 13-0-20. in F., - Counterbalanced, No Stays or Sliders.
Perzacco, Vr, Zovio, St Bartolomeo, **6**, 12cwt. in F#., - Counterbalanced, No Stays or Sliders.
Pescantina, Vr, B.V. della Pieta (Madonnina), **5**, 5-1-16. in Bb., - Counterbalanced, No Stays or Sliders.
Pescantina, Vr, St Lorenzo, **9**, 36-3-14. in B., - Counterbalanced, No Stays or Sliders.
Peschiera del Garda, Vr, St Martino Vescovo, **6**, 10-0-20. in F#., - Counterbalanced, No Stays or Sliders.
Pesina di Caprino, Vr, Costermano, St Gallo Abate, **5**, 16-1-12. in Eb., - Counterbalanced, No Stays or Sliders.
Piana di Valdagno , *Vi, 5, - Automatically Swing Chimed Only.*
Pieve , *Vr, Colognola ai Colli, Annunciazione di Maria, 6, 12cwt. in E., - Automatically Swing Chimed Only.*

Pigozzo, Vr, Verona, St Nazaro e St Celso, **5**, 9-0-10. in G., - Counterbalanced, No Stays or Sliders.
Pilastro, Vi, Orgiano, **3**, 10cwt. in G., - Counterbalanced, No Stays or Sliders.
Piovene , *Vi, Piovene Rocchette, St Stefano, 6, 19cwt. in Eb., - Automatically Swing Chimed Only.*
Piovezzano, Vr, Pastrengo, St Zeno, **6**, 10-1-12. in F#., - Counterbalanced, No Stays or Sliders.
Poiano di Valpantena, Vr, Verona, St Pietro e St Paolo, **6**, 16cwt. in Eb., - Counterbalanced, No Stays or Sliders.
Pojana Maggiore , *Vi, 5, 21-3-14. in Eb., - Automatically Swing Chimed Only.*
Pol, Vr, Pastrengo, **3**, 1-2-4. in F#., - Counterbalanced, No Stays or Sliders.
Polegge, Vi, Vicenza, St Giovanni Evangelista, **6**, 18-2-4. in Eb., - Counterbalanced, No Stays or Sliders.
Poleo , Vi, Schio, **8**, 21cwt. in D., - Counterbalanced, No Stays or Sliders.
Polpenazze, Br, Polpenazze sul Garda, **5**, - Counterbalanced, No Stays or Sliders.
Polverara , *Pd, St Fidenzio, 4, 27cwt. in Db., - Automatically Swing Chimed Only.*
Pontepossero , *Vr, Sorga, Ognisaanti, 5, 6-2-4. in Ab., - Automatically Swing Chimed Only.*
Ponti sul Mincio, Mn, St Antonio Abate, **5**, 8cwt. in Ab., - Counterbalanced, No Stays or Sliders.
Ponton di St Ambrogio, Vr, St Ambrogio di Valpolicella, **3**, 3-1-6. in Db., - Counterbalanced, No Stays or Sliders.
Portese, Br, St Felice del Benaco, **6**, - Counterbalanced, No Stays or Sliders.
Porto , *Vr, Legnago, St Maria, 6, 25-2-4. in Db., - Automatically Swing Chimed Only.*
Porto St Pancrazio, Vr, Verona, St Pancrazio e St Caterina, **3**, 3-3-6. in C., - Counterbalanced, No Stays or Sliders.
Posina , *Vi, 3, 24cwt. in D., - Automatically Swing Chimed Only.*
Pove del Grappa , *Vi, 3, 24cwt. in D., - Automatically Swing Chimed Only.*
Povegliano Veronese, Vr, St Martino Vescovo, **6**, 25-2-4. in Db., - Counterbalanced, No Stays or Sliders.
Povolaro , *Vi, 5, 24cwt. in D., - Automatically Swing Chimed Only.*
Pozzolengo, Br, St Lorenzo, **6**, 27cwt. in Db., - Counterbalanced, No Stays or Sliders.
Pozzoleone , *Vi, 5, 17-1-4. in E., - Automatically Swing Chimed Only.*
Pozzolo di Villaga , *Vi, Villaga, 5, 24cwt. in D., - Automatically Swing Chimed Only.*
Pradelle di Gazzo Veronese, Vr, Gazzo Veronese, St Prodocimo, **3**, 2-3-6. in Db., - Counterbalanced, No Stays or Sliders.
Presina, Vr, Albaredo D'Adige, Visitazione di Maria SS. ma, **5**, 4-1-12. in B., - Counterbalanced, No Stays or Sliders.
Pressana , *Vr, St Maria Assunta, 6, 27cwt. in D., - Automatically Swing Chimed Only.*
Prova di St Bonifacio, Vr, St Bonifacio, Presentazione di Maria SS ma, **5**, 3-1-12. in C., - Counterbalanced, No Stays or Sliders.
Prun, Vr, Negrar, St Paolo, **5**, 8-1-12. in Ab., - Counterbalanced, No Stays or Sliders.
Puegnago del Garda , *Br, 5, 30cwt. in C., - Automatically Swing Chimed Only.*
Pugnello , *Vi, Arzignano, 5, 13-0-12. in F., - Automatically Swing Chimed Only.*
Quaderni, Vr, Villafranca di Verona, St Matteo Apostolo, **5**, 11-3-10. in F#., - Counterbalanced, No Stays or Sliders.
Quargnenta , *Vi, 5, 26-3-0. in D., - Automatically Swing Chimed Only.*
Quinto di Valpantena, Vr, Verona, Nativita di St Giovanni Battista, **6**, 14-1-6. in Eb., - Counterbalanced, No Stays or Sliders.
Quinto Vicentino , *Vi, 4, 24cwt. in D., - Automatically Swing Chimed Only.*
Quinzano, Vr, Verona, Decollazione di St Giovanni Battista, **6**, 16-2-24. in E., - Counterbalanced, No Stays or Sliders.
Quinzano, Vr, Verona, St Giuliano, **3**, 1-2-24. in E., - Counterbalanced, No Stays or Sliders.
Raldon, Vr, St Giovanni Lupatoto, St Maria Maddalena, **5**, 16-2-24. in E., - Counterbalanced, No Stays or Sliders.
Rampazzo di Camisano, Vi, **6**, 19cwt. in Eb., - Counterbalanced, No Stays or Sliders.
Rancani di Tregnago, Vr, Tregnago, **3**, 12cwt. in F., - Counterbalanced, No Stays or Sliders.

Recoaro Terme, *Vi, 6, 17cwt. in E., - Automatically Swing Chimed Only.*
Revere, *Mn, Annuciazione della B.V. Maria, 5, 4cwt. in C., - Automatically Swing Chimed Only.*
Revere, *Mn, Torre Civica, 5, 32cwt. in C., - Automatically Swing Chimed Only.*
Riva del Garda, Tr, **4**, 20cwt. in D., - Counterbalanced, No Stays or Sliders.
Rivalta, Vr, Brentino-Belluno, St Giacomo, **6**, 5-1-12. in A., - Counterbalanced, No Stays or Sliders.
Rivoli Veronese, Vr, St Giovanni Battista, **5**, 17-2-16. in Eb., - Counterbalanced, No Stays or Sliders.
Rivoltella, *Br, Desenzano, 5, 10cwt. in G., - Automatically Swing Chimed Only.*
Roana, *Vi, St Giustina, 5, 30-1-12. in Db., - Automatically Swing Chimed Only.*
Rocca di Garda, Vr, Eremo Camaldolese, **3**, 6-2-24. in Ab., - Counterbalanced, No Stays or Sliders.
Romagnano, Vr, Grezzana, St Andrea Apostolo, **6**, 11-1-20. in F., - Counterbalanced, No Stays or Sliders.
Romano d'Ezzellino, Vi, Purificazione della B.V. Maria, **6**, 16cwt. in E., - Counterbalanced, No Stays or Sliders.
Ronca, *Vr, St Maria Annunciata, 5, 30cwt. in C., - Automatically Swing Chimed Only.*
Roncanova, Vr, Gazzo Veronese, St Filippo e St Giacomo, **5**, 5-0-20. in Bb., - Counterbalanced, No Stays or Sliders.
Ronco all Adige, Vr, St Maria, **6**, 22-1-12. in D., - Counterbalanced, No Stays or Sliders.
Roncoleva, Vr, Trevenzuolo, St Zeno Vescovo, **6**, 12cwt. in F#., - Counterbalanced, No Stays or Sliders.
Ronconi, Vr, St Anna d'Alfaedo, St Bartolomeo Apostolo, **6**, 8cwt. in A., - Counterbalanced, No Stays or Sliders.
Rosa, Vi, St Antonio Abate, **6**, 66-3-6. in A., - Counterbalanced, No Stays or Sliders.
Rosaro, Vr, Grezzana, St Barnaba Apostolo, **6**, 10cwt. in G., - Counterbalanced, No Stays or Sliders.
Rosegaferro, *Vr, Villafranca di Verona, St Girolamo, 6, 12-2-18. in F#., - Automatically Swing Chimed Only.*
Rota, Vr, Caldiero, St Lorenzo, **5**, 9cwt. in G., - Counterbalanced, No Stays or Sliders.
Rotzo, *Vi, 4, 35cwt. in C., - Automatically Swing Chimed Only.*
Rovegliana di Ricoaro, *Vi, 5, 24cwt. in D., - Automatically Swing Chimed Only.*
Roverchiara, *Vr, St Zeno Vescovo, 5, 20cwt. in D., - Automatically Swing Chimed Only.*
Roverchiaretta, Vr, Madonna del Carmine, **6**, 33-2-24. in C., - Counterbalanced, No Stays or Sliders.
Rovere Veronese, Vr, St Nicolo, **10**, 29cwt. in C., - Counterbalanced, No Stays or Sliders.
Roveredo di Gua, *Vr, St Pietro, 6, 33-2-4. in C., - Automatically Swing Chimed Only.*
St Ambrogio di Valpolicella, *Vr, St Ambrogio, 5, 34cwt. in C., - Automatically Swing Chimed Only.*
St Andrea, Vr, Badia Calavena, St Andrea Apostolo, **5**, 15cwt. in F., - Counterbalanced, No Stays or Sliders.
St Andrea, *Vi, Crespadoro, St Andrea, 3, 22cwt. in D., - Automatically Swing Chimed Only.*
St Andrea di Cologna, *Vr, Cologna Veneta, St Andrea, 5, 14-1-12. in Eb., - Automatically Swing Chimed Only.*
St Anna d'Alfaedo, *Vr, St Anna, 6, 22cwt. in D., - Automatically Swing Chimed Only.*
St Anna di Rosa, *Vi, 5, 8-2-20. in Ab., - Automatically Swing Chimed Only.*
St Bartolomeo delle Montagne, Vr, Selva di Progno, St Bartolomeo, **6**, 21cwt. in Eb., - Counterbalanced, No Stays or Sliders.
St Benedetto, Vi, Trissino, St Benedetto, **5**, 8cwt. in G., - Counterbalanced, No Stays or Sliders.
St Benedetto di Lugana, Vr, Lugana, St Benedetto, **3**, 4-0-20. in B., - Counterbalanced, No Stays or Sliders.
St Bonifacio, *Vr, St Bonifacio, 8, 31cwt. in C., - Automatically Swing Chimed Only.*
St Bortolo, Vi, Arzignano, St Bortolo, **6**, 14-2-4. in F., - Counterbalanced, No Stays or Sliders.

St Bortolo di Montagne, Vr, St Bortolo, St Bartolomeo Apostolo, **6**, 20-1-12. in D., - Counterbalanced, No Stays or Sliders.
St Briccio, Vr, Lavagno, St Briccio, **5**, 15-2-24. in E., - Counterbalanced, No Stays or Sliders.
St Carlo di Savena, Vi, Valli del Pasubio, St Carlo, **5**, 4-2-24. in B., - Counterbalanced, No Stays or Sliders.
St Caterina di Conco, *Vi, Conco, 3, 24cwt. in D., - Automatically Swing Chimed Only.*
St Colombano di Cazzano, Vr, Cazzano, **3**, - Counterbalanced, No Stays or Sliders.
St Croce di Albare, Vr, Costermano, St Croce, **3**, 2-0-20. in E., - Counterbalanced, No Stays or Sliders.
St Daniele di Chiampo, Vi, Chiampo, St Daniele, **5**, 2-1-12. in Eb., - Counterbalanced, No Stays or Sliders.
St Felice, Vr, Cazzano di Tramigna, St Felice, **3**, 3cwt. in D., - Counterbalanced, No Stays or Sliders.
St Fermo, *Vi, Lonigo, St Fermo, 3, 11-0-20. in G., - Automatically Swing Chimed Only.*
St Floriano, *Vr, St Piero in Cariano, St Floriano, 5, 26cwt. in Db., - Chimed Only.*
St Francesco, Vr, Rovere Veronese, St Francesco, **5**, 18-1-12. in D., - Counterbalanced, No Stays or Sliders.
St Germano dei Berici, Vi, St Germano, **6**, 17-0-12. in E., - Counterbalanced, No Stays or Sliders.
St Giacomo del Grigliano, Vr, St Giacomo, **3**, 4-2-4. in C., - Counterbalanced, No Stays or Sliders.
St Giorgio di Valpolicella, Vr, St Ambrogio di Valpolicella, Pieve di St Giorgio, **5**, 12cwt. in F., - Counterbalanced, No Stays or Sliders.
St Giorgio in Salici, Vr, Sona, St Giorgio, **10**, 18-1-8. in Eb., - Counterbalanced, No Stays or Sliders.
St Giovanni Ilarione, *Vr, St Caterina, 6, 21-3-6. in Eb., - Automatically Swing Chimed Only.*
St Giovanni Lupatoto, Vr, Madonnina, **6**, 9-0-20. in G., - Counterbalanced, No Stays or Sliders.
St Giovanni Lupatoto, *Vr, St Giovanni Battista in Nativtate, 6, 17cwt., - Automatically Swing Chimed Only.*
St Girolamo, *Pd, Padova, St Girolamo, 6, 12-1-6. in F#., - Automatically Swing Chimed Only.*
St Giuliana Santuario, *Vi, Recoardo Terme, St Giuliana, 5, 19cwt. in Eb., - Automatically Swing Chimed Only.*
St Gregorio, *Vr, Veronella, St Gregorio, 5, 25-2-4. in Db., - Automatically Swing Chimed Only.*
St Lorenzo di Chiampo, Chiampo, St Lorenzo, **6**, 4-0-10. in C., - Counterbalanced, No Stays or Sliders.
St Lucia ai Monti, Valeggio sul Mincio, St Lucia, **6**, 8cwt. in Ab., - Counterbalanced, No Stays or Sliders.
St Lucia Extra, Vr, Verona, St Lucia, **6**, 24-1-4. in D., - Counterbalanced, No Stays or Sliders.
St Marco dei Boschi, Vr, Boschi St Anna, St Marco Evangelista, **5**, 12-1-12. in F., - Counterbalanced, No Stays or Sliders.
St Margherita, *Vr, Ronca, St Margherita, 4, 3cwt. in D., - Automatically Swing Chimed Only.*
St Maria, *Vi, Camisano Vicentino, St Maria, 5, 11-2-4. in F., - Automatically Swing Chimed Only.*
St Maria delle Grazie di Costabissara, Vi, Costabissara, St Maria delle Grazie, **9**, 6-0-2. in A., - Counterbalanced, No Stays or Sliders.
St Maria di Negrar, Vr, Negrar, St Maria in Progno, **6**, 5-0-10. in Bb., - Counterbalanced, No Stays or Sliders.
St Maria di Tretto, Vi, Schio, St Maria, **3**, 7cwt. in A., - Counterbalanced, No Stays or Sliders.
St Maria di Zevio, Vr, Zevio, Nativita di St Maria, **5**, 9-2-4. in G., - Counterbalanced, No Stays or Sliders.
St Maria in Stelle, Vr, Verona, St Maria Assunta, **10**, 23cwt. in D., - Counterbalanced, No Stays or Sliders.
St Maria Valverde, Vr, St Maria, **6**, 4-3-2. in Bb., - Counterbalanced, No Stays or Sliders.

St Martino Buon Albergo, Vr, San Martino Buon Albergo, St Martino Vescovo, 6, 10-2-18. in F#., Counterbalanced, No Stays or Sliders.
St Massimo, Vr, Verona, St Massimo, 9, 29-2-22. in C., - Counterbalanced, No Stays or Sliders.
St Mattia, Vr, Verona, 3, 3cwt. in D., - Counterbalanced, No Stays or Sliders.
St Mauro di Saline, St Mauro Vescovo, 5, 18-1-12. in D., - Counterbalanced, No Stays or Sliders.
St Michele Angarano, Vi, Bassano del Grappa, St Michele, 5, 3-2-6. in C., - Counterbalanced, No Stays or Sliders.
St Michele Extra, Vr, Verona, St Michele Arcangelo, 6, 29-0-16. in D., - Counterbalanced, No Stays or Sliders.
St Peretto di Negrar, Vr, Negrar, St Pietro, 6, 3-1-12. in Db., - Counterbalanced, No Stays or Sliders.
St Pietro di Lavagno, Vr, Lavagno, St Pietro, 9, 29-2-4. in Db., - Counterbalanced, No Stays or Sliders.
St Pietro di Lagnago, Vr, Legnago, St Pietro Apostolo, 6, 15-2-22. in E., - Counterbalanced, No Stays or Sliders.
St Pietro di Montecchio Maggiore , *Vi, Montecchio Maggiore, 3, 24cwt. in D., - Automatically Swing Chimed Only.*
St Pietro di Morubio , *Vr, St Pietro e St Paolo, 6, 11-0-8. in F#., - Automatically Swing Chimed Only.*
St Pietro in Cariano , *Vr, St Pietro Apostolo, 6, 23cwt. in D., - Automatically Swing Chimed Only.*
St Pietro in Valle, Vr, Gazzo Veronese, St Pietro, 5, 6-0-20. in Ab., - Counterbalanced, No Stays or Sliders.
St Pietro Mussolino , *Vi, St Pietro, 5, 16-2-24. in E., - Automatically Swing Chimed Only.*
St Rocco di Madonna Campagna, Vr, Verona, St Rocco, 3, 1-0-4. in Ab., - Counterbalanced, No Stays or Sliders.
St Rocco di Piegara, Vr, Rovere Veronese, St Rocco, 5, 15cwt. in E., - Counterbalanced, No Stays or Sliders.
St Rocco di Quinzano, Vr, Verona, St Rocco, 6, 4-2-24. in B., - Counterbalanced, No Stays or Sliders.
St Sebastiano di Cologna Veneta , *Vr, Cologna Veneta, St Sebastiano, 5, 10cwt. in G., - Automatically Swing Chimed Only.*
St Sebastiano Oratorio, Vi, Valli Del Pasubio, St Sebastiano, 3, 6-3-8. in A., - Counterbalanced, No Stays or Sliders.
St Stefano di Zimella, Vr, Zimella, St Stefano, 9, 24cwt. in D., - Counterbalanced, No Stays or Sliders.
St Urbano di Montecchio Maggiore , *Vi, Montecchio Maggiore, 3, 23cwt. in Db., - Automatically Swing Chimed Only.*
St Valentino, Vr, Badia Calavena, St Valentino, 5, 8-1-12. in Ab., - Counterbalanced, No Stays or Sliders.
St Valentino , *Vi, Pozzoleone, St Valentino, 3, 16-1-12. in Eb., - Automatically Swing Chimed Only.*
St Vitale in Piano, Vr, Rovere Veronese, St Vitale, 5, 12cwt. in F., - Counterbalanced, No Stays or Sliders.
St Vito al Mantico, Vr, Negrar, St Vito, 6, 6-1-10. in Bb., - Counterbalanced, No Stays or Sliders.
St Vito di Leguzzano , *Vi, Leguzzano, 3, 36cwt. in C., - Automatically Swing Chimed Only.*
St Vittore, Vr, Colognola ai Colli, St Vittore e St Corona, 6, 22-0-20. in Db., - Counterbalanced, No Stays or Sliders.
St Zeno, Vr, Colognola ai Colli, St Zeno, 6, 7-3-6. in Ab., - Counterbalanced, No Stays or Sliders.
St Zeno di Montagna, Vr, St Zeno, 6, 29-2-4. in Db., - Counterbalanced, No Stays or Sliders.
St Zeno in Mozzo , *Vr, Mozzecane, St Zeno, 5, 7-1-12. in Ab., - Automatically Swing Chimed Only.*
St Zenone, Vi, Arzignano, St Zeno, 8, 8cwt. in Ab., - Counterbalanced, No Stays or Sliders.
St Zenone di Minerbe , *Vr, Minerbe, St Zenone, 5, 17-2-14. in E., - Automatically Swing Chimed Only.*

Sabbion di Cologna Veneta, Vr, Cologna Veneta, 3, - *Automatically Swing Chimed Only.*
Salcedo, Vi, 3, 24cwt. in D., - *Automatically Swing Chimed Only.*
Salionze, Vr, Valeggio sul Mincio, St Giovanni Battista, 5, 6-1-12. in A., - *Automatically Swing Chimed Only.*
Salizzole, Vr, St Martino Vescovo, **6**, 18-0-20. in E., - Counterbalanced, No Stays or Sliders.
Sanctuario St Giuliana, Vi, Recoardo Terme, St Giuliana, **5**, 19cwt. in Eb., - Counterbalanced, No Stays or Sliders.
San Dona di Piave, Vr, 6, 66-0-24., - *Automatically Swing Chimed Only.*
Sandra, Vr, Castelnuovo del Garda, St Andrea Apostolo, **6**, 17-2-4. in Eb., - Counterbalanced, No Stays or Sliders.
Sandrigo, Vi, St. M. Ass e St Filippo e St Giacomo, 5, 44-2-10. in B., - *Automatically Swing Chimed Only.*
Sanguinetto, Vr, St Giorgio, **6**, 16-2-4. in Eb., - Counterbalanced, No Stays or Sliders.
Santo di Thiene, Vi, St Sacramento, 5, 6-1-12. in A., - *Automatically Swing Chimed Only.*
Santorso, Vi, 5, 24cwt. in D., - *Automatically Swing Chimed Only.*
Santuario St Moro, Vr, St Mauro di Saline, St Moro, **2**, 6-3-6. in A., - Counterbalanced, No Stays or Sliders.
Sarcedo, Vi, St Andrea Apostolo, 6, 37-1-22. in C., - *Automatically Swing Chimed Only.*
Sarmego, Vi, 6, 36cwt. in C., - *Automatically Swing Chimed Only.*
Sasso, Vi, Asiago, **4**, 17-2-24. in E., - Counterbalanced, No Stays or Sliders.
Scardevara, Vr, Ronco all'Adige, St Filippo e St Giacomo, **5**, 10-0-20. in F#., - Counterbalanced, No Stays or Sliders.
Schiavon, Vi, 5, 10-2-18. in G., - *Automatically Swing Chimed Only.*
Schio, Vi, Duomo di St Pietro, 4, 30cwt. in C., - *Automatically Swing Chimed Only.*
Scorgnano, Vr, Tregnago, Madonna Addorata, **3**, 1-2-14. in F., - Counterbalanced, No Stays or Sliders.
Selva, Vi, Trissino, St Maria Maddalena, 5, 15-0-22. in F., - *Automatically Swing Chimed Only.*
Selva di Montebello, Vi, 3, 36cwt. in C., - *Automatically Swing Chimed Only.*
Selva di Progno, Vr, St Maria Assunta, **10**, 21-0-20. in D., - Counterbalanced, No Stays or Sliders.
Setteca, Vi, Vicenza, 3, 16-2-0 in Eb., *Automatically Swing Chimed Only.*
Settimo, Vr, Pecantina, St Antonio Abate, **6**, 9cwt. in G., - Counterbalanced, No Stays or Sliders.
Sezano di Valpantena, Vr, Verona, Padri Passionisti, **3**, 8cwt. in A., - Counterbalanced, No Stays or Sliders.
Sezano di Valpantena, Vr, Verona, St Lorenzo, **5**, 5-0-20. in Bb., - Counterbalanced, No Stays or Sliders.
Soave, Vr, Dominicani, **3**, 3-2-4. in C., - Counterbalanced, No Stays or Sliders.
Soave, Vr, St Lorenzo, **9**, 32cwt. in C., - Counterbalanced, No Stays or Sliders.
Soave, Vr, St Maria della Bassanella, **5**, 5-0-22. in Bb., - Counterbalanced, No Stays or Sliders.
Solane, Vr, Fumane, Santuario Monte Solane, 5, 4-2-4. in C., - *Automatically Swing Chimed Only.*
Sommacampagna, Vr, St Rocco, **13**, 24-0-10. in D., - Counterbalanced, No Stays or Sliders.
Sona, Vr, Visitazione di St Maria, **5**, 18-2-12. in D., - Counterbalanced, No Stays or Sliders.
Sorga, Vr, B.V. Maria Nascente, 6, 11-1-26. in F#., - *Automatically Swing Chimed Only.*
Sorio di Gambellara, Vi, Gambellara, 5, 14-1-12. in E., - *Automatically Swing Chimed Only.*
Sossano, Vi, 8, 31-0-10., - *Automatically Swing Chimed Only.*
Sovizzo, Vi, 6, 36cwt. in C., - *Automatically Swing Chimed Only.*
Sovizzo Colle, Vi, 5, 3-2-24. in C., - *Automatically Swing Chimed Only.*
Spiazzi (Madonna della Corona), Vr, Caprino Veronese, Madonna della Corona, **6**, 4-0-20. in B., Counterbalanced, No Stays or Sliders.
Spinimbecco, Vr, Villa Bartolomea, St Maria Assunta, **5**, 9cwt. in G., - Counterbalanced, No Stays or Sliders.
Sprea, 5, 10cwt., Counterbalanced, No Stays or Sliders.

Sprea di Badia Calavena, Vr, Selva di Progno, St Rocco, **6**, 8-1-2. in G., - Counterbalanced, No Stays or Sliders.
SS Trinita di Montecchio Maggiore, Vi, Montecchio Maggiore, SS Trinita, **6**, 20cwt. in D., - Counterbalanced, No Stays or Sliders.
Stallavena, Vr, Grezzana, St Stefano Protomartire, **6**, 5-1-12. in Bb., - Counterbalanced, No Stays or Sliders.
Staro, Vi, Valli del Pasubio, **6**, 9-2-4. in G., - Counterbalanced, No Stays or Sliders.
Stoccareddo di Gallio , Vi, Gallio, 5, 19cwt. in Eb., - Automatically Swing Chimed Only.
Sustineza, Vr, Casaleone, St Giacomo Maggiore, **5**, 8cwt. in Ab., - Counterbalanced, No Stays or Sliders.
Tarmassia, Vr, Isola della Scala, St Giorgio Martire, **6**, 11-1-12. in F., - Counterbalanced, No Stays or Sliders.
Terranegra, Vr, Legnago, **5**, 7cwt. in Ab., - Counterbalanced, No Stays or Sliders.
Terrazzo, Vr, St Paolo, **6**, 18-2-24. in D., - Counterbalanced, No Stays or Sliders.
Terrossa , Vr, Ronca, St Maria Maddalena, 5, 14cwt. in F., - Automatically Swing Chimed Only.
Tezze, Vi, Arzignano, St Agata, **10**, 15-0-10. in E., - Counterbalanced, No Stays or Sliders.
Tezze sul Brenta , Vi, 6, 36cwt. in C., - Automatically Swing Chimed Only.
Thiene , Vi, Duomo di St Gaetano, 5, 16cwt. in F., - Automatically Swing Chimed Only.
Toara di Villaga , Vi, Villaga, 5, 13cwt. in F., - Automatically Swing Chimed Only.
Tomba Extra, Vr, Verona, St Giovanni Battista, **6**, 22-1-12. in Db., - Counterbalanced, No Stays or Sliders.
Tombazosana, Vr, Ronco all'Adige, St Ambrogio Vescovo, **6**, 24-1-12. in D., - Counterbalanced, No Stays or Sliders.
Tombetta , Vr, Verona, St Teresa del Bambin Gesu, 9, 18-1-16. in Eb., - Automatically Swing Chimed Only.
Tonezza Del Cimone , Vi, Tonezza Del Cimone, 4, 21-1-12. in Eb., - Automatically Swing Chimed Only.
Torbe, Vr, Negrar, St Pietro Apostolo, **10**, 25-3-2. in D., - Counterbalanced, No Stays or Sliders.
Tormine, Vr, Mozzecane, St Antonio Abate, **5**, 4-0-20. in B., - Counterbalanced, No Stays or Sliders.
Torrebelvicino , Vi, 3, 24cwt. in D., - Automatically Swing Chimed Only.
Torreselle di Isola Vicentino , Vi, Isola Vicentino, 3, 24cwt. in D., - Automatically Swing Chimed Only.
Torri Del Benaco , Vr, Torri Del Benaco, St Pietro e St Paolo, 5, 17-2-4. in E., - Automatically Swing Chimed Only.
Torri Di Quartesolo , Vi, 3, 27-1-14. in Db., - Automatically Swing Chimed Only.
(Transportable), Capanni Mobile Tower, Capanni Foundry, **6**, 6cwt. in Bb., This Tower travells around the Area but may be in Rome, Counterbalanced, No Stays or Sliders.
Tregnago, Vr, St Egidio, **3**, 10cwt. in G., - Counterbalanced, No Stays or Sliders.
Tregnago, Vr, St Maria Assunta, **6**, 17cwt. in Eb., - Counterbalanced, No Stays or Sliders.
Trevenzuolo , Vr, St Maria Maddalena, 9, 15-0-20. in F., - Automatically Swing Chimed Only.
Trezzolano, Vr, Verona, St Andrea Apostolo, **5**, 13-1-12. in F., - Counterbalanced, No Stays or Sliders.
Trissino , Vi, St Andrea Apostolo, 6, 30cwt. in C., - Automatically Swing Chimed Only.
Vaggimal, Vr, St Anna d'Alfaedo, St Rocco, **6**, 6-3-8. in Ab., - Counterbalanced, No Stays or Sliders.
Vago, Vr, Lavagno, St Francesco d'Assisi, **6**, 12-1-26. in E., - Counterbalanced, No Stays or Sliders.
Valdagno , Vi, Duomo, 9, 39-0-24. in C., - Automatically Swing Chimed Only.
Valdiporro, Vr, Boscochiesanouva, St Antonio Abate, **6**, 24-1-12. in D., - Counterbalanced, No Stays or Sliders.
Valeggio sul Mincio , Vr, St Pietro, 9, 20-1-0. in D., - Chimed Only.

Valgatara, Vr, Marano di Valpolicella, St Fermo e St Rustico, **6**, 16-2-4. in Eb., - Counterbalanced, No Stays or Sliders.
Vallese, *Vr, Oppeano, St Giacomo e St Anna, 5, 5-1-12. in A., - Chimed Only.*
Valli Del Pasubio, *Vi, 5, 23cwt. in Eb., - Automatically Swing Chimed Only.*
Valstagna, *Vi, 5, 19cwt. in Eb., - Automatically Swing Chimed Only.*
Vangadizza, Vr, Legnago, St Maria, **6**, 22-0-26. in D., - Counterbalanced, No Stays or Sliders.
Velo d'Astico, *Vi, 5, 30cwt. in Db., - Automatically Swing Chimed Only.*
Velo Veronese, *Vr, St Giovanni Battista, 5, 25-2-4. in Db., - Automatically Swing Chimed Only.*
Venezia, Vr, San Marco, **5**, 72-2-0., - Counterbalanced, No Stays or Sliders.
Venice, Ve, Verona, St Elena, (G.F.), **6**, 40cwt. in B., - The Bells are at the top of the 250 Foot High Tower, Counterbalanced, No Stays or Sliders.
Verona, Vr, Cattedrale, **9**, 89-0-8. in Ab. -, All these Bells were cast by the Cavadini Bell Foundry in 1931, Counterbalanced, No Stays or Sliders.
Verona, Vr, St Anastasia, **9**, 35-2-18. in C., - Counterbalanced, No Stays or Sliders.
Verona, Vr, St Bernardino, **6**, 15-2-4. in E., - Counterbalanced, No Stays or Sliders.
Verona, Vr, St Carlo, **3**, 1-1-12. in F., - Counterbalanced, No Stays or Sliders.
Verona, *Vr, St Eufemia, 6, 12cwt. in F., - Automatically Swing Chimed Only.*
Verona, *Vr, St Fermo Maggiore, 6, 15cwt. in F., - Automatically Swing Chimed Only.*
Verona, Vr, St Fermo Minore (Filippini), **6**, 10cwt. in G., - Counterbalanced, No Stays or Sliders.
Verona, Vr, St Giorgio in Brida, **6**, 12-0-18. in G., - Counterbalanced, No Stays or Sliders, These Bells are the Oldest Ring in Italy.
Verona, Vr, St Giovanni in Foro, **2**, 3-0-20. in D., - Counterbalanced, No Stays or Sliders.
Verona, Vr, St Giovanni in Valle, **6**, 13cwt. in F., - Counterbalanced, No Stays or Sliders.
Verona, Vr, St Lorenzo, **5**, 5-0-20. in Bb., - Counterbalanced, No Stays or Sliders.
Verona, Vr, St Luca, **6**, 9cwt. in Ab., - Counterbalanced, No Stays or Sliders.
Verona, Vr, St Maria della Scala, **5**, 13cwt. in F#., - Counterbalanced, No Stays or Sliders.
Verona, Vr, St Maria in Organo, **6**, 14cwt. in E., - Counterbalanced, No Stays or Sliders.
Verona, Vr, St Maria in Paradiso, **6**, 6-0-12. in A., - Counterbalanced, No Stays or Sliders.
Verona, Vr, St Nazaro e St Celso, **6**, 22-2-14. in D., - Counterbalanced, No Stays or Sliders.
Verona, Vr, St Nicolo all arena, **6**, 37cwt in C., - Counterbalanced, No Stays or Sliders.
Verona, *Vr, St Paolo in campo marzio, 6, 10-1-4. in G., - Automatically Swing Chimed Only.*
Verona, Vr, St Stefano, **6**, 10-1-12. in F#., - Counterbalanced, No Stays or Sliders.
Verona, *Vr, St Teresa degli Scalzi, 5, 7-2-4. in Ab., - Automatically Swing Chimed Only.*
Verona, *Vr, St Tommaso Cantuariense, 10, 28-2-4. in D., - Automatically Swing Chimed Only.*
Verona, Vr, St Toscana, **5**, 3-1-12. in C., - Counterbalanced, No Stays or Sliders.
Verona, Vr, St Zeno in Oratorio, **4**, 1-1-12. in F., - Counterbalanced, No Stays or Sliders.
Verona, *Vr, SS Apostoli, 6, 8cwt. in Ab., - Automatically Swing Chimed Only.*
Verona, Vr, SS Trinita, **6**, 11-1-22. in F#., - Counterbalanced, No Stays or Sliders.
Verona, Vr, Stimate, **6**, 9-2-4. in G., - Counterbalanced, No Stays or Sliders.
Verona, Vr, Suore Valverde, **5**, 2-3-6. in D., - Counterbalanced, No Stays or Sliders.
Verona, Vr, Torre dei Lamberti, **4**, 84-1-2. in A., - Counterbalanced, No Stays or Sliders, The Tenor was cast in 1557.
Veronella, *Vr, St Giovanni Battista, 6, 8cwt. in A., - Automatically Swing Chimed Only.*
Vestenanuova, Vr, St Leonardo, **10**, 30-3-12. in Db., - Counterbalanced, No Stays or Sliders.
Vestenavecchia, Vr, St Zenone e St Urbano, **6**, 19cwt. in D., - Counterbalanced, No Stays or Sliders.
Vicenza, *Vi, Carmini, 3, 12-1-12. in F., - Automatically Swing Chimed Only.*
Vicenza, *Vi, Cattedrale, 5, 26cwt. in Eb., - Automatically Swing Chimed Only.*
Vicenza, Vi, Filippini, **12**, 10-3-4. in G., - Counterbalanced, No Stays or Sliders.
Vicenza, *Vi, Maddalene, 3, 12cwt. in F#., - Automatically Swing Chimed Only.*
Vicenza, Vi, Madonna dei Prati, **3**, 10cwt. in G., - Counterbalanced, No Stays or Sliders.
Vicenza, *Vi, Madonna dei Pace, 3, 21cwt. in D., - Automatically Swing Chimed Only.*

Vicenza, Vi, Madonna di Monte Berico, **12**, 45-1-8. in B., - Counterbalanced, No Stays or Sliders.
Vicenza , *Vi, St Agostino, 4, 4cwt. in Db., - Automatically Swing Chimed Only.*
Vicenza, Vi, St Caterina, **3**, 12cwt. in F#., - Counterbalanced, No Stays or Sliders.
Vicenza , *Vi, St Corona, 3, 14cwt. in F., - Automatically Swing Chimed Only.*
Vicenza , *Vi, St Domenico, 3, 5-1-4. in Bb., - Automatically Swing Chimed Only.*
Vicenza, Vi, St Felice e St Fortunato, **9**, 13-2-10. in F#., - Counterbalanced, No Stays or Sliders.
Vicenza, Vi, St Giuliano, **9**, 9-3-4. in G., - Counterbalanced, No Stays or Sliders.
Vicenza, Vi, St Lorenzo, **10**, 39-0-22. in C., - Counterbalanced, No Stays or Sliders.
Vicenza , *Vi, St Lucia, 3, 4-2-24. in B., - Automatically Swing Chimed Only.*
Vicenza, Vi, St Marco, **12**, 19-1-26. in Eb., - Counterbalanced, No Stays or Sliders.
Vicenza , *Vi, St Pietro, 3, 17cwt. in E., - Automatically Swing Chimed Only.*
Vicenza, Vi, St Rocco, **9**, 5-1-2. in Bb., - Counterbalanced, No Stays or Sliders.
Vicenza, Vi, St Stefano, **9**, 18cwt. in E., - Counterbalanced, No Stays or Sliders.
Vicenza, Vi, St Vincenzo, **2**, 4-1-12. in C., - Counterbalanced, No Stays or Sliders.
Vicenza , *Vi, Servi St Michele, 3, 7cwt. in F#., - Automatically Swing Chimed Only.*
Vigasio , *Vr, St Zeno, 6, 13-0-26. in F#., - Automatically Swing Chimed Only.*
Vigo , *Vr, Legnago, St Martino Vescovo, 5, 17-2-22. in Eb., - Automatically Swing Chimed Only.*
Villa D'Adige, Rv, Badia Polesine, **5**, 10cwt. in G., - Counterbalanced, No Stays or Sliders.
Villabalzana , *Vi, 3, 24cwt. in D., - Automatically Swing Chimed Only.*
Villabartolomea , *Vr, 5, 16cwt. in E., - Automatically Swing Chimed Only.*
Villafontana, Vr, Bovolone, St Agostino, **6**, 10-0-14. in F#., - Counterbalanced, No Stays or Sliders.
Villafranca di Verona , *Vr, St Pietro e St Paolo, 6, 12-1-24. in F#., - Automatically Swing Chimed Only.*
Villafranca Padovana, Pd, **10**, 31-0-20. in Db., - Counterbalanced, No Stays or Sliders.
Villaga , *Vi, 5, 13cwt. in F., - Automatically Swing Chimed Only.*
Villaganzerla , *Vi, 5, 30cwt. in Db., - Automatically Swing Chimed Only.*
Villanova , *Vr, St Bonifacio, Abbazia di St Pietro Apostolo, 6, 13cwt. in E., - Automatically Swing Chimed Only.*
Villaverla , *Vi, 3, 30cwt. in Db., - Automatically Swing Chimed Only.*
Vo, Vi, Brendola, **3**, 22cwt. in D., - Counterbalanced, No Stays or Sliders.
Volargne, Vr, Dolce, St Martino, **6**, 14-1-12. in E., - Counterbalanced, No Stays or Sliders.
Volon, Vr, Zevio, St Trinita e St Madonna del Rosario, **5**, 5cwt. in B., - Counterbalanced, No Stays or Sliders.
Volpino , *Vr, Zimella, St Maria Maddalena, 3, 7cwt. in A., - Automatically Swing Chimed Only.*
Zane , *Vi, 5, 17-1-26. in E., - Automatically Swing Chimed Only.*
Zane , *Vi, St Maria Immacolata, 6, 12-1-22. in F#., - Automatically Swing Chimed Only.*
Zevio , *Vr, St Pietro Apostolo, 6, 26cwt. in Db., - Automatically Swing Chimed Only.*
Zimella , *Vr, St Floriano, 3, 23-0-20. in D., - Automatically Swing Chimed Only.*

JAMAICA.

Montego Bay , (Anglican), St James Parish Church, **12**, in C, - Unringable, Cast by Whitechapel in 1959.

JAPAN.

Itami , *43, - Carillon.*
Kanzeonji , *Buddhist Temple, 1, - Hung Dead, This is the Oldest Temple Bell and was cast during the Nara Era, Japanise Shaped Bell a bit like a Wine Glass.*
Nagasaki , *Carillon Symphonica, (Bell Museum), 37, - Carillon, In the Museum there are over 300 Bells here from all over the world & there are some Bronze Bells made in China 3500 Years Ago.*

Rengein-Tanjyoji, Shigon-Ritsu Buddhist Temple, 1, 750cwt., - Hung Dead, Chimed with hitting the Bell with a Hammer, This Bell is called " Hiryu-No-Kane " or " Flying Dragon Bell " and was cast in Kyoto in 1977 and is a Japanise Shaped Bell a bit like a Wine Glass.
Shiga, Shinji Shimeikai Tower, 50, - Carillon.

KOREA.

King Songsok, Divine Temple, 1, - Hung Dead, This Bell was cast in 771 during the Unified Shilla Kingdom and is the Largest Temple Bell in Korea, This is the Divine Temple Bell of King Songsok, Korean Shaped Bell a bit like a Wine Glass.

LITHUANIA.

Kaunas, Bell Tower, 35, - Carillon.
Klaipeda, Post Office, 48, - Carillon.

MALAWA.

Likoma, Island of Likoma, Likoma Cathedral, 8, - Hung Dead, Hemispherical Bells cast by Mears and Stainbank in 1906.

MALTA.

Valleta, Memorial, 1, 214-1-24. - Swing Chiming Only, This Bell was cast by Taylors, Round Tower with the Bell open to the eliminates by Six Round Pillars.
Valleta, Pro-Cathedral Church of St Paul, **6,** 13cwt. - Unringable.

MEXICO.

Guadalajara, Mexico, Cathedral, 25, in C, - Automatic Carillon, Cast by Rincker.
Mexico City, Catedral Metropolitan (Metropolitan Cathedral), (South East Tower), **6,** 140cwt. - **Three** Bells Hung Dead and **Three** Bells Counterbalenced with No Wheels, The Tenor is called "Santa Maria de Ascention" and was cast in 1573. (South West Tower), **5,** 260cwt. in C. - Counterbalenced with No Wheels, The Tenor Bell is called "Santa Maria de Guadelupe" and was cast in 1791, The Belltower is open Daily between 10am - 8pm.
Mexico City, Basilica de la Virgin de Guadelupe (Basilica Sancta Maria de Guadelupe), 35, in F, Automatic Carillon, Detatched Tower, These Bells were cast by Eijsbouts in 1990.
Mexico City, Basilica de la Virgin de Guadelupe (Basilica Sancta Maria de Guadelupe), 19, in C, Chimed Only, These Bells were cast by Eijsbouts in 1989.
Mexico City, Iglesia San Filipe de Jesus, 35, in A, - Carillon, Cast by Petit and Fritsen in 1971.
Mexico City, Tlatelolco, Banco Nacional de obrass y Servicious, (Barnobras), 47, 94-1-18 in G, - Traditional Keyboard, Carillon, The Belltower is open at weekends at midday, Cast by Petit and Fritsen in 1963.
Puebla, Mexico, Catedral de Nuestra SeOora de la Immaculada Concepciun (Immaculate Conception Cathedral), **19**, 170cwt. in C., Eleven Bells are Clapper Chimed by Swinging the Clappers with a Rope, **Eight** Bells are Counterbalenced with No Wheels, The Tenor was cast in 1729, This is the Second Largest Cathedral in Mexico.
Tuxtla Gutierrez, Mexico, San Marcos Cathedral, Plaza San Marcos, 48, in C, - Traditional Keyboard Carillon, Cast by Petit and Fritsen in 1981.

NETHERLANDS.
In the Netherlands they have Two Main styles of Swing Chiming, The first is Lever Chiming (Flying Clapper) and the Second is Swing Chiming (Falling Clapper) and the Rope is around the top of the Wheel when the Bell is Down , The Headstock is called a Yoge., They ring the Bells by Schedules.

Aarle-Rixtel , Noord-Brabant, Klokkengieterij, 47, - Carillon.
Alkmaar , Noord-Holland, St. Laurens Toren, 35, - Carillon.
Alkmaar , Noord-Holland, Waag Toren, 47, - Carillon.
Almelo , Overijssel, St. Georgius Toren, 48, - Carillon.
Almere-Haven , Flevoland, Goede Rede Toren, 48, - Carillon.
Almere-Stad , Flevoland, Lichtboog Toren, 48, - Carillon.
Alphen a/d Rijn , Zuid-Holland, Advents Kerk, 47, - Carillon.
Amersfoort , Utrecht, O.L. Vrouwe Toren, 7, 56-0-20. in C., - Lever Chimed Only, These Bells were cast by Ricker in 2000.
Amersfoort , Utrecht, O.L. Vrouwe Toren, 58, 61-1-0. in G., - Carillon, Cast by Eijsbouts in 1997.
Amersfoort , Utrecht, Belgen Monument, 49, - Carillon.
Amsterdam , Noord-Holland, Munt Toren, 38, - Carillon.
Amsterdam , Noord-Holland, Oude Kerks Toren, 47, - Carillon.
Amsterdam , Noord-Holland, Koninklijk Paleis, 47, - Carillon.
Amsterdam , Noord-Holland, Plein 1940 - 1945, Vrijheids Carillon, 31, - Carillon.
Amsterdam , Noord-Holland, Vrije Universiteit, 37, - Carillon.
Amsterdam , Noord-Holland, Wester Toren, 50, 150cwt. - Carillon.
Amsterdam , Noord-Holland, Zuider Toren, 35, - Carillon.
Apeldoorn , Gelderland, Oude Raadhuis, 52, - Carillon.
Apeldoorn , Gelderland, Groot Schuylenburg, 47, - Carillon.
Appingedam , Groningen, Nicolai Toren, 51, - Carillon.
Arnhem , Gelderland, St. Eusebius Toren, 53, 184cwt. - Carillon, All these Bells were cast by Petit and Fritsen between 1958 - 1994.
Assen , Drenthe, Gemeentehuis, 38, - Carillon.
Asten , Noord-Brabant, Maria Presentatie Kerk, 56, - Carillon.
Axel , Zeeland, Stadhuis Toren, 35, - Carillon.
Barneveld , Gelderland, Jan van Schaffelaar Toren, 51, - Carillon.
Bellingwolde , Groningen, 2, - Swing Chimed, Steel Wheels, Both these Bells were cast by Yohan en Mamees Fremi in 1697.
Bergambacht , Zuid-Holland, St. Laurentius Toren, 51, 7-2-14. in D. - Carillon, All the Bells were cast by Eijesbouts between 1964 - 1999.
Bunde , Rheiderland, 2, - Lever Swing Chimed.
Bergen , Noord-Holland, Ruine Kerk, 26, - Carillon.
Bergen op Zoom , Noord-Brabant, St. Geertruids Toren, 48, - Carillon.
Beverwijk , Noord-Holland, St. Agatha Toren, 49, - Carillon.
Bolsward , Friesland, Stadhuis Toren, 44, - Carillon.
Boxmeer , Noord-Brabant, Stadhuis Toren, 25, - Carillon.
Boxtel , Noord-Brabant, St. Petrus Toren, 48, - Carillon.
Breda , Noord-Brabant, Heuvelbrink Carillon, 23, - Carillon.
Breda , Noord-Brabant, O.L. Vrouwe Toren, 49, - Carillon.
Brielle , Zuid-Holland, St. Catharijne Toren, 47, - Carillon.
Brunssum , Limburg, Bestuurs Centrum, 38, - Carillon.
Bussum , Noord-Holland, Raadhuis Toren, 47, - Carillon.
Cuijk , Noord-Brabant, Stadhuis Toren, 25, - Carillon.
Culemborg , Gelderland, St. Barbara Toren, 47, - Carillon.
De Lier , Zuid-Holland, St. Georgius Toren, 37, - Carillon.
Delft , Zuid-Holland, Nieuwe Kerks Toren, 48, - Carillon.

Den Bosch , Noord-Brabant, St. Jansbasiliek, 50, - Carillon.
Den Bosch , Noord-Brabant, Stadhuis Toren, 35, - Carillon.
Den Haag , Zuid-Holland, St. Jacobs Toren, 51, - Carillon.
Den Haag , Zuid-Holland, Vredespaleis, 47, - Carillon.
Den Helder , Noord-Holland, Zeehelden Monument, 49, - Carillon.
Deventer , Overijssel, St. Lebuinus Toren, 47, - Carillon.
Dinxperlo , Gelderland, N.H. Kerk, 50, - Carillon.
Ditzum , Rheiderland, 2, - Lever Swing Chimed, The Treble was cast by Bartold Klinge in 1479 and the Tenor is a Steel Bell.
Doesburg , Gelderland, St. Martini Toren, 47, - Carillon.
Doetinchem , Gelderland, St. Catharina Toren, 47, - Carillon.
Dokkum , Friesland, Stadhuis, 47, - Carillon.
Dordrecht , Zuid-Holland, Grote Kerk, 67, 196cwt. - Carillon, All the Bells were cast by Eijesbouts between 1965 - 1999.
Dronten , Flevoland, Gemeentehuis, 25, - Carillon.
Drunen , Noord-Brabant, Klokkestoel Lips N.V., 47, - Carillon.
Drunen , Noord-Brabant, St. Lambertus Toren, 47, - Carillon.
Edam , Noord-Holland, Speel Toren, 37, - Carillon.
Ede , Gelderland, Oude Kerk, 51, - Carillon.
Eindhoven , Noord-Brabant, Stadskirk St. Cathrien Philips-Beiaard, 61, - Carillon.
Eindhoven , Noord-Brabant, Stadhuis, 48, - Carillon.
Elburg , Gelderland, St. Nicolaas Toren, 47, - Carillon.
Emmeloord , Flevoland, Polder Toren, 48, 47-2-8. in D. - Carillon, Detatched Hexagonal Tower, All the Bells were cast by Eijesbouts between 1958 - 1959.
Enkhuizen , Noord-Holland, Dromme Daris, 39, - Carillon, Round Tower attached to a Round Church.
Enkhuizen , Noord-Holland, Zuider Toren, 52, 69-2-24. - Carillon.
Enschede , Overijssel, Universiteit Twente, Campusbeiaard, 49, - Carillon, Detatched Hexagonal Steel Tower.
Enschede , Overijssel, Oude Kerk, 49, - Carillon.
Epe , Gelderland, N.H. Kerk, 30, - Carillon.
Etten-Leur , Noord-Brabant, St. Lambertus Toren, 38, - Carillon.
Geldrop , Noord Brabant, St Brigida Kerk, 8, 12-2-24. in G. - Thur, These Bells are Hung Dead but are Chimed to Methods, in the future they may be rehung for Change Ringing, Also these Bells are Part of an existing Carillon of Forty-seven Bells.
Gersloot , Friesland, 2, - Lever Swing Chimed, Detatched Wooden Tower, The Treble was cast in 1300.
Goedereede , Zuid-Holland, St. Elisabeth Toren, 51, - Carillon.
Goes , Zeeland, Maria Magdalena Toren, 47, - Carillon.
Gorinchem , Zuid-Holland, St. Jans Toren, 47, - Carillon.
Gouda , Zuid-Holland, St. Jans Toren, 50, - Carillon.
Groenlo , Gelderland, St. Calixtus Kerk, 47, - Carillon.
Groningen , Groningen, Martini Toren, A-Tower , 3, - Swing Chimed, Steel Wheels, All these Bells were cast by Jan Crans in 1714.
Groningen , Groningen, Martini Toren, Martini-Tower , 12, - Swing Chimed, Steel Wheels, There is Also a Carillon of Forty-two Bells in the Same Tower.
Groningen , Groningen, Academie Toren, 25, - Carillon.
Haarlem , Noord-Holland, Bakenesser Toren, 26, - Carillon.
Haarlem , Noord-Holland, St. Bavo Toren, 47, - Carillon.
Haastrecht , Zuid-Holland, N.H. Kerk, 38, - Carillon.
Halsteren , Noord-Brabant, St. Martinus Toren, 47, - Carillon.
Harderwijk , Gelderland, Grote Kerk, 47, - Carillon.
Hasselt , Overijssel, St. Stephanus Toren, 42, - Carillon.

Hattem, Gelderland, St. Andreas Toren, 38, - Carillon.
Heerenveen, Friesland, Raadhuis Crackstate, 49, - Carillon.
Heerhugowaard, Noord-Holland, Raadhuis Toren, 35, - Carillon.
Heerlen, Limburg, St. Pancratius Toren, 47, - Carillon.
Heiligerlee, Groningen, Klokkengieterij Museum, 49, - Carillon.
Helenaveen, Noord-Brabant, Klokkestoel Kerkplein, 23, - Carillon.
Helmond, Noord-Brabant, St. Lambertus Toren, 47, - Carillon.
Hengelo, Overijssel, Raadhuis Toren, 47, - Carillon.
Heusden, Noord-Brabant, Stadhuis Toren, 48, - Carillon.
Hilvarenbeek, Noord-Brabant, St. Petrus-Banden Toren, 43, - Carillon.
Hilversum, Noord-Holland, Raadhuis Toren, 48, - Carillon.
Holtgaste, Rheiderland, 2, - Lever Swing Chimed, The Treble was cast in 1300 and the Tenor was cast in 1379.
Hoogeveen, Drenthe, Raadhuis Toren, 39, - Carillon.
Hoorn, Noord-Holland, Grote Kerk, 52, - Carillon.
Huissen, Gelderland, O.L. Vrouwe-ten-Hemelopnemings Toren, 48, - Carillon.
Hulst, Zeeland, St. Willibrordus Toren, 36, - Carillon.
IJsselstein, Utrecht, Oude N.H. Kerk, 50, - Carillon.
Joure, Friesland, N.H. Kerk, 39, - Carillon.
Kamerik, Utrecht, St. Hippolytus Toren, 35, - Carillon.
Kampen, Overijssel, Nieuwe Toren, 47, - Carillon.
Katlijk, Friesland, 2, - Lever Swing Chimed, Detatched Wooden Tower.
Katwijk, Zuid-Holland, Andries Toren, 36, - Carillon.
Laren, Noord-Holland, N.H. Kerk, 47, - Carillon.
Leeuwarden, Friesland, Stadhuiskoepel, 39, - Carillon.
Leiden, Zuid-Holland, Stadhuis Toren, 49, - Carillon.
Lochem, Gelderland, St. Gudula Toren, 49, - Carillon.
Maarssen, Utrecht, Heilig Hart Kerk, 40, - Carillon.
Maassluis, Zuid-Holland, Grote Kerk, 47, - Carillon.
Maastricht, Limburg, St. Sevaas Basiliek, 59, - Carillon.
Maastricht, Limberg, Stadhuis, 49, 15-1-2. - Carillon.
Meppel, Drenthe, Grote Kerk, 47, - Carillon.
Middelburg, Zeeland, Abdij Toren, 49, - Carillon.
Middelstum, Groningen, St. Hippolytus Toren, 30, - Carillon.
Middelstum, Groningen, 1, - Lever Swing Chimed, This Bell was cast by Johan Schonenborch in 1520.
Naaldwijk, Zuid-Holland, St. Adrianus Toren, 38, - Carillon.
Nieuwegein, Utrecht, Parkbeiaard, 47, - Carillon.
Nijkerk, Gelderland, Grote Kerk, 49, - Carillon.
Nijmegen, Gelderland, St. Stevens Toren, 48, - Carillon.
Nijverdal, Overijssel, Raadhuis, 30, - Carillon.
Oirschot, Noord-Brabant, St. Petrus-Banden Toren, 49, - Carillon.
Oldendorp (bij Ditzum), Rheiderland, 2, - Lever Swing Chimed, The Treble was cast in 1300.
Oldenzaal, Overijssel, St. Plechelmus Toren, 48, - Carillon.
Oosterbeek, Gelderland, Raadhuis Toren, 37, - Carillon.
Oosterhout, Noord-Brabant, St. Jans Basiliek, 49, - Carillon.
Oudega (Smallingerland), Friesland, 2, - Lever Swing Chimed, The Treble was cast in 1200.
Oudehorne, Friesland, 2, - Lever Swing Chimed, Detatched Wooden Tower.
Oudewater, Utrecht, St. Michaels Toren, 53, 14-2-0., - Carillon.
Pieterburen, Groningen, 1, - Lever Swing Chimed, This Bell was cast in 1553.
Raalte, Overijssel, Kruisverheffings Kerk, 37, - Carillon.
Rhenen, Utrecht, St. Cunera Toren, 47, - Carillon.
Ridderkerk, Zuid-Holland, Raadhuis Toren, 47, - Carillon.

Rijnsburg, Zuid-Holland, N.H. Kerk, 50, - Carillon.
Rijssen, Overijssel, Schild Kerk, 50, - Carillon.
Rijswijk, Zuid-Holland, Raadhuis Toren, 47, - Carillon.
Roermond, Limberg, Stadhuis, 47, - Carillon.
Roosendaal, Noord-Brabant, St. Jans Toren, 48, - Carillon.
Rotterdam, Zuid-Holland, Pelgrimvaders Kerk, 44, - Carillon.
Rotterdam, Zuid-Holland, Erasmus Universiteit, 47, - Carillon.
Rotterdam, Zuid-Holland, St. Laurens Toren, 49, - Carillon.
Rotterdam, Zuid-Holland, Stadhuis Toren, 63, - Carillon.
Scheveningen, Zuid-Holland, Oude Kerks Toren, 37, - Carillon.
Schiedam, Zuid-Holland, St. Jans Toren, 39, - Carillon.
Schijndel, Noord-Brabant, St. Servatius Toren, 49, - Carillon.
Schoonhoven, Zuid-Holland, Stadhuis, 50, 13-2-24. in G. - Carillon.
Sint-Maartensdijk, Zeeland, N.H. Kerk, 40, - Carillon.
Sluis, Zeeland, Stadhuis Toren, 38, - Carillon.
Sneek, Friesland, Martini Kirk, 47, - Carillon.
Son, Noord-Brabant, St. Petrus-Banden Toren, 48, - Carillon.
Spakenburg, Utrecht, Beiaard Toren, 42, - Carillon.
Spijkenisse, Zuid-Holland, Dorps Toren, 47, - Carillon.
Tholen, Zeeland, Stadhuis Toren, 37, - Carillon.
Tiel, Gelderland, St. Maartens Toren, 47, - Carillon.
Tilburg, Noord-Brabant, Heikese Toren, 50, - Carillon.
Utrecht, Utrecht, Buurtoren, 5, - Swing Chiming, Steel Wheels.
Utrecht, Utrecht, Domtoren, 14, 164-1-26 in F - Swing Chiming, Steel Wheels, The back Six Bells were cast by Geert van Wou in 1505, The Majestic Gothic Tower was built between 1321 - 1382.
Utrecht, Utrecht, Domtoren, 50, 140cwt. - Carillon, Thirty-four Bells were cast by the Hemony Brothers between 1663 - 1664 and Sixteen Bells were cast by Eijesbouts in 1972.
Utrecht, Utrecht, Geertetoren, 2, Swing Chiming, Steel Wheels.
Utrecht, Utrecht, Jacobitoren, 5, - Swing Chiming, Steel Wheels.
Utrecht, Utrecht, Nicolai Toren, 43, - Carillon, All the Bells were cast by the Hemont Brothers in the 17th Century.
Valkenswaard, Noord-Brabant, St. Nicolass Toren, 45, - Carillon.
Veendam, Groningen, N.H. Kerk, 42, - Carillon.
Veere, Zeeland, Stadhuis Toren, 47, - Carillon.
Velsen, Noord-Holland, Stadhuis Toren, 49, - Carillon.
Venlo, Limburg, St. Martinus Toren, 53, - Carillon.
Venray, Limberg, St. Petrus-Banden Toren, 50, - Carillon.
Vianen, Zuid-Holland, N.H. Kerk, 42, - Carillon.
Visvliet, Groningen, 1, - Lever Swing Chimed.
Vlaardingen, Zuid-Holland, Grote Kerk, 47, - Carillon.
Vlissingen, Zeeland, St. Jakobs Toren, 47, - Carillon.
Vlissingen, Zeeland, Stadhuis Toren, 47, - Carillon.
Vollen, Overledingerland, 2, - Lever Swing Chimed, The Treble was cast in 1330.
Voorburg, Zuid-Holland, Oude Kirk, 38, - Carillon.
Voorschoten, Zuid-Holland, N.H. Kerk, 38, - Carillon.
Vught, Noord-Brabant, St. Lambertus Toren, 47, - Carillon.
Waalre, Noord-Brabant, St. Willibrordus Toren, 35, - Carillon.
Wageningen, Gelderland, Grote Kerk, 50, - Carillon.
Wateringen, Zuid-Holland, N.H. Kerk, 38, - Carillon.
Weert, Limberg, St. Martinus Toren, 49, - Carillon.
Weesp, Noord-Holland, St. Laurens Toren, 38, - Carillon.

Wijnjewoude, Friesland, 3, - Lever Swing Chimed, Detatched Wooden Tower, All these Bells were cast by Petit and Fritsen in 1948.
Winschoten, Groningen, Olle Witte, 49, - Carillon.
Winterswijk, Gelderland, Jacobs Toren, 48, - Carillon.
Woerden, Utrecht, St. Petrus Toren, 47, - Carillon.
Zaltbommel, Gelderland, Gasthuis Toren, 35, - Carillon.
Zeerijp, Groningen, 2, - Swing Chimed, Steel Wheels.
Zeewolde, Flevoland, Open Haven Toren, 47, - Carillon.
Zeist, Utrecht, Raadhuis, 35, - Carillon.
Zierikzee, Zeeland, Stadhuis Toren, 36, - Carillon.
Zoetermeer, Zuid-Holland, Oude Kerk, 47, - Carillon.
Zutphen, Gelderland, Wijnhuis Toren, 47, - Carillon.
Zwijndrecht, Zuid-Holland, Konings Kerk, 37, - Carillon.
Zwolle, Overijssel, Peperbus, 47, - Carillon.

NETHERLANDS ANTILLES.

Aruba, Spritzer and Fuhrmann, Jewellers, 14, in C, - Chimed Only.
Filipsburg, Spritzer and Fuhrmann, Government House, 23, in C, - Automatic Carillon, All the Bells were cast by Petit & Fritsen in 1969.
Filipsburg, Spritzer and Fuhrmann, St Maarten, 23, in C, - Automatic Carillon, All the Bells were cast by Petit and Fritsen in 1969.
Oranjestad, Aruba, Shopping Mall, 12, in C, - Automatically Chimed Only, Cast by Eijsbouts in 1989.
Willemstad, CuraAao, Cito Bank, on Plasa Smeets, 18, in C, - Automatically Chimed Only, All these Bells were cast by Eijesbouts in 1989.
Willemstad, CuraAao, Cito Bank, 18, in C, - Automatically Chimed Only, Cast by Eijesbouts in 1991.
Willemstad, CuraAao, CuraAao Museum, on Van Leeuwenhoek Straat, 47, 20 cwt. in G, - Traditional Keyboard, Carillon, Hung Dead on the Roof Top of the Museum, Cast by Eijesbouts in 1951.
Willemstad, CuraAao, Spritzer and Fuhrmann, Jewellers, 13, in D, - Automatically Chimed Only, All these Bells were cast by Eijsbouts in 1954.
Willemstad, CuraAao, Spritzer and Fuhrmann, Jewellers, 23, in G, - Carillon, Cast by Petit & Fritsen in 1958.

NEW ZEALAND.

Auckland, North Island, St John's College, **1**, 4-0-24., - This Bell was cast by Whitechapel in 1872.
Auckland, North Island, Selwyn Village, 13, 10-0-23. in G., - Chimed Only, All These Bells were cast by Gillett and Johnson in 1911.
Blenheim, South Island, War Memorial, 5, 1-2-2., - Chimed Only, All these Bells were cast by Gillett and Johnson between 1900 - 1902.
Burnett C, 11, - Chimed Only, Hemispherical Bells, All these Bells were cast by Whitechapel.
Cambridge, North Island, St Andrew, 6, 15cwt., - Swing Chiming Only, Steel Bells, All these Bells were cast by Vickers in 1884, Wooden Church, Tues 7 - 8 pm.
Cambridge, North Island, Post Office, 5, 10cwt., - Chimed Only, Cast by Taylors in 1908.
Cambridge, North Island, St Peter's Archangel, **2**, 30-1-25. in F., - Cast by Gillett and Johnson in 1955.
Canturbury, South Island, **1**, 13-2-0., - This Bell was cast by Whitechapel in 1859.
Canturbury, South Island, Cust Church, **1**, 5-2-0., - This Bell was cast by Whitechapel in 1868.
Carterton, North Island, Post Office, 5, 10cwt., - Chimed Only, Cast by Taylors in 1906.

Christchurch, South Island, 8, 4-1-21. in D#. - *Chimed Only, Cast by Gillett and Johnson in 1926.*
Dargaville, North Island, Post Office, **1**, 4cwt., - This Bell was cast by Taylors in 1924.
Dunedin, South Island, (R.C.), **2**, 12-0-15., - These Bells were cast by Whitechapel in 1864 and 1911.
Gisborne, North Island, Post Office, 5, 6cwt., - *Chimed Only, Cast by Taylors in 1903.*
Gisborne, North Island, (R.C.), **1**, 3cwt., - This Bell was cast by Whitechapel in 1898.
Gore, South Island, C. of E., **1**, 5cwt., - This Bell was cast by Taylors in 1954.
Gore, South Island, Post Office, 5, 10cwt., - *All these Bells were cast by Taylors in 1905.*
Greymouth, South Island, Post Office, 5, 10cwt., - *All these Bells were cast by Taylors in 1907.*
Hastings, North Island, Post Office, 5, 12cwt., - *Chimed Only, Cast by Taylors in 1910.*
Hastings, North Island, (R.C.), **1**, 10cwt., - This Bell was cast in Dublin before 1916.
Hawks Bay - *See Hawkes Bay.*
Hawkes Bay, North Island, (R.C.), **3**, 13-1-5., - The Tenor was cast by Whitechapel in 1850, The Treble and Second was cast before 1916 in Dublin.
Levin, North Island, St Mary, 8, 5-2-0., - *Chimed Only, These Bells were cast by Taylors in 1955.*
Lower Hutt, North Island, Post Office, 5, 10cwt., - *Chimed Only, Cast by Taylors in 1906.*
Lower Hutt, North Island, St James, 8, 5-2-0., - *Chimed Only, Cast by Taylors in 1953.*
Lyttleton, South Island, St Savior, **1**, 2cwt., - This Bell was cast by Whitechapel in 1889.
Lyttleton, South Island, 4, 13cwt., - *Clock Bells, All these Bells were cast by Taylors in 1903.*
Marivale, South Island, Post Office, **1**, 5cwt., - This Bell was cast by Taylors in 1927.
Marivale, South Island, St Mary, 8, 6-0-11. in C., - *Chimed Only, Cast by Gillett and Johnson in 1950.*
Napier, North Island, Corporation Fire Station, 1, 5cwt., - *Chimed Only (Fire Alarm), This Bell was cast by Taylors in 1902.*
Napier, North Island, St John's Cathedral, 8, 12-3-0., - *Chimed Only, All Cast by Taylors in 1958.*
Nelson, South Island, Christ Church, **3**, 3-3-16., - These Bells were cast by Whitechapel in 1855.
Nelson, S. Island, Post Office, 5, 7cwt., - *Chimed Only, These Bells were cast by Taylors in 1906.*
Nelson, South Island, (R.C.), **1**, 10cwt., - This Bell was cast in Dublin before 1916.
Nelson, South Island, Cathedral, 8, 9-2-0., - *All these Bells were cast in 1965.*
New Plymouth, North Island, Post Office, 5, 10cwt., - *Chimed Only, All Cast by Taylors in 1907.*
Ngaio, 1, 9-0-20. in A., - This Bell was cast by Gillett and Johnson in 1936.
Oamaru, South Island, Post Office, 5, 40cwt., - *Chimed Only, Cast by Taylors in 1902.*
Otagu, University, 5, 10cwt., - *Chimed Only, All these Bells were cast by Taylors in 1930.*
Otahuhu, South Island, Kings College, **2**, 5cwt., - These Bells were cast by Taylors in 1954.
Paekakariki, North Island, St Peter, **1**, 4-2-0., - This Bell was cast by Taylors in 1947.
Palmerston North, North Island, Post Office, 5, 10cwt., - *Chimed Only, Cast by Taylors in 1906.*
Palmerston North, North Island, **1**, 4cwt., - This Bell was cast by Whitechapel in 1909.
Pokeno, North Island, St Mary, **3**.
Ponsonby, North Island, All Saints Church, 13, 6-2-0., - *Chimed Only, Cast by Taylors in 1958.*
Prebbleton, 5, 6-3-0., - These Bells were cast by Whitechapel in 1912.
Remuera, North Island, St Luke, **1**, 17-1-0., - This Bell was cast by Taylors in 1958.
Rotorua, North Island, Seddon Memorial (Clock Tower), 5, 9cwt., - *Hung Dead, Clock Chime, All these Bells were cast by Taylors in 1910.*
Rotorua, North Island, St Luke, **1**, 5-2-0., - This Bell was cast by Taylors in 1946.
St Heliers Bay, North Island, St Philip, **1**, 9cwt., - This Bell was cast by Taylors in 1960.
Stratford, North Island, Memorial Tower, 5, 10cwt., - *Chimed Only*, *Cast by Taylors in 1924.*
Stratford, North Island, (R.C.) St Taranaki, **1**, 4cwt., - This Bell was cast in Dublin before 1916.
Sydenham, South Island, Christ Church, **1**, 12cwt., - This Bell was cast by Taylors in 1915.
Taihape, North Island, Post Office, 5, 7cwt., - *Chimed Only, Cast by Taylors in 1907.*
The Bluff, South Island, Post Office, 4, 12cwt., - *Chimed Only, Cast by Taylors in 1902.*
Timaru, South Island, Chalmers Church, **1**, 13cwt., - This Bell was cast by Taylors in 1903.
Timaru, South Island, Post Office, 5, 11cwt., - *Chimed Only, These Bells were cast by Taylors in 1912.*

Wadestown, St Luke, **1**, 2-1-0., - This Bell was cast by Taylors in 1962.
Waimate, *Post Office, 5, 7cwt., - Chimed Only, All these Bells were cast by Taylors in 1912.*
Waipawa, (R.C.), **2**, 3-1-0., - These Bells were cast in Dublin before 1916.
Wairoa, *North Island, Post Office, 5, 5-1-15., - Chimed Only, Cast by Gillett and Johnson in 1920.*
Waitemata, (R.C.), **1**, 4-3-12., - This Bell was cast by Whitechapel in 1862.
Waiwhetu, *St Paul, 8, 5-2-0., - Chimed Only, All these Bells were cast by Taylors in 1960.*
Wanganui, *North Island, Clock Tower, 4, 12cwt., - Hung Dead, Clock Chime, Cast by Taylors in 1903.*
Waverley, *North Island, War Memorial, 1, 4cwt., - Chimed Only, Cast by Taylors in 1925.*
Wellington, North Island, Free Church, **1**, 3-0-16., - This Bell was cast by Whitechapel in 1856.
Wellington, *North Island, Masterton, Clock Tower, 4, 12cwt., - Hung Dead, Clock Chime, All these Bells were cast by Taylors in 1901.*
Wellington, *North Island, National War Memorial Carillon, 74, 250cwt. - Carillon.*
Wellington, North Island, New Church, **1**, 3-1-0., - This Bell was cast by Whitechapel in 1858.
Wellington, North Island, (R.C.), **1**, 11cwt., - This Bell was cast in Dublin in 1862.
Wellington, *North Island, St Peter, 8, 16cwt., - Chimed Only.*
Westport, *Post Office, 5, 12cwt., - Chimed Only, All these Bells were cast by Taylors in 1911.*
Woodbury, 1, 6cwt., - This Bell was cast by Taylors in 1936.

NICARAGUA.

Leon, *Leun, Cathedral of St Peter, 25, in A, - Traditional Keyboard Carillon, Cast by Petit & Fritsen in 1959, There is also 3 other Bells, One Hung Dead which weighs 12 cwt. &* **Two** *Bells that are Counterbalenced with No Wheels that weigh 30 cwt. These Bells were cast in Spain.*

NORWAY.

Drammen, *Brageernaes Kirken, 35, 12-2-24. in E. - Carillon,The Bells were cast by Bergholtz in 1961.*
Haugesund, *Var Frelsers Kirke, 36, 13-2-4. in G. - Hung Dead, Automatic Carillon, All the Bells were cast by Olsen-Nauen in 1988.*
Kristiansand, *Dom Kirken, 36, 13-2-4. in G. - Hung Dead, Automatic Carillon, All these bells were cast by Olsen-Nauen in 1990.*
Molde, *Dom Kirken, 26, 13-2-4. in G. - Carillon, All these Bells were cast by Olsen-Nauen in 1983.*
Oslo, *Radhuset, 49, 80cwt. in A. - Carillon.*
Sandefjord, *Kirken, 25, 25cwt. in E♯. - Carillon, All these Bells were cast by Schilling in 1931.*
Stavanger, *Dom Kirken, 49, 21-2-0. in E. - Carillon.*
Tonsberg, *Sems Sparebank, 25, 13-2-4. in G. - Hung Dead, Automatic Carillon, All these Bells were cast by Olsen-Nauen in 1971.*
(Transportable) Tonsberg, *Trans Porta Belt, 52, 21cwt. in F. - Hung Dead, Mobile Carillon, All these Bells were cast by Olsen-Nauen between 1972 - 1984.*
Trondheim, *Nidaros Dom Kirken, 37, 13-2-4. in G. - Carillon, All Cast by Olsen-Nauen in 1976.*

PAKISTAN.

Lahore, Cathedral Church of the Resurrection, **6**, 17-3-0. in F, - Unringable.

PERU.

Lima, *(R.C.), 25, in C, - Automatic Carillon, All the Bells were cast by VanBergen in 1954.*

Lima , *Iglesia de Nuestra Senora de Fatima, 25, in G, - Electric Keyboard, Carillon, Cast by Petit and Fritsen in 1957.*

POLAND.

Gdansk , *Catharine Churche, 49, - Carillon.*
Gdansk , *Ratusz, 37, - Carillon.*

PORTUGAL.

Mafra , *Palacio Nacional de Mafra, 53, 192cwt. - Carillon, All Cast by Willem Witlockx.*
Porto , *Torre da Igreja Dos Clerigos, 49, 180cwt. - Carillon, All Cast by Nicolas La Vache.*

PUERTO RICO.

Bayamon , *Collegia Santa Rita, 23, in C, - Carillon, Cast by Petit & Fritsen in 1962.*
Hato Rey , *San Juan, Polytechnic University de Puerto Rico, 47, in F, - Electric Keyboard, Carillon, All the Bells were cast by Petit and Fritsen in 1992.*
Rio Piedras , *San Juan, University de Puerto Rico, Franklin D.Roosevelt Tower, 25, - Automatic Carillon.*

RUSSIA.

Moscow , *Red Square, 1, 5000cwt., - This Bell is Cracked and you can walk through the Crack in the Bell, This Bell is placed on the Floor in the Square and is called the "Tsar-Bell", This is the Largest Bell in the World.*
St Petersburg (Ex Leningrad) , *Gatchina Palace, (Clock Tower), 3, 6-1-12, - Hung Dead, These Bells were cast at Voronezh Bell Foundry in Russia.*

SLOVAKIA.

Bardejov , *St Egidius Cathedral, 3, 80cwt , The Two Largest are Automatically Swing Chimed and the Smallest is Hung Dead.*
Kozany , *Uniate Church of Virgin Mary Patroness, 1, - Chimed Only, This is one of the Oldest Bells in Eastern Slovakia and was cast in 1406. Also this Church is made of Wood.*

SLOVENIA.

Sentjost , *Saint Jost, 3, 29-2-4., - Chimed Only, The Tenor Bell is Made of Iron and the Treble and Second are made of Bronze weighing 8-0-14 and 13-2-18.*
Ustje , *St Justusus, 3, - Automatic Chiming.*

SOUTH AFRICA.

Cape Town , *Cape of Good Hope, City Hall, War Memorial Carillon, 39, 47-1-13., Carillon, All these Bells were cast by Taylors.*
Durban , *Natal, City Hall, 12, - Clock Chime.*
Port Elizabeth , *Eastern Cape, Campanile, 23, - Chimed Only.*

SOUTH KOREA.

Inchon, *Leave Centre Chapel, 5, 0-1-2., - These Bells were hung for ringing in 1956 but maybe now in another tower, These bells are in a two tier frame with a mixture of Korean and English bells, This Chapel is under the Authority of the Royal Army Chaplains Department.*
Sole , Cathedral, 1, 40cwt., - Hung Dead, The Cathedral was built around the bell which was cast by Taylors.

SPAIN.

In Spain most the bells are rung full circle but they do not have a wheel, stay or slider the bells are couterbalenced so they hold them on the balance by holding the headstock, On the bigger bells they put four ropes around the headstock to control the bell, In some towers the bells are rung by automatic swing chime motors and they disconnect the motor to ring the bell manually, Also most of the bells are hung in the walls of the tower.

Abejuela , Parroquial, 2, - Chimed Only.
Ademuz , Ermita de St Miguel de val de Sabina, 1, 0-1-20., - Chimed Only.
Ademuz , Ermita de Sta Barbara deMas del Olmo, 1, 1-0-4., - Chimed Only.
Ademuz , Purisima de Sesga, 1, 1-0-20., - Chimed Only.
Ademuz , Stos Pedro y Pablo, 5, 11-0-22., - Chimed Only.
Ador , Ermita St Josep, 1, - Automatically Swing Chimed Only.
Ador, Ntra Sra del Loreto, **3**, 9cwt., - Counterbalanced, No Wheels.
Adsubia, St Bernat de Forna, **2**, 0-2-22., - Counterbalanced, No Wheels, Cast by Roses in 1949 and 1950.
Adsubia , St Vicent Ferrer, 3, 8-1-16., - Automatically Swing Chimed Only.
Agorreta , Iglesia Parroquial, 1, 2-2-6., - Chimed Only, This Bell was cast in 1450.
Agost , St Pere, 3, 10-3-4., - Automatically Swing Chimed Only, All the Bells were cast by Roses in 1791.
Agres , St Miquel, 3, 11-3-8., - Automatically Swing Chimed Only, All the Bells were cast by Roses in 1944 and 1955.
Aguilon , Parroquia, 1, 3-2-8., - Chimed Only.
Aigues , St Francesc, 2, 7-0-10., - The Tenor is Hung Dead in a Steel Archway leading into the Church. The Treble is Hung for Automatic Swing Chiming in the Tower and weights 1-1-16.
Ain , St Ambros, 3, 7-0-1., - Chimed Only.
Aincioa , Iglesia Parroquial, 1, 1-3-8., - Chimed Only, This Bell was cast in 1450.
Ainsa , Santa Maria, 5, 19-2-0., - Automatically Swing Chimed Only.
Alacant , Ajuntament (City Hall), 2, 28-1-20., - Hung Dead, Clock Bells.
Alacant , Bon Pastor, 3, 2-2-0., - Hung Dead on the Roof of the Public Building , Chimed Only, All the Bells were cast by Salva in 1971 and 1980.
Alacant, Catedral de St Nicolau, **8**, 34-2-0. -, Counterbalanced, No Wheel, There are Two other Bells in the Tower but they are Chimed only.
Alacant, Mare de Deu de Gracia, **3**, 2-1-8., - Counterbalanced, No Wheels, There is also Two other Bells in the Tower Automatically Swing Chimed Only, Octagonal Tower.
Alacant, Mare de Deu de les Virtuts de Tanger, **2**, 3-0-18., - Counterbalanced, No Wheels, These Bells were cast by Roses in 1941 and 1950.
Alacant , Mare de Deu del Rosari, 2, 2-0-14., - Automatically Swing Chimed Only on the Roof.
Alacant , Mare de Deu Dels Angels, 2, 4-3-4., - Chimed Only.
Alacant , Misericordia, 4, 3-3-12., - Automatically Chimed Only.
Alacant, Ntra Sra de los Angeles, **1**, 2-3-4., - Counterbalanced, No Wheel, Hexagon Tower.
Alacant , Ntra Sra del Carmen del Robolledo, 1, 0-2-18., - Chimed Only.
Alacant , Resurreccio del Senyor, 1, 5-3-8., - Chimed Only.
Alacant, St Antoni de Padua, **1**, 5-3-8., - Counterbalanced, No Wheel, Triangular Tower.

Alacant, St Joan Baptiste, 3, 10-3-4., - Automatically Swing Chimed Only, All the Bells were cast by Roses in 1949.
Alacant, St Josep de les Carolines, 3, 5-1-20., - Automatically Swing Chimed Only.
Alacant, St Josep de Vilafranquesa, 3, - Automatically Swing Chimed Only.
Alacant, Salvador, 1, 0-1-20., - Chimed Only.
Alacant, Santiago de l'Abufereta, 3, 1-1-16., - Hung Dead on Roof Chimed Only, All the Bells were cast in 1911.
Alacant, Sta Cruz de Vistahermosa, 2, 4-3-4., - Automatically Chimed Only.
Alacant, Sta Maria, 5, 20cwt., - Automatically Chimed Only.
Alacant, Sta Teresa d'Avila, 2, - Chimed Only, These Bells were cast by Cabrillo.
Alacant, Sts Joans de Bacarot, 1, 0-2-18., - Chimed Only.
Alaquas, Assumpcio, 3, 10-2-0., - Chimed Only.
Alaquas, Colegio Operarias Catequistas, 1, 0-1-8., - Chimed Only.
Alaquas, Stma Creu, 1, 2-2-6., - Chimed Only.
Alaquas, Virgen del Olivar, 5, 6-1-10., - Chimed Only.
Albacete, Catedral de San Juan, 4, 22-2-4., - Counterbalanced, No Wheels, All these Bells were cast by Roses Hnos in 1947.
Albaida, Assumpcio, 8, 25-1-16., - Chimed Only.
Albaida, Ermita St Joan, 1, - Counterbalanced, No Wheel, This Bell was cast in 1775, This Bell is Housed in an opening in the Wall.
Albaida, Ermita Sant Miquel, 1, - Counterbalanced, No Wheel, This Bell was cast in 1643, This Bell is Housed in an opening in the Wall.
Albaida, Ermita Verge de Gracia, 1, 0-3-0., - Lever Chimed Only.
Albal, Ermita Sta Anna, 1, 0-3-14., - Chimed Only, This Bell was cast by Lavina in 1723 and apears to have a Gun Shot Wound.
Albal, Mare de Deu dels Angels, 4, 10-3-4., - Chimed Only.
Albal, St Carles Borromeu, 1, 2-2-6., - Automatically Swing Chimed Only.
Albalat de la Ribera, Ermita St Roc, 1, 1-0-20., - Counterbalanced, No Wheel, This Bell was cast in 1748.
Albalat Dels Sorells, Sts Reis, 5, 13-1-12., - Chimed Only.
Albalat Dels Tarongers, Immaculada Concepcio, 4, 8-0-16., - Automatically Swing Chimed Only.
Albarracin, Catedral de El Salvador, 6, 20-2-0., - Counterbalanced, No Wheels, There are also Three other Bells in the Tower.
Albarracin, Sta Maria, 2, 4-3-4., - Counterbalanced, No Wheels.
Albatera, Santiago Apostol, 3, 14-0-18., - Automatically Swing Chimed Only.
Albentosa, Ntra Sra de los Angeles, 2, - Chimed Only.
Albinyana, St Bartomeu, 2, 11-2-2., - Chimed Only.
Albinyana, Segrat Cor de les Peces, 2, 5-3-8., - Chimed Only.
Albocacer, Assumpcio, 5, 20-2-0., - Chimed Only.
Albocacer, Ermita de St Pau, 1, 1-1-8., - Chimed Only, Hung in a Bellcote.
Albocacer, Ermita Ntra Sra de la Esperanca, 1, 0-1-20., - Chimed Only.
Albocacer, Ermita St Miquel, 1, 0-1-26., - Chimed Only, Hung in a Bellcote.
Albocacer, Sts Joans, 1, 0-2-18., - Chimed Only, This Bell was cast in 1685.
Alborache, Santiago Apostol, 4, 5-3-8., - Automatically Swing Chimed Only.
Alboraia, Assumpcio, 6, 18-0-6., - Automatically Swing Chimed Only.
Alboraia, Cementeri Parroquial, 1, 0-1-6., - Chimed Only.
Alboraia, Ermita Cristo de las Almaso de Vilanova, 2, 0-1-0., - Counterbalanced, No Wheels, The Tenor and Treble are the same weight.
Alboraia, Ermita de St Cristofol, 1, 0-0-24., - Chimed Only.
Alboraia, Ermita dels Peixets, 1, 0-1-2., - Chimed Only.
Albuixech, Ntra Sra de Albuixec, 7, 13-1-12., - Automatically Swing Chimed Only.
Albuixech, St Benito Abad de Mahuella, 2, 0-1-0., - Chimed Only, The Tenor was cast in 1650.
Alcacer, Convent Ma Auxiliadora, 2, 0-2-18., - Chimed Only.

Alcacer , *St Marti, 6, 20cwt., - Chimed Only.*
Alcala de Chivert , *Campanar Municipal (Clock Tower), 10, 18-0-6., - Automatically Chimed Only, Clock Bells, Detatched Octagonal Tower.*
Alcala de Chivert , *Ermita St Antoni de Cap i Corb, 1, 0-3-8., - Swing Chimed Only.*
Alcala de Chivert , *Ermita St Benet i Sta Llucia, 1, - Chimed Only in Bellcote.*
Alcala de Chivert , *Esglesia de Alcoceber, 1, 0-1-20., - Chimed Only.*
Alcala de Chivert , *Magatzem Municipal, 3, 9cwt., - Chimed Only, All the Bells were cast by Roses in 1906 and 1941.*
Alcala de Henares, Iglesia Magistral de los Santos Justo y Pastor, **2**, 8-0-16. - Counterbalanced, No Wheels.
Alcalali , *Ermita Mare de Deu del Calvali, 2, 0-3-8., - Chimed Only.*
Alcalali, *Nativitat, 1, 0-0-18., - Counterbalanced, No Wheel, There is also Three More Bells that are Automatically Swing Chimed Only with a Tenor of 6-3-2. and One Bell Hung Dead, The Treble was cast in 1450.*
Alcalali, Purissima Concepcio de La Llosa de Camatxo, **2**, 2-0-14., - Counterbalanced, No Wheels.
Alcanar , *Parroquia, 1, 7-0-10., - Chimed Only.*
Alacanter de Xuquer , *Immaculada, 3, 3-3-12., - Chimed Only.*
Alcocer de Planes , *St Josep, 8, 3-3-12., - Chimed Only, Four of the Bells were cast by Portilla in 2001.*
Alcoi , *Cor de Jesus, 2, 1-1-16., - Automatically Swing Chimed Only, These Bells were cast by Roses.*
Alcoi , *Ermita St Antoni Abad, 1, 0-1-2., - Chimed Only.*
Alcoi , *Mare de Deu dels Desemparats, 2, 1-0-4., - Chimed Only.*
Alcoi , *Nativitat de Sta Maria, 6, 36-2-22., - Automatically Swing Chimed Only, There is also Two more Bells in the Tower Hung Dead with a Tenor of 20cwt.*
Alcoi , *Sant Jordi, 4, 5-3-8., - Automatically Swing Chimed Only.*
Alcolecha , *Ermita Verge dels Desamparats de Beniafe, 1, 0-1-2., - Chimed Only.*
Alcolecha, St Vincent Ferrer, **5**, 8-1-16., - Counterbalanced, No Wheels.
Alcorisa, Santa Maria la Mayor, **3**, 8-0-16., - Counterbalanced, No Wheels, All the Bells were cast by Cabrillo Mayor of Salamanca in 1939, 1940 and 1952.
Alcublas , *St Antonio Abad, 4, 11-0-22., - Automatically Swing Chimed Only.*
Alcudia de Veo, Assumpcio de Veo, **2**, 1-3-8., - Counterbalanced, No Wheels, The Tenor was cast in 1777.
Alcudia de Veo , *St Miquel, 3, 4-0-14., - Automatically Swing Chimed Only.*
Aldaia , *El Salvador i Ntra Sra de la Salette, 3, 6-3-2., - Chimed Only, All the Bells were cast by Manclus Salvador of Valencia in 1967 and 1970.*
Aldaia , *Ermita del Pilar, 1, 0-1-16., - Chimed Only.*
Aldaia , *Ermita Ntra Sra de la Salette, 1, 0-1-20., - Chimed Only.*
Aldaia , *Ermita St Rafel, 1, 0-0-20., - Chimed Only, This Bell was cast in 1908.*
Aldaia , *Ntra Sra de l'Anunciacio, 5, 18-0-6., - Automatically Swing Chimed Only, There is also One Bell in the Church Hung Dead on the Wall and weights 0-0-4.*
Aldea Del Fresno , *Iglesia Parroquial, 3, - Automatically Swing Chimed Only.*
Aldehuela de Liestos, Asuncion, **2**, 2-2-0., - Counterbalanced, No Wheels.
Alfafar , *Col.Legi de la Inmaculada, 3, 0-0-22., - Chimed Only.*
Alfafar , *Mare de Deu del Do, 4, 8-1-16., - Automatically Swing Chimed Only, There are also Two more Bells in the Tower which are Chimed Only.*
Alfafara , *Transfiguracio del Senyor, 3, 8-1-16., - Chimed Only.*
Alfara de Algimia , *St Agusti, 2, 5-3-8., - Chimed Only.*
Alfara del Patriarca , *Fosforera Espanola, 1, 0-3-8., - Chimed Only.*
Alfara del Patriarca , *St Bertomeu, 5, 9-3-8., - Chimed Only, The Treble was cast in 1538 and the rest were cast by Roses in 1939.*
Alfarp , *St Jaume, 4, 8-2-16., - Automatically Swing Chimed Only.*

Alfauir, Ntra Sra del Roser, **2**, 3-2-8., - Counterbalanced, No Wheels.
Alfaz del Pi, St Josep, 3, 2-5-0., - Automatically Swing Chimed Only, The Second and Tenor are the same weight.
Alfondeguilla, St Bartolome, 4, 5-3-8., - Chimed Only.
Algar de Palancia, Ntra Sra de las Mercedes, 3, 7-0-10., - Chimed Only.
Algemesi, Ntra Sra del Pilar, 4, 3-3-12., - Chimed Only.
Algemesi, St Jaume, 5, 22-2-4., - Automatically Swing Chimed Only, There are also Three other Bells in the Tower Two Hung Dead and the Third Hung for Lever Chiming Only.
Algimia de Alfara, St Vincent Ferrer, 3, 1-1-24., - Chimed Only.
Algimia de Almonacid, St Juan Bautista, 4, 8-2-16., - Chimed Only.
Allande, Capilla de St Jose en Castello, Berducedo, 1, 1-0-4., - Chimed Only, This Bell was cast in 1698.
Allande, Parroquial (Celon), 2, 1-0-4., - Chimed Only, The Treble was cast in 1222.
Almassera, Stm Sacrament, 6, 17-0-14., - Chimed Only.
Almassora, Ermita Sta Quiteria, **1**, 0-2-18., - Counterbalanced, No Wheel.
Almassora, La Nativitat, 6, 24-1-0., - Chimed Only.
Almazan, St Miguel, 2, - Chimed Only, The Tenor was cast in 1717.
Almazan, Torre del Reloj, 2, - Chimed Only, The Tenor was cast in 1791.
Almedijar, Virgin de los Angeles, **3**, 5-3-8., - The Treble is Counterbalanced, No Wheel and weights 1-3-8. the rest are Automatically Swing Chimed Only.
Almeria, Catedral de Ntra Sra de la Encarnacion, **6**, 27-0-24., - Counterbalanced, No Wheels, There are also Two other Bells Hung Dead.
Almeria, San Jose, 2, 3-1-4., - Automatically Swing Chimed Only, Cast by Linares in 1945.
Almiserat, Nativitat de Ntra Sra, 2, - Chimed Only.
Almoines, St Jaume Apostol, 3, 7-3-4., - Automatically Swing Chimed Only.
Almoradi, Parroquia, 4, 25-1-16., - Automatically Swing Chimed Only.
Almudaina, St Bertomeu, 2, 8-2-16., - Automatically Swing Chimed Only.
Alpuente, Campo de Abajo, 1, 0-2-18., - Chimed Only in a Belcote.
Alpuente, Campo de Arriba, 1, 0-2-18., - Chimed Only in a Belcote.
Alpuente, Ermita de St Rogue de Baldovar, **1**, 1-1-16., - Counterbalanced, No Wheel, This Bell was cast by Roses in 1948
Alpuente, Ermita Madre Sacramento de la Carrasca, 1, 0-1-26., - Chimed Only.
Alpuente, La Almeza, 1, - Chimed Only in a Belcote.
Alpuente, Ntra Sra de la Piedad, 3, 13-1-12., - Automatically Swing Chimed Only, There is also Two Hemispherical Bells Hung Dead and the Tenor weighs 3-1-20, Octagonal Tower.
Alpuente, St Bernabe de Corcolilla, **3**, 5-0-8., - Counterbalanced, No Wheels, The Tenor was cast in 1773.
Alpuente, St Jose de la Cuevarruz, **2**, 1-1-16., - Counterbalanced, No Wheels, The Treble was cast in 1750.
Alpuente, St Miguel de El Collado, **2**, 3-0-2., - The Treble is Counterbalanced with No Wheel and weights 2-0-24. The Tenor is Automatically Swing Chimed Only, Cast by Roses in 1935 and 1942.
Alqueria D'Asnar, St Miquel, 2, 2-2-0., - Chimed Only.
Alquerias de nino Perdido, Convent Carmelites, 2, 0-0-22., - Chimed Only.
Altea, Mare de Deu del Consol, 3, 16-2-14., - Automatically Swing Chimed Only.
Altea, Sant Francesc, **2**, 1-1-24., - Counterbalanced, No Wheels.
Altea, Santa Anna d'Altea la Vella, **3**, 1-2-26., - Counterbalanced, No Wheels.
Altura, St Miguel Arcangel, 4, 17-2-4., - Chimed Only, Cast by Manclus in 1985 and 1989.
Altura, Santuario de la Cueva Santa, 2, 6-0-14., - Automatically Swing Chimed Only, The Tenor was cast by Mestre Miquel in 1641.
Alzira, Parroquia Ntra Sra de Lluch, 4, - Automatically Swing Chimed Only, All the Bells were cast by Manclus in 1963 and 1992.
Alzira, Santuari Ntra Sra de Lluch, 4, - Chimed Only.

Alzira, *Sta Caterina - Torre Campanar*, **2**, *- Counterbalanced, No Wheels, There is also One Bell on Display and another in the Church hung for Chiming Only.*
Alzira, *Sta Caterina - Torre Rellotge*, **5**, *5-3-8., - Chimed Only, The Back Three Bells were cast by Murua in 1940 and are Hung Dead.*
Andilla, Asuncion, **2**, 5-3-8., - Counterbalanced, No Wheels, These Bells were cast by Manclus in 1959.
Andilla, Purisima de Osset, **2**, 2-2-18., - Counterbalanced, No Wheels.
Andilla, Sta Paula de la Pobleta, **4**, 2-0-2., - Counterbalanced, No Wheels.
Andilla, *Virgin del Carmen de Artaj*, *1*, *0-0-20., - Chimed Only.*
Anna, *Ermita Stmo. Cristo de la Providencia*, *1*, *0-2-18., - Chimed Only.*
Anna, *Inmaculada Concepcion*, *4*, *19-2-0., - Automatically Swing Chimed Only.*
Ansoain, *Iglesia Parroquial*, *1*, *15-1-12., - Chimed Only, This Bell was cast in 1550.*
Aoiz, *Iglesia Parroquial*, *1*, *1-3-8., - Chimed Only, This Bell was cast in 1500.*
Aranuel, *St Miguel Arcangel*, *4*, *7-0-10., - Chimed Only.*
Aras de Alpuente, *Ermita Sta Catalina*, *1*, *0-2-22., - Chimed Only.*
Aras de Alpuente, *Ntra Sra de los Angeles*, *5*, *6-1-10., - Automatically Swing Chimed Only.*
Aras de Alpuente, *St Jose de Losilla de Aras*, *2*, *1-1-16., - Chimed Only, Cast by Manclus in 1987.*
Arcos de las Salinas, *Parroquial*, *4*, *- Chimed Only.*
Ares del Maestre, Assumpcio, **5**, 13-2-22., - Counterbalanced, No Wheels.
Ares del Maestre, *Ermita St Antoni del Mas de la val*, *1*, *0-1-2., - Chimed Only in a Belcote.*
Ares del Maestre, *Ermita Sta Elena*, *1*, *0-0-16., - Chimed Only in a Belcote.*
Argelita, *Sta Ana*, *4*, *8-1-16., - Automatically Swing Chimed Only.*
Artana, *St Joan Baptiste*, *5*, *13-1-12., - Automatically Swing Chimed Only.*
Aspe, *Ntra Sra del Socorro*, *7*, *22-2-4., - Automatically Swing Chimed Only.*
Ateca, *San Francisco del Barrio de San Martin*, *2*, *2-0-24., - Chimed Only.*
Ateca, Santa Maria, **4**, 15-1-12., - Counterbalanced, No Wheels.
Atzeneta D'Albaida, *Ermita Cristo de la Fe*, *3*, *- Automatically Swing Chimed Only.*
Atzeneta D'Albaida, *St Joan Baptiste*, *4*, *15-1-12., - Automatically Swing Chimed Only, All the Bells were cast by Roses Between 1966 - 1991.*
Atzeneta del Maestrat, *Col-legi Operaries Trinitaries Terciaries Descalces*, *1*, *0-0-10., - Chimed Only in a Belcote.*
Atzeneta del Maestrat, *Ermita de St Roc*, *1*, *0-0-18., - Chimed Only in a Belcote.*
Atzeneta del Maestrat, *Ermita del Castell*, *1*, *0-1-20., - Chimed Only in a Belcote.*
Atzeneta del Maestrat, *Ermita St Gregori*, *1*, *0-1-26., - Chimed Only in a Belcote.*
Atzeneta del Maestrat, *Ermita St Josep del Mas de la Vila*, *1*, *0-1-16., - Chimed Only in a Belcote, This Bell was cast by Roses in 1950.*
Atzeneta del Maestrat, *Ermita St Miquel de Torreselles*, *1*, *1-0-12., - Chimed Only This Bell was cast in 1721.*
Atzeneta del Maestrat, *Ermita Verge del Pilar del Pou de la Riba*, *1*, *0-1-16., - Chimed Only.*
Atzeneta del Maestrat, *Ermita Virgin del Loreto*, *1*, *0-1-16., - Chimed Only in a Belcote.*
Atzeneta del Maestrat, *St Betomeu*, *4*, *19-0-2., - Automatically Swing Chimed Only.*
Aviles, *Casa Consistorial*, *1*, *13-1-12., - Chimed Only, This Bell was cast in 1839.*
Avinyonet del Penedes, *St Salvador de les Gunyoles*, *2*, *3-3-12., - Chimed Only, The Treble was cast in 1701.*
Ayodar, St Vicente Ferrer, **3**, 10-2-0., - Counterbalanced, No Wheels.
Ayora, *Asuncion*, *5*, *28-1-20., - Automatically Swing Chimed Only exept Treble that is Chimed in a Belcote, The Third Bell was cast in 1496.*
Ayora, *Ermita St Anton*, *1*, *0-1-16., - Chimed Only, This Bell was cast by Moreno in 1949.*
Ayora, *Ermita St Blas*, *1*, *0-1-0., - Chimed Only.*
Ayora, *Ermita St Jose*, *1*, *1-1-8., - Chimed Only.*
Ayora, *Ermita Sta Lucia*, *1*, *0-1-16., - Chimed Only.*
Ayora, *Ermita Virgin del Rosario*, *1*, *1-1-0., - Chimed Only.*
Ayora, *Ex-Asilo de Sto Domingo*, *1*, *0-1-6., - Chimed Only.*

<u>Azkoitia</u>, *Ermita de los Stos. Emeterio y Celedonio*, 1, - Chimed Only, This Bell was cast by Erice Vidal (Pamplona) in 1881.
<u>Azuebar</u>, *St Mateo Apostol*, 3, 3-1-20., - Automatically Swing Chimed Only, The Second Bell was cast in 1795.
Baeza, Catedral de la Natividad de Nuestra Senora, 4, 39-3-2., - Counterbalanced, No Wheels, The Tenor was cast by Venero Bernardo in 1722.
<u>Bailo</u>, *Santa Barbara*, 1, - Chimed Only.
<u>Balaguer</u>, *Parroquia de Santa Maria*, 7, - Automatically Swing Chimed Only.
Balones, St Francesc d'Assis, 3, 9-2-4., - Counterbalanced, No Wheels, The Treble was cast by Casanova in 1643, The Second and Tenor were cast by Roses in 1882 and 1961.
Baneres, Ermita de St Jorge, 1, - Counterbalanced, No Wheel.
<u>Baneres</u>, *Ermita de Sta Maria Magdalena*, 1, - Chimed Only.
<u>Baneres</u>, *Ermita del Stmo Cristo*, 1, - Chimed Only.
<u>Baneres</u>, *Mare de Deu de la Misericordia*, 4, 17-2-4., - Automatically Swing Chimed Only, All the Bells were cast by Roses between 1940 and 1951.
<u>Banyeres del Penedes</u>, *Capella de St Miquel (Masies de St Miquel)*, 1, 1-1-16., - Chimed Only.
<u>Banyeres del Penedes</u>, *Ermita de St Ponc de Saifores*, 1, 0-2-18., - Chimed Only.
<u>Banyeres del Penedes</u>, *Sta Eulalia*, 2, 8-0-16., - Chimed Only, The Tenor was cast by Palles in 1773.
Barbastro, Catedral de la Asuncion de la Virgen, 4, 18-0-6., - Counterbalanced, No Wheels, There are also Two other Bells Hung Dead, Hexagonal Tower.
<u>Barcelona</u>, *Catalunya, Palau de la Generalitat de Catalunya, Carillo del Palau*, 49, - Carillon.
<u>Barracas</u>, *Ayuntamiento*, 1, 2-0-2., - Chimed Only, This Bell was cast by Cronos in 1967.
<u>Barracas</u>, *Ermita St Rogue*, 1, 0-1-2., - Chimed Only.
<u>Barracas</u>, *St Pedro Apostol*, 3, 4-2-12., - Automatically Swing Chimed Only.
<u>Barx</u>, *St Miquel Arcangel*, 2, 2-2-0., - Automatically Swing Chimed Only, Cast by Roses in 1898.
Barxeta, Stos Desposorios, 1, 1-3-8., - Counterbalanced, No Wheel, This Bell was cast by Roses in 1961.
<u>Bejis</u>, *Ermita del Loreto*, 1, 3-1-4., - Chimed Only, This Bell was cast by Garcia in 1763.
<u>Bejis</u>, *St Juan Bautista de Arteas de Abajo*, 1, 0-0-16., - Chimed Only, This Bell was cast in 1722.
<u>Bejis</u>, *Virgin de los Angeles*, 2, 7 1 8., - Chimed Only, These Bells were cast by Roses in 1944.
<u>Belgida</u>, *St Llorenc*, 3, 8-0-16., - Chimed Only.
<u>Bellreguard</u>, *St Miquel Arcangel*, 4, 18-0-6., - Automatically Swing Chimed Only, All the Four Bells were cast by Roses Hnos (Silla) between 1939 - 1945, There are also Two other Bells in the Tower.
<u>Bellvei del Penedes</u>, *Sta Maria*, 2, 7-0-10., - Chimed Only, These Bells were cast by Mestres in 1738.
<u>Benabarre</u>, *Castle*, 5, 20cwt., - Chimed Only.
<u>Benafer</u>, *Ermita St Roque*, 1, 0-0-18., - Chimed Only.
<u>Benafer</u>, *Sto Cristo del Salvador*, 4, 4-0-14., - Chimed Only, All the Bells were cast by Roses in 1948.
Benafigos, Ermita Virgin de la Ortisella, 1, 0-1-20., - Counterbalanced, No Wheel.
Benafigos, St Joan Baptiste, 1, 1-3-8., - Counterbalanced, No Wheel, This Bell was cast in 1691.
<u>Benageber</u>, *Ermita del Pilar (Embalse)*, 1, 0-1-20., - Chimed Only, This Bell was cast in 1730.
<u>Benageber</u>, *Ermita St Isidro*, 1, - Chimed Only.
Benageber, Purissima Concepcio, 3, 2-2-6., - Counterbalanced, No Wheels.
Benaguasil, Assumpcio de Ntra Sra, 6, 18-0-6., - *Counterbalanced, No Wheels, There is also Three other Bells in the Tower Hung Dead with a Tenor of 3-2-8.*
<u>Benaguasil</u>, *Gratia Dei*, 3, 2-5-0., - Automatically Swing Chimed Only.
<u>Benaguasil</u>, *Mare de Deu del Pilar*, 1, 0-0-24., - Chimed Only, Hung in a Belcote and was cast in 1772.
<u>Benaguasil</u>, *Montiel*, 1, 1-2-6., - Chimed Only, This Bell was cast by Manclus in 1972.
<u>Benasal</u>, *Assumpcio de Ntra Sra*, 7, 15-1-12., - Automatically Swing Chimed Only.

Benasal, Ermita de St Cristofol, 1, 2-1-8., - Chimed Only, Hung in a Belcote.
Benasal, Ermita de St Roc, **1**, 1-0-12., - Counterbalanced, No Wheel, Hung in a Belcote, This Bell was cast in 1598.
Benasal, Ermita St Libori, 1, 0-2-6., - Automatically Swing Chimed Only.
Benasau, St Pere, 3, 5-2-14., - Automatically Swing Chimed Only, The Treble was cast by Sainz in 1773.
Benasau, Sta Maria dels Angels d'Ares, **2**, 1-2-6., - Counterbalanced, No Wheels, The Treble was cast in 1700.
Benavites, Ntra Sra dels Angels, 3, 9-3-8., - Chimed Only, The Tenor was cast by Lavina Joan in 1779.
Beneixama, Ermita de la Divina Aurora, 1, - Chimed Only, Hung in a Belcote.
Beneixama, Ermita de St Vincent Ferrer, 1, - Chimed Only, Hung in a Belcote.
Beneixama, Ermita del Stmo Cristo, 1, - Chimed Only.
Beneixama, Escola Llar (Antic Convent), 1, - Chimed Only, Hung in a Belcote.
Beneixama, St Joan Baptista, 4, 14-2-2., - Automatically Swing Chimed Only, There is Also Two Bells Hung Dead with a Tenor weight of 10-2-0.
Benetusser, Institut Verge del Socorro, 1, 1-2-16., - Chimed Only.
Benetusser, Mare de Deu del Socorro, 3, 11-2-2., - Chimed Only, Cast by Roses in 1962.
Beniarbeig, St Joan Baptiste, **3**, 9-2-4., - Counterbalanced, No Wheels.
Beniarda, St Joan Baptiste, 4, 9-3-8., - Automatically Swing Chimed Only, All the Bells were cast by Roses between 1852 and 1990.
Beniarjo, Ajuntament, 3, 1-2-16., - Chimed Only, Hung Dead in a Steel Frame on the Roof, All the Bells were cast by Diez Moises in 1925 and 1926.
Beniarjo, St Joan Baptiste, 4, 13-1-12., - Automatically Swing Chimed Only, There is also another Bell in the Church Counterbalanced with No Wheel that is Swing Chimed Only this Bell was cast in 1700 and weights 0-0-14.
Beniarres, Ermita Sto Cristo Afligidos, **1**, 6-2-6., - Counterbalanced, No Wheel.
Beniarres, St Pere Apostol, 3, 11-2-2., - Automatically Swing Chimed Only, There is also Two Hemispherical Bells Hung Dead.
Beniatjar, Ntra Sra de l'Encarnacio, **3**, 14-0-18., - Counterbalanced, No Wheels.
Benicarlo, Ermita St Gregori, 1, 0-2-18., - Chimed Only, Hung in a Belcote.
Benicarlo, St Bertomeu, 5, 20cwt., - Automatically Swing Chimed Only, There is also Three other Bells Hung Dead with a Tenor of 10-3-4, Detached Hexagonal Tower.
Benicarlo, St Pere, 2, 0-2-18., - Chimed Only, Both Bells are the same weight.
Benicassim, Convent Agustines, 1, 0-3-8., - Chimed Only.
Benicassim, Convent de les Oblates, 2, 0-3-8., - Chimed Only, The Tenor was cast in 1690.
Benicassim, Convent dels Carmelites, 2, 0-1-26., - Chimed Only, The Treble was cast in 1657 and the Tenor was cast in 1732.
Benicassim, Ermita Desert de les Palmes, 1, 0-0-14., - Chimed Only, This Bell was cast in 1691.
Benicassim, Monestir del Desert de les Palmes, 3, 5-0-8., - Automatically Swing Chimed Only, Hung in a Belcote.
Benicolet, St Joan Baptista, 4, 8-1-16., - Chimed Only, The Treble was cast in 1550 and there is also another Bell Hung for chiming in the Church.
Benidoleig, Stma Sang, 4, 9-3-8., - Automatically Swing Chimed Only, The Treble was cast in 1777. The rest were cast by Roses in 1960, 1926 and 1897.
Benidorm, St Jaume, 5, 9-2-4., - Automatically Swing Chimed Only.
Benifaio, St Pere Apostol, 4, 18-1-26., - Automatically Swing Chimed Only, All the Bells were cast by Roses in 1940.
Benifairo de les Valls, Ermita Mare de Deu del Bon Succes, 1, 0-0-24., - Chimed Only, This Bell was cast in 1475.
Benifairo de les Valls, St Gil Abat, **4**, 9-3-8., - Counterbalanced, No Wheels.
Benifallim, St Miquel Arcangel, 3, 7-0-10., - Automatically Swing Chimed Only.
Benifato, St Miquel, 2, 4-0-14., - Chimed Only.

Benifla, St Jaume Apostol, 1, - Chimed Only in a Belcote.
Beniganim, St Miquel Arcangel, 8, - Chimed Only, Octagonal Tower.
Benigembla, St Josep, 3, 5-3-8., - Automatically Swing Chimed Only, The Treble was cast by Tormo in 1708.
Benijofar, Santiago Apostol, **2**, 4-0-14., - Counterbalanced, No Wheels.
Benilloba, Nativitat, 4, 9-3-8., - Automatically Swing Chimed Only.
Benillup, Ntra Sra del Rosari, 2, 2-2-18., - Automatically Swing Chimed Only, The Treble was cast in 1799.
Benimantell, St Vincent Martir, **2**, 5-3-8., - Counterbalanced, No Wheels, These Bells were cast by Roses in 1940 and 1947. There is also Two Hemispherical Bells in the Tower Hung Dead.
Benimarfull, Sta Anna, 4, 6-2-6., - Automatically Swing Chimed Only, All the Bells were cast by Roses between 1941 - 1963.
Benimasot, Purissima Concepcio, 2, 4-3-4., - Automatically Swing Chimed Only.
Benimeli, St Andreu, **2**, 4-0-14., - Counterbalanced, No Wheels, These Bells were cast by Roses in 1940. There is also Two other Bells Hung Dead with a Tenor of 10-2-0. These Bells were cast by Roses in 1892.
Benimodo, Purissima Concepcio, 5, 13-1-12., - Automatically Swing Chimed Only.
Benimuslem, Purissima Concepcio, **3**, 4-2-0., - Counterbalanced, No Wheels.
Beniparrell, Sta Barbera, 4, 9cwt., - Automatically Swing Chimed Only.
Benirredra, Esclaves del Cor de Jesus, 1, 0-1-2., - Chimed Only.
Benirredra, St Llorenc Martir, **4**, 11-2-2., - Counterbalanced, No Wheels, All the Bells were cast by Roses in 1941.
Benissa, Convent Franciscans, 3, 6-0-14., - The Treble is Chimed Only and the rest are Automatically Swing Chimed Only.
Benissa, Purissima Concepcio i St Pere (Torre Dreta), 5, 25-1-16., - The Front Three Bells are Automatically Swing Chimed Only. The Fourth and Tenor are Chimed Only, The Tenor was cast by Portilla in 2001. (Torre Esquerra), 4, 14-2-2., - Chimed Only, The Bells were cast by Portilla in 2001.
Benissano, Sants Reis, **4**, 8-2-16., - Counterbalanced, No Wheels.
Benlloch, Assumpcio, 5, 15-1-12., - Automatically Swing Chimed Only, There is also another Two Bells in the Tower with a Tenor of 2-0-2. Chimed Only.
Betera, Bancaixa, 1, 2-0-2., - Chimed Only.
Betera, Calvari, 1, 1-0-12., - Chimed Only.
Betera, Campament Militar, 1, 1-2-26., - Automatically Swing Chimed Only.
Betera, Carme, 1, 2-0-24., - Chimed Only, This Bell was cast by Quiles in 1888.
Betera, Castell, 2, 5-1-20., - Chimed Only, These Bells were cast in 1897.
Betera, Club de Golf Escorpion, 1, 0-1-0., - Chimed Only.
Betera, Mare de Deu dels Desemparats, 1, 2-0-24., - Hung Dead, Chimed Only.
Betera, Purissima, 4, 14-0-18., - Automatically Swing Chimed Only.
Betexi, Mare de Deu dels Angels, 7, 5-1-0., - Chimed Only.
Betexi, St Antoni, 1, 0-3-8., - Chimed Only.
Biar, Ermita de Sta Lucia, **2**, - Counterbalanced, No Wheels.
Biar, Ermita Ntra Sra de Loreto, 1, - Chimed Only.
Biar, Ermita St Roque, 2, - Chimed Only.
Biar, La Asuncion, 8, 27-3-2., - Automatically Swing Chimed Only, There is also a Hemispherical Bell Hung Dead and weights 24-1-0.
Biar, Santuario Ntra Sra de Gracia, 1, - Chimed Only.
Bicorp, St Juan Evangelista, 3, 7-3-4., - Automatically Swing Chimed Only.
Bilbo, Sta Iglesia Catedral Basilica del Sr Santiago, 11, 39-0-8., - Four Bells Hung Dead the rest are Automatically Swing Chimed Only, All the Bells were cast by Murua, Hijos de (Gasteiz/Vitoria) in 1916.
Binaced, San Marcos Evangelista, **3**, 8-1-16., - Counterbalanced, No Wheels.
Binefar, San Pedro, 1, - Chimed Only, This Bell was cast by Barnola in 1796.

Bocairent , Agustines Recoletes, 2, 1-3-8., - Automatically Swing Chimed Only, Cast by Roses in 1952.
Bocairent , Assumpcio, 7, 24-1-0., - Five Bells are Automatically Swing Chimed Only the Rest are Chimed Only.
Bocairent , Cementiri de Bocairent, 1, 1-0-4., - Chimed Only.
Bocairent , Ermita St Crist (Calvari), 2, 1-3-8., - Chimed Only, Cast by Roses in 1952.
Bocairent , Residencia d'ancians, 1, 0-0-24., - Chimed Only, This Bell was cast in 1750.
Bolbaite, St Francisco de Paula, **3**, 6-2-6., - Counterbalanced, No Wheels.
Bolulla , St Josep, **3**, 7-3-4., - Counterbalanced, No Wheels.
Bonastre , Sta Maria Magdalena, 4, 8-1-16., - Chimed Only, The Treble was cast in 1620.
Bonrepos I Mirambell , Ermita del Pilar de Cases de Barcena, 1, 0-1-2., - Chimed Only, This Bell was cast in 1790.
Bonrepos I Mirambell , Ermita St Joan Baptista de Mirambell, 2, 2-0-14., - Chimed Only, These Bells were cast by Roses in 1947.
Bonrepos I Mirambell , Mare de Deu del Pilar, 4, 7-3-4., - Automatically Swing Chimed Only, All the Bells were cast by Roses in 1945.
Botorrita , San Agustin, **2**, 4-3-4., - Counterbalanced, No Wheels.
Bufali , Ntra Sra de Loreto, **2**, 4-3-4., - Counterbalanced, No Wheels.
Bugarra , St Juan Bautista, 4, 4-1-4., - Automatically Swing Chimed Only, Hung in a Belcote.
Bunol , St Pedro, 3, 9-2-4., - Automatically Swing Chimed Only, The Second was cast in 1688.
Burgo De Osma, Catedral de San Pedro de Osma, **12**, 54-3-6., - Counterbalanced, No Wheels, There is also a Lever Chimed Bell in the Tower.
Burgos , Catedral de Burgos, 16, 61cwt., - Automatic Chimed Only, These Bells are Not all in one Tower there is Four in (Tower One), Four in (Tower Two), Four in (Tower Three), Three in a Hexagonal Tower and One on the Roof.
Burgos , Cerveceria Ojeda, 3, - Automatically Chimed Only.
Burjassot , Ajuntament, 1, 1-1-24., - Chimed Only.
Burjassot , Ermita St Roc, 1, 0-2-6., - Chimed Only.
Burjassot , Htas Desamparats, 1, 0-0-22., - Chimed Only, This Bell was cast in 1904.
Burjassot , Natividad de Cantereria, 3, 1-3-8., - Automatically Swing Chimed Only, The Treble is Hung on the Roof of the Tower.
Burjassot , St Joan de la Ribera, 2, 0-3-8., - Chimed Only, Cast by Roses in 1945 and 1954.
Burjassot , St Miquel Arcangel, 7, 15-2-26., - Chimed Only, The Front Three Bells were cast by Cronos in 1964. Three Bells were cast by Roses Between 1827 and 1943. The Fifth Bell was cast by Portilla in 1992.
Burjassot , Sgdo Corazon de Jesus, 2, 3-0-2., - Chimed Only, Cast by Roses in 1960 and 1964.
Burjassot , Trinitat, 1, 0-0-20., - Chimed Only, This Bell was cast in 1913.
Burriana , Col. Legi Salesians, 1, 0-3-0., - Chimed Only.
Burriana , Ermita de la Misericordia, 1, 0-1-26., - Chimed Only.
Burriana , La Merce, 3, 3-2-8., - Automatically Swing Chimed Only.
Burriana , St Blai, 1, 0-2-2., - Chimed Only, This Bell was cast by Martinez in 1891.
Burriana , Salvador, 9, 26-2-6., - Chimed Only, Octagonal Tower.
Busot , St Llorenc, **2**, 5-2-14., - Counterbalanced, No Wheels, These Bells were cast by Roses in 1944.
Cabanes , St Joan Baptiste, 1, - Chimed Only, This Bell was cast in 1650.
Calafell , Sta Creu, 2, 21-0-2., - Chimed Only, The Tenor was cast in 1818.
Calahorra, Catedral de Sta Maria, **7**, 29-2-20., - Counterbalanced, No Wheels, There are also Three Bells Hung Dead with a Tenor weighing 63-0-12., One of the Bells was cast in 1350 and is Elongated.
Calamocha , Sta Maria La Mayor, **4**, 13-1-12., - Counterbalanced, No Wheels, The Third and Tenor are the Same Weight.
Calig , Ajuntament, 2, 8-2-16., - Chimed Only, These Bells were cast by Metal Font in Madrid in 1913.

Calig, Convent de Trinitaries, 1, 0-1-2., - Chimed Only.
Calig, Ermita Mare de Deu del Socos, 1, 1-0-4., - Chimed Only in a Belcote.
Calig, St Llorenc, 1, 2-2-6., - Chimed Only, This Bell was cast in 1858.
Calles, Ermita de Sta Quiteria, 1, 0-1-20., - Chimed Only, Hung in the Walls of the Church above a Crossing.
Calles, Purisima Concepcion, 4, 10-3-4., - Automatically Swing Chimed Only, There is also Two other Bells in the Tower that are on Display.
Callosa d'en Sarria, Espadanya Restaurant Casa Marcos, 1, 0-0-14., - Counterbalanced, No Wheel Chimed Only on the Roof.
Callosa d'en Sarria, St Joan Baptiste, 5, 19-0-2., - The Treble is Chimed Only, The Rest are Automatically Swing Chimed Only.
Calp, Antic Ajuntament, 1, - Chimed Only, Hung Dead.
Calp, Ermita san Salvador, 1, 0-2-18., - Chimed Only.
Calp, Mare de Deu de les Neus, 4, 6-0-14., - The Second is Chimed Only the Rest are Automatically Swing Chimed Only.
Calzada de Valdunciel, Parroquia, 4, 10-2-0., - Chimed Only.
Caminreal, Parroquial, 2, 7-3-4., - Automatically Swing Chimed Only, These Bells were cast in 1829.
Campo de Mirra, Ermita St Bertomeu, 1, - Chimed Only in a Belcote.
Campo de Mirra, St Bertomeu, 4, 9-2-4., - Automatically Swing Chimed Only.
Camporrobles, Asuncion, 3, 3-3-12., - Counterbalanced, No Wheels, There is also another Bell in the Tower that is Chimed Only and weights 1-0-4.
Canada, Ermita Virgin del Carmen, 1, 0-1-20., - Chimed Only in a Belcote, This Bell was cast in 1892.
Canada, St Cristofol, 3, 5-0-8., - Automatically Swing Chimed Only.
Canals, Oratori dels Borgia, 1, 0-3-0., Counterbalanced, No Wheel.
Canals, St Antoni Abad (Torre Est), 2, 19-0-2., - Chimed Only, Hung Dead, (Torre Oest), 4, 20-2-0., - Automatically Swing Chimed Only.
Canals, St Jaume d'Aiacor, 2, 7-3-4., - Automatically Swing Chimed Only.
Candas, Capilla de St Roque, 1, 0-1-2., - Chimed Only, This Bell was cast in 1801.
Candasnos, Nuestra Senora de la Asuncion, 4, 5-0-2., - Chimed Only.
Canet d'en Berenguer, St Pedro Apostol, 3, 9-2-4., - Chimed Only, All the Bells were cast by Roses in 1943 and 1964.
Canet Lo Roig, St Miquel Arcangel, 4, 13-2-22., - Chimed Only.
Cangas del Narcea, Convento Predicadores de Corias, 1, 0-1-20., - Chimed Only, This Bell was cast in 1726.
Cangas del Narcea, Iglesia Colegiata, 3, 5-3-8., - Chimed Only, The Treble was cast in 1845. The Second was cast in 1550. The Tenor was cast in 1587.
Cangas del Narcea, Iglesia de Castanedo, Cibuyo, 2, 1-1-8., - Chimed Only, Cast in 1763 and 1819.
Cangas del Narcea, Parroquial Cibuyo, 2, 1-1-16., - Chimed Only, Cast in 1577 and 1806.
Cangas del Narcea, Parroquial de Besullo, 1, 1-1-24., - Chimed Only.
Cangas del Narcea, Parroquial de Corias, 1, 1-3-8., - Chimed Only, This Bell was cast in 1327.
Caravaca de la Cruz, Real Alcazar Santuario, 4, 5-2-14., - Chimed Only.
Caravaca de la Cruz, Salvador, 6, 25-1-16., - The **Fifth** and **Tenor** are Counterbalanced, No Wheels. The Two and Three are Automatically Swing Chimed Only the rest are Chimed Only.
Carcaixent, Assumpcio, 9, 27-0-24., - Chimed Only.
Carcaixent, Col. Legi de Maria Inmaculada, 1, 1-0-20., - Chimed Only.
Carcaixent, Convent de Dominiques, 1, 0-0-24., - Chimed Only.
Carcaixent, Convent St Francesc, 2, 0-2-18., - Chimed Only, The Treble was cast in 1731 and the Tenor in 1911.
Carcaixent, St Antoni de Padua, 1, 0-2-6., - Chimed Only, This Bell was cast in 1654.

<u>Carcaixent</u>, St Bartolome de Cogullada, 3, 6-1-10., - Chimed Only, The Treble and Second were cast by Roses in 1954 and 1803. The Tenor was cast in 1428.
<u>Carcaixent</u>, St Francesc de Paula, 1, 2-0-2., - Chimed Only, This Bell was cast in 1912.
<u>Carcaixent</u>, Virgin de Aguas Vivas de la Barraca, 1, 1-1-24., - Chimed Only.
<u>Carenas</u>, Santa Ana, 2, 5-3-8., - Chimed Only.
<u>Cartagena</u>, Santa Maria de Gracia, 3, 22-2-4., - Chimed Only, Hung Dead in a Bellcote.
<u>Casas Altas</u>, Stma Trinidad, 4, 3-0-2., - Chimed Only.
<u>Casas Bajas</u>, San Salvador, 3, 8-0-16., - Chimed Only.
<u>Cascante</u>, Basilica Ntra Sra del Romero, 1, - Chimed Only, This Bell was cast in 1425.
<u>Cascante del Rio</u>, Parroquia, 2, 9-1-3., - Chimed Only.
<u>Casinos</u>, Ermita de St Roc, 1, 0-0-24., - Chimed Only, This Bell was cast in 1770.
<u>Casinos</u>, Sta Barbera, 4, 6-0-14., - Automatically Swing Chimed Only, Octagonal Tower.
<u>Castalla</u>, Antic Convent de St Francesc, 3, 2-3-4., - Automatically Swing Chimed Only.
<u>Castalla</u>, Assumpcio, 4, 27-3-2., - Automatically Swing Chimed Only, There is also another Bell in the Tower that is Chimed Only.
<u>Castalla</u>, Ermita de la Sang, 1, 1-1-24., - Automatically Swing Chimed Only, Hung in the Wall of the Church, This Bell was cast in 1550.
<u>Castalla</u>, Ermita St Pasqual, 1, - Chimed Only, This Bell was cast in 1904.
<u>Castell de Cabres</u>, St Llorenc, 2, 7-0-10., - Chimed Only.
Castell de Castells, Sta Anna, 4, 5-2-14., - Automatically Swing Chimed Only, There is also **One More Bell** Counterbalanced, No Wheel and weights 0-2-6.
Castell de Guadalest, Campanar del Poble, **2**, 5-2-14., - Counterbalanced, No Wheels.
<u>Castell de Guadalest</u>, Ermita St Joaquim i Sta Anna de Gines, 1, 0-2-22., - Chimed Only, This Bell was cast in 1859.
<u>Castellet I La Gornal</u>, Mare de Deu de Montserrat de Clariana, 2, 5-2-14., - Chimed Only.
<u>Castellet I La Gornal</u>, St Marcal, 2, 3-3-12., - Chimed Only.
<u>Castellet I La Gornal</u>, St Pere de Castellet, 1, 3-0-18., - Chimed Only, This Bell was cast in 1929.
<u>Castellet I La Gornal</u>, St Pere de La Gornal, 2, 8-1-16., - Chimed Only.
<u>Castellfort</u>, Ermita Mare de Deu de la Font, 1, 2-0-14., - Chimed Only.
<u>Castellfort</u>, Ermita St Pere, 1, - Chimed Only.
Castellfort, Parroquia, **4**, 12-1-0., - Counterbalanced, No Wheels.
<u>Castellnovo</u>, Ermita St Cristobal, 1, 1-1-8., - Chimed Only.
<u>Castellnovo</u>, Stos Reyes, 5, 9-3-8., - Chimed Only, The Treble was cast in 1763. The Second was cast in 1806. The Third was cast in 1911. The Fourth was cast in 1662. The Tenor was cast by Belen de Fongueva in 1705.
Castello de la Plana, Campanar de la Vila (Bell Tower), **8**, 38-1-2., - Counterbalanced, No Wheels,
There are also Two other Bells Hung Dead, Detatched Hexagonal Tower wich was built between 1591 - 1604.
<u>Castello de la Plana</u>, Concatedral de Sta Maria, 3, 4-2-0., - Chimed Only, These Bells were cast by Roses in 1939 and 1941.
<u>Castello de la Plana</u>, Ntra Sra de la Esperanza, 2, 2-2-6., - Chimed Only, Cast by Paccard in 2000.
<u>Castello de la Plana</u>, St Agusti, 1, 6-3-2., - Chimed Only, This Bell was cast by Roses in 1939.
<u>Castello de la Plana</u>, St Jorge, 4, 21-0-2., - Chimed Only.
<u>Castello de la Plana</u>, St Josep Obrer, 1, 2-3-4., - Chimed Only.
Castello de la Plana, St Pere del Grau, 8, 20cwt., - Automatically Swing Chimed Only, All the Bells were cast by Rivera Dominguez in 2001. There is also **another Bell**, Counterbalanced with No Wheel this Bell was cast by Roses in 1945.
<u>Castello de la Plana</u>, St Vincent Ferrer, 1, 2-2-0., - Chimed Only.
<u>Castello de la Plana</u>, Santuari del Lledo, 2, - Chimed Only in a Belcote.
<u>Castello de la Plana</u>, Sgda Familia, 4, 8-2-16., - Chimed Only, All the Bells were cast by Roses in 1939, 1967 and 1969.

119

Castello de Rugat, Assumpcio, 5, - Chimed Only, The Back Three Bells were cast in 1768 and the Second was cast in 1950.
Castello de Rugat, Ermita Sta Barbera i St Antoni Abat i de Padua, 1, 0-2-18., - Chimed Only, This Bell was cast by Roses in 1960.
Castellonet, St Joan Apostol, **2**, 1-2-26., - Counterbalanced, No Wheels.
Castellvi de la Marca, St Sadurni, 1, 4-2-0., - Chimed Only.
Castellvi de la Marca, Sta Maria de la Munia, 2, 9-3-8., - Chimed Only.
Castielfabib, Ermita Virgin de Gracia, 1, 0-1-6., - Chimed Only, This Bell was cast in 1475.
Castielfabib, Ntra Sra de los Angeles, **4**, 9-2-4., - Counterbalanced, No Wheels.
Castielfabib, Purisima de Cuesta del Rato, 1, 1-1-16., - Chimed Only.
Castielfabib, St Joaquin y Sta Ana de Arrayo Cerezo, 1, - Chimed Only, This Bell was cast by Arcos Y Menezo in 1859.
Castielfabib, St Marcos de Los Santos, 2, 2-2-6., - Chimed Only.
Castielfabib, St Sebastian del Mas de Jacinto, 1, 0-3-8., - Chimed Only.
Castillo de Villamalefa, Iglesia (Cedraman), 1, 0-1-20., - Chimed Only in a Belcote.
Castillo de Villamalefa, St Pedro, 3, 10-2-0., - Automatically Swing Chimed Only.
Castropol, Capilla del Campo, 1, 1-1-16., - Chimed Only, This Bell was cast in 1661.
Castropol, Parroquial de Castropol, 1, 1-1-8., - Chimed Only, This Bell was cast in 1724.
Castropol, Parroquial de Presto, 1, 3-0-18., - Chimed Only, This Bell was cast in 1848.
Castropol, Parroquial de Seares, 2, 1-2-6., - Chimed Only, These Bells were cast in 1797.
Catarroja, St Antoni de Padua, 3, 2-2-6., - Chimed Only, The Treble was cast in 1782. The Second and Tenor were cast by Roses in 1934 and 1954.
Catarroja, St Miquel Archangel, 5, 17-0-14., - Automatically Swing Chimed Only, The Treble was cast in 1744. The rest were cast by Roses in 1900, 1924 and 1972.
Cati, Assumpcio, 3, 21-0-2., - Automatically Swing Chimed Only, The Treble and Second were cast by Linares Ortiz in 1911 and 1929. The Tenor was cast by Manes in 1833.
Cati, Ermita Mare de Deu del Avella, 1, 1-0-4., - Chimed Only.
Cati, Ermita Mare de Deu del Piar, 1, 0-1-2., - Chimed Only.
Cati, Ermita Sta Anna, 1, 0-1-2., - Chimed Only.
Caudete, Santa Catalina, 5, 19-0-2., - Automatically Swing Chimed Only.
Caudete, Virgin de Gracia, 3, 5-1 20., - Chimed Only.
Caudete de Las Fuentes, Natividad de Ntra Sra, 4, 7-2-6., - Automatically Swing Chimed Only, The Treble was cast in 1792.
Caudiel, Ayuntamiento, 1, 6-2-6., - Chimed Only, This Bell was cast by Monzo in 1858.
Caudiel, Convento Carmelitas Descalzas, 1, 1-1-0., - Chimed Only.
Caudiel, St Juan Bautista, 3, 12-1-0., - Chimed Only, The Tenor was cast by Roses in 1791.
Celadas, Santo Domingo de Silos, 3, 7-2-6., - Chimed Only, The Treble and Second were cast by Roses in 1945 and 1947. The Tenor was cast by Quintana in 1833.
Cerda, St Antoni Abat, 2, 4-2-0., - Automatically Swing Chimed Only.
Cervera, Parroquia de Santa Maria, **6**, - Counterbalanced, No Wheels, There is also Two more Bells that are Chimed Only and Hung Dead.
Cervera del Maestre, Assumpcio, 3, 18-0-6., - Chimed Only, The Treble and Tenor were cast by Roses in 1906 and 1940. The Second was cast by Blasco in 1957.
Chella, Ntra Sra de Gracia, 4, 13-1-12., - Automatically Swing Chimed Only.
Chelva, Convento Franciscanos, 1, 0-1-26., - Chimed Only, This Bell was cast by Roses in 1912.
Chelva, Ermita del Loreto, 1, 0-1-2., - Chimed Only, This Bell was cast in 1774.
Chelva, Ermita La Soledad de Benacira, 1, 0-0-12., - Chimed Only, This Bell was cast in 1943.
Chelva, Ermita Mas de Cavallero, 1, 0-3-0., - Chimed Only, This Bell was cast by Quintana in 1884.
Chelva, Ermita Ntra Sra de los Desamparados, 1, 0-1-2., - Chimed Only, This Bell was cast by Roses in 1952.
Chelva, Ntra Sra de los Angeles, **5**, 14-0-18., - Counterbalanced, No Wheels, There are also Three other Bells in the Tower that are Chimed Only.

Chelva, St Juan de Ahillas, 1, 0-1-6., - Chimed Only, This Bell was cast in 1890.
Chelva, Virgin de la Misericordia de Villar de Tejas, 1, 0-2-2., - Chimed Only, This Bell was cast in 1919.
Chera, Ntra Sra de los Angeles, 3, 4-2-12., - Automatically Swing Chimed Only.
Cheste, Ermita de la Soledad, 2, 0-2-12., - Chimed Only, The Treble was cast in 1750 and the Tenor in 1920.
Cheste, St Lucas, 6, 22-0-6., - Automatically Swing Chimed Only, The Third and Fifth were cast by Eijesbouts in 1990. The rest were cast by Lleonart in 1780. Hexagonal Tower.
Chiva, St Juan Bautista, 4, 19-0-2., - Automatically Swing Chimed Only, The Treble was cast by Palacios in 1882. The Second and Third were cast by Lleonart 1803 and 1776. The Tenor was cast by Roses in 1962.
Chodos, St Pere, 4, 2-2-6., - Chimed Only.
Chovar, Santa Ana, 1, 2-2-18., - Automatically Swing Chimed Only, This Bell was cast by Roses in 1943.
Chulilla, Balneario, 1, 0-1-0., - Chimed Only, This Bell was cast in 1890.
Chulilla, Ermita de Sta Barbara, 1, 1-1-8., - Chimed Only, This Bell was cast in 1719.
Chulilla, Ntra Sra de los Angeles, 4, 14-2-2., - Automatically Swing Chimed Only, The Treble and Tenor were cast by Palacios in 1881. The Second and Third were cast by Fenollera 1758.
Cimballa, Purificacion de Nuestra Senora, 2, 2-2-18., - Counterbalanced, No Wheels, These Bells were cast in 1767 and 1889.
Cinctorres, Ermita Mare de Deu de Gracia, 2, 1-1-16., - Chimed Only, The Treble was cast by Palles in 1855. The Tenor was cast by Roses in 1942.
Cinctorres, Ermita St Marc, 1, 0-1-6., - Chimed Only, This Bell was cast by Palles in 1855.
Cinctorres, Ermita St Pere, 1, 0-3-0., - Chimed Only, This Bell was cast by Palles in 1855.
Cinctorres, St Pere Apostol, 5, 19-0-2., - Counterbalanced, No Wheels, The Treble was cast in 1799 and the Fourth was cast in 1717.
Cirat, San Bernardo, 4, 4-2-12., - Automatically Swing Chimed Only, There is also another Bell in the Tower that is Chimed Only and weighs 5-2-14.
Cirat, Sta Maria Desamparadosde El Tormo, 2, 2-1-8., - Automatically Swing Chimed Only.
Ciudad Real, Santa Iglesia Prioral Basilica Catedral de las Ordenes Militares, 7, 31-0-8., - Counterbalanced, No Wheels, There is also another Bell Hung Dead in a Small Tower.
Ciutadella, Catedral de la Purificacio, 4, 22-2-4., - Counterbalanced, No Wheels, There is also another Two Bells Hung Dead.
Ciutat de Palma, Catedral de Santa Maria, 8, 92-2-8., - Counterbalanced, No Wheels, There is also Two other Bells in the Tower, The Treble was cast in 1310.
Cocentaina, Assumpcio, 4, 20cwt., - Automatically Swing Chimed Only, The Second was cast by Roses in 1940 and the rest were cast by Manclus in 1984.
Cocentaina, Ermita Sta Barbera, 1, 0-1-20., - Chimed Only.
Cocentaina, Miracle, 2, 1-2-6., - The Tenor is Automatically Swing Chimed Only and the Treble is Chimed Only, The Treble was cast in 1747.
Cocentaina, St Pere de L'Alcudia, 2, 0-3-8., - Counterbalanced, No Wheels, The Treble was cast by Rodes in 1884 and the Tenor by Roses in 1951.
Cocentaina, Salvador, 1, 0-0-14., - Chimed Only, This Bell was cast in 1550.
Cocentaina, Sant Sebastia, 3, 5-2-14., - Automatically Swing Chimed Only, The Tenor was cast by Manclus in 1979 and the rest were cast by Roses in 1940.
Cofrentes, Cas Los Pinares del Pilar, 1, - Chimed Only.
Cofrentes, Castillo, 1, - Chimed Only, This Bell was cast in 1849.
Cofrentes, Ermita del Calvario, 1, 0-0-10., - Chimed Only.
Cofrentes, Patriarca St Jose, 4, 10-0-24., - Chimed Only, Cast in 1849, 1861 and 2000.
Colombres, Parroquial, 1, 8-0-16., - Chimed Only, This Bell was cast in 1864.
Confrides, Sant Josep, 3, 7-2-6., - The **Treble** is Counterbalanced with No Wheel the rest are Automatically Swing Chimed Only. All the Bells were cast by Roses in 1940.
Confrides, Sant Vicent Ferrer d'Abdet, 2, 3-1-20., - Counterbalanced, No Wheels.

Cordoba, Catedral de Cordoba, **12**, 64-0-20., - Counterbalanced, No Wheels, These Bells are Hung in Circle Three Bells in each corner of the Tower, There are also Two other Bells in the Tower.
Cortes de Arenoso, Ermita St Cristobal, **1**, 0-2-18., - Counterbalanced, No Wheel.
Cortes de Arenoso, Iglesia (San Vicente de Piedrahita), **2**, 1-0-2., - Counterbalanced, No Wheels, Hung in a Bellcote on the Roof.
Cortes de Arenoso, Ntra Sra de los Angeles, **5**, 13-0-2., - Counterbalanced, No Wheels, There is also a Bell cast in 1627 on display and weights 0-2-18.
Cortes de Pallas, Ntra Sra de los Angeles, **4**, 6-3-2., - Counterbalanced, No Wheels, The front Three Bells were cast by Eijesbouts in 2001 and the Tenor was cast by Lleonart Josep (Valencia) in 1775.
Costur, *St Pere Martir, 2, 4-1-2., - Counterbalanced, No Wheels, There is also another Bell Hung Dead on the Wall and it is very Oddly Shaped.*
Crivillen , San Martin, 2, - Chimed Only.
Cudillero , Capilla Virgin de la China en Lamuno, St Martin de Luina, 1, 1-1-8., - Chimed Only, This Bell was cast in 1716.
Cudillero , Parroquia Soto de Luina, 1, - Chimed Only, This Bell was cast in 1691.
Cuenca , Catedral de San Julian, 1, 1-1-0., - Lever Chimed Only.
Culla , El Salvador, 3, 8-2-16., - Automatically Swing Chimed Only, The Treble was cast by Roses in 1921. The Second was cast in 1732 and the Tenor was cast in 1404.
Culla , Ermita de St Roc, 1, 0-1-26., - Chimed Only in a Belcote.
Culla , Ermita St Cristofol, **1**, 1-1-16., - Counterbalanced, No Wheel, Hung in a Belcote.
Cunit , St Cristofor, 2, 3-3-12., - Chimed Only, The Treble was cast by Pomarol in 1772 and the Tenor was cast by Diez Moises in 1912.
Daimus , St Pere Apostol, 6, - The Front Three Bells are Hung Dead above the Belcote in a Steel Frame above each other and the Back Three Bells are Automatically Swing Chimed Only in the Belcote.
Denia , Ajuntament, 1, 14-0-18., - Hung Dead as a Clock Bell in a Steel Frame on the Roof of a Public Building.
Denia , Assumpcio, 5, 28-1-20., - Automatically Swing Chimed Only, All the Bells were cast by Roses in 1942.
Denia , Jesus Pobre de Denia, 2, 4-1-4., - Automatically Swing Chimed Only, Cast by Roses in 1942.
Denia , Sant Antoni, **3**, 6-0-14., - Counterbalanced, No Wheels.
Denia , Sant Mateu de la Xara, **4**, 5-1-20., - Counterbalanced, No Wheels, All the Bells were cast by Roses in 1928 and 1965.
Domeno *, Santa Catalina, 3, 3-1-20., - The* **Treble** *and* **Second** *are Counterbalanced with No Wheel. The Tenor is Hung Dead, All the Bells were cast by Roses in 1914 and 1965.*
Donostia, Catedral de El Buen Pastor, **5**, 14-0-18., - Counterbalanced, No Wheels, There are also Five other Bells in the Tower Hung Dead with a Tenor weighing 31-2-20.
Eivissa , Catedral de Santa Maria la Major, 5, 12-1-0., - Chimed Only, All the Bells were cast by Ribot Pere between 1565 - 1670, Pentagon Shaped Tower.
El Campello , Santa Anna de la Platja de Muchavista, **1**, - Counterbalanced, No Wheel.
El Campello *, Santa Teresa, 3, 17-2-20., - Counterbalanced, No Wheels, There is also another Bell in the Tower Hung Dead and weighs 8-1-16.*
El Frago , Parroquia, 3, 9-2-4., - Chimed Only, The Second was cast by Ballesteros in 1869 and the Tenor was cast in 1604.
El Montmell , El Remei de la Joncosa, 2, 9cwt., - Chimed Only.
El Montmell , St Miquel de Marmellar, 1, 1-3-8., - Chimed Only.
El Montmell , St Pere d'Aiguaviva, 1, 0-2-18., - Chimed Only.
El Pinos , Torre del Rellotge, 3, 17-2-4., - Chimed Only in a Bellcote on the top of a Octagonal Tower.
El Pla del Penedes , St Jaume de Can Cerda de Palou, 1, 0-2-18., - Chimed Only.

El Pla del Penedes, Sta Magdalena, 3, 8-1-16., - Chimed Only, The Treble and Second were cast by Guitart in 1884 and the Tenor by Murua in 1941.
El Poble Nou de Benitatxell, Oratori Jaime Llobell, 2, 0-3-0., - Chimed Only, Cast in 1913.
El Poble Nou de Benitatxell, Sta Maria Magdalena, 2, 6-2-6., - Automatically Swing Chimed Only, These Bells were cast by Roses in 1924.
El Puig, Santa Maria del Puig, 5, 13-1-12., - Chimed Only, The Fourth Bell and the Tenor are the Same weight.
El Toro, Ermita St Roque, 1, 0-1-0., - Chimed Only.
El Toro, Ntra Sra de los Angeles, 3, 6-3-2., - Chimed Only.
El Toro - Calvia, Ntra Sra del Toro, **1**, 2-0-14., - Counterbalanced, No Wheel, This Bell was cast by Portilla in 2000.
El Vendrell, Ermita de St Salvador de St Salvador, 1, 0-1-2., - Chimed Only.
El Vendrell, St Salvador, 8, 19-0-2., - Chimed Only, The Treble was cast by Barnola in 1743.
El Vendrell, St Vicenc de Calders, 1, 5-2-14., - Chimed Only.
El Verger, Mare de Deu del Rosari, 5, 9-1-2., - Automatically Swing Chimed Only.
Els Poblets, Divino Salvador, 2, 1-1-16., - Automatically Swing Chimed Only in a Belcote, These Bells were cast by Roses in 1939 and 1970.
Els Poblets, Jesus Pobre, 2, 4-1-4., - Automatically Swing Chimed Only, Cast by Roses in 1942.
Els Poblets, Sant Josep de Miraflor, 2, 2-2-18., - Lever Chimed Only.
Elx, Basilica de Sta Maria, 4, 20-2-0., - Automatically Swing Chimed Only, The Treble was cast in 1654. The Second was cast by Manclus in 1984. The Third and Tenor were cast in 1719.
Elx, St Josep, **1**, 1-1-16., - Counterbalanced, No Wheel, This Bell was cast in 1475.
Emperador, Ntra Sra del Rosari, **2**, 0-2-6., - The **Tenor** is Counterbalanced with No Wheel and the Treble is Chimed Only, The Treble was cast in 1898 and the Tenor in 1784.
Enguera, Antiguo Convento, **2**, 0-3-8., - Counterbalanced, No Wheels, Hung in a Belcote, The Treble was cast in 1659 and the Tenor by Portilla in 1993.
Enguera, Asilo, 1, 0-2-2., - Chimed Only, This Bell was cast in 1806.
Enguera, Cementerio, 1, 0-1-18., - Chimed Only, This Bell was cast in 1780.
Enguera, Ermita St Antonio de Padua, 1, 0-1-20., - Chimed Only in a Belcote, This Bell was cast in 1704.
Enguera, Finca Torre Tallada de Navalon, 1, 0-1-16., - Chimed Only, This Bell was cast in 1856.
Enguera, Ntra Sra de Belen de Navalon, **4**, 3-3-12., - Counterbalanced, No Wheels.
Enguera, St Antonio de Padua de Beniali, 1, 0-1-20., - Chimed Only, This Bell was cast in 1989.
Enguera, St Miguel Arcangel, **6**, 25-1-16., - Counterbalanced, No Wheels, There are also Two other Bells in the Tower Hung Dead One is Hemispherical and the other is a normal Bell.
Erdozain, Iglesia Parroquial, 1, 1-1-16., - Chimed Only, This Bell was cast in 1500.
Erro, Iglesia, 1, 1-1-16., - Chimed Only, This Bell was cast in 1500.
Eslida, Calvari, 1, 0-2-18., - Chimed Only, This Bell was cast by Roses in 1944.
Eslida, Salvador, 2, 5-0-8., - Automatically Swing Chimed Only, The Treble was cast in 1686 and the Tenor in 1778.
Esnoz, Iglesia Parroquial, 2, 10-0-24., - Chimed Only, The Treble was cast in 1450 and the Tenor in 1350.
Espadilla, St Juan Bautista, **3**, 4-1-4., - Counterbalanced, No Wheels, The Treble was cast in 1703. The Second in 1858 and the Tenor in 1744.
Estivella, Ermita St Roc de Beselga, 2, 0-1-2., - Chimed Only.
Estivella, Sants Joans, 5, 14-2-2., - Automatically Swing Chimed Only, The Treble and Fourth were cast in 1764. The Second and Tenor were cast by Cases in 1821 and the Third was cast by Canobas in 1851.
Estopinan del Castillo, Parroquia, 3, 4-0-14., - Chimed Only, The Second was cast in 1683.
Estubeny, St Onofre, **3**, 5-1-20., - Counterbalanced, No Wheels, All the Bells were cast by Roses.
Facheca, Espiritu Santo, 3, 6-1-10., - Automatically Swing Chimed Only.
Famorca, St Cayetano, 2, 3-3-12., - Automatically Swing Chimed Only, These Bells were cast by Roses in 1941 and 1894.

Fanzara, Asuncion, 3, 6-0-14., - Automatically Swing Chimed Only, The Treble and Tenor were cast by Manclus in 1950 and 1966. The Second was cast by Massa in 1882.
Fanzara, Ermita Santo Sepulcro, 1, 0-2-18., - Chimed Only in a Belcote.
Faura, Ermita Sta Barbera, 1, 0-1-0., - Chimed Only.
Faura, Sants Joans, 4, 20-2-0., - Automatically Swing Chimed Only, There are also Five more bells in the Tower that are Chimed Only with a Tenor of 36-2-22.
Figueroles, St Mateu, 2, 3-2-8., - Counterbalanced, No Wheels.
Finestrat, St Bertomeu, 4, 7-2-6., - The Third is Hung Dead and Chimed Only the rest are Automatically Swing Chimed Only, These Bells were cast by Murua in 1979 and 1980.
Foios, Assumpcio, 4, 17-2-4., - Automatically Swing Chimed Only, There is also in the Church One Bell Hung Dead which weights 0-0-12. and which apears to be a big round wheel with 20 hand bell size bells attached to the edge of the wheel that you spin round.
Font - Rubi, St Pere i St Feliu, 2, 5-3-8., - Chimed Only, These Bells were cast by Murua in 1941.
Font - Rubi, Sta Maria de Bellver, 1, 3-3-12., - Chimed Only, This Bell was cast by Marco Y Ragel in 1887.
Forcall, Assumpcio, 7, - **Two** of the Bells are Counterbalanced with No Wheel, Three of the Bells are Automatically Swing Chimed Only the rest are Chimed Only, One of the Bells was cast in 1671 and another in 1696.
Fuente la Reina, Ntra Sra de los Angeles, 3, 2-2-18., - Counterbalanced, No Wheels, Hung in a Large Belcote.
Fuenterrobles, Santiago Apostol, 3, 3-1-20., - Counterbalanced, No Wheels.
Fuentes de Ayodar, St Roque, 3, 4-2-12., - Counterbalanced, No Wheels.
Gador, Virgin del Rosario, 3, 7-1-8., - Automatically Swing Chimed Only, All the Bells were cast by Roses in 1951 and 1963.
Gaianes, St Jaume, 3, 8-1-16., - Automatically Swing Chimed Only, There is also another Bell in the Tower that is Hung Dead, Also Three of the Bells were cast by Roses between 1930 - 1947.
Gaibiel, St Pedro, 5, 10-0-24., - Chimed Only.
Gandia, Colegiata de l'Assumpcio de Ntra Sra, 3, 40-2-1., - Automatically Swing Chimed Only, All these Bells were cast by Roses in 1847, 1923 and 1971.
Gandia, Crist Rei, 4, 12-1-0., - Automatically Swing Chimed Only, All the Bells were cast by Portilla in 1998.
Gandia, Esglesia de les Escoles Pies, 1, - Chimed Only.
Gandia, St Cristofol de Benipeixcar, 4, - Automatically Swing Chimed Only.
Gandia, St Josep del Raval, 3, 11-2-2., - Automatically Swing Chimed Only, All the Bells were cast by Roses in 1955.
Gandia, St Nicolau de El Grau, 12, - Chimed Only, Hung Dead in a Detatched Concrete Tower.
Gandia, Santa Ana, 1, - Automatically Swing Chimed Only.
Gandia, Sta Maria Magdalena de Beniopa, 3, 13-1-12., - Automatically Swing Chimed Only, Two of the Bells were cast by Roses in 1941.
Gasteiz, Catedral Vieja de Santa Maria, 6, 67-1-24., - Automatically Swing Chimed Only.
Gata de Gorgos, Ermita del Calvari, 1, 1-1-0., - Counterbalanced, No Wheel.
Gata de Geogos, St Miquel Archangel, 4, 15-2-26., - Automatically Swing Chimed Only, There is also another Bell in the Tower Hung Dead and weights 7-1-8.
Gatova, Ntra Sra de los Angeles, 2, 3-0-18., - Counterbalanced, No Wheels, The Treble was cast in 1765 and the Tenor by Calleja in 1776.
Gavarda, St Joan i St Antoni de Gavarda, 3, 3-1-4., - Counterbalanced, No Wheels, The Treble was cast by Manclus in 1967. The Second was cast in 1632 and the Tenor in 1796.
Geldo, La Misericordia, 5, 8-0-16., - The Treble is Chimed Only the rest are Automatically Swing Chimed Only, The Second was cast in 1739.
Gelida, St Pere, 2, 12-1-0., - Chimed Only.
Gelida, St Pere (Antiga Parroquia), 1, 1-0-4., - Chimed Only.
Genoves, Cristo, 1, - Automatically Swing Chimed Only in a Belcote.
Genoves, Ntra Sra dels Dolors, 2, 3-3-12., - Chimed Only, The Treble was cast in 1750.

<u>Gestalgar</u>, Purisima Concepcion, 3, 20-2-0., - Automatically Swing Chimed Only.
<u>Gijon</u>, Capilla de la Stma. Trinidad, 1, 1-1-24., - Chimed Only, This Bell was cast in 1674.
Gijon, Capilla de la Soledad, **1**, 0-2-18., - Counterbalanced, No Wheel, This bell was cast in 1666.
<u>Gijon</u>, Capilla de los Remedios, 2, 0-2-12., - Automatically Swing Chimed Only.
Gijon, Capilla de St Lorenzo de Tierra, **1**, 0-3-8., - Counterbalanced, No Wheel, This Bell was cast in 1450.
Gijon, Colegiata de St Juan Bautista, **2**, 3-2-24., - Counterbalanced, No Wheels.
Gijon, Oratorio Casa Natal de Jovellanos, **1**, 0-1-0., - Counterbalanced, No Wheel, This Bell was cast in 1750.
<u>Gijon</u>, Parroquial de la Inmaculada Concepcion, 1, 0-2-22., - Chimed Only.
<u>Gijon</u>, Parroquial de St Antonio de Padua, 1, 1-1-16., - Chimed Only.
<u>Gijon</u>, Parroquial de St Jose, 1, 0-0-10., - Chimed Only.
<u>Gijon</u>, Parroquial de St Lorenzo, 4, 10-3-4., - The Second is Chimed Only and the rest are Automatically Swing Chimed Only, All the bells were cast by Fabrica de Trubia in 1946.
<u>Gijon</u>, St Pedro Apostol, 3, 20cwt., - Automatically Swing Chimed Only, Cast by Murua in 1957.
<u>Gijon</u>, Sagrado Corazon, 4, 18-0-6., - The Second is Chimed Only and the rest are Automatically Swing Chimed Only.
Gilet, (R.C.), Convent del Sant Espirit, **4**, 5-1-0., - Counterbalanced, No Wheels, The Tenor was cast by Dencausse Pedro in of Barcelona in 1927, The Second and Third Bells were cast by Roses of Valencia in 1941., There is also another Bell Hung Dead in the Tower and weights 0-1-16.
<u>Gilet</u>, St Antoni Abad, 3, 7-1-8., - The Tenor is Automatically Swing Chimed Only and the rest are Chimed Only.
<u>Girona</u>, Catedral de Santa Maria, (G.F.), 6, 79-1-14., - The Treble and Tenor are Hung Dead, The Third has a rope attached to the Clapper and the rest are Lever Chimed, The Treble was cast by Se Va in 1717, The Tenor was cast by Sever Antoni in 1574 and the rest were cast by Barberi between 1941 and 1946.
<u>Godella</u>, Colegio Sgdo. Corazon, 1, 0-2-2., - Chimed Only.
<u>Godella</u>, Convento Carmelitas Descalzas, 2, 1-1-8., - Chimed Only.
<u>Godella</u>, El Salvador, 1, 1-2-26., - Chimed Only, This Bell was cast by Barberi in 1993.
<u>Godella</u>, Ermita de Campolivar, 1, 0-2-12., - Chimed Only.
<u>Godella</u>, St Bartolome, 4, 9-3-8., - Automatically Swing Chimed Only.
<u>Godella</u>, Seminari Terciaris Caputxins, 2, 0-2-6., - Chimed Only.
Gorga, Assumpcio, **4**, 10-3-4., - Counterbalanced, No Wheels, The Third was cast by Casanueva, Manuel de in 1777.
<u>Grado</u>, Parroquial de Castanedo, 1, 1-0-20., - Chimed Only, This Bell was cast in 1780.
<u>Grado</u>, Parroquial de Fresno, 1, 2-2-0., - Chimed Only, This Bell was cast in 1678.
<u>Granada</u>, Alhambra, 4, 24-3-0., - Chimed Only, The Front Three Bells were cast in 1795, 1795 and 1919. The Tenor was cast by Corona in 1773.
<u>Granada</u>, Ayuntamiento, 3, 5-1-20., - Automatically Chimed Only, Cast by Blasco Y Liza in 1933.
<u>Granada</u>, Capilla de St Cecilio, 1, 0-2-18., - Chimed Only.
<u>Granada</u>, Capilla del Transito de St Juan de Dois, 1, 3-1-4., - Chimed Only.
<u>Granada</u>, Capilla Real, 1, 5-1-20., - Chimed Only, This Bell was cast by Campo Y Vega in 1688.
<u>Granada</u>, Catedral de la Encarnacion, 18, 126-2-12., - Chimed Only, The Second was cast in 1495.
<u>Granada</u>, Colegio de las Siervas del Evangelio, 2, 1-1-16., - Chimed Only, Cast by Murua in 1957.
<u>Granada</u>, Colegio de las Vistillas, 1, 0-1-2., - Chimed Only.
<u>Granada</u>, Colegio de Mercedarais de la Caridad, 1, 3-3-12., - Chimed Only, This Bell was cast by Linares Perez in 1905.
<u>Granada</u>, Colegio de St Isidro, 1, - Chimed Only, This Bell was cast by Villanueva Saenz in 1930.
<u>Granada</u>, Colegio del Beaterio de Sto Domingo, 3, 2-1-8., - Chimed Only, These Bells were cast in 1900, 1816 and 1905.

Granada, Colegio del Beaterio del Santisimo, 1, - Chimed Only, This Bell was cast by Corona in 1750.
Granada, Colegio del Sanrado Corazon, 3, 3-0-18., - Chimed Only.
Granada, Convento de Carmelitas Calzadas, 2, 1-1-16., - Automatically Swing Chimed Only, Both Bells are the same weight.
Granada, Convento de la Concepcion, 2, 7-0-10., - Chimed Only, The Tenor was cast by Coronas in 1798.
Granada, Convento de la Encarnacion, 1, 1-2-6., - Automatically Swing Chimed Only.
Granada, Convento de la Piedad, 3, 1-2-26., - Chimed Only.
Granada, Convento de las Comendadoras de Santiago, 2, 2-0-14., - Automatically Swing Chimed Only, The Treble was cast in 1670.
Granada, Convento de las Esclavas del Stmo. Sto y de la Inmaculada, 1, 0-1-20., - Chimed Only.
Granada, Convento de los Angeles, 2, 0-3-14., - Automatically Swing Chimed Only.
Granada, Convento de P.P. Agustinos Calzados, 2, 3-1-4., - Chimed Only.
Granada, Convento de St Bernardo, 4, 2-2-6., - Counterbalanced, No Wheels, The Second was cast in 1693.
Granada, Convento de St Jose, 2, 0-1-26., - Chimed Only.
Granada, Convento de St Juan de la Penitencia, 3, 2-0-2., - Automatically Chimed Only, Hung Dead.
Granada, Convento de Sta Catalina de Siena - Realejo, 6, 3-3-12., - Chimed Only.
Granada, Convento de Sta Catalina de Siena - Zafra, 5, 7-0-10., - The Back Two Bells are Automatically Swing Chimed Only the rest are Chimed Only.
Granada, Convento de Sta. Cruz la Real, 4, 0-2-18., - The Tenor is Chimed Only the rest are Automatically Swing Chimed Only.
Granada, Convento de Sta. Isabel la Real, 3, 3-1-4., - Chimed Only, Cast in 1775, 1813 and 1588.
Granada, Convento de Sto. Tomas de Villanueva, 2, 3-0-18., - Chimed Only, Cast by Rivas in 1878.
Granada, Convento del Santo Angel Custodio, 2, 1-0-4., - Counterbalanced, No Wheels.
Granada, Convento Jesus y Maria, 2, 3-3-12., - Automatically Swing Chimed Only, These Bells were cast in 1753 and 1749.
Granada, Convento la Magdalena, 6, 3-0-18., Automatically Swing Chimed Only, The Treble was cast by Corona in 1786.
Granada, Diputacion Provincial, 3, 2-2-18., - Automatically Chimed Only, Hung Dead, These Bells were cast by Blasco Y Lisa in 1932 and 1933.
Granada, Ermita de St Isidro, 1, - Chimed Only, This Bell was cast by Corona in 1750.
Granada, Ermita de St Juan de Letran, 1, 1-0-20., - Chimed Only, This Bell was cast by Corona in 1767.
Granada, Ermita de St Miguel, 1, 1-2-6., - Chimed Only, This bell was cast in 1750.
Granada, Ermita de St Sebastian, 1, 0-3-8., - Chimed Only.
Granada, Ermita del Cristo de la Yedra (desaparecida), 1, - Chimed Only, This Bell was cast in 1750.
Granada, Ermita del Sto. Sepulcro, 1, 1-1-24., - Chimed Only.
Granada, Escuela del Ave Maria del Sacro Monte , 2, 1-0-20., - Chimed Only.
Granada, Hermandad de Ntra. Sra. de las Angustias, 4, 14-0-18., - Automatically Swing Chimed Only, The Treble was cast in 1671 and the Third in 1675.
Granada, Hogar Infantil Bermudez de Castro, 1, 0-0-16., - Chimed Only.
Granada, Hospital de la Caridad y del Refugio, 1, - Chimed Only, This Bell was cast by Corona in 1740.
Granada, Hospital de St Juan de Dios - Claustro, 1, 0-3-14., - Chimed Only.
Granada, Iglisia del Sagrario, 1, 3-0-2., - Chimed Only, This Bell was cast in 1525.
Granada, Institucion Benefica del Sagrado Corazon, 1, 1-0-20., - Automatically Swing Chimed Only.

<u>Granada</u>, Instituto General y Tecnico Padre Suarez, 3, 4-1-4., - Automatically Chimed, Hung Dead, These Bells were cast by Diez Moises in 1921 and 1922.
<u>Granada</u>, Monasterio de la Cartuja o de la Asuncion, 2, 5-1-20., - Chimed Only, These Bells were cast by Casares in 1845 and 1847.
<u>Granada</u>, Monasterio de St Jeronimo, 11, 5-0-8., - Eight of the Bells are Automatically Swing Chimed Only the rest are Chimed Only, The Treble was cast in 1475.
<u>Granada</u>, Ntra Sra. de Gracia, 2, 3-0-18., - Automatically Swing Chimed Only, These Bells were cast in 1657 and 1798.
Granada, Ntra Sra de la Asuncion de la abadia del Sacro Monte, **8**, 24-1-0., - Three of the Bells are Hung Dead and Automatically Chimed Only, Four of the Bells are Automatically Swing Chimed Only and **One** Bell is Counterbalanced with No Wheel, Two of the bells were cast in 1613 and One in 1660.
<u>Granada</u>, Ntra Sra de la Paz, 2, 4-0-14., - Chimed Only, The Tenor is Hung Dead, These Bells were cast by Roses in 1993.
<u>Granada</u>, Ntra Sra de las Angustias, 4, 10-0-24., - Automatically Swing Chimed Only, The Third was cast in 1757.
<u>Granada</u>, Ntra Sra de los Remedios, 4, 2-0-24., - Chimed Only.
<u>Granada</u>, Ntra Sra de Montserrat, 2, 3-0-18., - Chimed Only.
<u>Granada</u>, Palacio de la Chancilleria, 2, 15-2-26., - Automatically Chimed Only, Hung Dead, The Tenor was cast in 1500.
<u>Granada</u>, St Andres, 3, 8-1-16., - The Tenor is Automatically Swing Chimed Only the rest are Chimed Only.
<u>Granada</u>, St Bartolome, 2, 4-1-4., - Chimed Only, The Treble was cast in 1450.
<u>Granada</u>, St Cecilio, 4, 8-1-16., - Automatically Swing Chimed Only.
<u>Granada</u>, St Cristobal, 2, 4-2-12., - Chimed Only.
<u>Granada</u>, St Gregorio Betico, 1, 0-0-22., - Chimed Only.
<u>Granada</u>, St Gregorio Magno, 2, 2-2-6., - Chimed Only, These Bells were cast in 1757 and 1763.
<u>Granada</u>, St Ildelfonso, 4, 7-1-8., - Chimed Only, The Tenor was cast in 1550.
<u>Granada</u>, St Jose, 3, 9-1-2., - The Tenor is Chimed Only the rest are Automatically Swing Chimed Only, The Tenor was cast by Corona in 1784.
<u>Granada</u>, St Juan Bta y Ntra Sra del Amparo, 1, 1-2-6., - Automatically Swing Chimed Only.
<u>Granada</u>, St Juan de Avila, 2, - Automatically Swing Chimed Only.
<u>Granada</u>, St Juan de Dios, 7, 17-0-14., - Automatically Swing Chimed Only.
<u>Granada</u>, St Juan de los Reyes, 3, 5-0-8., - Chimed Only.
<u>Granada</u>, St Matias, 3, 13-1-12., - The Treble is Chimed Only, The Second is Automatically Swing Chimed Only. The Tenor is Automatically Chimed and Hung Dead.
<u>Granada</u>, St Miguel Arcangel, 2, 2-0-14., - Automatically Swing Chimed Only, Cast by Rosas in 1991.
<u>Granada</u>, St Nicolas, 3, - Chimed Only.
<u>Granada</u>, St Pedro y St Pablo, 4, 5-0-8., - Automatically Swing Chimed Only.
<u>Granada</u>, Sagrado Corazon, 5, 11-2-2., - Chimed Only.
<u>Granada</u>, Salvador, 8, 22-0-6., - The Back Three Bells are Automatically Chimed and Hung Dead. The rest are Chimed Only.
<u>Granada</u>, Seminario de St Cecilio, 1, - Chimed Only.
<u>Granada</u>, Sta Ana, 4, 17-2-4., - Chimed Only, The Treble was cast in 1450.
<u>Granada</u>, Sta Maria de la Alhambra, 4, 11-0-22., - Automatically Swing Chimed Only, The Treble was cast in 1450 and the rest were cast by Corona in 1773, 1755 and 1790.
<u>Granada</u>, Sta Maria Micaela, 3, 5-2-14., - The Treble is Chimed Only and the rest are Automatically Swing Chimed Only.
<u>Granada</u>, Stmo Corpus Christi, 5, 9-1-2., - Chimed Only.
<u>Granada</u>, Sto Angel Custodio, 1, - Chimed Only.
<u>Granada</u>, Stos Justo y Pastor, 7, 19-0-2., - The Treble, Second, Five and Tenor are Automatically Swing Chimed Only the rest are Chimed Only.

Graus , Santuario de la Pena, 5, 18-0-6., - *Chimed Only, The Fourth was cast by Alos in 1501.*
Guadaseauies , Mare de Deu de l'Esperanca, 2, 4-2-12., - *Automatically Swing Chimed Only.*
Guadaseauies , Nova Esglesia, 2, - *Chimed Only, These Bells were cast in 2000.*
Guadasuar , St Vincent Martir, 4, 18-1-26., - *Chimed Only.*
Guadix, Catedral de Guadix, **12**, 39-0-8., - *Counterbalanced, No Wheels, There are also Three other Bells Hung Dead.*
Guardamar , St Joan Baptista, **1**, - *Counterbalanced, No Wheel.*
Higueras , Purisima, 2, 1-1-24., - *Chimed Only.*
Higueruelas , Sta Barbara, 4, 6-1-1., - *Automatically Swing Chimed Only, There is also another Bell in the Tower Hung Dead, Clock Bell.*
Huesca , Catedral de Huesca, 7, 23-0-16., - *Automatically Chimed Only.*
Huesca , San Vicente Martir, 3, 10-2-0., - *Chimed Only.*
Ibdes , San Miguel Arcangel, **3**, 11-3-8., - *The Treble is Chimed Only the* **Second** *and* **Tenor** *are Counterbalanced with No Wheels.*
Ibi , Santiago Apostol, 2, 5-3-8., - *The Treble is Automatically Chimed Only and the Tenor is Chimed Only, This is a Modern Concrete Tower.*
Ibi , Transfiguracio del Senyor, 4, 11-2-2., - *Automatically Swing Chimed Only, There is also Two Hemispherical Bells Housed in another Tower.*
Igualada , Basilica de Sta Maria, 6, 56-3-4., - *The Tenor is Chimed Only and the rest are Automatically Swing Chimed Only, These Bells were cast by Bachert in 1990.*
Ilurdoz , Iglesia, 1, 18-0-6., - *Chimed Only, This bell was cast by Alli in 1500.*
Imoz , Iglesia de Latasa, 1, 5-1-20., - *Chimed Only, This Bell was cast by Muguiro in 1481.*
Iturmendi , Iglesia Parroquial, 1, 0-1-20., - *Chimed Only, This Bell was cast in 1611.*
Jaca , Ayuntamiento, 3, - *Chimed Only.*
Jaca, Catedral de San Pedro, **4**, 30-1-14., - *Counterbalanced, No Wheels, The Tenor was cast in the 14th Century, There are also Three other Bells in the Cathedral.*
Jaen, Catedral de Jaen, 9, 37-2-24., - *Automatically Swing Chimed Only exept the* **Tenor** *that is Hung for Ringing, Counterbalanced, No Wheel.*
Jalon , Ermita Sto Domingo, 1, 0-3-8., - *Chimed Only.*
Jalon , Santa Maria, 4, 14-3-14., - *Automatically Swing Chimed Only, These Bells were cast by Roses in 1941. There is also a Hemispherical Bell in the Spire, Octagonal Tower.*
Jarafuel, Sta Catalina Martir, 4, 8-0-16., - *Counterbalanced, No Wheels, There is also another Bell in the Tower.*
Javier , Museo de Castillo, 1, 3-0-18., - *Chimed Only, This Bell was cast in 1510.*
Jerica , Cristo de la Sangre, 1, 0-2-22., - *Chimed Only.*
Jerica , Ermita de St Miguel de Novaliches, 1, 1-0-20., - *Chimed Only.*
Jerica , Ermita del Loreto, 1, 0-1-0., - *Chimed Only.*
Jerica , Ermita St Roque, 1, 0-1-16., - *Chimed Only.*
Jerica , Sta Agueda, 1, 0-3-0., - *Automatically Swing Chimed Only.*
Jerica, Torre de las Campanas, **5**, 31-2-2., - *Counterbalanced, No Wheels, This Church was built between 1616 - 1628 and looks like a Castle with Battlements the Tower is Octagonal.*
La Bisbal del Penedes , Sta Maria, 2, 5-0-8., - *Chimed Only.*
La Canada de Benatanduz , Ntra Sra de la Asuncion, **1**, 8-1-16., - *Counterbalanced, No Wheels.*
Laciana , Parroquial de Rabanal de Abajo, 1, 1-3-8., - *Chimed Only, This Bell was cast in 1550.*
La Cuba , St Miguel Archangel, **2**, 8-2-16., - *The* **Treble** *is Counterbalanced with No Wheel and the Tenor is Automatically Swing Chimed Only.*
La Font de la Figuera , Ermita Sta Barbera, 1, - *Chimed Only.*
La Font de la Figuera , La Nativitat de Nostra Senyora, **4**, 11-3-8., - *Counterbalanced, No Wheel, The Treble was cast by Roses in 1776. The Second was cast in 1972. The Third and Tenor were cast by Sarrio in 1766.*
La Font D'en Carros , St Antoni Martir, 4, 14-0-18., - *Automatically Swing Chimed Only.*
La Granada , St Cristofor, 2, 8-1-16., - *Chimed Only, The Treble and Tenor are both the same weight, The Treble was cast in 1700 and the Tenor by Palles in 1831.*

La Granja de la Costera, St Francesc d'Asis, 2, 11-2-2., - Counterbalanced, No Wheels.
La Jana , Ermita de la Inmaculada, 1, 0-1-2., - Chimed Only in a Belcote.
La Jana , Ermita Sta Anna, 1, 0-1-2., - Chimed Only in a Belcote.
La Jana , St Bartolome, 4, 15-2-26., - Chimed Only, The Tenor was cast by Gvitarte in 1736.
L'Alcora , Antiga Carcel, 1, - Chimed Only, Clock Bell.
L'Alcora , Assumpcio de Ntra Sra, 6, 15-1-12., - Automatically Swing Chimed Only, Also there are Three more Bells in the Tower Hung Dead.
L'Alcora , Capella Residencia, 1, 0-2-18., - Automatically Swing Chimed in a Belcote.
L'Alcora , Ermita de St Cristofol, 1, 15-2-26., - Automatically Swing Chimed Only.
L'Alcora , Ermita del Calvari, 1, - Chimed Only in a Belcote.
L'Alcora , St Francesc, 1, 0-1-20., - Automatically Swing Chimed Only.
L'Alcora , St Miquel de la Foia, 2, 0-3-8., - Automatically Swing Chimed Only in a Belcote, Both Bells were cast by Roses in 1953 and 1967.
L'Alcudia , St Anreu Apostol , 4, - Chimed Only.
L'Alcudia de Crespins , Calvari, 1, - Automatically Swing Chimed Only.
L'Alcudia de Crespins , St Onofre Anacoreta, 4, 11-3-8., - Automatically Swing Chimed Only, There is also another Bell in the Tower Hung Dead it is shaped like the Cristmas Card Bell Style very weird Shaped and weighs 8-1-16.
L'Alqueria de la Comtessa , Sant Pere, 6, 14-0-18., - Four of the Bells are Automatically Swing Chimed Only and the rest are Chimed Only.
La Mata de Morella , Ntra Sra de las Nieves, 3, 8-1-16., - The **Treble** is Counterbalanced with No Wheel and the rest are Chimed Only.
La Nucia , Ermita, 2, - Chimed Only.
La Nucia , Purissima, 4, 7-3-4., - Automatically Swing Chimed Only.
La Pobla de Farnals , St Josep, 4, 12-2-8., - Chimed Only.
La Pobla de Vallbona , Ermita St Sebastia, 1, 0-0-8., - Chimed Only.
La Pobla de Vallbona , St Jaume Apostol, 2, 11-2-2., - Automatically Swing Chimed Only, There is also Two other Bells in the Tower that are Hung Dead and Chimed Only with a Tenor of 3-0-2.
La Pobla de Vallbona , Trinitat de Las Ventas, 7, 11-2-2., - Bells Four, Six and Seven are Automatically Swing Chimed Only. The Rest are Chimed Only.
L'Arboc , Capella St Ponc (Masia Papiol), 2, 1-1-16., - Chimed Only, Cast by Manclus in 1886.
L'Arboc , St Julia, 4, 13-2-22., - Chimed Only.
Larraun , Iglesia de Echarri, 2, 26-0-2., - Chimed Only, The Treble was cast by Muguiro in 1498 and the Tenor by Lecumberri in 1569.
La Seu D'urgell , Catedral de Santa Maria, 4, 19-0-2., - Automatically Swing Chimed Only, The Tenor was cast by Mestre in 1507.
La Torre de les Macanes , Santa Ana, 3, 6-2-6., - The Treble is Chimed Only and the rest are Automatically Swing Chimed Only, These Bells were cast by Roses in 1939 and 1940.
La Vall D'Uixo , Assumpcio, 5, 14-0-18., - Chimed Only.
La Vila Joiosa , Assumpcio, 4, 9-2-4., - Automatically Swing Chimed Only.
La Vila Joiosa , Casa Badia - Barri de Sant Antoni, 1, - Chimed Only.
La Vila Joiosa , Sant Antoni, 2, 2-3-4., - Automatically Swing Chimed Only, These Bells were cast by Roses in 1964 and 1942.
La Yesa , Ntra Sra de los Angeles, **4**, 9-2-4., - Counterbalanced, No Wheels, The Treble is Not Hung and is in the Tower.
La Zaida , Torre Nueva de la Iglesia de San Jose, 3, 3-0-18., - Automatically Swing Chimed Only.
Lecinena , Santa Maria, 5, 11-2-2., - Chimed Only.
Leliana , Ntra Sra del Carme, 4, 6-3-2., - Automatically Swing Chimed Only.
Lena , Capilla de St Bartolome de Fierros, 1, - Chimed Only.
Lena , Iglesia Tuiza (El Campo), 1, 0-2-18., - Chimed Only, This bell was cast in 1650.
Lena , Parroquial de Cabezon, 1, 1-0-4., - Chimed Only, This Bell was cast in 1752.
Les Borges del Camp , Esglesia Parroquial, 2, - Chimed Only.
Les Cabanyes , St Valenti, 1, 1-0-20., - Chimed Only.

Les Useres, Ermita Sta Waldesca, 1, 0-1-20., - Chimed Only in a Belcote, This Bell was cast in 1750.
Les Useres, Ermita Sto Cristo, 1, 0-2-18., - Chimed Only in a Belcote.
Les Useres, Ermita Virgin del Loreto, 1, 0-2-18., - Chimed Only in a Belcote.
Les Useres, Transfiguracio del Senyor, 3, 5-3-8., - Automatically Swing Chimed Only.
Llanera de Ranes, Crist de la Fe, 1, - Chimed Only.
Llanera de Ranes, St Joan Baptiste, 4, 10-0-24., - Automatically Swing Chimed Only.
Lleida, Parroquia de Sant Llorenc, 12, - Chimed Only, The Back Four Bells were cast by Eijesbouts.
Lleida, Seu Vella, 7, 92-2-8., - Automatically Swing Chimed Only, The Tenor was cast by Madam in 1418 and the Fifth by Mestre Nicolau Barrot in 1485. The rest were cast by Menezo in 1945.
Lliber, Sants Cosme I Damia, 4, 3-3-12., - Two of the Bells are Automatically Swing Chimed Only and the rest are Chimed Only, Hexagonal Tower.
Lliria, Assumpcio, 1, 0-2-6., - Chimed Only, This Bell was cast in 1940.
Lliria, El Remei, 4, 15-1-12., - Automatically Swing Chimed Only.
Lliria, Ermita St Vicent, 1, 1-1-16., - Chimed Only.
Lliria, La Sang, 6, 22-0-6., - Automatically Swing Chimed Only, There is also Two other Bells Hung Dead.
Lliria, Sant Francesc d'Assis, 5, 9-1-2., - Four of the Bells are Automatically Swing Chimed Only and the other one is Chimed Only.
Lliria, Santuari St Miguel, 3, 2-0-2., - The Tenor is Automatically Swing Chimed Only and the rest are Chimed Only.
Llocnou de Sant Jeroni, Sant Roc, 4, 10-3-4., - Chimed Only on the roof of the Tower, The Back Three Bells were cast by Eijesbouts in 2000.
Llorenc del Penedes, St Llorenc, 4, 15-1-12., - Chimed Only.
Llosa de Ranes, Calvari, 1, 1-1-8., - Chimed Only.
Llosa de Ranes, Nativitat de la Nostra Senyora, 3, 7-2-6., - Automatically Swing Chimed Only, These Bells were cast by Roses in 1910 and 1956.
Llutxent, Corpus Christi, 3, - Chimed Only, These Bells were cast in 1994.
L'Olleria, Santuario Virgin del Loreto, 4, 2-0-14., - These Bells are in the Ringing Chamer on the Floor and Not Hung.
L'Olleria, Sta Maria Magdalena, 6, 17-0-14., - The Two and Tenor are Hung Dead in a Steel Frame on the Roof. The rest are Automatically Swing Chimed Only.
Loriguilla, Ermita del Pla de Nadal, 1, 0-1-16., - Chimed Only.
Loriguilla, St Juan Bautista, 3, 1-2-6., - Chimed Only, These Bells were cast by Manclus in 1967.
L'Orxa, Sta Maria Magdalena, 3, 7-0-1., - Automatically Swing Chimed Only.
Losa Del Obispo, St Sebastian, 4, 4-2-12., - Automatically Swing Chimed Only.
Losar de la Vera, Santiago Apostol, 4, - Chimed Only.
Luarca, Palacio de los Riego, 1, 0-3-8., - Chimed Only.
Lucena del Cid, Assumpcio, 4, 17-2-4., - Automatically Swing Chimed Only, There is also Two more Bells in the Tower One is Lever Chimed and Counterbalanced, The Other is Hung Dead and Chimed Only.
Lucena del Cid, Ermita de St Antoni, 1, 0-1-20., - Chimed Only.
Lucena del Cid, Ermita de St Vincent Ferrer, 1, 0-2-18., - Chimed Only in a Belcote.
Lucena del Cid, Ermita del Calvari, 1, 0-0-18., - Chimed Only in a Belcote.
Ludiente, Ermita Virgin de Pilar, 1, - Chimed Only in a Belcote.
Ludiente, Nativdad, 2, 6-1-1., - Automatically Swing Chimed Only.
Lugar Nuevo de Fenollet, St Diego d'Alcala, **2**, 1-3-8., - Counterbalanced, No Wheels, The Tenor was cast in 1643.
Lugar Nuevo de la Corona, Ntra Sra del Rosari, 2, 0-2-2., - Chimed Only.
Macastre, Transfiguracion del Senor, 4, 8-2-16., - Counterbalanced, No Wheels, Chimed Only.
Madrid, Madrid, Catedral de la Almudena, 3, 30-1-14., - Chimed Only.

Madrid, Madrid, Catedral de San Isidro, **4**, 17-0-14., - Counterbalanced, No Wheels, The Treble was cast in 1586 and the rest were cast by Linares Viuda de in 1960.
Madrid, Madrid, Iglesia de San Francisco el Grande (The Royal Church), **8**, 8-2-0. in Ab. - Unringable.
Madrid , *San Jeronimo el Real, 3, 17-2-4., - Automatically Swing Chimed Only.*
Malaga, *Catedral de Malaga, 11, - Counterbalanced, No Wheels, There is also One Bell Hung Dead and Three Bells were cast by Mears and Stainbank in 1868 also Hung Dead.*
Manises , *Ermita St Antonio, 1, 0-0-12., - Chimed Only.*
Manises , *Inmaculado Corazon de Maria, 1, 3-0-2., - Chimed Only.*
Manises , *Ntra Sra del Carmen, 1, 0-2-22., - Chimed Only.*
Manises , *St Francisco de Asis, 1, 0-0-10., - Chimed Only.*
Manises , *St Joan Baptiste, 5, 17-2-4., - Chimed Only, The Second was cast in 1799.*
Manzanera , *Ayuntamiento, 1, 1-1-16., - Automatically Chimed Only.*
Manzanera , *El Salvador, 4, 5-1-20., - The Treble and Second are Counterbalanced and Lever Chimed, The Third and Tenor are Clapper Chimed Only, The Treble and Second were cast by Manclus in 1956, The Third and Tenor were cast by Portilla in 1967.*
Manzanera , *El Salvador de El Paul, 1, - Chimed Only.*
Manzanera , *Ermita de la Virgin del Loreto, 1, 0-0-8., - Chimed Only.*
Manzanera , *St Antonio de los Cerezos, 1, 1-1-20., - Automatically Swing Chimed Only.*
Manzanera , *Sta Barbara de los Olmos, 1, 0-1-20., - Automatically Swing Chimed Only.*
Manzanera , *Sta Quiteria de Alcotas, 2, 2-2-18., - Chimed Only, Cast by Manclus in 1952.*
Marines , *Cristo de las Mercedes de Marines Nuevo, 4, 3-0-2., - Chimed Only.*
Marines , *Cristo del Perdon de Marines Viejo, 3, 2-0-14., - Clapper Chimed Only.*
Masllorenc , *St Ramon de Penyafort, 2, 9cwt., - Chimed Only, The Treble was cast in 1605 and the Tenor in 1855.*
Massalfassar , *Sant Llorenc, 4, 4-0-14., - Chimed Only.*
Massamagrell , *Monestir de la Magdalena , 1, 1-0-4., - Chimed Only.*
Massamagrell , *St Joan Evangeliste, 5, 13-2-22., - Chimed Only, The Tenor was cast by Borras in 1761 and the rest by Roses in 1940.*
Massamagrell , *Terciarias Capuchinas, 1, 0-1-6., - Chimed Only, This Bell was cast in 1750.*
Massanassa , *Escoles de St Josep i St Andreu, 1, 0-1-12., - Chimed Only, This Bell was cast by Garcia in 1791.*
Massanassa , *St Antoni de Padua, 1, 1-0-12., - Chimed Only.*
Massanassa , *Sant Pere, 4, 19-0-2., - Automatically Swing Chimed Only, There are also Two other Bells in the Tower that are Chimed Only.*
Matet , *Ermita, 1, 0-1-2., - Chimed Only.*
Matet , *St Juan Bautista, 3, 6-0-14., - Chimed Only, Cast by Manclus in 1959 and 1966.*
Mediona , *St Joan de Mediona, 1, 7-1-8., - Chimed Only, This Bell was cast by Goma Roldegu in 1827.*
Mediona , *St Pere Sacarrera, 1, 0-2-18., - Chimed Only.*
Meliana , *Ermita de la Providencia, 1, 0-2-22., - Chimed Only.*
Meliana , *Ermita Ntra Sra Misericordia, 1, 0-2-6., - Automatically Swing Chimed Only, This Bell was cast in 1659.*
Meliana , *Ntra Sra de la Misericordia de Roca-Cuiper, 2, 1-1-16., - Chimed Only, The Treble was cast in 1750 and the Tenor by Manclus in 1970.*
Meliana , *Sts Joans, 6, 18-0-6., - Chimed Only.*
Millares , *La Transfiguracion, 4, 3-3-12., - Automatically Swing Chimed Only.*
Millena, *St Josep, 3, 6-0-14., - Automatically Swing Chimed Only.*
Miramar , *St Andreu Apostol, 4, 16-0-26., - Automatically Swing Chimed Only.*
Mislata , *Hnas Doc Cristiana, 5, 6-0-14., - Chimed Only, The Treble was cast in 1912 and the rest were cast by Manclus Salvador in 1957.*
Mislata , *Ntra Sra dels Angels, 4, 16-2-14., - Chimed Only, The Treble and Tenor were cast by Roses in 1970 and 1942, The Second was cast in 1798 and the Third in 1690.*

Mislata, St Francesc d'Asis, 1, 0-1-12., - Chimed Only.
Moixent, Ermita del Calvari, 1, 0-1-20., - Chimed Only in a Belcote.
Moixent, Purisima Concepcio, 1, - Chimed Only in a Belcote.
Moixent, Purissima de Mas de Rabossa, 1, - Chimed Only.
Moixent, St Pere Apostol, 5, 22-2-4., - Counterbalanced, No Wheels, The **Treble** can be Rung Full Circle and weights 0-2-6. The rest are Automatically Swing Chimed, Hexagonal Tower.
Moncada, Bancaixa, 1, 1-3-8., - Chimed Only.
Moncada, Casa Obreras de la Cruz, 1, 0-2-12., - Chimed Only.
Moncada, Convent Franciscanes Inmaculada, 5, 1-1-8., - Chimed Only.
Moncada, Ermita de St Josep, 4, 2-2-18., - Chimed Only.
Moncada, Iglisia St Isidro de Benagever, 3, 1-2-6., - Chimed Only, Cast by Manclus in 1980.
Moncada, Religiosas Oblatas, 1, 0-2-12., - Chimed Only.
Moncada, St Jaume, 7, 19-2-0., - The Tenor is Automatically Swing Chimed Only and the rest are Chimed Only.
Monforte del Cid, Ermita de la Aparicion - Orito, 1, 0-2-18., - Chimed Only in a Belcote.
Monforte del Cid, Ermita St Pascual Bailon, 1, 0-2-18., - Chimed Only in a Belcote.
Monforte del Cid, Ermita St Rogue, 1, 0-1-2., - Chimed Only in a Belcote.
Monforte del Cid, Ntra Sra de las Nieves, 4, 9-2-4., - The Treble is Hung Dead and the rest are Automatically Swing Chimed Only, The Third was cast in 1678.
Monover, St Joan Baptista, 5, 22-0-6., - The Treble is Counterbalanced and Lever Chimed, The rest are Automatically Swing Chimed Only, These Bells were cast by Roses in 1940, 1963 and 1971.
Montan, Convento Servitas, **1**, 0-1-6., - Counterbalanced, No Wheel, Hung in the Wall of the Building.
Montan, St Bernardo, 2, 8-2-16., - Automatically Swing Chimed Only.
Montanejos, Santiago Apostol, 3, 7-3-4., - Automatically Swing Chimed Only.
Montaverner, St Jaume i St Joan Evangeliste, 4, 12-1-0., - Automatically Swing Chimed Only.
Montesa, Assumpcio, **1**, 5-3-8., - Counterbalanced, No Wheels, There is also Three other Bells that are Automatically Swing Chimed, Also there are Two Bells on the roof Hung Dead one of the Bells is Hemispherical and the other is a normal bell, There is another Bell Hung Dead and Chimed by moving the clapper with a rope and One Bell on Display.
Montilla, Parroquia del Apostol Santiago, 10, 20-2-0., - Chimed Only, The Eighth was cast in 1550.
Monzon, Catedral de Santa Maria del Romeral, 3, 23-2-16., - Automatically Swing Chimed Only.
Morcin, Capilla Palacio de St Esteban, 1, 0-0-18., - Chimed Only, This Bell was cast in 1793.
Morella, La Llecua, 3, 0-0-8., - Chimed Only, The Treble was cast in 1697, The Second was cast by Corral in 1799 and the Tenor was cast in 1450.
Morella, Museu de Santa Maria, 2, 1-2-16., - Chimed Only.
Morella, Santa Maria, 6, 30-1-14., - Automatically Swing Chimed Only, The Tenor was cast by Mestres in 1756.
Moya, Santa Maria la Mayor, 3, 13-1-12., - Chimed Only, The Treble and Tenor were cast in 1757 and 1746, The Second was cast by Gargollo in 1815.
Moyuela, Nuestra Senora de la Piedad, 2, - Chimed Only.
Murcia, Catedral de Sta Maria, 25, 128-1-12., - Automatically Chimed Only, There is also Three Bells on Display including One cast in 1383 and Also a Hemispherical Bell Hung Dead cast in 1731.
Murcia, St Pedro, 4, 7-3-4., - Automatically Swing Chimed Only, The Treble was cast by Lopez, The Second was cast by Portilla in 2000, The Third was cast by Costa in 1940, The Tenor was cast by Murua in 1986.
Murcia, Santuario de Ntra Sra de la Fuensanta, 4, 5-3-8., - Automatically Swing Chimed Only.
Murcia, Virgin de los Peligros, 1, 0-1-20., - Chimed Only, This Bell was cast in 1684.
Murla, Ermita de la Sang, 1, 0-0-22., - Chimed Only in a Belcote.
Murla, Ermita St Sebastia, 1, 0-1-16., - Chimed Only.

<u>Murla</u>, St Miguel, 4, 14-2-2., - Chimed Only, Hexagonal Tower attached to a Castle Style Church.
<u>Muro de Alcoy</u>, Ermita Ntra Sra dels Desamparats, 2, 1-1-8., - Chimed Only in Two Small Belcotes.
<u>Murio de Alcoy</u>, Ermita St Antoni, 1, 0-0-18., - Chimed Only.
<u>Murio de Alcoy</u>, Maria de Gracia de Benamer, 1, 0-1-20., - Chimed Only in a Belcote.
Murio de Alcoy, St Francesc de Turballos, **3**, 2-2-0., - Counterbalanced, No Wheels, These Bells were cast by Roses in 1954 and 1989.
<u>Murio de Alcoy</u>, St Joan Baptista, 4, 17-2-4., - Automatically Swing Chimed Only, There is also Two more Bells in the Tower that are Chimed Only with a Tenor of 11-2-2.
<u>Murio de Alcoy</u>, St Joaquim de Cetla de Nunez, 2, 5-0-8., - Automatically Swing Chimed Only, these bells were cast by Roses in 1939 and 1940.
<u>Museros</u>, Assumpcio de Ntra Sra, 4, 9-3-8., - The Treble is Chimed Only and the rest are Automatically Swing Chimed Only, The Treble was cast in 1717.
<u>Museros</u>, Ermita St Roc, 1, 0-1-20., - Chimed Only, This Bell was cast by Roses in 1944.
<u>Mutxamel</u>, Convent Mercedares, 1, 1-1-8., - Counterbalanced, No Wheel, Clapper Chimed Only.
<u>Mutxamel</u>, El Salvador, 5, 22-2-4., - Automatically Swing Chimed Only, There is also Three Hemispherical Bells Hung Dead above each other outside the Church.
<u>Naquera</u>, Ermita, 1, 0-3-14., - Chimed Only.
<u>Naquera</u>, Mare de Deu de l'Encarnacio, 5, 2-2-18., - Treble, Three and Tenor are Automatically Swing Chimed Only, The Fourth is Counterbalanced with No Wheel and the Second is Hung Dead.
<u>Navajas</u>, Parroquial, 4, 9-1-2., - Chimed Only.
<u>Navarres</u>, Asuncion, 4, 13-1-12., - The Treble is Counterbalanced with No Wheel, Clapper Chimed and Hung in the Church, The rest are Automatically Swing Chimed Only.
<u>Navarres</u>, Ermita Cristo de la Salud, 1, - Automatically Swing Chimed Only.
<u>Navascues</u>, Ermita Ntra Sra del Campo, 1, 1-1-16., - Chimed Only, This Bell was cast in 1500.
<u>Novelda</u>, Museu Arqueologic, 1, 0-2-12., - Chimed Only, This Bell was cast by Plassa in 1678.
<u>Novetle</u>, Nosta Senyora del Rosari, 4, 4-0-14., - Automatically Swing Chimed Only.
<u>Nules</u>, Capella de la Mare de Deu dels Desemparats i Santa Rita, 1, 0-1-2., - Chimed Only.
<u>Nules</u>, Esglesia de l'antic Hospital de la Vila, 1, - Chimed Only, This Bell was cast in 1700.
<u>Nules</u>, Esglesia del Convent, 1, - Chimed Only, This Bell was cast in 1640.
<u>Nules</u>, St Bertomeu, 4, - Automatically Swing Chimed Only, There is also Four more Bells in the tower that are Chimed Only.
<u>Olerdola</u>, St Jaume de Moja, 2, 4-2-12., - Chimed Only, These Bells were cast in 1940.
<u>Olerdola</u>, St Miquel de la Plana Rodona, 2, 3-3-12., - The Tenor is Automatically Swing Chimed Only and the Treble is Chimed Only.
<u>Olerdola</u>, St Pere Molanta, 1, 2-2-18., - Chimed Only.
<u>Olesa de Bonesvalls</u>, St Joan Baptista, 1, 2-2-0., - Chimed Only.
<u>Olite</u>, Sta Maria, 1, 1-3-8., - Chimed Only, This Bell was cast in 1475.
<u>Oliva</u>, Arc de St Vicent, 1, - Chimed Only in a Belcote.
<u>Oliva</u>, Ntra Sra del Rebollet, 1, - Automatically Swing Chimed Only.
<u>Oliva</u>, St Roc, 5, 12-2-8., - Automatically Swing Chimed Only, The Third was cast by Manclus in 1960 and the rest were cast by Roses in 1960.
<u>Oliva</u>, Sant Francesc, 4, - Automatically Swing Chimed Only in a Modern Style Tower.
<u>Oliva</u>, Sta Maria la Major, 5, 22-2-4., - Automatically Swing Chimed Only, There is also Three more Bells Hung Dead.
Olocau, Mare de Deu del Rosari, **4**, 6-3-2., - Counterbalanced, No Wheels.
<u>Olocau</u>, Mas del Capella, 1, 0-1-0., - Chimed Only and Hung Dead.
Olocau del Rey, Ntra Sra del Populo, **1**, 1-3-8., - Counterbalanced, No Wheels.
<u>Ona</u>, Salvador, 4, - Chimed Only.
<u>Onda</u>, Assumpcio, 4, 15-1-12., - Chimed Only, The Treble was cast by Dencausse in 1917, The Second was cast by Arcos in 1739, The Third was cast by Linares in 1927 and the Tenor was cast by Roses in 1804.
<u>Onda</u>, Convent de Clarises, 3, 1-1-24., - Chimed Only.

Onda, St Bartolome, 1, 0-2-22., - Chimed Only.
Onda, Virgin de la Esperanza, 2, 5-1-0., - Chimed Only.
Ondara, Santa Anna, 2, 7-0-10., - Automatically Swing Chimed Only, Cast by Roses in 1940.
Ondara, Sants Abdon i Senent (Pamis), 1, 0-1-20., - Chimed Only.
Ondara, Soledat, 2, 1-1-16., - Automatically Swing Chimed Only, These Bells were cast by Roses in 1948 and are the same weight.
Ondara, Torre del Rellotge, 1, 9-2-4., - Clock Bell, Hung Dead in a Belcote on top of the Tower, This Bell was cast by Roses in 1823.
Onil, Convent, 1, - Chimed Only in a Belcote.
Onil, St Jaume, 4, 15-1-12., - Automatically Swing Chimed Only.
Ontinyent, Concepcio, **3**, 2-3-4., - Counterbalanced, No Wheels, These Bells were cast by Roses in 1942, 1948 and 1956.
Ontinyent, Convent de Carmelites Calcades, 2, 3-3-12., - Automatically Swing Chimed Only, These Bells were cast in 1602 and 1898.
Ontinyent, Convent de la Concepcio, (Torre Dreta), 1, 3-0-2., - Automatically Swing Chimed Only, This Bell was cast by Roses in 1941, (Torre Esquerra), 3, 10-3-4., - Automatically Swing Chimed Only.
Ontinyent, Ermita de Morera, 1, 1-2-6., - Chimed Only.
Ontinyent, Ermita Sta Anna, 2, 6-2-6., - Automatically Swing Chimed Only.
Ontinyent, Hospital de Beneficencia, 2, 0-2-6., - Automatically Swing Chimed Only.
Ontinyent, La Clariana, 1, 0-1-8., - Automatically Chimed Only.
Ontinyent, La Salut, 1, 0-2-22., - Chimed Only.
Ontinyent, St Carles Borromeu, 4, 25-1-16., - Automatically Swing Chimed Only, These Bells were cast by Roses in 1939, 1941 and 1956.
Ontinyent, St Esteve, 2, 0-3-8., - Chimed Only.
Ontinyent, St Francesc, 4, 8-2-16., - Automatically Swing Chimed Only.
Ontinyent, St Josep, 1, 0-3-8., - Automatically Chimed Only.
Ontinyent, St Miquel, 1, 1-1-16., - Chimed Only.
Ontinyent, St Rafael, 2, 1-0-20., - The Tenor is Automatically Swing Chimed Only and the Treble is Chimed Only, These Bells were cast by Portilla in 1996.
Ontinyent, Sta Maria, **10**, 29-2-2, - Counterbalanced, No Wheels, There is also in the Tower One Bell Lever Chimed and One Bell Hung Dead.
Orba, Naixement del Senyor, 3, 14-2-2., - Automatically Swing Chimed Only.
Orcheta, Sant Jaume, 3, 4-3-4., - Automatically Swing Chimed Only, Cast by Roses in 1940.
Orihuela, Asilo, 1, 1-2-6., - Chimed Only, This Bell was cast by Senac in 1921.
Orihuela, Carmen, 2, 2-3-4., - Chimed Only, These Bells were cast in 1709 and 1789.
Orihuela, Catedral de El Salvador, 6, 27-0-24., - Automatically Swing Chimed Only, Also there is Two other Bells in the Tower One Hemispherical and One Normal Hung Dead.
Orihuela, Colegio de Santo Domingo, 5, 9cwt., - Chimed Only, The Treble and Third was cast by Bou in 1888, The Second was cast in 1650, The Fourth and Tenor was cast by Roses in 1952.
Orihuela, Convento San Francisco, 3, 3-0-2., - Chimed Only.
Orihuela, Ermita de la calle de arriba, 2, 0-0-24., - Chimed Only.
Orihuela, Ermita de la Cruz Cubierta, 1, 1-1-24., - Chimed Only.
Orihuela, Ermita del Molino de la Ciudad, 1, 0-1-20., - Chimed Only.
Orihuela, Ermita del Pilar, 1, 1-0-4., - Chimed Only.
Orihuela, Ermita del Sagrado Corazon, 1, 0-1-20., - Chimed Only.
Orihuela, Monastrio de la Trinidad, 3, 2-0-14., - Chimed Only.
Orihuela, Monastrio de la Visitacion, 2, 2-1-8., - Chimed Only.
Orihuela, Monastrio de San Juan de la Penitencia, 4, 1-3-8., - Chimed Only, The Treble was cast in 1640.
Orihuela, Monasterio de San Sebastian, 3, 4-0-14., - Chimed Only, The Treble was cast in 1649, The Second and Tenor was cast by Senac in 1881.

Orihuela, Ntra Sra del Remedio de la Matanza-Orihuela, 2, 5-3-8., - Automatically Swing Chimed Only, The Treble was cast in 1804 and the Tenor by Manclus in 1979.
Orihuela, Oratorio Festivo, 2, 1-0-12., - Chimed Only, Cast by Roses in 1957 and 1959.
Orihuela, Reloj Municipal (Clock Tower), 1, - Hung Dead, Clock Bell, The Bell Tower is Triangular in Shape in a modern steel structure and looks like Half of a Pyramid.
Orihuela, San Agustin, 1, 6-1-10., - Chimed Only, This Bell was cast in 1723.
Orihuela, San Vicente Ferrer, 3, 2-0-14., - Chimed Only, These Bells were cast by Manclus in 1977.
Orihuela, Santas Justa y Rufina, 6, 33-0-14., - Chimed Only, The Third was cast by Manclus in 1975, The Tenor was cast by Lastra in 1644 and the rest were cast by Roses in 1802, 1889 and 1970.
Orihuela, Santiago Apostol, 5, 25-1-16., - Chimed Only, The Treble was cast by Lebrecht in 1782, The Second and Third was cast by Torre in 1587, The Fourth was cast by Roses in 1816 and the Tenor was cast in 1600.
Orihuela, Santuario de Monserrate, 3, 4-0-14., - Chimed Only, The Treble was cast in 1650, The Second by Roses in 1890 and the Tenor was cast in 1776.
Orihuela, Seminario, 5, 5-0-8., - Chimed Only.
Orpesa, Ntra Sra de la Paciencia, 3, 5-3-8., - Chimed Only, There is also Two Bells Hung Dead in a Steel Frame on the roof.
Os de Balaguer, Sant Miquel, 2, 0-0-12., - Chimed Only.
Oscos, Capilla de St Maria de Quinta en Barcia, 1, 0-2-12., - Chimed Only.
Oscos, Capilla del Palacio de Mon, St Martin, 1, - Chimed Only, This Bell was cast in 1790.
Oscos, Parroquia San Martin, 2, 2-0-2., - Chimed Only, These Bells were cast in 1777.
Oscos, Parroquial de Sta Eulalia, 2, 3-1-20., - Chimed Only, These Bells were cast in 1851.
Otos, Purissima Concepcio, 4, - Chimed Only.
Oviedo, Casa Consistorial, 2, 3-3-12., - Chimed Only.
Oviedo, Catedral, 13, 43-0-12., - Chimed by Putting Ropes on the Clappers and a couple set up for Lever Chiming Only.
Oviedo, Coleccion Tabvlarium Artis Astvriensis, 1, 0-0-6., - Chimed Only, This Bell was cast in 1300.
Oviedo, Iglesia Santullano de los Prados, 1, 3-2-24., - Chimed Only.
Oviedo, Parroquial de Loriana, 2, 3-3-12., - Chimed Only.
Oviedo, Parroquial de Naranco, 1, 4-3-4., - Chimed Only.
Oviedo, San Isidoro, 2, 3-0-18., - Chimed Only, These Bells were cast in 1500 and 1790.
Oviedo, San Pelayo, 1, 5-3-8., - Chimed Only.
Oviedo, San Tirso el Real, 2, 3-0-2., - Chimed Only.
Oviedo, Universidad, 2, 4-2-12., - Chimed Only, These Bells were cast in 1668.
Pacs, St Genis, 2, 3-1-20., - Chimed Only, These Bells were cast in 1698 and 1693.
Paiporta, San Jorge, 5, 18-1-26., - Chimed Only, The Treble was cast in 1662.
Paiporta, San Ramon Nonato, 3, 6-1-10., - Chimed Only, These Bells were cast by Portilla in 1998.
Palma de Gandia, St Miquel Arcangel, 4, 9cwt., - Automatically Swing Chimed Only.
Palmera, Purissima Concepcio, 4, 10-0-24., - Automatically Swing Chimed Only.
Palomar, St Pere Apostol, 3, 14-2-2., - Automatically Swing Chimed Only, All the Bells were cast by Roses between 1801 - 1828.
Pamplona, Catedral de Sta Maria del Sagrario, (Torre dcha, South Tower), **5**, 40-2-10., - Counterbalanced, No Wheels, There is also Two other Bells in the Tower that are Automatically Swing Chimed Only, (Torre Izquierda, North Tower), 4, 201-0-18., - Chimed Only, Clock Bells, These Four Bells were cast by Villanueva Pedro de between 1519 - 1584.
Parcent, Immaculada, 2, 11-0-22., - Chimed Only, There is also another bell in the Tower Hung Dead and weights 3-3-12.
Paterna, Col. Lege Imperial dels Xiquets de St Vicent, **4**, 4-0-14., - Counterbalanced, No Wheels.
Paterna, Convent de Sta Caterina de Siena, 1, 0-2-18., - Chimed Only.

Paterna, Mare de Deu dels Desamparats, 3, 4-0-14., - Chimed Only, Cast by Manclus in 1973.
Paterna, St Antonio Abad de St Antonio de Benagever, 1, 1-2-26., - Chimed Only.
Paterna, St Pere, 5, 17-0-14., - Chimed Only, These Bells were cast by Roses in 1941, 1961 and 1969.
Paterna, Stm Crist de la Fe de La Canada, 1, 2-2-18., - Chimed Only.
Pavias, Sta Catalina, 4, 7-2-6., - Chimed Only.
Pedralba, Purisima Concepcion, 6, 14-3-14., - The Third and Tenor are Automatically Swing Chimed Only and the rest are Chimed Only.
Pedreguer, Sta Creu, 4, 17-0-14., - Automatically Swing Chimed Only, There is also a Hemispherical Bell in the tower wich is Hung Dead and weights 3-0-18.
Pedroso de Armuna, Parroquia, 2, 11-3-8., - Chimed Only, The Tenor was cast in 1716.
Pego, Assumpcio, 4, 16-0-26., - Automatically Swing Chimed Only, There is also One Hemispherical Bell Hung Dead which weights 2-2-6., There is also Two more bells in the Tower that are Chimed Only with a Tenor of 16-0-26.
Pego, Ecce Homo, 1, 7-1-8., - Automatically Swing Chimed Only.
Pego, Ermita St Josep, 1, 1-1-8., - Chimed Only in a Belcote.
Pego, Ermita St Miquel, 1, 0-2-6., - Lever Chimed Only in a Belcote.
Pego, Residencia San Juan de Dios, 1, - Chimed Only in a Belcote on top of a Residencial Building.
Pego, Sagrada Familia, 3, 14-2-2., - Automatically Swing Chimed Only.
Penaguila, Ajuntament, 1, - Automatically Swing Chimed in a Belcote.
Penaguila, Assumpcio, 4, 18-0-6., - Automatically Swing Chimed Only.
Penarroya de Tastavins, Parroquia, 2, 8-1-16., - Chimed Only.
Peniscola, Capelleta Sta Anna, 1, 0-0-8., - Chimed Only in a Belcote.
Peniscola, Mare de Deu de l'Ermitana, 2, 5-3-8., - Chimed Only.
Peniscola, Ntra Sra del Socorro, 4, 4-2-0., - Chimed Only.
Pertusa, Parroquia, 1, 5-3-8., - Automatically Swing Chimed Only.
Petrer, Ermita St Bonifacio, 1, - Chimed Only.
Petrer, Ermita Sto Cristo, 1, - Chimed Only, This Bell was cast in 1661.
Petrer, St Bartolome, 6, 13-1-12., - Chimed Only.
Petres, Ermita de Sto Domingo, 1, 0 2-22., - Chimed Only.
Petres, Sant Jaume, 4, 9-1-2., - Chimed Only, These Bells were cast in 1915, 1730, 1891 and 1814.
Picanya, Ntra Sra de Montserrat, 4, 10-3-4., - Chimed Only.
Picassent, Casa de Chuan el Obrer, 1, 1-0-4., - Chimed Only.
Picassent, Esglesia de Venta de Espioca, 1, 0-1-26., - Chimed Only, This Bell was cast in 1733.
Picassent, La Milagrosa, 3, 8-2-16., - Chimed Only.
Picassent, Ma Agustinas, 2, 1-3-8., - Chimed Only.
Picassent, Mare de Deu de la Vallivana, 2, 2-1-8., - Chimed Only, Cast by Roses in 1940.
Picassent, Sant Cristobal Martir, 4, 17-0-14., - Chimed Only, Cast by Roses in 1939 and 1940.
Pilar de la Horadada, Ntra Sra del Pilar, 3, 7-1-8., - Automatically Swing Chimed Only.
Piles, Santa Barbera, 3, 15-1-12., - Automatically Swing Chimed Only.
Pina de Montalgrao, San Salvador, 4, 5-1-0., - Automatically Swing Chimed Only, These Bells were cast in 1736, 1842, 1475 and 1876.
Pinet, St Pere Apostol, 1, - Chimed Only.
Pintoria, Parroquial, 1, - Chimed Only, This Bell was cast in 1817.
Pitarque, Sta Maria la Mayor, **2**, 3-3-12., - The **Tenor** is Counterbalanced with No Wheel and the Treble is Automatically Swing Chimed Only, These Bells are the Same weight.
Planes, Assumpcio, **4**, 9-2-4., - Counterbalanced, No Wheels.
Planes, St Francesc de Margarida, 2, 3-0-18., - Automatically Swing Chimed Only.
Planes, St Joan de Benialfaqui, 1, 1-2-6., - Chimed Only in a Belcote, There is also another Bell in the Church which was cast in 1656 and weighs 0-0-22.
Planes, St Josep de Catamarruc, 2, 4-0-14., - Chimed Only.

Pola de Lena , *Capilla de la Flor, 1, 0-1-20., - Chimed Only, This Bell was cast in 1753.*
Polop de la Marina , *St Pere, 4, 8-0-16., - Automatically Swing Chimed Only, These Bells were cast by Roses in 1945 and 1989.*
Polop de la Marina , *St Ramon Nonat de Chirles, 1, 2-2-18., - Chimed Only.*
Pontons , *Sta Magdalena, 2, 7-0-10., - Chimed Only.*
Portell de Morella , *Assumpcio, 3, 9-2-4., - Chimed Only.*
Portell de Morella , *Ermita de l'Albereda, 1, 2-3-4., - Chimed Only.*
Portell de Morella , *Ermita de l'Esperanca, 1, 0-2-18., - Chimed Only.*
Potries , *Ermita Stm Crist de l'Agonia, 1, 0-1-0., - Chimed Only in a Belcote.*
Potries , *Sants Joans, 3, 6-3-2., - Automatically Swing Chimed Only.*
Pozuelo de Tabara , *Parroquia, 3, 9cwt., - Chimed Only.*
Pravia , *Parroquial de Pravia, 2, - Chimed Only.*
Pucol , *Convent Carmelites, 1, 0-3-0., - Chimed Only.*
Pucol , *Ermita Mare de Deu del Carme, 1, 0-1-0., - Chimed Only.*
Pucol , *Sta Marta, 1, 1-2-16., - Chimed Only.*
Pucol , *Sts Joans, 5, 18-1-26., - Chimed Only.*
Puebla de Arenoso , *Ermita Virgin del Loreto, 1, 0-1-0., - Chimed Only in a Belcote.*
Puebla de Arenoso , *St Mateo, 2, 4-3-4., - The Treble is Hung Dead and the Tenor is Automatically Swing Chimed Only, The Treble was cast by Roses in 1944 and the Tenor was cast by Moreno in 1909.*
Puebla de Arenoso , *Virgin del Rosario de Los Calps, 2, 1-3-8., - Chimed Only.*
Puebla de Benifasar , *Assumpcio de El Boixar, 1, 10-2-0., - Chimed Only, This Bell was cast in 1793.*
Puebla de Benifasar , *Assumpcio de Ntra Sra, 1, 3-2-8., - Chimed Only, This Bell was cast in 1797.*
Puebla de Benifasar , *El Salvador de El Ballestar, 1, 3-2-8., - Chimed Only.*
Puebla de Benifasar , *Monestir de Benifassar, 3, - Chimed Only, Cast by Arragon in 1900.*
Puebla de Benifasar , *St Jaume de Coratxar, 1, 0-2-6., - Chimed Only.*
Puebla de Benifasar , *Sts Abdo i Senent de Fredes, 1, 2-1-8., - Chimed Only.*
Puebla de San Miguel , *St Miguel, 3, 7-1-8., - The* **Tenor** *is Counter Balanced with No Wheel, The Rest are Chimed Only.*
Puebla Tornesa , *St Miquel, 3, 5-1-0., - Automatically Swing Chimed Only.*
Quart de les Valls , *Ermita Crist de la Agonia, 1, 0-3-0., - Chimed Only.*
Quart de les Valls , *Ermita del Populo, 1, 0-0-20., - Chimed Only, This Bell was cast in 1770.*
Quart de les Valls , *St Miquel Archangel, 3, 9-1-2., - Chimed Only, The Treble was cast in 1731.*
Quart de Poblet , *Hospital Militar, 2, 1-3-8., - Chimed Only, These Bells were cast by Roses in 1952.*
Quart de Poblet , *Purissima, 4, 9-3-8., - Chimed Only.*
Quart de Poblet , *St Onofre, 2, 0-2-18., - Chimed Only.*
Quart de Poblet , *Sgda Familia, 1, 0-3-0., - Chimed Only.*
Quart de Poblet , *Sta Cecilia, 1, 0-2-22., - Chimed Only.*
Quartell , *Sta Anna, 3, 11-0-22., - Chimed Only, The Treble was cast in 1725, The Second and Tenor was cast by Guillem in 1801.*
Quatretonda , *Capella del Cementeri, 1, 0-0-2., - Chimed Only.*
Quatretonda , *Ermita de St Josep, 1, 1-0-4., - Chimed Only in a Belcote.*
Quatretonda , *Sts Joans, 4, 9-3-8., - Automatically Swing Chimed Only, The Treble was cast by Diego in 1738, There is also Two Bells Hung Dead with a Tenor of 11-3-8. and another Bell on Display cast in 1750 which weights 0-0-16, Hexagonal Tower.*
Quesa , *St Antonio Abad,* **4**, *8-0-16., - Counterbalanced, No Wheels.*
Rafelbunyol , *St Antoni Abad, 6, 14-0-18., - Chimed Only.*
Rafelcofer , *St Antoni de Padua, 4, 10-0-24., - Automatically Swing Chimed Only.*
Rafelguaraf , *Naixement del Senyor, 3, 3-1-20., - Chimed Only.*
Rafol de Almunia , *St Francesc de Paula, 2, 5-1-0., - Chimed Only.*

Rafol de Salem , Ntra Sra dels Angels, 3, 8-1-16., - Automatically Swing Chimed Only.
Real de Gandia , Visitacio de Ntra Sra, 3, 6-2-6., - Automatically Swing Chimed Only, The Treble and Second were cast by Calleja de la in 1779. The Tenor was cast by Roses in 1847.
Relleu , St Jaume, **3**, 9cwt., - Counterbalanced, No Wheels.
Requena , Carmen, 2, 1-2-26., - Automatically Swing Chimed Only, Cast in 1785 and 1898.
Requena , Convento Agustinas Recoletas, 1, 0-1-12., - Chimed Only in a Belcote.
Requena , El Salvador, 6, 28-1-20., - Chimed Only, These Bells were cast by Roses in 1803 and 1969.
Requena , Inmaculada Concepcion de Casas de Eufemia, 1, 1-0-12., - Chimed Only.
Requena , Nra Sra del Milagro de Los Ruices, 1, - Chimed Only.
Requena , Ntra Sra de la Encarnacion de Los Duques, 1, - Chimed Only in a Belcote.
Requena , St Antonio Abad de Los Isidros, 2, 1-1-8., - Chimed Only, The Tenor was cast in 1692.
Requena , St Antonio de Padua de Casas del Rio, 1, 0-2-18., - Chimed Only.
Requena , St Antonio de Padua de Los Pedrones, 1, 0-1-6., - Chimed Only in a Belcote, This Bell was cast in 1670.
Requena , St Antonio de Padua de St Antonio, 2, - Chimed Only.
Requena , St Francisco, 1, 3-1-4., - Chimed Only, This Bell was cast in 1911.
Requena , St Juan Bautista de San Juan, 1, 1-2-6., - Chimed Only.
Requena , St Nicolas, **3**, 15-2-26., - Counterbalanced, No Wheels.
Requena , St Sebastian, 1, - Chimed Only.
Requena , Sta Maria, **4**, 30-1-14., - Counterbalanced, No Wheels, The Treble is a very weird shaped Bell.
Ribadesella , Parroquia Ucio, 1, - Chimed Only, This Bell was cast in 1775.
Riba-Roja del Turia , Assumpcio de Ntra Sra, 4, 14-2-2., - Automatically Swing Chimed Only.
Riba-Roja del Turia , Sant Gregori, 5, 1-0-20., - The Fourth and Tenor are Automatically Swing Chimed Only, The rest are Chimed Only, The Tenor was cast in 1550.
Riba-Roja del Turia , Xalet Hereus d'Artemi Molla, 1, 1-3-8., - Chimed Only.
Ribesalbes , St Cristofol, 4, - Chimed Only.
Rocafort , St Sebastia, 4, 7-0-10., - Chimed Only, The Treble was cast in 1792 and the rest were cast by Roses in 1944.
Rocafort , Sta Barbera, 2, 0-2-22., - Chimed Only, These Bells were cast by Manclus in 1980.
Roda de Isabena , Catedral de San Vicente Martir, 7, 14-2-2., - Automatically Swing Chimed Only, Octagonly Shaped Tower.
Rodenas , Sta Catalina, 3, 8-1-16., - Chimed Only, These Bells were cast in 1450 and 1750.
Rosell , St Jaume de Bel, 1, - Chimed Only, This Bell was cast in 1862.
Rosell , Sants Joans, 2, 13-2-22., - Chimed Only, These Bells were cast by Manclus in 1971.
Rotgla Y Corbera , Ermita Verge del Socors, 1, - Automatically Swing Chimed Only.
Rotgla Y Corbera , Sts Joans, 3, 13-0-02. - Automatically Swing Chimed Only.
Rotova , St Bartolome Apostol, 4, 10-0-24., - Automatically Swing Chimed Only.
St Cugat Sesgarrigues , 4, 9-3-8., - Chimed Only, The Treble and Second were cast by Dencausse in 1892, The Third and Tenor were cast by Mestres in 1950.
St Jaume dels Domenys , St Jaume, 2, 8-1-16., - Chimed Only, The Tenor was cast by Tarantino in 1800.
St Llorenc D'Hortons , St Joan Baptista de St Joan Samora, 2, 5-3-8., - Chimed Only, These Bells were cast by Murua in 1941.
St Llorenc D'Hortons , St Llorenc, 2, 5-3-8., - Chimed Only, These Bells were cast by Mestres in 1940.
St Marti Sarroca , Capella Mare de Deu de Montserrat, 1, 0-1-26., - Chimed Only, This Bell was cast by Barberi in 1948.
St Marti Sarroca , Sta Maria, 3, 10-0-24., - Chimed Only.
St Pere de Riudebitlles , St Pere, 3, 13-1-12., - Chimed Only, These bells were cast by Murua in 1949.

St Quinti de Mediona , *St Quinti, 3, 6-1-10.*, - *Chimed Only, The Treble was cast by Goma in 1698, The Second was cast by Dencausse in 1906 and the Tenor was cast by Forns in 1796.*
St Sadurni D'Anoia , *St Sadurni, 3, 17-2-4.*, - *Chimed Only, These bells were cast by Murua in 1941.*
Sacanet , *Santiago Apostol, 1, 1-2-26.*, - *Chimed Only.*
Sagra , *St Sebastia, 3, 6-0-14.*, - *Automatically Swing Chimed Only.*
Sagunt , *Col. Ntra. Sra. del Rosari, 1, 0-1-6.*, - *Chimed Only.*
Sagunt , *El Salvador, 3, 4-0-14.*, - *The Treble is Chimed Only and the rest are Automatically Swing Chimed Only, These Bells were cast by Roses in 1943.*
Sagunt , *Ermita de la Sang, 2, 0-1-2.*, - *Chimed Only.*
Sagunt , Ermita de Bon Succes, **1**, 0-1-2., - Counterbalanced, No Wheel.
Sagunt , *Ermita del Calvari, 1, 0-0-18.*, - *Chimed Only, This Bell was cast by Traver in 1860.*
Sagunt , *Ermita dels Dolors, 1, 0-1-0.*, - *Chimed Only.*
Sagunt , *Ermita Desamparats i St Roc, 1, 1-0-12.*, - *Chimed Only.*
Sagunt , *Ermita St Cristobal, 1, 0-1-2.*, - *Chimed Only.*
Sagunt , *Ermita Sant Miquel, 1, 0-0-20.*, - *Chimed Only.*
Sagunt , *Ermita Sta Alicia de Monte Picayo, 1, 0-3-0.*, - *Chimed Only.*
Sagunt , *Htas Ancianos Desamparados, 1, 1-0-12.*, - *Chimed Only.*
Sagunt , *Ntra Sra de Begona del Port de Sagunt, 2, 6-1-10.*, - *Chimed Only.*
Sagunt , *Ntra Sra del Carmen del Port de Sagunt, 5, 6-0-14.*, - *Chimed Only, The Treble was cast in 2000, The Second was cast in 1750 and the rest were cast by Roses in 1957.*
Sagunt , *St Josep del Port de Sagunt, 2, 1-1-16.*, - *Chimed Only.*
Sagunt , Santa Maria, **6**, 20cwt., - Counterbalanced, No Wheels, These Six Bells were All cast by Roses in 1948. There is also another Bell Automatically Swing Chimed Only.
Sagunt , *Sta Ana (Siervas de Maria), 2, 0-3-14.*, - *Chimed Only.*
Salas , *Iglesia Colegiata, 2, 5-1-20.*, - *Chimed Only, These Bells were cast in 1550 and 1808.*
Salas , *Parroquial de Bodenaya, 1, 3-1-4.*, - *Chimed Only.*
Salas , *Parroquial de La Espina, 2, 4-3-4.*, - *Chimed Only, These Bells were cast in 1799 and 1852.*
Salas , *Parroquial de Soto de los Infantes, 1, 1-1-0.*, - *Chimed Only, This Bell was cast in 1788.*
Salas Bajas , *San Vicente, 2, 10-3-4.*, - *Chimed Only.*
Salinas , *Reloj Municipal, 1,* - *Clock Bell, Hung Dead.*
Salinas , *St Antonio Abad, 4, 3-3-12.*, - *Automatically Swing Chimed Only, There is also another Bell in the Church that is Counterbalanced but is Chimed Only and weights 0-1-2.*
Salsadella , *Assumpcio, 3, 10-2-0.*, - *Chimed Only.*
Salsadella , *Ermita St Josep, 1, 0-2-18.*, - *Chimed Only.*
Salsadella , *Ermita Sta Barbera, 1, 0-0-8.*, - *Chimed Only in a Belcote.*
Salvatierra de los Barros , *Iglesia Parroquial, 2,* - *Chimed Only.*
San Juan de Alicante , *St Joan Baptista, (Torre de Campanas), 4, 16-2-14.*, - *Automatically Swing Chimed Only, These Bells were cast by Roses in 1939, 1959 and 1994., (Torre del Reloj), 2, 11-2-2.*, - *Chimed Only, Hung Dead, The Treble is a Hemispherical Bell which weights 1-1-16. and the Tenor is a very wide in the mouth normal Bell.*
San Juan de Alacante , *Santa Fac, 3, 5-2-14.*, - *The Treble is Hung Dead and Chimed Only, The rest are Automatically Swing Chimed Only, The Treble was cast by Rosdas in 1670, The Second was cast by Roses in 1940 and the Tenor was cast by Manclus in 1985.*
San Lorenzo de El Escorial , *Madrid, Monasterio de San Lorenzo el Real de El Escorial, 47,* - *Carillon.*
San Miguel de Salinas , *St Miguel, 2, 5-0-8.*, - *Chimed Only.*
San Pedro Manrique , *Plaza junto Ermita de la pena, 3,* - *Chimed Only, The Treble was cast in 1720.*
San Pedro Manrique , *St Martin, 5,* - *Chimed Only.*
San Rafael del Rio , *St Rafel, 2, 2-3-4.*, - *Chimed Only.*

San Vicente del Raspeig, St Vicent Ferrer, 3, 12-2-8., - *The Second is Chimed Only and the rest are Automatically Swing Chimed Only, These Bells were cast in 1801, 1968 and 1789.*
San Vicente del Raspeig, Sta Isabel, 2, 8-1-16., - *Automatically Swing Chimed Only, These Bells were cast by Manclus in 1985.*
Sanet Y Negrals, Sta Anna, **3**, 5-2-12., - Counterbalanced, No Wheels.
Sant Joan de Moro, St Antoni del Mas de Flors, 1, 0-1-8., - *Chimed Only.*
Sant Joan de Moro, St Joan Baptiste, 3, 5-2-14., - *Chimed Only.*
Sant Mateu, Arxiprestal de St Mateu, 4, 19-2-0., - *Automatically Swing Chimed Only, There is also Two more bells in the Tower that are Chimed Only with a Tenor of 1-1-8. and the Tenor was cast in 1730, Hexagonal Tower.*
Sant Mateu, Ermita St Cristofol, 1, 0-1-2., - *Chimed Only in a Belcote.*
Sant Mateu, Mare de Deu dels Angels, **2**, 2-2-0., - Counterbalanced, No Wheels, These Bells were cast by Cronos in 1952.
Sant Mateu, Monestir de Sta Anna, 1, 3-3-12., - *Chimed Only.*
Sant Mateu, St Pere, 1, 1-2-6., - *Chimed Only.*
Santa Cruz de Grio, San Blas, 2, 3-2-8., - *Chimed Only, The Treble was cast in 1773 and the Tenor was cast by Ballesteros in 1882.*
Santa Magdalena de Pulpis, Ajuntament, 1, 2-1-22., - *Automatically Swing Chimed Only, This Bell was cast in 1918.*
Santa Magdalena de Pulpis, Sta Magdalena, 2, 3-2-24., - *Chimed Only.*
Santa Maria de Palautordera, Santa Maria, 2, - *Chimed Only, Hexagonal Tower.*
Santo Domingo de la Calzada, Catedral de El Salvador y la Virgin de la Asuncion, **4**, 48-1-4., - Counterbalanced, No Wheels, There are also Two Bells Automatically Swing Chimed and Two Bells Hung Dead.
Sarratella, Ermita St Joan Nepomuceno, 1, 0-3-14., - *Chimed Only, This Bell was cast in 1764.*
Sarratella, St Miquel, 3, 1-2-16., - *Chimed Only, The Treble was cast in 1853, The Second was cast by Roses in 1950 and the Tenor was cast in 1685.*
Sax, Ermita Ntra Sra de la Soledad, 1, - *Chimed Only, This Bell was cast in 1816.*
Sax, Ermita St Blas, 1, - *Chimed Only.*
Sax, Ermita Sta Eulalia, 1, - *Chimed Only.*
Sedavi, Ntra Sra de Rosari, 5, 9-1-?, - *Chimed Only.*
Segart, Purissima Concepcio, 3, 1-3-8., - *Automatically Swing Chimed Only in a Belcote, The Treble and Second were cast by Manclus in 1990., The Tenor was cast in 1688.*
Segorbe, Casa Dr. Manuel Quixal, 2, 0-1-16., - *Chimed Only.*
Segorbe, Catedral de la Asuncion de Nuestra Senora, 7, 26-2-6., - *Counterbalanced, No Wheels, There are also Seven other Bells in the Tower that are Chimed Only, Trapezoidal Shaped Tower or an odd Square Shaped Tower.*
Segorbe, Convento de los Franciscanos, 1, 0-2-22., - *Chimed Only.*
Segorbe, Museo Catedralicio, 1, 0-0-24., - *On Display.*
Segorbe, St Fco de Asis de Villatorcas, 2, 1-1-0., - *Chimed Only.*
Segorbe, San Joaquin y Sta Ana, 2, 0-3-8., - *The Treble is Chimed Only and the Tenor is Automatically Swing Chimed Only, The Treble was cast in 1999 and the Tenor in 1628.*
Segorbe, San Martin, 3, 1-1-16., - *The Tenor is Automatically Swing Chimed Only and the rest are Chimed Only, The Treble was cast by Traver in 1886.*
Segrobe, San Pedro, 2, 0-3-8., - *Chimed Only, These Bells were cast in 1790 and 1701.*
Segrobe, Seminario, 1, 0-2-2., - *Chimed Only, This Bell was cast in 1883.*
Segrobe, Sta Maria, 2, 2-0-2., - *Chimed Only, The Treble was cast in 1779.*
Segrobe, Virgin de Cueva Santa de Penalba, 2, 0-1-26., - *Chimed Only, The Treble was cast in 1900 and the Tenor in 1719.*
Sella, Ermita, 1, 0-1-16., - *Chimed Only.*
Sella, Sta Anna, 2, 7-3-4., - *The Treble is Chimed Only and the Tenor is Automatically Swing Chimed Only.*
Sellent, Purissima, 1, - *Chimed Only, This Bell was cast in 1730.*

Senija , Sta Caterina, 4, 6-2-6., - Automatically Swing Chimed Only.
Serra , Ntra Sra dels Angels, **5**, 4-0-14., - The **Treble** is Counterbalanced with No Wheel and the rest are Automatically Swing Chimed Only, There is also another Bell in the Church that is Lever Chimed Only and weights 0-0-2.
Serra , Porta Coeli, 6, 4-1-4., - Chimed Only, These Bells were cast by Roses in 1948, 1949 and 1951.
Serra , Sant Josep, **1**, 0-0-12., - Counterbalanced, No Wheel.
Sevilla , Catedral de Sta Maria de la Sede, 24, 107-0-24., - Eighteen Bells are Automatically Swing Chimed and the rest are Hung Dead, Six of the Bells in the Tower were cast by Eijesbouts in 1998.
Sevilla , Hermanitas de los Pobres, 1, 3-3-12., - Automatically Swing Chimed Only, This Bell was cast by Oliva in 1892.
Sevilla , Museo Arqueologico, 1, 0-1-2., - Chimed Only, This Bell was cast in 1100.
Sevilla , Salvador, **8**, 79-1-14., - The Front **Six** Bells are Counterbalanced with No Wheels with a Tenor of 11-0-22. and the Back Two Bells are Chimed Only.
Siete Aguas , Centro Verbum Dei, 2, 2-2-18., - Chimed Only.
Siete Aguas , St Juan Bautista, 5, 9-3-8., - Chimed Only.
Siguenza , Santa Iglesia Catedral Basilica de Santa Maria la Mayor, 13, 56-3-4., - Ten Bells Automatically Swing Chimed, One Bell Counterbalanced with no Wheel and Hung for Ringing which weighs 0-1-12. and Also Three Bells Hung Dead.
Silla , Ntra Sra dels Angels, **5**, 22-0-6., - The Treble is Counterbalanced with No Wheel and weights 3-3-12. The rest are Automatically Swing Chimed Only.
Simat de la Valldigna, Capilla de la Mare de Deu de Gracia, **1**, - Counterbalanced, No Wheel.
Simat de la Valldigna , Monestir de Santa Maria de la Valldigna, 1, 10-2-0., - Automatically Swing Chimed Only, This Bell was cast by Eijesbouts in 1997.
Simat de la Valldigna, St Miquel Arcangel, **6**, 6-3-2., - The Treble and Third are Counterbalanced with No Wheel, The Second is Chimed Only and the Back Three Bells are Automatically Swing Chimed Only, The Second and Third were cast in 1682. The back Three Bells were cast by Roses in 1944 and 1964.
Sin , San Esteban, **3**, 8-2-16., - The Treble is Chimed Only, The **Second** and **Tenor** are Counterbalanced with No Wheels, These Bells were cast in 1941 and the Tenor in 1774.
Sinarcas , Santiago Apostol, **4**, 11-3-8., - Counterbalanced, No Wheels, The Third was cast in 1796 and the rest were cast by Roses in 1955.
Solsona, Catedral de la Marie de Deu de l'Assumpcio, **6**, 66-1-12., - Counterbalanced, No Wheels, There are also Three Bells on the Roof Hung Dead.
Soneja , St Fco Javier, 1, 0-0-20., - Chimed Only, This Bell was cast in 1691.
Soneja , St Miquel, 7, 23-0-16., - Chimed Only, The Treble and Sixth were cast by Roses in 1794, The Third was cast by Miguel in 1847, The Second was cast in 1380, The Fourth was cast in 1550, The Fifth and Seventh were cast in 1795.
Soria, Concatedral de San Pedro, **3**, 23-0-16., - Counterbalanced, No Wheels, There are also Four Bells Hung for Automatic Chiming Only.
Soria , Sto Domingo, 4, - Chimed Only, The Treble and Second were cast by Quintanilla in 1833, The Third was cast in 1721 and the Tenor in 1713.
Sot de Chera , Ermita de St Roque, 1, 0-1-16., - Chimed Only in a Belcote.
Sot de Chera , St Sebastian, 4, 3-3-12., - Automatically Swing Chimed Only, The Treble, Second and Tenor were all cast by Manclus Salvador of Valencia in 1976 and Third was cast by Palacios Pedro in 1881.
Sot de Ferrer , Ermita St Antonio, 2, 0-1-2., - Chimed Only, These Bells were cast in 1889 and 1748.
Sot de Ferrer , Inmaculada, 4, 9-1-2., - Chimed Only, Cast by Roses in 1939, 1944 and 1966.
Soto en Cameros , Parroquia, **4**, - Counterbalanced, No Wheels.
Sta fe del Penedes , Sta Fe, 2, 1-2-6., - Chimed Only.

Sta Margarida I Els Monjos, Ermita Mare de Deu del Castell de la Bleda, 1, 0-2-18., - Chimed Only.
Sta Margarida I Els Monjos, Sta Margarida de Els Monjos, 2, 8-1-16., - Chimed Only.
Sta Oliva, Capilla Mare de Deu del Remei, 2, 2-2-18., - Chimed Only, These Bells were cast by Manclus in 1961 and are the same weight.
Sta Oliva, Sta Maria, 1, 1-1-16., - Chimed Only, This Bell was cast by Cronos in 1948.
Subirats, Capilla de St Joan Sesrovires de Torre-ramona, 1, 0-0-18., - Chimed Only.
Subirats, Capilla St Joan Salerm de Can Bas, 1, 2-1-22., - Chimed Only.
Subirats, St Pau d'Ordal, 3, 7-3-4., - Chimed Only.
Subirats, St Pere de Lavern, 1, 2-1-22., - Chimed Only.
Sueca, Ntra Sra de Fatima, 3, 3-2-8., - Chimed Only in a Belcote, Cast by Roses in 1954.
Sueca, Ntra Sra del Carmen de El Perello, 1, - Chimed Only.
Sueca, St Pere, 10, 28-1-20., - The Fifth, Sixth, Eighth, Ninth and Tenor are Automatically Swing Chimed Only, The rest are Chimed Only, The Treble was cast in 1694.
Suera, Assumpcio, **4**, 14-3-14., - Counterbalanced, No Wheels.
Sumacarcer, Ermita del Calvari, 1, 0-1-16., - Chimed Only.
Tales, St Joan Baptiste, 4, 8-1-16., - Automatically Swing Chimed Only.
Tamarite, Santa Maria la Major, 3, 9-2-4., - The Treble is Chimed Only and the rest are Automatically Swing Chimed Only, The Treble was cast in 1942, The Second was cast by Querri in 1787 and the Tenor was cast by Erice in 1940.
Tarazona, Catedral de la Seo, 8, 18-1-26., - Chimed Only.
Tarbena, Sta Barbera, **1**, 10-3-4., - Counterbalanced, No Wheel.
Taroda, Iglesia Parroquial, 1, - Chimed Only.
Tarragona, Catedral de Santa Tecla, **8**, 39-0-8., - Counterbalanced, No Wheel, There is also **another Bell** on the Roof of the Cathedral which is Counterbalanced with No Wheel and weights 1-2-6., Also there is Six other Bells in the Tower including One Bell Hung Dead on the Roof of the Tower, Octagonal Tower.
Taull, Sant Climent, 1, 11-2-2., - Chimed Only, This Bell was cast in 1450.
Tavernes Blanques, Mare de Deu dels Desemparats de Carraixet, 2, 3-0-2., - Automatically Swing Chimed Only, The Treble was cast in 1716 and the Tenor in 1942,
Tavernes Blanques, Stma Trinitat, 1, 11-2-2., - Chimed Only, These Bells were cast by Roses in 1944, 1942, 1941 and 1969.
Tavernes de la Valldigna, Ermita Stm Crist del Calvari, 1, - Automatically Swing Chimed Only.
Tavernes de la Valldigna, St Pere Apostol, 5, 15-1-12., - Automatically SWing Chimed Only, There is also a Hemispherical Bell in the Tower which is Hung Dead and weights 7-2-6.
Tejeda, Nuestra Senora de Tejeda, 6, - Chimed Only.
Teresa, Ntra Sra de la Esperanza, 4, 8-1-16., - Chimed Only, Cast by Roses in 1953 and 1954.
Teresa de Cofrentes, Asuncion, **3**, 8-0-16., - The Treble is Counterbalanced with No Wheel and the rest are Automatically Swing Chimed Only, The Treble and Second were cast by Manclus in 1952 and 1968., The Tenor was cast in 1740.
Teresa de Cofrentes, Ermita St Apolinar, 1, 0-2-18., - Chimed Only.
Teruel, Catedral de Sta Maria de Mediavilla, **6**, 27-3-2., - Counterbalanced, No Wheels, There are also Two Bells hung for Automatic Swing Chiming and Two Bells Hung Dead.
Teruel, Salvador, 4, 17-2-4., - Chimed Only, The Treble was cast in 1950, The Second was cast by Corral in 1799, The Third was cast in 1550 and the Tenor was cast by Verruguer in 1593.
Teulada, Ermita de Benimarco, 1, 0-1-20., - Chimed Only in a Belcote.
Teulada, Ermita Divina Pastora, **1**, 1-0-4., - Counterbalanced, No Wheel, Hung in a Belcote.
Teulada, Ermita Font Santa, **1**, 0-1-20., - Counterbalanced, No Wheel, This Bell is Hung in the Wall of the Church and was cast in 1700.
Teulada, Ermita St Joan Baptista, 1, 0-1-20., - Chimed Only in a Belcote.
Teulada, Ermita St Vincent Ferrer, 1, - Chimed Only.

Teulada , *Mare de Deu dels Desemparats de Moraira, 3, 4-1-22.,* - *Automatically Swing Chimed Only, The Treble was cast by Roses in 1970, The Second and Third were cast by Eijesbouts in 1984 and 1983.*
Teulada , *Sta Caterina, 6, 10-2-0.,* - *Automatically Swing Chimed Only, The Third and Tenor were cast in 1736, Hexagonal Tower.*
Tibi , Santuari Maria Magdalena, **2**, 1-1-16., - Counterbalanced, No Wheels, Hung in a Belcote.
Tibi , *Sta Maria Magdalena, 3, 8-2-16.,* - *Automatically Swing Chimed Only, All the Bells were cast by Roses in 1914 and 1941.*
Tineo , *Parroquial, 1, 2-3-4.,* - *Chimed Only, This Bell was cast in 1857.*
Tineo , *Parroquial de Arganza, 1, 2-1-8.,* - *Chimed Only, This Bell was cast in 1832.*
Tineo , *Parroquial de Borres, 1, 0-2-2.,* - *Chimed Only, This Bell was cast in 1723.*
Tineo , *Parroquial de Troncedo, 1, 1-0-20.,* - *Chimed Only, This Bell was cast in 1801.*
Tirig , *Ermita Sta Barbera, 1, 0-1-2.,* - *Chimed Only in a Belcote.*
Tirig , *Mare de Deu del Pilar, 2, 4-0-14.,* - *Chimed Only.*
Titaguas , *Ermita del Remedio, 1, 0-2-6.,* - *Chimed Only.*
Titaguas , *Salvador, 5, 7-1-8.,* - *The* **Third** *and* **Tenor** *are Counterbalanced with No Wheels, The Treble is Chimed Only, The Second in Automatically Swing Chimed Only and the Fourth is Automatically Chimed Only.*
Todolella , *Ermita St Cristofol de Saranyana, 1, 2-1-22.,* - *Chimed Only, This Bell was cast in 1450.*
Todolella , *Ermitori de St Onofre, 1, 0-0-12.,* - *Chimed Only.*
Todolella , Esglesia Parroquial, **3**, 9-2-4., - Counterbalanced, No Wheels, The Treble was cast in 1598. The Second and Tenor was cast by Roses in 1947.
Toga , *Purisima Concepcion, 3, 11-3-8.,* - *Automatically Swing Chimed Only, The Treble was cast by Roses in 1930, The Second was cast by Corral in 1803 and the Tenor was cast by Manes in 1821.*
Toledo , *Catedral Primada, 9, 291-1-0.,* - *Swing Chimed, Counterbalanced, No Wheels,*
Tollos , St Antoni de Padua, **2**, 2-2-18., - Counterbalanced, No Wheels, Cast by Roses in 1841 and 1908.
Toras , Sta Quiteria, **2**, 7-1-8., - Counterbalanced, No Wheels.
Tormos , *St Lluis Bertran, 2, 3-3-12.,* - *Automatically Swing Chimed Only, These Bells were cast by Roses in 1940 and 1964.*
Torralba del Pinar , *El Salvador, 4, 9-2-4.,* - *Chimed Only.*
Torralvilla , *Parroquia, 3, 4-1-22.,* - *Chimed Only, The Treble and Second were cast in 1698 and 1669. The Tenor was cast by Quintana in 1833.*
Torre Embesora , *St Bertomeu, 2, 3-3-12.,* - *Chimed Only, These Bells were cast by Manclus in 1978.*
Torre Endomenech, Esglesia Parroquial, **3**, 7-0-10., - Counterbalanced, No Wheels, The Treble was cast in 1890 and the rest were cast by Roses in 1945.
Torrebaja , *Ermita St Jose, 1, 0-0-20.,* - *Chimed Only, This Bell was cast in 1750.*
Torrebaja , *Ermita St Roque, 1, 0-1-16.,* - *Chimed Only.*
Torrebaja , *Sta Ana de Torre Alta, 2, 0-2-18.,* - *Chimed Only, Cast by Manclus in 1980.*
Torrebaja , *Sta Marina, 2, 3-2-24.,* - *Chimed Only.*
Torreblanca , St Bertomeu, **3**, 8-2-16., - Counterbalanced, No Wheels, The Treble and Tenor were cast by Roses in 1929, The Second was cast by Manclus in 1972.
Torrechiva , *St Roque, 2, 3-2-8.,* - *Automatically Swing Chimed Only, The Treble was cast by Borras Bartolome in 1790 and the Tenor was cast by Roses in 1954.*
Torrella , *Calvari, 1,* - *Chimed Only.*
Torrella , *Ntra Sra dels Angels, 2, 2-0-14.,* - *Automatically Swing Chimed Only.*
Torrelles de Foix , *St Genis, 2, 13-1-12.,* - *Chimed Only, The Treble was cast by Guitart in 1896 and the Tenor was cast by Dencausse in 1899.*

Torrent, Assumpcio, 8, 21-0-2., - The Treble is Automatically Swing Chimed Only and the rest are Chimed Only, The Treble was cast in 1778.
Torrent, Buen Consejo, 3, 2-0-14., - Chimed Only.
Torrent, Capella Mare de Deu dels Desamparats, 1, 0-2-12., - Chimed Only.
Torrent, Convent de Dominiques de Betlem, 1, 0-1-20., - Chimed Only, This Bell was cast in 1670.
Torrent, Convent de St Josep i Sta Tecla, 1, 0-0-18., - Chimed Only, This Bell was cast in 1250.
Torrent, Convent Dominiques, 1, 0-3-8., - Chimed Only.
Torrent, Mont-Sio, 4, 7-1-8., - Chimed Only, The Treble was cast in 1743, This Tower is on the Top of the Building in a weird Triangular Shape.
Torrent, St Josep, 3, 4-3-4., - Chimed Only, The Treble was cast in 1780.
Torrent, St Lluis Beltran, 3, 7-1-8., - Chimed Only.
Torrent, St Vicent Ferrer del Mas del Jutge, 3, 1-1-24., - Chimed Only, The Treble was cast by Roses in 1970, The Second was cast in 1813 and the Tenor was cast by Garcia in 1755.
Torrent, Sta Maria de Monte Vedat, 7, 10-0-24., - The Treble is Chimed Only and the rest are Automatically Swing Chimed Only, The Treble was cast by Aleaciones in 1951 and the rest were cast by Portilla in 1994.
Torres-Torres, Ntra Sra dels Angels, 3, 11-0-22., - Chimed Only, The Treble was cast in 1691 and the rest were cast by Roses in 1787.
Torrijas, Santos Cosme y Damian, 2, 3-3-12., - Automatically Swing Chimed Only, The Tenor was cast in 1780, Octagonal Tower.
Tortosa, Catedral de l'Assumpcio de la Mare Deu, 8, 56-3-4., - Three Bells Automatically Swing Chimed and Five Bells Hung Dead, There is also another Bell Hung for Chiming in a Small Bellcote.
(Transportable), El Campanomobil, 4, 1cwt. - Counterbalanced, No Wheels, These Bells are housed at Sant Francesc Xavier in Valencia.
Traiguera, Assumpcio, 7, 30-1-14., - The **Back Three** Bells are Counterbalanced with No Wheels, The Fourth is Automatically Swing Chimed Only and the rest are Chimed Only, The Treble and Third was cast in 1428.
Traiguera, Ermita Mare de Deu de la Font de la Salut, 1, 0-3-14., - Chimed Only.
Traiguera, Ermita St Cristofol, 1, 0-1-2., - Chimed Only.
Traiguera, Ermita St Jaime, 1, 0-1-8., Chimed Only, This Bell was cast in 1781.
Triste, Iglesia, 2, - Chimed Only, The Treble was cast by Ballesteros in 1892.
Tudela, Catedral de la Virgin Maria, 4, 9cwt., - Counterbalanced, No Wheels, There is also Six other Bells in the Tower that are Automatically Chimed Only with a Tenor which weighs 39-3-2.
Tudela, Magdalena, 5, 15-1-12., - Chimed Only, The Treble was cast in 1768, The Second and Fourth was cast by Murua in 1891, The Third was cast in 1740 and the Tenor was cast in 1414.
Tuejar, Ermita, 1, 0-0-18., - Chimed Only, This Bell was cast in 1858.
Tuejar, Ntra Sra de los Angeles, 5, 13-1-12., - Automatically Swing Chimed Only, All the Bells were cast between 1739 - 1791.
Tunon, Iglesia Parroquial, 2, 1-1-0., - Chimed Only, These Bells were cast in 1627 and 1573.
Turis, Nativitat de Ntra Sra, 4, 23-0-16., - Automatically Swing Chimed Only, These Bells were cast by Roses in 1941 and 1998.
Ulzama, Iglesia de Lisazo, 1, 13-2-22., - Chimed Only, This Bell was cast by Muguiro in 1481.
Usechi, Iglesia, 1, 2-1-22., - Chimed Only, This Bell was cast in 1500.
Utiel, Ermita Ntra Sra del Remedio, 1, 0-1-16., - Chimed Only.
Utiel, St Jose Obrero de Casas de Utiel, **3**, 3-3-12., - Counterbalanced, No Wheels.
Utiel, St Pedro Apostol de Los Corrales, **4**, 4-1-22., - Counterbalanced, No Wheels.
Utiel, Virgin del Loreto de las Cuevas, **2**, 2-0-2., - Counterbalanced, No Wheels.
Valencia, Adoratrius, 5, 3-1-20., - Chimed Only.
Valencia, Ajuntament de Valencia, 1, 0-0-22., - Chimed Only.
Valencia, Ajuntament de Valencia - Torre del Rellotge, **7**, 13-1-12., - Counterbalanced, No Wheels, All these Bells were cast in 1930.
Valencia, Alqueria de l'Alba, 1, - Chimed Only, This Bell was cast in 1868.

Valencia, Angel Custodi, 2, 2-0-24., - Chimed Only, These Bells were cast by Roses in 1940.
Valencia, Assumpcio de Benimaclet, 4, - Chimed Only, Cast by Roses in 1939 and 1970.
Valencia, Assumpcio i Sta Barbera de Massarrojos, 4, 12-2-8., - Chimed Only.
Valencia, Bancaixa - Agencia 2a, 1, 1-1-0., - Chimed Only.
Valencia, Bancaixa - Glorieta, 3, 1-1-24., - Chimed Only, These Bells were cast by Roses in 1932.
Valencia, Bancaixa - Mercat Central, 1, 1-2-26., - Chimed Only.
Valencia, Bancaixa - Russafa, 1, 1-3-8., - Chimed Only.
Valencia, Beneficencia, 4, 5-3-8., - Chimed Only, The Third was cast by Tormo in 1793 and the Tenor was cast in 1739.
Valencia, Buen Pastor, 3, 0-2-6., - Chimed Only.
Valencia, Capitulet, 1, 0-0-8., - Chimed Only, This Bell was cast in 1853.
Valencia, Casa Cuna de Soternes, 1, - Chimed Only.
Valencia, Catedral de Santa Maria, **12**, 35-1-2. - Counterbalanced, No Wheels, one Bell was cast in 1305. There is also a Bourdon Bell hung Dead and weights 150-1-0., There are also Five other Bells in the Tower one was cast in the13th Century and the other in the14th Century, Octagonal Tower.
Valencia, Cementeri General - Capilla, 1, 0-1-20., - Chimed Only.
Valencia, Cementeri General - Porta Principal, 1, 0-1-20., - Chimed Only.
Valencia, Col-leccio Francesc LLOP i BAYO, 1, 0-0-8., - Chimed Only.
Valencia, Col-legi Salesians - C/ Sagunt, 3, 1-1-16., - Chimed Only, Cast by Dencausse in 1920.
Valencia, Companyia de Jesus, 4, 10-3-4., - Chimed Only, The Treble was cast in 1697 and the rest were cast by Roses in 1950.
Valencia, Confeccions Oltra, 2, - Chimed Only, The Treble was cast in 1750.
Valencia, Conselleria de Cultura, 4, 0-2-22., - Chimed Only, These Bells were cast by Roses in 1942.
Valencia, Convent - Agustines recoletes, 2, 0-3-0., - Automatically Swing Chimed Only, These Bells were cast by Manclus in 1960.
Valencia, Convent Corpus Christi, 3, 0-3-8., - The Treble is Chimed Only and the rest are Automatically Swing Chimed Only, The Second was cast in 1699.
Valencia, Convent de l'Encarnacio, 1, - Chimed Only.
Valencia, Convent de la Puritat - clarises, 3, 0-1-16., - Chimed Only.
Valencia, Convent de la Trinitat, 3, 4-0-14., - The Treble is Chimed Only and the rest are Automatically Swing Chimed Only.
Valencia, Convent de Sta Ursula, **2**, 1-0-4., - The Treble is Chimed Only and the **Tenor** is Counterbalanced with No Wheel, The Treble was cast in 1665.
Valencia, Convent dels Angels de Russafa, 3, 1-1-24., - Chimed Only.
Valencia, Convent Reparadores, 1, - Chimed Only, This Bell was cast in 1903.
Valencia, Convent St Cristofol - Canonesas, 3, - Chimed Only, The Tenor was cast in 1716.
Valencia, Convent St Josep - Carmelites, 3, 1-2-6., - Chimed Only, The Tenor was cast in 1697.
Valencia, Cooperativa de Casas Baratas - Archiduque Carlos, No 8 , 1, 1-3-8., - Chimed Only.
Valencia, Cor de Jesus de Patraix, 4, 5-1-20., - Chimed Only, Hexagonal Tower.
Valencia, Crist de l'Agonia del Forn d'Alcedo, 4, 4-1-4., - Automatically Swing Chimed Only, these Bells were cast by Roses in 1915 and 1927. There is also another Bell in the Church that is Chimed Only and weights 0-1-8. which was cast in 1787.
Valencia, Crist de la Providencia de la Creu Coberta, 2, - Chimed Only.
Valencia, Crist Rei, 2, 1-1-16., - Chimed Only, These Bells were cast by Roses in 1948.
Valencia, El Salvador, 4, 19-1-22., - Automatically Swing Chimed Only, The Second was cast by Solano in 1710 and the rest were cast by Lleonart in 1783 and 1799.
Valencia, Ermita de Vera, 1, 1-1-16., - Chimed Only.
Valencia, Ermita del Camp, 1, - Chimed Only, This Bell was cast by Empresa 2001 Tecnica Y Artesania in 1995.
Valencia, Ermita St Roc de Carpesa, 1, 0-1-16., - Chimed Only.
Valencia, Ermita Sta Ana de l'Alqueria del Pi, 1, 0-1-0., - Chimed Only.

Valencia, Escola de Graduats Socials, 3, 0-3-14., - Chimed Only.
Valencia, Escola Pia - campanar, 4, 7-1-8., - Chimed Only, These Bells were cast by Roses in 1948.
Valencia, Escola Pia - espadanya, 1, - Chimed Only, This Bell was cast in 1829.
Valencia, Escola Pia - espadanya rellotge, 3, - Chimed Only, These Bells were cast by Murua in 1940.
Valencia, Facultat de Teologia, 2, 3-3-12., - Chimed Only in a Belcote, Cast by Quiles in 1879.
Valencia, Franciscanes de la Immaculada - Carrer Doctor Sumsi, 1, 0-2-12., - Chimed Only.
Valencia, Franciscanes de la Immaculada - Casa Generalicia, 2, - Chimed Only, Cast by Quiles in 1891.
Valencia, Htas Desamparados, 5, 1-3-8., - The Treble is Chimed Only and the rest are Automatically Swing Chimed Only.
Valencia, Htas Desamparados de Massarojos, 1, 0-2-18., - Chimed Only.
Valencia, Inss - Antiga Casa del Xavo, 5, 6-0-14., - Automatically Chimed Only, The Fourth and Tenor are the same weight.
Valencia, Institut Lluis Vives, 2, 2-2-18., - On Display, The Treble was cast by Sesaro in 1585 and the Tenor was cast in 1319.
Valencia, Institut Psiquiatric " Pare Jofre ", 1, 0-2-18., - Chimed Only.
Valencia, Mare de Deu del Puig, 2, 5-3-8., - The Treble is Automatically Swing Chimed Only and the Tenor is Chimed Only.
Valencia, Maria Auxiliadora - salesians, 3, - The Treble is Chimed Only and the rest are Automatically Swing Chimed Only.
Valencia, Milagrosa, 3, 2-2-18., - Chimed Only, These Bells were cast by Quiles in 1884.
Valencia, Montolivet, 3, 4-0-14., - Chimed Only, These Bells were cast in 1771, 1877 and 1911.
Valencia, Nino Jesus del Huerto de El Palmar, 1, 1-0-4., - Chimed Only in a Belcote, This Bell was cast in 1774.
Valencia, Ntra Sra de Gracia de La Torre, **4**, 8-1-16., - The **Treble** and **Second** are Counterbalanced with No Wheels, The rest are Automatically Swing Chimed Only.
Valencia, Ntra Sra de la Buena Guia, 1, - Chimed Only.
Valencia, Ntra Sra de la Misericordia de Campanar, 7, 6-2-6., - Chimed Only.
Valencia, Ntra Sra de la Paz, 1, 1 0-4., - Automatically Swing Chimed Only.
Valencia, Ntra Sra de Lepanto de Castellar, 5, - Chimed Only.
Valencia, Ntra Sra de Montserrat, 1, - Chimed Only.
Valencia, Ntra Sra del Carme - carmelites, 4, 2-1-22., - The Treble is Chimed Only and the rest are Automatically Swing Chimed Only, The Treble was cast by Murua in 1961, The Second and Tenor were cast by Roses in 1941., The Third was cast by Fenollera in 1790.
Valencia, Ntra Sra del Rosari del Canyamelar, 4, 20cwt., - The Second is Chimed Only and the rest are Automatically Swing Chimed Only, The Treble was cast by Aleaciones in 1939 and the were cast by Roses in 1940.
Valencia, Ntra Sra del Sdo Corazon, 1, 0-0-16., - Chimed Only.
Valencia, Ntra Sra del Socorro, 2, - Chimed Only, These Bells were cast by Roses in 1946.
Valencia, Ntra Sra dels Angels del Cabanyal, 4, - The Third is Automatically Swing Chimed Only and the rest are Chimed Only.
Valencia, Ntra Sra Desamparats de Nazaret, 2, - The Treble is Chimed Only and the Tenor is Automatically Swing Chimed Only.
Valencia, Ntra Sra Desamparats del Fiscal, 1, 0-3-14., - Chimed only.
Valencia, Parroquia de Vera, 1, 5-3-8., - Chimed Only.
Valencia, Passio del Senyor, 3, 6-1-10., - Automatically Swing Chimed Only, Cast by Roses in 1960.
Valencia, Patriarca, 11, 14-2-2., - Chimed Only, The Fifth was cast by Galtero in 1678, The Sixth and Tenor was cast by Martinez in 1603 and 1606, The Seventh was cast in 1603.
Valencia, Patronat de la Juventut Obrera, 1, - Chimed Only.
Valencia, Pilar, 3, 6-1-10., - Chimed Only.

Valencia, Policia Autonomica, 1, - *Chimed Only.*
Valencia, Port - *Torre del rellotge, 1, 10-0-24., - Chimed Only.*
Valencia, Portal dels Serrans, 1, 1-0-20., - *Chimed Only, This Bell was cast in 1662.*
Valencia, Pouet de Sant Vicent, 1, 0-2-6., - *Chimed Only.*
Valencia, Purissima de la Punta, 4, - *The Tenor is Automatically Swing Chimed Only and the rest are Chimed Only.*
Valencia, Residencia Ntra Sra del Carme, 1, - *Chimed Only, This bell was cast in 1919.*
Valencia, St Augusti, 4, - *Chimed Only, The Treble was cast by Ruiz in 1863, The Second and Third were cast in 1848 and 1814, The Tenor was cast by Guillem in 1799, The Tower is Square at the Botton and Hexagonal at the Top.*
Valencia, St Andreu, 2, 2-1-22., - *Chimed Only, These Bells were cast by Roses in 1947.*
Valencia, St Antoni Abad, **4**, 3-2-24., - Counterbalanced, No Wheels.
Valencia, St Antoni de Padua d'En Corts, 3, - *Chimed Only, These Bells were cast by Roses in 1940.*
Valencia, St Bernat de Poble Nou, **2**, 2-1-8., - Counterbalanced, No Wheels, These Bells were cast by Roses in 1944 and 1952.
Valencia, St Domenec - capilla castrense, 7, 7-1-8., - *Automatically Swing Chimed Only, The Treble and Second were cast in 1820, The Third and Fourth were cast by Roses in 1935 and the Back Three Bells were cast by Eijesbouts in 1991.*
Valencia, St Domenec Savio, **1**, 0-1-20., - Counterbalanced, No Wheel.
Valencia, St Esteve, 5, 17-2-4., - *Automatically Swing Chimed Only, The Tenor was cast by Borras in 1761.*
Valencia, St Francesc de Borja, 2, - *Chimed Only, These Bells were cast by Manclus in 1946.*
Valencia, St Isidre, **4**, 5-3-8., - Counterbalanced, No Wheels, The Treble was cast in 1767.
Valencia, St Joan Baptista - Asil, 2, 5-0-8., - *Chimed Only, These Bells were cast by Quiles in 1872, There is also a Hemispherical bell Hung Dead.*
Valencia, St Joan de la Creu, antic St Andreu, **1**, - Counterbalanced, No Wheel.
Valencia, St Joan del Mercat - Campanar, 7, 36-0-2., - *Automatically Swing Chimed Only, The Tenor was cast in 1738 and the rest were cast by Roses in 1942.*
Valencia, St Joan del Mercat - Torre de la Facana, 1, 2-1-22., - *Chimed Only, Hung Dead, Triangular Tower.*
Valencia, St Joan i St Vicent, 2, 4-2-12., - *Chimed Only, The Treble was cast in 1750 and the Tenor by Roses in 1900.*
Valencia, St Jordi Martir, 1, - *Chimed Only, This Bell was cast by Roses in 1954.*
Valencia, St Josep - Col.legi Jesuites , **3**, - Counterbalanced, No Wheels.
Valencia, St Josep de la Muntanya, 4, 11-2-2., - *Automatically Swing Chimed Only.*
Valencia, St Llacer, 1, 0-2-6., - *Automatically Swing Chimed Only.*
Valencia, St Llorenc, 2, 2-1-22., - *Chimed Only, These Bells were cast in 1742 and 1718.*
Valencia, St Lluis de la Fonteta, 4, 11-2-2., - *Chimed Only.*
Valencia, St Marceli, 2, - *Chimed Only, These Bells were cast by Roses in 1959 and 1955.*
Valencia, St Marti, **6**, 17-0-14., - *The Treble and Second are Chimed Only, The Third is Automatically Chimed Only, The* **Fourth** *is Counterbalanced with No Wheel and the Back Two Bells are Automatically Swing Chimed Only.*
Valencia, St Martin de Porres de l'Oliveral, 1, - *Chimed Only.*
Valencia, St Miquel de Soternes, 1, 1-0-20., - *Chimed Only, This Bell was cast in 1718.*
Valencia, St Miquel i els Reis, **3**, 3-0-18., - *The* **Tenor** *is Counterbalanced with No Wheel and the rest are Chimed Only.*
Valencia, St Miquel i St Sebastia, **3**, 14-0-18., - Counterbalanced, No Wheels, These Bells were cast by Roses in 1915, 1956 and 1927.
Valencia, St Nicolau i St Pere Martir, 6, 18-1-26., - *Automatically Swing Chimed Only, The Fifth was cast by Guitarte in 1755.*
Valencia, St Pasqual Bailon, 5, 1-2-16., - *Chimed Only.*
Valencia, St Pasqual de El Saler, 2, - *Chimed Only.*

147

Valencia, *St Rafel Arcangel del Cabanyal, 1, - Chimed Only, This Bell was cast in 1903.*
Valencia, *St Roc de Benicalap, 4, 10-3-4., - Automatically Swing Chimed Only.*
Valencia, *St Thomas, 6, 19-0-2., - The Treble and Second are Chimed Only, The rest are Automatically Swing Chimed Only, The Second was cast in 1663, The Fourth was cast in 1697 and the rest were cast by Roses in 1920 and 1940.*
Valencia, St Valer de Russafa, **7**, 23-0-16., - Counterbalanced, No Wheels, All the Bells were cast by Roses in 1940 and 1965, Octagonal Tower.
Valencia, *St Vicent de la Roqueta, 7, 3-2-8., - Chimed Only.*
Valencia, *St Vicent Ferrer - basilica, 2, - Chimed Only, These Bells were cast by Roses in 1913.*
Valencia, *St Vicent Martir, 1, - Chimed Only, This Bell was cast in 1914.*
Valencia, *St Vicent Martir de Benimamet, 4, 9-3-8., - Chimed Only.*
Valencia, *Sagrado Corazon, 2, 3-3-12., - Chimed Only, These Bells were cast by Quintana in 1988.*
Valencia, Santiago Apostol de Beniferri, **2**, 1-3-8., - Counterbalanced, No Wheels, The Treble was cast by Quiles in 1888 and the Tenor was cast by Manclus in 1952.
Valencia, *Santiago Apostol de Marxalenes, 2, 3-3-12., - The Treble is Automatically Swing Chimed Only and the Tenor is Chimed Only.*
Valencia, *Sta Anna de Borboto, 5, 5-0-8., - The Treble is Chimed Only and the rest are Automatically Swing Chimed Only.*
Valencia, *Sta Anna, 1, - Chimed Only, This Bell was cast in 1959.*
Valencia, *Sta Caterina, 1, 2-1-8., - Automatically Swing Chimed Only, This Bell was cast by Manclus Salvador of Valencia in 1950, Hexagon Tower.*
Valencia, *Sta Cecilia, 3, 4-2-12., - Chimed Only, These Bells were cast by Portilla in 1992.*
Valencia, *Sta Clara, 2, 0-3-14., - Chimed Only, The Treble was cast by Roses in 1956 and the Tenor was cast by Dencausse in 1926.*
Valencia, *Sta Creu, 6, 22-2-4., - The* **Second** *is Counterbalanced with No Wheel and the rest are Automatically Swing Chimed Only, The Treble was cast in 1682, The Fourth was cast by Avin in 1504 and the rest were cast by Roses in 1941.*
Valencia, *Sta Llucia, 8, 0-2-12. in Si 4, - Automatically Chimed Only, Hung Dead, These Bells were cast by Paccard in 1996, There is also* **Two Bells** *that are Counterbalanced with No Wheels and are Hung in a Belcote with a Tenor of 1-0-20., - The Treble was cast in 1872 and the Tenor in 1786.*
Valencia, *Sta Llucia - Seu del Gremide Campaners Valencians, 1, 0-0-14., - This Bell is carried to the Association meeting and Chimed by the Chairman.*
Valencia, *Sta Maria de Jesus, 3, 3-1-20., - Automatically Swing Chimed Only, These Bells were cast by Roses in 1928 and 1950.*
Valencia, *Sta Maria del Mar, 6, 18-1-26., - Automatically Swing Chimed Only.*
Valencia, *Sta Monica i El Salvador, 7, 16-0-26., - The Treble is Chimed Only and the rest are Automatically Swing Chimed Only.*
Valencia, *Sta Rosa de Lima de Benicalap, 4, 4-0-14., - The Tenor is Chimed Only and the rest are Automatically Swing Chimed Only.*
Valencia, *Sts de la Pedra de Carpesa, 4, 15-1-12., - Chimed Only.*
Valencia, *Tabacalera, 4, - Chimed Only, The Front Three Bells were cast by Diez Moises in 1912 and the Tenor was cast in 1865.*
Valencia, *Trinitaries, 2, 5-3-8., - Chimed Only.*
Valencia, *Universitat - espadanya rellotge, 3, - Chimed Only, Clock Bells, Hung Dead, Hemispherical Bells.*
Vall D'Alcala, Beniaia, **2**, 1-2-26., - Counterbalanced, No Wheels, Cast by Roses in 1942 and 1943.
Vall D'Alcala, La Purissima d'Alcala de la Jovada, **2**, 4-0-14., - Counterbalanced, No Wheels, These Bells were cast by Roses in 1942.
Vall de Almonacid, *Parroquial, 5, 9-2-4., - Chimed Only.*
Vall de Ebo, *St Miquel, 2, 5-3-8., - Automatically Swing Chimed Only.*

Vall de Gallinera, Assumpcio de Benissili, **2**, 2-0-2., - Counterbalanced, No Wheels.
Vall de Gallinera, Assumpcio de Patro, **4**, 5-2-14., - Counterbalanced, No Wheels.
Vall de Gallinera , St Cristofol de Benirrama, *1, 2-3-4., - Automatically Chimed Only.*
Vall de Gallinera, St Francesc de Borja de Carroja, **2**, 1-1-8., - Counterbalanced, No Wheels, These Bells were cast by Manclus Salvador in 1953.
Vall de Gallinera, St Miquel de Benissiva, **2**, 1-2-6., - Counterbalanced, No Wheels, These Bells were cast in 1925 and 1941.
Vall de Gallinera , *St Roc de Beniali, 3, 8-1-16., - The Treble is Not Hung and the rest are Chimed Only.*
Vall de Laguart , *Ermita de St Josep de Campell, 1, 0-1-20., - Chimed Only.*
Vall de Laguart , *St Francesc de Borja de Fontilles, 2, 0-1-8., - Chimed Only in a Belcote, These Bells were cast in 1940.*
Vall de Laguart, St Pasquil Bailon de Fleix, **3**, 6-0-14., - Counterbalanced, No Wheels, These Bells were cast by Roses in 1940.
Vall de Laguart, Sta Anna de Campell, **2**, 5-0-8., - Counterbalanced, No Wheels.
Vall de Laguart , *Sts Cosme i Damia de Benimaurell, 1, 2-3-4., - Automatically Swing Chimed Only, This Bell was cast by Roses in 1941.*
Vallada , *Divi Jutge, 1, - Counterbalanced with No Wheel but Chimed Only in a Belcote.*
Vallada , *Ermita St Sebastia, 1, - Chimed Only in a Belcote, This Bell was cast in 1691.*
Vallada , *St Bartolome, 3, 12-1-0., - Automatically Swing Chimed Only.*
Vallanca , Ntra Sra de los Angeles, **1**, 10-3-4., - Counterbalanced, No Wheel, This Bell was cast by Gargollo in 1814.
Vallanca , *St Antonio de Padua de El Negron, 1, 0-1-16., - Chimed Only.*
Vallat , *St Juan Evangelista, 3, 3-2-24., - Automatically Swing Chimed Only.*
Vallbona de les Monges , *Santa Maria de Vallbona, 6, 15-1-12., - Chimed Only, The Fourth was cast by Barberi in 1946, The Fifth and Tenor were cast by Mestres in 1761 and 1784.*
Valles , *St Joan, 2, - Automatically Swing Chimed Only in a Belcote.*
Vallibona , *Esglesia, 3, 15-1-12., - Chimed Only.*
Vegadeo , *Parroquial de Pianton, 2, 3-0-2., - Chimed Only, These Bells are both the same weight, They were cast in 1850 and 1831.*
Venta del Moro , *Ntra Sra del Loreto, 2, - Chimed Only, Hung Dead.*
Vianos , *Torre del Reloj, 1, 3-3-12., - Clock Bell, Hung Dead above the Tower in a Twisty Steel Frame with a weather vain on the top.*
Vic, Catedral, **6**, 25-1-16., - Counterbalanced, No Wheels, There are also Four other Bells in the Tower.
Vilafames , *Assumpcio, 5, 15-2-26., - Chimed Only.*
Vilafames , *Ermita de la Sang, 1, 0-1-2., - Chimed Only.*
Vilafames , *Ermita de Sant Ramon, 1, 0-0-22., - Chimed Only but Counterbalanced with No Wheel, This Bell was cast in 1674.*
Vilafames , *Ermita St Miquel, 1, 0-2-2., - Chimed Only.*
Vilafranca del Penedes , *Basilica de Sta Maria, 7, 20cwt., - Chimed Only.*
Vilafranca del Penedes , *Capella de St Joan, 2, 1-1-24., - Chimed Only, The Treble was cast in 1944 and the Tenor in 1350.*
Vilafranca del Penedes , *St Francesc, 1, 1-0-12., - Chimed Only.*
Vilafranca del Penedes , *Stma Trinitat, 3, 8-1-16., - Chimed Only, Cast by Barberi in 1948.*
Vilagrassa , *Parroquia de Santa Maria, 2, 1-1-16., - Chimed Only, Cast by Blasco in 1954 and 1962.*
Vilamarxant , *Ermita de l'Assumpcio de Monte Horquera, 1, 0-0-24., - Chimed Only.*
Vilamarxant , *Mas de Teula, 1, 0-0-16., - Chimed Only.*
Vilamarxant , *Mas dels Frares, 1, 0-1-0., - Chimed Only.*
Vilamarxant , *Sta Caterina Martir, 5, 18-0-6., - The Second is Hung Dead and Chimed Only, The rest are Automatically Swing Chimed Only.*

Vilanova D'Alcolea, Sant Bertomeu, 2, 13-1-12., - The Treble is Automatically Swing Chimed Only and the Tenor is Chimed Only.
Vilanova I La Geltru, Sant Antoni, 3, 22-0-6., - The Tenor is Automatically Swing Chimed Only and the rest are Automatically Chimed Only, The Treble and Second were cast in 1677, The Tenor was cast by Roses in 1969.
Vila-Real, Arxiprestal de St Jaume, **8**, 28-1-20., - The **Treble** is Counterbalanced with No Wheel and the rest are Automatically Swing Chimed Only, The Treble was cast in 1650, The Fifth and Sixth were cast by Manclus in 1978, The Rest were cast by Roses in 1940, 1941 and 1942, Octagonal Tower.
Vila-Real, Basilica de St Pasqual - Campanar de les Campanes (Est), 12, - Automatically Swing Chimed Only, These Bells were cast by Paccard.
Vila-Real, Basilica de St Pasqual - Campanar de Carrillo (Oest), 71, 43-3-12. in D, - Carillon, These Bells were cast by Eijesbouts in 1997.
Villa del Prado, Parroquia, **6**, - Counterbalanced, No Wheels, The Second was cast in 1693 and the Fourth was cast in 1603.
Villafranca del Cid, Ermita Pobla St Miquel o Pobla de Bellestar, 1, 0-1-20., - Chimed Only, This Bell was cast by Roses in 1964.
Villafranca del Cid, Ex-Cvto Consolacion, 1, 0-2-22., - Chimed Only.
Villafranca del Cid, Mare de Deu del Llosar, 3, 2-2-18., - Chimed Only in a Belcote.
Villafranca del Cid, Sta Maria Magdalena, 5, 14-0-18., - The Treble and Third are Chimed Only, The rest are Automatically Swing Chimed Only.
Villahermosa del Rio, Nativadad de Ntra Sra, 4, 11-2-2., - Automatically Swing Chimed Only.
Villalonga, Ermita St Antoni, 1, - Automatically Swing Chimed in a Belcote.
Villalonga, Ermita St Josep, 2, 0-1-6., - Automatically Swing Chimed on the roof of the Church in a Steel Frame.
Villalonga, Ermita St Llorenc, 1, - Chimed Only in the wall of the Church.
Villalonga, Ermita St Vicent Ferrer (La Llacuna), 1, 0-2-18., - Chimed Only in a Belcote.
Villalonga, Sants Reis, 4, 15-1-12., - Automatically Swing Chimed Only.
Villalonga, Santuari Verge de la Font, **3**, 4-1-4., - The **Treble** is Counterbalanced with No Wheel and the rest are Automatically Swing Chimed Only.
Villamalur, Sto Domingo de Guzman, 4, 5-0-8., - The Third is Chimed Only and the rest are Automatically Swing Chimed Only.
Villanueva de Viver, St Antonio, 4, 2-2-6., - The Second is Chimed Only and the rest are Automatically Swing Chimed Only.
Villar de Canes, St Llorenc, **2**, 4-3-4., - Counterbalanced, No Wheels.
Villar del Arzobispo, Convento Franciscanas, 1, 0-1-0., - Chimed Only.
Villar del Arzobispo, Ntra Sra de la Paz, 4, 28-1-20., - Automatically Swing Chimed Only, There is also Two Hemispherical Bells Hung Dead in a Belcote above the Tower.
Villargordo del Cabriel, St Roque, 3, 3-0-2., - Chimed Only.
Villarluengo, Asuncion de Montoro de Mezquita, **2**, 4-3-4., - Counterbalanced, No Wheels, These Bells were cast by Cabrillo Mayor in 1941.
Villarluengo, Ntra Sra de la Asuncion, 3, 4-3-4., - The Treble is Counterbalanced with No Wheel, The Second is Hung Dead and Chimed Only, The Tenor is Automatically Swing Chimed Only, Octagonal Towers.
Villaviciosa, Capilla en Arbazal, Puelles, 1, 0-2-18., - Chimed Only, This Bell was cast in 1756.
Villaviciosa, Parroquial de Cazanes, 2, 2-1-22., - Chimed Only.
Villena, Ermita St Anton, 1, 0-0-18., - Lever Chimed Only in a Belcote, This Bell was cast in 1723.
Villena, Ermita St Bartolome, 1, - Chimed Only.
Villena, Ermita St Isidro - La Zafra, 1, - Chimed Only.
Villena, Ermita St Jose, 1, - Chimed Only.
Villena, Santiago, 6, 49-0-22., - Chimed Only, The Second was cast in 1700, The Third was cast in 1727, the Fourth was cast in 1650, The Fifth and Tenor were cast in 1572.
Villores, Parroquia, 2, 4-1-22., - Chimed Only, These Bells were cast in 1955.

Vilobi del Penedes, Sta Maria, 2, 5-3-8., - Chimed Only, These Bells were cast by Barberi in 1940.
Vinalesa, Col.legi Santa Joaquina, 2, 0-1-20., - Chimed Only.
Vinalesa, Ermita Sta Barbera, 1, 1-0-4., - Chimed Only.
Vinalesa, Fabrica de la Seda, 1, 1-1-8., - Chimed Only, This Bell was cast in 1777.
Vinalesa, St Honorat, 3, 14-3-14., - Chimed Only, The Treble was cast in 1875, The Second was cast by Roses in 1915 and the Tenor was cast by Lavina in 1779.
Vinaros, Arxiprestal de l'Assumpcio, 5, 22-2-4., - Automatically Swing Chimed Only, There is also another Two Bells Hung Dead.
Vinaros, Ermita St Roc, 1, 0-1-2., - Chimed Only.
Vinaros, Ermita St Sebastia, 1, 0-3-8., - Chimed Only in a Belcote.
Vinaros, Ex-Convent St Agusti - Auditori, 1, 1-0-4., - Chimed Only.
Vinaros, Magdalena, 1, 0-3-8., - Chimed Only.
Vistabella Del Maestrazgo, Assumpcio de Ntra Sra, **4**, 15-1-12., - Counterbalanced, No Wheels.
Vistabella Del Maestrazgo, Ermitori de St Joan de Penyagolosa, **2**, 2-1-22., - Counterbalanced, No Wheels, The Treble was cast in 1751 and the Tenor was cast by Palacios in 1888.
Viver, Ermita St Roque, 1, 0-0-22., - Chimed Only.
Viver, Ntra Sra de Gracia, 2, 11-0-22., - Chimed Only, Cast by Roses in 1963 and 1941.
Viver, St Francisco de Paula, 1, 0-2-12., - Chimed Only.
Xabia, Loreto del Port, **7**, 1-3-8., - The **Third** is Counterbalanced with No Wheels, All the Bells are Automatically Chimed Only, A Modern Style Triangular Tower.
Xabia, Sagrado Corazon de Jesus, 2, - Chimed Only in Two Belcotes.
Xabia, Sant Bertomeu, 4, 26-2-6., - Automatically Swing Chimed Only.
Xativa, Antic Convent de Sant Agusti, 2, 3-0-18., - Chimed Only.
Xativa, Antic Hospital, 1, - Counterbalanced with No Wheel but Chimed Only.
Xativa, Ermita Calvario Alto, 1, 0-1-8., - Chimed Only, This Bell was cast in 1776.
Xativa, La Merce i Santa Tecla, 4, 9cwt., - Automatically Swing Chimed Only, Cast by Roses in 1940.
Xativa, Nostra Senyora de la Consolacio, 2, - Chimed Only.
Xativa, Nostra Senyora del Carme, 3, 6-2-6., - Automatically Swing Chimed Only, These Bells were cast by Barberi in 1992, These are Hung in a Modern Tower.
Xativa, Sant Feliu, 1, - Chimed Only.
Xativa, Sant Josep i Santa Barbara, **2**, 2-2-18., - Counterbalanced, No Wheels, Cast by Roses in 1942.
Xativa, Sant Onofre, 1, - Chimed Only.
Xativa, Sant Pere, 4, 7-2-6., - The Treble is Chimed Only and the rest are Automatically Swing Chimed Only.
Xativa, Sants Joans, **1**, 3-2-8., - Counterbalanced, No Wheel.
Xativa, Santuario Dulce Nombre de Maria, 1, 0-2-22., - Chimed Only.
Xativa, Seu de Sta Maria, 4, 43-0-12., - Automatically Swing Chimed Only, The Tenor was cast by Eijesbouts in 1998, There is also Two Bells Hung Dead that are Chimed Only, The Treble was cast in 1665 and weights 35-1-2. The Tenor of the Two Bells weights 40-2-10., There is also another Bell on display which was cast by Trilles in 1520, There is also a Carillon of Twenty Bells in the Tower with a Tenor of 8-2-16.
Xeraco, Ermita del St Crist, 1, - Automatically Swing Chimed Only.
Xeraco, Ntra Sra de la Encarnacio, 5, 7-2-6., - The Second and Fourth are Hung Dead and the rest are Automatically Swing Chimed Only, The Treble was cast in 1450.
Xeresa, Ermita de la Trinitat, 1, - Automatically Swing Chimed Only.
Xeresa, St Antoni de Padua, 3, 14-2-2., - Automatically Swing Chimed Only, There is also Two more Bells in the Tower that are Hung Dead the Treble is Hemispherical and weights 1-2-16, The Tenor is a Normal Bell and weights 6-1-10.
Xert, Assumpcio, 2, 9-2-4., - Chimed Only.
Xert, Capilla de Anroig, 1, 0-1-26., - Chimed Only.

Xert, *Ermita St Marc de la Barcella, 1, 1-0-12., - Lever Chimed Only in a Belcote, This Bell was cast in 1736.*
Xert, *Esglesia Vella, 7, 11-2-2., - Chimed Only, The Third was cast by Roses in 1961. The rest were cast by Portilla in 1988, 1989 and 1990.*
Xirivella, *Ermita de la Salud, 1, 0-1-20., - Chimed Only.*
Xirivella, *Mare de Deu de la Salud, 4, 10-0-24., - Chimed Only.*
Xirivella, *St Ramon Nonat, 3, 3-0-18., - Chimed Only.*
Xirivella, *St Vicent Ferrer, 2, 1-3-8., - Chimed Only.*
Xirivella, *Sant Francesc de Paula, 3, 6-2-6., - Automatically Swing Chimed Only, These Bells were cast by Portilla in 1991.*
Xixona, *Assumpcio, 6, 8-1-16., - The Treble and Second are Chimed Only, The rest are Automatically Swing Chimed Only, There is Also Two more Bells in the Tower that are Hung Dead the Treble is a Normal Bell and the Tenor is Hemispherical and weights 12-2-8.*
Zabaldica, *Iglesia, 1, 4-1-4., - Chimed Only, This Bell was cast in 1377.*
Zaragoza, *Catedral de El Pilar, 15, 123-1-2., - Automatically Chimed Only.*
Zaragoza, Catedral de la Seo, 7, 52cwt., - Counterbalanced, No Wheels, The Treble was cast in 1450.
Zaragoza, *San Felipe, 5, 1-0-12., - Chimed Only, The Fourth was cast in 1714 and the Tenor in 1768.*
Zaragoza, *San Miguel Arcangel de Monzalbarba, 4, 5-1-20., - The Treble is Automatically Chimed Only and the rest are Chimed Only, The Tenor was cast by Asin in 1709.*
Zaragoza, *San Nicolas, 4, 6-0-14., - Chimed Only, The Treble was cast in 1739, The Second was cast in 1450, The Third was cast by Manclus in 1961 and the Tenor was cast in 1773.*
Zaragoza, *Santa Engracia, 2, - Automatically Swing Chimed Only.*
Zaragoza, *Santo Sepulcro, 1, 1-1-24., - Chimed Only, This Bell was cast in 1721.*
Zarra, Sta Ana, **4**, 5-1-0., - Counterbalanced, No Wheels, All the Bells were cast by Manclus Salvador of Valencia in 1965 and 1987, Detatched Tower.
Zucaina, *Ermita Calvari, 1, 0-2-12., - Chimed Only in a Belcote.*
Zucaina, Ermita de Sta Ana, **1**, 0-2-6., - Counterbalanced, No Wheel.
Zucaina, Ermita de Sta Barbara, **1**, 1-1-0., - Counterbalanced, No Wheel, This Bell was cast in 1923.
Zucaina, San Salvador, **3**, 12-1-0., - Counterbalanced, No Wheels, All the Bells were cast by Roses in 1912 and 1941.

SURINAME.

Paramaribo, *Toren op Valliantsplein, 25, in G, - Traditional Keyboard Carillon, All these Bells were cast by Eijsbouts in 1976.*

SWEDEN.

Gavle, *Radhuset, 36, 5-2-14. in C. - Carillon, All these Bells were cast by Bergholtz in 1972.*
Gislaved, *Kirken, 24, 5-2-14. in C. - Hung Dead, Automatic Carillon, All the Bells were cast by Bergholtz in 1970.*
Goteborg, *Kristine Kyrka, 42, 5-2-14. in C. - Carillon, All these Bells were cast by Bergholtz in 1961.*
Harnosand, *Dom Kyrka, 37, 5-2-14. in C. - Carillon, All these Bells were cast by Bergholtz in 1981.*
Kalmar, *Tva Systrars Kapel, 37, 5-2-14. in C. - Hung Dead, Automatic Carillon, All the Bells were cast by Bergholtz in 1981.*
Karlskrona, *Frederiks Kyrka, 35, 12-2-24. in G. - Carillon, The Bells were cast by Bergholtz in 1965.*

<u>Karlstad</u>, *Dom Kirken, 25, 5-2-4. in C. - Hung Dead, Automatic Carillon, All the Bells were cast by Bergholtz in 1990.*
<u>Kiruna</u>, *Radhuset, 23, 31-2-4. in D. - Hung Dead, Automatic Carillon, All the Bells were cast by Bergholtz in 1962.*
<u>Kumla</u>, *Kirken, 24, 5-2-14. in C. - Hung Dead, Automatic Carillon, Cast by Bergholtz in 1972.*
<u>Landskrona</u>, *Sofia Albertina Kyrka, 43, 12-2-24. in G. - Carillon, Cast by Bergholtz in 1967.*
<u>Linkoping</u>, *Sct. Lars Kyrka, 36, 5-2-14. in C. - Carillon, All these Bells were cast by Bergholtz in 1972.*
<u>Malmoe</u>, *St Paul, 3, - Hung Dead.*
<u>Mariestad</u>, *Dom Kirken, 20, 5-2-14. in C. - Hung Dead, Automatic Carillon, All these Bells were cast by Bergholtz in 1972.*
<u>Molmo</u>, *Radhuset, 48, 12-2-24. in G. - Carillon, Detatched Tower, All Cast by Petit and Fritsen in 1970.*
<u>Nassjo</u>, *Radhuset, 25, 5-1-12. in C. - Hung Dead, Automatic Carillon, All Cast by Bergholtz in 1986.*
<u>Norrkoping</u>, *Radhuset, 48, 13-2-4. in G. - Carillon, All Cast by Bergholtz between 1963 - 1983.*
<u>Nykoping</u>, *Sct. Nicolai Kirke, 37, 5-1-12. in C. - Hung Dead, Automatic Carillon, All these Bells were cast by Bergholtz in 1986.*
<u>Ostersund</u>, *Radhuset, 26, 5-2-12. in C. - Hung Dead, Automatic Carillon, All the Bells were cast by Bergholtz in 1986.*
<u>Oxelosund</u>, *Sct. Botvids Kirke, 24, 8cwt. in A#. - Hung Dead, Automatic Carillon, All these Bells were cast by Bergholtz in 1969.*
<u>Sodertalje</u>, *Radhuset, 24, 5-2-14. in C. - Hung Dead, Automatic Carillon, All the Bells were cast by Bergholtz in 1964.*
<u>Stockholm</u>, *Adolf Fredriks Kirke, 24, 5-2-14. in C. - Hung Dead, Automatic Carillon, All the Bells were cast by Bergholtz in 1977.*
<u>Stockholm</u>, *Sct. Gertruds Kyrka, 25, 15cwt. in F. - Carillon, All the Bells were cast by Ohlsson in 1921.*
<u>Stockholm</u>, *Sct. Clara Kyrka, 35, 31-0-20. in D. - Carillon, The Bells were cast by Bergholtz in 1965.*
<u>Stockholm</u>, *Hedvig Eleonora Kyrka, 24, 5-2-14. in C. - Carillon, Cast by Bergholtz in 1968.*
<u>Sundby-Berg</u>, *Fredens Kirke, 24, 5-2-14. in C. - Hung Dead, Automatic Carillon, All the Bells were cast by Bergholtz in 1973.*
<u>(Transportable) Sigtuna</u>, *Trans Porta Belt, 35, 5-2-14. in C. - Carillon, All the Bells were cast by Bergholtz in 1968.*
<u>Uppsala</u>, *Gattsunda Kirken, 25, 9-2-14. in A. - Hung Dead, Automatic Carillon, All the Bells were cast by Bergholtz in 1980.*
<u>Vaseras</u>, *Radhuset, 47, 44cwt. in C. - Carillon, All these Bells were cast by Eijesbouts in 1960.*
<u>Vaxjo</u>, *Dom Kyrka, 28, 11-2-4. in G#. - Carillon, All these Bells were cast by Bergholtz in 1962.*
<u>Visby</u>, *Dom Kyrka, 45, 13-2-4. in G. - Carillon, All these Bells were cast by Bergholtz in 1960.*
<u>Ystad</u>, *Ohlssons Klockgjuteri, 24, 1-2-24. in G. - Hung Dead, Automatic Carillon, All these Bells were cast by Petit and Fritsen in 1968.*
<u>Ystad</u>, *Sct. Maria Kirke, 36, 9-0-1. in A. - Hung Dead, Automatic Carillon, All these Bells were cast by Petit and Fritsen in 1970.*

SWITZERLAND.

<u>Econe</u>, *(R.C.), Seminary of Saint Pius X, 4, 9cwt., - Automatically Chimed Only.*
<u>Lens</u>, *Valais, Eglise Saint-Pierre-aux-Liens, 24, - Carillon.*
<u>Zofingen</u>, *Aargau, Stiftsturm, 24, - Carillon.*

TRINIDAD.

Port of Spain, Cathedral Church of Holy Trinity, **8**, in C, - Unringable, now Chimestand Chimed by external Clappers on the outside of the Bells. Cast by Mears & Stainbank between 1819 - 1880 and installed in 1880.

URUGUAY.

Montevideo, Beffroi de la Mairie Communale, Cerro Colorado, 23, in C, - Traditional Keyboard, Carillon, Cast by Petit & Fritsen in 1962, This Carillon is Owned by Dr Gallinal Heber.
Montevideo, 99, in C, - Carillon, All these Bells were cast by Michiels.

UNITED STATES OF AMERICA.

Abilene, Texas, (Episcopal) Church of the Heavenly Rest, **25**, in F. - Electric Keyboard, Carillon, these Bells were cast by Eijesbouts in 1982, *Six* Bells in the Carillon are hung for ringing, 6-1-0. in B.
Abilene, Texas, McMurry University (formerly McMurry College), Radford Auditorium, 35, in A#, - Traditional Keyboard, Carillon, All the Bells were cast by Petit and Fritsen and installed in 1952.
Abiquiu, New Mexico, (R.C.), Monastery of Christ in the Desert, 1, 6cwt, Lever Chimed Only.
Aiken, South Carolina, St Thaddeus Episcopal Church, 23, in C, - Traditional Keyboard, Carillon, All the Bells were cast by Petit and Fritsen in 1964.
Akron, Ohio, North Clock Tower, Goodyear Tire & Rubber Company, East Market Street, 12, 30 cwt in D, - Chimestand Chimed, Detached Tower, These Bells were cast by Meneely of Troy in 1920.
Albany, New York, City Hall, Pine and Eagle Streets, 49, 97-2-23 in G, - Traditional Keyboard, Carillon, These Bells were cast by Taylors in 1928 and 1986, The Keyboard is made of Ivory.
Alfred, New York, Alfred University (South Campus), Davis Memorial Carillon, 47, 9-1-9 in D, Traditional Keyboard, Carillon, Detached Steel Tower,This is the Only Pre 19th Century Carillon in North America.
Allendale, Michigan, Grand Valley State University, Cook Carillon Tower, 48, 26-2-0 in D#, - Traditional Keyboard, Carillon, Detached Tower, All the Bells were cast by Eijsbouts in 1994.
Alliance, Ohio, Christ United Methodist Church, 13, in D, - Chimed Only, Cast by McShane in 1919.
Alstead, New Hampshire, Estate of Chas N Vilas, 12, in D, - Electric Keyboard Chimed, These Bells were cast by Meneely of Troy in 1930.
Amarillo, Texas, First Baptist Church, 10, in D#, - Electric Keyboard Chimed, Cast by Meneely of Troy in 1930.
Ames, Iowa, Iowa State University, Campanile, Stanton Memorial Carillon, 50, 35 cwt in A#, - Traditional Keyboard, Carillon, Detatched Tower, Cast by Taylors in 1899, 1929, 1956 and 1967.
Amherst, Massachusetts, Stearns Steeple, Amherst College, 9, in E, - Chimestand Chimed, These Bells were cast by Wm Blake & Co in 1871, Detatched Tower.
Amherst, Massachusetts, Old Chapel, University of Massachusetts, 12, 15 cwt in F, - Baton Keyboard Chimed, These Bells were cast by Eijesbouts in 1999.
Andover, Massachusetts, Phillips Academy, Memorial Tower, Samuel Lester Fuller Carillon, 37, in E, Traditional Keyboard, Carillon Currently Unplayabe, Eighteen of The Bells were cast by Petit and Fritsen in 1966 The rest were cast by Taylors in 1923 and 1926, Detatched Tower.
Ann Arbor, Michigan, Kerrytown Chime, Kerrytown Shops, 407 North of 5th Avenue, 17, 9cwt in B, - Chimestand Chimed, Ten of the Bells were cast by Gillett and Johnson in 1928, The rest were cast by Eijesbouts in 1997, These Bells are open at noon for the public to play.
Ann Arbor, Michigan, University of Michigan, Main Campus,Charles Baird Carillon, 55, 216-3-12 in D#, - Traditional Keyboard, Carillon, Cast by Taylors in 1936 and 1976, Detatched Tower.

Ann Arbor, Michigan, University of Michigan, North Campus, Ann and Robert H Lurie Carillon, 60, 98-0-21 in G. - Traditional Keyboard, Carillon, Cast by Eijsbouts between 1995 - 1996.
Anniston, Alabama, Church of St Michael and All Angels, 12, 38-2-27 in C, - Electric Keyboard Chimed, These Bells were cast by McShane in 1889.
Ardmore, Oklahoma, First Presbyterian Church, 11, in E,- Chimed Only, Cast by Meneely & Wvit in 1919.
Arlington, Virginia, Netherlands Carillon Gardens, The Netherlands Carillon, beside Arlington National Cemetery, (Jefferson Davis Highway of U.S. Highway 50), 50, 112-3-14 in G, - Traditional Keyboard, Carillon, All the Bells were cast jointly and anonymously in 1949 by All three Dutch Founders (VanBergen, Eijsbouts, Petit & Fritsen), Detatched Steel Tower.
Astoria, New York, Long Island City, Episcopal Church of the Redeemer, 10, in E, - Electric Keyboard Chimed, These Bells were cast by Jones in 1873.
Athens, West Virginia, Concord College, Joseph F Marsh Hall (Administration Building), The Marsh Family Memorial Carillon, 48, in C, - Traditional Clavier Keyboard,Carillon,Cast by Paccard in 1997.
Atlanta, Georgia, Fulton County Government Centre, 23, in C, - Hung Dead, Automatic Carillon, These Bells were cast by Eijesbouts in 1988.
Atlanta, Georgia, First Presbyterian Church of Atlanta, Devereaux McClatchy Carillon, 47, 30 cwt in C, - Electric Keyboard, Carillon, Cast by Petit & Fritsen.
Atlanta, Georgia, Galleria Parkway, Galleria Speciality Mall, 27, in C, - Automatic Carillon, These bells were cast by Eijesbouts in 1985.
Atlanta, Georgia, Oglethorpe University, Lupton Hall, 42, 55 cwt in C, - Electic Keyboard, Carillon, Hung on the Roof of the Hall Open to the Eliments in a Steel frame.
Atlanta, Georgia, Ousley Methodist Church, 15, - Chimed Only, These Bells were cast by VanBergen.
Atlanta, Georgia, St Bartholomew's Episcopal Church, 8, in D#, - Electric Keyboard Chimed, These Bells were cast by Taylors in 1963.
Atlanta, Georgia, Sandy Springs Methodist Church, 15, 10 cwt, - Electric Keyboard Chimed, These Bells are hung in Three Separate Towers with Five Bells in each Tower, Cast by VanBergen.
Atlanta, Georgia, University, 10, in G, - Automatically Chimed Only, Cast by Eijesbouts in 1953.
Augusta, Georgia, First Baptist Church, 15, - Chimed Only, These Bells were cast by Paccard.
Augusta, Georgia, St Paul's Episcopal Church, 14, in D#, - Electric Keyboard Chimed, Eleven of the Bells were cast by Meneely of Watervliet in 1923, The rest were cast by Paccard in 2001.
Augusta, Georgia, St Mark's Episcopal Church, 11, in D#, - Chimed Only, Cast by Meneely of Watervliet in 1925, There is also another **bell** in the Tower cast by Meneely of Troy in 1850, Hung for Ringing.
Austin, Texas, The Burleson Bells, Bass Concert Hall Plaza, The University of Texas, 11, 8 cwt, - Keyboard Chimed, Unplayable, Hung in a Concrete Structure, Cast by Paul Garnier in Paris in 1929.
Austin, Texas, The University of Texas, Main Building, Kniker Carillon, 56, 65-2-6 in Bb, - Traditional Keyboard, Carillon, Seventeen Bells cast by Meneely of Watervliet in 1936, the rest cast by Petit & Fritsen in 1987.
Baltimore, Maryland, Martin Luther Ev. Luth. Church, 11, - Keyboard Chimed Only, These Bells were cast by McShane in 1890.
Baltimore, Maryland, New Refuge Deliverance Cathedral, (Formerly Christ Church) 13, in C, - Electric Keyboard Chimed, These Bells were cast by McShane in 1908, Before this Chime was installed there was Ring of bells, 6, 12cwt. These Bells were cast by Mears and Stainbank in 1803, The Bells were removed and hid from the British Army during the War of 1812 but Three Bells were lost and never recovered Maybe are still hidden.
Baltimore, Maryland, Our Saviour Lutheran Church, 18, - Chimed Only, Cast by McShane.
Baltimore (Huntingdon), Maryland, St John's Episcopal Church, 11, - Chimed Only, Cast by McShane.

Baltimore, Maryland, St Pauls Episcopal Church, 24, in G, - Electric Keyboard, Carillon, Cast by Petit and Fritsen in 1990.
Baltimore, Maryland, York Road Development Project, 16, - Chimed Only, Cast by Petit & Fritsen in 1979.
Bangor, Maine, First Universalist Church, 10, in F#, - Chimestand Chimed, These Bells were cast by Meneely of Troy in 1919.
Baraboo, Wisconsin, Ringling Bros (Bell Wagon), Circus World Museum, 550 Water Street, 9, 10 cwt, - Chimestand Chimed, The Only Chime Cast by Gardiner Campbell & Sons, Centennial Bell Foundry, Milwaukee in 1892, This Wooden Wagon is pulled by Horses.
Bar Harbor, Maine, St Saviour's Episcopal Church, 10, in F - Electric Keyboard Chimed Only, These Bells were cast by Meneely of Troy in 1938.
Barrington, Illinois, St Michael's Episcopal Church, 12, in A, - Electric Keyboard Chimed Only, These Bells were cast by Petit and Fritsen in 1955.
Bay City, Michigan, Trinity Episcopal Church, 10, - Chimed Only.
Belmont, North Carolina, First Presbyterian Church, William James Pharr Carillon, 48, in C, - Traditional Keyboard, Carillon, All the Bells were cast by Eijsbouts in 1984.
Belmont, North Carolina, Lutheran Church of the Holy Comforter, Lineberger Memorial Carillon, 40, in C, - Carillon.
Benton Harbor, Michigan, First Congregational Church, 15, in D#, - Chimed Only, These Bells were cast by Meneely of Troy in 1920 and 1927.
Berea, Kentucky, Berea Colledge, Phelps Stokes Chapel, 10, in F, - Electric Keyboard Chimed, These Bells were cast by Meneely of Troy in 1917.
Berea, Kentucky, Berea Colledge, Draper Building, 56, 24-1-27 in D#, - Traditional Keyboard, Carillon, Cast by Petit and Fritsen in 2000.
Berkeley, California, (Private House), 18, in C, - Automatically Chimed, Cast by Eijsbouts in 1985.
Berkeley, California, University of California at Berkeley, Class of 1928 Carillon, 61, 93-2-19 in G, - Traditional Keyboard, Carillon, Detached 307' Tower, Twelve Bells were cast by Taylors in 1917, The rest were cast by Paccard in 1979 and 1983.
Bethlehem, New Hampshire, Ivie Memorial Chapel of the Messiah, 10, in F, - Electric Keyboard Chimed Only, These Bells were cast by Meneely of Troy in 1930.
Birmingham, Alabama, First Presbyterian Church, 37, in F#, - Traditional Keyboard, Carillon, Twenty-five Bells were cast by Taylors in 1924 and the rest were cast by VanBergen in 1961.
Birmingham, Alabama, Hartwell Goodwin Davis Library, Rushton Memorial Carillon, 60, in C, - Traditional Keyboard, Carillon, These Bells were cast by Eijsbouts in 1968 and 1980.
Birmingham, Alabama, Highlands United Methodist Church, 13, in D, - Chimed Only, Cast by McShane in 1921, Octagonal Tower.
Birmingham, Alabama, Methodist Church, 10, - Chimed Only, Cast by Meneely of Watervliet.
Birmingham, Michigan, St James Episcopal Church, 35, in A, - Electric Keyboard, Carillon, Cast by Petit and Fritsen in 1965.
Bloomfield Hills, Michigan, Beautiful Saviour Lutheran Church, 35, in C, - Electric Keyboard, Carillon, These Bells were cast by Petit and Fritsen in 1966.
Bloomfield Hills, Michigan, (Episcopal), Christ Church Cranbrook, The Wallace Carillon, 50, in A#, - Traditional Keyboard, Carillon, These Bells were cast by Taylors in 1928 and 1978.
Bloomfield Hills, Michigan, (Presbyterian), Kirk on the Hills, The Children's Bells of Blessing, (Over west Entrance), 12, in F, - Automatically Chimed, These Bells were cast by Petit and Fritsen in 1965.
Bloomfield Hills, Michigan, (Presbyterian), Kirk in the Hills, The Tower of the Apostles, 77, 104-1-5 in G, - Traditional Keyboard, Carillon These Bells were cast by Petit and Fritsen in 1960.
Bloomington, Indiana, Indiana University, Arthur R Metz Memorial Carillon, 61, in A#, - Traditional Keyboard, Carillon, All the Bells were cast by Eijsbouts in 1971, Detached Tower.

Bloomington, Indiana, Indiana University, Music School Building, School of Music Carillon, 42, in C, - Traditional Keyboard, Carillon, All the Bells were cast by Eijsbouts in 1971, Hung on the Roof.
Bloomington, Indiana, Indiana University, Student Building, 14, 20 cwt in E, - Chimestand Chimed, These Bells were cast by Petit and Fritsen in 1991.
Boston, Massachusetts, (Episcopal), All Saints Church, 11, in E, - Chimestand Chimed, Cast by McShane in 1926.
Boston, Massachusetts, (Unitarian-Universalist) Arlington Street Church, Phillips Chime, 16, in D, - Ellacombe Chimed, The Notes of the Bells are G, A, B, C, C#, D, D#, E, F, F#, G, A, B, C, C#, D, Cast by Henry N Hooper & Co of Boston in 1860.
Boston, Massachusetts, (Christian Science Mother Church) First Church of Christ, 18, in D, - Baton Keyboard Chimed, These Bells were cast by Eijesbouts in 1984.
Boulder, Colorado, St John Episcopal Church, 9, in F, - Chimestand Chimed Only, This Octave includes a Flat Seventh, These Bells were cast by Meneely of Troy in 1905.
Bristol, Connecticut, Lake Compounce, New Gateway for New England's Oldest Amusement Park, 9, 8 cwt, Clock Chime, Children of the world appear in the windows.
Bronx, New York, St Peter's Episcopal Church, 10, in F#, - Chimestand Chimed Only, These Bells were cast by Meneely of Troy in 1923.
Bronxville, New York, (Dutch Reformed Church), The Reformed Church of Bronxville, 8, in C, - Baton Keyboard Chimed, These Bells were cast by Taylors in 1927.
Bronxville, New York, Village Lutheran Church, Wyman Memorial Carillon, 24, in G, - Electric Keyboard, Carillon, All these Bells were cast between 1960 - 1963 by VanBergen.
Brookings, South Dakota, First Lutheran Church, 12, - Chimed Only.
Brooklyn, New York, Reformed Church of Flatbush (Originally Reformed Dutch Church), 10, in D#, - Chimestand Chimed, These Bells were cast by Meneely of Troy in 1913, There is also separate **Bell** in the Tower dated 1796 when the Church was built which is Hung for Ringing.
Brooklyn, New York, St Mark's Evangelist Lutheran Church, 16, in C#, - Chimestand Chimed.
Brunswick, Maine, Bowdoin College, Bowdoin Chapel, 11, in G, - Electric Keyboard Chimed, These Bells were cast by Meneely of Watervliet in 1923.
Bryan, Ohio, Wesley United Methodist Church, Markey Memorial Carillon, 49, in G, - Electric Keyboard, Carillon, These Bells were cast by Petit and Fritsen in 1970.
Bucyrus, Ohio, Aumiller Park, Bucyrus-Navada Road, The John Q Shunk Memorial, 14, in A, - Automatically Chimed, Eleven Bells cast by Meneely of Watervliet in 1940, The rest Cast by Petit & Fritsen in 1968, Detatched Tower.
Buffalo, New York, St Paul's Episcopal Cathedral, **14**, 22-1-4. in Eb. - Unringable, Electric Keyboard Chimed, **Tenor** Only Hung for Ringing, Ten of the Bells were Cast in 1856 & 1857 including Extra Treble & Flat Second, They were the Only Meneely of Watervliet Bells Hung for Change Ringing, in 1924 Four Bells were Cast by Meneely of Watervliet and hung around the frame.
Burlington, Vermont, St Paul's Episcopal Cathedral, 8, in F, - Electric Keyboard Chimed, These Bells were cast by Meneely of Troy in 1895.
Calistoga, California, Sterling Winery, Streling Vineyards, 1111 Dunaweal Lane, **8**, - *(Tower One)* **Six** Bells are hung for Ringing with Small Wheels, No Stays or Sliders, (Tower Two) One Bell Hung Dead, (Tower Three) One Bell Hung Dead, Cast by Taylors in 1951 and 1972.
Cambridge, Massachusetts, Christ Church in Cambridge, 13, in D, - Ellacombe Chimed Only, These Bells were cast by Willian Blake in 1860.
Cambridge, Massachusetts, Lowell House, Harvard University, 17, 260 cwt in G, - Zvon Chimed Only, These Bells were cast between 1790 - 1890 and were installed in 1930. These Bells were previously housed in Danilov Monastery in Moscow.
Cambridge, New York, (Eastern Orthodox), New Skete Monastery, 17, 12 cwt, - Chimed Only, Twelve of the Bells were cast by Gillett and Johnson in 1968, Detatched Wooden Tower.
Camden, Maine, St Thomas Episcopal Church, 11, in G, - Chimed Only, Cast by Meneely of Watervliet in 1939.

Camp Hill, Alabama, Shopping Centre, 14, in C, - Automatically Chimed, Cast by Eijsbouts in 1985.
Canajoharie, New York, Canajoharie United Methodist Church (Originally First Methodist Church) 11, in F, - Electric Keyboard Chimed, These Bells were cast by Meneely of Watervliet in 1922.
Canton, Ohio, Garden Center Park, 3043 Fulton Road, 14, - Chimed Only.
Carlisle, Pennsylvania, First United Church of Christ, 11, in D, - Electric Keyboard Chimed, Including a Sharp Fourth and Flat Seventh, The Bells were cast by McShane in 1930.
Catasauqua, Pennsylvania, Catasauqua Presbyterian Church, 11, in D, - Chimestand Chimed, Including a Sharp Fourth and Flat Seventh, These Bells were cast by McShane in 1925.
Cedar Falls, Iowa, University of Northern Iowa, Campanile, 47, 80cwt. in C. - Traditional Keyboard, Carillon, Eleven Bells cast by Meneely of Watervliet in 1926, Rest cast by Petit & Fritsen in 1968, Detatched Tower.
Centralia, Illinois, Tower Park, The Centralia Carillon Tower, 65, 98-0-21. in G. - Traditional Keyboard, Carillon, Detatched Tower, Cast by Paccard Fouderie de Cloches between 1982 - 1983.
Champaign, Illinois, University Lutheran Church and Student Centre, Trinity Tower, 25, in F, - Traditional Keyboard, Carillon, These Bells were cast by Petit and Fritsen in 1953.
Chapel Hill, North Carolina, Morehead-Patterson Bell Tower, University of North Carolina, 14, 31-0-25 in D, - Automatically Chimed, Detatched Tower, Twelve Bells cast by Meneely of Troy in 1931, The rest were cast by Petit and Fritsen in 1997.
Charleston, South Carolina, First Church, 16, - Chimed Only, Cast by Wm Blake & Co in 1868.
Charleston, South Carolina, St Matthew Evangelical Lutheran Church, 10, in E, - Chimed Only, These Bells were cast by Meneely of Watervliet in 1901.
Charleston, South Carolina, The Citadel (Military College), The Thomas Dry Howie Tower, The Thomas Dry Howie Carillon, 59, 39-1-0 in C, - Traditional Keyboard, Carillon, All the Bells were cast by VanBergen in 1955.
Charlestown, Massachusetts, First Church, 16, in D, - Chimed Only, Cast by Wm Blake & Co in 1868, This Church was built in 1632.
Charlotte, North Carolina, Covenant Presbyterian Church, 48, in D, - Traditional Keyboard, Carillon, These Bells were cast by Petit and Fritsen in 1966, 1969 and 2002.
Charlotte, North Carolina, Myers Park Presbyterian Church, 27, in C, - Traditional Keyboard, Carillon, These Bells were cast by Taylors in 1985 and 1997.
Charlotte, North Carolina, Myers Park United Methodist Church, 23, in E, - Electric Keyboard, Carillon, Fourteen bells were cast by Gillett & Johnson in 1945, The rest were cast by Taylors in 1995.
Charlotte, North Carolina, The Charlotte Museum of History, located between the Hezekiah Alexander Homesite & Charlotte Museum of History, 1, 140 cwt. in F#, - Hung Dead on Display in Park.
Charlottesville, Virginia, Christ Episcopal Church, 23, in G, - Traditional Keyboard, Carillon, All the Bells were cast by Gillett and Johnson in 1947.
Chattanooga, Tennessee, St Paul's Episcopal Church, 11, in D, - Chimed Only, Cast by McShane in 1911.
Chautauqua, New York, Chautauqua Institution, Miller Bell Tower, 14, in D#, - Chimestand Chimed, Three Bells were cast by Petit & Fritsen in 1967, The rest were cast by Meneely of Troy in 1885, This Tower is on the Water Front.
Cherryville, North Carolina, First United Methodist Church, Beam Pratt and Brawley Carillon, 23, in C, - Electric Keyboard, Carillon, These Bells were cast by VanBergen in 1974.
Cheyenne, Wyoming, St Mark's Episcopal Church, 11, in D, - Chimed Only, Cast by McShane in 1927.

158

Chicago, Illinois, (Columbian Exposition in 1893), 1, 116-0-7 in G, - Hung Dead & low to the Ground, Cast in the likeness of the Liberty Bell at the request of the Daughters of the American Revolution, Cast by Meneely of Troy in 1893, This Bell Disappeared after the Exposition.
Chicago, Illinois, Michigan Avenue Baptist Church, 17, in D, - Chimed Only, Cast by Jones in 1870.
Chicago, Illinois, St Chrysoston's Episcopal Church, Crane Memorial Carillon, 43, in C, - Traditional Keyboard, Carillon, These Bells were cast by Gillett and Johnson in 1927.
Chicago, Illinois, St James Catholic Church, 20, in C, - Chimestand Chimed, Cast by McShane in 1895.
Chicago, Illinois, St James Episcopal Cathedral, James Carter Memorial Chime, 10, in D#, - Electric Keyboard Chimed, These Bells were cast by Meneely and Kimberley of Troy in 1876.
Chicago, Illinois, University of Chicago, Rockefeller Memorial Chapel, The Laura Spelman Rockefeller Memorial Carillon, 72, 330-1-2. in C#., - Traditional Keyboard, This is the Second Heaviest Carillon in the World, The Bells were cast by Gillett and Johnson in 1932.
Cincinnati, Ohio, Old St Mary's Catholic Church, 8, - Chimed Only, Cast by Petit & Fritsen in 1992.
Cincinnati, Ohio, St Francis de Sales, **1**, 330-1-7. in Eb, - Counterbalenced & Recessed into the Headstock, No Stay or Slider, Cast by Vanduzen & Co in 1896.
Cincinnati, Ohio, St Gregory Street Project, Mount Adams Neighbourhood, 14, - Chimed Only, Cast by Petit & Fritsen in 1988.
Cincinnati, Ohio, St John's United Church of Christ, 35, in A, - Electric Keyboard, Carillon, Cast by Petit and Fritsen in 1967.
Cincinnati, Ohio, (R.C.), St Peter in Chains Cathedral, 12, in F, - Electric Keyboard Chimed, Cast by Petit & Fritsen in 1955.
Cincinnati, Ohio, (R.C.), St Teresa of Avila, 11, 12 cwt, - Chimed Only, Detatched Octagon Tower, Cast by Vanduzen in 1955.
Cincinnati, Ohio, Westwood United Methodist Church, 10, 16-3-12, - Chimestand Chimed, Cast by Vanduzen in 1905.
Circleville, Ohio, Pickaway County Courthouse, William Foresman Chime, 11, in F, - Chimestand Chimed, Cast by Meneely of Watervliet in 1926.
Clearwater, Florida, Episcopal Church of the Ascension, Dimmit Memorial Carillon, 49, in C, - Traditional Keyboard, Carillon and these Bells were cast by Eijsbouts in 1982.
Clemson, South Carolina, Clemson University, Tillman Hall, 47, 39-0-16 in C#, - Traditional Keyboard, Carillon, All the Bells were cast by Paccard in 1987.
Clemson, South Carolina, Holy Trinity Episcopal Church, 16, in E, - Chimed Only, These Bells were cast by VanBergen in 1967.
Cleveland, Ohio, (R.C.), Immaculate Conception Church, 11, in D, - Automatically Chimed, Cast by Meneely of Troy in 1899.
Cleveland, Ohio, St Patrick's Roman Catholic Church, 11, in D, - Chimed Only, Cast by Meneely of Watervliet in 1899.
Cleveland, Ohio, (Presbyterian), The Church of the Covenant, The McGaffin Carillon, 47, in D#, Traditional Keyboard, Carillon, All the bells were cast by Eijsbouts in 1968.
Cleveland Heights, Ohio, Church of the Savior, Arter Memorial Carillon, 47, 47-0-14 in C, - Traditional Keyboard, Carillon, These Bells were cast by Petit and Fritsen in 1952 and 1954.
Cleveland Heights, Ohio, St Ann's Catholic Church, 10, in D, - Chimed Only, Cast by Meneely of Troy in 1952.
Cleveland Heights, Ohio, St Paul's Episcopal Church, Harry A and Mariah H Seabrook and Thomas Family Memorial Carillon, 25, in F, - Traditional Keyboard, Carillon, Eight of the Bells were cast by Gillett and Johnson in 1929, The rest were cast by VanBergen in 1952 and 1953.
Clinton, Tennessee, Anderson County Court House, 11, in F, - Electric Keyboard Chimed, These Bells were cast by Meneely of Troy in 1937.
Clinton, Illinois, Clinton United Methodist Church, 9, - Chimed Only, Cast by Vanduzen.

Clinton, South Carolina, First Presbyterian Church, Bailey Memorial Carillon, 35, in C, - Electric Keyboard, Carillon, These Bells were cast by VanBergen in 1973.
Clinton, Iowa, First United Methodist Church, 9, - Chimed Only, These Bells were cast by Jones.
Cohasset, Massachusetts, St Stephen's Episcopal Church, The Cohasset Carillon, 57, 100-2-15 in G, - Traditional Keyboard, Carillon, Sixteen Bells were cast by Gillett and Johnson in 1924, 1925 and 1928, The rest were cast by Taylors in 1990.
College Station, Texas, Texas A & M University, Albritton Tower Carillon, 49, in C, - Electric Keyboard, Carillon, Detached Tower,These Bells were cast by Paccard in 1984.
Columbia, Maryland, Wharf Bell Tower, 14, in G, - Automatically Chimed, Cast by Petit & Fritsen in 1977.
Columbus, Nabraska, Columbus Quincentenary Belltower, Pawnee Park, 10, 10 cwt in F, - Automatically Swing Chimed, Hung in Ten Individual Belltowers.
Columbus, Ohio, King Avenue United Methodist Church, **10**, 17 cwt in F, - Chimestand Chimed, **Tenor** Only Hung for Ringing, Cast by Meneely of Troy in 1921.
Columbus, Ohio, Ohio State University, Orton Hall, 12, 75 cwt in D#, - Electric Keyboard Chimed, Cast by McShane in 1915, Round Tower.
Columbus, Ohio, (Episcopal), Trinity Church, All Saint's Tower, Trinity Chime, 10, in D#, - Chimestand Chimed, Cast by Meneely of Troy in 1910.
Concord, New Hampshire, St Paul's School, Chapel of St Peter and St Paul, Houghton Memorial Carillon, 23, in E, - Traditional Keyboard, Carillon, Cast by Gillett and Johnson in 1933.
Concord, North Carolina, Evangelical Lutheran Church of St James, Coltrane Memorial Carillon, 28, 6 cwt in C, - Electric Keyboard, Carillon, These Bells were cast by Vanbergen in 1966 & 1970.
Concord, New Hampshire, St Paul's Episcopal Church, 9, in F, - Chimestand Chimed, These Bells were cast by Meneely of Watervliet in 1868.
Corpus Christi, Texas, Church of the Good Shepherd, Memorial Carillon, 48, in G, - Traditional Keyboard Carillon.
Corpus Christi, Texas, First Baptist Church, Glasscock Memorial Carillon, 51, in F, -Traditional Keyboard, Carillon, All the Bells were cast by Eijsbouts in 1976.
Covington, Kentucky, Goebbel Park, The Carrol Chimes Philadelphia Street at West 6th Street, 43, 22 cwt in A,- Traditional Keyboard, The Carillon is rarely played by hand but the Automatic play accompanies Jacquemarts acting out the Pied Piper Story, Cast by Petit & Fritsen in 1979, Detatched Tower.
Covington, Kentucky, Trinity Episcopal Church, 10, in F, - Electric Keyboard Chimed, Including Flat Seventh, These Bells were cast by McShane in 1888.
Crisfield, Maryland, Asbury United Methodist Church, 11, in F#, - Chimestand Chimed, These Bells were cast by Meneely of Watervliet in 1923.
Culver, Indiana, Culver Military Academy, Memorial Chapel, **51**, in B, - Traditional Keyboard, Carillon, All the Bells were cast by Gillett and Johnson in 1951 & was the last Complete Carillon Cast by the Foundry, The **Tenor** is Hung for Ringing, No Stay or Slider.
Cumberland, Maryland, Allegany Community College, Main Campus, 12, - Automatically Chimed Only, These Bells were cast by Petit and Fritsen.
Cumberland, Maryland, St Paul's Lutheran Church, 14, in A, - Electric Keyboard Chimed, These Bells were cast by Petit and Fritsen in 1963.
Dallas, Texas, Church of the Incarnation, 30, in A, - Electric Keyboard, Carillon, These Bells were cast by VanBergen in 1964.
Dallas, Texas, Church of the Transfiguration, 8, 5 cwt in C, - Electic Keyboard Chimed, There is also another **bell** Hung for Ringing in the Tower & weighs 11-2-0 in Gb, Cast by Taylors in 1996.
Dallas, Texas, (Episcopal), Church of St Michael and All Angels, 19, - Electric Keyboard Chimed, These Bells were cast by Taylors in 1996 and 2001.
Dallas, Texas, Highland Park United Methodist Church, Porter Memorial Carillon, 48, 40cwt. in C. - Traditional Keyboard, Carillon, All the Bells were cast by Paccard and installed in 1985.
Dallas, Texas, Park Cities Baptist Church, 28, in C, - Carillon, Cast by Paccard in 1986.

Dallas, Texas, Southern Methodist University, Foundren Science Building, 25, 80 cwt in A#, - Electric Keyboard, Carillon, These Bells were cast by Petit and Fritsen in 1952.
Dallas, Texas, St James Episcopal Church, **3**, 5cwt. - All the Bells were Cast by Taylors in 1997.
Danbury, Connecticut, St James Episcopal Church, Bulkley Memorial Carillon, 25, 22-1-4. in E. - Traditional Keyboard, This was the First American Made Carillon & was totally refurbished in 1987, These Bells were cast by Meneely of Watervliet in 1928 and 1936.
Danville, Kentucky, Lexington Avenue Baptist Church, 11, in C, - Chimed Only, These Bells were cast by Meneely of Watervliet in 1941.
Danville, Virginia, Main Street United Methodist Church, 11, in F, - Chimestand Chimed, These Bells were cast by Meneely of Watervliet in 1909.
Davenport, Iowa, Palmer College of Chiropractic, 9, 8-0-3. in A., - Chimed Only, These Bells were cast by Meneely of Troy in 1921.
Dayton, Ohio, Deeds Memorial Tower, Carillon Historical Park, South Patterson Boulevard at Carillon Boulevard, 57, 62-2-0 in A#, - Traditional Keyboard, Carillon, These Bells were cast by Petit and Fritsen in 1988 and 1992, Detatched Tower.
Dayton, Ohio, First (English) Lutheran Church, 11, in D, - Electric Keyboard Chimed, Nine Bells were cast by the Niles Works in Cincinnati in 1868 & the rest were cast by Vanduzen in 1907.
Dayton, Ohio, (The Bell Wagon), American Guild of English Handbell Ringers, 18, in B, - Quasi-Baton Keyboard Chimed, Cast by Taylors.
Decatur, Illinois, First United Methodist Church, 11, in C, - Electric Keyboard Chimed but not played often due to the Tower being Unsafe, These Bells were cast by McShane in 1910.
De Land, Florida, John B Stetson University, Hulley Tower, The Eloise Chimes, 11, 26-2-22. in D. - Chimed Only, Detatched Tower, All the Bells are Rough Cast and were cast by McShane in 1901.
Delaware, Ohio, Ohio Wesleyan University, Stuyvesant Hall, 15, - Chimestand Chimed.
Delaware, Ohio, (R.C.), St Mary's Church, 12, in D#, - Chimed Only, Cast by McShane.
Denver, Colorado, (Episcopal), Cathedral of St John in the Wilderness, 15, in A, - Chimed by Vertical Cast Iron Levers, Fourteen Bells hung in the (W.Tower) and the Tenor hung in the (E.Tower) Cast by Petit and Edelbrock of Germany in 1905.
Denver, Colorado, Central Christian Church, 24, 12-0-3., - Hung Dead, Automatic chime in Detatched Tower, All these Bells were cast by Taylors.
Denver, Colorado, Chapel of our Merciful Saviour, 9, in F, - Chimed Only, These Bells were cast by Meneely of Troy in 1904.
Denver, Colorado, City and County Building, Civic Centre, 10, in C, - Electric Keyboard Chimed, Cast by Meneely of Troy in 1932 & 1950.
Denver, Colorado, Colorado Women's Collage of the University of Denver, 30, 8-0-25 in A#, - Traditional Keyboard, Carillon, Cast by VanBergen at Heiligerlee in 1961, Detatched Hexagon Tower.
Denver, Colorado, Daniel L Ritchie Centre for Sports and Wellness, University of Denver, 65, 120 cwt in G, - Traditional Keyboard, Carillon, Cast by Eijsbouts in 1999, The Spire is Covered with Gold.
Denver,Colorado,(R.C.),Immaculate Conception Cathedral, (E.Tower), **15**, 40 cwt in C#, - Chimestand Chimed, including **Four Bells** hung for Ringing, No Stays or Sliders, Cast by McShane in 1912.
Des Moines, Iowa, (Episcopal), Cathedral Church of St Paul, 23, in D#, - Traditional Keyboard, Carillon.
Detroit, Michigan, (Episcopal), Christ Church Detroit , 9, in D#, - Chimed Only, These Bells were cast by Jones in 1864.
Detroit, Michigan, (R.C.), Church of the Precious Blood, 12, in A, - Electric Keyboard Chimed, These Bells were cast by Petit and Fritsen in 1956.
Detroit, Michigan, (R.C.), Holy Redeemer Church, 10, in F, - Chimed Only, These Bells were cast by Meneely of Troy in 1926.

161

Detroit, Michigan, Historic Trinity Lutheran Church, 11, in F, - Electric Keyboard Chimed, These Bells were cast by Taylors in 1930.
Detroit, Michigan, Jefferson Avenue Presbyterian Church, 23, 20-2-0 in E, - Traditional Keyboard, Carillon, All the Bells were cast by Gillett and Johnson in 1926.
Detroit, Michigan, (R.C.), Ste Anne de Detroit, 10, in E, - Chimed Only, Cast by McShane.
Detriot, Michigan, St Charles Borrowmeo, 1, 19cwt. - Swing Chiming Only.
Detroit, Michigan, (R.C.), St Peter and St Paul, 9, in E, - Electric Keyboard Chimed, Cast by Jones in 1879.
Detroit, Michigan, St Stephen's (Polish) Catholic Church, 10, in E, - Chimed Only, Cast by McShane.
Detroit, Michigan, (R.C.), Sweetest Heart of Mary, (N.Tower), **3**, in Eb, - Unringable.
Detroit, Michigan, Trinity Episcopal Church, 10, in E, - Chimed Only, Cast by McShane.
Dorchestor, South Carolina, St Georges Church, 4, - These Bells were Cast by Thomas Rudhall in 1751 and 1753.These Bells were the Second Ring to be installed in America but the Town was laid waste by the British Army during the American Revolution. The Bells Survived and were later hung in the New Church the Present Cathedral in Charleston. The Bells were later cast into One Large Bell which was Destroyed or maybe Melted Down during the Civil War.
Dover, New Jersey, First Memorial Presbyterian Church, 12, in C, - Chimestand Chimed, These Bells were cast by Petit and Fritsen in 1971 and 1973.
Dover, New Hampshire, St John's United Methodist Church, 12, - Chimed Only,Cast by Jones in 1875.
Drexel Hill, Pennsylvania, Collenbrook United Church, 15, 12 cwt in E, - Baton Keyboard Chimed,
These Bells were cast by Meneely of Watervliet in 1928, Detatched Tower.
Dubuque, Iowa, St Luke's United Methodist Church, 11, in D, - Chimed Only, Cast by McShane in 1913.
Duluth, Minnesota, First United Methodist Church, 10, in F#, - Chimed Only, These Bells were cast by Meneely of Troy in 1921.
Durham, North Carolina, Duke Memorial United Methodist Church, (East Tower), 10, in F#, - Chimestand Chimed, These Bells were cast by Meneely of Watervliet in 1907.
Durham, North Carolina, (United Methodist), Duke University Chapel, Allen and Perkins Carillon, 50, 99-2-4. in G. - Traditional Keyboard, Carillon, All these Bells were cast by Taylors in 1932.
East Lansing, Michigan, Michigan State University, Beaumont Tower, 49, 50 cwt in C, - Traditional Keyboard, Carillon, Twenty-seven Bells were cast by Gillett and Johnson in 1928, 1930, 1935 and 1959, The Four Largest bells were cast by Gillett and Johnson using Taylors Bellfoundry, The rest were cast by Eijsbouts in 1996, Detatched Tower.
East Northfield, Massachusetts, Northfield and Mount Hermon Schools, Sage Chapel, McRoberts Memorial Carillon, 47, in C, - Traditional Keyboard, Carillon, Not Played because the Tower is Unsafe, These Bells were cast by Paccard in 1966.
East Orange, New Jersey, Church of the Holy Spirit & Our Lady Help of Christians, 14, in E, - Baton Keyboard Chimed, Cast by Gillett and Johnson in 1926, This Church is in a Rough Neighbourhood.
Eau Claire, Wisconsin, Christ Church Cathedral, 15, - Electric Keyboard Chimed,Cast by Petit & Fritsen.
Eau Claire, Wisconsin, Grace Lutheran Church, 11, in D, - Chimed Only, Cast by McShane.
Edgerton, Ohio, Trinity Church, 9, - Chimed Only, Cast by Meneely of Watervliet.
Elsah, Illinois, Principia Colledge Chapel, The Jean L Rainwater Carillon, 39, 18 cwt in A#, - Traditional Keyboard, Carillon, All the Bells were cast by Eijsbouts in 1999.
Emmitsburg, Maryland, Pangborn Memorial Campanile, The National Shrine of our Lady, 14, in G, Electric Keyboard Chimed, These Bells were cast by Petit and Fritsen in 1964, Detatched Stone Tower with a Statue of a French Saint on the Top of the Tower.

Erie, Pennsylvania, The Behrend College, Larry & Kathryn Smith Chapel, Floyd & Juanita Smith Carillon, 48, 12 cwt in D#, - Traditional Keyboard, Carillon, All the Bells Cast in 2002 by Meeks & Watson except the Four Tenors were Cast by Whitechapel.
Evanston, Illinois, St Mark's Episcopal Church, 9, in F, - Chimestand Chimed, Cast by Meneely of Watervliet in 1901.
Evanston, Illinois, (Episcopal), Seabury-Western Theological Seminary, Laurance Hearn Armour Memorial Carillon, 35, in A, - Traditional Keyboard,Carillon, Cast by Petit and Fritsen in 1954.
Evergreen, Colorado, International Bell Museum, 23, 20 cwt, - Carillon, Open to the public Tues-Sun 10am-5pm, They have an outdoor collection of 80 Bells from 12" to 48" in Diameter both iron and bronze but mostly American made, There are over 5000 Bells in the Museum.
Faribault, Minnesota, (Episcopal), Cathedral of our Merciful Saviour, Bishop Whipple Memorial Tower, 10, in C, - Chimestand Chimed, These Bells were cast by McShane in 1902, There is Also another **Bell** Hung for Ringing cast by Meneely of West Troy in 1869 which weighs 32-0-14.
Fayetteville, North Carolina, First Presbyterian Church, 14, in F#, - Chimed Only, Cast by Meneely of Watervliet.
Ferrum, Virginia, Ferrum Colledge (formerly Ferrum Junior College), Vaughn Memorial Tower, 23, in C, - Electric Keyboard, Carillon, These Bells were cast by VanBergen in 1970.
Flint, Michigan, First Baptist Church, 12, in D, - Electric Keyboard Chimed, Cast by Petit & Fritsen in 1952.
Flint, Michigan, First Presbyterian Church, 10, in F, - Chimed Only, Cast by Meneely of Troy in 1928.
Flint, Michigan, Kettering University (Formerly General Motors Institute), Alumni Tower, 47, 20 cwt in G, - Electric Keyboard, Carillon, These Bells were cast by Petit and Fritsen in 1969.
Fond du Lac, Wisconsin, (Episcopal), Cathedral Church of St Paul, 15, - Chimed Only, Eight of the Bells were cast by Gillett and Johnson in 1927 and the rest were cast by Paccard in 1993.
Fort Collins, Colorado, St Luke's Episcopal Church, Mary Lee Townsend Memorial Carillon, 23, in F, Electric Keyboard, Carillon, These Bells were cast in Greenwood by VanBergen in 1967.
Fort Dodge, Iowa, First United Methodist Church, 11, in D#, -Chimed Only, Cast by McShane in 1915.
Fort Smith, Arkansas, Westark Colledge, Donald W Reynolds Tower, 42, 12-2-10. in F. - Electric Keyboard, Carillon, Detatched Tower, These Bells were cast by Paccard in 1995.
Fort Washington,Whitemarsh, Pennsylvania, St Thomas Church, Catherine Colt Dickey Memorial Carillon, 48, in D, - Traditional Keyboard, Carillon, All the Bells were cast by Petit and Fritsen in 1974.
Fort Wayne, Indiana, Emmaus Evang. Lutheran Church, 12, in D#, - Baton Keyboard Chimed, These Bells were cast by Meneely of Watervliet in 1922.
Fort Wayne, Indiana, First Presbyterian Church, 10, in D#, - Electric Keyboard Chimed, These Bells were cast by Meneely of Troy in 1920.
Fort Worth, Texas, First Presbyterian Church, 14, in D, - Chimed Only, Cast by McShane in 1911.
Fort Worth, Texas, St John's Episcopal Church, 14, in B, - Chimed Only, Cast by Petit & Fritsen in 1965.
Frankenmuth, Michigan, Bavarian Inn, 713 South Main Street, Glockenspiel Tower, 35, 1 cwt - Electric Keyboard, The Carillon is Manual and Automatic Play, It Plays at 11am, 12pm, 3pm, 6pm, 9pm and 10pm for 15 Minutes with animation of the legend of the Pied Piper of Hameln in Germany, These Bells were cast by Eijsbouts in 1967, Hung in a small tower attached to the restaurant.
Frederick, Maryland, Baker Park, The Joseph Dill Baker Memorial Carillon, West Second & Bentz Streets, 49, in D, - Traditional Keyboard, Carillon, Fourteen Bells were cast by Meneely of Watervliet in 1941, Nine bells were cast by Eijsbouts in 1967, The rest were cast by Petit & Fritsen in 1995, Detached Tower.
Frederick, Maryland, Trinity Chapel, Evangelical Reformed Church, **10**, in E, - Chimestand Chimed, These Bells were cast by McShane in 1893, **Tenor** Hung for Ringing but Unringable.

Fredericksburg, Virginia, St George Episcopal Church, 11, - Chimed Only, Cast by Meneely of Watervliet.
Gainesville, Florida, University of Florida-Gainesville, Century Tower, 49, 62-2-0. in A#. - Traditional Keyboard, This Carillon was cast by Eijsbouts in 1979, Detatched Tower.
Gainesville, Georgia, First United Methodist Church, 24, in G, - Hung Dead, Automatic Carillon, These Bells were cast by Eijsbouts in 1987.
Galveston, Texas, Trinity Episcopal Church, 10, in D#, - Chimed Only, Cast by Meneely of Troy in 1929.
Gambier, Ohio, Kenyon Colledge, Colledge Chapel, Church of the Holy Spirit, **10**, 16-1-0 in F, - Chimestand Chimed, The **Tenor** is also Hung for ringing with No Stay or Slider, Cast by Meneely of Troy in 1879 & 1941.
Garden Grove, California, The Crystal Cathedral, Crean Tower, Arvella Schuller Carillon, 52, in C, - Traditional Keyboard, Carillon, All the Bells were cast by Eijsbouts in 1990, Detatched Tower.
Gastonia, North Carolina, First Presbyterian Church, The Memorial Carillon, 49, 37 cwt in G, - Traditional Keyboard, Carillon, All the Bells were made by Eijsbouts in 1973, There is also another Bell Hung for Swing Chiming which was cast by Vanduzen in 1895.
Gastona, North Carolina, First United Methodist Church, 23, in C, - Electric Keyboard, Carillon, These Bells were cast by VanBergen in 1974.
Gates Mills, Ohio, Church of St Christopher-by-the-River, 23, in D, - Traditional Keyboard, Carillon, Eight of the bells were cast by Gillett and Johnson in 1927 and the rest were cast by Taylors in 1964.
Gaylord, Michigan, Glens Market (The Alpine Village), 23, 0-1-0, - Automatic Carillon, Hung at the front of a Swiss style building under the clock.
Gering, Nabraska, Gering National Bank and Trust Company, 24, in C, - Electric Keyboard, Carillon, These Bells were cast by Petit and Fritsen in 1982.
Glencoe, Illinois, Chicago Botanic Garden, Lake-Cook Rd off east of Edens Highway, 48, 40 cwt in C, Traditional Keyboard, Carillon, These Bells were cast by Petit and Fritsen in 1986, Detatched Tower.
Glendale, Ohio, Convent of the Transfiguration, Chapel Tower, 36, in A#, - Traditional Keyboard, Carillon, Cast by Petit & Fritsen between 1950 -1951 this was the First Traditional Carillon in North America by this Founder.
Glendale, Ohio, (Episcopal), Christ Church, 11, - Cast by McShane in 1915.
Gloucester, Massachusetts, (R.C.), Church of our Lady of Good Voyage, (W.Tower), 31, in D#, - Traditional Keyboard,This was the first modern attuned carillon in the U.S.A. in 1924, These Bells were cast by Taylors in 1922 and 1924, The Church is modelled on a Church in Azores in Portugal.
Grand Rapids, Michigan, (Non Denominational), Fountain Street Church, 8, - Chimed Only, These Bells were cast by Petit and Fritsen, These Bells are Chimed to Methods (Change Ringing).
Grand Rapids, Michigan, (R.C.), Cathedral of St Andrew, 10, in D, - Chimed Only, Cast by McShane.
Grand Rapids, Michigan, Grand Valley State University, DeVos Centre, Beckering Family Carillon Tower, 48, in C, - Traditional Keyboard, Carillon, All the Bells were cast by Paccard in 2000.
Granville, Ohio, Swasey Chapel, Denison University, 10, in F, - Chimed Only, These Bells were cast by Meneely of Troy in 1924.
Green Bay, Wisconsin, First Evangelical Lutheran Church, Kaap Memorial Carillon, 47, in C, - Traditional Keyboard, Carillon, All the Bells were cast by Petit and Fritsen and installed in 1957.
Greencastle, Indiana, DePauw University, Performing Arts Centre, Alpha Chi Omega Memorial Carillon, 37, 10 cwt in A, - Traditional Keyboard, Carillon, Cast by Petit and Fritsen in 1976.
Greensboro, North Carolina, Our Lady of Grace Catholic Church, 14, in A#, - Chimed Only, These Bells were cast by Petit and Fritsen in 1976.

Greenville, South Carolina, Furman University (New Campus), The Burnside Carillon, 60, in D, Traditional Keyboard, Carillon, All the Bells were cast by VanBergen in 1966, Detatched Tower.
Greenville, South Carolina, Westminster Presbyterian Church, Niven Memorial Tower, Niven Memorial Carillon, 24, in C, - Electric Keyboard, Carillon, Cast by VanBergen in 1964.
Greenwood, South Carolina, Callie Self Memorial Baptist Church, 35, in D#, - Electric Keyboard, Carillon, These Bells were cast by VanBergen in 1941 and 1948.
Greenwood, South Carolina, First Baptist Church, 37, in C, - Electric Keyboard, Carillon, Cast by VanBergen in 1970 & 1977.
Greenwood, South Carolina, Greenwood Building and Loan Company, 18, in F, - Automatically Chimed Only, These Bells were cast by VanBergen.
Greenwood, South Carolina, Lander College, Laura Lander Hall, 35, in C, - Electric Keyboard, Carillon, Cast by Paccard in 1978.
Grosse Pointe, Michigan, Christ Church, 35, - Carillon, The practice keyboard was made by Taylors.
Grosse Pointe Farms, Michigan, (Episcopal), Christ Church, 35, in D, -Traditional Keyboard, Carillon, Thirty Bells cast by Gillett & Johnson in 1935 & 1938, The rest were cast by Taylors in 1988.
Grosse Pointe Farms, Michigan, (Presbyterian), The Grosse Pointe Memorial Church, Memorial Tower, 47, in C#, - Traditional Keyboard, Carillon, Eight of the bells were cast by Gillett and Johnson in 1927, The rest were cast by Petit and Fritsen in 1952.
Hampton, Virginia, The Memorial Church, Hampton University, 9, in F, - Electric Keyboard Chimed, Including Sharp Fourth, These Bells were cast by Meneely of Troy in 1887.
Hanover, New Hampshire, Baker Memorial Library, Dartmouth College, 16, 22-1-4 in C, - Electric Keyboard Chimed, These Bells were cast by Meneely of Troy in 1928 - 1929.
Harrisburg, Pennsylvania, Zion Lutheran Church, 11, in F, - Electric Keyboard Chimed, These Bells were cast by Jones in 1868 - 1869, Rehung in a New Frame in 1980.
Hartford, Connecticut, Trinity Colledge, Chapel Tower, Plumb Memorial Carillon, 49, 50 cwt in B, - Traditional Keyboard, Carillon, These Bells were cast by Taylors in 1932 and 1978.
Hastings, Nebraska, First United Methodist Church, 10, in E, - Chimestand Chimed, Including Flat Seventh, Cast by McShane in 1916.
Haverhill, Massachusetts, Trinity Episcopal Church, 10, in F, - Ellacombe Chimed, Including Extra Treble & Flat Seventh, The **Tenor** and **Sixth** are hung for Ringing but Unringable, Nine of the Bells Cast by Blake in 1869.
Helena, Montana, (R.C.), St Helena's Cathedral, (North Tower), 15, in D#, - Electric Keyboard Chimed exept the **Four Largest Bells** which are hung for Ringing, Cast by McShane in 1914.
Henderson, North Carolina, First Baptist Church, 16, in C, - Electric Keyboard Chimed, These Bells were cast by Paccard in 1979.
Hereford, Texas, (R.C.), St Anthony, 10, in A#, - Electric Keyboard Chimed, Cast by Petit & Fritsen in 1951.
High Point, North Carolina, Wesley Memorial United Methodist Church, 13, in D, - Chimed Only, These Bells were cast by McShane in 1920.
Hingham, Massachusetts, The Old Ship Church of First Parish, 1, 5 cwt, - Unringable, Hung in a Wooden Bellcote above the Church, This is the Oldest Church in the USA.
Hinsdale, Illinois, The Union Church of Hinsdale, 9, in F, - Electric Keyboard Chimed, These Bells were cast by Meneely of Troy in 1902.
Holland, Pennsylvania, Trinity Reformed Church, Henry D Schneider Memorial Carillon, 49, 20 cwt in D#, - Traditional Keyboard, Carillon, Twenty-five Bells were cast by Meneely of Watervliet in 1930, The rest were cast by Petit and Fritsen in 1955 and 1976.
Houston, Texas, Hillside Village (Shopping Centre), near Westview Drive and Wirt Road, Spring Branch, Bell Tower Centre Carillon, 53, in G, - Traditional Keyboard, Carillon, Cast by Eijsbouts in 1986 and 1991.
Houston, Texas, (R.C.) St Mary's Seminary, Chapel Tower, 23, in A, - Electric Keyboard, Carillon, These Bells were cast by Petit and Fritsen in 1954.

Houston, Texas, St John the Divine Episcopal Church, 42, in F, - Traditional Keyboard, Carillon, These Bells were cast by Petit and Fritsen in 1952 and 1962.
Houston, Texas, St Paul's United Methodist Church (Upper Belfry), 10, 15 cwt in D#, - Electric Keyboard Chimed, These Bells were cast by Meneely of Troy in 1908, (Lower Belfry), 8, 11-0-3. in G. - These Bells were cast by Whitechapel in 2001.
Houston, Texas, (R.C.), St Vincent de Paul Church, 14, 8-3-8 in A, - Electric Keyboard Chimed, These Bells were cast by Petit and Fritsen in 1968.
Houston, Texas, Trinity Lutheran Church, Theresa Mohnke Memorial Carillon, 25, in A#, - Traditional Keyboard, Carillon, All the Bells were cast by Petit and Fritsen and installed between 1954 - 1957.
Howell, Michigan, St Alexander Nevsky Church, 11, in G, - Automatically Chimed Only, These Bells were cast by Eijsbouts in 1985.
Huntington, Indiana, First M.E. Church, 11, in F, - Chimestand Chimed, Cast by Meneely of Troy in 1915.
Huntington, West Virginia, James E Morrow Library, Marshall University, 16, 10 cwt in C, - Electric Keyboard Chimed, These Bells were cast by Paccard in 1983.
Huntsville, Alabama, First Baptist Church, 48, in C#, - Traditional Keyboard, Carillon, Cast by Petit and Fritsen in 1987, Hung in a Sixty-one Bell frame with space on the Keyboard also for more bells.
Hyannis, Massachusetts, Christmas Tree Shops,(655 Route 132), 25, 30 cwt in C, - Automatic Carillon, These Bells were cast by Petit and Fritsen in 1989, Detatched Tower.
Indianapolis, Indiana, (Episcopal), Christ Church Cathedral, 9, in E, - Including a Flat Seventh, These Bells were cast by Meneely of Watervliet in 1860 & 1890, These Bells are Regularly Swing Chimed to Methods, These Bells have Full Wheels, No Stays or Sliders.
Indianapolis, Indiana, (Masonic) Scottish Rite Cathedral, 54, 100 cwt. in G, - Traditional Keyboard, Carillon, Twenty-four Bells were cast by Taylors in 1929 and the rest were cast by Paccard in 1965.
Indianapolis, Indiana, St Paul's Lutheran Church, 10, - Hung Dead, Keyboard Chimed Only.
Iowa City, Iowa, (R.C.), St Mary of the Visitation Church, 17, - Electric Keyboard Chimed Only, Fifteen Bells were cast by Henry Stuckstede & Co of St Louis in 1854, One Bell cast by Francis Mayer of St Louis in 1834, One Bell Cast by Jones & Co of Troy in New York in 1867.
Ithaca, New York, Cornell University, Uris Library, McGraw Tower, The Cornell Chimes, 21, 20 cwt in C#, - Chimestand Chimed, Most regularly played Chime on any American Campus.
Jackson, Tennessee, First Presbyterian Church, The Jackson Memorial Carillon, 47, in C, - Traditional Keyboard, Carillon, All the Bells were cast by Paccard in 1954.
Jackson, Mississippi, St Andrew's Episcopal Cathedral, 17, in F#, - Electric Keyboard Chimed, Eleven of the bells were cast by Meneely of Watervliet in 1937 the rest were cast by Verdin Bell Co in 1999.
Jacksonville, Florida, St John's Episcopal Cathedral, 10, in F, - Chimed Only, These Bells were cast by Meneely of Watervliet in 1948.
Jamestown, New York, St Luke's Episcopal Church, 12, - Electric Keyboard Chimed, Cast by Vanduzen.
Janesville, Wisconsin, First Congregational Church, 10, in D, -Chimestand Chimed, Cast by McShane.
Jefferson, Iowa, Mahanay Memorial Carillon Tower, Court House Square, 14, 20 cwt in C, - Electric Keyboard Chimed, Cast by Petit and Fritsen in 1966, There are also 32 Tubular Bells cast by Deagan, Detatched Tower.
Jim Thorpe, Pennsylvania, Episcopal Parish of St Mark and St John, 12, in D#, - Electric Keyboard Chimed, Nine Bells were cast by Jones in 1876, The rest were cast by Meneely of Troy in 1947, Before 1954 this town was called Mauch Chunk & the other side of town was called East Mauch Chunk.
Johnstown, Pennsylvania, First Lutheran Church, 11, in D#, - Electric Keyboard Chimed.

Jordanville , New York, Holy Trinity Russian Orthodox Monastery, Church, 12, - Zvon Chimed Only, Hung Dead in a balanced gable of the Monastery Church.
Jordanville , New York, Holy Trinity Russian Orthodox Church, Gatehouse Tower, 18, 117-3-1. - Zvon Chimed Only, Hung Dead, Fourteen of the Bells were cast by Eijesbouts in 1988.
Kalamazoo , Michigan, (Episcopal), Cathedral of Christ the King, 47, in G, - Electric Keyboard, Carillon, These Bells were cast by Eijsbouts in 1969.
Kansas City , Missouri, (R.C.), Cathedral of the Immaculate Conception, 11, in C, - Electric Keyboard Chimed Only, These Bells were cast by McShane.
Kansas City , Missouri, (Disciples of Christ), Independence Boulevard Christian Church, 11, in D, Chimestand Chimed, Including Sharp Forth & Flat Seventh, These Bells were cast by McShane in 1919.
Kansas City , Missouri, (R.C.), Visitation of the Blessed Virgin, 10, in F, - Electric Keyboard Chimed, These Bells were cast by McShane.
Kearney , Nabraska, University of Nabraska at Kearney, Memorial Carillon Tower, 24, 5 cwt in C, - Automatic Carillon,These Bells were cast by Paccard, Detatched Tower.
Kennett Square , Pennsylvania, Longwood Gardens, (off U.S. Highway 1 at Penn.Route 52), 62, 61-2-11 in A#, - Traditional Keyboard, Carillon, All the Bells were cast by Eijsbouts in 2001, (0-0-20 in C, 0-0-20 in B, 0-0-20 in A#, 0-0-20 in A, 0-0-20 in G#, 0-0-20 in G, 0-0-20 in F#, 0-0-20 in F, 0-0-22 in E, 0-0-22 in D#, 0-0-22 in D, 0-0-22 in C#, 0-0-26 in C, 0-0-26 in B, 0-0-26 in A#, 0-0-26 in A, 0-1-1 in G#, 0-1-1 in G, 0-1-3 in F#, 0-1-3 in F, 0-1-5 in E, 0-1-5 in D#, 0-1-7 in D, 0-1-9 in C#, 0-1-12 in C, 0-1-12 in B, 0-1-17 in A#, 0-1-22 in A, 0-1-27 in G#, 0-2-4 in G, 0-2-9 in F#, 0-2-14 in F, 0-2-19 in E, 0-3-6 in D#, 0-3-11 in D, 0-3-21 in C#, 1-0-3 in C, 1-0-18 in B, 1-1-5 in A#, 1-1-25 in A, 1-2-17 in G#, 1-3-14 in G, 2-0-16 in F#, 2-1-18 in F, 2-3-2 in E, 3-0-14 in D#, 3-2-10 in D, 4-1-5 in C#, 5-0-17 in C, 6-1-1 in B, 7-1-8 in A#, 8-2-27 in A, 10-1-25 in G#, 12-2-2 in G, 14-3-11 in F#, 17-2-25 in F, 21-0-16 in E, 25-0-26 in D#, 30-0-22 in D, 36-0-20 in C#, 43-1-2 in C, 61-2-11 in A#,) Detatched Round Tower.
Key West , Florida, St Pauls Episcopal Cathedral, (North Tower), 10, in F#, - Chimestand Chimed, These Bells were cast by McShane in 1891 and 1919, The original Eighth Bell Cracked when a Hurricane destroyed the Cathedral in 1909.
Knoxville , Tennessee, Second Presbyterian Church, 10, in D, - Chimed Only, Cast by McShane.
La Grange , Georgia, 1st Baptist Church on the Square, Fuller B Callaway Memorial Carillon, 49, in C, - Carillon.
Lake Charles , Louisiana, First Presbyterian Church, 23, in F, - Electric Keyboard, Carillon, Cast by Petit and Fritsen in 1954.
Lake Wales , Florida, Bok Tower Gardens, Bok Singing Tower, 60, 214-1-0. in D#. - Traditional Keyboard, Carillon, Detatched Tower, The Gardens are open daily between 8am - 6pm and on moonlight recital evenings closes at 9.30pm, All the Bells were cast by Taylors in 1928.
Lakewood , Ohio, Faith Lutheran Church, 9, - Chimed Only.
Lakewood , New Jersey, Winkelmann's Restaurant, (US Highway 9), 25, in C, - Electric Keyboard, Carillon, These Bells were cast by Petit and Fritsen in 1986.
Lansing , Michigan, Central United Methodist Church, Christopther Hansen Memorial Carillon, 36, in B, - Traditional Keyboard, Carillon, All the Bells were cast by Petit and Fritsen in 1951.
Lapeer , Michigan, (R.C.), Immaculate Conception of the Blessed Virgin Mary, 10, - Chimed Only.
Laramie , Wyoming, St Matthew's Episcopal Cathedral, 11, in F, - Electric Keyboard Chimed, Cast by Meneely of Watervliet in 1917, This is the Highest Episcopal Cathedral in the World at 7165' in elevation.
Latrobe , Pennsylvania, St Vincent Colledge, 3, 14-1-0. - Chimed Only.
Laurinburg , North Carolina, St Andrews Presbyterian Colledge, Katherine McKay Belk Bell Tower, 18, - Chimed Only, These Bells were cast by VanBergen, Detatched Tower.
Lawrence , Massachusetts, (R.C.), St Mary and Immaculate Conception, 16, in D, - Electric Keyboard Chimed, These Bells were cast by Wm Blake & Co in 1874.
Lawrence , Kansas, University of Kansas, World War II Memorial Campanile, 53, 120 cwt in F#, - Traditional Keyboard, Carillon, All the Bells were cast by Taylors in 1951, Detatched Tower.

167

Lawrenceville, Georgia, First Baptist Church, 18, - Chimed Only, These Bells were cast by VanBergen and were previously part of a Carillon at the VanBergen Bell Foundry in Greenwood.
Lebanon, Pennsylvania, (Presbyterian), Christ Church, 10, 18-0-3 in F, - Chimed Only.
Lebanon, Tennessee, First Presbyterian Church, 25, in C, - Hung Dead, Automatic Carillon, These Bells were cast by Eijsbouts in 1995.
Leechburg, Pennsylvania, First Evangelical Lutheran Church, 23, in F, - Electric Keyboard, Carillon, Ten of the Bells were cast by Meneely of Watervliet in 1910, The rest were cast by Petit and Fritsen.
Lewiston, Maine, St Joseph's Catholic Church, 12, in F, - Electric Keyboard Chimed, Cast by Meneely of Watervliet.
Lexington, Kentucky, (Episcopal) Christ Church Cathedral, 10, in D, - Chimed Only, These Bells were cast by Meneely of Troy in 1915.
Lincoln, Nabraska, First-Plymouth Congregational Church, Tower Carillon, 57, in C, - Traditional Keyboard, Carillon, Twenty Bells were cast by Taylors in 1931 and the rest were cast by Whitechapel in 1988 and there are 24 ornamental Bells in a Belfry Screen.
Lincoln, Nabraska, First-Plymouth Congregational Church, Chapel (Indoors), Chamber Carillon, 29, in A#, - Electric Keyboard, This Carillon is Unplayable, Twenty-four Bells were cast by Taylors in 1989 and the rest were cast by Whitechapel, These Bells are Hung Inside the Chapel.
Lincoln, Nebraska, (United Methodist Church), St Paul, 10, in F, - Chimestand Chimed, These Bells were cast by Meneely of Troy in 1902.
Little Falls, New York, Holy Family Parish (formerly St Mary RC Church), 14, in D#, - Electric Keyboard Chimed.
Lock Haven, Pennsylvania, Lock Haven University of Pennsylvania, Fredericks Family Memorial Carillon, 47, 24 cwt in C, - Electric Keyboard, Carillon, Cast by Paccard in 2000, Detatched Tower.
Longview, Washington, Longview Community Church, 11, in E, - Chimed Only, Cast by McShane in 1926.
Los Angeles, California, Hollywood Forever Memorial Park, (Cemetery), Otis Memorial Chimes, (The Bells of Hollywood), Santa Monica Boulevard between Gower and Van Ness Avenue, 12, in D#, - Chimestand Chimed, These Bells were cast by Vanduzen in 1908, Detatched Ivy Covered Tower.
Los Angeles, California, Holman United Methodist Church, 10, in C, - Electric Keyboard Chimed, These Bells were cast by Petit and Fritsen in 1957.
Los Angeles, California, Music Centre of Los Angeles County, Dorothy Chandler Pavilion, Stage Left, 32, in B, - Electric Keyboard, Carillon, The Bells are indoors and Amplified from individual contact microphones, These Bells were cast by VanBergen in 1968.
Los Angeles, California, St Agnes Catholic Church, 12, in D#, - Chimed Only, Cast by McShane in 1907.
Los Angeles, California, St Brendan's Catholic Church, 15, in A, - Chimed Only, Cast by Taylors in 1958.
Los Angeles, California, St Paul's Catholic Church, 9, in A#, - Chimed Only, Including a Flat Seventh, These Bells were cast by Taylors in 1956.
Louisville, Kentucky, (R.C.), Cathedral of the Assumption, 35, in C, - Electric Keyboard, This Carillon used to be owned by Pepsi-Cola Limited between 1970-1982 and was known as the (Mobile) Pepsi Carillon, These bells were cast by Petit and Fritsen in 1982, There is Also One Other Bell in The Tower cast by William Kaye of Louisville in 1852 it was a Gift from the Archbishop of Mexico Monsignor la Batisda and it weighs 50cwt.
Louisville, Kentucky, Walnut Street Baptist Church, 10, in C, - Electric Keyboard Chimed, These Bells were cast by McShane in 1902.
Lowell, Massachusetts, St Anne's Episcopal Church, 11, in E, - Chimestand Chimed, Cast by Jones in 1857.
Lowell, Massachusetts, (R.C.), St Patrick's Church, 11, in D, - Chimestand Chimed, Cast in 1906.

Lubbock, Texas, Texas Tech University, Administration Building, (West Tower), Charles and Georgia Robertson Baird Memorial Carillon, 36, in B, - Traditional Keyboard,Carillon, Fifteen Bells were cast by VanBergen in 1974 and the rest were cast by Paccard in 1976. (East Tower), 2, 8-0-3, - Donated by the Class of 1936.
Lubbock, Texas, First United Methodist Church, Overton Memorial Bell Tower, 25, 80 cwt in G, - Electric Keyboard,Carillon, The **Tenor** is Hung for ringing, recessed into Headstock, No Stay or Slider, All the Bells were cast by Taylors in 1995.
Luray, Virginia, Luray Singing Tower, Luray Caverns, West Main Street (off U.S. Highway 211), 47, in A, - Traditional Keyboard, Carillon, All the Bells were cast by Taylors and installed in 1937.
Lynchburg, Virginia, Court Street United Methodist Church, 10, in F#, - Chimestand Chimed, These bells were cast by Meneely of Watervliet in 1908.
Madison, Wisconsin, Grace Episcopal Church, 23, in E, - Electric Keyboard, Carillon, Nine of the bells were cast by Jones in 1874, The rest were cast by Petit and Fritsen in 1975.
Madison, Wisconsin, University of Wisconsin, Campanile, Memorial Carillon, 56, 60-3-7 in A#, - Traditional Keyboard, Carillon, Twenty-four Bells were cast by Gillett and Johnson in 1936 and the rest were cast by Eijsbouts in 1973, Also Ivy growing up the Detached Tower.
Magnolia, Arkansas, Southern Arkansas University, Water Tower, 14, - Automatically Chimed Only.
Manchester, New Hampshire, Brookside Congregational Church, 9, in F, - Chimed Only, These Bells were cast by Meneely of Troy in 1878.
Manistee, Michigan, (R.C.), Guardian Angels Church, 12, in C, - Chimed Only, These Bells were cast by Meneely of Watervliet in 1910.
Maple Heights, Ohio, Lutheran Church of the Covenant, 25, in A#, - Electric Keyboard, Carillon, Cast by VanBergen in 1961.
Mariemont, Ohio, Thomas J Emery Memorial Carillon Tower, Mary M Emery Memorial Carillon, Dogwood Park, 49, in C#, - Traditional Keyboard, Carillon, Twenty-three Bells were cast by Gillett and Johnson in 1929, The rest were cast by Petit and Fritsen in 1969.
Marietta, Ohio, First Congregational Church, 10, in F, - Chimed Only, Cast by Meneely of Troy in 1922.
Marietta, Georgia, Life University College of Chiropractic, The Chiropractic Memorial Bell Tower, 16, 8 cwt, - Chimed Only, Detached Tower.
Marion, Indiana, First Presbyterian Church of Grant County, 11, in E, - Electric Keyboard Chimed, These Bells were cast by Meneely of Watervliet in 1910.
Marysville, Ohio, First United Methodist Church, 12, in F, - Electric Keyboard Chimed, Ten Bells were cast by Meneely of Troy in 1920, The rest were cast by Eijsbouts in 1985.
Masonville, New Hampshire, Shopping Centre, 20, in C, - Automatically Chimed Only, These Bells were cast by Eijsbouts in 1985.
McAdenville, North Carolina, City of McAdenville, 14, - Chimed Only.
McDonogh, Maryland, McDonogh School, Target Memorial Chapel, The McDonogh Carillon, 48, in D, - Traditional Keyboard, Carillon, All the Bells were cast by Petit and Fritsen in 1978.
Medford, Massachusetts, Grace Episcopal Church, 9, 15 cwt in F, - Unringable, Electric Keyboard Chimed, These Bells were cast by William Blake of Boston in 1873.
Medford, Massachusetts, Tufts University, Goddard Chapel, Bowen-Tilton Memorial Carillon, 25, in C, - Electric Keyboard, Carillon, Ten of the Bells were cast by Meneely of Troy in 1926, The rest were cast by Petit & Fritsen in 1965.
Memphis, Tennessee, Idlewild Presbyterian Church, 48, 30 cwt in C, - Traditional Baton Keyboard, Carillon, These Bells were cast by Paccard in 1981, 1983 and 1999.
Menomonie, Minnesota, Stout University, 5, 39-3-8. in D., - Hung Dead, Clock Chime.
Mercersburg, Pennsylvania, Mercersburg Academy, Chapel, Barker Tower, The Henry Bucher Swoope Carillon, 49, 64 cwt in Bb, - Traditional Keyboard, Carillon, Forty-three Bells were cast by Gillett and Johnson in 1926, The rest were cast by Meeks and Watson in 1996, The Practice Keyboard was made by Taylors in 1973.

<u>Mesa</u>, Arizona, Las Sendas, The Centre, 48, in G, - Electric Keyboard, Carillon, All the Bells were cast by Petit and Fritsen in 1995, Also it Automatically Plays between 6.30pm-8.30pm Sat and Sun.
<u>Middlebury</u>, Vermont, Middlebury College, Mead Memorial Chapel, 48, in E, - Traditional Keyboard, Carillon, Nine of the bells were cast by Meneely of Watervliet in 1915, Twelve Bells were cast by VanBergen in 1959 and the rest were cast by Paccard in 1986.
<u>Middletown</u>, Ohio, (Episcopal), Church of the Ascension, The Sidney Case McCammon Memorial Carillon, 35, in D#, - Traditional Keyboard, Carillon, Cast by Petit and Fritsen in 1964.
<u>Middletown</u>, Connecticut, (Episcopal), Church of the Holy Trinity, 10, in F, - Chimestand Chimed, Cast by Meneely of Troy in 1902.
<u>Middletown</u>, Connecticut, Wesleyan University, South College Building, Cupola, 16, 30 cwt in E, - Baton Keyboard Chimed, These Bells were cast by Whitechapel in 1918 and 1966.
<u>Midland</u>, Michigan, The Memorial Presbyterian Church, 15, in E, - Electric Keyboard Chimed, These Bells were cast by Eijsbouts in 1951.
<u>Milford</u>, New Hampshire, First Congregational Church, 10, in F#, - Chimed Only, These Bells were cast by Meneely of Troy in 1942.
<u>Millwood</u>, Virginia, (Episcopal), Christ Church, Cunnington Chapel Parish, 12, in G, - Electric Keyboard Chimed, These Bells were cast by Petit and Fritsen in 1963.
<u>Milwaukee</u>, Wisconsin, Capitol Drive Lutheran Church, 10, 8 cwt in A#, - Electric Keyboard Chimed Only, Hung Dead,These Bells were cast by Petit and Fritsen in 1956.
<u>Milwaukee</u>, Wisconsin, Marquette Building, Rooftop Belfry, The Marquette University Carillon, 48, 65 cwt in C, - Traditional Keyboard, Carillon, All the Bells were cast by Paccard and installed in 1967.
<u>Milwaukee</u>, Wisconsin, Milwaukee City Hall, 1, 220 cwt. - Clock Bell, Cast by G. Campbell & Sons of Milwaukee in 1896.
<u>Milwaukee</u>, Wisconsin, St James Episcopal Church, 9, - Electric Keyboard Chimed, These Bells were cast by Jones in 1876.
<u>Minneapolis</u>, Minnesota, Breck School, Chapel of the Holy Spirit, 23, 15 cwt in C, - Electric Keyboard, Carillon, These Bells were cast by Paccard in 1986.
<u>Minneapolis</u>, Minnesota, (R C.), Church of St Olaf, 9, in D#, - Electric Keyboard Chimed, These Bells were cast by Meneely of Troy in 1882.
<u>Minneapolis</u>, Minnesota, Minneapolis City Hall, Hennepin County Courthouse, 4th Street Tower, 15, 65-0-17 in A#, - Hung Dead, Electric Keyboard Chimed Only, Four-teen Bells were cast by Meneely of Troy in 1924 the Treble was cast by Petit & Fritsen in 1972.
<u>Minneapolis</u>, Minnesota, North Hennepin Community College, 25, in F, - Electric Keyboard, Carillon, Cast by Petit and Fritsen in 1994, Detatched Steel Tower sculptured to honour Sheep & Potatoes.
<u>Minneapolis</u>, Minnesota, St Mark's Episcopal Cathedral, 14, in C, - Electric Keyboard Chimed, These Bells were cast by Paccard in 1998.
Mishawaka, Indiana, First United Methodist Church, **11**, in E, - Chimestand Chimed exept the **Tenor** which is hung for Ringing, These Bells were cast by Meneely of Watervliet in 1912.
<u>Missoula</u>, Montana, University of Montana (formerly Montana State University), Main Hall, Ellis Tower, 47, 20 cwt in F, - Traditional Keyboard, Carillon, Cast by VanBergen in 1953.
<u>Modesto</u>, California, St Stan's Brewery and Restaurant, 821 'L' Street, 9, in E, - Automatically Chimed Only These Bells were cast by Eijsbouts in 1990.
<u>Monrovia</u>, California, St Luke's Episcopal Church, 11, in G, - Electric Keyboard Chimed, These Bells were cast by Meneely of Watervliet in 1931.
<u>Montgomery</u>, Alabama, St John's Episcopal Church, 9, in F#, - Chimestand Chimed, These Bells were cast by Meneely of Troy in 1885.
Montpelier, Vermont, Trinity United Methodist Church, 10, in F, - Chimestand Chimed, Cast by McShane, There is also another **Bell** Hung for Ringing cast by Meneely & Kimberley in 1872.

Morgan City, Louisiana, Brownell Memorial Park, (4 Miles NE on SR 70), 61, 42-0-23. in C. - Traditional Keyboard, Carillon, Hung Dead, Detatched Hexagonal Tower, This carillon is not regularly used by hand but the Automatic play goes every Half an Hour and the park is open every day between 9am - 5pm, These Bells were cast by Petit and Fritsen in 1971.

Morganton, North Carolina, First Baptist Church, 23, in C, - Electric Keyboard, Carillon, Cast by Paccard in 1991.

Morgantown, West Virginia, Wesley United Methodist Church, 11, - Ellacombe Chimed Only but Unplayable, These Bells were cast by Vanduzen.

Morgantown - See Morganton.

Morristown, New Jersey, St Peter's Episcopal Church, 49, in C, - Traditional Keyboard, Carillon, This was the Largest Carillon in the USA when it was installed in 1924, Thirty-three Bells were cast by Taylors, Fourteen Bells were cast by Bigelow in 1955, Two Bells cast by Petit and Fritsen in 1993.

Moundsville, West Virginia, Simpson United Methodist Church, 10, in E, - Chimestand Chimed, These Bells were cast by McShane in 1914.

Muncie, Indiana, Ball State University, Shafer Tower, 48, in C, - Traditional Keyboard, Carillon, Cast by Paccard in 2001.

Muncie, Indiana, First United Presbyterian Church, 15, - Chimed Only, Cast by McShane in 1926.

Naperville, Illinois, Riverwalk, Aurora Rd West of Eagle Street, Millennium Carillon, 72,120 cwt in G, - Traditional Keyboard,Carillon, Detatched Tower, All the Bells were cast by Eijsbouts in 2000.

Nashua, New Hampshire, (Congregational), The First Church, 15, in C, - Chimestand Chimed, These Bells were cast by Vanduzen in 1893 and were originally displayed at the Chicago Exposition in 1893.

Nashua, New Hampshire, St Patrick's Church, 12, - Chimed Only.

Nashville, Tennessee, Belmont University (formerly Belmont College), 23, in G#, - Traditional Keyboard, Carillon, Cast by Petit & Fritsen and installed in the Tower in 1986.

Nashville, Tennessee, Bicentennial Capitol Mall, The Tennessee Bicentennial Bells, 48, in C, - Electric Keyboard, The Larger of the two similar Carillon's collectively Housed in 50 individual cylindrical Towers arranged in two concentric circles, All the Bells were cast by Petit & Fritsen and installed in 1999.

Nashville, Tennessee, Bicentennial Capitol Mall, The Tennessee Bicentennial Bells, 47, in C, - Electric Keyboard, The Smaller of the two similar Carillon's collectively Housed in 50 individual cylindrical Towers arranged in two concentric circles, All the Bells were cast by Petit & Fritsen and installed in 1999.

Nashville, Tennessee, Lipscomb University (formerly David Lipscomb University), Allen Bell Tower 35, in C, - Traditional Keyboard, Carillon, Cast by Petit & Fritsen and installed in the Tower in 1999.

Nashville, Tennessee, St Georges Episcopal Church, 8, in F, - Electric Keyboard Chimed Only, These Bells were cast by Whitechapel.

Nashville, Tennessee, Tulip Street United Methodist Church, 10, in D#, - Chimestand Chimed, These Bells were cast by Vanduzen in 1897, The Church was damaged by a Tornado in April 1998.

Neillsville, Wisconsin, United Church of Christ, 15, 2 cwt, - Electric Keyboard Chimed Only, Cast by Ruetschi Aarau in Switzerland in 1966, Hung in a Double A-Frame Detatched Steel Tower.

Newark, New Jersey, Cathedral Basilica of the Sacred Heart, (West Tower), 14, in C, - Electric Keyboard Chimed, These Bells were cast by Daciano Colbachini e Figli, Padula, Italy in 1953, Also This is the Fifth Largest Cathedral in the U.S.A.

Newark, Ohio, Second Presbyterian Church, Flory Memorial Carillon, 35, in C, - Traditional Keyboard, Reportedly the Lightest Hand-Playable Carillon in the World, Cast by Petit & Fritsen in 1964.

<u>New Bern</u>, North Carolina, Christ Episcopal Church, 25, in C, - Electric Keyboard, Carillon, Cast by Paccard in 1996.
<u>New Britain</u>, Connecticut, (Congregational), First Church of Christ, Robert S Buol Tower, 37, 12-2-0. in G.- Traditional Keyboard, Carillon, All the Bells were cast by Petit and Fritsen in 1967.
<u>New Britain</u>, Connecticut, South Congregational and First Baptist Church, 14, in C, - Baton Keyboard Chimed, These Bells were cast by Meneely of Watervliet in 1904.
<u>New Brunswick</u>, New Jersey, New Brunswick Theoligical Seminary (Reformed Church in America), Charavay Memorial Carillon, 25, in C, - Electric Keyboard, Carillon, Cast in 1938 at Heiligerlee.
<u>New Canaan</u>, Connecticut, St Mark's Episcopal Church, The Dana-Barton Carillon, 30, 27-3-10. in D#. - Traditional Keyboard, Carillon, Thirteen Bells were cast by Meneely of Watervliet in 1948, The rest were cast by Paccard in 1962 and 1965.
<u>New Glorus</u>, Wisconsin, Bank of New Glorus, 501 First Street, 18, in C, - Automatically Chimed Only, These Bells were cast by Eijsbouts in 1977, In 1969 the Bank was rebuilt as a Swiss Style Building.
<u>New Haven</u>, Connecticut, Suburban Home School, Dixwell Avenue, 9, in D#, - Chimed Only, These Bells were cast by Jones in 1860.
<u>New Haven</u>, Connecticut, Yale University, Battell Chapel, (Southwest Tower), 8, - Chimed Only.
<u>New Haven</u>, Connecticut, Yale University, Harkness Tower, Yale Memorial Carillon, 54, 120 cwt in F#, - Traditional Keyboard, Carillon, These Bells were cast by Taylors in 1921 and 1966.
<u>New Milford</u>, Connecticut, Canterbury School, Chapel of our Lady, Jose M Ferrer Memorial Carillon, 23, 10cwt. in A. - Traditional Keyboard, Carillon, These Bells were cast in 1931 by Gillett and Johnson.
<u>Newnan</u>, Georgia, Newnan Presbyterian Church, 15, - Chimed Only, Cast by McShane.
<u>New Orleans</u>, Louisiana, Grace Episcopal Church, 15, in F#, - Chimed Only, Cast by Taylors in 1955.
<u>New Orleans</u>, Louisiana, (R.C.), Holy Name of Jesus Church, 13, in C#, - Chimed Only, Cast by McShane in 1921.
<u>New Orleans</u>, Louisiana, (R.C.), Sacread Heart of Jesus, 13, in A, - Electric Keyboard Chimed, These Bells were cast by Petit and Fritsen in 1953.
Newport, Rhode Island, 3, 57-0-25., - The Tenor is Counter Ballenced & Recessed into the Headstock, complete with a Stay and a Slider, The Tenor is inscribed "The Gift of Sophia Augustia Brown in Memory of her Dear Son Harold Brown", All the Bells were cast by Whitechapel in 1903.
<u>Newport</u>, Kentucky, Millennium Monument, 1, 589-1-0. in A,, - Automatically Swing Chimed Only,This Bell was cast by Verdin Company of Cincinnati, Ohio & inscribed "World Peace Bell", Also this is the Largest Swinging Bell in the World.
<u>Newport News</u>, Virginia, (R.C.), Our Lady of Mount Carmel Church, 10, - Automatically Chimed Only.
<u>Newton</u>, Massachusetts, Grace Episcopal Church, 9, in C, - Chimed Only, These Bells were cast by William Blake in 1873.
<u>New Ulm</u>, Minnesota, Schonlau Park Plaza, Ted Schonlau Memorial Carillon, 4th North and Minnesota, 37, 8 cwt in C, - Automatic Carillon, The Carillon is played Automatically every day at 12pm, 3pm and 5pm with the animated glockenspiel,Cast by Eijsbouts in 1980, Detatched Tower.
<u>New Wilmington</u>, Pennsylvania, Westminster College, Old Main, Armington Memorial Carillon, 35, 30 cwt in A#, - Traditional Keyboard, Carillon, Eight Bells were cast by Meneely of Watervliet in 1935, The rest of the Bells were cast by Petit and Fritsen in 1978.
<u>New York</u>, New York, Most Holy Redeemer Catholic Church, 8, in C, - Chimed Only, Two Bells were cast by Meneely & the rest were cast by Constance.
<u>New York</u>, New York, (Non-Denominational) Riverside Church, Riverside Drive at 122nd Street, Laura Spelman Rockefeller Memorial Carillon, 74, 365-1-13. in C. - Traditional Keyboard, Carillon,Cast by Gillett & Johnson in 1925 &1931,Two Bells cast by VanBergen in 1956,Heavyest Carillon in the World.

<u>New York</u>, New York, St Martin's Episcopal Church, 122nd Street at Lenox Avenue, 42, in D#, - Traditional Keyboard, This was the first Carillon the be installed in the USA after WW II and All the Bells were cast in 1949 by VanBergen.
<u>New York</u>, New York, (Episcopal), St Thomas Church, 21, in B, - Baton Keyboard Chimed, Cast by Taylors in 1929.
New York, New York, 213 West 82nd St, (R.C.) Holy Trinity Church, **3**, 13cwt., - Cast by Whitechapel in 1854.
New York, New York, St Pauls Chapel, **1**, 10 cwt, Recessed into the Headstock, No Stay or Slider, Cast by Mears & Stainbank in 1797, Hung in a Wooden Tower.
New York, New York, Wall Street, Trinity Church, **10**, 30cwt. in D. - This Tower was the Fourth ring of **Eight** in America but after time they were converted for Automatic Chiming with Hammers and the Back Eight Bells are now Hung without Wheels, Three Bells were cast by Mears and Stainbank in 1797, Six Bells were cast by Whitechapel in 1845 & 1849, One Bell cast by Meneely of Watervliet in 1909.
<u>Norfolk</u>, Virginia, Freemason Street Baptist Church, 10, in F, - Chimestand Chimed, These Bells were cast by Meneely of Troy in 1917.
<u>North Adams</u>, Massachusetts, St Francis of Assisi Catholic Church, 9, in E, - Electric Keyboard Chimed, These Bells were cast by Jones in 1872.
<u>Northampton</u>, Massachusetts, Smith Colledge, College Hall Tower, Dorothea Carlile Carillon, 47, 25 cwt in D#, - Traditional Keyboard, Carillon, These Bells were cast by Paccard in 1957 and 1977.
<u>North Andover</u>, Massachusetts, First-Calvary Baptist Church, 25, in F, - Electric Keyboard, The Carillon Player mechanism was destroyed by a Fire in 1988 but the Bells are intact, Cast by Petit & Fritsen.
Northfield, Minnesota, Carleton Colledge, Willis Hall, **5**, 11cwt. in G#. - **One Bell** is Hung for Ringing but Unringable wich was cast by C H Meneely the Rest are Clock Bells which were cast by W.Blake and Co. in 1886 but they are Hung Dead.
<u>Northfield</u>, Vermont, Norwich University, Jeannie Porter Adams Memorial Tower, Charlotte Nichols Green Memorial Carillon, 47, 10-2-15 in D#, - Traditional Keyboard, Carillon, Fourteen Bells were cast by Michiels in 1956 and the rest were cast by Paccard in 1959, Detached Tower.
<u>North Manchester</u>, Indiana, Administration Building, Manchester College, 10, in D#, - Chimed Only, These Bells were cast by McShane in 1925.
<u>Norwalk</u>, Ohio, St Pauls Catholic Church, 10, in E, - Chimed Only, Cast by McShane.
<u>Norwood</u>, Massachusetts, Norwood Memorial Municipal Building, (Soldiers Memorial WW 1), Walter F Tilton Memorial Carillon, 50, in A#, - Traditional Keyboard, Carillon, All the Bells were cast by Gillett and Johnson in 1928 exept for two were recast in 1983 by Taylors.
<u>Notre Dame</u>, Indiana, (R.C.), University of Notre Dame, Basilica of the Sacred Heart, (Main Quadrangle), 23, 140cwt. in A. - Traditional Keyboard, Carillon, Hung Dead except Tenor that is now Automatic Swing Chimed & was cast in 1867 the rest were cast in 1856 all by the same founder E BollEe (or BollEe et Fils).
<u>Nyack</u>, New York, (Russian Orthodox), Holy Virgin Protection Church, (G.F.), 10, in C, - Zvon Chimed Only, These Bells were cast by Eijesbouts in 1987.
<u>Oakland</u>, California, El Campanil, Mills Colledge on the MacArthur Boulevard Oakland, 10, 22-1-4 in E, - Chimed Only, Cast by VanBergen in 1893, Hung in Seven openings in this Spanish style Detatched Bell Tower.
<u>Oak Park</u>, Illinois, Grace Episcopal Church, 10, in D, -Chimed Only, Cast by Meneely of Watervliet in 1922.
Oklahoma City, Oklahoma, First United Methodist Church of Oklahoma City, **11**, in C, - Chimestand Chimed, Also the **Tenor** is hung for Ringing, These Bells were cast by McShane in 1922, This Church was seriously damaged by the Federal Building Bombing, **Wed 5pm**.
<u>Oklahoma City</u>, Oklahoma, Penn Square Mall, Northwest Expressway and Pennsylvania Avenue, 14, in C, - Automatically Chimed Only, Cast by Eijsbouts in 1981, Shopping Mall open Mon - Sat 10am - 9pm & Sun 12pm - 6pm.

173

<u>Oklahoma City</u>, Oklahoma, St Luke's United Methodist Church, V V Harris Memorial Carillon, 42, in D#, - Traditional Keyboard, Carillon, All the Bells were cast by Petit and Fritsen in 1956.
<u>Oklahoma City</u>, Oklahoma, Westminster Presbyterian Church, Westminster Carillon, 42, in F, - Traditional Keyboard, Carillon, Cast by Petit and Fritsen in 1954 and 1956.
Omaha, Nebraska, (Episcopal), Trinity Cathedral, **10**, 30 cwt in D#, - Electric Keyboard Chimed, exept the **Tenor** is Hung for Ringing, These Bells were cast by McShane in 1885.
<u>Omaha</u>, Nebraska, University of Nebraska at Omaha, Henningson Memorial Campanile, 47, 39-0-25 in C, - Traditional Keyboard, Carillon, All the Bells were cast by Paccard in 1988, Detatched Tower.
<u>Orange</u>, California, Immanuel Evang. Lutheran Church, 11, in F#, - Baton Keyboard Chimed, Cast by Taylors in 1937.
<u>Orange</u>, New Jersey, Orange Valley Congregational Church, 10, in E, - Chimed Only, Cast by Jones in 1880.
Orlando, Florida, Cathedral, **1**, 4cwt.
<u>Oshkosh</u>, Wisconsin, Trinity Episcopal Church, 11, in F, - Chimed Only, Cast by Meneely of Watervliet in 1917.
<u>Oskaloosa</u>, Iowa, St James Episcopal Church, 10, in F, - Chimed Only, Cast by Meneely of Watervliet in 1902.
<u>Oxford</u>, Ohio, Miami University, Beta Bell Tower, 4, 26-2-22 in Eb, - Clock Chime, Cast in 1939, Detatched Tower.
<u>Oxford</u>, Ohio, Miami University, Molyneaux Western Bell Tower, 14, 18 cwt in E, - Electric Keyboard Chimed, Detatched Steel Tower.
<u>Oxford</u>, Ohio, Miami University, Pulley Bell Tower, 50, - Electric Keyboard, Carillon, Cast by Petit and Fritsen in 2001, Detatched Tower.
<u>Pacific Palisades</u>, California, St Matthew's Episcopal Church, 15, in C, - Baton Keyboard Chimed, These Bells were cast by Petit and Fritsen in 1986, Detatched Tower.
Paducah, Kentucky, (R.C.), St Thomas More, **1**, 18-2-19. in D.
<u>Palm Beach</u>, Florida, (Episcopal), Bethesda-by-the-Sea, 14, in E, - Chimed Only, These Bells were cast by Meneely of Watervliet in 1927.
<u>Palos Heights</u>, Illinois, The Evangelical Lutheran Church of the Good Shepherd, 14, 3 cwt, - Electric Keyboard Chimed, Detatched Tower.
<u>Panama City Beach</u>, Florida, Carillon Beach, Panama City Beach, 35, 35 cwt in C, - Traditional Keyboard, Carillon, Cast by Petit and Fritsen in 1993, Detatched Tower.
<u>Park Forest</u>, Illinois, Faith United Protestant Church, 12, 8 cwt in F, - Electric Keyboard Chimed, These Bells were cast by Petit and Fritsen in 1963, Detatched Tower.
<u>Pasadena</u>, California, Pasadena Presbyterian Church, 11, 20 cwt in F, - Electric Keyboard Chimed, These Bells were cast by Meneely of Watervliet in 1908, Detatched Modern Tower.
<u>Pella</u>, Iowa, Franklin Place, 5, 3 cwt, - Clock Chime, Cast in Holland.
<u>Pensacola</u>, Florida, First Presbyterian Church, 24, in C, - Electric Keyboard, Carillon, Cast by Petit and Fritsen in 1985.
<u>Pensacola</u>, Florida, Pensacola Christian Colledge, 43, in F, - Electric Keyboard, Carillon, Cast by Petit and Fritsen in 1989, Detatched Tower.
<u>Peterborough</u>, New Hampshire, All Saints Episcopal Church, 12, 14-3-6 in F#, - Electric Keyboard Chimed, Ten of the Bells were cast by Gillett and Johnson in 1923, The rest were cast by Petit & Fritsen.
<u>Petersburg</u>, Virginia, St Paul's Episcopal Church, 9, in E, - Electric Keyboard Chimed, These Bells were cast by Meneely of Watervliet in 1860.
Pewaukee, Wisconsin, **8**, 9-2-0. in G#., - Cast by Whitechapel in 1995 and are awaiting construction of a Tower.
<u>Philadelphia</u>, Pennsylvania, Cathedral Church of the Saviour, 13, in D, - Chimed Only, These Bells were cast by McShane in 1912.

Philadelphia, *Pennsylvania, (Episcopal) Christ Church, 11, 18-0-24. in F. - Baton Keyboard Chimed, These Bells were cast by Lester and Pack in 1754 and were the Second Oldest Ring of Eight in America but These Bells became Unringable in the 1939 when a Large Pipe Organ was put in the Ringing Chamber, Then in the 1950 Three more Trebles were cast by Paccard and the Bells were converted to Ring by a Carillon Type Apparatus, There is also a Service Bell cast in 1695 which is automatically swing chimed.*

Philadelphia , Pennsylvania, (Episcopal) Church of the St James-the-Less, 15, in B, - Chimestand Chimed, There is also a Deagan Tubular Chime hung surrounding the Bellframe, These Bells were cast by McShane in 1909.

Philadelphia , Pennsylvania, (Episcopal) Holy Trinity Church, 25, in D, - Electric Keyboard, Carillon, These Bells were cast by VanAerschodt in 1883.

Philadelphia , Pennsylvania, First United Methodist Church of Germantown, Shelmerdine Memorial Carillon, 50, in A#, - Traditional Keyboard, Carillon, Cast by Taylors in 1948, The rest were cast by Petit and Fritsen in 1990.

Philadelphia , Pennsylvania, Independence National Park Visitors Center, Market Street between 5th and 6th Streets, 1, 17-3-1., - Hung Dead on Display, "Liberty Bell", The Bell Cracked and was re-cast in 1753 by John Pass and John Stow, It arrived in Philadelphia in 1915 after travelling around the Country helping heal the rifts after the Civil war and remained in Philadelphia ever since.

Philadelphia , Pennsylvania, Independence National Park Visitors Center Tower, Third Street between Chesnut & Walnut Streets, 1, 111-0-12 in G, - Clock Bell, Cast by Whitechapel in 1976.

Philadelphia , Pennsylvania, Independence Hall, Chesnut Street between 5th & 6th Streets, 1, 116-0-7 in G, -Hung Dead on Display, "Centennial Bell", Cast by Meneely of Troy in 1876, Hall open 9am - 5pm.

Philadelphia , Pennsylvania, (R.C.), Miraculous Medal Shrine, St Vincent's Seminary, 47, in D, - Traditional Keyboard, Carillon, Twenty-six Bells were cast by Paccard in 1900, Eighteen Bells were cast by Bigelow in 1947 and Three Bells by Paccard in 1952.

Philadelphia , Pennsylvania, PNB First Union Bank, North Broad Street & Penn Square, 3, 53-2-1 in C, Chimed Only on the roof top of the Bank, Cast by Gillett & Johnson in 1926.

Philadelphia , Pennsylvania, The Lutheran Home of Germantown, Harrison Bell Tower, 28, in C, Electric Keyboard, Carillon, Seventeen bells were cast by Schilling in 1930 & the rest were cast by Eijsbouts in 1980.

Philadelphia , Pennsylvania, St Barnabas Roman Catholic Church, 25, in F, - Electric Keyboard, Carillon, All the Bells were cast by Petit and Fritsen in 1952.

Philadelphia , Pennsylvania, St Francis de Sales Catholic Church, 11, in E, - Chimestand Chimed, Including Sharp Fourth and Flat Seventh, These Bells were cast by Meneely of Watervliet in 1916.

Philadelphia , Pennsylvania, St Mark's Church Frankford, 14, in C, - Chimed Only, These Bells were cast by Meneely of Watervliet in 1915.

Philadelphia, *Pennsylvania, St Mark's Episcopal Church, 8, 17-3-18 in F, - Cast by Mears & Stainbank in 1876 & 1878, There is a Angelus Bell, Hung Dead which weights 6-0-25, Cast by Eijsbouts in 1999.*

Philadelphia, *Pennsylvania, (Episcopal), St Martin-in-the-Fields, (Upper Belfry), 9, in E, - Ellacombe Chimed Only, Cast by Whitechapel in 1889, (Lower Belfry), 8, 4-2-8. in D., - Cast by Whitechapel in 1980,* **Wed 7.30 - 9pm***.*

Philadelphia , Pennsylvania, St Mary's at the Cathedral Episcopal Church, 12, 21-0-7. in Eb., - Chimed Only, These Bells were taken out of the Tower and are now in the Cathedral Basement and the Tenor is on Display, All these Bells were cast in Whitechapel by Mears and Stainbank in 1896, These Bells will hopefully be hung for full Circle Ringing in the Future.

Philadelphia, *Pennsylvania, (Episcopal), St Peter's Church, 8, 15-1-25. in G. - Unringable, The Tower was Declared Unsafe for Ringing in 1848, All the Bells were tied down with Steel wires to stop them moving then a Ellacombe Chime Apparatus was fitted. Cast by Mears and Stainbank in 1842.*

175

<u>Philadelphia</u>, Pennsylvania, St Timothy's Episcopal Church, 12, 19-0-23 in F, - Ellacombe Chimed, Ten Bells cast by Meneely of Watervliet in 1897, The rest cast by Petit & Fritsen in 1959.
<u>Philippi</u>, West Virginia, Alderson-Broadus College, Wilcox Chapel, 32, in D, - Electric Keyboard, Carillon, These Bells were cast by Taylors in 1978.
<u>Pittsburgh</u>, Pennsylvania, Calvery Episcopal Church, 11, in D, - Electric Keyboard Chimed, These Bells were cast by Meneely of Troy in 1907, The Church was built in 1906 - 1907, Designed by the Architect Ralph Adams as his first major commission.
<u>Plainfield</u>, New Jersey, Grace Episcopal Church, 47, in E, - Traditional Keyboard, Carillon, Twenty-three Bells were cast by Gillett and Johnson in 1923 and the rest were cast by Paccard in 1969.
Plainfield, Illinois, Plainfield United Methodist Church, **10**, 20 cwt in F#, - Chimestand Chimed, These Bells were cast by Meneely of Watervliet in 1906, The **Tenor** is Hung for Ringing.
<u>Portola Valley</u>, California, Christ Episcopal Church, 35, 10 cwt in A, - Electric Keyboard, Carillon, Cast by Eijsbouts in 1965, Detatched Tower.
<u>Portsmouth</u>, New Hampshire, 8, - Chimed Only, These Bells were cast by McShane.
<u>Portsmouth</u>, Ohio, Holy Redeemer Catholic Church, 11, in E, - Chimed Only, Cast by Meneely of Watervliet in 1914.
<u>Port Townsend</u>, Washington, Fire Bell Tower, 1, 13-1-11., - Chimed Only, This is a Solid Brass Bell that has been Painted Purple with White Dots.
<u>Pottsville</u>, Pennsylvania, Trinity Episcopal Church, 9, in E, - Chimed Only, Cast by Jones in 1874.
<u>Princeton</u>, New Jersey, Princeton University, Graduate College, Grover Cleveland Tower, The Class of 1892 Bells, 67, 115-0-23 cwt in G, - Traditional Keyboard, Carillon, Twenty-five Bells were cast by Gillett and Johnson in 1927, Forty-one Bells were cast by Paccard in 1965 and 1968, The Other was cast by Petit and Fritsen in 1993.
<u>Proctor</u>, Vermont, Union Church of Proctor, 10, in G, - Electric Keyboard Chimed.
<u>Providence</u>, Rhode Island, (Episcopal), Grace Church in Providence, 16, 30 cwt in D, - Chimestand Chimed, Nine Bells Cast by Blake in 1861 & the rest cast by Meneely of Watervliet in 1940.
<u>Provo</u>, Utah, Brigham Young University, BYU Centennial Carillon Tower, BYU Centennial Carillon, 52, 39 0-1 in C, - Traditional Keyboard, Carillon, This Tower is Denominated to the Church of Jesus Christ and Latter-Day Saints (Mormon), Cast by Petit and Fritsen in 1975, Detatched Tower.
<u>Quincy</u>, Illinois, St John's Episcopal Church, 11, - Chimed Only, These Bells were cast by Vanduzen.
<u>Racine</u>, Wisconsin, St Luke's Episcopal Church, 9, in F, - Chimed Only, Cast by Meneely of Troy in 1887, The Tower is attached to the Church by one corner at 45 degrees from the main entrance.
<u>Rancho Palos Verdes</u>, California, (Swedenborgian), Wayfares Chapel, 16, - Chimed Only.
<u>Reading</u>, Pennsylvania, Christ Episcopal Church, 10, in D#, - Chimestand Chimed, These Bells were cast by Meneely of Watervliet in 1874.
<u>Reading</u>, Pennsylvania, Schwarzwald Lutheran Church, Bells of Joy, 24, in A, - Traditional Keyboard, Carillon, All the Bells were cast by VanBergen at Heiligerlee in 1964.
<u>Reading</u>, Pennsylvania, Trinity Lutheran Church, 10, in G, - Electric Keyboard Chimed, These Bells were cast by Petit and Fritsen in 1952.
<u>Reading</u>, Pennsylvania, Wesley United Methodist Church 10, in F, - Electric Keyboard Chimed, All the Bells were cast by McShane in 1923.
<u>Red Bank</u>, New Jersey, St James Catholic Church, 11, in E, - Chimestand Chimed, Including Sharp Fourth & Flat Seventh, All the Bells were installed in 1925.
<u>Reno</u>, Nevada, Trinity Episcopal Church, Bonnie Jean Richardson Carillon, 35, in A, - Electric Keyboard, Carillon, These Bells were cast by Petit and Fritsen in 1973.
<u>Richmond</u>, Virginia, Centenary United Methodist Church, 12, 35-2-15 in C#, - Electric Keyboard Chimed, These Bells were cast by McShane in 1882.

<u>Richmond</u>, Kentucky, Eastern Kentucky University, 37, in A, - Electric Keyboard, Carillon, Cast by Petit and Fritsen in 1971.
<u>Richmond</u>, Virginia, James Centre, 18, in G, - Automatically Chimed Only, Cast by Eijsbouts in 1987.
<u>Richmond</u>, Indiana, Reid Memorial United Presbyterian Church, 14, in F, - Electric Keyboard Chimed, Ten Bells were cast by Meneely of Troy in 1906, Four Bells were cast by Petit & Fritsen in 1969, 1977 & 1978.
<u>Richmond</u>, Virginia, Virginia Soldiers War Memorial (WW I), off Pump House Road and Blanton Avenue (Virginia Highway 161), 53, 100 cwt. in G, - Traditional Keyboard, Carillon, These Bells were cast by Taylors in 1932 and 1970, Detatched Tower.
<u>Riverside</u>, California, First Congregational Church, 24, in C, - Electric Keyboard, Carillon, Automatically plays at 12pm, These Bells were cast by Paccard in 1989.
<u>Riverside</u>, California, Mission Inn, Between Main and Orange Streets, 25, - Tubular Bell Carillon, Keyboard Disconnected, Cast by Deagan, Also over 800 Bells from all over the world in the Museum, Open daily from 9.30am - 4.00pm.
<u>Riverside</u>, California, University of California, Carillon Tower, 48, in C, - Traditional Keyboard, Carillon, Automatically Plays on the hour strike " O God Our Help " first phase only exept at 12pm the full tune, These Bells were cast by Paccard in 1966, Detatched Tower.
<u>Riverside</u>, Missouri, Red-X General Store, 2401 NW Platte Road (Off Hwy 9), This Shop has a collection of over 20 Tower Bells on display from all over the world.
<u>Roanoke</u>, Virginia, Greene Memorial Methodist Church, 10, in D#, - Chimed Only, Cast by McShane.
<u>Roanoke</u>, Virginia, Hollins University, Jessie Ball DuPont Chapel, (off Highway 11), 47, in D#, - Traditional Keyboard, Carillon, All the Bells were cast by Paccard and installed in 1959.
<u>Rochester</u>, Minnesota, Plummer Building, Mayo Clinic, The Rochester Carillon, 56, in A#, - Traditional Keyboard, Carillon, Twenty-three Bells were cast by Gillett & Johnson in 1928,The rest were cast by Petit & Fritsen in1977, 7pm Mon, 12pm Wed & Fri.
<u>Rochester</u>, New York, University of Rochester, River Campus, Rush Rhees Library, Hopemen Memorial Carillon, 50, 12-2-0 in A#, - All the Bells were cast by Eijsbouts in 1973, Round Tower.
<u>Rugby</u>, North Dakota, Niewoehner Funeral Home, 15, 11-2-4., - Chimed Only, Hung in a Detatched Steel Tower only 30 foot High and has Six American Flags attached to the Tower.
<u>Rumson</u>, New Jersey, (Episcopal Church) St George's-by-the-River, 26, 42 cwt in C, - Traditional Keyboard, Carillon, These Bells were cast by Taylors in 1934 and 2001.
<u>Rutland</u>, Vermont, Grace Congregational Church, 11, in D#, - Chimed Only, Ten Bells were cast by Meneely of Troy in 1947, One Bell was cast by Petit & Fritsen in 1973.
<u>Sackets Harbor</u>, New York, United Presbyterian Church, The Dewitt C. Hay Memorial Tower & Library, 10, in F#, - Chimed Only, Including Sharp Fourth & Flat Seventh, Cast by Meneely of Watervliet in 1899.
<u>Saint Albans</u>, Vermont, St Luke's Episcopal Church, 10, in G, - Electric Keyboard Chimed, These Bells were cast by Meneely of Troy in 1925.
<u>Saint Johns</u>, Michigan, First United Methodist Church, 11, in D#, - Chimed Only, Cast by McShane in 1916.
<u>Saint Louis</u>, Missouri, Concordia Seminary, Chapel of the Holy Apostles, Luther Tower, 49, 50 cwt in C, - Traditional Keyboard, Carillon, Cast by VanBergen in 1971.
<u>Saint Louis</u>, Missouri, Pilgrim Congregational Church, 10, in D#, - Electric Keyboard Chimed Only, These Bells were cast by Meneely of Troy in 1876.
<u>Saint Louis</u>, Missouri, Zion Lutheran Church, 16, in C, - Electric Keyboard Chimed Only, These Bells were cast by The Henry Stuckstede Bell Foundry Co, St Louis in 1895.
<u>Saint Mary-of-the-Woods</u>, Indiana, Church of Immaculate Conception, St Mary-of-the-Woods College, 10, in D, - Chimed Only, These Bells were cast by McShane in 1910.
<u>Saint Paul</u>, Minnesota, (R.C.), Holy Childhood Church, 12, in F, - Electric Keyboard Chimed, These Bells were cast by Petit and Fritsen in 1957.

<u>Saint Paul</u>, Minnesota, House of Hope Presbyterian Church, Noyes Memorial Carillon, 49, in C, - Traditional Keyboard, Carillon, Three Bells were cast by Michiels in 1928, Ten bells were cast by Petit and Fritsen in 1951, Twenty Bells by Biglow in 1951 and Fourteen Bells by Paccard in 1959 and 1985, The other two are unknown.
<u>Saint Petersburg</u>, Florida, First United Methodist Church, 12, - Electric Keyboard Chimed, Cast by Meneely of Troy in 1926.
<u>Salina</u>, Kansas, Christ Episcopal Cathedral, 11, in E, - Electric Keyboard Chimed, These Bells were cast by Meneely of Watervliet in 1906.
<u>Salisbury</u>, Maryland, Trinity United Methodist Church, 10, in E, - Chimestand Chimed, Cast by McShane in 1921.
<u>San Anselmo</u>, California, San Francisco Theological Seminary, 13, in D, - Chimed Only, These Bells were cast by McShane in 1923.
<u>San Antonio</u>, Texas, Central Christian Church, Nordan Memorial Carillon, 48, in D, - Traditional Keyboard, Carillon, These Bells were cast by Petit and Fritsen in 1953 and 1986.
<u>San Diego</u>, California, First United Methodist Church, 11, 4 cwt in F, - Chimed Only, These Bells were cast by Meneely of Watervliet in 1908, Detatched Wooden Pyramid Tower.
<u>San Fernando</u>, California, Mission San Fernando Rey, 35, in A, - Hung Dead, Automatic Carillon and The Bells were cast in 1932 by VanAerschodt, Open 9am - 4.30pm.
<u>San Francisco</u>, California, Gazibo, Ghirardelli Square, North Point Street between Larkin and Polk Streets, 15, in G - Electric Keyboard Chimed Only, These Bells were cast by Taylors in 1986.
<u>San Francisco</u>, California, (Episcopal), Grace Cathedral, (North Tower), 44, 120cwt. in C. - Electric Keyboard, Carillon, These Bells used to be housed at the Tower of the Sun at the Golden Gate Exposition, Also these Bells were cast by Gillett and Johnson in 1938.
<u>San Francisco</u>, California, (Eastern Orthodox), Holy Trinity Cathedral, 7, 51-1-19., - Chimed Only, Zvon Style, These Bells were donated by Czar Alexander III in 1888.
<u>San Francisco</u>, California, St Patrick's Catholic Church, 11, in E, - Chimed Only, These Bells were cast by Meneely of Watervliet in 1874 and 1904.
<u>San Jose</u>, California, (Episcopal), Trinity Cathedral, Trinity Chime, 18, in G#, - Baton Keyboard Chimed, Hung Dead exept the Tenor that is hung for Swing Chiming, Before & After 10am Sunday Service.
<u>San Juan Bautisa</u>, California, San Luis Rey De Francia Mission, 3, - Chimed in open Belcote.
San Juan Capistrano, California, San Juan Capistrano (New Church), **8**, 8 cwt in C, - Counterbalenced, No Wheels, These Bells were cast by Petit and Fritsen in 1983.
<u>San Juan Capistrano</u>, California, Mission San Juan Capistrano (Old Church), 4, 2 cwt, - Clapper Chimed, Cast in Spain in 1775, Hung in the Wall of the Church.
<u>San Mateo</u>, California, St Matthew's Episcopal Church, 15, in A#, - Electric Keyboard Chimed, These Bells were cast by Taylors in 1964.
<u>San Rafael</u>, California, First Presbyterian Church, 10, 8 cwt in E, - Electric Keyboard Chimed, Cast by McShane in 1915, Hung Dead in a Wooden Structure.
<u>San Simeon</u>, California, Hearst San Simeon State Historical Monument, Hearst Castle Towers, 36, in G, - Electric Keyboard, Carillon, Hung evenly in both Towers, Cast by Michiels in 1937.
<u>Santa Barbara</u>, California, University of California, Publication Building, 61, in C, - Traditional Keyboard, Carillon, These Bells were cast by Petit and Fritsen in 1969.
<u>Santa Monica</u>, California, (Episcopal), St Augustine by-the-Sea, 8, in C#, - Chimed Only, These Bells were cast by Whitechapel in 1970.
<u>Santa Paula</u>, California, St Sebastian's Catholic Church, 15, - Chimed Only, Cast by Petit and Fritsen.
<u>Sault Sainte Marie</u>, Michigan, St James Episcopal Church, 11, in D, - Chimed Only, These Bells were cast by Meneely of Watervliet in 1905.
<u>Savannah</u>, Georgia, St John's Episcopal Church, 47, in E, - Electric Keyboard, Carillon, Forty-six Bells were cast by Paccard in 1990, The other was cast by Meneely of Watervliet.
<u>Scarborough</u>, New York, Chapel, 6, 15 cwt, - Ivory Keyboard Chimed, Hung Dead.

Scituate, Massachusetts, The Lawson Tower (Originally Observatory Tower, Dreamwold, Egypt), 10, 26-2-22 in D, - Chimestand Chimed, The Bells weigh 2-2-11, 4-0-1, 4-1-18, 4-3-7, 5-2-24, 7-2-22, 11-2-4, 13-1-11, 17-3-1, 26-2-22, The Tower and Belfry were built to conceal a water tank (Now Disused) for Dreamwold in 1902, The estate of Thomas W Lawson in the village of Egypt is now part of Scituate, Also the Detached Round Tower resembles a 15th Century Roman Tower, Cast by Meneely of Watervliet in 1902.

Scottdale, Pennsylvania, First Regular Baptist Church, 11, - Chimed Only, Cast by Vanduzen.

Seattle, Washington, The Washington State Centennial Bell Garden, Washington State Convention & Trade Center, 8th Avenue & Pike Street, 39, - Automatic Carillon, Mixture of Iron & Bronze Bells.

Seattle, Washington, Washington State Convention and Trade Centre, 8th Avenue and Pike Street, 8, - Automatically Chimed Only, Galleria open daily 5am - 12am.

Sellersville, Pennsylvania, Schulmerich Carillons Incorporated, (off Penn. Highway 152), 23, in G#, Traditional Keyboard, All the Bells were cast by Gillett and Johnson in 1952.

Selma, Alabama, St Paul's Episcopal Church, 10, in F, - Electric Keyboard Chimed, These Bells were cast by Meneely of Troy in 1888 and 1938.

Seneca, South Carolina, Trinity Baptist Church, 16, - Chimed Only, Cast by VanBergen in Greenwood.

Sewanee, Tennessee, The University of the South, All Saints Chapel, Shapard Tower, Leonidas Polk Memorial Carillon, 56, 66-3-12 in A#, - Traditional Keyboard, Carillon, Cast by Paccard and in 1958.

Sharon, Pennsylvania, St John's Episcopal Church, Henry B Forker III and Henry B McDowell Jr Memorial Carillon, 35, in G, - Traditional Keyboard, Carillon, Cast by Eijsbouts in 1969.

Shelby, North Carolina, First Baptist Church, 16, - Chimed Only, Cast by VanBergen in Greenwood.

Sherman, Texas, Austin College, Wynne Chapel, 24, in G, - Traditional Keyboard, Carillon, All the Bells were cast by VanBergen at the Greenwood Foundry in 1967.

Shreveport, Louisiana, First Baptist Church, 13, in D, - Electric Keyboard Chimed, Cast by McShane in 1921.

Simsbury, Connecticut, Simsbury United Methodist Church, The Foreman Carillon, 55, 42-0-23. in C. Traditional Keyboard, Carillon, All the Bells were cast by Petit and Fritsen in the Netherlands in 1986.

Sioux City, Iowa, First United Methodist Church, 11, in E, - Chimed Only, Cast by McShane in 1916.

Sitka, Alaska, St Michael's Orthodox Cathedral, 8, - Zvon Chimed Only, Cast by Petit & Fritsen in 1976.

South Yarmouth, Massachusetts, Christmas Tree Shops, Whites Path, 24, - Carillon.

Spartanburg, South Carolina, (Episcopal), Church of Advent, 10, in F, - Chimed Only, These Bells were cast by Meneely of Troy in 1926.

Spencer, Iowa, Grace United Methodist Church, 14, - Chimed Only, Ten Bells cast by Petit & Fritsen, Four Bells cast by Meneely of Troy.

Spokane, Washington, Cathedral of St John the Evangelist, Bishop Cross Tower, Carillon in Thanksgiving for the life and work of George Frederick Jewett, 49, 44-2-8 in C, - Traditional Keyboard, Carillon, All the Bells wee cast by Taylors and installed in 1968.

Springfield, Illinois, (R.C.), Immaculate Conception Cathedral, 11, in D#, - Electric Keyboard Chimed, These Bells were cast by Meneely of Troy in 1928.

Springfield, Illinois, Washington Park, West Fayette Avenue, Thomas Rees Memorial Carillon, 66, 150cwt. in Gb. - Traditional Keyboard, Carillon, Detached Tower, All the Bells were cast by Petit and Fritsen Ltd in Aarle-Rixtell in the Netherlands in 1962.

Springfield, Massachusetts, Hillcrest Park Cemetery, Parker Street, 25, in B, - Traditional Keyboard, Carillon, All The Bells were cast by Taylors in 1936, Detached Tower.

Springfield, Massachusetts, Trinity United Methodist Church, Trinity Singing Tower, 48, in A, - Traditional Keyboard, Carillon, All the Bells were cast by Taylors in 1928.

<u>Springfield</u>, Missouri, Southwest Missouri State University, Duane G Meyer Library, Jane A Meyer Carillon, 48, 52-2-6 in C, - Traditional Keyboard, Carillon, Cast by Eijsbouts in 2001.
<u>Stamford</u>, Connecticut, First Presbyterian Church, Maguire Memorial Tower, Walter N Maguire Memorial Carillon, 56, 60-3-14. in B. - Traditional Keyboard, Carillon, Detatched Steel Tower, Twenty-two Bells were cast by Gillett and Johnson in 1947 and the rest were cast by Paccard in 1968.
<u>Stanford</u>, California, Stanford University, Hoover Tower, Hoover Institute Carillon, 48, 50 cwt in C, - Traditional Keyboard, Carillon, Thirty-five Bells were cast in 1938 in Tournai in Belgium by Michiels and the rest were cast by Eijsbouts in 2001.
<u>Staten Island</u>, New York, St John's Episcopal Church, 10, - Chimed Only, Cast by Meneely of Watervliet.
<u>Stillwater</u>, Minnesota, (R.C.), St Michael's, 11, in D#, - Electric Keyboard Chimed, Cast by McShane in 1883.
<u>Storm Lake</u>, Iowa, Buena Vista University, 12, in A, - Electric Keyboard Chimed, Cast by Petit and Fritsen in 1963.
<u>Storrs</u>, Connecticut, St Mark's Episcopal Chapel, (University of Connecticut), 10, in C, - Chimed Only, These Bells were cast by Petit and Fritsen.
<u>Storrs</u>, Connecticut, Storrs Congregational Church, Austin Cornelius Dunham Memorial Carillon, 31, 25 cwt in E, - Traditional Keyboard, The Carillon is Owned by the University of Connecticut, Cast by the Meneely of Watervliet Foundry in 1931, Also They Play Methods on the Carillon by Numbers.
<u>Tallahassee</u>, Florida, St John's Episcopal Church, 14, in F, - Chimestand Chimed, Two Bells were cast by Petit & Fritsen in 1991, The rest were cast by McShane.
<u>The Woodlands</u>, Texas, Trinity Episcopal Church, 8, in F, - Automatically Chimed Only, These Bells were cast by Whitechapel in 1984.
<u>Tiffin</u>, Ohio, First English Lutheran Church, 10, in A#, - Chimed Only, Cast by Petit & Fritsen in 1964.
<u>Toledo</u>, Ohio, St Joseph's French Church, 11, in D, - Chimed Only, Cast by Meneely of Watervliet in 1900.
<u>Toledo</u>, Ohio, Trinity Episcopal Church, 12, 30 cwt in C#, - Chimed Only, Cast by Meneely of Troy in 1943.
<u>Torrance</u>, California, Broadway Mall, Entrance 11 (East) interior Lobby, Del Amo Fashion Centre and Square, Clock Tower, 31, in C, - Electric Keyboard, Carillon, These Bells are not used and the clock drives a speaker system with tubular-chime sound, Cast by Petit and Fritsen in 1982.
<u>Towson</u>, Maryland, Church of Immaculate Conception, 3, - Hung for Automatic Chiming Only in Detatched Bell Tower.
<u>(Travelling)</u>, Pottstown, Pennsylvania, (CariBelle) America's Only Travelling Carillon, This Carillon Travells with (Cast in Bronze) Musical Group, 35, 5 cwt in C, - Traditional Keyboard, Carillon, Hung Dead but Moves Location, All the Bells were cast by Petit & Fritsen in 1980.
<u>Troy</u>, New York, St John's Episcopal Church, 11, 31-0-25 in Eb. - Chimestand Chimed, Cast by Meneely of Troy in 1870, This Town used to be called Watervliet before being renamed as West Troy and then renamed again as Troy.
<u>Tuscaloosa</u>, Alabama, University of Alabama, Main Quadrangle, The Denny Chimes, 25, 22 cwt in G, Automatic Carillon, Cast by Eijsbouts in 1986, Detatched Tower.
<u>Upper Montclair</u>, New Jersey, St James Episcopal Church, 11, in D, - Chimestand Chimed, These Bells were cast by McShane in 1919.
<u>Upper Montclair</u>, New Jersey, The Presbyterian Church of Upper Montclair, 16, in D, - Baton Keyboard Chimed, Cast by Meneely of Watervliet in 1929, Also The Tower is Difficult to Access.
<u>Urbana</u>, Illinois, University of Illinois, Altgeld Hall, (Upper Belfry), The Senior Memorial Chime, 15, 26-2-22 in D. - Chimestand Chimed, Cast by the McShane Belfoundry in Baltimore, Maryland in 1920.

Valley Forge , Pennsylvania, (Episcopal) Washington Memorial Chapel, Valley Forge National Historical Park, Washington Memorial National Carillon, 58, in A#, - Traditional Keyboard Carillon, Twenty-eight Bells were cast by Meneely of Watervliet in 1926 and 1931, The rest were cast by Paccard in 1953 and 1963.
Valparaiso , Indiana, Chapel of the Resurrection, Valparaiso University, 12, 10 cwt, - Chimed Only, Detatched Tower.
Valrico , Florida, St Stephen Catholic Church, 10, - Electric Keyboard Chimed.
Van Wert , Ohio, St Mark's Lutheran Church, 10, in D#, - Chimestand Chimed, Cast by McShane in 1913.
Vicksburg , Mississippi, St Paul Catholic Church, 10, in F, - Electric Keyboard Chimed, Cast by McShane.
Victoria , Texas, Trinity Episcopal Church, 10, 8 cwt in A#, - Chimed Only, Hung Dead, Cast by Petit and Fritsen in 1961, Detatched Tower.
Waco , Texas, Baylor's University, Pat Neff Hall (Administration), McLane Carillon, 48, 39-0-1 in C, Traditional Keyboard, Carillon, All the Bells were cast by Paccard and installed in 1988.
Waco , Texas, St Alban's Episcopal Church, 36, in C, - Traditional Keyboard, Carillon, All the Bells were cast by Petit and Fritsen and installed in 1953.
Wallingford , Connecticut, First Congregational Church of Wallingford, 14, 14 cwt in E, - Baton Keyboard Chimed, Including a Sharp Fourth and Flat Seventh, Cast by Meneely of Watervliet in 1927.
Wapakoneta , Ohio, St Mark's Evangelist Lutheran Church, 24, in C, - Electric Keyboard, Carillon, These Bells were cast by Petit and Fritsen in 1981.
Warren , Pennsylvania, Bicentennial Bell Tower, 3, 15-3-18, Hung Dead, These Bells are hung on a steel structure outside the City Building and can be remotely chimed from the Police Station, The weights of the Bells are 6-0-25, 10-2-15, 15-3-8, The Second was cast by the Cincinnati Bell Foundry & is a Iron Bell , The rest were cast by Meneely of Troy in 1868 & 1864.
Warren , Pennsylvania, Charles Warren Stone Museum, 4, 16-3-12, - Hung Dead in a Steel Structure, The Third Bell is Steel & the rest are Bronze.
Warren , Pennsylvania, First United Methodist Church, 11, in D, - Chimestand Chimed, These Bells were cast by McShane in 1926.
Warren , Pennsylvania, North of Fourth Avenue in the Park, 8, 49-3-23 in C, - Hung Dead, Cast by the Mcshane Bell Foundry in Baltimore, Maryland in 1884, Hung in a Steel Structure.
Warren , Pennsylvania, on the Corner of Fourth Avenue and Beech Street, 3, 12-2-0, Hung Dead, These Bells are hung under each other from largest at the top and smallest at the bottom on a Steel Structure, The weights of the Bells are 3-0-12, 5-1-7, 12-2-0, All the Bells are Iron.
Warren , Pennsylvania, North side of Fourth Avenue, Near Union Street, 3, 11-0-16, Hung Dead,Hung in a Steel Structure, These bells look like a Bell Tree, The weights of the Bells are 2-0-23, 5-1-7, 11-0-16, The Second was cast by Jones in 1868 & the rest were cast by McShane in 1882.
Warren , Pennsylvania, 419 West Third Avenue, 3, 9-2-26, Hung Dead, in a Steel Structure, The weights of the Bells are 2-2-11, 4-0-1, 9-2-26, Cast by Meneely of Troy in New York.
Washington , D.C., (Episcopal), Church of the Epiphany, 15, in C, - Electric Keyboard Chimed, Also Old Chimestand in the Tower, These Bells were cast by Meneely of Watervliet in 1922.
Washington , D.C., National Shrine of the Immaculate Conception, Knights Tower, 56, in A#, - Traditional Keyboard, Carillon, These Bells were cast by Paccard in 1963.
Washington , D.C., St Luke's United Methodist Church, 30, in C, - Electric Keyboard, Carillon, These Bells were cast by VanBergen in 1969.
Washington , D.C., Taft Memorial, Constitution Ave and New Jersey Ave, 27, in C, - Electric Keyboard, Carillon, Hung Dead except the Tenor that is Hung for Automatic Swing Chiming, Cast by Paccard in 1959.
Washington , D.C., The Pelzman Glockenspiel, near the pedestrian entrance at the National Zoo, 35, in F, - Traditional Keyboard, Carillon, These Bells were cast by Petit and Fritsen in 1976.

Washington , D.C., (Scientist) Third Church of Christ, 20, 10 cwt in F, - Electric Keyboard Chimed Only, These Bells were cast by VanBergen in 1971, Hung Dead outside the Church on the wall.
Washington , D.C., Washington National Cathedral (The Cathedral Church of St Peter and St Paul), Gloria in Excelsis Tower (Lower Belfry), 53, 214-1-0 in D#. - Traditional Keyboard, Carillon, (Upper Belfry), **10**, 32-0-4. in D., All the Bells were cast by Taylors in 1963.
Waterloo , Iowa, First Presbyterian Church, 11, in D, - Electric Keyboard Chimed.
Wayne, Penns, Presbyterian Church, **1,** 8cwt. - Unringable, No Stay or Slider.
Wellesley , Massachusetts, Wellesley Colledge, Green Hall, Galen L Stone Tower, 32, 14-1-0 in G, Traditional Keyboard, Carillon, Thirty Bells were cast by Gillett and Johnson in 1931 and the rest were cast by Taylors in 1990.
West Hartford , Connecticut, (Congregational), First Church of Christ, Gordon Stearns Memorial Carillon, 50, 7-2-20. in A#. - Traditional Keyboard, Carillon, Cast by Whitechapel in 1969 and 1985.
Westminster , Colorado, City Hall, 24, 3-0-4. in C. - Automatic Carillon in Detatched Tower, These Bells were cast by Petit and Fritsen in 1986 and 1998.
West Point , New York, West Point Military Academy, The Cadet Chapel, 12, 31-0-25 in D, - Chimed Only, Cast by Meneely of Troy.
White Salmon , Washington, City Hall, North Main Avenue and Jewett Boulevard, 14, 2 cwt, - Chimed Only, Cast by Petit and Fritsen in 1977, The Building is made of Wood in a Half Timbered Style.
Wichita , Kansas, Immanuel Lutheran Church, 14, in F, - Chimed Only, Including Sharp Fourth and Flat Seventh, These Bells were cast by Gillett and Johnson in 1939.
Wichita Falls , Texas, Midwestern State University, Hardin Administration Building, 35, in C, - Traditional Keyboard, Carillon, All the Bells were cast by Petit and Fritsen and installed in 1952.
Willard , Ohio, Willard Christian Reformed Church, 12, in F, - Electric Keyboard Chimed, Cast by Petit & Fritsen in 1954.
Williamsport , Pennsylvania, Trinity Episcopal Church, 9, in E, - Chimestand Chimed, Including Flat Seventh, Cast by Jones in 1875.
Williamsville , New York, Calvary Episcopal Church, The Niederlander Carillon, 44, in C, - Traditional Keyboard, Carillon, Thirty-seven Bells were cast by VanBergen in 1959 and 1966, The rest were cast by Petit and Fritsen in 1995 and 1996.
Wilmington , Delaware, Alfred I duPont Institute Children's Hospital, Nemours Carillon, 30, in C, Electric Keyboard, Computerised Carillon with no Clappers, Cast by Meneely of Watervliet in 1936, Detatched Hexagonal Tower.
Wilmington , North Carolina, Fifth Avenue United Methodist Church, 10, in D#, - Chimed Only, These Bells were cast by McShane.
Wilmington , Delaware, Grace United Methodist Church, 16, in C#, - Chimestand Chimed, These Bells were cast by Meneely of Watervliet in 1920.
Wilmington , Delaware, Old Swedes Church, **1**, 4 cwt, - Church Constructed in 1698 - 1699.
Wilmington , North Carolina, St Andrews-Covenant Presbyterian Church, 16, - Chimed Only.
Wilmington , Delaware, Trinity Episcopal Church, 14, in E, - Quasi-Baton Keyboard Chimed, These Bells were cast by Meneely of Watervliet in 1925.
Wilmington , Delaware, Westminster Presbyterian Church, 20, in E, - Baton Keyboard Chimed, Ten Bells were cast by McShane in 1913 and Ten Bells were cast by Petit and Fritsen in 1980.
Wilmington , Ohio, Wilmington College, Collett Mall, Simon Goodman Memorial Carillon, 35, in A, - Traditional Keyboard, Carillon, Cast by Petit & Fritsen in 1958 with a denomination of Quaker.
Winamac , Indiana, (R.C.), St Peter, 25, in C, - Automatic Carillon, These Bells were cast by Petit & Fritsen.
Winchester , Virginia, Grace Evangelical Lutheran Church, 10, in E, - Chimed Only, These Bells were cast by McShane in 1917.

Winnetka, Illinois, Christ Episcopal Church, 11, in D#, - Chimestand Chimed, These Bells were cast by Meneely of Watervliet in 1912.
Winona, Minnesota, Central United Methodist Church, 11, in D#, - Chimestand Chimed, Including Sharp Fourth and Flat Seventh, These Bells were cast by Meneely of Watervliet in 1907.
Winston-Salem, North Carolina, Wake Forest University, Walt Chapel, Janet Jeffery Carlile Harris Carillon, 48, in C, - Traditional Keyboard, Carillon, Cast by Paccard in 1978 and 1981.
Yoakum, Texas, James F. Neumann Residence, (101 Coke), 25, in C, - Hung Dead, Automatic Carillon, All the Bells were cast by Meeks and Watson between 1997 - 1998 and installed in 2000.
Yonkers, New York, St Paul's Episcopal Church, 25, in C, - Electric Keyboard, Carillon, Cast by Paccard in 1963.
Youngstown, Ohio, Boardman United Methodist Church, 23, in G, - Electric Keyboard, Carillon, These Bells were cast by Petit and Fritsen in 1953 and 1967.

VENEZUELA.

Caracas, Church, 9, in E, - Hung Dead, Automatically Chimed Only, All Cast by Eijesbouts in 1969.
San Cristobal, Iglesia de los Recolletos, 23, in C, - Traditional Keyboard, Carillon, Cast by Petit and Fritsen in 1963.

WEST INDIES.

Granada, St George, Isle of Spice, (R.C.) St Georges Cathedral, **3**, 2-2-0. - Unringable.
Kingstown, Island of St Vincent, St Georges Cathedral, **3**, 12cwt. - Unringable, These Bells were originally a Warner Three but the Treble was recast by Taylors in 1959, The Second was recast by Whitechapel in 1925 and the Tenor was cast by Warner's in 1820, These Bells were Rehung in 1959 in a Locally Made Timber Frame.
Montserrat, St Peter, Island of St Vincent, St Peter, 1, 2cwt - Swing Chiming Only, Rehung in 2001.

ENGLAND COUNTY LIST.

AVON.

Bath, Farrington Gurney, Great Badminton,

BEDFORDSHIRE.

Edworth, Milton Bryan,

BERKSHIRE.

| Aldworth, | Bisham, | Boveney, | Combe, | Fawley, | Hurley, |
| Inkpen, | Letcombe Basset, | Sulhamstead Abbots, | Sunninghill, | Thatcham, | Tidmarsh, |

BUCKINGHAMSHIRE.

Addington,	Ashendon,	Aston Sandford,	Astwood,	Boveney,	Buckland,
Chearsley,	Chesham Bois,	Chilton,	Cold Brayfield,	Donton,	Dorton,
Dunton,	Edgcott,	Fawley,	Great Hampton,	Grendon Underwood,	Hardmead,
Haversham,	Hoggeston,	Hulcot,	Ickford,	Lillingstone Dayrell,	Lillingstone Lovell,
Little Brickhill,	Little Marlow,	Little Woolstone,	Medmenham,	Middle Clayton,	Newton
Blossomville, Oakley,	Over Winchendon,	Oving,	Penn Street,	Pitstone,	Radclive,
Ravenstone,	Saunderton,	Stoke Hammond,	Stokenchurch,	Thornton,	Walton (Aylesbury),
Westbury,	Worminghall,				

CAMBRIDGESHIRE.

Abbots Ripton,	Bury,	Caldecote,	Cambridge (All Saints),	Cambridge (St Matthew),	Chesterton,
Covington,	Diddington,	Ellington,	Etton,	Eye,	Farcet,
Grafham,	Grantchester,	Great Eversden,	Haddon,	Hail Weston,	Harlton,
Hauxton,	Helpston,	Hildersham,	Houghton,	Impington,	Kennett,
Kingston,	Little Addington,	Little Gransden,	Little Wilbraham,	Lolworth,	Maddingly,
Milton,	Molesworth,	Newton,	Offord Darcy,	Paston,	Pidley,
Steeple Gidding,	Stuntney,	Tadlow,	Tilbrook,	Upwood,	Waresley,
Water Newton,	Whaddon,	Yelling,			

CHESHIRE.

Eaton, Ince, Over Peover, Swettenham,

CORNWALL.

| Colan, | Mawnan, | Otterham, | Perranuthnoe, | Philleigh, | Quethiock, |
| St Just in Penwith, | St Levan, | Sithney, | | | |

CUMBRIA.

Brigham,	Caldbeck,	Casterton,	Crosby Ravensworth,	Dacre,	Edenhall,
Gosforth,	Grasmere,	Ings,	Keswick,	Long Marton,	Lowick,
Moreland,	Ravenstonedale,	Skirwith,			

DERBYSHIRE.

Allestree,	Barrow-on-Trent,	Beeley,	Brackenfield,	Chaddesden,	Egginton,
Elmton,	Fenny Bentley,	Hartington,	Kirk Hallam,	Kirk Ireton,	Mackworth,
Marston Montgomery,	Mickleover,	Monyash,	Morley,	Newton Solney,	Norby,
Radbourne,	Rosliston,	Scropton,	Shirley,	Snelston,	Stoney Middleton,
Swarkestone,	Thorpe,	Tissington,	Twyford,	Walton-on-Trent,	Weston on Trent,
Whitwell,					

184

DEVON.

Abbots Bickington,	Alverdiscott,	Ashbury,	Axmouth,	Brushford,	Bushford Barton,	
Butterleigh,	Combe Pyne,	Combe Raleigh,	Cookbury,	Countisbury,	Doddiscombsleigh,	
Dunchideock,	Dunterton,	Eggesford,	Exeter (St Stephen),	Exeter (St Mary Arches),Farway Street,		
Gittisham,	Harford,	Highampton,	Hockworthy,	Hollacombe,	Honeychurch,	
Horwood,	Huish,	Huntshaw,	Instow,	Kennerleigh,	Kingswear,	
Loxbeare,	Luffincott,	Moreleigh,	Newton St Petrock,	Parracombe,	Puddington,	
Ringmore,	Salcombe Regis,	Sheldon,	Stockleigh Pomeroy,	Templeton,	Twitchen,	
Venn Ottery,	Wembworthy,	West Ogwell,	Woodbury Salterton,	Woodland,	Woolfardisworthy,	

DORSET.

Beer Hacket,	Chaldon Herring,	Charmouth,	Chetnole,	Chettle,	Church
Knowle,	Edmonsham,	Fifehead Magdalen,	Langton Long,	Maddington,	Poyntington,
Puncknowle,	Purse Caundle,	Ryme Intrinseca,	Shaftesbury,	Sispenny Handley,	Stapehill,
Tarrant Crawford,	Tarrant Gunville,	West Stafford,	West Stour,	Winterbourne Abbas,	Winterbourne Houghton,
Winterbourne Strickland,	Worth Matravers,				

DURHAM.

Aycliffe,	Easington,	Newton Aycliffe,

ESSEX.

Ashen,	Bowers Gifford,	Bush End,	Langford,	Panfield,	Wicken Bonhunt,
Widdington,					

GLOUCESTERSHIRE.

Abenhall,	Badminton,	Church Westcote,	Coberley,	Coln Rogers,	Dowdeswell,
Diffield,	Eastleach Martin,	Farmington,	Hawling,	Highnam,	Little
Barrington,	Lower Swell,	Notgrove,	Oxenhall,	Rodmarton,	Sapperton,
Sevenhampton,	Somerford Keynes,	Staverton,	Stoke Gifford,	Syde,	Tibberton,
Westcote,					

GREATER LONDON.

Bethnal Green,	Feltham,	Hampstead,	Homerton,	Kenley,	London (Lombard St),
North Cray,					

HAMPSHIRE.

Alton,	Botley,	Braishfield,	Bullington,	Chalton,	Chilbolton,
Compton,	East Tisted,	Ecchinswell,	Faccombe,	Farley Chamberlayne,	Greywell,
Hannington,	Harbridge,	Headbourne Worthy,	Herriard,	Hinton Ampner,	Holybourne,
Houghton,	Martin,	Martyr Worthy,	Michelmarsh,	Newnham,	Northington,
Portchester,	Shipton Bellinger,	South Warnborough,	West Tytherley,	Winchfield,	

HEREFORDSHIRE.

Acton Beauchamp,	Ballingham,	Birley,	Brampton Abbots,	Brimfield,	Brinsop,
Brockhampton,	Bulmer,	Byford,	Canon Frome,	Castle Frome,	Credenhill,
Dinedor,	Dormington,	Downton on the Rock,	Edvin Loach,	Evesbatch,	Hope under Dinmore,
Knill,	Letton,	Leysters,	Little Hereford,	Middleton-on-the-Hill,	Ocle Pychard,
Pencoyd,	Putley,	Richards Castle,	Rowlestone,	St Margarets,	Thornbury,
Vowchurch,	Westhide,				

HERTFORDSHIRE.

Buntingford,	Eastwick,	Little Wymondsey,	Nettleden,	Puttenham,	Ridge,
Sacomb,	Stanstead Abbots,				

HUMBERSIDE.

Alkborough,	Amcotts,	Barnetby Le Wold,	Beeford,	Bilborough,	Bishop Burton,
Bishop Wilton,	Bonby,	Brandesburton,	Bottesford,	Bridlington,	Burnby,
Burton Pidsea,	Carnaby,	Cherry Burton,	Crowle,	East Halton,	Etton,
Everthorpe,	Fimber,	Full Sutton,	Garton on the Wolds,	Goodmanham,	Habrough,
Harpham,	Hibaldstow,	Holme on the Wolds,	Horkstow,	Humbleton,	Keyingham,
Kilnwick,	Kirkburn,	Longesborough,	Long Riston,	Low Catton,	North Dalton,
North Frodingham,	North Newbold,	Old Clee (Cleethorpes),	Otteringham,	Preston,	Rudston,
Sancton,	Saxby All Saints,	Scartho,	Scorborough,	Seaton Ross,	South Cave,
South Dalton,	Scawby,	Sigglesthorne,	Skipsea,	Sledmere,	Sutton upon Derwent,
Wansford,	Warlaby,	Warter,	Wawne,	Wetwang,	Whitgift,
Worlaby,	Worlaby,	Wrawby,			

CHANNEL ISLANDS.

Guernsey (Castle), Guernsey (St Marrinde la Bellouse), Guernsey (St Peters Port), Guernsey (St Philip du Torteval), Guernsey (St Savior), Jersey (St Aubin),

KENT.

Bicknor,	Boughton Malherbe,	Brenzett,	Bridge,	Broomfield,	Chalk,
Davington,	Deptford,	Fairfield,	Faversham (Preston),	Graveney,	Hoath,
Loose,	Lower Halstow,	Milstead,	Monkton,	Nonington,	Old Romney,
Orlestone,	Otham,	Patrixbourne,	St Paul's Cray,	Snave,	Stelling,
Teston,	Thurnham,	Tonbridge,	Tong,	Upper Hardres,	West Farleigh,
West Peckham,					

LANCASHIRE.

Barnoldswick,	Billinghay,	Blackburn,	Bolton-by-Bowland,	Bolton-le-Sands,	Lancaster (Warton),
Over Kellet,	Pilling,	St Michael on Wyre,	Tatham,	Tunstall,	Westhead,

LEICESTERSHIRE.

Ab Kettleby,	Ashby Magna,	Ashby Parva,	Bardon,	Beeby,	Braunstone,
Bruntingthorpe,	Carlton Curlieu,	Catthorpe,	Chadwell,	Clipsham,	Cold Garthorpe,
Overton,	Coston,	Dunton Bassett,	Edmonthorpe,	Frolesworth,	Little Dalby,
Goadby Marwood,	Grimston,	Gumley,	Horninghold,	Keyham,	Ragdale,
Loddington,	Long Whatton,	Lowesby,	Nether Broughton,	Owston,	Shackerstone,
Ravenstone,	Rearsby,	Saxelbye,	Scalford,	Seagrave,	Twycross,
Slawston,	Stockerston,	Teigh,	Thornton,	Thorpe Langton,	
Worthington,	Wycombe and Chadwell,				

LINCOLNSHIRE.

Alvingham,	Anwick,	Aslackby,	Barholme,	Baumber,	Benniworth,
Binbrook,	Boothby Graffoe,	Boothby Pagnell,	Bottesford,	Bratoft,	Burton-Le-Dowsby,
Coggles,	Carlton-Le-Moorland,	Castle Bytham,	Donington on Bain,	Dorrington,	Gate Burton,
Edlington,	Evedon,	Faldingworth,	Fenton,	Fotherby,	Hemingby,
Grainthorpe,	Grayingham,	Gunby,	Hainton,	Harrington,	Lenton,
Hundleby,	Huttoft,	Irby in the Marsh,	Kirkby la Thorpe,	Kirkby Underwood,	Mavis
Little Bytham,	Ludborough,	Mareham le Fen,	Market Stainton,	Marshchapel,	North
Enderby,	Normanton,	North Kelsey,	North Scarle,	North Somercotes,	Rothwell,
Thoresby,	North Willingham,	Orby,	Potterhanworth,	Ranby,	Sutton on Sea,
Sand Hutton,	Sausthorpe,	Sixhills,	South Cockerington,	Stroxton,	Utterby,
Swayfield,	Syston,	Tetney,	Theddlethorpe St Helens,	Trusthorpe,	
Welton le Wold,	West Ashby,	Wickenby,	Wilsford,	Yarburgh,	

NORFOLK.

Boughton,	Bradwell,	Bramerton,	Earsham,	East Reynham,	Feltwell,
Fritton,	Haveringland,	Merton,	North Runcton,	Norwich (St Stephen),	Sparham,
Stradsett,	Weeting,	Wendling,	West Raynham,	West Rudham,	Wimbotsham,
Yelverton,					

NORTHAMPTIONSHIRE.

Abington,	Brockhall,	Cinderhill,	Clay Coton,	Denton,	Glapthorne,
Great Billing,	Great Harrowden,	Great Oakley,	Greatworth,	Loddington,	Overstone,
Sywell,	Tansor,	Thorpe Mandeville,	Tiffield,	Wakerley,	Winwick,

NORTHUMBERLAND.

Lowick,   Matfen,

NOTTINGHAMSHIRE.

Askham,	Beckingham,	Bole,	Bramcote,	Carlton-in-Lindrick,	Caunton,
Clarborough,	Cromwell,	Darlton,	Eakring,	Edwalton,	Egmanton,
Elkesley,	Finningley,	Hawksworth,	Hockerton,	Kelham,	Keyworth,
Kirklington,	Kneesall,	Kneeton,	Low Marnham,	Maplebeck,	Marnham,
Minsterton,	Normanton on Trent,	North Clifton,	North Leverton,	Papplewick,	Scarrington,
Screveton,	Scrooby,	Skegby (St Andrew),	Skegby (All Saints),	Sneinton,	South Leverton,
South Muskham,	Thurgarton,	Tollerton,	Tresswell,	Walesby,	Walkeringham,
Wellow,	Weston,	Wysall,			

OXFORDSHIRE.

Asthall,	Banbury,	Chesterton,	Claydon,	Didcot,	Drayton,
Emmington,	Fifield,	Finmere,	Fringford,	Fulbrook,	Heythrop,
Holton,	Idbury,	Kiddington,	Lyford,	Minster Lovell,	Mixbury,
Moulsford,	North Stoke,	Oakley,	Oddington,	Ramsden,	Shilton,
South Hinksey,	Stoke Lyne,	Sydenham,	Upper Heyford,	Westcott Barton,	

SHROPSHIRE.

Beckbury,	Bucknell,	Buildwas,	Clungunford,	Cullmington,	Harley,
Kynnersly,	Leighton,	Loppington,	Myddle,	Neen Sollars,	Quatford,
Stanton Long,	Stowe,				

SOMERSET.

Aisholt,	Blackford,	Brean,	Charlton Musgrove,	Cloford,	Compton
Pauncefoot,	Downhead,	Hornblotton,	Keinton Mandeville,	Lamyatt,	Lovington,
Middle Chinnock,	North Wooton,	Oare,	Pitcombe,	Priddy,	Raddington,
Rimpton,	Shepton Montague,	South Barrow,	Sparkford,	Stocklynch Ottersay,	Stoke Pero,
Stoke St Michael,	Stowell,	Statton-on-the-Fosse,	Stringston,	Sutton Montis,	Tolland,
Treborough,	Weston Brampfylde,	Withiel Florey,	Yarlington,		

STAFFORDSHIRE.

Armitage,	Blore,	Blymhill,	Bramshall,	Dunstall,	Farewell,
Harlaston,	Stafford (Castle Church),	Stafford (Baswich),	Tatenhill,	Weston under Lizard,	Wetton,
Whitmore,					

SUFFOLK.

| Barningham, | Brockley, | Hawstead, | Ipswich (St Peter), | Ipswich (St Stephen), | Rede, |
| Westerfield, | | | | | |

SURREY.

| Compton, | East Clandon, | Elstead, | Mitcham, | Peper Harow, | Reigate, |
| Thursley, | West Horsley, | | | | |

EAST SUSSEX.

Brighton (Preston),   Chalvington,

WEST SUSSEX.

| Arundel, | Botolphs, | Fernhurst, | Northchapel, | Storrington, | Stoughton, |

TYNE and WEAR.

Heworth,   Ovingham,   Wallsend,

WARWICKSHIRE.

Beaudesert,	Bedworth,	Bishops Tachbrook,	Bourton-on-Dunsmore,	Chesterton,	Curdworth,
Fenny Compton,	Harborough Magna,	Lea Marston,	Marton,	Middleton,	Newton
Regis,	Old Milverton,	Pillerton Hersey,	Preston-on-Stour,	Priors Hardwick,	Princethorpe,
Ratley,	Stockton,	Tidmington,	Ufton,	Wappenbury,	Warmington,
Whatcote,	Willey,	Wishaw,	Wormleighton,	Wroxall,	

WEST MIDLANDS.

Bournville, Coventry (Foleshill),

WILTSHIRE.

Allington,	Alton Priors,	Ashley,	Atworth,	Baverstock,	Baydon,
Berwick Bassett,	Bishopstone,	Blaydon,	Bowerchalke,	Cherhill,	Codford St Mary,
Coombe,	Corsham,	Cricklade,	Easton Grey,	Easton Royal,	Figheldean,
Fugglestone,	Hartham Park,	Leigh,	Little Linton,	Little Somerford,	Little Drew,
Monkton Farleigh,	Netherhampton,	Nunton,	Odstock,	Old,	Orcheston,
Pewsey,	Pitton,	Poulshot,	Pouny,	Rushall,	Stratford Tony,
Sutton Mandeville,	Swallowcliffe,	Teffont Evias,	The Leigh,	Tidcombe,	Tilshead,
Upton Lovell,	Upton Scudamore,	Whiteparish,	Wilsford,	Wingfield,	Winsley,
Winterbourne Basset,					

WORCESTERSHIRE.

Bricklehampton, Great Malvern, Kington, South Littleton,

NORTH YORKSHIRE.

Acklam,	Allerston,	Allerton Mauleverer,	Ampleforth,	Arkengarthdale,	Arncliffe,
Birdsall,	Blubberhouses,	Bolton Percy,	Brayton,	Brompton,	Brotherton,
Broughton with Elslack,	Bulmer,	Burythorpe,	Cayton,	Clapham,	Coverham,
Cowton,	Crambe,	Coxwold,	Crathorne,	Crayke,	Croft,
Dalton Holme,	Danby,	Danby Wiske,	Dunnington,	East Cowton,	East Gilling,
East Hauxwell,	East Heslerton,	East Marton,	Ebberston,	Eggborough,	Egton,
Farnham,	Fewston,	Folkton,	Forcet,	Foston,	Foxholes,
Gate Helmsley,	Hackness,	Hambleton,	Hampsthwaite,	Harrogate,	Harteshead,
Harwood Dale,	Hauxwell,	Healaugh,	Helperthorpe,	Holtby,	Hubberholme,
Hunmanby,	Husthwaite,	Hutton Buscel,	Kettlewell,	Kilburn,	Kirby
Fleetham,	Kirkby Grindalythe,	Kirkby Knowle,	Kirkby Malham,	Kirkby Misperton,	Kirkby
Overblow,	Kirkby Wharfe,	Kirkleatham,	Kirk Leavington,	Kirklington,	Kirk
Smeaton,	Lastingham,	Long Marston,	Long Preston,	Manfield,	Marrick,
Marton in Craven,	Middleton Tyas,	Myton on Swale,	Nafferton,	Newton Kyme,	Nunnington,
Old Malton,	Osmondthorpe,	Osmotherley,	Pannal,	Patrick Brompton,	Pixhill,
Ramsgill (Patley Bridge),	Raskelf,	Redcar,	Rillington,	Rufforth,	Ruston,
Rylstone,	Saxton,	Seamer,	Sessay,	Settle (Stainforth),	Settrington,
Sheriff Hutton,	Sinnington,	Skelton,	Sleights,	South Cowton,	South Otterington,
Spennithorne,	Stainton,	Staintondale,	Stanwick-St-John,	Staveley,	Stillingfleet,
Stillington,	Stonegrave,	Terrington,	Thirkleby,	Thormanby,	Thornton Dale,
Thornton Watlass,	Tockwith,	Ugglebarnby,	Warthill,	Weaverthorpe,	Weeton,
Well,	Wensley,	Westerdale,	West Gilling,	Westow,	West Witton,
Whenby,	Whitby,	Wighill,	Wintringham,	Wistow,	Womersley,
Wormersley,	Yarm,	York (St Mary),	York (St Denys),	York (Goodramgate),	York (Pavement),

SOUTH YORKSHIRE.

Aston,	Bamburgh,	Bolton upon Dearne,	Brodsworth,	Burghwallis,	Hickleton,
High Melton,	Hooton Pagnell,	Laughton-en-le-Morthen,	Loversall,	Maltby,	Marr,
Mexborough,	Rossington,	Skelbrook,	South Anston,	Tankersley,	Thorpe
Salvin, Todwick,	Wickersley,	Worsbrough,			

WEST YORKSHIRE.

Bardsey,	Birkin,	East Hardwick,	Featherstone,	Harewood,	Ledsham,
Leeds (St George),	Leeds (St John the Evan),	Leeds (New Briggate),	Methley,	Normanton,	North Featherstone,
Roundhay,	South Elmsall,	Thorpe Arch,	West Bretton,	Whitkirk,	Whitwood (Hightown),

188

WALES TOWER LIST.

Bangor	Bettisford,	Bettws Cedewain,	Bodfari,	Bosherston,	Caergwrie,
Cardiff (Lisvane),	Carno,	Castle Caereinion,	Cilgerran,	Cilybebyll,	Clynnog
Fawr, Evancoyd,	Gwenddwr,	Henllys,	Kerry,	Llanbedrog,	Llandeilo
Graban, Llangefni,	Llangwm Uchaf,	Meifod,	Mitchell Troy,	Panteg,	Pennant,
Rockfield,	Rudry,	Trefeglwys,	Wenvoe,	Whitford,	Wolvesnewton,
Ysciefiog,					

SCOTLAND TOWER LIST.

Edinburgh (Colinton),	Golspie,	Kirkcudbrught,	Millport,

OVERSEAS TOWER LIST.

AUSTRALIA.

Alice Springs,	Appotsford,	Ballarat,	Kalgoolie,	Melbourne,	Melbourne,
Mount Leonora,	Perth,	Rockhampton North,	Sandgate,	Toowoomba,	Waanambool,

CANADA.

Calgary,	Ottawa,	Qubec,

NEW ZEALAND.

Hawkes Bay,	Nelson,	Pokeno,

U.S.A.

Detroit,	Dallas,	Newport,	New York,

WEST INDIES.

Granada,	Kingstown,

SUMMARY OF RINGS.

ENGLAND	3 Bells.
Avon:	3
Bedfordshire:	2
Berkshire:	12
Buckinghamshire:	44
Cambridgeshire:	45
Cheshire:	4
Cornwall:	9
Cumbria:	15
Derbyshire:	31
Devon:	48
Dorset:	25
Durham:	3
Essex:	7
Gloucestershire:	24
Greater London:	7
Hampshire:	29
Herefordshire:	31
Hertfordshire:	8
Humberside:	63
Channel Islands:	6
Kent:	31
Lancashire:	12
Leicestershire:	43
Lincolnshire:	68
Norfolk:	19
Northamptonshire:	18
Northumberland:	2
Nottinghamshire:	45
Oxfordshire:	29
Shropshire:	14
Somerset:	33
Staffordshire:	13
Suffolk:	7
Surrey:	8
East Sussex:	2
West Sussex:	6
Tyne and Wear:	3
Warwickshire:	28
West Midlands.	2
Wiltshire.	49
Worcestershire.	4
North Yorkshire.	141
South Yorkshire.	21
West Yorkshire.	18
Total.	989

WALES	3 Bells.
Total.	31

SCOTLAND.	3 Bells.
Total.	4

OVERSEAS.	3 Bells.
Australia.	12
Canada.	3
New Zealand.	3
U.S.A.	4
West Indies.	2

Cathedrals.

Wales, Bangor,	3 Bells
West Indies, Kingstown,	3 Bells

Greek Orthodox.

Bournville	3 Bells

Roman Catholic Churches.

Arundel	3 Bells
Banbury	3 Bells
Bedworth	3 Bells
Blackburn	3 Bells
Gosforth	3 Bells
Princethorpe (Colledge)	3 Bells
Storrington	3 Bells
Stapehill	3 Bells
Australia, Appotsford,	3 Bells
Australia, Ballarat,	3 Bells
Australia, Mount Leonora,	3 Bells
Australia, Rockhampton North,	3 Bells
Canada, Calgary,	3 Bells
Canada, Quebec City,	3 Bells
New Zealand, Hawkes Bay,	3 Bells
U.S.A., Detroit,	3 Bells
U.S.A., New York	3 Bells
West Indies, Granada (Cathedral)	3 Bells

Octagonal Tower.

Sancton	3 Bells
York (St Mary)	3 Bells

Round Towers.

Bradwell	3 Bells
Fritton	3 Bells
Guernsey	3 Bells
Haveringland	3 Bells
Merton	3 Bells
Weeting	3 Bells

Steel Bells.

Bicknor	3 Bells
Downton on the Rock	3 Bells
East Hardwick	3 Bells
Gate Burton	3 Bells
Lowick	3 Bells
Reigate	3 Bells
Shaftsbury	3 Bells

Secular Towers.

Little Woolstone (Community Music Centre)	3 Bells
Stapehill (Heritage Centre)	3 Bells
Australia, Kalgoolie (Town Hall),	3 Bells
Australia, Sandgate (Town Hall),	3 Bells
Australia, Toowoomba (Town Hall),	3 Bells